D0686933

The Money Game in Old New York

The Money Game in Old New York

DANIEL DREW AND HIS TIMES

Clifford Browder

THE UNIVERSITY PRESS OF KENTUCKY

Frontispiece, Daniel Drew in the 1860s.
From *Harper's Weekly*, April 11, 1868.

Scholarly publisher for the Commonwealth, serving Bellarmine
College, Berea College, Centre College of Kentucky, Eastern
Kentucky University, The Filson Club, Georgetown College,
Kentucky Historical Society, Kentucky State University, Morehead
State University, Murray State University, Northern Kentucky
University, Transylvania University, University of Kentucky,
University of Louisville, and Western Kentucky University.

Editorial and Sales Offices: Lexington, Kentucky 40506-0024

LIBRARY OF CONGRESS CATALOGING-IN-PUBLICATION DATA

Browder, Clifford, 1928–
   The money game in old New York.

   Bibliography: p.
   Includes index.
   1. Drew, Daniel, 1797–1879. 2. Capitalists and
financiers—United States—Biography. 3. Wall Street—
History. I. Title.
HG172.D74B76 1986   332'.092'4 [B]   85-17938
ISBN 0-8131-1573-6

Contents

Illustrations follow page 56

Acknowledgments

I am indebted to many persons for help in my research; I cannot possibly mention all of them here.

For genealogical information on Daniel Drew and his forebears, I am grateful to Dr. Robert Drew Simpson of Chatham, N.J., and to Ralph D. Phillips of Nassau, N.Y. For invaluable information about Putnam County local history, I thank Mrs. Charles Franklin, historian, of the Putnam County Historical Society; Mrs. Paul R. Fitchen of the Landmarks Preservation Committee of Southeast Museum, Brewster, N.Y.; and Mrs. Alvin Behr, the town historian of Kent, who also gave me a personal tour of the area associated with Drew and his family.

For help in my research generally, I am indebted to the staff of the New York Public Library, and especially of the Local History and Genealogy Room and the Annex, where the old newspapers are kept. I thank Mrs. Dorothy Illingworth Pearsall of Hamden, Conn., for passing on to me several family stories about her great-grandfather, Daniel Drew, and thank her son and grandsons for the same.

I am grateful to Donald C. Ringwald of Loudonville, N.Y., for generously sharing with me his vast knowledge of Hudson River steamboating, and to the staff of the National Archives in Washington, D.C., for access to the old federal steamboat records. I thank the secretary of the Canada Southern Railway Company for access to the old Canada Southern board minutes; the secretary of the Penn Central Transportation Company for access to the board minutes of the Hudson River, New York and Harlem, and New York Central railroads; and the Pennsylvania State Archives in Harrisburg for access to the old records of the New York and Erie Railroad and the Erie Railway.

vii

For permission to consult the old records of their respective churches, I am grateful to the Rev. Raeburn Cameron of the Mount Carmel Baptist Church of Carmel, N.Y.; the Rev. Richard Guice of the Drew United Methodist Episcopal Church of Carmel, N.Y.; the Rev. Joseph G. Bailey of the First United Methodist Church of Brewster, N.Y.; and the Rev. Robert E. Richmond of the Saint Paul and Saint Andrew Methodist Church of New York, which has the records of the Mulberry Street Methodist Church and the Saint Paul's Methodist Episcopal Church.

Dr. Arthur E. Jones, Jr., director of the Drew University library, and his wife, Rachel M. Jones, the university archivist, have given me access to the board minutes of Drew Theological Seminary and other records, and have assisted my research in every possible way. Susanne M. Javorski, the special collections and archives assistant of Wesleyan University, gave me information about Drew and Wesleyan University.

Joan Doherty of the New Jersey Room of the Jersey City Public Library helped me in researching the New Jersey aspects of Drew's career, and Mary Kenton of Dayton, Ohio, shared with me her master's thesis on Bouck White and answered numerous queries about White and the *Book of Daniel Drew.*

I am especially grateful to my friend Robert Lagerstrom of New York, a trained reference librarian, for his unending assistance in pursuing many murky avenues of research.

I am indebted to Dr. Wendell Tripp of the New York State Historical Association for help in finding a publisher.

Finally, I am grateful to the New York State Police for not arresting me when, during my first field trip to Putnam County, they picked me up, a suspicious stranger, on a highway north of Carmel, where, having despaired of ever finding a motel, I was trying to hitchhike back to Carmel, heavy suitcase in hand.

Prologue

Wall Street, July 1865. On the pavement excited speculators were talking vociferously; having sold the stock of the Erie Railway short, they expected to make a killing. On the steps of a broker's office nearby stood a plainly dressed old man, tall but slightly stooped, his face cross-hatched with wrinkles and fringed with whiskers, watching them with twinkling steel-gray eyes.

"Happy creeturs," he said with a nasal twang, "how merry they be! Wal, I guess I must pinch 'em."[1]

Within a short while a heavy demand for Erie developed, the stock surged, the speculators rushed to cover losses, and Uncle Daniel Drew—known also as the Speculative Director, the Old Bear, the Merry Old Gentleman of Wall Street, and several unprintable epithets—was (as he might have put it) as happy as a pig in pea straw. This time by bulling instead of bearing the market, he had skinned the boys yet again and was richer by tens of thousands of dollars. All in a day's work for Uncle Daniel.

Madison, New Jersey, November 6, 1867. The formal opening of Drew Theological Seminary was attended by all nine bishops of the Methodist Episcopal church, four college presidents, plus leading ministers and laymen—the largest group of Methodist intellectuals and theologians ever assembled. When a lady asked to see the founder of the seminary, she was told that the most unobtrusive elderly gentleman present would be Mr. Drew. It was true that among this distinguished assemblage the first Methodist millionaire, whose unprecedented gift of half a million dollars had made the occasion possible, appeared modest

1

and unassuming, a kindly, pious gentleman, reticent and humble to a fault.

Yet when he was next expected on the campus—at an all-important board meeting on April 23, 1868, at which the seminary's new charter was to be accepted, officers elected, and deeds transferred—Brother Drew was unable to appear. He sent his regrets not from his New York City mansion but from Taylor's Hotel in Jersey City, where, fearing lest he be kidnapped by his onetime friend and arch foe Cornelius Vanderbilt, he was being guarded by an army of toughs. He shared these quarters with the unprincipled Jay Gould and the garish and most immoral Jim Fisk. All three were fugitives from the state of New York, where if they dared to set foot they risked immediate arrest at the command of a magistrate subservient to Vanderbilt, whom they had just milked of millions through the sale of an unconscionable amount of watered Erie stock. The dramatic struggle between Drew and his confederates on the one hand and the furious Commodore on the other had already embroiled Wall Street and the New York State judiciary and engulfed two state legislatures in a tidal wave of farce and corruption. All of this was awkward for the Methodists, who admitted to having little grasp of Wall Street.

Five years later Daniel Drew was severely compromised in the Panic of 1873; eight years later he was bankrupt. Deprived of his largess, Drew Seminary survived, barely. In 1879, still honored by Methodists but a has-been on Wall Street, Drew died. Since then, he has been seen less and less as a benefactor and more and more as a robber baron.

In April 1910 his image was dramatically confirmed when Doubleday, Page & Company in New York published Bouck White's *Book of Daniel Drew*, purportedly the much-edited and much-amplified diary of Daniel Drew rediscovered by a grandniece then living in the city. In a rich rustic idiom the book candidly revealed how Drew prospered by cheating others while praying to God devoutly on Sundays, thus presenting the very image of the Sunday Christian—sanctimonious, hypocritical, and treacherous.

Immediately Drew's only son, William H. Drew, denounced the book as a fraud, demanding that the Manhattan district attorney stop its distribution and bring charges of criminal libel against White. Author and publisher defended the diary's authenticity. In newspaper interviews White, a radicalized minister turned social reformer, even invited Drew Seminary to change its name and return its original endowment to the plundered Erie Railway—something that the seminary, though much embarrassed, was not inclined to do. Then, without explanation, William H. Drew allowed the matter to drop, permitting White to declare himself vindicated—although the "vindication" does not bear scrutiny (see

Appendix). Within two years Drew's son died, and White went on to a brief but flamboyant career as a revolutionary socialist, then lapsed in silence and oblivion. His book remains.

Today Daniel Drew is largely forgotten. The few who remember him—local historians, railroad and steamboat buffs, and chroniclers of Wall Street—accept the image crystalized in Bouck White's pages: the cunning robber baron who hid his misdeeds with piety. In 1973, when invited by a local landmark-preservation society to help restore the abandoned cemetery where Drew lies buried, the students of Drew University emphatically refused; "Let him rot" proclaimed a headline in their newspaper.

But Daniel Drew should not be forgotten. First, he has been much lied about, and the record should be put straight. Second, for all his faults, he is a far richer and more complex character than the caricature conveyed by White. Finally, in understanding him in his entirety, one gets a hold on the time and place that produced him, the yesterday that engendered the America of today.

The following account attempts to separate truth from myth, the likely from the certain. All direct quotations, including words ascribed to Drew and others, are documented in endnotes; more general documentation is included in the chapter-by-chapter bibliography. The writer has taken one liberty: to relax slightly the faultless grammar and diction that certain sources attributed to Drew in quoting him, since it is no service to truth to credit this colorful semiliterate with a correctness of speech totally alien to him.

This, then, is the story of Daniel Drew, who in his own lifetime gave his name to a theological seminary, a female seminary, at least two churches, three steamboats, one locomotive, a professorship of Greek, and an ox; a man who knew railroads, steamboats, cattle; a man whose career is inseparable from the epic of the city and the nation in which he lived; a man who did much good and much ill, and who in all his varied roles—astute money manager, suffering repentant sinner, cheat, philanthropist, and bankrupt—was so human it hurts, so American it agonizes.

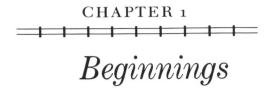

CHAPTER 1

Beginnings

Daniel Drew was born on July 29, 1797, on a rocky, thin-soiled farm in a remote area of southern Dutchess County (now Putnam County), New York, about fifty miles north of New York City. His father, Gilbert Drew, then sixty-five, was a vigorous old man who, at an age when most men would have given up farming and gone to live with their grown children, had stuck to his farm, remarried to a Scottish woman named Catherine Muckelworth, and started a second family. Daniel was the first child of this late second marriage, and he had a brother, Thomas, some fifteen months Daniel's junior.

Gilbert Drew had lived for about a quarter of a century in this sparsely settled corner of the county, off the main roads and far to the east of the Hudson River, the chief north-south artery of the day. Of his earlier life, little is known. He was born about 1732—perhaps, like many settlers of the area, in Massachusetts, although no local records there have been found to include his name. Quite possibly he is the apprentice Gilbert Drew mentioned in 1741 in the will of one John Hedger of Westchester County, New York, and almost certainly he is the Gilbert Drew of Yorktown in Westchester, a weaver, who married Sarah Hunt of the same place on July 5, 1753. Thereafter he became a farmer, and over the next twenty years he fathered at least five sons and four daughters, the half-brothers and half-sisters of Daniel Drew. By June 1771, when his name first appears on the yearly tax lists of southern Dutchess County, Gilbert Drew had moved his large family north to that same hilly, wooded area, perhaps to the very farm in what is now Putnam County's township of Kent, where Daniel Drew was born. Probably Gilbert became a tenant, or even the tenant of a tenant, of the Philipse family of New York City, who owned most of what is now Putnam County.

At the outbreak of the American Revolution, the farmers of this quiet, isolated area had rushed to arms. Gilbert Drew served as a sergeant and his three eldest sons served as privates in Colonel Henry Ludington's Seventh Dutchess County Militia Regiment, which during the war saw much action in Westchester County to the south. By the time peace came and the militiamen went back to their farms full time, Gilbert's children were marrying and setting up house for themselves. At some point Gilbert's first wife Sarah died. Although many of their children left the area, Hannah, the one unmarried daughter, remained with her father. Thereafter the old man made a fresh start, marrying Catherine Muckelworth.

Gilbert Drew's second wife had been born in Scotland on September 9, 1758. According to the tradition of a Lawrence family of New York City, she and her brother set sail for America with their parents, both of whom died on shipboard and were buried at sea. When the ship reached port, the captain arranged through church societies to have the two children placed in the home of the Lawrences, who brought them up. Nothing more is known of Catherine until 1790, when her name appears as Catherine Muckelworth on the rolls of the Mount Carmel Baptist Church of Carmel, New York, to which, thereafter under the name Catherine Lawrence, she belonged for the rest of her life. She was not an educated woman (she made a mark for her name on legal papers), and being in her middle thirties she may well have assumed that the time for marriage had passed. But at some point in the mid-1790s Gilbert Drew married her and took her to live with him on his farm in southeast Kent, where she bore two sons, Daniel and Thomas.

By local tradition, the house where Daniel Drew was born stood on the wooded knoll now occupied by a house built in 1836 by the Northrup family, to make room for which the earlier house, a simple frame structure, was demolished.[1] There young Daniel grew up in a household that included his mother, father, and younger brother Thomas, his unmarried half-sister Hannah, and a slave. His mother was a woman of strong, simple feelings who gave her son much love and was an example of piety that he treasured all his life. In later years Daniel had little to say of his father; to the young boy, a father in his early seventies may have seemed awesome and remote.

Given the father's advanced years and the fact that he may have been the only man on the farm (it is not known if the slave was a man or a woman), Gilbert surely expected his young sons to pitch in from an early age. The farm lay in a wild, rugged area traversed by thickly wooded ridges with rock ledges and by narrow valleys whose shallow stony soil could be made productive only with effort. Although farmers there grew buckwheat, corn, and rye, the land was suited chiefly to the raising of livestock. Doubtless it was from his father on the farm, then, that Daniel first learned about cattle. Since in those days the cattle in the area roamed free, identified only by the owner's earmark, Daniel and Tom must have spent much time hunting cows in the woods, guided only by the tinkling of a distant cowbell. This and other chores left little time for school, though in winter the boys did attend irregularly. Otherwise, their chief contact with the outside world was Carmel, a mere cluster of houses two miles away, where their mother attended church on Sundays and where news could be gleaned from travelers spending the night at the local inn.

By 1807 Gilbert Drew, now seventy-five years old, had relinquished the farm in Kent and bought another a few miles away. Consisting of 120 acres, it lay on the middle branch of the Croton River at the western limit of the township of Southeast, in the area later known as Drewville. The new farm differed only in degree from the old one. Here, too, wooded ridges running north and south abounded, but between them lay wider and more level valleys whose soil, although stony, was more suitable for crops and pasture. Acquiring it must have given the old man great satisfaction: having been a tenant all his life, at long last he had a farm of his own. Yet the work was still arduous, and as the aging father began to fail, his growing sons must have taken on more and more of it. As Daniel worked with his brother prying rocks out of the fields and stone-boating them over to the fields' edges to make fences, this smart youngster must have sensed early that he was not cut out to be a farmer.

Soon after the Drews moved there, the town of Southeast was witness to the most wrenching, draining, humbling, and exalting, not to say just downright exciting, experience that a remote rural area of the time could hope for: a Methodist revival. In encouraging backcountry populations to "git religion," no one was more adept than the Methodists. Their unique system of itinerant ministers serving scattered settlements throughout a lengthy circuit enabled them to spread the gospel in sparsely settled regions where churches were few. As early as 1791, Methodist circuit riders from Connecticut had preached in Southeast. Then in 1809 the Cortlandt Circuit was organized, embracing much of Westchester and southern Dutchess counties. From then on, the counties were visited regularly by the circuit riders: earnest, fervent men of scant education and overpowering conviction, firm in their resolve to outpreach, outpray, and outlove the competition (Baptists, Presbyterians, Shakers, and Universalists) in an impassioned effort to reconcile sinners to their God.

One itinerant preacher converted the entire family of Major Lemuel Clift, a Connecticut-born veteran of the Revolution who lived some two miles east of the Drews and whose house became a Methodist preaching place. There and elsewhere, loud and zealous meetings were held, resulting in spectacular conversions: Molly Nixon, who so took to heart Methodist strictures against fancy and extravagant apparel that she attended meetings in a petticoat and short gown; Sally Seymour, who on occasion fell under "the Power" and lay helpless for forty-eight hours; and many others. It was what Methodists called a great melting time, when sinners were pricked to the heart and souls melted down in love.

News of these heady events reached young Daniel Drew, who was only fourteen at most—years later, he remembered the time as 1811— when he attended one of the meetings at the home of Major Clift. Such gatherings often began with group prayers and shouts of "Praise Jesus!" and "Hallelujah!" and the singing of heartfelt hymns, but the Methodists brought their big guns up in the sermon. Invariably, those present were informed that Satan was in their homes and hearts; that they were guilty of blasphemy, intemperance, false pride, card-playing, adultery, and dancing; that before the year was out many of them—especially the young folk present, so smug in their vain thoughts and fripperies—might be roasting in hell, cast down for all eternity among the heathen, Mahometans, and Papists. At this point, as sobs and groans escaped from the audience and as many a young girl was swooning, the preacher made his climactic appeal: there was still hope, God was merciful, and Satan could be foiled of his prey; one had only to come forward, renounce one's sins, and accept Jesus into one's heart. As fervent cries of "Come! Come! Come!" resounded, the sinners staggered forward, sobbing and trembling, to the Mourners' Bench, where they entreated God for deliverance. Each mourner traversed a fierce gamut of emotions, running from remorse and terror through anguished supplication to incipient hope, then assurance and triumphant joy as amid cries of "Amen!" and "Glory!" from the others, he felt himself redeemed; Jesus lived enshrined in his heart.

The effect of such a scene on an impressionable boy of fourteen, predisposed to religion by the teachings and example of his mother, was irresistible. Placed between Satan and the fiery pit on one side and the merciful Savior on the other, young Daniel knew which way to jump. Falling under the conviction of sin, he implored his Redeemer, became a struggling Jacob, a prevailing Israel, felt God's grace, and was saved.

It marked him for life. Although this first conversion was by no means permanent—by his own account, after three years he lost his religion— it awakened in his down-to-earth nature a profoundly emotional strain. Religion for him would always be a matter of keen feeling rather than sober thought, a blend of anguish and yearning quickened by a whiff of brimstone, sin-ravaged, tearful, and ardent. And Methodist as well. Although his mother was a devout Baptist, years later he would say that he dearly loved the Baptist church but thought of himself always as a Methodist. In his younger years his "backslidden" periods would be lengthy, but in his heart lurked the germ of faith. As for Catherine Lawrence, rejoicing in her son's first awakening, she prayed for God to make him like Daniel of old.

Meanwhile Gilbert Drew was failing at last. In February 1810, being "weak in body but of sound and perfect memory blessed be Almighty God for the same," he made his will and had his neighbors witness it. On March 26, 1812, he died at the age of eighty. His will left Daniel and Thomas, then fourteen and thirteen respectively, eighty dollars each; made provisions for his unmarried daughter Hannah; and gave his widow two of the best feather beds and bedding, and a horse, saddle, and bridle. The estate was to be kept and improved by the executors (his widow and two others), so as to support and educate his two youngest sons until they should be twenty-one. Then, when all debts and legacies had been paid, the remainder was to be divided equally among all seven sons and four daughters.

Whatever Gilbert Drew's estate included, besides the farm and a slave, it cannot have amounted to much. The provisions of his will notwithstanding, after their father's death both boys, perhaps as much from choice as necessity, left school forever to work full time on the farm. Daniel had barely learned to write and had not mastered spelling, so that a quaintness of speech, flavored by a droll Yankee dialect rich in diphthongs and devoid of grammar, would characterize him all his life. But this did not matter to him in the slightest; he was eager to work, to be doing things. At first he seems to have helped his brother on the farm, then to have worked on other farms in the neighborhood, hiring out as a day laborer and driving a team of mules. But since none of this could have satisfied his enterprising nature, he had his eye out for something that would bring in more money.

In the summer of 1814, it came. For two years the United States had been at war with Great Britain. Now at last, as Napoleon's fortunes waned in Europe, Britain was tightening the coastal blockade and threatening a seaborne invasion. To bolster New York City's inadequate defenses, Governor Daniel D. Tompkins had ordered all New York State militia readied for immediate service, and on August 4 he summoned four thousand men from the Hudson River counties to New York. All able-bodied white male citizens between eighteen and forty-five years old were liable for militia service, but of those actually called, many avoided duty quite legally by hiring a substitute. Although under age, the Drew boys were tall and sturdy for their years, and they calculated that in view of the emergency recruiters would not be finicky. Probably prompted less by patriotism (in all his long life, Daniel Drew was never accused of it) than by the lure of money and excitement, they decided to hire themselves out.

So it was that on September 6, 1814, having deposited his substitute money with his mother, Daniel, aged seventeen, became a private in a company of the Sixty-first New York State Militia Regiment. He replaced one Daniel Wilson of Carmel, who had been drafted for a term of three months and under whose name he served. At the same time his brother Thomas, not even sixteen years of age, entered a different company of the same regiment as a substitute for another man. The regiment's point of rendezvous was presumably Peekskill, which could be reached by road from Carmel. The brothers set out each equipped with a musket, ammunition, and a uniform and blanket for which they had put out good money. According to claims filed later, they had each spent forty-six dollars, which was no small outlay for two farm boys from Putnam County[2] who would earn only eight dollars a month as militia privates.

It may or may not have been the Drew boys' first visit to Peekskill, but it was certainly their first trip downriver to New York City. At the Peekskill landing Private Daniel Drew was marched aboard a Hudson River sloop, one of those graceful little single-masted, large-sailed vessels that in the days before steamboats carried passengers and freight on the river. Although in later years he showed little sensitivity to nature, it is hard to believe that, as a young man on his first trip down the Hudson, Daniel was not awed by the river's majesty. Off to the north, he would have seen the huge rounded humps of the Highlands and, as the flotilla of sloops headed southward, the broad reaches of Haverstraw Bay and the Tappan Zee; next, as the river narrowed, the sheer basalt walls of the towering Jersey Palisades; and then at last, the goal also of other squadrons of troop-filled sloops whose white sails dotted the water, Manhattan Island, and at its southernmost end, the city.

Numbering nearly one hundred thousand people, New York in 1814 was the biggest port in the nation. Along the docks bristled the masts of sailing vessels idled by the British blockade, their bowsprits lunging over the waterfront streets. The city itself was a mass of two- and three-story frame houses where merchants still lived above their shops, and in the business district downtown, of red-brick buildings with dormer windows protruding from steeply pitched roofs. There were warehouses, banks, stores, roofed markets, churches, hotels, and coffee houses—more buildings, streets, and people than Daniel had ever dreamed existed. And it was a metropolis under siege at that, with horsemen dashing here and there, armed sentinels in the streets, pitched tents in the very midst of the city, and troops marching about, while parties of civilian volunteers labored feverishly to complete essential earthworks. The worst was anticipated; every man was needed.

Under these circumstances Daniel Drew's first glimpse of the city must have been brief. Upon landing on Manhattan's west side at the foot of Fulton Street, his company would have been marched off promptly to the north. Crossing Canal Street, an open sewer devoid of houses and spanned by only two bridges, and the sparsely settled area above it, the company reached Fort Gansevoort, near the foot of the present Gansevoort Street, about a mile to the north of the city. Built recently, this oblong structure of whitewashed stone enclosed a battery with magazines, an arsenal, and extensive barracks. One end of it rested on a spit of land jutting into the Hudson, which its cannon commanded to both the north and the south.

Here Daniel had the good luck to be assigned to a barracks, although most militiamen lived in tents. His brother's company, which must have come down by sloop at the same time, was also stationed here, so that young Thomas, the "kid" of his outfit and remembered as such years later by his comrades, was lodged in a barracks nearby. Together, then, the brothers had their first taste of the discipline theoretically in force. Reveille was beaten by the drums at daybreak, followed by roll call, inspection, and drill. There were more roll calls and drill throughout the day, then retreat at sunset and the tattoo at nine, whereupon all men retired to their quarters for the night.

Hard work and simple living were nothing new to young Daniel, but given the carelessness of dress and manner that characterized him all his life, one suspects that he was a rather slovenly soldier. Meanwhile, as the weeks passed and there was news of victories on the northern frontier and at Baltimore, but in New York no sign of the enemy, dissatisfaction in the militia grew. Many of the boys were underequipped, ill housed, and ill supplied, and they found that real military discipline— so different from muster days back home, when they paraded before the ladies, and the captain stood the company to drinks—did not agree with their tastes. Worse still, it was harvest time; their families were shorthanded on the farm, while they were stuck in the city with not a single redcoat in sight. Requests for furloughs grew, and desertions multiplied.

Private Daniel Drew was no exception. The company muster roll reports Daniel Wilson, under whose name he served, as having deserted as of October 17, 1814, only to rejoin the company from November 2 until December 6. Probably, like many others, he went A.W.O.L. to help with the work on the farm, then came back to the city to resume his service. For this semi-desertion he may have been given extra duty and certainly forfeited all pay prior to his return. Meanwhile Thomas had not returned home, but when his shorter term of service expired, he joined another regiment at Harlem Heights and did a second stint as a substitute.

By late November it was clear that John Bull, who was well informed about the improved state of the city's defenses, had decided not to visit New York. Consequently, when the militiamen's three-month terms began to expire, they were permitted to go back home. Honorably discharged at the barracks in New York City on December 3, Daniel Drew received $9.33 for one month and five days' service and returned to Putnam County, presumably with his company and again by sloop. When word of peace arrived in February 1815, to be greeted deliriously throughout the state, both he and his brother were long since back on the farm.

But Daniel had no intention of staying there. How could he, once he had been to New York and seen ships, docks, stores, banks, and market places, all teeming with the lust and rumpus of a thriving, sprawling city? And a hungry city, as he had noticed the high price of meat.

"I want my substitute money, Mother," he announced one day. "I'm going to buy cattle and sell 'em in New York." Catherine Lawrence was a shrewd and cautious woman. "Are you sure you'll make money by it?" she asked. "I'm sure I'll make money."[3] And so Daniel Drew became a cattle drover, a profession that would shape his existence for years, his temperament for life.

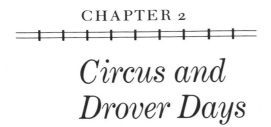

CHAPTER 2

Circus and
Drover Days

To be a successful drover, one had to be a keen judge of "critters," a good talker, a shrewd haggler, a tough boss, at least a seasonal vagrant, and more than just a bit of a gambler. The profession had come into its own only recently, when the booming growth of certain Eastern cities, New York among them, had outstripped the supplies nearby. Someone had to ride out to distant areas to buy up cattle, pigs, sheep, or even turkeys, then drive them in herds to the city and sell them to butchers in the marketplace. Lying fifty miles north of New York and on the same side of the Hudson, Putnam County, especially the eastern part of it with its stony soil suitable for grazing, had become a source of the city's beef. Surely young Daniel had noticed how certain of his neighbors were buying up cattle and driving them off to New York, then returning a fortnight later with flashing smiles and fat wallets or muttering darkly about the "beneathenest" prices in the city. Being competitive and risky, this was not a trade for just anyone; but to a young man hankering for money and excitement and determined to live by his wits rather than his muscles, it must have seemed just the thing. By the age of nineteen, Daniel Drew was a drover.

Years later the story would be told how young Daniel, barefoot and clad in unbleached linen clothing, his trousers climbing above his ankles and with an old straw hat on his head, first brought a flock of bleating spring lambs to New York, cutting so awkward a figure as he drove them down the Bowery Lane that children in the street made fun of him. Doubtless the story is apocryphal, some latter-day invention to feed the legend of the rags-to-riches self-made millionaire. Yet in it there must

13

lurk a germ of truth. Naturally he dressed, talked, and acted like a rube, and having meager capital, he must have started out with small droves of lambs or calves. Bouck White at this point described him as a buyer of bob calves—spindly newborn creatures that the farmers were glad to get rid of—and said that he had to rush them to market before they could sicken and die; but there is no authority for this. Daniel's business start was probably humble but legitimate; if he got ahead, it was by dint of hard work and saving.

At some early point, Drew's career as a drover was interrupted while he worked for a circus. Perhaps on one of his calf-buying trips he heard that the outfit, wintering nearby but about to begin its spring tour, could use a bright young man who knew animals, and the fun and excitement lured him. Uncharacteristically, he may have acted on the spur of the moment, and in so doing he defied the puritanical condemnation that all the early rolling shows provoked from pulpits. If there was action in droving, Daniel must have reasoned, there was even more action in a circus!

In itself, this new departure is not so surprising, for Daniel had grown up and was working in the very area—eastern Putnam County, northeast Westchester, and adjoining western Connecticut—that was the birthplace of the American traveling show, and where it was common for a local farmer to have put in at least a short hitch with a circus in his youth. It had all begun in or before 1808, when Hackaliah Bailey of Westchester had imported an elephant for experimental use in farm work. Upon observing the reaction of his neighbors, who crowded round to gape at Old Bet in wide-eyed astonishment, Bailey began to exhibit her in barns and charge admission. This he did quite successfully, then added other animals, and so created a menagerie caravan that toured through all New England and even as far as Maine, where in 1816 Old Bet was shot and killed by a crank. Meanwhile, struck by Bailey's success, other men in the area had created traveling shows of their own that combined a menagerie with performers, and in so doing recruited still others, including one Phineas Barnum of Bethel, Connecticut. Prominent among these early showmen were four neighbors of North Salem in Westchester—John J. June, Lewis B. Titus, Caleb Sutton Angevine, and Jeremiah Crane—who combined forces to establish the June, Titus, Angevine & Crane Circus, which by 1820 was playing small towns in the vicinity of New York and Philadelphia. This was the circus that Daniel joined.

If it was typical of the rolling shows of the time, the outfit comprised a handful of bright red wagons housing animals in cages: perhaps a leopard or jaguar, a camel, a polar bear, and a rhinoceros that could be advertised as a unicorn. Heralded by the clown, the wagons would parade into a town and proceed to the exhibition site, around which the company would erect a canvas screen of six- to ten-foot walls stretched between poles. Inside it they would put together a makeshift platform of boards where the performers—a few riders, tumblers, ropewalkers, contortionists, and the clown—would entertain a standing audience. In those days there was no tent or ring, no female performers in tights, and no seats either, unless fetched from a tavern for the ladies. The only music was a fiddle or a hurdygurdy. Two hundred fifty spectators, each paying a quarter, was considered a very good house.

Being smart and handy, young Daniel won the esteem of his colleagues during the time he stayed with the circus (by one account, three seasons), and he was advanced in position and pay. Probably he served in many capacities—animal feeder, wagon driver, ticket taker, canvas man—and became the clown and advance agent for certain. As clown, dressed in some bizarre costume and ringing a loud bell, he would ride into the village in advance of the caravan, whose arrival he announced with fanfare, then gave the time and place of the performance. Promoted to advance agent (his capacity for handling money as well as animals had been noted), he would arrive by horseback several days ahead of the company to hire the performance grounds, pay any necessary fees, put up printed posters, and speak glowingly to the villagers of the fantastic spectacle to come. In the absence of local newspapers, such promotional work was essential; so well did he do it that further advancement in the company seemed likely, and in time perhaps even a partnership.

However, it was not to be. Quite by chance, near one of the towns where the circus played, a revival was in progress and Drew attended. Perhaps it was one of the great outdoor meetings that the Methodists held in the summer, where at night the torchlight and flickering glow of candles on forest foliage created an awesome setting. Once again, wrought upon by sermon, hymn, prayer, and exhortation, young Daniel felt himself convicted of sin, confessed his backsliding, repented tearfully, and reached through the agony to God. His prayers were heard, and when the penitent had found peace at last, he poured forth a heartfelt testimonial so impressive that the preacher in charge asked him afterward if he felt a call to the ministry. He did not, but having reenlisted in the Army of Zion, he took a fresh look at circus life, at its glitter, fanfare, and hokum, and saw in it the hand of the devil. Immediately he gave it up, returned to Putnam County, and resumed his profession of drover. God had straightened him out, to the extent that in his life thereafter the circus experience seems to have left hardly a trace.

Now a dealer in full-grown animals, each spring and fall over the next few years Drew rode about Putnam and Dutchess counties, asking the farmers how they were fixed for fat cattle, exchanging pleasantries, then looking over the stock. When he liked what he saw, he initiated the time-honored ritual of bargaining, in the course of which the seller allowed repeatedly as how he hadn't oughter sell, and the buyer as how he hadn't oughter buy, inevitably resulting in a sale. Probably Drew bought a great deal on credit, and most certainly, as throughout his life, he kept his accounts in his head.

With his cattle bought and assembled, Drew set out for New York. Although the details of this part of his career are meager, one can imagine him a typical drover in a floppy hat, linsey breeches, and top boots, mounted on a mare, snapping over the heads of the cattle, as they plodded strung out along the road in front of him, a long blacksnake whip with linen strips on the tip that crackled in the air like rifle fire. In the early years he must have worked alone; later, as his capital increased and the droves got larger, he would have a couple of hired men or boys to help him, one guiding the lead ox with a rope and crying "sukey, sukey" or "suboy" while the other prodded laggards, fetched strays from cornfields, and at a crossroads urged the herd in the right direction. All this took place under the eye of the "boss," ever watchful lest the drove get tangled in another passing herd or take alarm at a village blacksmith's pounding or at Sunday morning church bells, either of which could cause a stampede.

The route he took was an old stage road from Vermont, known locally as the Great Way, which ran south across the easternmost part of Dutchess and Putnam counties, then southwest across Westchester and down the Harlem valley to the King's Bridge, which spanned the Harlem River at the northernmost tip of Manhatten. Since cattle on the road averaged only ten to twelve miles a day, from Putnam County to the city must have taken at least four days. Each night the cattle were pastured at drove stands: inns or large farmhouses that catered specially to drovers. Even when the drove had crossed the King's Bridge, there remained a full day's drive down the length of rural Manhattan before reaching the Bowery Lane, the only road that led into town.

In the city his destination was the Bull's Head Tavern in the Bowery, just above the present Canal Street, which for decades had been the city's cattle market. A rambling old structure with two low stories, and three dormer windows poking out of a third-story attic, it was quite run down, but still popular with its clientele. With its adjacent stockyards and slaughterhouse, it was the center of the butchers' district, known as the Bowery Village, on the northern fringe of the town. In the spacious ground-floor taproom or in the bustling cobbled yard in the rear, young Daniel rubbed elbows with butchers, drovers, farmers, and stage drivers. Here customers were met by chance or by arrangement, prices discussed, and deals consummated. His cattle sold, Drew would ride back to Putnam County, the whole operation—driving the herd down, selling it, collecting the money, and returning home—having taken about two weeks.

Even at this point, when he was just hitting his stride in the business, Drew was not wholly committed to the tough, grubby life of a drover. Lured by the city, he tried to get permanent work there. In the wake of the Panic of 1819, however, there were few opportunities, so he continued in the cattle trade.

That trade was by its nature an unsettled one, and the men who followed it were known for rough talk, drink, and gambling. Although Daniel escaped the worst of these vices, which years later he attributed to the influence of his mother's piety, while in such company he drifted from the means of Grace. It was not easy to attend church and respect the Sabbath when driving cattle, and after a long day's work in the sun, how could a fellow not wet his whistle with the boys at a tavern? Once again young Daniel backslid. But if Daniel Drew had forgotten his Maker, his Maker had not forgotten Daniel.

One day—the date is uncertain, but it seems to have been not long before his marriage—he went on business in a gig with another man, riding out from New York to Manhattanville, a small rural village on the Hudson at what is now 125th Street. There, having fastened the horse under a whitewood tree, the two men walked into a field to examine some cattle. Suddenly a thunderstorm came up, and they hastened back to the gig for shelter. Scarcely seated, Daniel was dazzled by a blinding flash of lightning, then oblivion. When he came to, he and his companion were lying together on the ground, stunned but unharmed, while in front of them the horse lay dead in the harness. For Daniel it was a miraculous and providential escape, the meaning of which could not be mistaken; to this perennial backslider, God had spoken with the fire of lightning. Immediately Daniel recalled his past sins and resolved to mend his ways. Although as long as he remained in the cattle trade, his associations and itinerant existence kept him in a "backslidden" state, he never forgot the incident. Indeed, he told the story all his life, so vividly that it became a family tradition; a century and a half later, his descendants were still recounting it.

In the days before railroads, drovers worked in spring and fall but not in winter because roads became impassable and the hard ice injured the cattle's hooves, nor in summer because the heat could sweat pounds of meat off the animals. In his off-seasons Daniel returned to Putnam County to help his brother on the farm or to hire out to others as a laborer. At the beginning these were lean periods. Late in life, pointing to a shabby outbuilding near his country home, he told a visiting Methodist professor how he had once boarded there for a dollar a week and had found the money hard to raise.

Meanwhile Thomas Drew continued as a farmer. With his older brother keeping him posted on city cattle prices, he probably turned early to stock raising, a specialization that he pursued in later years with profit. His father's farm was now his, deeded to him by the other heirs, who except for Daniel all had land of their own. By now, his half-sister Hannah and the slave were gone, although his mother still lived on the farm. Even so, the household was growing. On Christmas Day of 1816 Thomas had married Abigail Mead, the daughter of John Mead, a poor farmer who lived in the vicinity. Over the next fifteen years Abigail bore him two sons and five daughters.

In farming areas in those days, winter was a social season, and since for him it was also an idle time, Daniel surely participated. Here, White's fictional account is probably not wide of the mark: sleigh rides and paring bees, nut-cracking parties and candy-pulls, with refreshments of cake, new cider, apples, and hickory nuts; and kissing games too for the young, where even a very practical fellow—his head all business, perhaps a bit shy with the girls, and an off-and-on Methodist to boot— might manage to join in. The result was not surprising: after a brief courtship during the preceding winter, on March 5, 1820, Daniel Drew married Abigail Mead's younger sister Roxanna. He was twenty-two, she was twenty.

Little is known of the bride. Like most farm girls of the area, she was uneducated; when her husband sold some property in 1827, she had to sign the deed with her mark, although in later years, being called on to sign documents frequently, she learned to write her name. In marrying her one suspects that Daniel, chastened by the bolt of lightning, had decided to straighten up; as a traveling man who had to keep rough company, he wanted a good, decent woman and a cozy hearth to come home to. These were conventional needs, but adventure he got from his business life. As for Roxanna, she must have seen in her husband, for all his lack of refinement, plainness if not shabbiness of dress, and lack of property, a thrifty, enterprising fellow who, being alert, diligent, and shrewd, was bound to go far, although how far she never could have dreamed.

They lived at first with his brother, and in a year or so she bore a daughter, whom they named Catherine after Daniel's mother. In time they may have boarded nearby, until in 1827 Daniel bought a part of the old Clift farm, which at his death in 1821 Major Clift had left to two of his sons. Although it was good to have land of one's own, the new householder did not intend to settle down in Putnam County. All his thoughts and energy were harnessed to the city to the south.

In the early 1820s, with New York City bursting at the seams and its craving for beef insatiable, throughout the Hudson valley the roads were clogged with droves heading south. By 1825, estimates of the number of cattle driven to market yearly in the city were ranging as high as two hundred thousand.

It was the heyday of the drovers and the highways. Shunning the turnpikes, the cattlemen used the softer side roads, which were easier on the cattles' hooves, less crowded, and free from tolls. In dry weather, urged on by the crack of the boss's blacksnake, each plodding herd kicked up clouds of choking dust, while ahead of it and behind it more dust rose from other herds. Indeed, even the shunpikes could be crowded, for half of America seemed to be on the move. Besides the cattle men, there were grimy pig pelters, aristocratic horse drovers, emigrant families jammed with their belongings in canvas-covered wagons heading west, and sweaty teamsters riding beside laden wagons.

At the drove stands, having pastured their cattle, the tired drovers "liquored," gulped down ample meals, swapped gossip of the trade, and argued politics, then stumbled into bed and slept till daybreak, when they awakened to a symphony of neighing horses, lowing cattle, bleating sheep, and the grunting of corn-fed pigs. Quickly, having breakfasted and paid their bill, they got their herds under way, on to New York, the city that never stopped growing, the huge ravenous belly that consumed all the beeves they could provide, then called for more.

New York was the goal and test of the drovers, the climax of the trip. Far more important than buying the stock and getting it to market was the last stage of a drover's work, the one that could make him or break him—dickering in the cattle yard of the Bull's Head with the butchers of New York City.

In those days the city butchers were a close-knit group with their own district (the Bowery), their own association, and their own traditions. Stubborn, vigilant, shrewd, and jealous of their privileges, these men were tough to deal with in a cattle yard, all the more so in that the advantage lay generally with them, since on a given day they could choose to buy or not buy. The drover, on the other hand, after a trek of from thirty to two hundred miles, was pretty much committed to selling. He could pasture his drove with a farmer to await better prices, but those prices might not come, and he would still be out the cost of the pasture. Nor could foresight protect him, since he usually arrived in the city ignorant of the prices prevailing. Decidedly, selling cattle in New York was no job for the greenhorn; at times even old hands had the bitterest of luck.

So how did Daniel Drew fare, when bargaining with the butchers at the Bull's Head? Over the first several years, not so well, since by his own account he merely broke even. But, once he had learned his trade, he did remarkably well indeed. One suspects that, although by nature reticent, under at least two circumstances he enjoyed great liberty of speech: when fresh under the spell of religion, and when touting his stock in a cattle yard. In time, the butchers learned that this skinny young man from Putnam County—a hick in appearance, but alert and agile, and with piercing steel-gray eyes—usually had good cattle and knew it, and that he was a tight fellow to deal with, one who knew which end was up.

Eventually Drew came to do business with the town's foremost butcher, Henry Astor, the elder brother of John Jacob Astor, the fur magnate who by then was one of the richest men in America. According to tradition, Drew cheated old Henry outrageously.

For a bit of chicanery, Henry was no mean target. The son of a German butcher, in 1776 he had come to New York as young Heinrich Ashdour, a sutler accompanying the Hessian troops brought over by the British. Likable and thrifty, he had prospered, and when permitted to remain after the war, he became a citizen and persuaded his younger brother to emigrate as well. In 1785 Henry bought the Bull's Head Tavern, with its adjoining cattle yards and slaughterhouse, but left the tavern's management to others. As his fortune grew, Butcher Astor delighted in dressing his wife Dorothy in finery; in later days he would tell associates, "Dolly vass de pink of de Powery." Although he never amassed John Jacob's millions, he did well, thanks partly to hard work and thrift and partly to sharp practice. As regards the latter, an 1801 butchers' petition accused him and several others of riding out of the city to meet incoming droves of cattle and buy the pick of them, thus obliging fellow butchers, if they wanted choice meat, to buy from them at higher prices. By the time Daniel Drew became a drover, old Henry reigned as king of the butchers, thrifty as ever, opinionated, earthy, astute—the very image of the American self-made man.

Yet time had wrought its changes. In 1822 Henry Astor retired, becoming something of a banker, loaning out money at interest. By then, as the city expanded north along the Bowery, the butchers' district— with its smelly cattle yards and slaughterhouses and steers that on occasion ran amok, broke windows, and trampled or gored passers-by—had become an encumbrance. Accordingly, in 1825 Henry Astor sold the property to a company that tore the tavern down and built the Bowery Theater. The cattle market moved uptown to the new Bull's Head at Third Avenue and Twenty-fourth Street, which opened in May of that year. Clearly, although Henry's reign was drawing to a close, he was still a man of substance and shrewdness (he would leave an estate of half a million dollars); he was still a man worth knowing and worth dealing with, and certainly worth cheating.

According to White, Daniel capped his career as a drover by fleecing Henry Astor through a monumental piece of deceit: the famous stock-watering scheme. According to White, Drew hit on the idea of feeding his drove quantities of salt. This he did stealthily at night, then the next day, having kept the thirst-crazed animals from water, allowed them to drink just before Astor, summoned by messenger, arrived to look them over. Upon viewing Drew's hefty cattle, each of which had drunk so greedily as to take on fifty pounds of weight, Astor conceded that they were "tolerable good," and after a stretch of hard bargaining, he bought the whole lot at the high price of three cents a pound.

As White has Drew tell the story, a day or two later, when they chanced to meet in town, Astor confronted Drew furiously, whereupon Drew eluded him and made off for Putnam County. When they met again a few weeks later, Astor, much calmer, quite civilly declined to buy more cattle, but referred Drew to a competitor of his who did. Deceived by watered cattle in turn, this second butcher introduced Drew to a third who, when tricked similarly, referred him to still a fourth. So it went, until most of the local butchers had been cheated by the wily Drew, which explains the origin of the Wall Street expression "watered stock."

This story of White's has become famous, and many sober historians, with due allowance for White's fictional conversations, have accepted it as true. Did it really happen? Probably not. First of all, by the time in question Henry Astor, then in his seventies and without a market stall, was almost certainly not buying cattle. Moreover it is unlikely that he and the other New York butchers would have been deceived by so gross a stratagem, and even more unlikely that each of them, saying nothing, would have set up a colleague in turn. Nor is it probable that Drew, a practical businessman, would have jeopardized his future operations, all of which involved the New York butchers, for the sake of a momentary gain. Drew's reputation among the butchers was obviously excellent, because a few years later they permitted him to become the proprietor of the new Bull's Head Tavern, which they owned through an association. Furthermore, frank as they were about Drew's Wall Street operations, not one of the New York dailies' obituaries mentioned the cheating of Henry Astor; on the contrary, they stated that Drew had been an honest and trustworthy drover.

In his later years Drew's name was indeed linked to stock watering— the kind that Wall Street indulged in—and the ex-drover was credited with inventing the term. One version is recounted by the historian William Pelletreau, who says that when a broker tried to sell him some inflated stock, Drew replied: "That stock makes me think of old farmer Brooks up in 'Put,' who used to salt and water his stock to make his cattle weigh heavy when he sold them!" The broker then told the anecdote in Wall Street, where it became an adage.[1] In time, however, the practice itself was attributed to Drew as a drover, in which form White elaborated the story. When White's book was published, Drew's son discounted the story, but his statement has proved far less durable than White's printed word. Of all White's inventions, the cheating of Henry Astor is surely the most enduring, the most entertaining, and the most dubious.

In 1830 the proprietorship of the Bull's Head Tavern fell vacant. To Drew it seemed like the perfect opportunity. As the manager of the city's only cattle market, the proprietor of the Bull's Head would be at the center of business and business talk, with plenty of opportunities for profit. He applied for the position at once. Although without experience as an innkeeper, he had stayed in countless drove stands and knew both the butchers and the drovers, and they in turn knew him. Consequently, the butchers' association that owned the tavern allowed him to lease it. At long last he could sell his farm and move to the city. No longer just a drover, he now became the king of the drovers, a long stride ahead in his career.

CHAPTER 3

King of the Bull's Head Tavern

The year 1830, when Daniel Drew took over at the Bull's Head, was the second year of the administration of Andrew Jackson, the hero of New Orleans. His election to the presidency had been bally-hooed by his supporters—promoters of one of the most successful political myths of all time—as the ultimate American success story. In him, they saw the triumphant progress of the common man, by dint of iron will and genius, from the log cabin to the White House, shattering in the process the combined forces of aristocracy, privilege, and corruption. Just how far the new egalitarianism could go had become apparent at the public reception at the White House following the inaugural address, when throngs of frontier well-wishers snatched refreshments from the waiters, broke glass and chinaware, climbed on the damasked chairs with muddy boots, and when wine and ice cream were removed to the garden outside, leaped through the windows in pursuit.

Jacksonian America was bursting with crude, vital energy, intoxicated by new land, new power, new technology, new businesses, and new uto-pias. America was a nation of pushers and doers whose coarse manners the English visitor Mrs. Trollope chronicled with fascinated horror, not-ing how the masculine half of Democracy put its feet up on the table, bragged, drank, chewed, swore, and spat, while its feminine counter-part, relegated to making sweetmeats and darning stockings, talked vap-idly of sermons and dyspepsia pills, or attended camp meetings and re-vivals where orgies of repentance ensued, and overwrought adolescent females (as she noted with alarm) swooned beside handsome young min-isters. Although it appalled Mrs. Trollope, this raw new society that had put Old Hickory in the White House—a man who reputedly misspelled three words in four—constituted the perfect setting for another self-made man in the making, a farm boy turned cattle drover whose affinity for money and excitement launched him into tavern-keeping, then large-scale cattle-buying, steamboats, stocks, and banking.

For such ventures, he could not have been better located. A mecca for hucksters and hustlers, the city of New York, through a combination of luck, imagination, hard work, easy credit, and sheer unrelenting go-aheaditiveness (the word actually appeared in the press), had made itself the foremost port in the nation. Swelled by newcomers from both sides of the Atlantic, the population doubled every sixteen years. Irresistibly the city spread northward, imposing on Manhattan's topography a rigid gridiron of streets as farmlands were bought up, orchards chopped down, valleys filled, hills leveled, and ponds and cemeteries obliterated to make way for a booming metropolis, slum-ridden and riot-prone already, that each year grew richer, bigger, brasher, denser, and grimier; and hungrier, as well. To feed the city's tens then hundreds of thousands, drovers had to bring in cattle from more and more distant areas, and they pastured and sold them at the Bull's Head, all of which meant profits for Daniel Drew.

In those days the Bull's Head Tavern was a large three-story frame structure with an attic standing on the northwest corner of Third Avenue and Twenty-fourth street, with its gable end facing Twenty-fourth Street and a brick front along the avenue. The signboard, featuring a grim bull's head, swung from a post at the corner, while beneath it hung the dinner bell with a rope attached. Adjoining it at its northwest corner was an annex, which probably served as a dining hall. Behind the tavern was a large barn with one end abutting Twenty-fourth Street, said to have been a low Dutch stable with a wooden pump and trough in front of it. The land owned by the butchers' association included most of the two large blocks bordered by Lexington and Third avenues on the west and east, and by Twenty-third and Twenty-fifth streets on the south and north, affording ample room for cattle yards with a capacity of fifteen hundred head, as well as various outbuildings, and pens for pigs and sheep.

The location was in fact semirural, since most of the city remained below Fourteenth Street, although a thin line of buildings stretched north along Third Avenue, the main route north to Harlem. To the west of the Bull's Head was a pleasant woodland where people from the city came to picnic, while on the other side of Third Avenue there were slaughterhouses and sheds, and in time two rival hostelries: the Black Swan and the smaller Bull's Head Junior. The whole area was known as the Bull's Head Village and constituted the northernmost limit of the city, as evidenced by the common saying "from Bull's Head to the Battery." Here cattle from the north could be brought in, sold, slaughtered, and the meat distributed with minimum inconvenience to the city. But cattle from the west, upon arriving by ferry from New Jersey, had to pass through the city's streets to get there, an increasingly frequent spectacle as trans-Allegheny drives multiplied in the 1830s.

Monday was the main market day at the Bull's Head, which meant that, at some cost to respect for the Sabbath, an average of seven hundred head of cattle, plus calves, sheep, and pigs in smaller numbers, would be driven into the pens by Sunday evening, while the tavern's guests might be lodged two or three to a room or even two strangers to a bed. If an excess of cattle appeared, the drovers often called a meeting at which each of them agreed to send a quota of cattle to pasture, to await the secondary market on Thursday. Thus prepared, Monday morning presented the liveliest spectacle. The tavern and yard thronged with butchers and drovers doing business, plus keen-eyed speculators, farmers looking for cattle to pasture, and a crowd of onlookers. In the single sale lot, all the cattle were mixed together, urged this way or that by running, shouting, prodding cattle boys, as by mark or by appearance the sellers identified their animals. On the fringe of things, hawkers sold clothing, jewelry, watches, soap, and knives, while thimbleriggers in beaver hats and fancy vests tried their sleight of hand on the unwary. The whole vivid scene unfolded to the constant music of whinnying, lowing, grunting, and bleating animals.

At midday the dinner bell rang, precipitating a pell-mell rush to the dining saloon, where the patrons grabbed a seat, helped themselves at once, and dined voraciously. Those too polite, slow, or faint of heart to secure seats at the first service fared shabbily at the second, following which trading resumed. The finest cattle were usually sold the first thing in the morning; by afternoon, butchers would be leading their purchases away, while drovers who had made few sales would be sacrificing stock at low prices, or making arrangements to pasture them over till Thursday. If sales had gone well, the drovers would be standing friends to drinks at the bar; if they had gone badly, they would be calling it "the meanest kind of a market" and proclaiming themselves "dead broke."

Over all these proceedings Daniel Drew presided as host and manager, as mediator and pacifier if need be, and as banker, too. In the absence of banks it was the practice of many innkeepers to carry large accounts for drovers who wished to avoid the expense and delay of a week's further stay in the city until they got the money for their animals. Setting himself up as a collector, Drew cashed the drovers' bills on the butchers, who had thirty days' credit, and for his trouble took one percent interest. In addition, any guest with large quantities of cash on hand—a drover who had just been paid or the winner in a game of chance—might deposit his funds with the host, who placed them in an iron safe built into the brick wall of the taproom, which served as the tavern's office. Money management came natural to Drew, who became the banker of more than half the drovers in the city, one of several circumstances that led directly to his Wall Street career.

To help him run the Bull's Head, in 1830 Daniel Drew had living in the house his wife Roxanna (no innkeeper's wife was ever idle), at least one white assistant and bartender, and six free blacks—three men and three women. Roxanna, who probably supervised the maids and kitchen help, and his little daughter Catherine were the only white women on the premises. Among the blacks who worked for him was Orrin Hutchinson, whose mother was a convert highly esteemed among the Methodists of Southeast; later Orrin would work for Drew as a steward on his steamboats, too. From the outset, Drew was inclined to hire friends and relatives, a practice that for him, thanks to his judgment of character, always bore excellent results.

If his life as a drover had led Drew to lose his religion, his life as an innkeeper made him stray even farther from the fold. In those days, when the first words of two strangers who had just met were apt to be, "Let's liquor," no innkeeper could have prospered without maintaining a first-rate taproom. At the Bull's Head, whenever the cattle market was not in operation, the patrons made a beeline for the bar, where butchers, drovers, rough farmers, and refined gentlemen mingled readily, smoking, spitting, arguing, telling tall tales, and toasting or damning the president. The favorite drinks were apple jack, brandy and water, and cider, dispensed at six cents a tumbler, though the Bull's Head was also known for its superior Jamaica rum.

Gambling too was common at the Bull's Head, which was just a bit awkward for Drew, who as a tavernkeeper was forbidden by law to tolerate any form of it, at the risk of losing his license. It would have taken more than admonitions from the host, however, to keep the patrons of the Bull's Head from gathering each evening around a long table in the taproom to throw dice for small stakes, or from risking big ones in the game of "crack-a-loo," in which the pot was won by the player who tossed a coin nearest a designated crack in the floor. Fair-weather diversions would have included quoits and horseshoes, weight-lifting, impromptu wrestling matches, and horse racing up Third Avenue. In addition, noisy revels were not unknown at the Black Swann just across the road, but if in her younger years Roxanna Drew harbored even a fraction of the severity that dominates the portrait done of her in later years, now hanging at Drew University, one suspects that such roistering was rare at the Bull's Head.

Although trusted and esteemed by his patrons, Drew himself was never a glad-hander, a hearty mixer drinking with the boys, backslapping and swapping jokes. Rather, they knew him as a competent manager who ran a comfortable and economical house, a man whose orderly and businesslike ways benefited both his guests and himself. Years later they would remember him in the dim light of the taproom, oblivious to the chatter and drinking all around him, pacing solemnly back and forth in a blue, brass-buttoned swallow-tail coat, his hands clasped behind him, his reflective eyes shaded by the rim of a bell-shaped hat, as he pondered some business scheme. Indeed, his mind was elsewhere: on real estate and cattle speculations, on steamboats, and ultimately on Wall Street. For Daniel Drew, the Bull's Head was only a stepping stone.

In moving to the Bull's Head, Drew had not severed his ties with Putnam County. All his life his interests oscillated between his home county and New York City. Feeling a warm regard for his mother, in the 1830s he must have visited her often, taking a steamboat up the Hudson to Peekskill, then traveling overland to Carmel or, when winter ice closed the Hudson, going the whole way by stage. During these visits he kept his eye out for good local farmland, since as a seasoned cattleman he wanted to raise stock as well as trade in it. In 1833 he bought from one of Major Clift's sons the bulk of the old Clift farm, another slice of which he had already owned and sold; he paid $17,000 and assumed a mortgage.

Supplemented by another forty acres, this fine pastureland became the 386-acre farm that belonged to Drew for thirty years and to his family for the balance of the century; it later received the name of Drewsclift.[1] Immediately he hired John Mead, the youngest of his wife's three brothers, to move onto the property (the site of his first conversion) and to live there as superintendent. Thereafter John Mead, with his brothers Harry and Charles Mead, worked the farm for him, although he himself supplied the stock and kept it under close inspection. Owning a big farm "up in Put" and paying his in-laws to look after it must have shown the home folks how Daniel was getting on in the city. At the same time, it let him keep his hand in the one kind of farming that appealed to him, the fattening of beeves for market.

Fat beeves and where to find them were much on Drew's mind in the early 1830s, for managing the Bull's Head had not made him give up droving. With the city's demand ever growing, competition keen, and supplies within the state inadequate, once again he enlarged his operations. First, taking other men as partners, he moved into eastern Pennsylvania, where farmers were fattening on corn limited numbers of three-year-old steers that had been brought over the mountains from Ohio. From these farmers, if not from drovers in the taproom of the Bull's Head, he learned of vast herds of corn-fattened cattle in the rich bottom lands of the distant Scioto Valley of Ohio, a large new supply, virtually untapped, that could be had (so they said) for a song. Of course there was a catch, and a big one. These cattle were not easy to bring to market by water, because shipping livestock via the Erie Canal was slow, awkward, and expensive. But the land route to the Eastern markets, a good five hundred miles of country, was blocked by bad roads, unbridged streams, and the mighty barrier of the Alleghenies. Given these obstacles, drovers on both sides of the mountains had concluded that too much stock would be lost along the way and that whatever animals did reach the coast would be too thin to market profitably. But the more he thought about those fat, cheap cattle grazing lushly in distant Ohio, the more Drew yearned for them and for the prices they would fetch in New York. He made up his mind that he would show the boys the thing could be done.

All his life Drew was fond of telling how he had been the first to drive Western cattle over the mountains to the East, a claim that, unless qualified, cannot be allowed. As early as 1805 George Renick of Chillecothe, Ohio, had driven sixty-eight cattle from the Scioto Valley over the Cumberland Road to Baltimore, thus initiating the cattle trade between Ohio and the eastern seaboard. Because of the problems involved, this trade was slow in developing, but as cattle multiplied in the West and demand soared in the East, the more venturesome drovers kept trying. In June 1817 the first drove reached New York—over a hundred cattle from Chillecothe that were sold at the old Bull's Head for the excellent price of sixty-nine dollars a head. Yet not until 1824 did the next Ohio droves reach New York, and they appeared sporadically at best thereafter. By the early 1830s, however, the time was ripe.

When Daniel Drew got the idea of bringing cattle over the mountains to New York, it still seemed a daring, even a foolhardy, notion. To be profitable at all, it would have to be an extensive operation, requiring partners and capital. As regards capital, he was thinking big. In an age when a drover setting out with four thousand dollars was considered an important operator, Drew wanted ten or even twenty times as much, although to obtain this amount in loans he had no security to offer. Accordingly, he went to Henry Astor, the retired butcher now turned banker, presented his scheme, and asked for a loan. Old Henry pondered: he knew the cattle business, he knew the dangers, and he knew Daniel Drew. "I'll take the risk!" he declared.[2]

It was spring in the early 1830s when Drew's party, perhaps only two or three in number, since hands could be hired in the West, set out by stage coach, crossed New Jersey and Pennsylvania, traversed the Alle-ghenies, and finally reached central Ohio. At this time it was a jouncing, tiring trip over roads that got worse all the way. But it was worth it, for in the middle Scioto Valley they found a drover's dream come true—thousands upon thousands of cattle being fattened annually. Wintered on corn and grazed in the summer on bluegrass, there were perhaps twelve thousand head in all, including quantities of fat, solid beeves ripe for market.

As newcomers all the way from New York, with cattle on their minds and sound Eastern bank notes in their pockets, Drew and his partners must have evoked a hearty welcome from the Buckeyes. Doubtless the leading cattlemen informed them of the local herds available and intro-duced them around. For several weeks they must have visited the farms, buying cattle, after which, since by New York standards the cattle were cheap, they may have extended their operations southward into the bluegrass region of Kentucky, another great cattle-feeding area. In all, they purchased some two thousand head, which with the help of hired hands they gathered in droves and moved toward the mountains, cover-ing perhaps ten miles a day over unpaved roads that became a clayey morass when it rained and swirls of dust in the heat. Surely it was the largest cattle operation in a single season ever seen in Pennsylvania or Ohio.

In Pennsylvania, Drew and his men took the cattle over the moun-tains a hundred at a time. Probably, heading southeast from Pittsburgh toward Chambersburg, they followed a cutoff preferred by cattlemen called the Three Mountain Trail. Within a distance of about ten miles, this rugged, winding track climbed over three parallel ridges with inter-vening deep, narrow valleys. This was the most arduous stretch of all, consisting of a rocky trail never more than twenty feet wide, dusty in dry weather unless summer rains reduced it to a quagmire, with steep banks where cattle plunged readily to their death, and wilderness where the animals went astray or fell victims to wolves at night. Traversed in the late spring or early summer, the region would have been a mountain paradise with morning mist, pure air, and bird songs, surrounded on all sides by blue tops of ridges capped by clouds. These were vistas that Drew, one suspects, gave little thought to, preoccupied as he was with his drove's safety, with the "shrink" being sweated off his beeves, and with the price they would bring in New York. Well might he have wor-ried, since hundreds of cattle, perhaps a sixth or a fifth of the whole, were lost on the way, mostly through straying in the forests and moun-tains.

After nearly two months on the road, Drew at long last ferried his drove over the Hudson and brought it into the Bull's Head, thus confounding the skeptics. His cheap Western cattle brought a good price on the market, so that despite the heavy losses on the road, he made tens of thousands of dollars and repaid Henry Astor's loan.

If this was not the first cattle drive over the mountains, it was surely the first successful one of this magnitude, and it established Drew as the foremost cattle dealer in the city. Yet more than just business was involved. Having overcome mud, dust, ruts, swollen streams, wilderness, and towering mountains to bring his Western beeves to New York, Daniel Drew had had a hand in the making of America, an achievement that this least heroic of men delighted to recount all his life. It was his one physical exploit, and he relished it.

In the course of the 1830s, Drew and his associates made more cattle-buying trips to the West, visiting not only Ohio but also Kentucky, Indiana, and Illinois, where at one time or another they probably reached all the major cattle-feeding ranges of the area. Their drives from these regions to New York involved investments of at least thirty or forty thousand dollars at a time, and eastward treks of up to ten weeks, but the profits were always substantial.

Of course they were not the only ones engaged in such trade. Organized by Western drovers, trans-Allegheny drives became common in the 1830s. Leaving Ohio, or even Kentucky, Indiana, or Illinois, between mid-February and June (the first drives got under way as soon as the roads were passable), typical herds of from one hundred to two hundred head, accompanied by three attendents, so clogged the mountain roads that by early summer the dust never settled. When the Westerners reached New York between mid-April and mid-August, weary from their six to ten weeks on the road, they found a ready welcome at the Bull's Head, where Drew himself, if not absent on a venture of his own, might greet them at the door, ask what they would have to drink, and recommend his excellent Jamaica rum.

But not all the drovers reached New York. Often at Harrisburg or other points in eastern Pennsylvania, with the arduous mountain crossing well behind them, the cattlemen, sweat-soaked, tired, and ragged, encountered gentlemen sitting comfortably in gigs. These were speculators who had driven out from New York, Philadelphia, or Baltimore to intercept the incoming herds, which they offered to buy in their entirety and accompany with their own crews the rest of the way. Being ignorant of current prices in the city, the drovers faced the difficult decision either to take the price offered or press on and run the risks of the market. Often they sold, although they might regret it keenly afterward.

By the late 1830s Daniel Drew was one of these speculators sitting snugly in a gig, meeting incoming droves three or four days out from the city. Now that others were bringing Western beeves over the mountains, why should he go to all that risk and trouble himself? With ever greater funds at his disposal, on occasion he even went to Philadelphia, bought up entire herds, and secured a corner on the market. Within just a few years he had ceased to be a drover involved firsthand in the trade and had become a large-scale capitalist, a manipulator. Gone forever was the Daniel of the epic mountain crossings, the drover pioneer. It was not in him to be heroic for long; nor did he have to be. He was a money manager now and had his eye on Wall Street.

Two unhappy events marred Drew's last years at the Bull's Head. In May of 1836, fifteen years after the birth of their first child Catherine, Roxanna Drew gave birth to a second daughter, Josephine. However, this new daughter died on April 20, 1837, at the age of eleven months.

Meanwhile Catherine, the other daughter, was fast maturing. Still probably the only white girl on the premises, she was not long in finding a husband. The young man was named Roswell Willcox Chamberlain. He was her father's assistant at the Bull's Head, perhaps bartending a bit and looking after the place whenever the boss was away. Probably in 1838, when he was twenty-eight and she about seventeen, Roswell married Catherine, following which the young couple continued to live at the Bull's Head. On October 20, 1838, Roswell Chamberlain died of what the doctor termed a bilious fever, leaving his young wife about two months pregnant.

Perhaps his daughter's widowhood was a further inducement for Drew to leave the Bull's Head. At any rate, by May of the following year he had relinquished the tavern's proprietorship and moved into the city, leasing a house at 42 Bleecker Street and an office in Wall Street. It was surely at the Bleecker Street residence that on May 20, 1839, his first grandchild was born, a boy who was named Daniel Drew Chamberlain.

For his wife Roxanna, this first grandchild would have been the second great event of the season. The first was the new residence itself, a three-story row house on elegant Bleecker Street that was only one block from Bond Street, the most desirable address in the city. To exchange the Bull's Head Tavern, with its atmosphere of tobacco, cattle dung, and whiskey, for the quiet of a refined interior, with carpets underfoot and drapes flanking tall front windows, may well have slightly dazed Roxanna. Yet it was time for a crack at gentility. Her husband was launching a career in Wall Street and had long since become a major operator of steamboats on the Hudson. The move to Bleecker Street confirmed that the ex-drover and the farm girl from Putnam County had "arrived."[3]

CHAPTER 4

=╤═╤═╤═╤═╤═╤═╤═╤═

Into Steamboating

In September 1814 when Daniel Drew, as a wide-eyed young Putnam County militiaman, first sailed down the Hudson to New York, he must have gaped in wonder at one or another of Robert Fulton's early steamboats, which for seven years had been plying between New York and Albany. These were flush-decked little sidewheelers with masts and sails, awnings fore and aft to shelter passengers, the engine and boiler amidships, and a single funnel emitting clouds of smoke and sparks, of which the latter, cast off by dry pine wood fuel, created breath-taking patterns at night. But neither then nor later, when he was driving cattle to the city, did young Daniel have any reason to anticipate involvement, other than occasionally as a passenger, with these impressive fire-breathing boats.

Yet New York City, where he resided as of 1830, was all but predestined to a dominant role in the steamboat's evolution. Its large, protected harbor, with adjacent sheltered waterways leading toward Philadelphia and Boston, and the deep, navigable channel of the Hudson stretching far north into the interior, where it connected with routes to Canada and the West—everything, in short, about the city's geography—seemed ideal for steamboat navigation. That the city should undertake the construction and operation of steamboats with a keen sense of Yankee "go-ahead" was further encouraged by several major events. First, in 1824 and 1825 federal and state courts annulled the monopoly on state waters that the legislature had granted Fulton and Robert R. Livingston. Then, in October 1825, came the much-celebrated opening of the Erie Canal, which, by establishing a water link between the Hudson River valley and the Great Lakes, secured for the port of New York access to a vast commercial hinterland in the West. Immediately, with state waters open to everyone and commerce thriving, there had followed a wild stampede of independent steamboat operators to obtain the freight and passenger business of the river.

The passenger business had proved especially lucrative, for Americans liked to travel fast but in comfort, conditions met by neither sailing vessels nor stages. Even at the risk of boiler explosions that on occasion hurled victims from one state to another, passengers flocked to the boats, so that prodigious profits were realized by aggressive owners. To enter steamboating did not require excessive capital, since nature had provided the thoroughfares; to exploit them, a number of partners need only pool their resources to procure and operate a boat. As a result, this exciting new business lured many small capitalists wholly without experience on the water, but amply endowed with such traditional Yankee virtues as initiative, energy, and greed.

Daniel Drew was just such a man, yet his first involvement in steamboating came about by chance. In the summer of 1831 his friend Hackaliah Bailey of Westchester, whose elephant Old Bet had been instrumental in launching the American circus many years before, came to him with a business proposition to invest in Bailey's new steamboat, the *Water Witch*. That same year Bailey and Charles Davison of new London, Connecticut, had had the *Water Witch* built in New York; with Davison as master, on July 30 it had begun operating on Long Island Sound between New York and New London. Almost immediately, however, certain residents of the lower Hudson valley had invited Bailey to put his vessel on the run between New York and Peekskill. These residents were organizing a joint stock company to finance a boat on the route, for which they thought the *Water Witch* ideal.

This invitation was prompted by circumstances connected with a recent calamity. On June 7, 1831, Captain Jacob Vanderbilt's steamboat *General Jackson*, which for two years had been plying the Hudson between New York and Peekskill, had been demolished by a boiler explosion at a landing in Haverstraw Bay. The explosion killed at least seven or eight and scalded many more, but Jake Vanderbilt himself, on shore at the time of the accident, survived unscathed and moments later was said to have exclaimed, "Ain't I a lucky dog?" This remark, when reported, provoked much comment, given the wreckage and maimed bodies lying all about at the time. Furthermore, when the steamboat *Albany* passed the wreck an hour later, Vanderbilt left the wounded to hop aboard and hasten to New York, ostensibly to fetch help but more likely, it was thought, to find a replacement for his vessel, lest some other operator take over the route. When he showed up the following day with his brother Cornelius's old boat *Bellona*, the indignant citizens of Peekskill refused to let him land at the dock. Convinced that Captain Jake had long overcharged them, they and other residents of the area now concluded that he was callous as well and, in view of the accident, probably negligent to boot. Assailed in both the Albany and New York press, Jake Vanderbilt published a lengthy statement defending his vessel, his crew, and himself, while branding the lucky dog story "a base and atrocious falsehood."[1] Meanwhile, with the *General Jackson* out of service pending repairs, he asked his elder brother Cornelius to switch other boats to the route.

His former patrons, however, wanted no more of Captain Jake and his vessels, which they pelted with eggs and drove from the landings. Determined to form a company to finance a rival boat of their own, the local residents learned that their neighbor Hackaliah Bailey had a new boat that was bigger, better, and faster than the *General Jackson* or any of the boats replacing it. They urged Bailey to place the *Water Witch* on the Peekskill run, and Bailey, seeing the whole region up in arms against Jake Vanderbilt, recognized a unique opportunity. He in turn asked Daniel Drew, installed for over a year at the Bull's Head, if he cared to participate. Since Bailey lived in the Westchester township of Mount Pleasant, he was probably looking for an on-the-spot co-owner who could manage the boat's daily operations. Drew seemed ideal for the job, all the more so since he surely knew the Peekskill run from his numerous trips between New York and Carmel, and since, as an ex-drover, he was well known to the Putnam and Westchester residents whom the line would serve. About the steamboat business itself, to be sure, Drew knew even less than he had about tavern-keeping when he began at the Bull's Head, but this did not hold him back. Having a keen nose for profits and excitement, he accepted Bailey's offer and invested a thousand dollars in the *Water Witch*. The lower Hudson valley citizens' revolt against a cruel and wicked monopoly had found its hero, or at least its agent.

The new vessel of which Drew was now part owner was enrolled at the New York Custom House (as required by federal law) at 134 feet in length and 207 tons, substantial dimensions for its time. In appearance it was a typical Eastern river boat, a shallow-drafted, long, narrow vessel adapted to sheltered waterways, with a large low-pressure engine and sidewheels, built for speed. If its arrangements were typical, they included in the hold a gentlemen's cabin that doubled as a dining room; toward the stern on the main deck above, a ladies' cabin; and over that, a promenade deck exposed on all sides, either open above or roofed with an awning. Forward amidships sat the boxlike pilot house, behind which, flanked on either side by the rounded housings of the paddle wheels, loomed the iron walking beam, and somewhat farther astern, the two towering funnels. Long hailed as floating palaces, such vessels were miracles of technology, sleek aristocrats beside whom their freight-laden, clumsy Western cousins, the river boats of the Ohio and Mississippi valleys, looked like wedding cakes mounted on scows. At the sight of such engineering triumphs, foreigners who deprecated Yankee manners marveled unstintingly.

An advertisement in the *Evening Post* of August 12, 1831, announced that the *Water Witch* would leave the foot of Warren Street at 7:00 A.M. daily for Sing Sing and Peekskill, touching at all the intermediate landings, and then return the same day, leaving Peekskill at 1:00 P.M. "No pains will be spared," the public was informed, "to render every accommodation to the travelling community on this rout [*sic*] with the hope to merit their patronage." At the sight of his first vessel in actual operation, with its decks stacked with wood, its funnels belching smoke, the walking beam oscillating, and the paddle wheels churning, Drew must have felt a special thrill of ownership. No longer just a cattleman, he was launched in steamboating, a career that he was to pursue all his life.

And he was launched in a fight as well. Leaving New York daily for Peekskill, and Peekskill for New York, at the same time as the *Water Witch* was the steamboat *Flushing*, owned and operated by Captain Curtis Peck of Flushing, Long Island. The *Flushing* had been on the route for over a month, chartered by Cornelius Vanderbilt until his own *Cinderella*, being built in New York that year, could be completed and placed on the run. Certainly the Vanderbilt brothers had no intention of forfeiting the route to outsiders, and just as certainly Daniel Drew, the *Water Witch's* managing owner, was determined to make them do precisely that. When Drew scheduled his boat to depart at the same time as the *Flushing*, he issued the most blatant of challenges. A rate war resulted, pitting him against Cornelius Vanderbilt in the first fight between two men who would be friends and enemies, allies and rivals over the next forty-six years.

Three years Drew's senior, Cornelius Vanderbilt had been born on Staten Island, the son of a plodding farmer of Dutch descent and a shrewd Yankee mother. A husky, self-reliant youth, at the age of sixteen he had acquired his own periauger—a flat-bottomed little two-masted sailing vessel—with which he initiated a highly successful ferry service to the city. Over the next few years he became the ablest boatman in the harbor, adroit, hard-working, combative—he liked to "wrastle"—and renowned equally for rough language and a physical courage exhibited in several daring rescues at sea. In 1818, convinced that "b'ilers" had it over sails, he sold his sailing vessels and went to work for Thomas Gibbons, the independent New Jersey steamboat operator who was then at war with the Fulton-Livingston monopoly. Regularly over the next several years, in open violation of the laws of New York State, Vanderbilt brought Gibbons's steamboats over to New York, where by one trick or another he almost always eluded the constables sent to arrest him. After Gibbons's victory in the United States Supreme Court in 1824, ending the monopoly on interstate waters, Vanderbilt started a steamboat line of his own in New Jersey, engaging in cutthroat competition with the Stevens family of Hoboken, who in desperation bought him off the route. Anxious to get a foothold on the Hudson, he was determined to keep the Peekskill route for his brother and himself. Especially himself, one suspects. Given the state of public opinion, he surely advised Jake to transfer his talents to Long Island Sound.

During the ensuing rate war Cornele Vanderbilt often met Drew on the docks. Outwardly the two could not have differed more. The blue-eyed, square-jawed Vanderbilt was tall, handsome, erect, striking in speech and manner, and richly profane—a big-boned, rangy fellow with great physical presence and an air of potency. In rapid succession he fathered nine daughters and four sons with his wife Sophia, exhausting her in the process, and he still had libido to expend on other women. Drew on the other hand, although tall as well, gave no hints of such presence or prowess. A quiet, thin-voiced man with dark hair and a dark complexion, and perhaps already traces of the pinched face of his later years, he was plain at best, low-keyed, and reserved, as devious, discreet, and unobtrusive (surely he had never "wrastled") as his opponent was direct, forthright, and bold. Quickly they sized each other up. Although it was said of Vanderbilt that he could measure a man from his crown to his toes by looking at him, in Drew's case he made a mistake. A veteran of over twenty years on the water, Vanderbilt simply could not conceive that this cattle-driving, tavern-keeping landlubber knew what he was about. Repeatedly he told Drew on the dock, "You have no business in this trade. You don't understand it and you can't succeed!"[2]

Daniel Drew was not used to being informed that he could not succeed; it nettled him. If this crusty, big-limbed wharf rat wanted a fight, he would give it to him. Relentlessly, he slashed the rates on the *Water Witch*, forcing his opponent to match them, till by October both boats were carrying passengers at twelve and one-half cents a head. Meanwhile Drew and his partners, depicting the Vanderbilts as outsiders, monopolists, and rate gougers, exploited local loyalties for all they were worth. A *Water Witch* ad in the *Morning Courier and New-York Enquirer* of October 4, 1831, announced that the vessel was now being operated by the newly organized Westchester and Putnam County Steam Boat Company, a joint stock company owned chiefly by the inhabitants of Westchester, Putnam, and Rockland counties. In the same ad the *Water Witch's* management promised in the name of safety never to race the other boat (the *General Jackson* explosion had made the public wary), and they pledged themselves to a maximum rate of only fifty cents, while warning that if they failed to get public support, travelers would be charged exorbitant rates and forced to travel in small and unsafe boats. (It goes without saying that Vanderbilt's *Cinderella*, which had appeared on the run in September, was of smaller dimensions than the *Water Witch*.)

The campaign was a stunning success. With the entire lower Hudson valley rallying behind the antimonopolists, the *Water Witch* carried from three hundred to six hundred passengers a day and was welcomed by tumultuous, cheering crowds at every landing. The *Cinderella*, on the other hand, carried only twenty or thirty, and at times only a solitary patron who hid from the hostile gaze of the locals; at best, its master encountered sullen resentment at the wharves and sometimes, when a rope was cast ashore to make fast, not a single hand that would take it. Vanderbilt, faced with daily receipts as low as twelve and one-half cents, knew he had been bested, but even so resolved to stick it out. Grudgingly, he had to concede that the cattle drover had a head for business and, like himself, a fair amount of obstinacy. When he met Drew now on the docks, although he might joke a bit about Drew's inexperience in steamboats, he quickly turned serious and put it to him straight: since the rate war was ruinous to both of them, in the name of good sense alone, Drew ought to abandon the route. But Drew refused.

The *Water Witch* ran to the very end of the season, until ice blocked the river in December. Its last advertisement, in the *Evening Post* of December 16, 1831, announced that it had discontinued service for the winter, but would resume it at the opening of navigation, refitted for improved accommodations and speed. The evil monopoly had been trounced, and Daniel Drew was a hero. Exultant, the *Water Witch's* patrons looked forward to another season of cheap, safe, and speedy transportation.

In early March of 1832, however, when service between Peekskill and New York resumed, to the patrons' astonishment it was the *Cinderella* that provided it, and at the higher rate originally prevailing. With the *Water Witch* nowhere in sight, they had to give their business to the enemy. Then in April the *Water Witch* reappeared at last, but running not to Peekskill but Albany, and in the service of none other than Cornelius Vanderbilt. A few days later, when the boat reverted to the Peekskill run, it was still in Vanderbilt's service, skippered by one of his captains and charging the higher fare. The local citizens, many of whom held stock in the boat, were beside themselves with rage and dismay. What had happened?

To begin with, although it had reaped much glory, because of its low fare the *Water Witch* had ended the previous season about ten thousand dollars in debt. Sick of the enterprise, for twenty thousand dollars Hackaliah Bailey sold his interest in the boat to Daniel Drew and four other New Yorkers; Charles Davison likewise sold out and returned to operations on the sound. The stockholders of the company then entrusted Drew and James Smith, a New York shipmaster, with the vessel's management, whereupon, at either his initiative or their own, Drew and Smith secretly opened negotiations with Vanderbilt. Cornelius too was weary of battle, and so he embraced the solution that the Stevenses had adopted when dealing with him in New Jersey: to buy the enemy off. He proposed that Drew and Smith leave the route, in effect, that they abandon the battlefield at the very moment of victory, betraying honor and consistency, and the trust invested in them by the citizens of three counties, all for the mere sake of money, to which Drew and Smith, without consulting or even informing the shareholders, agreed. Furthermore, so attuned now were they to Vanderbilt's desires, that as controlling managers they even placed their boat at his disposal, under which arrangement it ran first to Albany, then to Peekskill, and later on other routes in New Jersey.

Although in early steamboating quick shifts of alliance among operators were probably more the rule than the exception, this about-face (not to say double cross) by Drew and Smith was a prime bit of rascality, an early foreshadowing of Uncle Daniel's wiles on Wall Street. An astute, cool-headed businessman, Drew had weighed the advantages of alliance with his enemy against loyalty to the stockholders and found the latter sadly deficient. More than that, he was probably a bit dazzled by Vanderbilt, humbly born and illiterate like himself, but a comer if there ever was one, in the splendor of whose ruthless ego mere ordinary mortals— one's fellow shareholders, for instance—paled to irrelevance. To encounter such a fellow was stimulating; to walk in step with him, inspiring. All his life Drew, even while bucking and beguiling him, would see in Vanderbilt a man to admire and emulate.

In dumping his allies for Vanderbilt, Daniel Drew gave proof of the peculiarly Yankee quality of "smartness." Almost universally admired throughout America (with the notable exception of pulpits), "smartness" was shrewdness in business pushed to, and often a good bit beyond, the limits of legality and honesty. It was evidenced by all Yankee peddlers and "hoss" traders; by almost any drover dickering with a farmer, or any butcher dickering with a drover; by capitalists, promoters, lawyers, showmen, and thieves. When Mrs. Trollope complained to her hotel waiter in New York of being overcharged by a hackman, but admitted that she had failed to make a bargain in advance, she was told with a triumphant look, "Then I expect the Yankee has been too smart for you."[3] And when Charles Dickens, visiting America in 1842, asked time and again why certain men known to be "dishonourable, debased, and profligate" were tolerated and abetted by the citizens, he was always told, "Well, sir, he is a smart man."[4] In evangelized, church-going America, smartness was an essential weekday trait geared to the twin imperatives of go-ahead and get-more. It led easily from sharp practice to chicanery; in Drew's case, from the bluff and cajolery of a cattle dicker to unequivocal deceit and betrayal. From this time forth, Daniel Drew showed evidence of being a very smart man.

This perception afforded little solace to the minority owners of the *Water Witch*, who protested vehemently and threatened legal action. Few of them, however, owned more than a hundred dollars' worth of stock, and since Drew and Smith had functioned legally as managers, there was little the protesters could do but sell their shares at a great loss to the Vanderbilts. No doubt they cursed Drew as well, but he shrugged it off. After all, the soreheads were mostly from over near the river, which was not even his end of the county! As for the *Water Witch*, over the next few years it plied various routes, especially between New York and Hartford, where with Jake Vanderbilt as captain it acquired a great reputation for speed. Drew remained part owner until 1836, when Cornelius Vanderbilt at last bought him out.

So ended Drew's first venture into steamboating, so instructive for all concerned. Hackaliah Bailey learned that steamboats are more complicated than elephants; Cornelius Vanderbilt, that Daniel Drew of the Bull's Head was "smart" enough to take a large bite out of him; Drew, that Vanderbilt was a worthy foe and even worthier ally; and numerous residents of the lower Hudson valley, what happens to small fry when the big fish get together. It had been a splendid start for Daniel on the Hudson, so he decided to expand his operations.

Even while competing on the Peekskill run, Drew and Vanderbilt must have had an eye on the most lucrative route of all, the run 145 miles up the Hudson to the state capital of Albany, and five miles farther to Troy, Albany's arch rival, at the head of navigation. This was a much-traveled route with stage connections for Canada and the West, for which the biggest operators and the finest boats were contending. Under the original Fulton-Livingston monopoly, the fare to Albany had been fixed at five dollars, but after the monopoly's dissolution intense competition had driven it down to one dollar, to fifty cents, and even to twenty-five cents, although meals were extra and the price of drinks at the bar might soar.

Prominent among the Hudson River operators were Robert L. and James Stevens of Hoboken, whose father John Stevens had built the second successful steamboat in America. Well on their way to dominating the New York-Philadelphia traffic through their control of the Camden & Amboy Railroad in New Jersey, the Stevenses were powerful on the Hudson as well, especially Robert, a brilliant marine engineer whose technical innovations had revolutionized the Eastern river boat. Having bought Vanderbilt off in New Jersey, the Stevenses could hardly have been pleased when, in the spring of 1832, he began competing with them on the Hudson as well, sending first the *Water Witch* and then his new boat the *Westchester* to Albany, until an outbreak of cholera so deterred people from traveling that he had to withdraw his vessels.

By October 1832 the chief operators on the Hudson had come to realize the disastrous effects of racing and rivalry. Therefore, after a bit of preliminary bickering, they agreed to cease competition and form a monopoly, the Hudson River Steamboat Association, which thereafter ran both day and night boats to Albany and Troy at a fixed fare of three dollars. Each owner managed his own boats independently, but the profits were pooled; when the expenses of all the boats had been deducted, the remainder was divided proportionally. Unlike the original Fulton-Livingston monopoly, this arrangement had no official backing from the state; it was simply a private agreement. Still, throughout 1833 it worked smoothly since fewer boats, each carrying more passengers at a higher rate, meant bigger profits for everyone. Having brought peace and order to the river and a fortune to themselves, the members could sit back and enjoy their snug arrangement.

But not for long. It was later said, and rightly, of Cornelius Vanderbilt that in his younger days he would buck against anyone with wealth and power to divide, and where his newfound ally led the way, Daniel Drew was quick to follow. This time, in attacking the Stevenses and their associates, Vanderbilt probably had a special ax to grind, because in October 1833, while traveling on their Camden & Amboy Railroad, he had almost been killed in an accident, sustaining painful injuries that required months to heal and that would affect him all his life. As for Drew, no such personal animus goaded him; he just wanted a bit of the action. But to get it he would have to be patient, since when Cornele Vanderbilt set his mind to something, it behooved his friends to help him if he asked for it, but otherwise to keep out of the way. While doing so, of course, one could watch Cornele and pick up some pointers.

The assault began quietly in March and April 1834 when the *Westchester*, now sold by Vanderbilt to three men in Connecticut, ran again to Albany as a day boat, charging a fare of two dollars. Although he later denied it, the boat may have been chartered back secretly to Vanderbilt, so he could test the route's profitability and the monopoly's reaction without risk of reprisal on his other routes. Then, in July of that year, Drew entered the picture. Quietly teaming up with the boat's master, Capt. Alanson P. St. John of Connecticut, and with several other men, he arranged to run the *Westchester* to Albany in opposition to the Hudson River Steamboat Association, a venture undertaken certainly with Vanderbilt's knowledge and blessing and probably with his connivence as well, since Cornelius may have wanted a stalking-horse again. Running to Albany three times a week at a fare of two dollars, the *Westchester* soon slashed its fare to one dollar, compelling the association to cut theirs to two.

With the *Westchester* hurting them again, the association members speculated as to who was behind it. That fellow Vanderbilt had owned and operated the boat in the past, surely it was he. They accused him of it to his face, but Vanderbilt denied it. Him? Certainly not. Why, he wanted no contest with anyone! Unconvinced, the monopoly sent the steamboat *Citizen* to compete with Vanderbilt on the Peekskill run, whereupon Vanderbilt reacted with a bang. On August 27, 1834, the *Morning Courier* announced a new People's Line by day to Albany, with a fare of one dollar, consisting of the steamboats *Nimrod* and *Champion*, which Vanderbilt had fetched from the sound. Three days later, on the first page of the *Evening Post*, "C. VanDerbilt" (helped by some clerk, since he was no more literate than Drew) addressed a stirring appeal to the public. Because the "aristocratic" monopoly had "wantonly" attacked him, he explained, in self-defense he had organized an independent line to Albany. The North River belonged to everyone, not just to the monopolists; let the public support him, a lone individual, against this "gigantic combination."

Never had the chords of outraged innocence and lonely heroism been made to vibrate so nobly and adroitly. With this resonant appeal—echoing the rhetoric of President Jackson himself, then at war with another alleged citadel of privilege, the Bank of the United States—Cornelius Vanderbilt launched a full-scale attack on the monopoly. And the moment he did so, bringing his *Champion* and *Nimrod* to the Hudson, the *Westchester* was whisked away to a minor run to Glen Cove on Long Island Sound, while St. John became the captain of the *Nimrod*, which was a strange coincidence, unless Daniel Drew was working hand in glove with Vanderbilt. All of which, given Vanderbilt's denial of any interest in the *Westchester*—he had even published a sworn affidavit—would seem to make him a liar. (In his later years, when he deemed it to his interest in business, Cornelius not only lied but told whoppers.) And if Drew deftly stepped to one side, it was not out of great love for Cornele, but because Cornele had made him see that, financially or otherwise, to do so was in his own interest.

The remainder of the season was a lively one. Writing in his diary of a trip on the association's boat *Champlain* when it raced the *Nimrod*, Philip Hone, the aristocratic ex-mayor of New York, complained that debarking passengers and their luggage were "pitched ashore like bundles of hay." He would rather, he insisted, spend three or four days en route to Albany on a sloop than "be made to fly in fear and trembling, subject to every sort of discomfort, with my life at the mercy of a set of fellows whose only object is to drive their competitors off the river."[5] Far from being driven off the river, however, by late October Vanderbilt had fetched the *Westchester* back from the sound—he only had to whistle to get it—and teamed it up with his *Union* to establish a daily night line as well. Charging a fare of only fifty cents, he challenged the monopoly both by day and by night, until winter ice put an end to navigation in December.

Bruised by such relentless competition, the "gigantic combination" determined to buy Vanderbilt off, finally agreeing to pay a reported $100,000 plus $5,000 annually, in return for which Vanderbilt promised to leave the Hudson for a decade. That the heroic Cornelius's antimonopolist zeal should deflate so suddenly shows exactly what it was worth. And that the association should pay this astonishing price shows both how profitable the Albany run was, and how desperate they were to be rid of him. Pay it they did, and with Vanderbilt's energies deflected toward the sound and with the Albany fare restored to three dollars, once again the Hudson River Steamboat Association settled back to enjoy their tidy arrangement.

In mid-March, however, even before navigation had resumed to Albany, their old nemesis was back. The steamboat *Westchester*, under Captain St. John and charging one dollar, announced that it would run as a day boat to Albany or as far as the ice would permit. One can imagine the association's rage. They had paid a high price to be rid of that damned rascal Vanderbilt. How dare he break his word? But it was not Vanderbilt, it was Drew. Having waited all this time in the wings, now at last he wanted a crack at the monopoly, too. At the end of the previous season, when its Connecticut owners offered the *Westchester* for sale, Drew and several others had bought it in order to launch an opposition line of their own. As the smartest and most aggressive of the group, Drew was the leader from the start. His associates included the boat's master, St. John, and probably two men from Carmel, New York—Eli Kelley, an enterprising farmer, and James Raymond, a successful menagerie operator who owned real estate in the city. If 1834 had been Vanderbilt's year to shake up (or shake down) the monopoly, these men were determined that 1835 would be theirs.

It was. Running to Albany at a fare of one dollar three times a week, the *Westchester* proved so successful that by summer the partners had resolved to put on a second boat in order to offer service daily. But in New York City, probably because of the monopoly's heavy hand, there was no boat to be had. They consulted Vanderbilt. "The *Emerald* is running from Philadelphia to Wilmington," he told them, "you can buy her."[6] An old boat recently rebuilt, the *Emerald* belonged to a former partner of Vanderbilt's on the Delaware. Drew hastened to Philadelphia in July, bought the *Emerald* for twenty-six thousand dollars, enrolled it with himself as owner, and brought it back to New York. With antimonopolism still radiating fiercely from the White House, Drew and his partners adopted the name of the People's Line—so American, so democratic—which had not originated with Vanderbilt, but had been used earlier by others in New Jersey. Under this name, the new line was announced in the *Commercial Advertiser* of July 21, 1835. The announcement lacked the fanfare of Vanderbilt's just one year before, but behind it lay a cool determination: Daniel Drew had come to the Hudson to stay.

Over the months and years that followed, Drew and the monopoly fought it out through the bitterest of rate wars. All up and down the river, runners selling tickets solicited travelers boisterously on the piers, praising their employer's steamboats while decrying those of the rival line, whose boilers, they liked to tell nervous ladies, were anything but safe. Yet when a steamboat approached, no passenger at an intermediate point dared assume there would be contact between the vessel and the landing, or even between the vessel and himself. If the boat was racing it often shot right past, or failing that, executed a "landing on the fly." This was a maneuver whereby it lowered a small boat that, joined to it by a rope, was propelled by the vessel's momentum to the dock, where the boat hastily discharged and took on passengers, then was drawn back alongside the steamboat by a windlass on the steamboat's deck, the vessel having lost little time in the process. Quite legally, fly landings were performed even at night, at considerable risk to the passengers.

Like most steamboat owners, Drew probably condoned such practices, just as he condoned the racing that was in his captains' blood. After all, the first boat to the landing got the passengers. With this in mind, in August 1836 he put a new boat on the Albany run, the *Rochester*, which he and Eli Kelley had had specially built in order to eclipse all other boats on the river. Repeatedly it raced the association's new boat *Swallow* in contests that aroused keen excitement. The rivalry was climaxed by a special nonstop race without passengers on November 8, 1836, which the *Rochester* won by five minutes, a victory whose legitimacy the *Swallow*'s backers heatedly denied. Never had there been such intense competition on the river; Drew relished it.

But the Hudson River Steamboat Association did not. Basically, what its members wanted most were profits, peace, and stability, whereas this venturesome cattle drover yearned for a fight and excitement. He had sunk his teeth deep in their hide, and there seemed no way to make him let go. Or was there? Wearily, desperately, they swallowed their pride and invited him to join the association, whose profits he would then share proportionally. But would this arch antimonopolist, who had named his line the People's Line, forsake his principles for money? Absolutely. When the price they named was right, he was delighted to pocket their money and put the rate back up to three dollars. While the public complained but resigned itself, Drew gloated. A steamboat upstart from nowhere, he had forced himself on the mighty and now was one of them.

What did it cost the association to maintain the three-dollar fare? In its issue of May 3, 1839, James Gordon Bennett's *New York Herald* tried to get at the truth. If numerous steamboats lay idle at the wharves and their captains lounged about the city contentedly, while the monopoly ran only a few of its own boats to Albany, overcrowded and ill-serviced, at three dollars a head, it was because of massive payoffs. These allegedly included a bonus of $100,000 to Vanderbilt plus $5,000 annually; $50,000 to the People's Line plus $10,000 annually; and other sums to other boats, totaling in all $250,000 in bonuses plus $50,000 in yearly payments. These figures indicate how immensely profitable an undisturbed monopoly could be. Of course the People's Line had not suspended operations, but the sums cited may indicate the price exacted, at a given time, for "limiting" its efforts.

Having let him join the club and having bribed him, the association members naturally assumed that they had got rid of Drew at last. This was naive: one never got rid of Daniel Drew. A story was later told how Drew, having joined the monopoly, put an opposition boat on the route under the alleged ownership of the captain's brother. At a meeting, the association decided to buy the boat off and sent Drew to deal with the owner. Drew walked around the block, then came back and reported that the owner's price was $8,000. The others agreed, so Drew walked around the block once again and returned to announce the offer had been taken. He pocketed the $8,000 and his colleagues were never the wiser. It is a good story, unverified but not implausible. One thing is clear: when you bought Vanderbilt off, he stayed off, but with Drew, you could never be certain.

Purchases, alliances, payoffs—nothing had availed the Hudson River Steamboat Association in its attempt to eliminate or control competition. By the late 1830s the association was beginning to disintegrate, whereas Daniel Drew, running the *Rochester* and the new *Utica* to Albany with a connecting boat to Troy, was getting stronger and more self-confident. In point of fact, the association members were neither rich, smart, bold, nor mean enough to dominate the river. If in the decade that followed, when rivalry on the Hudson achieved climactic intensity, Drew emerged from the struggle triumphant, and in the process revolutionized Hudson River steamboating, it was because he had allied himself with one of the shrewdest, toughest men on the river: Isaac Newton.

CHAPTER 5

Top Dog on the River

A native of Rensselaer County, New York, just across the Hudson from Albany, Isaac Newton had been named for the great English physicist but ever since the age of thirteen, when he had witnessed the first trip of Fulton's *Clermont* up the river, he had shown a marked interest not in physics but in steamboats. Newton began his career as a sloop captain, but in 1826, seeing the opportunities created by the completion of the Erie Canal, he joined with others to form the first company operating steam towboats on the Hudson, and within a year's time he established himself in New York City as the agent of the Albany and New York Line of Towboats. A gifted ship designer, he supervised the construction of dozens of sloops and barges and then of passenger steamboats, which by the late 1830s were his chief concern. By then, too, in recognition of his mounting reputation, he had been admitted to the Hudson River Steamboat Association.

As as experienced river man Newton was smart, practical, opinionated, and aggressive. In the spring of 1840 the opposition boat *Napoleon*, a small, ill-furnished vessel skippered by its pugnacious owner, Joseph W. Hancox, challenged Drew's line and the association on the Albany run, forcing the rate down to one dollar. The struggle engendered much bitterness, with mutual charges of berth stealing and harassment. Hancox flooded the papers with antimonopolist tirades, and in moments of confrontation on the waterfront, he flourished a pistol. Hancox was that rarest of independents, a man who could not be bought off. So Newton, as part owner of the association's boat *De Witt Clinton*, proposed a practical demonstration of the simplest way to eliminate a rival.

45

Late on the afternoon of Saturday, June 13—within full view of spectators who lined the waterfront, drawn there by rumors of an impending incident—Isaac Newton watched and waited as the *Napoleon*, laden with passengers, left its dock and headed up the river. Then, when Hancox's boat came abreast of the *De Witt Clinton's* berth, Newton had the *De Witt Clinton*, its steam up, break away from the dock and head straight for the other boat. Hancox signaled the *De Witt Clinton* frantically and when it still bore down, whipped out his revolver and fired three shots at the other boat's pilothouse, hitting no one but forcing the pilot to duck. Moments later the *De Witt Clinton* rammed the *Napoleon* aft of the pilothouse, causing it to careen violently amid the screams of passengers, after which the *Napoleon* righted itself and continued on its way. Had the 500-ton *De Witt Clinton* struck its 179-ton rival square amidships as it had evidently intended, the *Napoleon* would surely have sunk. Yet it was not the *De Witt Clinton's* captain who was arrested in Albany, but Hancox, on a warrant sworn out by the association. Pleading self-defense in the shooting, Hancox was exonerated in triumph, following which he slashed his fare to fifty cents and continued the war in the newspapers. At the time of the collision, Isaac Newton had been standing on the *De Witt Clinton's* forward deck, no doubt to oversee the operation.

Presumably it was Newton's ability to design ships, not demolish them, that led Drew to pick him as a partner. In 1840 Newton had built for himself and some associates the steamboat *North America*. Like its consort *South America*, built by him and Drew in the following year, it was an immediate success on the river. These vessels burned anthracite coal, an improvement long contemplated by operators but never before successfully applied. Hitherto, steamboats had depended for fuel on bulky and increasingly expensive pine wood, which on long runs had to be stacked on the deck, giving the departing vessel the appearance of a floating lumberyard. Freed of this burden, the Eastern river boat rapidly evolved further in size and speed, affording the public more comfort and the owners more profits. Just in time to preside over these new developments together, in the winter of 1840-41 Drew and Newton effected their alliance. It was a shrewd move for each of them because Drew was an astute money manager and Newton a brilliant ship designer; their talents meshed.

First announced in the *Commercial Advertiser* of February 25, 1841, the expanded People's Line declared its vessels unmatched in the world for speed and elegance—no idle claim, given the reputation of the *North America*, *South America*, and *Rochester*, all of which became renowned as racers. Joined by the new *Knickerbocker* in 1843, over the next few years these vessels ran as day boats or night boats to Albany in a lively drama that recurred with variations each year. First, in late February, March, or early April, there was the breakthrough to Albany, a task for the sturdiest and not the swiftest vessels, since the ice could close up again and trap the first venturers, or sink them outright, or in its dissolution carry them off downriver with pier ends and warehouses and spans of bridges on a rushing flood. Next, with the river free of ice, came a rising tempo of traffic, with the fare plummeting to fifty or twenty-five cents or a shilling if opposition boats appeared and returning to three dollars if they withdrew. Throughout the summer, a heavy schedule of both day and night boats carried hordes of travelers and excursionists, till in the autumn, slackening crowds meant fewer day boats. Finally, there were the meager schedules of December, with the last boats bumping their way through the ice, finally landing passengers at points below Albany with stage or sleigh connections, until the entire channel was blocked for the season.

Then followed the time for maintenance and refurbishing (always of great concern to the People's Line), for selling off or demoting old boats to secondary runs and later, under different owners, to the towing of canal boats, coal barges, and cattle boats. Winter was a time too for designing and acquiring better vessels, for hatching new plans, new schemes, and new alignments in a business that each year got more crowded and competitive.

The alliance of Drew and Newton was the final blow to the old Hudson River Steamboat Association, which in the early 1840s broke up at last, some members withdrawing from the Albany run or from the Hudson altogether (the Stevenses retired to the Delaware), while others allied themselves with the People's Line. Drew and Newton were now top dog on the river, and many owners flocked to join them. Their triumphant People's Line acquired new prestige and resources when on July 1, 1843, Drew, Newton, Kelley, St. John, Vanderbilt, and eighteen others organized a joint stock company named the People's Line Association to carry passengers and freight between New York, Albany, and Troy. Capitalized at $360,000, the company had its nine boats and other assets divided into 360 shares at one thousand dollars each, of which Drew and Newton were the largest holders. Three trustees and five directors were to be elected annually, the trustees to manage the company's daily affairs and declare dividends, and the directors to meet monthly to examine its operations and acquire or dispose of vessels as necessary. The agreement was to run until January 1, 1849, at which time the association, unless a majority interest voted to continue it, was to be dissolved, its boats and property sold at public auction, and the proceeds divided proportionately among the shareholders.

This new organization of the People's Line suited Drew and Newton to a T. Never before had they controlled such abundant resources, both money and boats. At the same time they eliminated potential rivals, since now it would be against their own interest for shareholders to compete with Drew and Newton on the river. And since nobody was as inventive as Newton at the drawing board, as deft as Drew with money, or as decisive as the two of them in action, they ran the whole operation from the start. Reelected year after year as two of the three trustees and five directors, they made the decisions, negotiated deals, secured alliances, and invariably got what they wanted from their fellow managers and the stockholders. And as the People's Line prospered, still more operators became allied with it. First, it was joined by the Troy and New York Steamboat Association, which had once been allied with the old monopoly. Then, in 1845, many steamboat men from Albany bought into the association directly, most of them acquiring stock from Drew, who in selling it relinquished personal control of the company, a move that he would later regret.

Having supplanted the old association on the river, Drew found himself, with Newton, decried in turn as a monopolist and as such plagued by opposition boats. Some of these could be readily bought off and others not, these last being operated by such perennial upstarts as Hancox. In coping with rivals, however, Drew and Newton fared better than the old monopoly, whom they far surpassed in stamina, money, and initiative. It was an age of capitalism in the raw, of free-for-all free enterprise with only a hint of regulation. Having plenty of boats and capital in reserve, Drew and Newton could counter each opposition vessel with one of their own, offering the same schedule and fare. Furious rate wars resulted, with fares at times fluctuating daily to the vast confusion of the public who, when expecting Tuesday's fare of fifty cents, might find on Wednesday, when no rival boat was running, that they had to pay a dollar. On one occasion the opposition vessel *Belle*, finding her berth stolen by a boat of the People's Line, retaliated by carrying passengers to Albany free, a response that not even Drew and Newton could top.

Racing too continued unabated, even after the loss of the *Swallow*, then two-thirds owned by the People's Line, when it ran aground in 1845 while contending with two other boats and sank with a loss of fifteen lives. Certain owners played the game for all it was worth, staging special contests like that of June 1, 1847, when Vanderbilt pitted his luxurious new *C. Vanderbilt* against the speedy *Oregon* of his pugnacious rival George Law, a canal construction contractor turned banker and railroad man, who was branching out into steamboats as well. During the race on the Hudson, Vanderbilt in his excitement seized the wheel from the pilot and mismaneuvered his vessel, while Law, out of fuel, hurled furniture and costly fittings into the furnaces and so sailed on to win.

Such passion was beyond Daniel Drew, who first and foremost was a schemer, a calculator. He never knew the gut feeling of a river man, the skipper's fervent identification with his vessel, his assurance that it was the best damn boat on the river and he'd race anyone fool enough to doubt it. One cannot imagine Drew planting himself on a forward deck just prior to a planned collision. As for hurling sofas into a furnace during a race, why good heavens, those things cost money!

But if Drew himself never raced, his captains did, and with risk. During many seasons vessels of the People's Line had to be withdrawn for repairs, following machinery breakdowns and damage to their hulls from collisions. Such casualties were inevitable, for the racing urge impelled captains to leave before their scheduled departures, to skip landings, to subject passengers to "fly" landings, and to keep a supply of fireworks handy in order to blazon every victory in the sky. At the same time pilots crowded rivals onto shoals, and engineers, to force the last ounce of speed from their engines, tied down safety valves and plugged steam gauges, so that they had no idea what pressure their panting boilers carried, and the lives of all were endangered.

What did Drew reply when protesting letters appeared in the newspapers and when editorialists decried these practices? Nothing: he was just the money man. And what did Newton reply? Surely, that the People's Line boats were the best and therefore the safest on the river (true enough); that the line had never lost a passenger to date (also true); and that it considered safety a prime concern, although it was also aware that its patrons wanted to reach their destination fast. All of this the captains knew how to interpret. Discreetly then, like most owners, Drew and Newton winked at a lot. After all, if you could not buy a rival boat or its owner, or charter it and send it to the Delaware— policies on which they routinely spent vast sums—little remained but to steal its berth and its passengers, to race it, to crowd it, and to smash it. Having muscled their way to the top of the heap, they were not about to be pushed off again like that poor old tired association. So let their enemies watch out.

Yet there were defter ways to compete, and they knew it. Since freight on the Hudson was still relegated to sloops and towboats, it was passengers they needed to attract. From the very start, Hudson River steamboats had done this through luxurious appointments that foreign visitors had never failed to praise. Although Drew and Newton were country boys who had evolved by way of the freight barge and the cattle yard, they grasped how the key to success in Hudson River steamboating was luxury; how, rivaling their lust for speed, nothing so possessed their democratic countrymen as the longing for regal elegance—the craving of egalitarian, homespun America for palatial opulence such as few citizens could afford in their private lives, but that they might hire briefly for the price of a hotel room ("palace" hotels were becoming all the rage) or of a steamboat ticket. Very well, then, if the public wanted luxury, luxury they would have, with a vengeance. To achieve it, in the mid-1840s the managers of the People's Line undertook to construct a series of vessels that would truly merit the already hackneyed term *floating palace* like no previous craft. To this end they marshaled the skills and resources of the superb East River and Brooklyn shipyards for the hulls, the great iron works of the metropolis for the engines, and for the rest, the massed talents of the carpenters, plumbers, painters, gas fitters, upholsterers, furniture and glass makers, and provisioners—not to mention journalists—of New York City.

In October 1845 they opened the first of these marvels to the press and public, the mammoth *Hendrik Hudson*, officially enrolled at 330 feet in length and 1,186 tons.[1] A night boat, this new giant was advertised as having berths for 620 people and other accommodations for 2,000. (This latter was a fanciful figure, since practitioners of go-ahead were not above inflating their statistics.) When the public flocked aboard to inspect it, a *Tribune* reporter, surveying the illuminated interior with its grand saloons flanked by staterooms, likened it to Cleopatra's royal yacht at night. As the new vessel began running to Albany amid unstinted admiration, her creators could well believe they had achieved the ultimate in steamboat construction.

The ultimate, that is, for 1845. Exactly one year later, in October 1846, their second giant lay moored at the end of Liberty Street, ready for inspection. The *Isaac Newton*, registered at 322 feet (they told the newspapers 340) and 1,332 tons, had the biggest engine ever built in America, with a piston stroke of 12 feet. Although Newton had originally designed it as a day boat, Drew had objected that the summer season was too short to operate so costly a vessel. Obstinately, Newton had stuck to his plans but, as construction progressed, realized that Drew was right and therefore altered the design, finishing it as a night boat with berths for 500 and accommodations (again, as advertised) for a not wholly credible 2,000.

On October 9, 1846, when the *Isaac Newton* left its dock and headed up the river, besides six hundred passengers it carried a hundred invited guests—dignitaries, merchants, journalists—whom Newton and Drew hosted personally at a splendid supper that included turkey, chicken, woodcock, and snipe. Riding smoothly but swiftly, above West Point the vessel caught up with the smaller *Empire* and passed her, whereupon the crew fired rockets and the passengers cheered. The celebration was premature, however, since the *Empire* then regained her lead and held it all the way to Albany. Well, the People's Line managers explained, on this first trip they were not really trying to make time. Besides, the *Isaac*

Newton had been supplied, inadvertently, with the wrong kind of fuel. Genially they waved their guests on to a closer scrutiny of the interior: the white and gold ladies' saloon with curtains of French satin damask; the main or upper-deck saloon with a stained-glass dome overhead; and the superb staterooms, including one with a bed in the form of a chariot and another, the Bridal Room, with carpeting said to be from the drawing room of King Louis-Philippe of France, and over the bed a painted altarpiece featuring a cupid holding two doves over an altar, which a spellbound *Tribune* journalist hailed as "one of the most splendid achievements of taste."[2]

Could such taste be topped, such magnificence exceeded? In the go-ahead age, if one had eclipsed all others, what remained but to eclipse oneself? In June 1849 the day boat *New World* appeared. Her stated overall length of 382 feet caused her to be hailed as the longest and largest river steamboat ever built, and her engine's enormous piston stroke of 15 feet would for a river boat never be equaled. Visitors treading deliciously on thick carpets were invited to take note of satin damask chairs, marble tables from Italy, Corinthian pillars, and real oil paintings on the walls; to marvel at how steam from the engines was made to pass beneath the pantry stands, so that all the dishes would reach the table piping hot; and to applaud the new arrangement whereby passsengers would be served at small tables on the European plan, each party ordering separately, and not at the long tables where diners had hitherto been obliged to feed together. (On the line's night boats, also in imitation of the European style, private staterooms now replaced the communal sleeping saloons that had previously accommodated gentlemen on one deck and ladies on another.)

The *New World* was a stunning success, a "magnificent aquatic movable hotel," proclaimed the *Tribune*. On its first trip up the river on June 12 it was saluted on land and water the full length of its run, and then greeted in Albany by twenty thousand people thronging boats and wharves, who waved handkerchiefs and cheered while bells tolled and cannon boomed. For his improvements in steamboats, prophesied the *Herald*, Isaac Newton's fame would equal that of the great scientist whose name he bore.

Such were the plaudits garnered by the two masterminds of the People's Line for having given Everyman his palace, marrying Old World elegance to New World ingenuity in an ornate mishmash of styles. To experience these wonders, the paying public flocked aboard the "aquatic movable hotels" of the People's Line eight hundred, nine hundred, or a thousand at a time, until on September 4, 1850, when a state fair was luring unprecedented multitudes to Albany, the giant *New World* on a single trip broke all records by carrying an astonishing twelve hundred passengers. Grandiose was the vision, abundant the recompense—the profits of the People's Line soared.

But not the dividends. So costly had been the new boats' construction that since September 1844 not a penny had been paid to the shareholders. Indeed, by September 1845 the company, burdened with the building costs of the just completed *Hendrik Hudson* and the unfinished *Isaac Newton*, was close to a financial crisis, resolved only through a loan from Cornelius Vanderbilt, who imposed the condition that the company buy back his stock. Thereafter, however, with the *Hendrik Hudson* and the *Isaac Newton* in service, bringing in ample earnings, there was still no hint of dividends.

All of which must have struck Abraham Van Santvoord of Albany, a veteran of the Hudson River shipping and freighting business, as one hell of a way to run a company. Van Santvoord was president of the Hudson River Steamboat Company, which operated steam towboats on the river and itself paid a regular dividend. On behalf of his company, in 1845 he bought stock in the People's Line and a one-fourth interest in the *Hendrik Hudson*. By late 1847, however, he and his son Alfred, another People's Line shareholder, had become disenchanted with Drew and Newton's management. Alfred began urging other shareholders from Albany to leave the People's Line and join with him in a new line based in their own city. In early 1848 Abraham Van Santvoord, in the name of the Hudson River Steamboat Company, brought suit against the People's Line stockholders, charging that Drew and Newton, in purchasing George Law's *Oregon* for the association and converting the *Hendrik Hudson* to a day boat, had acted illegally and against his company's interest, for which two actions he demanded compensation.

Van Santvoord's lawsuit marked the beginning of dissension within the People's Line. Although the other Albanians did not rally behind the Van Santvoords, some among them—and other shareholders, too—began to wonder if the People's Line was not being run by two smart operators far more adept at lining their own pockets than at passing along profits to others. After all, these malcontents pointed out in private and in public, no dividends had been declared in over three years. Certainly not, Newton and Drew explained, for the company had always lacked the necessary nine thousand dollars surplus, as stipulated in the articles of association. Was the company then mismanaged? Not at all, the two trustees insisted: to date, it had earned over $300,000, which the managers had wisely plowed back into the business, to build and buy boats. So had the value of the company's property increased? Absolutely. To how much? Well, about $600,000.

To a small shareholder beginning to get suspicious of the management and starved for dividends, $600,000—or more, perhaps much more, since some claimed that the figure was grossly understated—sounded like a very big pie to divvy up. And if a majority interest should not vote to continue the company after its expiration date of January 1, 1849, divvying up the pie was exactly what the articles of association called for.

Drew and Newton liked the People's Line just the way it was, docile to their own good management and affording them the means to beat out competition on the river. On the other hand, a sale of the assets at public auction might bring only a fraction of their value, with the added risk that some of the finest boats on the Hudson might pass into other hands. In their view, consequently, divvying up the pie was unthinkable. However, the growing shareholder revolt caught them by surprise. In a rare lapse of judgment, Drew had sold much of his stock to the Albanians, so that he and Newton together still fell far short of controlling the company. Obviously, decisive action was called for. Rallying their allies at the annual meeting in New York on November 1, 1848, they got themselves reelected managers and had a resolution passed by a majority to continue the association for another year.

But the dissidents refused to knuckle under. Continuing their protests, they won over other stockholders and caused further meetings to be held, at which various resolutions failed for want of a majority. Finally, at a meeting on January 2, 1849, Drew, Newton, and their ally Eli Kelley came richly armed with powers of attorney and proxies—many of them contested—from absent stockholders and so obtained a vote for continuance of 224 ayes (just slightly more than a majority) versus 97 noes. Over the protests of certain members, Newton and Drew declared the matter settled and prepared for another year of operations.

But the matter was not settled, not by a long shot. On February 6, 1849, Drew was served with a summons to appear before the State Supreme Court in Albany to answer the complaint of one George Monteath, plaintiff. Also named in the summons and complaint were Newton and thirty-three other defendants, all the stockholders of the People's Line but one. The attached complaint—six very long pages of very small print—alleged that Drew and Newton had repeatedly assumed the authority of all three trustees of the company and all five directors; that they had failed to make monthly accountings or to declare dividends, so that the shareholders received nothing from the property; that in numerous transactions they had systematically defrauded the company; that although the People's Line Association had expired on January 1, 1849, they had refused to let go of its property; and more. The plaintiff, as a stockholder in the association, asked the court to name a receiver to take possession of all property of the People's Line and divide its assets among the shareholders according to their rights and interests.

Drew of course remembered George Monteath. He was a seventy-one-year-old Scottish-born Albanian who had begun his long career on the Hudson as a master and owner of sloops and had subsequently acquired a fortune as an operator of steam towboats. Along with twenty other Albanians, he had bought People's Line stock from Drew in 1845, and like many of them he had since become disillusioned with the company. Upon failing to meet a promissory note payment, Monteath had forfeited his ten shares to Drew. Through his lawyer, on January 2 Monteath had protested against the association's vote for continuance, calling it improper and illegal. Of all the dissidents it was he and he alone who had brought the action, which marked him as a determined loner, cantankerous, aggrieved, and perverse.

Clearly, the year 1849—distinguished otherwise by the appearance of the dazzling *New World* (happily, owned by Newton and not by the People's Line)—boded ill for Newton and Drew. Moreover, on February 2, the same day that Monteath signed his complaint, the Hudson River Steamboat Company, whose case against the People's Line was still in progress, asked the court to enjoin Drew, Newton, and the other "assumed" officers from using the association's boats and to name a receiver not in Monteath's case but its own, which, so Van Santvoord argued, was entitled to preference.

A fine legal donnybrook followed as Drew and Newton answered Monteath; as Van Santvoord, a defendant in Monteath's case, answered Monteath; and as Monteath, a defendant in Van Santvoord's case, answered Van Santvoord. Drew and Newton countered Monteath's charges point by point, insisting that their actions as managers had been entirely authorized and proper; that they had misappropriated no funds whatsoever, but on the contrary often used their own money in the company's behalf; that a majority of shareholders had voted twice for continuation, so that the association still existed; and that the appointment of a receiver would be destructive to the shareholders' interests.

Regarding the company's continued existence, however, the decision of the Supreme Court in Albany was prompt and unequivocal: the People's Line Association had expired of its own limitation on January 1, 1849, in consequence of which the court on March 9 named a receiver to take possession of all People's Line property and sell it at a public auction. This was a decision that should have left Drew and Newton reeling, but who was named to this stern function? None other than Eli Kelley, Drew's longtime partner and crony, it having no doubt occurred to the defendants that if there must be a receiver, they might as well have a friendly one. Surprisingly, this was agreeable to the court and the plaintiff. In April, receiver Kelley took possession of all the association's boats and other property, the sale of which, however, was postponed until December 26, 1849, so that it would fall near or after the close of navigation. In the meantime, under court orders the receiver operated the association's boats, so that the public remained unaffected. When the case came up on June 16, it was referred to a referee, before whom both this suit and the one brought by the Hudson River Steamboat Company were subsequently argued.

These proceedings were still under way when at noon of December 26, in the high-domed Merchants' Exchange on Wall Street, the entire property of the association was auctioned off, including seven steamboats, three-fourths interest in an eighth steamboat, one-half interest in three others, two barges, plus canal boats and scows; securities, unexpired leases, office fixtures, groceries, pig iron, and lumber; and the contents of two coal yards, including coal, fences, scales, tubs, and barrows. It was surely the greatest sale of a steamboat company's assets that the nation had ever seen, the whole of it bringing not $600,000 but, as the embattled managers had warned, just slightly over $330,000. For Drew and Newton, seemingly the worst had come to pass, since their beloved People's Line had been extinguished. Their toil of five years appeared to have been frustrated, and their dominance of the river wiped out.

But anyone who believed this even for a minute hardly knew the gentlemen in question. First of all, the sale was administered by a congenial receiver. Furthermore, only a few buyers turned up, prominent among them Drew himself, who on his and Newton's behalf bought the steamboats *Isaac Newton*, *Oregon*, *Columbia*, and *New Jersey*; a three-fourths interest in the *Hendrik Hudson*; a half interest in the Troy Line boats *Empire*, *Troy*, and *John Mason*; most of the association's coal; and stock in another line at half of par value. Only three steamboats escaped him. The *South America* and *Rochester* were purchased by Capt. William B. Dodge of New York, who operated a freight and passenger line between New York City and Rondout on the Hudson, while the *North America* was acquired by Alfred Van Santvoord. Moreover, not only did Drew get the lion's share, but he got it cheap. For the splendid *Isaac Newton*, built for $180,000, for instance, he paid only $127,000, and for the *Oregon*, bought by the People's Line from George Law for $100,000, only $36,000. "To them that have, shall be given, and from them that have not, shall be taken, even that which they have," observed the *Evening Post*, seeing in the whole transaction the cynical game of the steamboat sale forced upon such terms that only the largest stockholders could protect themselves.[3]

In snapping up bargains, furthermore, Drew and his partner had been not only nimble but cagey. When the *South America* and *Rochester* were enrolled a few days later at the Custom House, the owner proved to be not Capt. William B. Dodge but Daniel Drew, who, taking no chances, had employed Dodge as his agent at the auction. So only one boat really eluded Drew and Newton, the aging *North America*, purchased by Alfred Van Santvoord. Yet even this transaction may well have been sanctioned in advance, since on December 27, just one day after the sale, Drew settled with Abraham Van Santvoord, his father, buying up his company's shares in the association and its one-fourth interest in the *Hendrik Hudson* for $42,000, following which Van Santvoord dropped his case against the People's Line. So no one need weep for Drew and Newton, who acquired in their own name, and cheap, all but one of the company's boats, which they continued to operate. The joint stock company known as the People's Line Association was dead, but the People's Line went on.

As did the litigation. Its complexities were further compounded when Elijah Peck of Flushing, the third trustee of the People's Line, petitioned the court to become a co-plaintiff with George Monteath, whose charges he claimed he could prove. While receiver Kelley settled the association's debts and periodically disbursed the proceeds of the sale to the shareholders, the case dragged on, its affidavits and petitions teeming, its files thickening. At long last the referee submitted his report, following which the court announced its decision on March 18, 1851. The People's Line Association had indeed expired on January 1, 1849, but the trustees were deemed to have fully accounted for all of its property, nor had any fraud, misconduct, or bad faith been proved against Newton and Drew.

So ended the tangled case of *George Monteath* v. *Isaac Newton, Daniel Drew, and others*. George Monteath savored the satisfaction of having forced the breakup of the biggest steamboat company on the Hudson; yet for all that, having forfeited his shares to Drew, he was not one whit the richer, although his lawyer was. Rudely inconvenienced, Drew and Newton had maneuvered defeat into victory, salvaging their good name and their boats. The minority stockholders of the association received their share of the company's assets, sold for a little more than half their estimated worth, which even so left them better off than the minority stockholders of the *Water Witch* some twenty years before. All of which meant little to the public, since throughout the litigation and afterward, the gilt and damask palaces of the People's Line plied between New York and Albany as smoothly and profitably as ever. Not even a maze of lawsuits and the sale of their boats out from under them could dislodge Drew and Newton. Tough and foxy, their vessels sumptuous and their purses fat, they were still top dog on the river.

Pouring hotshot into Satan's ranks: an outdoor revival meeting of the 1820s. From an 1829 print in the Library of Congress.

Roxanna Mead Drew, from a portrait of the 1860s. Drew University Library.

The new Bull's Head Tavern at Third Avenue and Twenty-fourth Street. From Samuel Hollyer, *Old New York: Views by S. Hollyer*, 1909. U.S. History, Local History and Genealogy Division, the New York Public Library, Astor, Lenox, and Tilden Foundations.

Above, the new *Dean Richmond* passing the Jersey Palisades. From *Frank Leslie's Illustrated Newspaper*, August 12, 1865. Below, the two-tiered grand saloon of the *Drew:* splendor that no railroad could match. From Benson J. Lossing, *The American Centenary*, 1876. Jersey City Public Library.

Above, Cornelius Vanderbilt in the 1860s. Drew admired him
greatly and cheated him vastly. Below, Wall Street in the 1850s,
looking east. The massive building with columns in the background
is the Merchants' Exchange. From William Thompson Bonner,
New York, the World's Metropolis, 1623/4-1923/4, 1924. Jersey
City Public Library.

Right, Daniel Drew in the 1850s. From Wheaton J. Lane, *Commodore Vanderbilt: An Epic of the Steam Age*, © Alfred A. Knopf, Inc., 1942. Used with permission of the publisher.

Below, Jim Fisk (left) and Jay Gould (center) plan the 1869 corner in gold. At the right is Fisk's broker, William Belden. From W.W. Fowler, *Ten Years in Wall Street*, 1870. General Research Division, the New York Public Library, Astor, Lenox, and Tilden Foundations.

A March 1872 gamble that was the talk of the Street. Above, Drew contracts
to deliver 50,000 Erie at 55. Below, Erie speculators check the ticker tape
at Delmonico's in Broad Street during lunchtime. Both from *Frank Leslie's
Illustrated Newspaper*, April 13, 1872. General Research Division, the New York
Public Library, Astor, Lenox, and Tilden Foundations.

The *Daily Graphic* of April 3, 1873, thought Uncle Daniel
must be hard up for money to finance his seminary, since
his Wabash pool had ended with a loss. But it was the
pool that had a loss, not Drew. Drew University Library.

Mead Hall at Drew Theological Seminary in Madison, New Jersey. The seminary's
rustic tranquility was shattered by the founder's bankruptcy. Drew University Library.

The Clift farm near Brewster in Putnam County, New York. Here Drew recovered his physical but not financial health. From F.W. Beers, *Atlas of New York and Vicinity*, 1867.

CHAPTER 6

=|=|=|=|=|=|=|=

Wall Street

"I had been wonderfully blessed in moneymaking," said Daniel Drew later of his career. "I got to be a millionaire afore I know'd it, hardly."[1] In boosting his fortune to the million dollar mark, steamboats and cattle helped, but it was Wall Street that accomplished it. By the 1840s, when "the Street" became his preferred habitat, it already had its reputation. A *Tribune* journalist of the time hailed it as "the great purse-string of America—the key of the Union," but spoke as well of "the million deceits and degradations and hypocrisies and miseries played off there as in some ghostly farce," likening it to the valley of riches described by Sindbad the Sailor, "where millions of diamonds lay glistening like fiery snow, but which was guarded on all sides by poisonous serpents, whose bite was death and whose contact was pollution."[2]

Yet the place that inspired such rhetoric from press and pulpit was a simple and rather narrow cobblestoned street that in the early morning, when frequented by dogs and grunting pigs, for stretches still had a distinct small-town air. Beginning on the west at Broadway in front of Trinity, the city's chief Episcopal church, it ran eastward for less than half a mile to South Street and the anchored sailing vessels of the East River docks. Even in colonial times auctions of merchandise and public subscriptions for loans had been held there out of doors. Its traders had prospered as the craze for canal stocks in the 1820s and for rail stocks in the 1830s attracted vast amounts of both domestic and foreign capital. By the late 1830s Wall Street had at last edged out its rivals, Boston and above all Philadelphia, to become the foremost money center in the country, luring capitalists eager to finance new ventures and all those

57

with an urge to trade or speculate, to lend or borrow, to manage or mismanage money. That Daniel Drew should have gravitated there is not surprising. As a born money manager with an itch for action, how could he have stayed away?

Yet he came there at a most inauspicious time, close on the heels of the Panic of 1837, a devastating financial collapse that had been brought on by excessive land and cotton speculation and by the proliferation of new banks issuing quantities of worthless paper money. In New York as elsewhere, bankers and merchants failed by the hundreds, and when the banks suspended specie payment, mobs thronged Wall Street and troops had to be called out. Inevitably, stocks plunged, bank note circulation contracted, and foreign money fled back to Europe, while American investors shunned the markets, and a prolonged depression set in.

Hard hit by the panic was the country's currency, which in those days consisted not of uniform bills backed by the federal government, but of notes issued by the local banks of each of the states, subject to the latter's widely differing laws and regulations. Even under normal circumstances, such a system verged on chaos, owing to doubts about the issuers' willingness and ability to redeem their notes in coin. As a result such notes, if accepted at all in regions far removed from the issuing bank, were honored at a discount, the amount of which, fluctuating constantly and varying throughout the country, could be determined only by consulting the bank note tables in the local papers. Thoughtful financiers denounced this system, or lack of system, but it continued unreformed for years. At the height of the panic it collapsed for a while altogether, and bank notes were shunned by everyone. Even after a measure of calm returned, the notes were often viewed with distrust.

For Drew, however, a national catastrophe could be a major opportunity. All around him at the Bull's Head he had seen drovers from distant regions who in their wanderings had accumulated large amounts of uncurrent money, in the form of notes issued by obscure country banks that no one in New York would accept, even though the issuers were not necessarily verging on insolvency. Was there no way, for a price, to help these poor fellows out? By the spring of 1838, just a year after the panic had erupted, Drew joined with Edward B. St. John, a Wall Street banker and broker, to form the partnership of St. John & Drew, with offices at 53 Wall Street. As the junior partner, Drew put up only a small amount of money, but his participation assured the firm's success. Hearing that Dan Drew of the Bull's Head, who had banked for them so often in the past, was buying uncurrent money on Wall Street, cattle drovers flocked to the firm's offices to unload their notes, happy to be rid of them even at a sizable discount. St. John & Drew took in quantities of notes and held them patiently, until at last a chance came to sell them at a profit.

Countless other dealers were doing the same thing, but Drew's contacts with the drovers gave his firm an edge.

For Drew, then, it had been only a short hop from tavern-keeping to banking. Yet all did not go well. Without consulting him, his partner endorsed the extension notes of a friend, which brought the firm a loss of over thirty thousand dollars. Probably this was why the partnership was dissolved on August 30, 1839—this and the fact that, for Drew, it went against the grain to be number two in any operation. He was soon casting about for new partners, however, since not even the nation's worsening depression could keep him out of Wall Street.

Within a few months Drew had established the new banking house of Drew, Robinson & Company, which in late November 1839 moved into a basement office at 40 Wall Street, just opposite the Merchants' Exchange, where it announced that it would buy all kinds of uncurrent bank notes, certificates of deposit, and the like, and make collections in Albany, Buffalo, Detroit, and other places. As senior partner, Drew contributed his experience in banking acquired at the Bull's Head and in Wall Street, as well as most or all of the capital. His partners were Nelson Robinson and Robert Weeks Kelley, both of Putnam County, New York.

Eleven years Drew's junior, Nelson Robinson, of the township of Patterson, was a smart, vigorous self-made man without formal education and somewhat rough of manner. In his younger days he had been a cattle dealer and a speculator in wild beasts for shows. Like Drew, he had also spent some time with a circus, where he performed on horseback elegantly costumed with spangles and drove one of the wagons on the road. Drew knew him from a previous business connection, perhaps one of his Western cattle ventures, and took him as a partner even though he had no capital to contribute. This was a shrewd choice, as soon became apparent.

Drew's other associate, Robert Weeks Kelley, was the eldest son of Eli Kelley of Carmel, Drew's longtime partner in steamboating. Not yet twenty years of age, young Robert probably began as a clerk with the promise of a partnership, which he obtained within a few years. He too may have contributed little or no capital (although perhaps his father did), but he was recommended on another basis. In 1840 he married Drew's widowed daughter Catherine, following which the young couple lived for several years with Drew and his wife in their new home on Bleecker Street. Meanwhile Robert's father Eli Kelley also moved to New York and for a time had an office with the partners on Wall Street, where he worked as a broker but never became a member of the firm.

Six days a week throughout the 1840s, Daniel Drew commuted from his Bleecker Street residence to Wall Street. Sometimes he drove down in a simple one-horse chaise, dressed soberly in black and looking like a country parson, an appearance that in later years earned him the nickname of the Deacon. Often, however, he probably took a Broadway omnibus, the common public stage of the day, to be jounced downtown over rough cobblestones, getting out close by the soaring spire of Trinity Church, from which he would have headed east down Wall Street past rows of brokerage houses, insurance companies, and banks. There, just across from the dome-topped granite mass of the new Merchants' Exchange, that true symbol of the city's commercial preeminence, was the basement office of Drew, Robinson & Company, in the plain-fronted City Bank building at 40 Wall Street.

Awaiting Drew daily at his office was news to digest, decisions to make, customers to advise or console. Although he retained overall control of the firm, he left the details of the business to his partners, since an ex-drover of scanty education was hardly inclined to the minutiae of paper work. What did fire him up was moneymaking, and with this in mind he determined that Drew, Robinson & Company would also trade in stocks. To this end he got Nelson Robinson elected to the prestigious New York Stock and Exchange Board (as the New York Stock Exchange then called itself), an exclusive body of brokers holding closed sessions in a large hall of the Merchants' Exchange. Thereafter, twice daily Robinson attended the exchange's formal auctions, where the listed stocks were called out in order and seated members leaped to their feet to trade amid a frenzied babble decipherable only to the board's habitués. To this frantic scene the ex-cattleman took like a steer to pasture, becoming a sharp and aggressive trader.

With one of them a member of the Stock Exchange, Drew and his partners crossed the magic line separating "insiders" from "outsiders," that is, separating members of the brokerage community from the general public, who paid them commissions to buy and sell stock on their account. In the 1840s outsiders were conspicuous by their scarcity on Wall Street, since in the aftermath of the Panic of 1837, stricken with sanity, they had stampeded from the market. Of the chastened few who remained, many clung to sound state and federal bonds and to "solids," stable stocks that paid steady dividends, and so did little to enhance their brokers' fortunes. Happily for the latter, however, even the lackluster market of the forties drew speculators who traded heavily in "fancies," the widely fluctuating stocks of troubled companies, which offered ample opportunity for big gains and catastrophic losses.

When Daniel Drew became aware of Wall Street's fancy stocks, it was love at first sight, and the infatuation lasted all his life. Let others marry staid bonds and sober income stocks—he always chased the fancies, which promised excitement, risk, and big money. In their daily fluctuations on the market, the fancies reflected the war between the "bulls" and the "bears," those who bought now in expectation of a rise and those who sold short, contracting for future delivery of a stock that they hoped to buy at lower prices later. From the outset Daniel Drew, a down-to-earth fellow who for years had dealt in real cattle that one could see, hear, touch, and smell, was fascinated by the practice of selling short. This was an exercise in unreality whereby a trader, often using money that he did not own, bought pieces of paper that he never took possession of, representing ownership in a company whose property he never saw and of whose operations he might well be ignorant. Such a transaction produced this tangible result: if successful, the transfer of real money out of someone else's pocket into his own; if unsuccessful, the transfer of the same in reverse. All of this struck Drew and his partner Robinson as the most exciting and challenging of ventures, even though, under a state law not repealed till 1858, short contracts were not legally binding, a technicality that Wall Street cheerfully ignored.

Much, in fact, seemed to get ignored on Wall Street, where in the shadow of their legitimate operations, the financing of public and private enterprises, the professionals made of stock speculation a passionate, subtle, complex game that they pursued with an arsenal of ploys and maneuvers. Using false tips, planted rumors, and fictitious wash sales to inflate or depress a stock as desired, insiders not only routinely fleeced the public but also fleeced each other. The supreme coup—the dream of every Wall Street speculator—was a "corner," to achieve which a pool of operators secretly bought up the entire floating supply of a stock, so that trapped short sellers would be forced to buy at their prices. This was a maneuver not unfamiliar to Drew who, like Henry Astor before him, had done the same in the cattle market. While corners were difficult and risky to effect, some remarkable examples could be cited, each of which had brought profits and glory to the one side, bankruptcy and ruin to the other. Although in such transactions the contracts were not legally enforceable, by a rule of the Stock Exchange any member who failed in his contracts was suspended. Such failures and suspensions were common, the most hopelessly insolvent of the outcasts seeking refuge in the outdoor curbstone market, the receptacle of the Street's sorriest casualties and rejects, inveterate gamblers to the end.

Yet there were those who succeeded, and magnificently. Each day on Wall Street, because their offices were only a few doors apart, Drew must have passed a tall, slender, sloping-shouldered man, smooth-faced, careless in his dress, and with a tense, preoccupied look—the Street's most famous trader, Jacob Little. A money broker since 1822, Little was credited with inventing the short sale, which he had practiced effectively throughout the Panic of 1837 and after, reaping vast profits while others went to ruin. Now at the height of his fame, he lived for one thing only, the buying and selling of stocks for profit, which he pursued obsessively six or even seven days a week. From this prodigy as from no one else—from this man who by the end of his career was said to have made and lost nine fortunes (an exaggeration—it was only three or four)—Drew could have learned to speculate, and to speculate grandly. Known now as Ursa Major and the Great Bear of Wall Street—titles to which Drew would in time fall heir—Little could impart to one of Drew's temperament any number of invaluable lessons, such as the use of the manipulated short sale, whereby one not only anticipated declines in stocks but engineered them; the technique of working secretly through other brokerage houses so as to mask one's operations; the delicious satisfaction, when cornered, of turning a convertible issue into stock just in time; and a supreme example of how to ignore the tumult of the Street, keep one's own counsel, and prosper.

Drew of course was prospering already. Under his general direction, within a few short years Drew, Robinson & Company became one of the major houses on the Street, transacting a very large business. Thanks to Drew's judgment and Robinson's abilities as a trader, the firm was consistently successful—remarkably so, given its heavy dealings in the most notorious fancies of all, the volatile stocks of mismanaged railroads. By Drew's own account, no large operation of the firm ever proved a mistake except one, a loan of nearly one million dollars that, contrary to his advice, was made to a trust company in 1846. Yet even this was no disaster, since the securities for the loan, including a mortgage on a Western railroad, were so well managed that years later he anticipated no ultimate loss. Thus when a self-proclaimed "reformed stock gambler" named William Armstrong published a book on Wall Street in 1848, he ranged the firm among the Street's leading houses and conferred on it his ultimate in praise: "Never compromised." Yet his estimate of its worth at over one million dollars was certainly short of the mark.

Guessing the wealth of one's neighbors, however inaccurately, was a favorite pastime—one might say an obsession—of the day. In New York in the 1840s and early 1850s, the most popular tabulation was a pamphlet entitled *Wealth and Biography of the Wealthy Citizens of New York City*, put out by Moses Yale Beach, the publisher of the *New York Sun*. It was an annotated roster of all persons with an estimated wealth of $100,000 or more that went through thirteen editions. Drew and his two partners were included, their wealth estimated, inconsistently from one edition to another, at between $100,000 and $300,000 each. Also mentioned were Jacob Little, Eli Kelley, Isaac Newton, and Vanderbilt. Credited with over one million dollars, the Commodore—as Vanderbilt now delighted to be called—rated an ever lengthening commentary that praised his energy and "go-aheaditiveness," while Drew was summarized as "a shrewd, keen money-making man." Yet the front runner by far in the American money race was the aging fur and real estate magnate John Jacob Astor, appraised successively at between fourteen and twenty-five million dollars. He was the richest man in America and also, if reports were true, the stingiest.

By the 1840s the hustling businessmen of New York had renounced fastidious midday dining at home. Instead, they hazarded a quick descent into the steamy atmosphere and clatter of a downtown eating house—a phenomenon that appalled out-of-towners—where at no small gastric peril scores of patrons bolted stringy meats and insipid vegetables, all the while talking and thinking business. Then, soon after 3:00 P.M., when the Stock Exchange's short afternoon session ended, there was a general exodus of merchants, bankers, brokers, and their clerks, most of whom crowded aboard a northbound omnibus to be jounced back up the cobblestones of Broadway to the serenity of Above Bleecker. This was the residential refuge of the wealthy, who by now had abandoned the whole of Manhattan below Bleecker Street to commerce and the lower orders.

Above Bleecker for Daniel Drew was the three-story house at 52 Bleecker Street itself, at the corner of Mulberry, that he had leased in 1839 and purchased three years later. Like most of the homes lining the area's quiet tree-lined streets, it was in the Federal style, with a handsome red-brick facade, a low stoop leading to the door, and a steep roof with two dormer windows. Several servants also resided in the house, although after a year or two Robert Kelley and Catherine moved into a home of their own on Tenth Street, where their family multiplied. While the neighborhood was elegant and exclusive, Drew and his wife, being country-born and simple in their tastes, were not out to make a shine in society. This was just as well since, in the high-toned parlors of their neighbors, an ex-drover's quaint speech and manners might have grated on many a sensitivity. Probably the Drews' entertaining was confined to dinners for partners and relations, teas for ministers, and modest receptions for members of the Mulberry Street Methodist Episcopal Church.

For Daniel was back in the church. When he first moved to Bleecker Street in 1839, he was not a churchgoer, since as he put it, the "cares of this world had choked the Word" in him, so that he "became unfruitful."[3] Now, however, with his drover and tavern-keeping days behind him, he was leading a more settled existence. Having noticed a church just around the corner in Mulberry Street, he occasionally worshiped there simply because of its convenience and the providential fact that it was Methodist. In 1841 the pastor held a prolonged revival that Drew attended at night from curiosity, and there God tracked him down. Powerful preaching wrenched the backslider's heart, and he was wrought upon by the Spirit, heard the Divine Voice, and obeyed. Some eight or ten times he went to the altar as a suppliant until, reclaimed from his sins at last, he received the seal of forgiveness. Soon afterward he brought his wife in, too, and both of them joined the church. This time it stuck. After three awakenings and a bolt of lightning, he was in God's pocket.

News of her son's conversion must have gladdened the heart of Catherine Lawrence, who at an advanced age still lived with her other son in Putnam County. Daniel declared that his coming to the church was the late fruition of the piety sown in him long ago by his mother. They were as close as ever; the love he bore her was surely the deepest feeling of his life. When she died in August 1842, at the age of eighty-four, he was at her side. Years later he told his close friend, the Rev. John Parker, "If ever a saint died in triumph, it was my mother," and then he broke down and wept.[4] For the rest of his life he enshrined her memory, which nourished and strengthened his faith.

But if the church that Daniel Drew joined dispensed the gospel of his childhood, it did so with a difference. The Methodism of the Mulberry Street Church was not that of Putnam County thirty years before, nor even that of New York City fifteen years before, when drably clothed congregations, the sexes segregated, sat on hard benches in gloomy buildings with bare, whitewashed walls. Ministering to a congregation already leavened by incipient sophistication and wealth, the Mulberry Street Church boasted a polished mahogany pulpit backed by drapery, cushioned family pews, a carpeted floor, and finally—after some hesitation—a rented organ.

Despite the apparent relaxation of some strictures, however, church membership was still a serious commitment. All members came under the rules of the *Discipline*, which forbade Sabbath-breaking, profanity, intemperance, the putting on of costly apparel and gold, and the laying up of treasure on earth. As was incumbent upon new members, Drew and his wife for years attended weekly class meetings—she on Friday afternoons and he on Sunday mornings—where theology and practical religion were discussed. In addition, Daniel often attended the church's Wednesday evening prayer services where over the years, as well as at the class meetings and periodic revivals, the eminent steamboat operator and man of Wall Street was heard to confess his shortcomings copiously. Weeping like a child until the eyes of all were moist, he entreated, "O Lord, thy poor servant is so unworthy! Do not let me slip away!"[5] At such times he was again the anguished suppliant of the first conversion, humble and penitent, fearful of ultimate perdition. But when, in 1844, at the age of forty-five, Roxanna bore him a son at last, how could the sinner not have taken it as an exceptional sign of God's grace?

To have in their fold a Wall Street man so fervently contrite, and generous as well, was a boon to the Mulberry Street Church. In 1843 Drew was elected a trustee, in which capacity he served for many years. Always open to appeals for worthy causes, he became the financial mainstay of the church. Small wonder, then, that the Methodists were disinclined to censure Brother Drew's dual service in the ranks of God and Mammon. Far less than Drew himself did they question whether this thriving penitent could squeeze through the eye of the needle. In that day when commercial prosperity was fast creating a whole new class of rich men, most of whom attended church—Nelson Robinson, Isaac Newton, and the Kelleys were all good Baptists—few churches could resist encroaching affluence. Although its sermons still bore a whiff of brimstone, evangelical Methodism was already succumbing with the others to an insidious process of accommodation that would culminate, at the turn of the century, in a straightfaced pronouncement by Bishop William Lawrence of the Episcopal church, a friend of J.P. Morgan, that "it is only to the man of morality that wealth comes. . . . Material prosperity is helping to make the national character sweeter, more joyous, more unselfish, more Christlike."[6]

Back in his Wall Street office on a weekday morning, Drew made no pretense of being sweet and Christlike, or humble or remorseful either; he was confident, astute, energetic. And by the mid-1840s, as his resources and expertise grew, he was not content, like Jacob Little, to merely trade in the stock of companies. He was out to control them.

Drew's first ventures in this direction came in 1846, in connection with his steamboats. Probably it was Elijah Peck of Flushing, then friendly to him and a fellow trustee of the People's Line, who came to him with a proposition. Peck was president of the New York, Providence and Boston Railroad, more commonly known as the Stonington line, a little forty-seven-mile road linking Providence, Rhode Island, to Stonington, Connecticut. This line was the central link in an important rail-and-water route between Boston and New York, connecting at Providence with the Boston and Providence Railroad and at Stonington with the New Jersey Steam Navigation Company, which operated steamboats on Long Island Sound. The Stonington railroad, being financially weak, had always been imposed on and scorned by its partners, who were ever tempted to dispense with it altogether by connecting directly at Providence. At last, in March 1846, they announced that they would do just that. Left high and dry, Peck was anxious to secure a new link by boat to New York, since his railroad would get little business without it. So he proposed that Drew, having more boats than he could use on the Hudson, establish a new line between Stonington and New York. Since there was just as much money in the New York to Boston passenger business as in that between New York and Albany, Drew agreed.

On April 1, 1846, when the New Jersey Steam Navigation Company diverted its boats to Providence as announced, service to Stonington was assumed by the People's Line steamboat *Knickerbocker* and George Law's luxurious new *Oregon*, probably the fastest steamboat in the country. It was smart of Drew to switch these boats to the Stonington run, where they could offer more comfort, speed, and splendor than travelers had ever known on the sound. And it was even smarter of him, by negotiating with the coarse-featured Law, a heavyset giant of a man, to get the *Oregon* away from the Hudson, where it had a nasty habit of challenging his People's Line boats to races that they might not win. With one foot planted in the sound, it further occurred to Drew that he might snap up the New Jersey Steam Navigation Company itself and so be rid of it as competition. Operating under a corporate charter would have its advantages, and while the company's boats were inferior to his own, the bigger ones could serve as replacements. So Drew, Robinson, and Eli Kelley bought up the company's stock and took it over at the annual meeting in Jersey City on June 23, at which point Daniel Drew, as the company's new president, had both feet planted in the sound.

He had the steamboat company—what about the railroad? Granted, it was a poor, spindly thing, too hobbled with debt to have ever paid a dividend; milked and bullied by its connecting lines; and denied a much-needed direct junction with the Boston and Providence Railroad at Providence, owing to that city's fierce determination to lose no business to the rival port of Stonington. Yet to Drew's penetrating eye the road revealed certain advantages: the fine, deep harbor of Stonington, which unlike the port of Providence could accommodate the big new boats of the day; the directness of the route, shorter by an hour than any other to Boston; and its avoidance of the turbulent sea passage to Providence around Point Judith. The Stonington route, then, could offer travelers a swift, smooth trip to Boston, while rival lines subjected them to dingy old tubs and slow trains, and maybe got them there seasick to boot. What the Stonington road cried out for, Drew concluded, was money, brains, and spunk, to supply which it occurred to him to join forces with Cornele Vanderbilt, an old hand on the sound whom it was far better to have with you than against you.

Drew and Vanderbilt were now good friends, meeting often to relax in each other's company, talk boats and money, and manhandle the language with impunity. Drew had employed Vanderbilt's son William as a clerk in his Wall Street office until ill health had forced William to leave, and he had even named his own son for William, as a compliment to William's father. So Drew had no trouble getting Vanderbilt's ear, persuading him that together—steamboat men though they were, and therefore hardly partial to railroads—they could toughen up this weakling of a road and make the Stonington route the smoothest, quickest, and best line to Boston, and the most profitable.

When Drew and Vanderbilt teamed up, things began to happen. During the summer of 1846 they bought a controlling interest in the Stonington. Then on September 29 they took it over, at first retaining Elijah Peck as president. Thereafter, the steamboats of the New Jersey Steam Navigation Company docked not at Providence but at Stonington; the magnificent *Oregon* was joined by Vanderbilt's splendid new *C. Vanderbilt*, permitting schedules that beat all rival lines by an hour; the Stonington railroad flourished and declared a dividend; and the city of Providence was argued, pressured, and cajoled—doubtless for a price—into permitting a direct rail link with the Boston and Providence Railroad, so that passengers could at last ride all the way from Stonington to Boston without a change of train. When this direct service was inaugurated on May 1, 1848, the Stonington's transformation was complete.

Having given the world a lesson in how to make a railroad shipshape, the two steamboat men—each of whom served as president, Vanderbilt for nearly two years and Drew briefly thereafter—soon lost interest in the road. By September 1850 Vanderbilt, preoccupied now with building a canal in Nicaragua to capture the California gold rush traffic, had severed his connection with the Stonington. A year later Drew also sold out. For many years, however, he continued as president of the New Jersey Steam Navigation Company, running in its service some of the finest boats of the day, including Vanderbilt's *C. Vanderbilt* and *Commodore* (Vanderbilt's ego required that a fleet of vessels be named for him), both of which Drew finally bought. Like the People's Line itself, with which Drew often interchanged his vessels on the sound, the Stonington route became for him simply a nice little sideline business. For excitement, he looked elsewhere.

By the late 1840s, Wall Street offered plenty of excitement, since the stock market was finally waking up. It had resolutely ignored the new economic expansion that began in 1844 and the growing prosperity that accompanied the Mexican war. But late in 1848 came news from California of something that Wall Street could never ignore: gold. Immediately the newspapers teemed with ads announcing vessels to San Francisco and Panama, aboard which flocked throngs of young men armed with picks, axes, shovels, pans, and sifters. Then the first ships arrived actually bearing gold dust and nuggets, and wild tales from the West fired the imagination not only of the thousands dashing off to California, but of investors on both sides of the Atlantic, whose skepticism born of the previous panic succumbed at last—and feverishly—to new hopes and new illusions. Over the next decade California gold poured into New

York at the rate of $50 million a year, while stocks advanced, railroads spread, banks multiplied, credit expanded, and Wall Street profits soared. At long last, a new boom was on.

Not for an instant did Drew and his associates contemplate joining the booted, rough-coated hordes en route to California, it being the style and genius of Wall Street not to run off to gold fields but to make the gold come to it. Drew, Robinson & Company did precisely that, becoming a major recipient of California gold dust and prospering accordingly. Yet in the late winter of 1851-52, with the boom in full swing, their profits surging, and their outlook bright, the partners decided amicably to dissolve their partnership. Probably the prime motivation was Drew's. Recently, for the first time in his life, he had been seriously ill, so much so that for a while it was thought that he might die. Now, although fully recovered, he was of a mind to contract his daily labors in the banking business. So as of March 1, 1852, the firm of Drew, Robinson & Company ceased to exist.

Partly, at least, for reasons of health, Drew now felt a nostalgia for rural living. Perhaps, too, he and his wife wanted their son to grow up in the country as they had. Fortunately, commutation between Putnam County and New York had now become feasible, since in 1849 the New York and Harlem Railroad had finally reached Southeast. As a final determinant, Drew and his wife must have noticed their neighborhood's decline. By the late 1840s, fine shops and hotels had begun replacing houses along Broadway in the Bleecker and Bond Street area, where dentists' offices appeared soon afterward. In the flux that was New York City, the farsighted discerned the signs of decay: shops today, dentists tomorrow, the Irish the day after that. Clearly, it was time to get out.

In the exodus that followed, most of Drew's fashionable neighbors moved uptown to handsome brownstones around lower Fifth Avenue and Madison Square, which was the new preserve of the wealthy, far removed from the city's festering slums, those reputed breeding grounds of riots, cholera, grog shops, and popery. But for Drew, God's country lay a good fifty miles farther north. In May 1852 he went to Putnam County and bought a farm of 150 acres near the home of his brother Thomas in Drewville. Returning to the city, he sold the Bleecker Street house for a substantial profit in June and moved his family up to the farm. Thereafter, commuting weekly by the Harlem Railroad, he gave one day in seven to family, God, and his cattle. But the other six held him in the city, where there were stocks to buy, steamboats to sell, and railroads to compete with or to control. It was a fierce, giddy time, rank with opportunities and change; not for anything would he have missed it.

CHAPTER 7

Enter the
Iron Horse

In late September 1849 the lower Hudson valley was vexed along its eastern shore by an unwonted commotion: a chugging, snorting, screeching monster of iron with a jutting cowcatcher and a bulbous funnel that belched smoke as the machine's giant wheels sped northward over level track, with a tender and cars in tow. The unthinkable had happened: the railroad had come to the Hudson.

Unthinkable, to be sure, only on the Hudson, that serene avenue of proud, swift steamboats, since elsewhere throughout mid-nineteenth century America railroads, as they said at the time, were spreading like measles in a boarding school. Indeed, how could they not, when their logic was compelling and their promise dazzling. Unlike steamboats, which could go only where nature had provided accessible waterways, locomotives could go wherever the hand and brain of man directed them, reaching into every corner of the land to bind together, with cheap, speedy, year-round transportation, the huge, sprawling continent of America. Inevitably, from one end of the country to the other there raged a fever of railroad promotion and construction, matched on Wall Street by a fever of speculation. For Drew the Wall Street operator this meant new excitement and new opportunities, but for Drew the steamboat man, preoccupied already with rival operators and dissident stockholders, it meant trouble.

Specifically, the trouble took the form of the Hudson River Railroad, an enterprise first conceived in 1842 by businessmen from Poughkeepsie and other river towns, who were frustrated by seeing quantities of goods piled up on their wharves and in their warehouses for three long months

69

each winter, trapped by the river's freezing, a seasonal blockade that only a railroad could eliminate. Yet it was a daring notion, to challenge the steamboats of the Hudson. It had been too daring for the promoters of the New York and Harlem Railroad, chartered in 1831, who in extending their line north from Harlem stayed well to the east of the Hudson, thus confining themselves to an area limited in resources and without large towns, so that meager revenues resulted. The backers of the Hudson line were men of bolder vision, yet they soon learned just how complicated organizing a railroad could be. For while a steamboat line could be launched on a shoestring, even the shortest railroad cost millions, since it had to build its own right of way. This meant massive financing that required a corporate structure, which meant extracting a charter from the state legislature, which meant wooing legislators whom rival interests—canal, turnpike, and steamboat men, landowners along the proposed route, and other railroads—could woo just as winningly. In 1842 it was the steamboat men who fought the railroad and won; no charter was forthcoming.

In 1845, however, the railroad promoters tried again, this time under the plucky leadership of James Boorman, a prominent New York City merchant who, both as a champion of progress and an importer of iron, had long been an advocate of railroads. By now times had changed. With a jealous eye on Boston, which in the race for Western markets had pushed through a rail link to Albany and achieved connections all the way to Buffalo, the New York State Legislature shook off its smug confidence in state waterways at last. In May 1846, this time over the opposition of the rival Harlem line, the lawmakers passed an act incorporating the Hudson River Railroad Company, which was to build a line along the east bank of the Hudson from New York to Albany, where it would connect with existing rail links to Buffalo.

The Hudson River Railroad's choice of a route that closely paralleled the Hudson not only put it in direct competition with the steamboats, but also necessitated cutting through the flinty rock of the Hudson Highlands, whose massive humps rose up sheer from the river. Led by Boorman, a group of backers had argued persuasively for this route, pointing out that, whatever the risks and the costs, it was the most direct and gradeless. Work began in 1847, but required more time and money than anticipated as it pressed slowly north toward Poughkeepsie, delayed endlessly by the arduous task of tunneling through Anthony's Nose and Breakneck Hill. When the railroad's first president, discouraged by the cost and obstacles, proposed that the line stop at Poughkeepsie, Boorman and his allies ousted him and Boorman himself became president. As honest as he was determined, Boorman served without salary and decreed that his own firm should have no contracts with the railroad.

Headstrong, pushy, and obstinate, he vowed to dig, sweat, bridge, and blast his way to Albany: the railroad would be built!

All of this gave Daniel Drew plenty to think about. He knew what railroads were. They lurched and screeched and flung cinders in the eyes of their patrons, but they were faster than any steamboat. Was it conceivable that, by speed alone, Boorman's snorting machines would displace the queenly steamboats on the Hudson, just as the steamboats had displaced the poky river sloops?

The first hint of an answer came on September 29, 1849, when the railroad opened forty-two miles of track from New York to Peekskill. During this first season of the line's operation, a survey showed that while the railroad charged fifty-five cents to Peekskill as against thirty-seven and one-half cents on the boats, five passengers out of six took the train. Although the local boats slashed their fare to a quarter, they could not compete against the faster railroad and had to abandon the route. Three months later, the railroad opened as far as Poughkeepsie, the halfway point to Albany, with the same result: patronage of the boats so declined that operators stopped running them to Poughkeepsie and the nearby landings.

As a further jolt, the federal government, desiring the fastest possible service for the mails, took its contract for the northern mail away from the People's Line and gave it to the Hudson River Railroad. With tracks in service only as far as Poughkeepsie, however, the trains obviously had to connect with steamboats, so President Boorman turned to the two top men on the river. Throughout 1850 the People's Line joined forces with the railroad and ran certain boats to connect at Albany and Poughkeepsie with the trains, Drew and Newton being of a mind to hang on while they could to a slice of the government subsidy. But Boorman was no fool: under the terms of their agreement he made the steamboat men maintain their all-water fare between New York and Albany at two dollars—the same as on the rail-and-water route—and insisted on posting agents on their boats. Clearly it was a strained alliance, so in 1851 Boorman arranged other connections. By then, with the worst construction problems behind him, he was feeling downright cocky. "On the opening of the road to Albany," he informed Drew jauntily, "you can bid good-bye to your steamboats!"[1] Many of Drew's friends agreed.

Boorman's triumph came on October 8, 1851, when the railroad was formally opened to Greenbush, its terminus just across the Hudson from Albany. Seeing his task as completed, he had resigned the presidency the day before, but at the sumptuous dinner that the company gave in the depot for the governor, other dignitaries, and stockholders, he was hailed with cheers and applause. Far more ominous for the steamboat men, however, was the unprecedented time to Greenbush of the excursion train that had brought the guests from New York, a scant three hours and fifty-five minutes as compared with seven and one-half hours to Albany by boat.

Yet Drew did not bid his steamboats good-bye. Instead, he threw himself into the toughest fight of his steamboat career. Because the railroad was stealing away a lot of his passengers, he decided to handle more freight. Because the railroad had grabbed most of the local business, he suspended service to all intermediate points along the river. Because the railroad was reaching for the biggest prize of all, the through business to Albany and Troy, he competed fiercely, running his elegant boats—those marvels of mahogany and stained glass and lace—through the romantic scenery of what was called the American Rhine, offering through service amid unparalleled comfort and luxury, with fine dining and seemingly motionless travel that on the night boats guaranteed a good night's sleep. So what if the railroad was faster? It jammed its patrons into cramped quarters on hard wooden benches, gave them meager views through smudged windows, and subjected them to bumps, jolts, cinders, and soot, and to insipid food gulped down in dingy restaurants. Let the public decide. Were not the waterways God's own highway, composed, as the canal men used to argue, of the fluid that comes straight from heaven, whereas the railroad, with its smoke, dirt, and fire, stemmed from hell? Then, too, it occurred to him, the Hudson line was burdened with debt, so perhaps it could be nudged into receivership. Which to an old river man suggested an immediate solution: cut your fares and bleed 'em through a rate war.

Within eight days of the railroad's opening, the People's Line lowered its Albany fare from one dollar to fifty cents and maintained this low rate to the end of the season. By the following spring the railroad was running six trains a day to Albany at rates of from $1.25 to $2.50, in competition with which Drew and Newton operated no less than three lines of Albany night boats, all with a fare of fifty cents. Hard-pressed, on June 3, 1852, the Hudson River line reduced the rate on all Albany trains to $1.50, or about one cent a mile. Commenting on the line's frequent delays and accidents, Henry V. Poor's *American Railroad Journal* had already called the Hudson River road a disappointment and was frankly skeptical about a line whose unique distinction it was to combine the highest construction costs with the lowest rail fares in the country. Confirming this judgment was the railroad's next annual report, announcing net receipts that failed to meet the interest on its debt, much less offer hope of a dividend. It seemed the gracious steamboats were winning.

But were they safe? On July 21, 1852, the day boat *Henry Clay* caught fire on the Hudson and burned to the water's edge with a loss of some seventy lives. This disaster was so clearly the result of racing that a great public outcry arose, causing Congress to hastily pass the Steamboat Inspection Law of 1852, providing for more rigorous testing of boilers and the licensing of all passenger-steamboat engineers and pilots. To be sure, the *Clay* did not belong to the People's Line, whose safety record to date had been excellent. But on July 1, 1853, while the giant *New World* lay at her dock just prior to departing for Albany, the flue of one boiler collapsed, killing six crewmen and scalding two others. An investigation revealed excessive steam pressure resulting from deranged steam gauges and safety valves, for which the *New World's* chief engineer had his license revoked. Obviously, in flagrant violation of the steamboat law, the *New World* had been getting up extra steam to race the *Francis Skiddy*, a crack new opposition boat, on their first run of the season together.

So the boats were not always safe, and no matter how fast they went, they could never beat the trains. The diarist George Templeton Strong, a devoted patron of the steamboats, loathed "that filthy railroad," but admitted that it was aggravating "to see the trains come squealing and stinking after us as we lounge up the river and rush past and out of sight as if our meek little steamboat were at anchor."[2] By 1853 not only the day boat *New World*, designed to carry passengers only, but Drew's night boats as well, although still charging only fifty cents, were steadily losing business to the railroad. In April 1853 the *American Railroad Journal* announced that, even at one cent a mile, the railroad had a chance of success, and in May declared outright, "Public favor has turned unmistakably upon this road."[3] In early October, with the steamboat rates still at fifty cents, the railroad raised its Albany fare to two dollars, clearly in proclamation of victory.

But the battle was far from over. Connecting at Albany with both the steamboats and the Hudson River Railroad was the New York Central, an important carrier created in July 1853 by the merger of ten small railroads operating between Albany and Buffalo. Since the steamboats could not provide a year-round connection, the Central seemed inclined to an alliance with the Hudson line and already had four of its directors on the board. Some steamboat men might have resigned themselves to this situation, but not Drew and Newton, who must have approached the Central bristling with arguments as to why it would do better to join forces with the People's Line. For instance, since the Central was in keen competition with the New York and Erie Railroad, it needed to offer the lowest fare possible between New York and Buffalo. By teaming up with the steamboats, whose rates were lower than the Hudson River Railroad's, the Central could do just that. Also, the Central carried a lot of freight, hence needed the partner that could handle freight best. Boats could carry more than the trains, especially the vessels of the People's

Line, which henceforth would have an entire deck reserved for this purpose. And finally, what about connections to the West? Isaac Newton, the nation's top steamboat designer, could build new palace steamboats to ply between Buffalo and Detroit, the like of which the Great Lakes had never seen. They would link the Central with the Michigan Central Railroad and give it a connection all the way to Chicago. In the face of such prospects, what could Boorman's screeching little monsters offer?

These arguments won the day. Henceforth the New York Central gave the bulk of both its freight and passenger business to the People's Line. Then in 1854 Newton with great success designed and built two sidewheelers, the swiftest and most sumptuous ever seen on Lake Erie, that in plying between Buffalo and Detroit completed the new through line to Chicago of which the People's Line was the easternmost link. In a bold bid to participate in the ever widening transportation network that was rapidly tying the nation together, Drew and Newton could now offer through tickets to Buffalo, Cleveland, Chicago, and the other important cities of the West. Of course, when ice closed the Hudson the New York Central suddenly remembered the Hudson River Railroad and cordially consigned to it its freight and passenger business, although only for the balance of the winter. This policy so irked the Hudson that at its annual election of June 16, 1854, the four New York Central directors were ousted. Yet among their replacements, who should come in as a representative of the New York and Erie Railroad but Drew's former partner Nelson Robinson. Getting one up on Drew was not easy.

With the New York Central diverting most of its business to the People's Line, Boorman had changed his tune. Coming to Drew at a time when the boats were charging a dollar to Albany, he suggested that the People's Line raise its rate to two dollars, so that boat and rail passengers would pay the same and Drew's own profits double. Replied Drew, "My company's making money enough at a dollar the passage, and then the public too is better satisfied. But there's one way by which you can regulate the rate of passage." "How?" asked Boorman eagerly. "Why, buy out the People's Line," said Drew with a chuckle. "But you haven't got money enough to buy us out!"[4]

What remained to put the final pinch on the railroad? First, to incorporate, so as to give the People's Line greater legal protection and durability, but not in New York State, where politicking and payoffs would be necessary, and where hostile steamboat and railroad interests might work all kinds of mischief. So Drew and Newton applied for a charter in New Jersey, using as incorporators a bunch of unknowns and as a corporate name the New Jersey Steamboat Company, which hardly smacked of the Hudson. Probably few if any of the Jersey legislators knew or cared who or what they were incorporating by their special act of March 2, 1854, following which Newton became the president and Drew the treasurer of the new corporation, whose stock they held in very tight hands, and to which they sold their four finest boats, the *Oregon, Hendrik Hudson, Isaac Newton*, and *New World*, for a not ungenerous half million dollars.

And then the *New World*. Since the incorporated company, still operating under the name of the People's Line, renounced day service and intermediate stops completely to run night express boats to Albany and Troy, this giant had become a lavish embarrassment. What does one do with a 1,313-ton day boat if this marvel has been deserted by the public? Answer: you convert it to a 1,676-ton night boat with berths for eight hundred; you give it sumptuous furnishings, including gas-fitted chandeliers whose crystal pendants will never rattle, so smooth is the movement of the vessel; and finally, more dazzling yet, you create a grand saloon that rises through two stories to the ceiling above, and add a new second tier of staterooms that open onto a gallery overlooking that grand saloon below—an effect without precedent on river boats, suggestive of the theater or opera house, and well calculated to remind the public just how cramped, jolting, drab, and cinder-ridden even the finest railway coach must be.

It was a daring move by the managers of the People's Line, to try the gambit of luxury again and pour hundreds of thousands into it. The renovated *New World* resumed service to Albany as a night boat on September 5, 1855, and instantly became the talk of the river. When in a year's time it was joined by the *Isaac Newton*, similarly rebuilt with a second tier of staterooms and a grand saloon rising through two decks (features that thereafter became standard on Eastern river boats), the managers of the People's Line had doubled the stakes in their gamble, and the gamble paid off. In the war between the steamboats and the railroad, renewed each spring and fought doggedly, neither side won nor did either lose. In the end there was business for both, since travelers who wanted speed took the railroad, while those who relished comfort took the boats. Yet perhaps the boats had an edge. If they now carried only half as many passengers as before, there was freight to compensate. When the *New World* docked at Albany on May 1, 1858, it held a record 500 tons of it, which with the passenger receipts yielded earnings on a single trip of over twenty-two hundred dollars. Meanwhile the Hudson River Railroad, although heavily patronized, was also heavily mortgaged. Struggling along with its debt, troubled by accidents, and slighted by the New York Central, it was forced to stringent economies and only in 1862 declared its first dividend, at a meager 3 percent. If this was a draw, it was the kind that Drew liked.

As a hard-nosed steamboat man, Drew had been shrewd to tie his vessels into the great transportation links being forged throughout the country. And just as he had put out one finger to Boston via Stonington and another to Chicago via Albany, so now it occurred to him to put out still another to the north. In December 1848 the Saratoga and Washington Railroad had been completed, linking Saratoga Springs to Whitehall, the southern terminus of the steamboats operating on Lake Champlain. Since another little railroad already linked the town of Troy on the Hudson to Saratoga, and since a Canadian railroad connected with the Lake Champlain steamboats at the northern end of the lake, there was the dazzling new prospect of a through rail-and-water route connecting New York to Montreal. Since such a route was bound to be profitable, it struck Drew, already half owner of the vessels of the Troy line, how pleasant it would be to control the other water link as well. Suddenly he conceived a great hunger for the Champlain Transportation Company.

Incorporated in Vermont in 1826, the Champlain Transportation Company had competed fiercely with its rivals and absorbed them all, until it owned every steamboat on the lake. By 1849, however, the founders, still in control after twenty-three years, were running the company in a lackadaisical fashion, leaving the details of the business to the captains. So matters stood when in the summer of 1849 a group of New York financiers headed by Daniel Drew and Nelson Robinson bought out certain of the directors and so acquired control of the company. One glance at the line's operations must have revealed to these knowing Gothamites an old-fogy, slowpoke way of doing things that cried out for a little Wall Street flair.

At the next meeting of the board, in 1850, Drew, Robinson, and Robert Kelley all became directors, and they elected a local man as president. Immediately they hiked the dividend and raised the president's salary from eight hundred to ten thousand dollars. Negotiations with the connecting railroads to establish a north-south through line began. Furthermore, when the Swedish soprano Jenny Lind came to America in that same year of 1850, to sing to packed houses rendered feverish with anticipation through the promotional efforts of P.T. Barnum, the new managers contrived to sluice some of the profits their way. To patrons in the Lake Champlain area the Champlain Transportation Company proposed an inspired early version of the package deal. This included a ticket offering combined boat-and-rail passage from any point on the lake to New York, a ticket to the Jenny Lind concert on Friday night, October 25, an allowance of up to three days in New York, and return passage via boat and train to the original point of departure. Whatever their ignorance of Swedish coloratura singing, when it came to profits, the boys at Drew, Robinson & Company fairly sizzled with fresh ideas.

Not that all their ideas worked out. One failure was the Great Northern Mail and Express Route, the new north-south route that they organized in conjunction with the Troy steamboats and the neighboring railroads. With great fanfare, the route went into operation on June 2, 1851, offering through tickets from New York to Montreal for only five dollars, with a travel time of less than forty hours, and a fare and schedule that were enthusiastically hailed in the press. Yet after August 19 the ads disappeared and the service ceased, without any explanation to the public. Perhaps the recent organization of a new all-rail route to Montreal by the New York and New Haven Railroad and some New England lines— a route that would not be closed by ice in the winter—had something to do with it; or perhaps some of the cooperating lines had found the arrangement unsatisfactory. But whatever the reason, the new rail-and-water route to Montreal died almost as soon as it was born.

As a consequence, the Champlain Transportation Company was beginning to look like a lemon. By now, Drew and his colleagues may well have been asking themselves why they had ever cast an eye on the frigid regions of the North. But all was not lost, for in 1852 the company received an offer for the company's boats and equipment from the Rutland and Burlington Railroad of Vermont, which proposed to tie the boat line into a system of its own. By this time Drew was no longer on the board, but his associates dominated it. At a special meeting on August 31, they voted to accept the railroad's offer of $125,000 for the company's five steamboats and other property, although they held on to its charter.

The next two years brought boundless grief to the railroad. Like many other lines of the day, the Rutland and Burlington had underestimated construction costs and overestimated traffic, so that it failed to meet the interest on its mortgage bonds and passed into the hands of trustees. Meanwhile the debt-free Champlain Transportation Company, having retained its charter, could still operate boats on the lake, and when two new ones were launched in Whitehall, snapped them up and put them into service. As a result, while the railroad foundered, the steamboat company prospered. So in 1854, when the railroad's trustees resolved to get rid of its steamboats, they offered them to the very company from which they had first been acquired. Graciously the Champlain Transportation Company consented to repurchase most of its property, paying only $48,200; the railroad had been had.

By now, Drew and his partners were ready to bid the northland adieu. In 1856 they sold their controlling interest in the company to a group of Troy steamboat men who had a hand in the local railroads as well. So ended Drew's involvement in Lake Champlain steamboating, a venture that through luck or foresight had proved a remarkable success. So it usually went with Drew and his partners; money just stuck to their fingers.

For several years, after buying the Drewville farm in May 1852 and moving his family there, Drew lived during the week in the city at the new St. Nicholas Hotel on Broadway at Spring Street. This was a vast palatial establishment with a white marble facade, velvet carpets, sofas upholstered in Flemish tapestry, ornate mirrors, and gold leaf overlaying everything—a profusion of the same rich magnificence that Drew himself had lavished on his steamboats. Even so, he must have cut a curious figure there, this tall, lean, pinch-faced man, somberly and negligently dressed.

On the weekend he was off to Putnam County, borne there by the New York and Harlem Railroad, the Hudson line's not remarkably successful competitor. Still, the railroad's coming to Southeast in 1849 had produced something of a miracle: there, at the base of a steep, wooded hill, a depot and houses had sprung up, then a store, a screw factory, a lumber yard, and a solid block of handsome brick buildings. Known henceforth as Brewster's Station or Brewster's (later Brewster), this thriving village mined iron ore and shipped milk and cattle to the city. Its commerce was the wonder and despair of Carmel, the county seat four miles away, which, being untouched by the railroad, remained virginally rustic, undeveloped, and somnolent.

South of Carmel and west of Brewster lay the quiet little hamlet of Drewville, its name derived from long association with the Drews. There Daniel rejoined his wife and son on the farm and kept in touch with his brother Thomas, now a neighbor, whose married daughters and grandchildren likewise lived in the vicinity. Throughout the year, Sunday was Daniel's one full day there, when he worshiped at the Methodist church either in Carmel or near Brewster, then inspected every acre of his farms and every head of livestock on them. He had two farms now in Drewville, on one of which he lived quite modestly, as well as the larger Clift farm south of Brewster that he still retained as a stock farm, tended now by his brother-in-law Harry Mead, who lived there as a tenant. How it must have pleased him on his weekly tours, with Wall Street and railroads out of mind, to take along with him his son Billy and his grandson Danny, so as to teach the boys about critters, striding from pasture to pasture in dew-soaked trousers, his boots caked with dung, and leaping nimbly over the old stone walls that intervened. (Or not so nimbly: in May 1859, while jumping from just such a wall, he fell and dislocated his shoulder.) Then on Monday, refreshed by this brief rustic idyll, he hastened back to New York.

Meanwhile Drew's daughter Catherine had been widowed again. On February 27, 1853, Robert Kelley died in New York of typhus at the age of thirty-three. Left a wealthy woman with five small daughters, Catherine moved back to Putnam County, where she built and furnished a Methodist chapel on her father's land at Drewville and adjoining it another building to house the Drewville Institute. This was a small private school that she founded at her own expense to give her children and those of local friends and relatives (Drew's own son, her brother, among them) free instruction in matters intellectual, spiritual, and moral. Surely it was deemed fitting by all when in June 1857 this local benefactress, the most desirable match in the township, married in that very chapel the Rev. William S. Clapp of Danbury, Connecticut, a widower who thereafter, when called to the Baptist church of Carmel, took it laboriously upon himself to improve spiritually and otherwise that not wholly enlightened corner of the county. As for Catherine, remarried at thirty-six with two stepchildren to care for and another son soon to follow, she was still extending a rather full gamut of experience, having had as husbands a tavern barkeep, a Wall Street broker, and now the worthiest of Baptist clergymen.

Like father, like daughter, the neighbors must have reflected, since as the first Methodist millionaire Daniel had been a generous donor to Wesleyan University in Connecticut, the Concord Bible School in New Hampshire, and Troy University at Troy, becoming a trustee of all of them. Closer to home, he and Nelson Robinson were both trustees of the Raymond Collegiate Institute of Carmel, the area's chief stab at female education. And when the Methodist church in Carmel required renovation in 1853, Brother Drew's subscription of a hundred dollars kicked off the drive to raise funds. When it was announced that all but twenty-five dollars of the total sum needed had been raised, out of whose pocket should it come but his own, volunteered at once with a smile? Not for years had he been so close to the home folks, this benign capitalist who soon afterward served on a church committee to superintend tables at the July 4 Methodist Ladies' Sewing Circle Fair.

To be esteemed for one's good deeds was fine, but what most tickled the old man (he was pushing sixty and looked it) was to be known among his neighbors as the finest judge of critters in the county. Facilitated by the railroad, cattle trading was still big business in Putnam, where drovers like Thomas Drew took from a dozen to seventy head to the city by rail every week. Thanks to the railroad, Daniel too could keep his hand in. Each May he visited the Upper Bull's Head, New York City's chief cattle market at Forty-fourth Street and Fourth Avenue. There, in the glut of cattle from the West, brought now in a week's time by rail, his practiced eye singled out those animals best suited for rapid fattening on grass. Shipped by rail to Southeast, these cattle were grazed on his farms throughout the summer, then in October or November were shipped back to the drove yards in the city, where, ponderously fleshed, they were admired by all and fetched a top price. In 1858 Drew sold 120 cattle from his farms, of which a hundred weighed one thousand pounds each and some of them a good twelve hundred. Small wonder that the

Tribune's weekly Cattle Market Report extolled his results, obtained by grass feeding only, and recommended the practice as the best possible use of the rough grazing lands of eastern New York.

But Drew's supreme delight surely came not in the drove yards of the city, but at the county fair held in late September or early October at the fairgrounds near the village of Carmel. Flocking there in buggies, past roadside stands that hawked watermelons, sweet cider, and pastry or that offered Negro minstrelsy or a shrill performance by real whooping Indians from a circus, came people from every end of the county to survey, in a huge tent topped by Old Glory, the products of the enterprise of Putnam, including needlework, cabbages, and apples, harnesses and sewing machines, and all manner of livestock, viewing which in the glory of an Indian summer, one could almost forget the bloody strife of slaveholders and Abolitionists in Kansas.

In the fair's cattle section, Drew himself must have viewed with swelling pride and excitement the brawny working oxen, the hefty cows and bullocks, the entire lots of fine fat steers that he had bought at three hundred pounds and in six months tripled or quadrupled in weight, to be sold at a hundred dollars a head. Year after year these animals sent him home with top prizes, such as a diploma or a silver cup, *Stevens's Book of the Farm,* or the colored plates of the *Horticulturalist,* publications that thereafter (one suspects, in pristine condition) loomed prominently among the scanty volumes, mostly Methodist hymnals and the Good Book, that constituted his library. For all the time he had spent in the city, then, the old man still knew critters.

Yet when it came time to return to New York, he was always ready. Fat cattle, county fairs, and clean country living were all very fine in their way, but they did not make his brain tick or his pulse quicken. Seated in a Harlem coach en route to the city, he could hardly wait to get back: the Wall Street pot was boiling.

CHAPTER 8

The Best Friend a Railroad Ever Had

On October 11, 1853, Daniel Drew got married to the New York and Erie Railroad, whose board of directors he joined at that date and remained a member of for fifteen years, long enough to constitute, in speculative circles, a marriage. It was, however, a most cynical union, for the groom's intentions were anything but pure, while for her part the lady had a past; in fact, she was notorious.

Incorporated in New York State in 1832, the New York and Erie Railroad had embodied the sublimest of visions: a bond of iron linking the Atlantic to the Great Lakes, and the port of New York to the vast regions of the trans-Allegheny West; a railroad that would be one of the longest trunk lines in the world, guaranteeing forever to the port of New York, to the exclusion of her jealous rivals, the commerce of that immense hinterland that she had first secured by means of the Erie Canal. In an age when the construction of a railroad only fifty miles in length was considered a major undertaking, the Erie promoters had proposed a line nine times as long, part of it through forbidding mountainous terrain—a project so grandiose as to be conceivable only as a supreme act of faith.

From the outset, this vison was plagued by calamities. In December 1835, only one month after the first ground was broken, a great fire in lower Manhattan ruined many of the original backers, and of those then spared, many more went under in the Panic of 1837. Over the decades that followed, the work proceeded haltingly, hampered by a depleted treasury; by underestimated costs and overconfidence; by state and local rivalries, unreliable contractors, a restrictive charter; and by false and not-so-false accusations of managerial fraud and incompetence. President after president resigned in defeat or was ousted, while the line's backers despaired, took hope, and despaired again. The engineering problems alone were staggering. There were vast distances to be spanned, torrents and chasms to be bridged, and rocky precipices to be hewn through, the financing of which required millions, although at one point in those days before gaslight, the directors could not even afford candles for their meetings. All too often, colossal blunders were committed by the management. Of all the enemies arrayed against the Erie—man, nature, and God seemed among them—one of the foremost was the Erie itself.

What did Daniel Drew, the shrewdest of money men, see in this child of vision and disaster? At first, just another fancy to manipulate. But in 1851 this changed. With its charter's twenty-year limit about to expire, the Erie, through a desperate burst of energy and debt, managed to complete 445 miles of track between Piermont, twenty-five miles north of New York on the Hudson, and Dunkirk on Lake Erie (both termini in themselves insignificant, their choice another blunder). On May 14 and 15, 1851, two special trains bearing President Millard Fillmore and other dignitaries rode the full length of the line, following which at Dunkirk, amid pealing church bells and a barbecue, Director William B. Dodge announced triumphantly, "The Empire City and the great West, the Atlantic Ocean and the inland seas, are by this ligature of iron made one!"[1]

Daniel Drew did not attend the opening ceremonies. His chief contribution to the Erie saga to date had been, in company with most of Wall Street, some nimble trading in the railroad's stock. But a completed railroad was another thing; suddenly, this tawdriest of Wall Street jades seemed appealing. And when the "Ayrie" as he called it reported rising earnings, declared a dividend, and secured both a connection to Buffalo and a Jersey City terminus just across the Hudson from New York, the old drab looked positively glamorous. Now both he and Nelson Robinson were eager to get on the board, not because they believed in Erie's promise (although perhaps, to an extent, they did), but because the Erie was a setup for sustained speculation. Headquartered in New York, it had a large capitalization and was actively traded, with much stock available on the Street. Better still, there was no strong hand at the helm, so that the company's fortunes oscillated between shimmering hopes and tangible disasters, producing those wide fluctuations in stock so dear to a speculator's heart. The only thing lacking, in the eyes of these cynical appraisers, was the inside knowledge that would assure their operations of success, which was why they began wooing Erie.

Nor could Erie turn them down. Having begged loan after loan from the state and piled mortgage on top of mortgage, the company needed desperately the support of financiers like Robinson and Drew, whose resources and acumen were respected, and who in any event could not be kept out, given their heavy holdings of the stock. On July 27, 1853,

Robinson became the company's treasurer, and when the annual election of October 11 brought some new faces to the board, among them were Drew, Robinson, and several of their Wall Street allies. On March 14 following, when Robinson resigned for reasons of health, Drew became the company's treasurer and, as such, a power in the road.

To be sure, some Erie stockholders may have questioned the propriety of the new treasurer's presence in their midst. After all, Drew's steamboats were allied now with the New York Central, Erie's great rival in competing for the traffic of the West. If the Central undercut the Erie's rates consistently, it was because of the boats' low fares. To cope with this situation, in October 1853 the Erie for $100,000 had bought a controlling interest in the *Francis Skiddy*, thought by many to be the finest and fastest boat on the Hudson, and had run it up the river to Newburgh, to connect there with an Erie branch line. By this route, the Erie ads claimed, passengers would reach Buffalo and the West eight hours ahead of those leaving at the same time on the People's Line. All of this must have been awkward for Drew, who had just joined the Erie board. Drew, however, probably reflected that railroad men, especially Erie men, knew precious little about operating steamboats. Sure enough, by the following spring the *Francis Skiddy* had brought the railroad a loss of over $14,000, so that the company was dying to get rid of it. Now the treasurer, Drew was only too happy to help, so in May 1854 the *Skiddy* was sold to Eli Kelley and Vanderbilt, who promptly sold it to him. Obviously, sitting in Erie's councils could be useful: golden crumbs came your way.

In those days, they seemed to be coming everybody's way but Erie's. Real gold kept arriving on ship after ship from California, as if to fuel forever the economy of a lusty young nation that wanted more land, more cities, more mines, more beaver hats, silk dresses, cigars, and champagne—and most of it on credit. The Stock Exchange was feverish, money easy, hopes high, and for speculation one had the choice of stocks, land, guano, sugar, cotton, tobacco, lead, gold mines, and fancy poultry. Central to all ambitions and illusions were the railroads, those binders of the nation whose projected conquest of the wilderness glib promoters were touting with dizzying success throughout Europe. By the early 1850s, their stocks were at an all-time high.

In July 1854, however, there was a jolting discovery. Robert Schuyler, the socially prominent New Yorker who was president of the New York and New Haven Railroad, had forged twenty thousand shares of New Haven stock and sold it for two million dollars. Exposed, he absconded with the money to Canada. Then the Harlem line's secretary confessed to similar forgery and misappropriation, and it was learned in turn that a large number of other companies had also been looted by insiders. The bull market sagged grievously as banks tightened up on loans, and the dismayed public grasped that some of the most dazzling go-ahead artists were capable of outright fraud.

This upset was ruinous to Erie, whose stock, having hit 82 in March, by late summer had dropped to the low thirties—a plunge that Treasurer Drew surely worked for all it was worth in the market. Not that doubts about Erie were unjustified, since track and roadbed were deteriorating, laborers remained unpaid, and earnings were being ravaged by a rate war with the Central, while in this time of sudden stringency the company could not make loans to meet the interest on its mountain of debt. James Gordon Bennett's *Herald*, voicing its owner's caustic view of Wall Street, was ruthless in denouncing the "rottenness and insolvency of the Erie," which it blamed on years of mismanagement. By August the road was desperate, since semiannual interest of $337,000 on certain bonds was due September 1, and other huge debts were due soon thereafter, with no prospect of obtaining the money by loans. The affluent gentlemen of the board, generous in the past, refused to help the road in this crisis, and to top it off, three of them went bankrupt. Was there no hope, then? Yes, a glimmer. Erie's treasurer announced that he knew a man who, if properly approached, might help—Cornelius Vanderbilt.

Dressing elegantly in top hat and stock, his graying hair and ample sideburns neatly ranged, the dapper Vanderbilt of the 1850s was as resourceful and aggressive as ever, authoritarian to the core, respected but not loved, square-jawed, rough-tongued, and ruthless. Determined to open a route to California via Nicaragua, he had gone to Nicaragua himself, and to convince his own engineers it could be done, had bounced, scraped, and hauled a steamboat up a jungle river over rocks and through churning rapids. The route had indeed been opened, in consequence of which Drew had become co-owner with Vanderbilt of the steamship *North America*, plying between Nicaragua and California. This was surely Drew's farthest venture from home and not a happy one, since the ship, wrecked on the coast of Mexico, begot much litigation. Thereafter, in 1853 Vanderbilt had sailed off to Europe in his steam yacht the *North Star*, the biggest and most luxurious private yacht in the world, to create a sensation on both sides of the Atlantic by this unprecedented tour of the Old World by a self-made man of the New. Returning a celebrity, he discovered that in his absence two associates had seized control of his Nicaragua interests. Immediately he wrote them, "The law is too slow—I'll ruin you," and set plans in operation to do so. This was no idle threat, given his means; in wealth he ranked second only to William B. Astor, the son of John Jacob, a rating that he had vowed to improve.

It was to this giant of finance, a man whose brain swarmed with grandiose plans, and who would soon make the acquaintance of presidents, that Daniel Drew turned as an old friend and associate in Erie's hour of need. This was not, to be sure, an appeal to sentiment, for such an approach would have been wasted on Vanderbilt; Drew spoke as one businessman to another. As a result, on August 29, 1854, the Commodore endorsed Erie's short-term notes to the amount of $400,000, taking as security a mortgage on the company's entire rolling stock, plus $40,000 for his name. Yet the *Herald* was unimpressed, noting that most of this money would be paid out immediately as interest on the bonds, while the company's floating debt continued to mount. As if in answer, on August 31 Drew himself agreed to endorse Erie notes for up to one million dollars, of which he immediately endorsed $200,000, taking a mortgage on all Erie property that was still mortgageable. With two such endorsements behind them, Erie's five-month notes were taken at last by the banks, who advanced the railroad $600,000. Erie was saved, at a price.

This rescue provoked varied comments from the press, derisive from the *Herald*, more positive from the *Tribune*, which defended the board's "purity of character," while Poor's *American Railroad Journal*, hearing that Vanderbilt was boasting that he and the bondholders would soon get the road, decried him as a "sordid and grasping Shylock." As for Erie's troubled stockholders, it occurred to some of them to campaign for a change in management. At the annual election on October 10, however, the same group remained in power; Homer Ramsdell, a merchant of Newburgh, New York, was reelected president, and Drew continued as treasurer. Thereafter, in a fit of self-scrutiny, the company instituted reforms, then placed a new loan and satisfied the mortgages. Drew was officially thanked for his aid, and Vanderbilt did not get the road. So ended the Erie crisis of 1854.

Surprisingly, revelations of stock fraud did not halt the great boom of the 1850s, which got under way again as business conditions improved and the public recovered confidence. Speculations in land and commodities continued as frenzied as ever, and while railroad stocks declined steadily owing to a return of foreign capital to Europe, gold mine issues hit new highs. Everywhere, men met excitedly to trade securities, at the Stock Exchange, outdoors on the curb, at small rival exchanges, and even in hotel rooms after dinner.

No stock trader was more frenziedly active than Nelson Robinson, Drew's partner in a hundred coups. A daring speculator and a brilliant strategist, this former circus man and cattle dealer was now a giant of the exchange, a striking example of the self-made man in the rough. In 1854, however, a stroke struck him down in his office, and his condition was so serious that he could not be taken home for several days. Thereafter, heeding the pleas of his family and doctor, he retired for a while to the country, where his health improved. But with the market still at a fever pitch, he could not stay away. On Wall Street fellow brokers hailed his return, and the leading fancy stocks yielded to his deft manipulations. But again the strain told. Warned by his physician and beseeched by his young wife, he promised to wrench himself away: in May 1856 he would take his family on a European tour. On Sunday March 23, after a week of strenuous exertion, he attended church as usual, then went in his carriage to pick up his mother at another church. Just as he opened the door for her he was stricken again and collapsed. Taken at once to his Union Square mansion, he was borne up the stoop to the door, weeping as he announced, "I'm afraid I'm paralyzed."[2] Soon afterward he lost consciousness; a few hours later he was dead. The next morning the Board of Brokers passed resolutions of condolence and suspended the afternoon session. Only forty-eight years old, he left a fortune of over one million dollars.

Calm amid the frenzy of others, Drew mourned his ex-partner and bought his house. Some might have considered the house unlucky. The Suydam family, the wealthy merchants who had built it in 1849, had sold it to Robinson after suffering financial reverses, and now Robinson had died there. But 41 Union Square was a mansion worthy of a money king. It was a four-story brownstone with a high stoop on the west side of Union Square, at the corner of Broadway and Seventeenth Street, with a deep lot joined in the rear by another lot which, running back from Seventeenth Street, contained a private stable. And the neighborhood was the finest. Across the street lay Union Square, an elliptical park ringed by an iron fence and laid out with walks, shrubbery, and a fountain, while all around the park stood imposing hotels, churches, and costly private mansions. Drew of course knew the brownstone from visits, and on June 1, 1857, bought it from Robinson's executors for $60,000, and moved his family back to the city. Five years in Putnam County had been enough for him; New York was where he longed to be, had to be.

One of his prime concerns was the New York and Erie Railroad, whose recovery from its previous crisis had been thwarted by renewed blows from nature, man, and fate. First, the tunneling through a mass of solid rock called Bergen Hill—necessary to give better access to the new terminus in Jersey City—was swallowing up vast sums of money. Next, there was a ruinous strike by engineers. Then in January 1857, snowstorms that blocked traffic for days at a time were followed by riots of unpaid laborers and ice floods in the Delaware that swept away bridges which, rebuilt, were swept away again. Inevitably, the stock slumped in the market, its decline accelerated by the startling revelation in the *Herald* that, in late March of 1857, the Erie managers, desperate for money, had secretly sold five thousand new shares of stock through E. D. Stanton & Company, the brokerage house of Treasurer Drew. From a January high of 63, Erie stock plunged to a June low of 30 and under, a circumstance that provoked in the company's treasurer not dismay but serene satisfaction. With his new partner Edmund D. Stanton (a former clerk of his), he had shorted Erie heavily in the market, and he now covered his contracts to take a profit of substantial proportions.

When news of these operations got about, certain Erie shareholders thought it not altogether seemly that the attitude of the company's treasurer to the company should approach that of a leech to its victim. Why should he be treasurer anyway, they pointed out, when he still had a hand in the People's Line, whose low fares let the debt-free New York Central offer a bargain rate that the Erie could not match? It was high time this fellow chose either his steamboats or the Erie.

Treasurer Drew was heartsore to hear such murmurings. Why, he was a good friend to railroads. Just a few weeks before, he and Vanderbilt had joined the Harlem board and together endorsed the notes of that troubled line to the amount of $650,000. Could he do any less for the "Ayrie," which was desperate again to meet the interest on its floating debt? Certainly not! In late June he endorsed Erie's notes for $1.5 million, so that it could obtain bank loans to meet its obligations. Of course, for this loyal gesture he took as security three separate mortgages on the company's engines, cars, land, tracks, bridges, piers, buildings, walls, fences, fixtures, and all other unmortgaged property, and for his name alone, an absolute guarantee with the banks, received $25,000.

Alas, even as he was rescuing the railroad, another rate war with the Central broke out. Unfortunately for Erie, its only rail connection with the West was the little Buffalo and State Line Railroad, joining it at Dunkirk, which Erie and the Central had built jointly to connect with both. The Buffalo and State Line, however, was dominated by the Central, and in this new round of warfare refused to honor through tickets via the Erie Railroad and charged passengers who held such tickets double. Naturally, Erie shareholders were outraged. And who was one of the largest stockholders in the Buffalo and State Line Railroad? Why, none other than their very own treasurer! Wherever one turned, he seemed to have his finger in the pie, especially in pies inimical to Erie. Drew himself, however, showed proper indignation, promptly writing the Buffalo and State Line president on June 27 to protest against this policy, which continued regardless. To retaliate against the Central, on July 1 the Erie had to cut its rates once again.

With Erie's affairs fast deteriorating, the stockholders demanded changes at the top. For years now, as the *American Railroad Journal* and the *Herald* had long pointed out, the directors had waxed fat by looking each to his own private interests—Wall Street speculations, real estate deals, lucrative contracts, or rebates—always to the detriment of Erie. Homer Ramsdell, the president, was also a merchant, banker, and contractor, while dabbling in land speculation on the side. Assailed by criticism, he now suddenly offered to resign, recommending as his successor Erie director Charles Moran, a New York banker of high reputation, who two years before had restored Erie's credit by placing its last big loan in Europe. Summoned home from abroad for consultation, Moran was urged by the board to take over. Reluctant, he agreed, but on condition that he receive the unprecedented sum of $25,000 a year, matching the salary of the president of the United States. There were those who wondered if a railroad that often lacked funds to pay its laborers could afford a president at such a price, especially, as the *Herald* pointed out, a president who was just as ignorant as his predecessor of the practical workings of a railroad. The board, however, agreed, and on July 18, 1857, Moran became president, supremely confident that he could straighten out Erie's affairs.

What now of Treasurer Drew? With the departure of his good friend Ramsdell and the advent of Moran—who on the first day of his tenure arrived at his office at 6:00 A.M.—he sensed the chill breath of reform. Moran had roundly denounced the company's policy of obtaining special loans from individual lenders like Vanderbilt and Drew, which he thought disastrous for the company's reputation and credit. In addition, the treasurer was still under fire from stockholders for his divided loyalties. So Daniel reflected, if they wanted him to *git*, he would *git*. On July 20 he submitted his resignation as treasurer, at which news Erie's stock rallied on the market. But if treasurer no more, Drew was still thrice bound to the company as director, as speculator, and as mortgagee.

Meanwhile, if Erie had problems, so did the rest of the country. By July it was apparent that the nation's spring trade had fallen sharply, suggesting that the boom was at an end. Some observers like the *Herald* issued warnings, but public confidence remained unimpaired. Then, on the morning of August 24, 1857, the New York branch of the Ohio Life and Trust Company, an important and respected firm, announced that it had failed. This collapse, brought on by a cashier's embezzlements, hit Wall Street without warning, and stocks plummeted. Dangerously overextended, the New York bankers immediately contracted their loans, denying credit to customers whose operations depended on it. Since the New York banks were a source of credit throughout the country, the whole nation reeled with shock and dismay. It was the onset of the Panic of 1857, known otherwise as the Great Western Blizzard.

Within forty-eight hours of Ohio Life's suspension, seven New York country banks failed. Stocks declined, the banks continued to tighten up on credit, rumors of failures proliferated, and by September those rumors became failures in fact. Writing in his diary of the grim battles being fought in counting rooms, offices, and bank parlors by his distressed contemporaries, the New York lawyer George Templeton Strong expounded puritanically:

> They are fighting hard for the grand, ugly house in the Fifth Avenue; for the gold and damask sofas and curtains that are ever shrouded in dingy coverings, save on the one night of every third year when they are unveiled to adorn the social martyrdom of five hundred perspiring friends. They are agonizing with unavailable securities, and pleading vainly for discount with stony-hearted directors and inflexible cashiers, . . . that they may still yawn through *Trovatore* in their own opera boxes; that they may be plagued with their own carriage horses and swindled by their own coachman instead of hiring a comfortable hack when they want a ride.[3]

But they were fighting for much more than that—for the hopes, dreams, and illusions of a generation; for the assurance that their lives were more than flotsam in a storm; for the belief that progress was not just a game, a slick promotion, that they had not simply gambled and lost.

Amid this atmosphere of chaos and calamity, the new president of Erie proposed nothing less than a fourth mortgage loan of $6 million. At a meeting of stock and bondholders in New York on September 23, Moran expounded the company's perilous situation, warned that under his mortgages Drew could now seize the road at any time, lauded Erie's potential, and appealed to the assemblage to subscribe to the new issue of bonds. By October 1, when Erie's stock, which had once sold in the nineties, was down to 10, subscriptions totaled $600,000—a far cry from $6 million. Inevitably, on October 10 Erie joined the host of firms that had failed in their obligations. His back to the wall, Moran summoned the stock and bondholders to yet another emergency meeting.

By now, the panic had reached climactic nationwide proportions. Since the government held determinedly aloof (President Buchanan was convinced that he lacked authority to act), all eyes turned to New York, where the leading banks insisted that they would not suspend specie payment, even as the weaker banks were closing. Then on the morning of Tuesday October 13, the panic burst. As rumors of bank closings spread throughout the city like wildfire, distraught depositors scribbled checks and rushed downtown, and holders of paper money cleaned out their money boxes, cash drawers, and tills, and all hastened on foot or jammed the Broadway omnibuses in a wild dash down to Wall Street, where they scurried up the steep steps of banks to find out what hard-metaled reality, if any, lay behind those tall doors flanked with Grecian columns. Called upon to pay out hundreds of thousands of dollars worth of gold, bank after bank suspended. By now all Wall Street, from Water Street to Broadway, was jammed with depositors and spectators, the crowd orderly, never violent, but gripped with fear, anger, disbelief, and stupor. By 3:00 P.M. eighteen banks had suspended, and that evening the remaining thirty-three announced that, by mutual agreement, specie payments had been suspended by every bank in the city. Sober men approved, and a sense of relief came over everyone. Since the worst had happened, matters now could only improve.

The crowds thronging Wall Street at the height of the panic included men of moderate means, little means, and no means. Were the giants of finance there as well? The newspapers do not say, but a painting executed some months later, and noted for its accuracy of detail, shows a throng of capitalists in shiny top hats gesturing and talking earnestly on the sidewalk outside the Merchants' Exchange at exactly 2:30 P.M. of the fatal day, among whom Cornelius Vanderbilt and Jacob Little have been identified. Quite possibly Drew was also on hand, lured from E.D. Stanton & Company's nearby office at 22 William Street to witness all around him and to imprint on his bearish sensitivity that shrill peak of crisis when confidence and sanity are shattered, currency becomes mere paper, and the only thing that counts is gold. Yet if Drew was there, he was certainly one of the coolest on the scene, for he was not excitable by nature or inclined to fret. Indeed, when a friend asked him during this period if he could "sleep in these times" he answered, "I've never lost a night's rest on account of business in my life!"[4]

Daniel Drew slept easy while others lost their shirts and their dreams, because he himself was no dreamer and had never lived high on the hog. Neither of his steamboat companies was burdened with debt, while in the market his bearish inclinations probably kept his losses to a minimum. At a time when trust had almost vanished, his credit was intact, his signature a sterling guarantee.

In October 1857 Drew's solvency seemed to offer little hope to the Erie, whose shareholders bore in mind President Moran's warning that under his three mortgages Drew could seize the road at will. To be sure, Drew had rescued the Erie in the past, but not in times like these. Besides, since his last major act of largess, the stockholders had been so indiscreet as to oust him as the company treasurer. What could they expect now from this master of veiled purposes and mixed loyalties, this genius of manipulation? He held the company in the hollow of his hand.

On the evening of October 28 the Erie stock and bondholders trooped again to an emergency meeting, this one at the Mercantile Library in Astor Place. There the chairman of the finance committee reviewed the company's desperate condition, defended the president's outsized salary, and then announced that Daniel Drew, far from foreclosing as some had intimated, had assured him that if the company could pay him $1 million toward canceling that much of his endorsements, he would cheerfully—yes, *cheerfully*—take the remaining $500,000 in those fourth-mortgage bonds that the company was having a devil of a time getting rid of. Applause burst forth, as joy and relief enveloped the assembly. A resolution was quickly passed expressing confidence in the board of directors, "and especially Mr. Drew," who for the company's sake had incurred such vast liabilities. Daniel Drew was the best friend a railroad ever had.

For corporations, it was a time when friends were not easy to come by. Throughout the country—with specie payment suspended, construction halted, trade at a standstill, and tens of thousands out of work—the spirit of go-ahead had at last been stopped dead in its tracks. Along Broadway in New York, shells of buildings loomed frozen in mid-construction, while radical agitators fomented a march on city hall by the jobless and a mob attack on the subtreasury that was thwarted only by the intervention of the military. Meanwhile, getting no aid from Washington, decent citizens looked for help from on high. Church attendance rose, revivalism revived, and the *Journal of Commerce*, when advised of a newly instituted noonday prayer meeting for businessmen, urged its readers to

> Steal awhile away from Wall Street
> and every worldly care,
> And spend an hour about mid-day
> in humble, hopeful prayer.[5]

With time, stock prices recovered modestly, bank deposits rose, and gold flowed in from California and Europe, so that on December 12 the New York banks resumed specie payment, to be followed by the rest of the country. The panic was over, but the depression lingered. Hard hit, the commercial North recovered vigorously, yet remained shaken by "the late revulsion." The agrarian South, having suffered less, declared that "Cotton is king!" and predicted that if it came to an armed conflict over slavery, she would win.

On Wall Street the panic proved a watershed, a great winnowing out of fortunes and men. Down to ruin had gone the trusting, the overconfident, the careless, the tired, and the unlucky, while the shrewd and the unscrupulous survived. Among the victims was Jacob Little, who in the course of a year had failed and resumed, failed and resumed again, his fortune ebbing as he overstayed his genius or his luck. The young English-born broker Henry Clews, who had just forced the Stock Exchange to accept him as a member, saw the Great Western Blizzard as sweeping away old fogyism and making room for a younger element— presumably, men like himself. To the fore now pressed the leaders of the decade to come—bold, aggressive "Young America," like Daniel Drew, aged sixty.

CHAPTER 9

Wartime

In 1860 Daniel Drew was a director of three railroads, the president of two steamboat companies, and a trustee of three Methodist institutions of higher learning. For a millionaire he dressed soberly, although he spruced up for church on Sundays or a Matthew Brady photograph and could be seen in the streets, sometimes in a coach and sometimes in a calash, driving a stylish pair of bays with a plated harness and making, as the *Herald* put it, "a very fine show."[1] His residence at 41 Union Square was likewise impressive: a high-stooped, three-parlor brownstone that, when such embellishments became the rage in the sixties, he adorned with balconies and with a mansard roof featuring ornate dormer windows and a picturesque iron cresting on the top. Yet he never affected the sumptuous life style of many money kings, being still too much the frugal farm boy, the drover, the Methodist.

For the Methodists, indeed, he was the ideal layman benefactor, goodhearted, unobtrusive, generous, and a major contributor to their missionary funds, charities, and schools. In 1857, when the Mulberry Street Church congregation had decided to remove from their deteriorating neighborhood to a more fashionable site uptown, Brother Drew donated heavily toward the new edifice. The result, dedicated in May 1858, was St. Paul's Methodist Episcopal Church, a massive white-marble Romanesque structure at Fourth Avenue and Twenty-second Street, topped by a towering spire. Here the city's wealthy Methodists flocked to worship in comfortable pews, amid surroundings far more indicative of their sect's flourishing, genteel present than the severity and zeal of its past.

At the time of the removal, Drew's pastor was Dr. John McClintock, a brilliant scholar and educator, although infirm and inclined to hypochondria, whose fervent eloquence in the pulpit attracted multitudes and made the new church an immediate success. Becoming a close friend of Drew and his family, McClintock discovered in this homespun financier, so unlike himself in background, occupation, and temperament, a classic instance of the American self-made man, further enhanced in his eyes by piety, humility, and charity, as well as a robust health that he probably envied. In order that this first Methodist millionaire become a beacon unto others, McClintock took it upon himself to interview Drew and write a biographical sketch of him that appeared, with a portrait, as the lead article in the September 1859 issue of the *Ladies' Repository*, a Methodist monthly of wide circulation. In this article McClintock proclaimed the man of commerce as the hero of the age, and Daniel Drew as a model of the type, a flattering portrait to which Drew himself contributed no little through a tactful silence regarding such matters as his desertion from the militia in 1814, his brief circus career, the betrayal of the *Water Witch* stockholders, *Monteath v. Newton* and other legal embarrassments, and the mores of Wall Street. Inevitably, Drew emerged as a paragon of virtue, a "living example of peaceful and yet active piety."[2] The good doctor had been just a bit taken in.

Now in his sixties, even Drew conceded that it was time for honor, in the form of a crack new sidewheeler that would bear his name. He was president now of the New Jersey Steamboat Company. Isaac Newton, his steamboat partner of eighteen years, had died in New York on November 22, 1858—his passing hailed on the day of his funeral by flags at half mast in the harbor, and in Albany by tolling ships' bells, and artillery on Steamboat Square that fired salutes for an hour. With Newton gone, some river men and members of the public may have wondered if the new president, even with Capt. Alanson P. St. John as superintendent and treasurer to back him up, could maintain the company's prestige. As if to answer them and to serve notice that the People's Line would no longer renounce the day business to rival boats and the railroad, Drew contracted with the shipbuilder Thomas Collyer of New York for a new day boat to be named for himself.

Built in 1860 with the specific aim of outstripping all other river vessels in accommodations and speed, the 670-ton *Daniel Drew* did exactly that. Since the day boat *Armenia* was considered the fastest on the river, Drew immediately challenged its owner to a race. On June 4, 1860, in a run without passengers to Newburgh, the *Daniel Drew* beat her rival by seven minutes and was proclaimed the swiftest boat in the country. All summer she ran between New York and Albany, making excellent time, and on October 13, on her last through trip of the season, claimed a record running time of six hours and fifty minutes, an astonishing performance for a steamboat. Drew had made his point, that even without Isaac Newton the People's Line was still number one.

He yearned for a further accolade. That summer and fall the nineteen-year-old Prince of Wales, who later reigned as Edward VII, was touring the United States well chaperoned by a platoon of British peers, enduring with good grace the boisterous acclaim that democratic America always showered upon distinguished foreign guests. Of course he would pass through New York, and of course New York, which had hailed Lafayette, Dickens, Jenny Lind, the Erie Canal, and the Atlantic cable with enthusiasm, would give him the heartiest of receptions. Already city officials were preparing welcomes, the firemen a torchlight parade, the socially prominent a fancy dress ball. It occurred to Drew that as the owner of the newest, fastest, best boat on the river, he might place it at the prince's disposal and capture his illustrious person for the entire trip up the Hudson via West Point to Albany.

It was a daring idea; perhaps he got carried away. He offered the boat gratis to the mayors of New York and Albany and, upon learning that his offer was accepted, engaged Charles A. Stetson, the proprietor of the Astor House, to provide a splendid collation, and invited a hundred guests. On Thursday October 11, when the U.S. revenue cutter *Harriet Lane* brought the royal party over from New Jersey, Drew was on board as a member of the Committee of Invitation along with other dignitaries, and so got his first glimpse of the prince in the scarlet uniform of an English colonel. The prince then proceeded up Broadway to be acclaimed by a crowd of two hundred thousand. On the following evening he was honored by a grand ball at the Academy of Music, a glittering crush beneath which a section of the floor collapsed, while ladies who despaired otherwise of contact with the princely presence so contrived, it was said, to bump, jostle, squeeze, and pinch him, that his alarmed attendants almost whisked him away. Such was the spell cast by this lion of lions, in anticipation of whose visit fresh carpets were being laid on the *Daniel Drew*, cabin paintwork touched up, and new crockery supplied, while Stetson put in several days preparing his collation. The most gala of entertainments was anticipated.

Suddenly, late on Sunday the fourteenth, the very eve of the event, the Duke of Newcastle announced, courteously but firmly, that the invitation could not be accepted. It was the policy of the royal party, he explained, to pay its own way; they would travel by the *Harriet Lane* as far as West Point, and only thereafter by the *Daniel Drew*, without guests and at their own expense. Why the sudden change in plans? Rumors abounded, some alleging a difficulty between the duke and Mayor Fernando Wood of New York, while others said someone had warned Newcastle that the excursionists would include, self-invited, the entire New York City Common Council, certain uncouth members of which would bring the party into disrepute. Whatever the reason, Drew had to cancel the whole affair at once, to the intense disappointment of his guests. In compensation, however, he got the royal party to agree to tour his steamboat *New World*, which he then sent up specially to Albany. It is quite conceivable that, unknown to the foreign visitors, he had loaded it up with his disinvited guests, who thus still hoped to get a crack at the prince. And as the *Daniel Drew*'s owner, he himself, with his family, could hardly be barred from the boat.

So it was that on the morning of Tuesday October 16, 1860, the *Daniel Drew* lay waiting at a wharf near Cozzens' Hotel, about a mile below West Point Academy. There in the late morning it received the royal party, who the day before had inspected the academy installations. A crowd had gathered, flags were displayed, and when the cadets' band rendered "Home, Sweet Home," an earl in the suite dabbed his eyes and the embarking prince sighed heavily. What minimal greeting passed between Drew and his guests has not been recorded. All the way up the Hudson the royal party marveled at the frost-nipped autumn foliage, while bunting-bedecked boats saluted them with screeching whistles and clanging bells, as at landing after landing the prince was hailed by flags, booming cannon, and the shouts and waving handkerchiefs of multitudes.

Regarding the prince's own actions, however, two accounts exist. According to the newspaper reports of the day, the youthful prince, more boyish than his portraits indicated, appeared on deck wearing a dark blue frock coat with a velvet collar, a black beaver hat, and yellow kid gloves, and bowed gracefully to the repeated ovations. According to a tradition of Drew's own family, on the other hand, a story still told by his descendants today, during much of the trip to Albany the real prince lay indisposed in his cabin below, while on deck his place was hastily assumed by Drew's own son Billy, then sixteen, who bore a striking resemblance to the prince and bowed grandly to cheering crowds who never knew the difference.

At Albany the real prince was greeted by yet another exuberant reception. There, the *Daniel Drew* pulled up alongside the *New World*, which lay between it and the dock, an arrangement that, whether by chance or calculation, exposed the prince to the *New World*'s swarm of visitors. The prince, however, having grasped the situation at a glance, canceled his tour of the *New World* on the spot, strode across its deck to the dock, stepped into a carriage with the mayor, and drove off amid the cheering of multitudes. So ended Drew's first and only brush with royalty.

The visit of the Prince of Wales had afforded but momentary distraction from the impending national crisis. In November 1860 Abraham Lincoln triumphed in the national elections, whereupon one by one the Southern states seceded. Fearful of losing the vast sums that Southern merchants owed them, New York businessmen urged compromise. In April 1861, however, when Confederate batteries fired on Fort Sumter and the new president issued a call to arms, New York City poured forth men and money, the Stock Exchange passed resolution after resolution of loyalty, and Horace Greeley's *Tribune* announced exultantly, and prematurely, that a "sordid, grasping, money-loving people" had been redeemed by patriotism.

What was Daniel Drew's reaction in the wake of Sumter, when flags appeared everywhere, recruiting stations proliferated, baggy-trousered Zouaves with fezzes strutted in the streets, and on April 20 one hundred thousand citizens—reputedly, the largest assemblage ever seen on the continent—convened just across the way in Union Square to march, cheer, and orate in defense of the Union? Even in this feverish atmosphere, one suspects that his patriotism burned with a low, small flame. He was not one for huge enthusiasms, nor had the slavery issue ever wrenched his vitals. Although his friend John McClintock and other leading Methodists had long been abolitionists, throughout the 1850s he had remained preoccupied with business, and like most businessmen—especially in New York, with its strong commercial ties to the South—had probably deplored war talk as the rhetoric of extremists. Now, however, the war had come and of course he was routinely loyal, but no hothead, and immune to incandescent fervors.

Just as incombustible were his family, not one of whom succumbed to martial ardor. His young son would soon marry and live snugly as a gentleman farmer in Drewville, while his grandson entered Wall Street, and the husbands of two granddaughters likewise cleaved to business, none of them fearful of the draft legislated in 1863 since, if summoned, these affluent young men could buy substitutes. Nor was such an attitude uncommon, least of all after the North's initial burst of zeal had deflated. As the war dragged on over the months and the years, vast segments of the Northern mercantile classes stuck to their conviction that enlistment was for greenhorns and fools.

Not that they were indifferent to the war. The Union forces required uniforms, arms, munitions, and bunting, to supply which factories worked to capacity, new plants sprang up, and railroads were strained to the utmost, their revenues soaring. Contractors reaped unbelievable profits, some of them by supplying pasteboard shoes, shoddy uniforms, rotten blankets, tainted pork, and glued knapsacks that came apart in the rain. Begotten by this boom was a new wave of parvenus who gloried in imported luxuries and liveried servants, the so-called shoddy aristocracy, especially conspicuous in New York. Parading down Fifth Avenue on Sundays or in shiny equipages in the new Central Park, the women displayed brocaded silks and thousand-dollar camel's-hair shawls, while their escorts sported velvet coats, gold chains, breast pins, and rings as ample proof that war could be a very good business.

For steamboat men, the conflict was a godsend. With the military desperate for vessels to convey seaborne expeditions, all kinds of old hulks could be patched together, dusted off, and chartered or sold to the government. In 1862, when McClellan's Peninsula Campaign against Richmond required vast quantities of shipping, Drew chartered the *Knickerbocker* and the *Commodore* to the Quartermaster's Department, receiving for the first seven hundred, and for the second eight hundred dollars a day, which was not a bad rate for two vessels, aged nineteen and fourteen years respectively, that were nearly obsolete. A half interest in another such, the old People's Line boat *North America*, was acquired in 1861, probably with help from Drew, by his twenty-two-year-old grandson Daniel Drew Chamberlain, the co-owner being none other than Capt. Joseph W. Hancox, the pistol-flaunting skipper of the *Napoleon*, who after two decades on the river was as feisty and mettlesome as ever. On several occasions the two owners leased their boat to the government, then in 1863 sold it outright to the Quartermaster's Department for $55,000, no small bit of luck (if luck it was), since only three months later it was condemned as unseaworthy in Louisiana and destroyed there.

But what were these transactions, compared with those of the Commodore, who in 1861 chartered four steamships to the desperate government at the astonishing rate of two thousand dollars a day? Subsequently Vanderbilt incurred stiff criticism in Congress when some vessels hired by subordinates of his for an expedition to New Orleans proved so decrepit that they nearly sank on the way. Not that Vanderbilt's loyalty or courage were in question. At Lincoln's personal invitation, in March 1862 he undertook to destroy the much-feared rebel ironclad *Merrimac*, based at Norfolk, by ramming her with his unarmored steamship *Vanderbilt*, an encounter that the *Merrimac* avoided, but which, had it occurred, would probably have resulted in the obliteration of either the *Merrimac* or Cornelius Vanderbilt.

Flimsy uniforms and old vessels—dealing in these, as wartime profits went, was tame. For excitement, there was gold and securities.

Gold was hoarded from the outset of the war by a public beset with uncertainties, in consequence of which specie payment was stopped by both the banks and the government. Then, unable to sell its bonds to the public and pressed by creditors, the government began to issue greenbacks: paper currency unsecured by gold, backed only by the credit of the government, in effect, money by fiat, that starting in February 1862 flooded the country to inflate the currency, raise prices, and stimulate business. Instantly, Wall Street took note. Gold was esteemed but in hiding, whereas the greenbacks were plentiful but dubious, their value dependent on a Union victory that would let the government redeem them in gold, whereas in the event of defeat they might be repudiated. The relative value of the greenbacks and gold, then, must fluctuate inversely, varying with the military fortunes of the North. In terms of greenbacks, in other words, gold would fluctuate just like a stock or a commodity, and one could trade in it. *Gold!* The very word made the blood race, the brain quicken. Excitedly, even as armies clashed and bled on the battlefields, Wall Street initiated the most dramatic of its wartime operations, the speculation in gold.

By the third year of the war, Daniel Drew was up to his ears in it. How could he not be, when every fresh bulletin from the battlefields sent the price of gold plunging or soaring, and fortunes that had once been amassed over decades or years could now be made in months, weeks, and days or lost in hours or minutes? How could he not, when a federal law designed to suppress the speculation backfired and had to be repealed? The gold traders, driven from the Stock Exchange, took refuge in an ill-lit den called the Coal Hole, then in Gilpin's News Room nearby, and finally, by the war's last winter, in a home of their own called the Gold Room. There, packed masses traded frantically while outside on the street, ankle-deep in slush, more speculators gathered, their eyes riveted on an overhead price indicator, to whose fluctuations they had pinned their fortunes, their dreams, and their sanity.

Drew of course was not among them. Dry-shod and snug, he operated from a cozy back room in his broker's office in William Street, where messenger boys rushed in with the news and out with his orders. In speculating, he relied on his instincts as a bear, shorting gold when others were bulling it. In the process he seems to have forgone the ultimate finesse of certain operators, who planted agents at the front to wire back the battle news at once and so achieved an intelligence network on both sides of the lines that far surpassed those of the armies. Perhaps such indifference to technology worked to his detriment: in February 1863, when the price of gold climbed to 172½, meaning that to buy $100 in gold certificates required $172.50 in greenbacks, Drew suffered losses said to amount to half a million dollars. At this point other bears settled their contracts and retired from the field in defeat, whereas Drew stuck to his campaign. Thereafter, in the wake of unexpected Union victories, gold fell for several months, permitting Drew to recover much of his losses. Ironically, since to short gold was to hope for a Union success, in these operations he had assumed the stance of a patriot.

Such patriotism did not impress the president in the White House. "What do you think of those fellows in Wall Street, who are gambling in gold at such a time as this?" he asked Governor Andrew G. Curtin of Pennsylvania in April 1864. "They are a set of sharks," replied Curtin. "For my part," said Lincoln, banging his clenched fist on a table, "I wish every one of them had his devilish head shot off.!"[3]

Not gold, however, but the stock market was the hub of Drew's existence. After a brief panic at the war's outbreak, followed by months of doldrums, in 1862 it snapped to life with the first Union victories, and for the balance of the war churned with the same speculative fever that raged in gold. Lured by tales of riches, outsiders flocked to Wall Street— merchants, clerks, waiters, steamboat captains, dowagers, and clergymen—and as volume surged, exchanges multiplied until there were markets for gold, mining stocks, and petroleum issues, an Open Board that provided continuous daytime trading of stocks, countless minor fly-by-night markets, and a number of evening exchanges that gave to New York, alone of all the cities in the world, facilities for trading stocks twenty-four hours a day. Successful speculators learned to dine regularly at Delmonico's on partridge stuffed with truffles, but only too often were seen a few months later shuffling in seedy clothes, breakfasting on hash and coffee, or panhandling. It hardly mattered, because for every warrior who perished on the Wall Street battlefield, there were a dozen fresh recruits to take his place.

No one colossus overstrode the market, as Jacob Little had in his day, but a set of lesser titans inspired it: the genial, high-living Leonard Jerome; his elder brother Addison, who in 1863 was hailed as the Napoleon of the Open Board; Henry Keep, a master of pools, who lived up to his name by retaining all his fortune to the end; and above all Anthony W. Morse. A jaunty redheaded adventurer of small stature and huge daring, for one solid year Morse set the market ablaze with his spectacular corners in rail stocks, only to be wiped out in a single disastrous operation in Fort Wayne, following which he vanished from the Street, took to gambling, fell sick, and died months later in a shabby rooming house whose landlady, it is said, refused to surrender the body until some of his old friends paid the rent.

These men and their followers were mostly bulls. From 1862 on, the bear contingent congregated daily in William Street, roosting on iron railings in the sun or standing about dolefully (the market was not being kind to them) near the entrance to Number 15, the offices of David Groesbeck & Company, their headquarters. There, toward late morning, their acknowledged leader arrived in his one-horse chaise, a tall, stooped gentleman dressed drably in an ordinary suit, who when he alighted walked with a catlike tread. His pinched face—square, with high cheekbones—was a labyrinth of wrinkles, out of which shone twinkling steel-gray eyes charged with vitality and cunning. In appearance he struck contemporaries variously as a hardheaded old farmer, a cross between a cartman and a petty tradesman, and a country deacon or, since like the rail-splitter in the White House he had renounced the cleanshaven look of the fifties for a fringe of whiskers, as a dishonest Abraham Lincoln. No one would have called him handsome; some thought him ugly or grotesque. In witness of his age, Wall Street now referred to him as Uncle Daniel (he himself addressed younger men as "my son" and "sonny"), "uncle" being a term of affection widely used for elderly rustics at the time, although in this case with a tinge of irony. Probably he did not mind the name, and for his own purposes even played the part a bit. Nicknames in fact seemed to stick to him; he was known also as the Old Man, Ursa Major, the Old Bear, and the Deacon.

Groesbeck & Company had been set up by Drew in 1862 expressly to serve as his brokerage house, following the semiretirement of Edmund D. Stanton, his partner of the 1850s. As a new associate, David Groesbeck, called Grosy by his customers, was a natural choice, having worked for many years as a clerk in the office of Jacob Little, who then had launched him in an office of his own, that he might assist Little in his operations. Trained in bear techniques by the master, Groesbeck had both won and lost heavily, and by now he was quite content to amass profits strictly through commissions. Although Drew himself was not a member of the firm, the junior partners included his grandson Daniel Drew Chamberlain, who had just graduated from New York University (the first college graduate in the family), and William W. Everett, a Putnam County farmer's son who had married Drew's eldest granddaughter. Whenever possible, Uncle Daniel liked to keep things in the family.

Groesbeck's offices consisted of four snug rooms. The customers gathered in one room, or for congratulations or discreet consoling were summoned into another small one on the side. Behind a railing in a third room a half dozen clerks sat computing, and there too, in quiet moments, the firm's junior members, all sporting young gentlemen, could be seen strolling about "talking horse." As for Ursa Major, in times of heavy trading his presence was indicated by a steady stream of visitors in and out of a small room in the back, whence emanated clouds of cigar smoke and where, at intervals, he could be glimpsed through a half open door sitting cross-legged on a sofa, closeted with Grosy or an Erie director, or perhaps some eminence of the Street. In this little back room at Groesbeck's, schemes and speculations were ripened, pools formed, corners conceived, and rumors hatched and circulated. Here too Uncle Daniel sold "puts" and "calls"—contracts that let the holder sell to Drew or buy of him, respectively, given amounts of a stock—and here the esoteric "straddle," consisting of a put and call combined, may have first been offered, since Drew claimed to have invented it. But when not engaged in such arcana, the Old Bear could be seen puttering about in the offices, making occasional homely comments in a twang, or humorous remarks punctuated with short bursts of a hen-cackle laugh. Indeed, in all his operations he kept in mind the fun of the thing, thus earning himself yet another nickname, the Merry Old Gentleman of Wall Street. Obviously, like most Wall Streeters, he had marvelously adjusted to the war.

By the spring of 1863 the Merry Old Gentleman had his eye cocked most seriously, although intermittently, on the stock of the New York and Harlem Railroad, which having sold at 9 in 1860, had recently begun to rise, touched 61 in April, then fell back, rose, fell, and rose again. Wall Streeters were mystified, for they had long considered Harlem stock the tiredest of fancies, its certificates fit only for wrapping paper. The railroad had always been unprofitable because its roundabout route to Albany traversed a rural area providing little business and because it was surpassed by the Hudson River Railroad in speed and by the steamboats in economy of fare and comfort. Yet obviously there was something behind the stock's new vitality, and as an insider Drew knew that the something was Cornelius Vanderbilt.

Drew and Vanderbilt had first joined the Harlem board in May 1857 in a financial rescue operation that had failed to turn the railroad around. Thereafter, Vanderbilt had shown but little interest in the road and rarely attended the meetings of the board. By late 1862, however, in the most dramatic turn of his career, the Commodore began shifting his attention from shipping interests to railroads, and he discerned in Harlem a mismanaged property that, if reorganized, could surely become profitable. Since the Harlem was already operating horsecars below Twenty-sixth Street at a profit, and since its charter gave it the right, subject to the approval of the New York City Common Council, to lay tracks anywhere in the city, it occurred to Vanderbilt that operating a horsecar line down the full length of Broadway might transform this ailing railroad into a gilt-edged property. Under his leadership, in March 1863 the Harlem directors opened secret negotiations with the Common Council, a body whose talent for corruption was boundless, as a result of which the city fathers joined the Vanderbilt clique in purchasing the stock, which surged to 75 when the council approved the Harlem's street franchise petition in April, and to 116 in May, when at the annual election the Vanderbilt party took over the company and elected the Commodore president.

This transformation of the despised Harlem stock into one of the hottest issues on the market must have been watched by Drew with interest. Probably because he had other fish to fry—gold, for instance, and Erie—he had not joined forces with the bulls, although at the election he voted his modest 505 shares for Vanderbilt and was himself reelected a director. Now, however, with Harlem at 116, he surely yearned to sell the stock short. He did not, but there were others who did. Having rushed to take their profits, the city councilmen, in hopes of another scoop on the down side, shorted Harlem and then rescinded the franchise, a colossal double-cross of the Commodore, who avenged himself by cornering the stock and driving it ever upward through July even as Vicksburg surrendered, as Lee was being repelled at Gettysburg, and riots against the draft convulsed the city. In August the bleeding bears settled their contracts with disastrous losses, while Harlem peaked at 179. So ended the First Harlem Corner, with profits to the Vanderbilt camp of at least one million dollars.

Like the rest of Wall Street, Drew must have marveled. In his very first crack at the Street, Cornele had shown the touch of a master. Furthermore, the Commodore had also joined with some friends of his to smash a second bear attack, this one on the Hudson River Railroad, whose stock they hoisted from 123 to 180 in another huge massacre of shorts. And this from a fellow who claimed he was not even a speculator and whose advice to others was, "Don't you never buy anything you don't want, nor sell anything you hain't got!"[4]—which would rule out half the dealings on the Street! So the Commodore had marched onto the Old Bear's stomping ground and put himself at the top of the heap.

Having avenged himself on the shorts, Vanderbilt settled down to the serious business of reorganizing a railroad (and incidentally watering its stock). In mid-October, however, Harlem stock plunged to 93 when the State Supreme Court ruled that the projected Broadway line was not an extension of the Harlem but an independent route not covered by the Harlem's charter. To build his line, then, the Commodore would have to apply to the state legislature, an institution every bit as graft-prone as the council. Apply to it he did, dispatching well-heeled lobbyists to Albany whose suasions had the desired effect: early in 1864 the coveted Broadway railroad bill was introduced in the Senate. Thereafter, when the Senate Committee on Railroads opened hearings, what could Uncle Daniel do, as a loyal Harlem director, but accompany four fellow board members to Albany where on March 15, testifying before the committee, Vanderbilt's son-in-law Horace F. Clark proclaimed the Broadway railroad "an imperious public necessity." Swayed by Vanderbilt's attentions, the committee seemed inclined to agree, so much so that certain lawmakers joined Vanderbilt's friends in purchasing the stock, which having sold at 90 in January, by March reached 149. Wired by his agents that all was going well, the Commodore looked for a price of 200.

Meanwhile Drew reflected: Harlem was at 149! This worn-out fancy that he had known to trade at 50, at 30, at 9, even at 3, was sustained by one thing only—high hopes for its last chance at the franchise. He longed to sell it short and send it tumbling, but if he did so, it would make muddy water between him and the Commodore. Not for years had they tangled head-on. Quite the contrary, together, they had transformed the Stonington and rescued the Harlem itself and the Erie, teaming up so often that other railroad and steamboat men knew that to enlist the aid of the one was usually to get the help of the other. Such a relationship with the nation's biggest money king was not to be tossed away lightly. Then too, they were old friends, cronies. Why, he had even named his own son for Cornele's eldest! And finally, he knew the Commodore's wrath. Countering these forceful arguments, what was there but the pure joy and profit of a coup, reinforced perhaps by a further teasing thought: it was time Cornele got a twist in the market. In the scales of his mind, then, when balanced against pure joy and profit and the teasing thought, how did loyalty, friendship, and prudence weigh up? Like feathers. Of course he would sell Harlem short!

Others were like-minded. Perhaps Uncle Daniel put out feelers to them even while in Albany, or perhaps he joined the campaign later. In either case he reinforced a powerful army of bears that included his fellow Harlem director Addison Jerome, who after huge losses in the market was desperate to remake his fortune; President Erastus Corning and Superintendent Chauncey Vibbard of the New York Central Railroad, who hoped that by depressing Harlem stock they could facilitate a takeover of Harlem by the Central; certain legislators; and the powerful Republican politician Thurlow Weed. The original conspirators agreed that all would short Harlem in the market, following which the legislators would see to it that the Senate committee's report on the bill was negative. Thus the statesmen of Albany were undertaking against Vanderbilt precisely the maneuver that their confrères in Gotham had attempted just one year before, the results of which had prompted Wall Street to coin a new saying, "He went short of Harlem," to indicate that a man had been ruined. That this new team of short sellers so blithely disregarded the fate of their predecessors can be explained only by Ursa Major's inherent and persistent bearishness, and hubris inflicted by the gods.

About the third week in March, the legislators who held Harlem stock took their profits. Then, joining with the other bears, including fellow legislators and officers of the Custom House whom they had generously let in on the secret, they proceeded to sell Harlem short. On March 23, contrary to the general expectation, the Senate Committee on Railroads reported the bill adversely. Two days later, with Harlem hovering at 136, the chamber voted 27-2 to accept this negative report, while in the Assembly a similar bill was sent to committee, to gather dust until the end of the session. Harlem's friends were aghast; the stock sank to 101.

Caught unawares by this second double-cross, Vanderbilt was furious. If Daniel Drew wanted to go against him in the market, that was *his* business; he'd just as soon take money off of Dan'l as off of any man. But the legislators—*that* was something else again. Why, they were bought-and-paid-for allies! Against them, his rage waxed hot. They had betrayed him, therefore he would break them. And if Drew got in the way, by God he would break him, too!

Immediately he sent for his old friend John M. Tobin, a former gatekeeper at the Staten Island ferry house, who through recent speculations and bluff—on the Street he had hinted mysteriously of connections with Vanderbilt—had parlayed a small sum into $3 million. A bull in the First Harlem Corner, Tobin is said at that time to have wandered about Wall Street looking haggard, while his friends whispered that he was overcome with anxiety because of his heavy holdings of Harlem, thus prompting the bears to step up their short sales imprudently. In 1864 Tobin was a Harlem bull again, and like Vanderbilt a victim of the bears.

"They stuck you too, John," said Vanderbilt. "How do you feel about it?" Although obviously unhappy, Tobin said that he had no losses unless he sold. "Shall we let 'em bleed us?" asked Vanderbilt. "John, don't them fellows need dressing down?" Tobin agreed that they did. "Let's teach 'em never to go back on their word again as long as they live. Let's try the Harlem corner!"[5]

So they agreed to corner Harlem again, Tobin supplying a million and the Commodore and some other men the rest. Since Vanderbilt's approach to the stock market was the same as his technique for getting a steamboat up a rock-filled jungle river—make sure you can do it, then full speed ahead—orders went out to his lieutenants at once to buy all the Harlem offered, whether on seller's or buyer's option, for cash or otherwise, but *buy!*

Meanwhile the bears, reluctant to take profits when the stock had hit 101, held on for lower prices and continued to put out shorts. Under the barrage of Vanderbilt purchases, however, the stock began to go up—by April 6, to 156. Every day the tall, lithe form of Tobin was seen at the wildcat Public Board or in the street, his face pale with excitement and his eyes ablaze, buying thousands of shares of Harlem.

"No feeling, John!" shouted the stubborn bears, as the stock surged. "I'll make you feel!" cried Tobin.[6]

Above 150 the bears began to feel, and acutely, for it was around that price that they had first begun to sell short. By now Leonard Jerome had joined the Vanderbilt camp, playing the opposite side of the market from his brother Addison, while the anxious bears, still shorting, squelched incipient doubts with the knowledge that Uncle Daniel, the shrewdest of the ursine persuasion, had contracted to sell 30,000 shares of Harlem in the form of "calls": thirty- or sixty-day options permitting the holders to demand from him a certain amount of the stock at a given price. Naturally he had sold the calls expecting the stock to decline below the price stipulated, in which case the calls would be of no use to the holders, who would be out the price they had paid for them. However, since calls sold by operators of proven means were often used by the holders as margin to sell the stock short, Drew had in fact extended his credit to others, in the amount of millions, to continue selling Harlem short. Accordingly, his calls were snatched at by bulls and bears alike, the first in order to hold them for a rise, and the second to use them as margin. For a while, Harlem short sellers were legion. Big-time and petty speculators, insiders and outsiders, and even sober brokerage houses rushed to get in on the game, so that a broker with Harlem stock on hand could lend it for short sales at any hour of the day.

Unflinchingly, Vanderbilt and his friends continued to take every share offered, pushing the price up to 190. Then in mid-April, in an attempt to squelch the speculation in gold, Secretary of the Treasury Salmon P. Chase came to New York to sell millions in gold and lock up greenbacks and in the process precipitated a panic in stocks. In the face of this unlooked-for crisis, even Vanderbilt blanched, but Tobin convinced him that they should support Harlem regardless. For several days Vanderbilt rose at 5:00 A.M. to go to his office, where he wore a troubled look and barked at anyone who disturbed him, but on April 18, when the panic culminated in a calamitous decline, Harlem sold off only to 183 and afterward resumed its advance. By April 23, the day the legislature adjourned, it had reached 220.

Having kept a careful count of their transactions, Vanderbilt's lieutenants now reported to him that they held stock, or contracts for stock, for 27,000 more shares than the entire capitalization of the company: to cover their contracts, the shorts must buy Harlem from the only parties now holding it, Vanderbilt and his friends, who could set what price they pleased. "Put it up to a thousand!" cried the vengeful Commodore. "This panel game is being tried too often!"

But Tobin and Leonard Jerome urged prudence, since as Jerome pointed out, "It would break every house on the Street."[7]

So Vanderbilt relented; he would tighten the screws only to a point.

Watching closely, the *Herald* announced that the Harlem corner was nearing culmination, and even named the more prominent victims.

Drew was one of them. Far from making a killing, he was trapped, his calls for 30,000 shares dooming him to a loss of well over a million at the least. Under such circumstances the protocol of Wall Street prescribed a visit by the loser to the winner, to arrange to settle up. But when the Old Bear went to the Commodore, he threw himself on Vanderbilt's mercy, pleaded ancient friendship, and probed slyly for whatever scant reservoirs of sentiment existed in that ironbound heart. No use; Vanderbilt asked pointedly how much mercy he himself could have expected, had the tables been reversed.

"Dan'l," he told the suppliant, "don't go for to plead the baby act, anyhow. Come up like a man and settle!"[8] Instead, Drew charged conspiracy—he had been trapped by false representations, cruelly tricked—and when this made no impression, tried another tack: "Them contracts merely say that you may *call* upon me for so much stock— they say nothin' about me deliverin' the stock. Call, then, and keep callin'—I ain't obliged to deliver any stock!"[9]

And so, in Wall Street parlance, Drew "lay down" or "squatted" on his contracts: he refused to honor them and furthermore threatened litigation. Those calls, he insisted, were not legal, since all the stock was held by the very men to whom the calls had been sold. In guileless innocence, he claimed, he had been seduced into selling what he could not possibly deliver. This was a bit flimsy, perhaps, but he was well aware how Wall Street abhorred litigation.

Meanwhile the annual Harlem election came round. At the meeting on May 17, just ten stockholders assembled to vote 105,873 shares of stock, most of which was held by three men: Vanderbilt, Tobin, and one of Vanderbilt's brokers. Inevitably, Vanderbilt was reelected president, while Drew and Addison Jerome, both absent, were thrown off the board. That same day the stock attained 280, then on June 1 hit 285; the corner had achieved its climax.

For weeks now, one by one the defeated shorts had been presenting themselves at the offices of Vanderbilt's brokers, where in settling their contracts they received little mercy. Ruined, most of the smaller operators were never seen again on the Street. As for the Old Bear, as late as May 17, the very day of the Harlem election, he alone still refused to respond to his calls. But compromise was in the air. Almost daily, Tobin and Leonard Jerome were negotiating with him in the back room at Groesbeck & Company, haggling, threatening, arguing, and cajoling, until at last a settlement was reached. Only the parties concerned knew how much the old man paid—by one report, sixty cents on the dollar— but the Street reckoned his losses at between half a million and a million. "These calls are nasty things," said Uncle Daniel.[10]

Harlem stock remained close to 280 until the last short contracts had been settled. Then, being completely in the hands of the bulls, it ceased to be traded altogether. So ended the Second Harlem Corner, with scores of speculators wiped out and Vanderbilt's prestige at new heights. By his own account, the Commodore had made $2 million, not to mention his lieutenants. "We busted the whole legislature," he later reminisced, "and scores of the honorable members had to go home without paying their board bills!"[11] As for Drew, he was in great grief of mind since all the Street knew that "they had taken a slice out him." It was galling to lose, especially to lose to Vanderbilt. The Old Bear yearned for revenge.

CHAPTER 10

The Virtuoso of Erie

On the afternoon of March 14, 1864, to a city so little gripped by wartime austerity that it could indulge itself in lace, velvet, Brussels carpets, theater, balls, and receptions, Daniel Drew offered yet another sumptuous experience: the inspection, at the foot of Cortlandt Street, North River, of the newly completed steamboat *St. John*. Named for Capt. Alanson P. St. John, whose service to the People's Line as senior captain, superintendent, and treasurer left President Drew free for the more exhilarating distractions of Wall Street, the new vessel was a $400,000 marvel of marine construction that the newspapers described as being to river steamboats as the *Great Eastern* was to ocean steamers, the Fifth Avenue Hotel to hostelries, and St. Peter's in Rome to the churches of Christendom.

With the *St. John* in service, the replacement program of the People's Line was triumphantly under way. This program was long overdue, since by the early 1860s the *Hendrik Hudson*, *Isaac Newton*, and *New World* were aged and ripe for retirement. Because the People's Line was thriving, Drew could well afford to inaugurate a new series of three giant sidewheelers designed to maintain the company's dominance of the night line. In July 1865, when the second of these palaces was exhibited to the public—the $600,000 *Dean Richmond*, named for the new president of the New York Central Railroad, long an ally of the People's Line—the *Times*, having surveyed its lavish furnishings, declared that what remained exclusive in monarchical Europe had become common in republican America.

Ironically, the millionaire creator of this new fleet of luxury steamboats—who for tax purposes reported an income in 1864 of over $101,000—remained as personally frugal as ever, often carrying as a cane the stripped shaft of an old umbrella. When, during an inspection tour of a railroad out West, he learned that a lengthy telegram that he wished to send to his wife was going to cost twelve dollars, he was shocked. This frugality carried over into business as well. He never insured his steamboats, insisting instead on vigilance and proper upkeep, a policy that served him well for years, accidents being rare on his line and passenger deaths unknown. In December 1863, however, when a boiler explosion destroyed the *Isaac Newton*, a number of passengers died from scalding, while two years later a similar explosion on the *St. John* killed eleven. Even without insurance, however, Drew made good all claims from passengers and shippers. When the *Dean Richmond* collided with another boat in 1867, he is said to have paid out nearly $300,000 without a single lawsuit and still considered it a bargain, in that insurance for his boats would have cost him half a million.

To his employees he was a good boss; they remained in his service for years. Captains Peck and Roe, of the *St. John* and *Dean Richmond* respectively, had been with him since the 1840s, and his partner St. John, now the number two man in the company, since 1834. Behind his back the river men called him Raw Hide—presumably, a comment on his wrinkled, dark-complexioned features—but in his presence they were respectful, and politic as well. The story is told how on one occasion, when he was traveling on one of his boats, he chanced to meet the captain in the bar. Both were surprised, but the captain put on a bold face, talked business as he drank his whiskey, then conspicuously plunked down a quarter on the counter. "What?" said Drew. "Do you have to pay for your drinks on this boat?" "Always," said the captain. "Fact is, Mr. Drew, I find it the best means of interposing a most desirable restraint on natural tendencies."[1]

Drew left satisfied that his captain, if he had to pay steamboat prices, was a moderate drinker, while the thirsty skipper had the satisfaction of knowing he had bluffed his boss and the assurance that the bartender, if he valued his job, would return the quarter posthaste.

In steamboating Drew no longer aspired to be more than a good boss and an efficient manager, channeling all his ambitions into Wall Street. Noting the high wartime prices for boats, in September 1863 he sold his interest in the day boat *Daniel Drew*, and in December of that year he pulled out of the sound altogether, selling three of his New Jersey Steam Navigation Company's vessels to a company newly formed in Connecticut. Finally, in September 1864 Drew and the other New Jersey Steam Navigation Company directors and shareholders sold the company's remaining two boats, then running between New York and Troy, to Drew's

New Jersey Steamboat Company (Uncle Daniel's left hand was selling to his right) and divided the company's assets, of which Drew's share was a handsome half million. In their haste to pocket the money, however, they made no provision for the company's outstanding liabilities, an oversight which led to litigation that lasted for eleven years. But in steamboat circles, such contretemps were not unusual: a lawsuit arising from the loss of the *Francis Skiddy* in 1864 dragged on for all of fourteen. Although more sued than suing, Drew always kept the lawyers busy.

Reputedly, the sale of Drew's three boats on the sound was arranged through the good offices of James Fisk, Jr., of Boston, who brought the two parties together. This was Drew's first contact with Fisk, a twenty-eight-year-old Vermont-born Yankee peddler turned war contractor turned cotton smuggler (in the *New York City Directory* he was listed as "imp." for importer) who, having sought Drew out in his office, surprised and entertained him with his grandiose views on steamboats, railroads, stocks and finance, and just about everything else. Although usually reserved, Drew took a quick liking to this pudgy, sandy-haired rollicker, all flash and go-ahead, who like Drew had done a stint in the circus. Unlike him, however, Fisk had a vast craving for champagne, diamonds, checked suits, fast women, and attention. He was also a great joker and clown, a free spender, a fast talker, a born entrepreneur, and a super-salesman who above all was selling Jim Fisk. The Old Bear was a good judge of character: beneath all the flash and buffoonery, he sensed a smart operator, a judgment that was soon confirmed by Fisk's efficient handling of the steamboat sale. Uncle Daniel could use such a fellow in Wall Street.

Wall Street was the playground and killing ground, the torment and elysium of Daniel Drew. And of all the opportunities it offered, none so exercised his ingenuity as the stock of the New York and Erie Railroad or, as lately resurrected, the Erie Railway. For the old New York and Erie was no more; despite Drew's own canny generosity in 1857 and President Charles Moran's prodigious salary and confidence, the company's affairs had deteriorated until at last, in 1859, it defaulted on all five mortgages. On August 2, 1859, a foreclosure suit was brought against the railroad by the trustees of the fourth mortgage and by Daniel Drew as bondholder and mortgagee. The Erie passed into receivership, whereupon the directors slashed President Moran's salary and he resigned.

Over the next three years the Erie remained in receivership, while appointed trustees negotiated with the bondholders to induce them to exchange their bonds for preferred stock in the newly created Erie Railway Company, under which guise the road was finally reorganized in the spring of 1861, with both Vanderbilt and Drew on the board. Erie's rebirth was hailed with enthusiasm by the *American Railroad Journal*, which declared a repetition of its past misfortunes "almost beyond the reach of possibility."[2] With some exceptions, however, the gentlemen resuscitating Erie were precisely those who had presided over its decline and demise.

Further grounds for caution was provided by the stock's amazing vicissitudes in 1860. Early in the year it hovered between 8 and 10, the company's woes being known. Then suddenly the outlook changed. The creditors, it seemed, were being conciliated, and the costly Bergen Hill tunnel was completed, while the magnificent Long Dock property in Jersey City now provided deep-water terminal facilities unequaled in the world, which the company's own ferries joined to New York. Whatever its past, then, Erie's future seemed positively brilliant. The stock climbed steadily for months, until on October 2 it hit 42¾. At this point Drew and certain associates, having acquired a huge block of it at 10 and below, sold out, whereupon it dropped to 25. Insider Drew's profits were estimated as high as $2 million, which shows how he got the nickname of the Speculative Director, and why, through thick and thin, he cleaved to the board of the Erie.

The Erie's reorganization was completed just in time for the new company to share in the wartime boom. When the South's secession closed the Mississippi to navigation, the great east-west trunk lines of the North suddenly found themselves handling a huge traffic that taxed their capacity to the limit but sent earnings soaring. Inconceivably prosperous, in July 1863 the Erie shattered precedent by paying a dividend. Meanwhile the common stock, having sold below 8 in 1859, surged to 65 in 1862 and to 122 the following year. Erie's promise, it seemed, had at last been fulfilled.

Since these flush times were a boon to steamboats, too, in March 1862 Uncle Daniel induced the Erie board to sell him its five Lake Erie boats for $110,000 and to pay him a substantial sum to operate them in exclusive connection with the Erie trains. This he did, and profitably, under the name of the Erie Railway Steamboat Company, a vestpocket enterprise that he incorporated with just three directors: himself as principal stockholder and president, his grandson as secretary, and a vice-president to supervise the actual operations. Handily headquartered at Drewville, the company operated a growing fleet of first-class screw-propeller vessels that plied between the Dunkirk terminus and Cleveland, Sandusky, and Toledo, with connections to Chicago, as another of those lucrative little sidelines that Drew was so adept at organizing.

In the new Erie as in the old, Drew's influence was paramount; he served on both the executive and finance committees and was well thought of by President Nathaniel Marsh. Once when some English investors who were interested in Erie bonds came to New York to examine the company's affairs, Marsh introduced Drew as the bonds' expositor. Put off by Uncle Daniel's homespun ways, the visitors informed Marsh that this was not the sort of man with whom they wished to negotiate. Marsh, however, urged them to withhold judgment until they knew him better, which they agreed to do. Several interviews later the visitors' chief spokesman announced, "Mr. Marsh, I owe you an apology for my remark concerning Mr. Drew. Now we know more about him, and if anyone takes him to be green, they will catch a *trump*, sir, yes a *trump*!"[3] To celebrate their newfound congeniality, all parties concerned dined together at the sumptuous St. Nicholas Hotel.

Long in failing health, President Marsh died suddenly on July 18, 1864. The next regularly elected Erie president was Robert H. Berdell, a prominent director and friend of Cornelius Vanderbilt, whom Vanderbilt—himself a director since 1859—imposed on the board by buying off a rival. Marsh had been a diligent servant of the railroad; his death removed a major obstacle to the daring schemes entertained by certain members of the board. Over the next four years the Speculative Director in Erie was going to play trump after trump.

The summer of 1864 brought dark days for the North with Grant stalled in Virginia, Sherman all but stymied in Georgia, the president doubtful about his reelection, and gold at an all-time high. Meanwhile Director Daniel Drew felt obliged to make some dire predictions of his own regarding Erie, whose stock was selling well above 100 or par. "Them Ayrie sheers are a-sellin' naow for a leetle more'n they're wuth," he informed the boys on the Street. "It costs a heap naow to pay runnin' expenses. The Ayrie has to pay up'ards of twenty thousand for an injyne what cost only ten thousand afore the war. Coal and iron has riz, so has men. Whar are dividends a-comin' from? You boys better not be too fond of your sheers."[4] He spoke from knowledge, for soaring costs in men and machinery had so raised the road's operating expenses that they had outpaced the increase in earnings. By September a general bearish sentiment prevailed. Despite the news of Sherman's capture of Atlanta, the uncertainties of the coming election bore the market downward, until on October 5 "them air Ayrie sheers" were selling at 86½.

At this point, it would seem, the Old Bear received a business visit from Tobin and Jerome, the recent agents of his agony in Harlem. The two formed a curious pair. Tobin was of the same rough origins as Vanderbilt, with something of the Commodore's crusty pluck and obstinacy. On the other hand Jerome, the future grandfather of Winston Churchill, was a high-living fashionable who was fond of horses, theater, opera, and female opera singers, and who on Sabbath mornings delighted to drive a carriage full of elegantly dressed and gaily laughing friends up Fifth Avenue to the Park, shocking churchgoers all along the way. Having made and lost one fortune, he had made another and wanted to increase it. Although surprised by their visit, Uncle Daniel was surely cordial. Yes, the boys had pinched him in Harlem, but he bore no grudges. So what could he do for them?

What the Harlem victors had in mind was to repeat their coup by cornering Erie. This would be no mean feat, since Erie was the special preserve of Uncle Daniel, and furthermore there was a lot of it around. By an act of the state legislature of May 4, 1864, the company had been authorized to increase its capitalization by $8 million, which translated into 80,000 shares of new stock that, some legally, some not so legally, might find their way to the Street. How, then, did Tobin and Jerome propose to go about it, they who were operating now on their own hook, without the benefit of Vanderbilt's millions? Quite simply, they proposed to strike a deal with Uncle Daniel, the man most capable of advancing or thwarting their designs.

The Old Bear was delighted by the offer. Certainly he had no objections. Not only would he agree not to sell the stock above a certain price, but he would even stake them, on terms of course and at interest, to a handsome loan.

That recent enemies should become allies was not surprising on Wall Street; it happened every day. And so, the deal concluded, the campaign to corner Erie began. All through October Tobin and Jerome bought large amounts of stock in the nineties, following which it rose above par and on November 9, upon news of Lincoln's reelection, surged to 104. Strangely enough, however, at these high prices there seemed to be an abundance of Erie, which naturally they were forced to absorb. In time, they learned that, in blatant disregard of their agreement, Uncle Daniel was selling it! And he had plenty to sell, because, with the Erie election over, he could dispose of stock bought to assure his reelection and because the company, doubtless at his own suggestion, had authorized him to sell on its behalf 7,000 shares of the new stock, which he unloaded on Tobin and Jerome at close to 102, costing them over $700,000. With what befuddlement, frustration, and rage Tobin and Jerome greeted the news of this betrayal is not known. Quite possibly they stormed into the little back room at Groesbeck's to accuse the culprit to his face, only to hear him deny the whole thing in tones of injured innocence seasoned with a spidery charm, or to argue cagily, in a whiny twang, that their agreement did not include stock sold by the "Ayrie" itself, which he of course had to sell if the executive committee instructed him to do so. In any event, they were out their hundreds of thousands.

Doggedly, the two cornerers persisted. Over the winter, as the North pressed closer to victory, Erie declined with the market, it being Wall Street's opinion that if war had brought a boom to the railroads, peace would necessarily bring a bust. Then in early January of 1865, with Erie selling in the low eighties, a familiar scenario was enacted. Pressed by rising costs and debt, the company borrowed $3 million for a year from Director Drew, who received 900 mortgage bonds and 28,000 shares of new stock as collateral. Because Drew, heedless of legal technicalities, might or might not dump this stock on the market, Erie sagged, then broke below 70 on various rumors that seemed to emanate from William Street, where Ursa Major was busily selling short. Locked into the stock at a loss and unable to corner it, Tobin and Jerome were paying Drew interest on a borrowed fortune that, with repeated assists from the lender, grew steadily less each day. Then Uncle Daniel turned the final screw. Having restricted the money market, he called upon Jerome and Tobin to repay him the loan, whereupon those two harried bulls were forced to dump their Erie on the market, which depressed the stock still further. So ended the campaign of the would-be cornerers, said to have cost them a million dollars in all. This disaster helped Jerome toward the loss of the bulk of his fortune. The Harlem score was settled, in part.

Not that Drew was resting on his laurels. He had put out short contracts in Erie, so the stock must be depressed. All through March, as Grant hammered at the gates of Richmond, the Old Bear pounded Erie in the market, till it hit 50 on the twenty-eighth. At this point Drew covered his contracts for a large profit, then switched to the bull side and began buying Erie. Locked in battle now with Uncle Daniel, as Richmond fell and the South's defenses crumbled, was the chief bear, Edward B. Ketchum, a young speculative banker and well-known member of the Stock Exchange. In late March Ketchum sold Drew 10,000 shares of Erie at 49 with a seller's option of sixty days for delivery, Drew betting that for two months he could keep the stock above 49, while Ketchum bet that he could depress it to that price and lower. A fierce struggle ensued, against a background of the extraordinary news of Lee's surrender on April 9 in Virginia, followed five days later by the murder of the president. This last was a real impediment to trading since, in an unprecedented gesture, Wall Street partially suspended business for a week. Thereafter, as the nation grieved, Drew and Ketchum fought on while Erie rose to the seventies, buoyed by Wall Street's revised opinion that peace might not be so terrible after all. By June 1 Drew had won. Ketchum, his sixty days expiring, covered his short contracts at a loss of $250,000. Uncle Daniel had adjusted splendidly to peace.

Yet his store of wiles was far from exhausted. Since the bears could not conceive that Ursa Major had really turned bull, he encouraged their delusion, got them to short heavily, then in late July lifted the stock to 97, whereupon Groesbeck called on the shorts for 35,000 shares that he had loaned them, forcing them to cover at a loss. As Erie churned in the nineties, the bulls were jubilant, until Drew unloaded his stock and sent the price plummeting. The market was now awash with Erie, and the bulls in turn cried swindle, having trusted Uncle Daniel's assurances that the stock was scarce and likely to remain so. "The unscrupulous manner in which this stock is being played with on the Stock Exchange," affirmed the *Herald* of July 30, "is a disgrace to American railway management . . . and before three years elapse such trickery . . . will be as impossible as it is dishonest, for the reason that investors will protect their own interests." Alas, not by any strain of the imagination could the writer conceive of Erie's condition three years hence.

For nearly a year now, Drew had manipulated Erie masterfully. It was a performance that might well have inspired the saying that Bouck White invented, but attributed to traders in the Street: "Daniel says 'up'—Erie goes up. Daniel says 'down'—Erie goes down. Daniel says 'wiggle-waggle'—it bobs both ways!" How had Ursa Major done it? Through tactical expertise unsurpassed on Wall Street; through patience and daring, vast liquidity, small conscience, deceit, flexibility, and cunning; but most of all through knowledge. For Uncle Daniel *knew*. Almost daily he visited the company's offices and, more than any other director, closely watched its affairs. As an active member of the executive and finance committees with access to the company accountants, he knew beforehand every rise or fall in the Erie's monthly earnings and the prospects of a dividend; he knew the state of its debt, and whether or not it was ripe for yet another compromising loan; he knew the mood of the officers and directors—which ones were manageable and which ones were bent on reform. Friendly with the transfer clerk, on any given day he knew almost to a share where the stock was lodged—how much in his own account and those of the other directors, how much in the company's coffers, how much in Europe, and how much loose on the Street. Finally and above all, he knew the twists of his own mind. Knowledge is power, and power begets profits. He made hundreds of thousands, millions.

But even Drew could be taken by surprise. On August 15, 1865, just two weeks after his last great coup in Erie, a quiet Wall Street forsaken by vacationing operators was stunned to learn of the failure of Ketchum, Son & Company, in consequence of gold certificate forgeries and stock thefts by Edward B. Ketchum, the junior member, that totaled several million dollars. Undone by his ruinous speculations, young Ketchum had absconded (he was arrested ten days later), in the wake of which his broker failed as well, stocks plunged, and a "general smash" was predicted, reports of which, telegraphed to Newport and Saratoga, stampeded traders back to the city.

What they found on Wall Street, however, was not a panic but a lull, and in the midst of it the Speculative Director in Erie, calm and smiling, not only buying his favorite stock but selling puts in it, offering options permitting the holder to sell him Erie at a price just below the current market, suggesting that he was confident Erie would go up. Reassured, the nervous bulls snatched at these options and then bought Erie aggressively, knowing that if a decline ensued, the options would limit their losses. The whole market steadied, and Erie inched upward through the eighties, further helped by rumors that the stock would soon be in demand and rise to par or 150, because Drew's control of the company was being challenged by a clique of distinguished foreign personages whose arrival in the city was imminent: noted English capitalists, the Duke of Salamanca, the Marquis of Something-or-Other, the mere mention of whose names inspired further heavy purchases of Erie. Presently, a group of English capitalists—sans Duke or Marquis—did indeed arrive in New York, but for a tour of the American railroads and not for any contest over Erie. Thereafter, Erie neither soared nor plunged, but fluctuated narrowly in the eighties, so that no huge profits were realized, nor were those quantities of puts ever used. On Ursa Major's furrowed features, the subtlest of grins could be discerned. What had he been up to?

Being in the city when the Ketchum scandal broke, he had first snapped up at bargain prices much of the Erie that Ketchum's broker dumped on the market. At the same time, however, he found himself saddled with large amounts of other stock that Ketchum had contracted for, stock that, if sold at current prices, meant a loss. Consequently, he undertook to stem the panic, whence his heavy sales of puts to the bulls and the picturesque rumors about Erie. Then, as the market steadied and rose, he slid out of the stocks he was stuck with, while bobbing Erie narrowly until the options expired, each little twist bringing further profits to himself. Such control was easy, since he and his friends had by now acquired the bulk of the stock, with an eye to the October 10 election. At that election the old board was unanimously reelected, for this—and not profits—had been Drew's chief concern over the entire two months preceding. Inscrutable were the ways of Uncle Daniel.

What an extraordinary year 1865 had been! He had coped with war, peace, assassination, and fraud; had chastised Tobin and Jerome, outfought Ketchum, clipped bulls and bears alike, stopped a panic, and renewed his domination of the Erie. How he relished skinning the boys on the Street, rallying them on their losses, and when least expected, stand-

ing the whole market on its ear! It was "as good as nuts and cheese" to
him when he was working up a corner, or when on a high market he had
put out a heavy line of shorts. Yet even while matching his wits and purse
with giants, he routinely set traps for small game, too. Like all the successful men on the Street, he was a magnet for petty operators and
greenhorns who flocked to him with tips and schemes, hoping to join
him in a "dicker" or pick up a "point" or two. If, however, deceived by
his insinuating manner, sweet smile, and quaint, rustic ways, they put
faith in his "p'ints of sheers" or otherwise presumed upon a scant acquaintance, their fate was likely to be enshrined in yet another of the
Uncle Daniel stories told on the Street.

Those stories were legion. According to one told by the marine engineer Charles Haswell in his *Reminiscences*, a young lawyer friend had
recovered some money for Drew through litigation, whereupon Drew
advised him to use his remuneration to buy Erie on margin. "Sonny, you
did it. I like to see young men go ahead. I knew your father. Now, as you
have got some money, you had better go into the market and buy some
stock. It's low now, and if you'll be advised by an old friend of your father's, buy Ayrie. It's safe, very safe. Now, sonny, do as I say." The young
man followed his advice, bought Erie, saw it decline, and learned too
late that Drew himself had been selling him the stock. "In reference to
the transaction," Haswell adds, "my friend's words are not restricted
either by Webster or the Decalogue."[5]

Indeed, nothing brought more glee to the Old Bear's craggy features,
or made his gray eyes glint more merrily, than the knowledge that he
was unloading on a dupe. Henry Clews tells how once on Wall Street,
after being severely squeezed in the market, Drew was made the butt of
much jesting, especially by a group of young operators who literally
laughed in his face. One evening he appeared at a club that the young
men frequented, where he seemed to be looking for someone whom he
failed to find. Intensely preoccupied, time and again he drew forth from
his pocket a big white handkerchief to wipe his brow. Just before he left,
one last flurry of the handkerchief tossed out a small piece of paper that,
apparently unseen by him, fluttered to the floor, where one of the young
men covered it at once with his foot. After Drew had left, they examined
it and found an order to his broker to buy all the Oshkosh stock he could
get. The young men were electrified: here was advance warning of a big
rise in Oshkosh! Immediately they formed a pool and bought 30,000
shares the next day, following which the stock plummeted, giving them
a fearful loss. Of course the slip of paper had been planted and the stock
had come from Drew.

Once at least, however, Drew outreached himself. Overburdened
with Erie, he recommended to Capt. Joseph W. Hancox, his friend of

sorts and rival on the Hudson, that he buy a few thousand shares of the stock on the "p'int" that Drew's pool was about to put it up. Taking his advice, Hancox purchased Erie in several blocks, commiting the bulk of his fortune, then quite by accident discovered that his Erie had come from Groesbeck & Company, which meant that Uncle Daniel was selling the very stock he had urged him to buy. Immediately, having stopped payment on his latest check, Hancox strode over to Groesbeck's in high dudgeon and confronted Drew, informing him that unless he got all his money back, he would retain the last lot of Erie, that on which he had just stopped payment, and fight the matter in the courts. Groesbeck, seeing that he must either forfeit the stock or litigate, reasoned with Drew. As a result, Hancox was relieved of his Erie and thereafter took no more points from Uncle Daniel—a happy ending for all concerned, Drew included, given Hancox's propensity for brandishing revolvers on the river.

Needless to say, not all the Uncle Daniel stories should be believed. They were the stock in trade of Wall Street's losers, whose scribbled anathemas upon Drew, Vanderbilt, and other major operators covered the walls of the trading room at the Stock Exchange. In the case of one story, the process of distortion can be traced. Bouck White tells how during the war a young greenhorn named California Parker came to Drew and offered to boost Erie for him, if Drew would advance him some money when he needed it. Drew agreed, but then unloaded his own stock on Parker and callously refused him the loan, so that Erie declined, Parker was ruined, and his family left destitute, while Drew raked in more money. When published in 1910, this account especially incensed Drew's son, who denied that his father had been cruel. Indeed, White's sources tell it differently. According to Henry Clews's version, published in 1887, Drew simply took advantage of a brainless amateur, while W.W. Fowler's account, published in 1870, absolves Drew completely, stating that Parker was a young fool with $300,000 who in July 1863 conspired with friends to corner Drew in Erie, but was himself ruined in a sudden two-day panic in September. Probably Parker was the unnamed outsider whom the *Herald* of September 7 mentions as having been forced to sell 2,000 Erie at 100 to a "prominent banker and lender" (surely Drew) who shortly before had refused him a five-day loan on it even at an exorbitant rate of interest. All of this says more about the follies of speculation, especially by amateurs, than about the ruthlessness of Daniel Drew.

One Uncle Daniel story, recounted by Fowler, is in a different vein. A well-known bear was dead broke by the spring of 1865, inspiring some of the Street's big operators to a rare mood of pity. Drew sent for the man and informed him that "a few sheers of Ayrie" wouldn't hurt him.

"But," said the man, "I have no money to buy them." "Never mind that," said Drew. "Send in five thousand sheers to me and I'll take care of 'em."[6] The speculator did so and within a few days was on his feet again with fifty thousand dollars in his pocket.

Yet against this story one has to set a dozen others of how the old man tricked this one or cheated that one so as to dump his "Ayrie" on some unsuspecting victim. Unflattering stories circulated about other operators, too—how Leonard Jerome unloaded on an old acquaintance, how Vanderbilt milked his friends by manipulating Central, and how Henry Keep issued more Michigan Southern stock so as to ruin Addison Jerome—yet somehow these stories never overwhelmed the reputation of the men involved. But wherever Uncle Daniel ventured in the Street, fresh tales of his deceit and treachery proliferated; they stuck to him like burrs.

Given the likely number of his victims, one wonders why he was never assailed by shouted insults in the street or even physically assaulted, as happened later to Jay Gould, who was forced to hire bodyguards. Probably Drew was protected by his victims' chagrin at being duped, by their propriety (one did not assault old men), and by his own quiet, homespun manner—so rustic, so quaint—which one could learn to distrust but hardly hate. Suspect he certainly became, in the eyes of his Wall Street contemporaries: Henry Clews recorded his deceptively bland manner and cunning; James K. Medbery, his lack of popularity, owing to an alleged readiness to sacrifice his friends; while W. W. Fowler called him "vulpine." But Fowler perhaps said it best when he described Drew and Vanderbilt alike as being "unscrupulous, within the law."[7] Indeed, how could they not be, in a society that idolized go-ahead and condoned "smartness." And of course the law could be bent.

CHAPTER 11

A Seminary, an Injunction, and a Loan

"Generous," "liberal," "large-souled," "noble," "benefi-cent"—so the Methodists routinely described Brother Daniel Drew, who as the sect's first millionaire was continually solicited on behalf of worthy Methodist causes, to which he rarely failed to contribute. By the mid-1860s, the tide of his bounty ran high. When the Methodists of Southeast decided to build a larger structure nearer the center of the village of Brewster, Brother Drew immediately made a substantial do-nation and promised to pay half the total cost. The result, built in 1863 for $16,000, was a handsome frame building with a lofty spire, in which Drew and his grandson rented pews for years. Similarly, when the Meth-odists of the village of Carmel reared a sturdy new stone edifice that was dedicated in 1865, Drew served on several committees and donated more than three-quarters of the total cost of $40,000, in gratitude for which the new structure was named the Daniel Drew Methodist Epis-copal Church. And in that same year he gave Wesleyan University his bond for $25,000, thus founding the Drew Professorship of Greek. This was no mean contribution from a benefactor whose faulty English, when it impinged on learned ears, could at best be characterized as "quaint."

Motivating his generous donations to institutions of learning, no doubt, was the pained awareness of his own lack of education. The extent of that lack is illustrated by a story told in his own time, picked up by Bouck White, and subsequently confirmed by Drew's son. On leaving his office one evening, Drew changed the combination of the safe. The next morning he was detained at home, and the clerks in the office needed to open it. When they sent word, he informed them that he had set the combination at the letters that spelled "door." Presently they sent word again that they had tried "door," but the safe would not open.

"Door," Drew insisted. "An ordinary house door, barn door, stable door—any kind of a door!" "But," said the messenger, "there are five letters to the combination of our safe. Are you sure it's the word 'door'? We've tried it—several ways." "Of course I'm sure," said Drew. "Turn to those letters and it will work!" But still the safe would not open, so Drew himself had to go to the office, where for him it opened at once. "There!" he said. "It opens as easy as an old sack. Just D-O-A-R-E!"[1]

Daniel Drew's orthographic deficiencies did not trouble the Methodists, who saw in him not just a dependable source of largess, but a model for young businessmen in the city and aspiring plowboys on the farm. He was proof of what hard work and ambition could do, tempered by humility and piety. And some of them knew his fervor firsthand. They knew how when a revival was held in the schoolhouse at Drewville, for instance, daily for six weeks he commuted fifty miles by rail from the city and three miles by carriage from the station, so that after a hasty supper he could attend the meeting, where his tearful prayers and exhortations proved every bit as moving as the sermons. In time of sickness or doubt, he summoned his pastors for continuing counsel and prayer. And at love feasts and prayer meetings no sinner abased himself more contritely than he, tears flowing down his face as he confessed his backslidings copiously. Veteran class leaders discerned in him the periodic agony of a man who, in these laxer and more affluent times, relived the anguished longing and uncertainty of the sin-convicted boy of fourteen. If not a soul in triumph—on weekdays Mammon reclaimed him—here at least was a soul in struggle.

Yes, on weekdays Mammon reclaimed him, greedily, obsessively. But few Methodists were conversant with the wiles of Wall Street, and if any of them were troubled by Brother Drew's money-getting ways, such reservations were singularly inappropriate during the church's frequent fund-raising drives. Yet one Methodist—no bishop or eminent educator, but a simple pastor—had long since taken this matter very much to heart. Born in England, John Parker had emigrated to America in 1847 at the age of twenty-two. As a young preacher on trial at Princeton, New Jersey, new to the country, friendless, and unknown, in the winter of 1848 he had come to the Mulberry Street Church in New York in quest of funds for his church and there participated in a two-week revival meeting. No sooner had he finished his first sermon, when Drew came up to him, thanked him for the sermon, and invited him to his home. Thereafter they had become close friends, Drew treating him with the tenderness of a father, while the young Englishman, as he matured in his vocation, came more and more to be the older man's spiritual adviser and confessor.

Over the years, on many occasions Drew spoke feelingly to John Parker of his mother, of the influence of her piety upon him, and of the effect of her death on his life. More than any other living person, Parker was aware of how intensely Drew's two overriding passions, business and religion, clashed in his inner life. Once when the younger man was visiting Drew in his mansion on Union Square, Drew had taken his arm and said, "Come, let's go out and have a walk." As they walked around the square, Drew seemed peculiarly depressed. "Brother Parker," he said, "I begin to be afraid I shall lose my soul in these terrible fights in which I am engaged. Somehow I feel as if I was tied to business and don't dare to break the cord. This diminishes my love and joy in religious things."[2]

Because of such confessions, Parker had taken Drew's soul in charge. Years later he recalled:

> More than forty times have I met with him alone in prayer. I felt it was my duty to do so. I felt I owed a great deal to him. I loved him. I saw the peril in which he was placed, and I resolved years ago that when I called upon him, unless I found him surrounded by businessmen, or unless the arrangements of his family would make it inconvenient or improper, I would never leave without talking quietly with him about his soul, and having a season of prayer with him. I have kept that promise; and I think not more than four or five times in the twenty-five years that I have met him in this way have I failed to kneel with him in prayer.[3]

According to Parker's later testimony, one of their colloquies had given birth to a momentous idea. In the spring of 1857 Drew went to Albany, where Parker was stationed, and persuaded him to become his pastor at the little church near Brewster, and the following year at Carmel and Drewville. One day in the summer of 1857 Drew called him out for a ride in the vicinity. On this occasion, being close to sixty, Drew told him that he had been thinking of giving up business and spending the rest of his life using his money in the service of God. "Brother," said Parker, "do it!"

"I have long thought," said Drew, "I would like to do something for the church that has taken such an interest in me. My mother was a Baptist, and I love the Baptist church, but somehow the Methodist church has got a large place in my heart, and I want to do something for the Methodist church."[4]

Parker at once suggested that he found a school nearby for the sons of Methodist preachers and a Drew Theological Seminary either there or in New York. Both ideas appealed to Drew, who mentioned them to Dr. McClintock, his pastor at the time in New York. Within a few short weeks, however, came the Panic of 1857 and this alone, in Parker's opinion, had prevented these plans from maturing.

To be sure, Drew had not retired from business, but the idea of a seminary that would serve God's purposes while perpetuating his own humble name on earth had lurked in the back of his mind. By Methodist standards this was a rather liberal notion, for oldtime Methodists had been leery of an educated clergy, feeling that ministers should be called by God, not trained in a seminary. After considerable debate, however, the General Conference of 1856 had cautiously sanctioned such studies at last. Progressive Methodists like Parker and the learned McClintock were now convinced that, given the growing sophistication of the people, ministers must have a certain amount of scholarship and culture. Their opinions had surely influenced Drew, who seems to have mentioned the seminary project to Methodist friends on various occasions, although the turmoil of the war years imposed a further delay.

Even before the war had ended, however, prominent Methodists were busy planning for the Centenary of American Methodism in 1866. This was to be a nationwide celebration of a full century of formal Methodist meetings in America, which church leaders hoped to make a time of great spiritual awakening and of massive fund-raising in support of missionary and educational efforts. What could be more fitting than to found a new theological seminary in the vicinity of New York? And with regard to financing it, what could be more appropriate than to approach Brother Daniel Drew, who was reportedly predisposed to the idea and who in the midst of love feasts had been known to rise in his place and announce humbly, "All I am that is worth anything to the world I owe to the Methodist Episcopal Church under God."[5]

They would approach him, then, but with tact, since in matters of giving he was known to have a mind of his own. Solicited once by the Chamber of Commerce to help sustain the market in a panic, he was said to have replied, "Gents, I'd luff to do it, but I've sporn as much money as I kin."[6] That, of course, was business. On another occasion, however, when the question of finishing a mission chapel had been raised at a meeting of the trustees of his church, a fellow trustee was said to have announced, "We expect a generous sum from Brother Drew." Turning to Drew, he asked, "Brother Drew, I put it to your conscience. Don't you see your way clear to give us ten thousand dollars?" "No, I do not," answered Drew, which ended the discussion.[7] Decidedly, tact was in order.

Three members of the Central Centenary Committee, all known to the prospective donor, were appointed to a subcommittee to call on Drew. They were Dr. George R. Crooks, editor of the New York-based weekly, the *Methodist*; Charles C. North, a prominent layman interested in ministerial education; and Drew's close friend McClintock, who had twice been his minister at St. Paul's and who during the war had served as pastor of the American Chapel in Paris, a significant and sensitive post. Late in 1865 they visited Drew at his home to ask what offering he intended to make in connection with the centenary celebration. Immediately and with what Crooks later termed "the utmost simplicity," Drew announced, "I am willing to give two hundred and fifty thousand dollars for the endowment of a theological seminary at Carmel, Putnam County, in the state of New York, for the use of the Methodist Episcopal Church."[8]

So there it was—a quarter of a million dollars, bluntly but generously offered in an interview that had lasted all of five minutes. Yet it was only a start. On the evening of January 25, 1866, when prominent Methodist clergy and laymen flocked into St. Paul's Church, at the corner of Fourth Avenue and Twenty-second Street, for the official inauguration in New York of the Centenary of American Methodism, John McClintock, in his appeal for funds, announced: "I think it right to say that one of your members has set you a noble example. I pray that Daniel Drew's life be spared to see the erection of a theological seminary to which he has consecrated a quarter of a million of dollars, and to which he will give as much more before it is finished. It is a grand start."[9] McClintock slipped it into his address almost casually, although applause had greeted the announcement. Daniel Drew, who as a vice-president of the Centenary Committee was present and sitting on the platform, had not only already offered a quarter of a million for the buildings and grounds of a seminary, but also would donate "as much more" for a permanent endowment fund—in other words, half a million dollars in all. The banker Stephen Girard at his death in 1831 had left $6 million to found Girard College in Philadelphia, but rarely if ever had anyone in America given a school a half million all at once in his lifetime. Mindful no doubt that he was fast approaching the biblically allotted three score years and ten, Brother Drew had topped Brother Drew.

Drew's only conditions were that the school be located at his home town of Carmel, that it be named for him, and that McClintock become its first president. This last was a burden for McClintock, who being weary and ill had retired from the ministry in 1865; he consented, however, in order to assure the gift. Sixteen incorporators, half clergy and half laymen, were presently selected, among them Drew and his grandson, to whom, on April 16, 1866, the state legislature granted a charter. The great work was at last under way.

For John Parker the tangible plans for a Drew Theological Seminary must have been encouraging proof that the donor's soul had been nudged a bit nearer salvation. On Wall Street, to be sure, no such conviction prevailed, although a saying circulated that if Daniel Drew had a soul, it would assume the exact shape of a dollar sign. But it was not greed that motivated Drew. When Parker once urged him to retire from business with his millions, Drew explained: "I continue in business not because I want to make money. People don't understand me. They think I love money. I tell you, Brother Parker, it ain't so. I must have excitement or I should die. And when I get among these money kings, I go in because I don't want them fellows to feel that they can have everything their own way. And when I go in, I go in to win, for I love the fight!"[10]

During the immediate postwar period Wall Street still offered plenty of fight and excitement, albeit chiefly among the professionals, since the general public had retired from the Street following the war. In December 1865 the flourishing New York Stock Exchange had moved into a new building at 10 and 12 Broad Street, where its formal auctions of listed stocks continued in a rented hall on the second floor, while downstairs in a large hall known as the Long Room, the Open Board maintained a continuous market in securities. Appropriately, in the exchange's elegant hall lined with green damask, hung a portrait of Jacob Little, who on March 28 preceding had died in near-poverty of a liver disease, having already, it was said, been left demented by softening of the brain. Remembering his dazzling although finally futile career, the Board of Brokers had adjourned to attend his funeral and now set his gilt-framed likeness to survey the operations of his heirs and disciples.

Prominent among the latter was Drew, the Ursa Major of a later day, who on January 12, 1866, got the year off to a bearish start by buying a call for 2,000 shares of Old Southern (the Michigan Southern and Northern Indiana Railroad), permitting him to purchase the stock at 65 within the next ninety days. The seller of the call was the banker Henry Keep, surnamed Henry the Silent for his reticence regarding market operations. A master of pools, Keep excelled in manipulating railroad stocks and in particular Old Southern, of which he was the treasurer. Drew concluded that if Henry was selling calls—options to buy from him at the current market price—on easy terms, Henry must be bearish on the stock. Consequently, like many on the Street, he bought the call and used it as margin to sell the stock short. With Keep committed to the bear side, Old Southern was sure to fall below 65.

But it did not fall; instead, it went up. Astutely, having worked in a large bear interest by selling calls in the sixties, Keep encouraged bulls in the stock by liberally selling puts in the seventies and so by the end of March had forced the price up to 84½. Then on April 4 he and his allies suddenly demanded delivery of all stock loaned to the shorts, who now discovered that scarcely any shares were immediately available. Old Southern, having sold the day before at 89, hit 98 by the end of the day.

Rarely had a corner been engineered so ingeniously; it was worthy of the Old Bear himself.

Hoodwinked like a greenhorn, Drew was trapped. On April 4 the brokerage house of Scott, Capron & Company called on Drew's broker, Groesbeck, to return the 2,000 shares of Old Southern borrowed of it, to buy which at the current market would have meant a heavy loss for Drew. Groesbeck managed to put Scott, Capron off for one day, but to no avail. On the morning of April 5 Old Southern sold at between 97 and 101. At the office of Groesbeck & Company at 30 Broad Street, Grosy informed Drew that Scott, Capron had called again for the stock, threatening to have it bought in at the market price for Drew's account, unless Drew delivered it at once. Slouching in his easy chair in the back room, the Old Bear assumed a most lugubrious look and for a moment ruminated. "We must injine 'em! We must injine 'em!" he declared and over Groesbeck's protest betook himself to the courts.[11]

That afternoon, at the 2:30 session of the Stock Exchange—the time at which, under the rules of the exchange, any stock due that day but not delivered could be bought in for the account of the defaulting party—an injunction issued by a Superior Court judge at the petition of Mr. Daniel Drew was served on the presiding officer, enjoining Scott, Capron from buying in the stock for Drew's account. In an affidavit sworn to by him that day, Drew declared himself the victim of "a fraudulent combination and conspiracy between divers persons many of them not known to the plaintiff"[12]—Scott, Capron & Company being allegedly among them—to corner the stock of the Michigan Southern Railroad, double its price artificially, and so defraud him. He not only asked the court to enjoin the defendants from buying in the 2,000 shares, but also demanded damages of $50,000 (the likely amount of his loss at current prices) and a settlement at a "fair" value of the stock.

Confusion engulfed the exchange. Drew's action was declared unprecedented, unfair, dishonorable, perplexing, and unsportsmanlike—one simply did not enjoin the Stock Exchange—and he himself a bad loser, a cheat, and a conniver. Fortunately, the immediate dilemma was resolved when Groesbeck ordered that the 2,000 shares be bought in for his own account, not Drew's, which was promptly done at a price of 98½, Groesbeck being warmly commended by all for his action. Drew, however, then lodged a supplementary complaint, charging that the injunction had been violated, on which grounds he had Groesbeck in turn served with an injunction, to restrain him from using Drew's money in the settlement. At this, Wall Street was scandalized anew: one simply did not enjoin one's own broker! Then, to Uncle Daniel's disgust, Groesbeck paid Scott, Capron on his own account, assuming full responsibility for cajoling his obstinate customer into a settlement.

By April 6, the corner having culminated, Old Southern was abundant again on the market, where it sold for 82. Drew's recourse to litigation, however, continued as the prime topic on the Street and in the press. "As his influence *now* stands," announced the *Times* of April 7, "and with the prevailing feeling against his conduct in Wall Street, it seems doubtful whether he will be suffered to have things his own way much longer, even in the Erie direction"—a prediction of colossal naiveté. When Drew's case against Scott, Capron came up in court April 14, it was continued pending the filing of additional briefs by both parties. No more of it was heard thereafter, so presumably it was dropped, Drew having effected some kind of compromise with Groesbeck, who continued as his broker. Ursa Major, however, had been stung grievously in Old Southern and reacted in an untypical fit of pique. For years to come, his cry "We must injine 'em!" remained one of the jokes of the Street.

By January 1866 the price of Erie had been hoisted to the upper nineties by a pool of bull operators headed by the Speculative Director, who even at this lofty level proclaimed the stock cheap. By early April, however, when it had declined to the low seventies, he declared it overpriced, citing the company's declining peacetime earnings, fierce competition, a burdensome floating debt, and an imperiled dividend. Unknown to the rest of the pool at the time, he had gone heavily short of the stock around 90, calculating that his profits on his own as a bear would far outweigh his losses in the pool as a bull. By May Erie was trading in the sixties, although the market was calm and money easy, with higher stock prices generally anticipated.

Suddenly, on May 28, Wall Street was startled to learn that Groesbeck & Company was settling Drew's short contracts in Erie with brand-new certificates of stock. As rumors of all kinds abounded, traders rushed in droves to dump Erie, which fell ten points to 57, recovered to 62, then the next day plunged to 57 again. The *Times* printed the names of Drew's fellow directors in Erie, from whom it urged Erie shareholders to demand an explanation, while the *Herald* observed laconically, "The conduct of the Wall Street director is severely animadverted upon."[13] All eyes were on the Erie board meeting held that day, following which the newspapers reported that Drew had advanced millions to the hard-pressed Erie Railway Company and received as security vast amounts of convertible bonds and the equivalent of 58,000 more shares that he might at any moment throw on the market. This was a coup so staggering as to leave his fellow operators (many of whom still held Erie) green with jealousy and black with rage.

The facts of the case proved not quite so astounding, but disquieting even so. By the act of May 4, 1864, the state legislature authorized the company to increase its capitalization by $5 million to pay for equipment and construction, and by $3 million more to retire its first-mortgage bonds, whereupon the company created 50,000 new shares of common stock and 3,000 bonds convertible into stock at par. Of the 50,000 shares of stock, 22,000 were sold on the market, chiefly through the good offices of Uncle Daniel and to the discomfit of his enemies, while the remaining 28,000 shares were pledged to him as collateral for the loan of January 1865, which had not been repaid on maturity. Ever since, the thought of those 28,000 shares pledged to the Speculative Director haunted the market like a phantom. Not totally impervious to criticism, Erie finally negotiated a loan in London, repaid half the debt, and recovered 14,000 shares of the collateral.

So matters stood when in the spring of 1866 the Erie executive committee tackled the perennial problem of the company's floating debt, now totaling $3.5 million. Not surprisingly, no creditor would lend it any money, except the Speculative Director who, as three times already in the past, generously stepped forward with the offer of a loan, the terms of which were formally proposed on May 25. Drew would lend the company, at any time within the next four months, up to $3,480,000 in such sums as the company requested, each loan to be secured by the company's convertible bonds or stock at its option. It was stipulated, however, that Drew need not return the specific collateral given, but rather the same in kind and amount, including stock if the bonds should be converted. This astonishingly liberal arrangement left Drew free to play fast and loose with the loan's collateral. This contract was submitted to the full board on May 30 and approved, following which the details of it broke in the press.

When it was understood that the Erie board had agreed to hand over the equivalent of 58,000 shares of stock to the man whom many considered the Street's most unscrupulous operator, there rose up on all sides a cry of shock, disbelief, and outrage. "Very discreditable financiering," declared the *Herald*, while the *Commercial Advertiser* denounced "a shameless recreancy to weighty trusts" by a "corrupt and imbecile management."[14] The *Times's* criticism was blunted slightly when President Berdell invited its representative to the company office for more accurate information, explaining that the company would probably not borrow the full amount and that it hoped to recover the collateral at an early date. While the *Times* noted with satisfaction that the stock held around 60 and therefore disappointed short sellers who looked for 55 or 50, it still joined the rest of the press in denouncing Drew's stockjobbing and the board's complicity in what it labeled a "monstrous iniquity." Commented on by everyone was the remarkable way in which almost all of the $8 million increase in Erie's capitalization granted by the state legislature in 1864 had now been made to serve, in one fashion or another, the ends of Director Drew.

But the most pointed question of all, raised repeatedly by the entire press in chorus, was how such reputable men as Drew's fellow directors could lend themselves to this dubious transaction, or for that matter tolerate Drew's sly maneuverings over the past thirteen years. The men on the Erie board had solid reputations. Dudley S. Gregory had been three times mayor of Jersey City, had founded two banks there, and was important in New Jersey politics; J.C. Bancroft Davis, the road's counsel, was a lawyer of considerable reputation; J.F.D. Lanier was a noted banker and railroad promoter; Ralph Mead was a successful wholesale grocer and, with Drew, a pillar of the St. Paul's Methodist Episcopal Church; and the road's respected vice-president, Gen. Alexander S. Diven, was a longtime railroad promoter, contractor, and politician, an organizer of the Republican Party who had raised a regiment and fought in the war, and a leading citizen and later mayor of Elmira, New York. As for Robert H. Berdell, the president, prior to his present office he had headed the Long Dock Company in Jersey City, which operated the Erie's eastern terminus, and had managed that company's difficult affairs with success. And so on down the list of the entire sixteen fellow directors, all honorable men, successful, affluent, and esteemed, who capped their habitual tolerance of Drew's rascality by approving this extraordinary loan. Why had they done it?

Ostensibly, Erie's credit was so flimsy that no other lender was available. This begs the question, however, since the loan from Drew was only a temporary expedient. As always, more crises lay ahead, with the company's reputation further impaired by the surrender of its securities to Drew. Some of Drew's fellow directors may have been following his lead in the market, while others were no doubt preoccupied with their own self-serving ends—lucrative contracts or special rates from the railroad—and for this reason turned a blind eye to Uncle Daniel's misdeeds, on condition that he overlook their own. Still others, perhaps even the majority, were honest, but too immersed in their own affairs to keep abreast of developments in Erie, at whose board meetings they voted docilely for whatever the president and the executive committee recommended. As for Director Cornelius Vanderbilt, he rarely attended meetings at all; having other pressing matters to attend to, he resigned from the board in September.

Under these circumstances, with no strong personality dominating Erie as Vanderbilt now dominated Harlem, control of the company's affairs rested with the seven-man executive committee and the president, so that Drew, always on hand with his persistent liquidity and charm, had only to win over the president and two or three fellow directors to determine policy. In President Berdell, as in Homer Ramsdell before him, Drew had either a willing confederate or what the *Times* of June 9 termed a "soft customer." Certainly he was easily managed or got round, even to the point that (and it was told as a joke on the Street) when Berdell had recently issued a bullish statement on the company's affairs, Drew, having consulted an Erie accountant, put out a bearish report of his own. And when William Evans, the Erie director in London, queried Berdell in mid-June about the stock's recent plunge to 57, the president wrote him that Erie had been the victim of "a desperate raid" based on false and exaggerated rumors, yet failed to name Drew as the culprit, an omission so astounding that Berdell cannot escape the charge of complicity.

Indeed, they were all "soft customers" and accomplices, these board members who for over a decade had tolerated Drew and even abetted him, while with only one notable exception, in 1857, the stockholders acquiesced in their actions. Given the perennial slackness and indifference in Erie, one concludes that over the long run the Erie stockholders deserved the management they got, and the management deserved Daniel Drew. Without the endless pliancy and passivity of others, Uncle Daniel could not have been Uncle Daniel.

Ironically, Drew's 1866 coup in Erie was not the unmitigated success that his contemporaries described and denounced. To be sure, in the heavy trading of May 28 and 29, when Erie plunged to 57 twice, he covered his short contracts for a vast profit, the fresh certificates then delivered being presumably some or all of the collateral for the earlier loan. However, with the new loan pending but not yet known to the Street, he continued to short Erie in expectation of a further decline. At these low prices his contracts were taken eagerly by a ring of bulls just formed by a speculator named William H. "Billy" Marston, whom a contemporary described as "a portly gentleman, with a twinkling eye and great fondness for bidding stocks up five per cent at a leap." [15] Marston, in the face of Uncle Daniel's rumors and wiles, bought Erie heavily, so that it did not collapse at the announcement of Drew's new loan but held steady throughout June and actually began to rise in July. What had become of Drew's "coup"?

Probably it had been more fiction than fact. Some of the 58,000 shares had already been used to close out his earlier contracts in May, and much of the remainder quite possibly had not yet come into his possession, since it was to be delivered only if and when Erie requested installments of the loan. The 58,000 shares of stock were, in other words, a bluff, and Marston and his friends boldly called it. They kept buying, no avalanche of shares hit the Street, the stock rose to the seventies, and by mid-July Drew had been cornered in Erie. His triumph had turned to ashes.

Or had it? Suddenly the Old Bear made terms with Marston and his ring, compromised his contracts at a loss, and secretly joined with them in putting Erie up. (The switch was not without difficulties; claiming that Drew had welshed on $100,000, Marston brought suit until a settlement was reached.) In early October Erie hit 96, at which point the ring took its profits, of which Marston's share was close to a million. Drew, however, made sure that his broker went to the election on October 9 amply armed with stock, and to appease the board's belated scruples, handed over to Erie $1 million in securities as a guaranty of his collateral on the loan. As a result, rumored opposition evaporated, the election passed quietly, and the old direction remained in control.

Meanwhile, Billy Marston's twinkling eye had never gleamed so bright. All that fall he and his fellow bulls strode merrily in fashionable attire through the halls of the elegant Fifth Avenue Hotel, a favorite haunt of speculators, and quaffed champagne at Delmonico's. Yet their alliance with the Old Bear, which continued through the winter, was not an easy one, for who could trust Daniel Drew? Bouck White tells an anecdote, unverified, that if authentic must date from this period.

As the story goes, Marston, suspecting (and rightly so) that Drew, his supposed partner, had been saddling him with Erie in the market, went one morning to meet Drew in Drew's office, and upon entering, immediately locked the door. He then informed Drew that he had told his brokers to buy Erie, and while they did so he was going to keep Drew under lock and key, so as to find out once and for all if it was Drew who kept mysteriously supplying him with stock. Drew protested, Marston insisted, and a heated argument ensued, with Drew pounding his fist repeatedly on the table. Finally, when trading at the exchange had ended, Marston unlocked the door and went to get a report from his brokers, the contents of which Uncle Daniel could readily anticipate. Expecting trouble from Marston, he had instructed a clerk to stand outside the door to his office, and every time he heard a blow on the table, to send word to his brokers to sell a thousand Erie. In this fashion Marston had been stuck with quantities of Erie, far more than he had the means to absorb. Drew had to let him off with paying only part, and in so doing revealed the trick and had a good laugh.

Maybe in some form it happened, maybe not. It is known for certain that in the winter of 1866-67 Marston bought heavily in the stock of several railroads, Erie included, gambling hugely on a rise. In late January a panic swept the market, and the clique of Erie bulls was wiped out. Marston is said to have failed for $600,000—by one account, because Drew had sold him 20,000 Erie at top prices, breaking the ring and pocketing a million. Thereafter Billy Marston was still to be seen on the Street, more fertile in schemes than resources, being in the Street's parlance a "dead duck"; he filed for bankruptcy in 1870.

Reckoning up his accounts for 1866, Uncle Daniel, in view of the Old Southern corner and Marston, had to concede some reverses. But there were consolations: he had endowed a seminary, skinned the Street on both sides of the market, bounced back from a loss, and still had Erie on a tether. Sitting in the back room at Groesbeck's, his feet on the mantel, before a grate of glowing coal in the fireplace, the old man purred with contentment: all his eggs had two yolks.

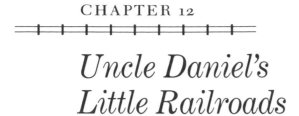

CHAPTER 12

Uncle Daniel's Little Railroads

Punctually at 6:00 P.M. on Tuesday, April 23, 1867, the last and most splendid of the new trio of People's Line night boats put out for the first time from its North River dock amid a chorus of steamboat whistles and in the failing sunlight, with the air cool and lazy under a clear sky, headed up the river toward Albany. In honor of a gentleman whom the *World* termed "one of the fathers of navigation enterprise on the Hudson,"[1] this new $800,000 marvel had been christened the *Drew*. Appropriately, the People's Line president and his family were aboard, occupying the two elegant bridal rooms. On board also, in addition to passengers, were over a hundred invited guests, including members of the press and the contractors who had provided the boat's lavish furnishings, for whose entertainment a champagne supper was provided, and after that, cigars and wine for the gentlemen.

When not so occupied, the guests could feast their eyes as well on a ladies' saloon in the "Pompeian style"; on a main saloon in the "Alhambric style"; and on the main saloon's ornate entrance, where, passing between a pair of bronze statuettes designated Seedtime and Harvest, they could mount a magnificent staircase with a balustrade of Santo Domingo mahogany, and on the first landing behold a portrait of imposing dimensions, paneled on either side with ebony and satinwood: the life-sized head and shoulders of Uncle Daniel himself, his pinched face with its thin fringe of whiskers looking fearfully solemn and distinguished.

Portrait, staircase, and saloon received ample praise on the leisurely run up to Albany, where the *Drew* was visited by more gaping throngs and was hailed on departing by a chorus of shrill-whistled tugs and ferryboats, and by a lusty little cannon that belched forth a salute from the dock. It would have been only human if the vessel's owner took the reception as a gesture toward himself, and even more human if he reveled in the thought of the thousands of travelers who for years (in actual fact, decades) would admire his boat and his portrait. Vanderbilt's massive ego had long since required a flotilla of river and ocean vessels bearing his name. Surely it was fitting that a second floating palace be named for the president of the People's Line.

Honor greeted him in Methodist circles too, as the great benefactor of the church's centenary. In Port Jervis, New York, a Methodist congregation composed chiefly of Erie Railway employees and their families had named a new church for him in 1866. But honor was his most of all in Old Put, where he was esteemed as the ragged farm boy turned drover of another era who was now worth a reputed $13 million; esteemed also as the area's biggest landowner, who throughout the decade was buying stock farms in Carmel and Southeast and installing tenants; and esteemed finally and above all as the chief local benefactor who in 1866 had established the Drew Female Seminary, situated on high ground just south of Carmel village with a fine view over Lake Gleneida, an idyllic setting for the instruction of Christian young ladies. And of course the theological seminary was anticipated.

Honor and esteem had embraced all the Drews and their relations who peopled that corner of the county. Thomas Drew was now the respected president of a bank newly organized in Brewster by a banker son-in-law. Drew's daughter Catherine lived in Carmel village as the self-effacing wife of the Rev. William S. Clapp, the indefatigable Baptist minister of Carmel, who through sermons, a library committee, lectures, and midwinter baptisms by full immersion through the pierced ice of Lake Gleneida, sought to achieve the spiritual, moral, social, cultural, economic, and even political betterment of what he candidly described, in a statement to the local paper, as "this rather indifferent and backward community."[2]

Less of a moral shadow was cast by the younger generation, including Drew's son and namesake grandson, and his granddaughters and their affluent husbands, these last a gilded youth new to the county, drawn there by the urban itch for rusticity and the convenience of the Harlem Railroad. So far, Drew's son Bill, having married his young cousin in 1862, seemed quite content to live in Drewville as a farmer. Daniel Drew Chamberlain, Drew's eldest grandchild, having thrived on Wall Street from the commissions on his grandfather's wartime speculations, had bought the Clift farm from his grandfather in 1863, torn down the old Clift farmhouse (the site of Daniel's first conversion), and raised in its stead an ample Italian-villa-style mansion where he lived as a weekend country gentleman. But if he kept fine horses that he raced at the new trotting park on the fairgrounds, there was no cause for alarm, since Danny was a good churchgoing Methodist who gave generously to the local churches and library, and at twenty-six was a trustee of Wesleyan University. In all Drew's progeny, morality and respectability ran deep.

Still, the old man might have resented this smoother generation, who surely viewed him as a distinctly rough article. His own youth and early manhood had been bleak and gritty, and his religion had involved no spruced-up Sabbath gentility, but glimpses of the fiery pit climaxed by a thunderbolt. Yet Daniel was an indulgent father and grandfather, not an autocrat like Vanderbilt, who tyrannized everyone around him and who for two decades banished his unpromising eldest son to a Staten Island farm. Milder and kindlier, Drew sought to help the young men of his family, not judge and challenge them. He had fixed up Danny and William Everett, the husband of the eldest granddaughter, with good jobs at Groesbeck's in Wall Street. And in 1867, when Danny decided that he would prefer a smaller estate, Drew gave him a note for $100,000 and had him deed the 386-acre Clift farm to Bill, whom he thus set up as the most prominent gentleman farmer in the district. Daniel himself still visited the vicinity on weekends and holidays, and for longer stretches in the summer, living modestly on a farm southwest of Drewville. He liked to see his kin and chitchat in the Brewster barbershop, while keeping an eye out for stock farms for sale. Plain old Dan Drew, but still the biggest man in the county.

If local esteem, seminaries, and steamboats were the soup and nuts of Daniel Drew's existence, railroads were the meat and potatoes. These included not just the Erie but also lesser lines, those frail little enterprises, long on hope and short on finances, that sprang up in abundance in the sixties, promoting themselves as vital links or strategic feeders for the bigger systems, as highways to untapped resources: ingenious little pie-in-the-sky concoctions that fired up local interests, sucked in funds by the millions, trapped the unwary, and enriched a few.

Such was the Adirondack Company, chartered in 1863 as a land and development company authorized to acquire a million acres of state land—one-fifth of the Adirondack Mountains—in order to develop the iron ores and minerals found there. Although not among the original corporators or subscribers, Drew was one of a number of prominent financiers soon recruited for the board by the company's chief promoter. This was Dr. Thomas C. Durant of New York City, the railroad contractor, stock market operator, and prime illusionist whose vision and dogged persistence was forcing the Union Pacific Railroad to completion, but who found time on the side to launch this grandiose endeavor in the North.

To tap the vast mineral resources that presumably awaited its coming, in the spring of 1864 the Adirondack Company began constructing a railroad north from Saratoga Springs to it was not quite clear just where—maybe Canada, in order to bind that nation commercially to the United States. The project was highly regarded. Henry V. Poor's *American Railroad Journal* recommended it, and the *Times* declared that it would make the Adirondacks "a suburb of New York."[3] At a cost of $2 million, by 1865 the company had exactly one engine and six freight cars in operation on twenty-five miles of track, nothing more being possible in the face of fearsome winters, rugged terrain, soaring expenses, and overwhelming debt. So the truth filtered out that the Adirondack Company was a huge overblown fantasy, a dubious, debt-ridden venture building a railroad from nowhere to nowhere, with its prospects hazy, its promotion close to fraudulent, and its profits nil. Inevitably, it defaulted on its bonds and on November 1, 1865, was seized by trustees.

In the mid-1860s, however, dreams died hard. To reinflate the venture, financial wizardry was called for and an expert was at hand. Throughout the following winter Daniel Drew, as the new head of the board of directors, labored with the trustees to salvage the enterprise. Did he really believe in it? Perhaps; but long experience with the Erie had made him a past master at resuscitating moribund railroads on terms beneficial to himself. By dint of great effort the most pressing debts were paid, more money was raised, construction was resumed, and hopes revived. By 1871 the line had advanced sixty miles to the crude little village of North Creek, the last town of any consequence in the upper Hudson valley, where, for lack of funds, construction stopped once and for all. The fabled riches of the Adirondacks remained inviolate, while in 1873 the company collapsed again in the panic. But Uncle Daniel was not inconvenienced, having left the board by 1869.

If the Adirondack Company had dreamed of iron in the mountains of upstate New York, the Buffalo, Bradford, and Pittsburgh Railroad yearned for coal in the mountains of northern Pennsylvania. Although the original promoters had hoped someday to link Buffalo to Pittsburgh, they at first projected a mere twenty-four-mile railroad running south from Carrollton, New York, on the Erie line, to the coal mines of Lafayette Township in McKean County, Pennsylvania, a modest effort that even so was only half completed when the outbreak of the Civil War made further financing impossible. For nearly three years the little line stagnated, until President Nathaniel Marsh of the Erie discovered it. Indignant at the high wartime prices for coal exacted by producers, he thought he had found the ideal solution for the Erie in this little railroad and the coal lands adjoining it. At his suggestion, in 1863 he, Drew, and three other Erie men bought the road, finished it, and acquired some nine or ten thousand acres of adjacent coal lands, all for a cash outlay of a million dollars or less.

Immediately, the Erie signed a contract with the Buffalo, Bradford, and Pittsburgh for the supply and transportation of coal. Announcing the line's opening, Erie's annual report of 1864 fairly glowed: coal, iron, and timber were to be obtained in almost inexhaustible quantities and Erie's own fuel supply assured. Then, in a moment of prudence, President Marsh sent Erie's assistant general superintendent to inspect this little gem of a property, and he received a startling report: whether the mines had been misrepresented or their working had proved impracticable, there was no coal there to be had.

What does one do with a heavily mortgaged twenty-four-mile railroad built to fetch coal, when there is no coal to be fetched? President Marsh dodged the issue by dying suddenly on July 18, 1864, leaving his fellow investors to cope. Led by Drew, they coped. Above all, they observed a marvelous reticence regarding the nonavailability of the coal, although the truth may have begun to leak out. Just in a nick of time, then, Uncle Daniel brought his suasive abilities to bear on the Erie. As a result, on January 5, 1866, the Erie Railway Company signed a 499-year lease of the Buffalo, Bradford, and Pittsburgh line, assuming its $2 million mortgage and guaranteeing the interest on its bonds. This was a remarkable bit of financial legerdemain in which Drew and his partners figured as both lessor and lessee, and one among them as the counsel of both railroads and the smaller line's trustee. Coal or no coal, the original purchasers of the useless little railroad now had only to sit back and divide up their guaranteed $140,000 a year—unless as Erie directors they chose, under a new state law, to convert the leased railroad's securities into stock of the Erie, which someday the Speculative Director just might find it handy to do. No wonder he was fond of little railroads.

In striking contrast with the visionary schemes of Durant and others was Drew's own pet project, the Saratoga and Hudson River Railroad, which was incorporated on April 16, 1864, with a capitalization of $1.5 million, a practically conceived venture that he promoted in the most hardheaded way. This was a thirty-eight-mile road projected from a point near Schenectady on the line of the New York Central, with whose encouragement it was surely undertaken, to the Greene County village of Athens, on the west bank of the Hudson thirty-five miles below Albany. The object of this little branch railroad was to establish a more southerly terminus for the People's Line that would be free of ice longer each winter and that would avoid the shoals just south of Albany that in times of low water hampered navigation. Also, by laying tracks right to the water's edge, the new line could eliminate the delays inevitable at Albany in transferring passengers and freight between the boats and the trains. Furthermore, by linking up with the Schenectady and Saratoga Railroad, it could offer a faster service to and from Saratoga, New York State's most fashionable resort. So sound was the project's conception that Drew got the ungullible Cornelius Vanderbilt—and this at the very time when the Second Harlem Corner had set them at odds in the market—to subscribe to 3,301 of the original 15,000 shares and to serve as a director. Drew himself, the company's future president, took 3,700 shares, probably with the understanding that between them they could control the company. And with Vanderbilt behind it as well, how could the project fail?

All through 1865 work on the little railroad proceeded, so that by March 1866 the track was laid, two locomotives were in operation ("No. 94" and the "Drew"), and the line was ready for business. Jutting into the Hudson one mile north of Athens was a 1,845-foot pier, on which stood a freight warehouse and a richly furnished passenger depot. Nearby, the streets of a new village were being laid out, and a complete gas manufactory was being built to supply the People's Line night boats with their requirements for illumination. With the world suddenly pounding on its door, sleepy little Athens had awakened and braced itself for imminent prosperity.

At the opening of navigation, however, no steamboats came to Athens; throughout the season they plied to Albany as always. No explanation was given to the public, but it was whispered in financial circles that the delay was the work of one man, a financial giant whose own evolving interests now made of him a deadly adversary of Daniel Drew's little railroad, which he had vowed to destroy. The man was Cornelius Vanderbilt.

Over the past few years, while the Old Bear had been dabbling with little railroads and manipulating Erie, the Commodore had been building an empire. In amassing it, he evidenced not only shrewd business instinct, blunt determination, ever widening vision, and flexibility, but also an acute sense of timing. Having scorned and ignored the railroads in their infancy, in their troubled adolescence he had utilized them chiefly as extensions and connections of shipping routes. Only in the 1860s, with their necessity and potential apparent, and the time for consolidation at hand, had he committed himself to them fully. Just as young Cornele years before had sensed when to get out of sails and into steam, so now the mature Vanderbilt, pushing seventy, knew when to desert steam vessels for the transcendent promise of the rails.

Vanderbilt's operations in Harlem stock in 1863 and 1864 were not speculative in origin, but the result of a shrewd decision to acquire and operate the New York and Harlem Railroad, which, even without the Broadway franchise, he had immediately set about to transform into a paying property. Once the shabbiest of fancies, Harlem stock soon came to be highly regarded on Wall Street. And since the Commodore viewed competition from the Hudson River Railroad as the chief obstacle to the Harlem's prosperity, in June 1864 he and his allies took over the Hudson line too, of which he became president a year later. Competition between the two roads ceased, and rates and schedules were adjusted. "I tell Billy," the old man was fond of saying, "that if these railroads can be weeded out and cleaned up and made shipshape, they'll both pay dividends."[4] Both did, and regularly, at 8 percent.

Master of the Hudson and Harlem, Vanderbilt now found his interests in direct conflict with those of Drew, whose People's Line also carried passengers and freight between New York and Albany. For years the People's Line and the New York Central Railroad had enjoyed a cozy alliance whereby the railroad, for eight or nine months of the year, gave to the People's Line the bulk of its traffic from the West, relying on the connecting railroads only in winter when the river was closed. This irked Vanderbilt, especially when he learned that Central employees routinely altered the markings on eastbound goods from "all rail" or "carriage by railroad" to "PL" for People's Line. As for Drew's new little branch line, built with the Central's blessing and sure to steal traffic from his own roads, the very thought of it galled the Commodore, especially since, owing to an appalling lack of foresight on his own part, it had been financed with nearly a third of a million dollars from himself. Clearly, something had to be done about the Central and about that little branch line, too. He said so in a very loud voice.

Daniel Drew was heartsore to learn that his old friend Cornele Vanderbilt was aggrieved by his little thirty-eight mile railroad, but he happened to think it a peach of a line, and so did the New York Central. Vanderbilt bought some stock in the Central and worked out an agreement with it that gave his Hudson line a share of the freight, but he could only fume and bluster when, in late May of 1866, the Central took a perpetual lease on the Saratoga and Hudson River Railroad at $120,000 a year. Financially, Drew was now sitting pretty. Whatever the fate of his branch line, he was sure of an income from the Central.

Mysteriously, that year the branch line never opened nor did its organizer complain of the delay. Perhaps Vanderbilt had been lucky: Drew and the Central had failed to reach an agreement regarding the connection of the boats with the trains. Or maybe Vanderbilt had been lucky like a fox, paying Drew not to send his boats to Athens for the season. After all, Drew may have reasoned, since he had unloaded the branch line on the Central, why turn a cold nose to some cash from the Commodore? Yet for one so competitive, such docility would be surprising. Vanderbilt, meanwhile, was swearing that the line would never open, and with this in mind he whipped up the citizens of Albany and Troy, who, fearful of losing business to Athens, talked down the cutoff as impractical and dubbed it the "White Elephant road."

In December 1866 a faction headed by the Wall Street speculator Henry Keep took control of the New York Central. Keep had battled Drew in the stock market, but as one of the original backers of the Saratoga and Hudson River Railroad, he was furious at Vanderbilt for his hostility to the branch line. Consequently it was he, not Drew, who squared off with the Commodore, canceling all the Central's agreements with Vanderbilt and throwing his representatives off the board. It was midwinter, however, and Vanderbilt retaliated by severing the Hudson line's connection with the Central at Albany, so that passengers had to cross the frozen Hudson on foot in the severe cold and a snowstorm. This arbitrary act quickly brought the Central to terms, despite denunciations of Vanderbilt by the public, politicians, and the press. Summoned to testify before the state assembly at Albany, Vanderbilt informed the assemblymen: "I for one will never go to a court of law when I have got the power in my own hands to see myself right. Let the other parties go to law if they want, but by God I think I know what the law is; I have had enough of it."[5] (This candid statement the journalists of the day transformed into a much-quoted declaration—"Law! What do I care about law? I got the power, hain't I?"—that Vanderbilt almost certainly never made.) Asked about the Athens road, the Commodore admitted that it "was one of the foolish acts of my life, but I don't cry about it," and asserted that he didn't care if they built forty roads to Athens, since the Hudson line could take care of itself.[6]

Rankling from his recent humiliation by Vanderbilt, President Keep of the Central declared that he would open the Athens branch and the Commodore be damned! Uncle Daniel was willing, but he balked when Keep demanded that he commit his best boats to the run, including the prestigious new *Drew*. This lavish vessel was costly to operate; would the cutoff provide enough business? When Keep insisted, however, Drew agreed.

At long last, on May 13, 1867, the *Dean Richmond* and the splendid new *Drew* began connecting nightly at Athens with a special New York Central express train bound for the North and the West, while two other People's Line vessels maintained the service to Albany. Some observers pronounced the new route an immediate success, and as if to confirm it, on June 27 the board of the New York Central voted to exchange Central stock for that of the leased line, thus giving both Drew and Vanderbilt about a half million dollars' worth of a highly esteemed security. Once again Uncle Daniel had turned a risky little railroad into gold.

But Vanderbilt was not done with it. Angrily he was telling all and sundry that the People's Line could only lose money by running two separate night lines and that if he had his way the branch line would be discontinued and its track ripped up. Cries of triumph erupted in Albany when on May 20, after only one week on the run to Athens, the luxurious *Drew*, apparently for want of business, was switched back to the Albany route, being replaced on the new run by an older and smaller vessel. Then in June Capt. Joseph W. Hancox, that enduring thorn in Drew's side, announced that his newly organized night line to Troy and Albany had slashed its rate to one dollar, which forced the People's Line to do the same. Rumor had it that Vanderbilt was financing him. All summer Hancox urged the Albanians to support his boats so as to force the People's Line to abandon Athens for Albany, while his *Connecticut* raced the *Drew* repeatedly. This challenge ended abruptly in September, when a chain of mishaps disabled all three of his vessels.

The calamities of the Troy line, however, were of little help to the White Elephant, which prematurely suspended passenger service as of September 25, when the People's Line resumed operations to Albany exclusively. Vanderbilt, it seemed, had been right: there was not enough business to support service to both Athens and Albany. "Huge as an elephant though it was," declared the *Albany Evening Journal*, "it has from the first been white as a ghost, and doomed to die. The friends of the deceased have our heartiest sympathies."[7]

In the face of such taunts, Drew and Keep may well have determined to give the branch line another try the next season, but across their plans fell the lengthening shadow of Vanderbilt, who was steadily acquiring stock in the Central. While the assembly's Railroad Committee had branded Vanderbilt's severing of his connection with the Central a "high-handed and uncalled-for act," certain prominent stockholders of the Central had drawn other conclusions—namely, the advantages of a consolidation of their line with the Hudson and Harlem under the mighty hand of the Commodore. As a result, in the December 11 election Henry Keep and his friends were swept out and Vanderbilt men were swept in. Central stock surged on the market; Vanderbilt became the president; and the Central and Hudson lines functioned thereafter as a unit. Commodore Vanderbilt had taken over railroad number three.

For Daniel Drew, the consequences were grave. Dead for all time was his comfortable arrangement with the Central, giving the People's Line priority in passengers and freight. Dead too was the through route via Athens. Restricted thereafter to local freight traffic, the White Elephant did a meager business at best while the little village of Athens lapsed into somnolence.[8] Having received a half million's worth of New York Central stock, Drew had not suffered financially from his Athens investment. But in view of these fresh setbacks—the loss of business to

Vanderbilt's railroads, and Vanderbilt's killing off of his pet little scheme of a branch line—Uncle Daniel, still smarting from his Harlem defeat of four years before, felt something less than affection toward the Commodore. His grievances, however, were soon to increase, and for the most startling of reasons: Vanderbilt had set his eye on railroad number four—the Erie.

CHAPTER 13

The Great Erie War: Preliminaries

The reason why I bought Erie [Vanderbilt later explained] was, there was a lot of people in the Street that called themselves my friends, came up to me and pressed me very hard to go in with them. It is altogether out of my line. "Damn your pools, I don't know anything about it anyhow." But I declined going in the pools. I says, "If you want me to help you, I will." I had some loose money. "If you want me to help you along with your Erie, I will help you along." And they got me engaged in it, and I bought a pretty large amount of Erie—but on no such idea as ever taking possession of the Erie road—not the slightest.[1]

All of which makes of Cornelius Vanderbilt, that prodigious consolidator of railroads, a prodigious liar.

Vanderbilt's interest in the Erie resulted from an inexorable process of logic. Master now of the Central, the Hudson, and the Harlem, in only four short years he had acquired the biggest railroad empire in the country. In so doing, he probably acted only half consciously, motivated at each step by an obscure but sound instinct. To make the Harlem pay, he must have the Hudson; to make the Hudson pay, he must have the Central. Therefore, to make the Central pay, he must have—what? Ultimately, perhaps a connection to Chicago; already there was talk of it. But for the moment he was a New York-Buffalo carrier and as such had one major rival for the traffic of the West, with whom the Central had already waged innumerable and costly rate wars—the mismanaged, debt-ridden Erie. Yes, to make the Central pay, he must have the Erie.

143

Not that he intended to seize outright control of the Erie. Given its stock capitalization of over twenty-five million dollars, this would have been extremely difficult, and in any event it was not his style. His initial goal was simply to acquire enough shares to give him a voice in its management. This he undertook to do in the late summer of 1867, even before he had consolidated his hold on the Central. That the Central would soon be his he had little doubt; therefore it was time to take its rival also in hand. And so he began buying Erie.

To take Erie in hand, however, was to challenge Drew on Drew's own preserve. This was a perilous undertaking that would have deterred many men, but not Cornelius Vanderbilt. The Commodore declared his intervention to be a moral necessity. Even though, during his many years on the Erie board, he had remained immune to stockholders' complaints of mismanagement, he now suddenly endorsed the opinion that the company had paid too high a price for Drew's moneyed friendship. Indeed, he could not agree more with those who thought it scandalous that the company's stock was now shunned as a serious investment and abandoned to Wall Street operators, in witness of which, being "on the Street," Erie was known as the Scarlet Woman of the Stock Exchange. Clearly, to make an honest woman of her, it was necessary once and for all to throw Drew, President Berdell, and all their associates out; the time for reform had come.

These noble sentiments were likewise voiced by a group of Boston capitalists who had also acquired a large block of Erie stock. These gentlemen were associated with the Boston, Hartford, and Erie (B,H & E) Railroad. Projected as a feeder and connection for the Erie, this line was to run from Boston via Hartford to Fishkill on the Hudson, where it would be linked by ferry with Newburgh, the terminus of a branch of the Erie. Theoretically, immense benefits would redound to both railroads upon effecting this connection, which would tie Boston to the Pennsylvania coal fields and the West while bypassing New York, at the same time giving the Erie a New England rail connection comparable to the one possessed by its rival, the Central. With this in mind, in December 1865 the B,H & E proposed that several Erie directors join its board (to which Erie had generously consented), and then, in June 1867, that the Erie guarantee the interest on $6 million of its bonds on the security of future traffic, the receipts of which would be set aside to repay the Erie.

This proposal came from a railroad of which nearly a third of the track had yet to be laid, a railroad burdened with no less than ten mortgages, and which, having cost $20 million already and incurred $10 million of debt, in 1867 would earn exactly $369,577. The Boston, Hartford and Erie Railroad was more fiction than fact, and infinitely more ailing than the Erie, whose own strained resources it was grasping for in bumptious desperation. To his credit, Robert H. Berdell was hostile to the notion from the start. Nevertheless, on June 5, 1867, an amended proposal to guarantee $4 million of bonds was endorsed by a board vote of 9-6, Drew being among those approving. The contract between the two railroads, however, had yet to be signed, nor would it be prior to the Erie election, which gave the Boston adventurers a large stake in the contest and especially in the ousting of Berdell.

It was ill news for Uncle Daniel that with the election approaching, not one but two parties were in the field against him: Vanderbilt and the B,H & E clique. As it happened, no one of the three contending groups could control the election, but any two by banding together could overwhelm the third. Although in the past he had often allied himself with Drew, Vanderbilt was not inclined to do so now, given Drew's bearish propensities in Erie and the fact that Drew, by producing a money stringency, had recently impeded his own bullish moves in the market. So Vanderbilt joined with the Boston men to draw up an opposition slate of directors with B,H & E president John S. Eldridge as president of the Erie, while excluding Drew, Berdell, and most of their cronies. To further their cause, the Vanderbilt party even prepared to petition the courts for an injunction to restrain Drew from voting the 58,000 shares of stock that he had received as collateral for the 1866 loan.

As the date of the election neared, both sides solicited proxies energetically—in fact paid for them, since many Erie shareholders, or the brokers in whose name their shares were held, offered them to the highest bidder. Collecting proxies for the Drew-Berdell ticket was their fellow director Frederick A. Lane, a lawyer and market operator who had forced his way onto the board by amassing proxies in the previous election. Having accumulated proxies once again, however, Lane attempted to extort payment for his continued loyalty and when he failed to get it, sold the proxies to Vanderbilt, an act of treachery that many on Wall Street thought rather a good joke on Drew. Uncle Daniel's defeat now seemed assured. Some few of the old directors might be suffered to remain, announced the *Times* (whose financial editor was actively working for Vanderbilt), but only on condition that they not oppose a thorough reform of the road's finances. New days indeed for Erie.

That at long last he should be divorced from his corporate spouse of fourteen years was inconceivable to Daniel Drew. What other money tree could he shake so handily? His discomfitures in Old Southern and Harlem were telling proof of the pitfalls awaiting him, once he set foot beyond this magical terrain. And so, with the election scheduled for Tuesday, October 8, on the preceding Sunday he went to see Vanderbilt at the Commodore's handsome red-brick Greek Revival residence at 10 Washington Square. Vanderbilt started the meeting off on a merry note by showing Drew the complaint and proposed injunction that he was prepared to use against him. There followed on Drew's part an outpouring of whines, cajolery, and appeals to sentiment, seasoned with promises of good behavior and the offer of an alliance in Erie (he would end his speculations in the stock or let Vanderbilt in on them), the whole of it well calculated to tug the Commodore's heartstrings and enlist his self-interest. Sentiment may or may not have softened Vanderbilt, but it occurred to him that Drew might be less dangerous on the inside as a friend than on the outside as an enemy, and that if secured as an ally, this veteran operator could be played off against the Boston clique to the Commodore's advantage. Vanderbilt therefore agreed to let Drew remain on the board and even assume the office of treasurer, on condition that his bear raids cease once and for all and that he serve as a loyal ally. To all this Drew readily assented and went home reassured.

That evening, when Eldridge and one of his allies, a young New York broker named Jay Gould, were summoned to 10 Washington Square to hear of Vanderbilt's change of heart, they reacted with astonishment and outrage. Strong words and hot argument ensued. Still later that Sunday they all convened at 41 Union Square, where Vanderbilt consulted secretly with Drew in the back-parlor dining room, while the others waited in another parlor in front. After a lengthy discussion, the dissidents were brought round by a threat from Drew and Vanderbilt to join forces against them and leave them out in the cold. That same evening a written agreement was drawn up and signed, stipulating that, to save appearances, since the Eldridge clique had committed themselves to the ousting of Drew, the new board should be elected without him, following which a Vanderbilt man would resign, so that Drew could replace him and at the same time be elected treasurer. That night, when his visitors had left, the Old Bear slept better. Although he had grievously broken the Sabbath, he had also shattered the conspiracy against him, or rather wormed his way inside it.

On Tuesday October 8 the Erie election proceeded as arranged. Drew, Berdell, and most of the old board were ousted as the "reformers" took over and elected Eldridge president. The first act of the new board was to approve unanimously the contract with the B, H & E, immediately following which one of the Vanderbilt men resigned, whereupon Drew was chosen to replace him and was elected treasurer. All of this left Wall Street confused. The *Times*, in a quick flipflop, approved of Drew's election as treasurer, while the *Herald* proclaimed the proceedings a "farce."

Among the old faces on the board were Drew, Vice-president Alexander S. Diven, and the treacherous Lane. Among the new faces were Eldridge and three other Boston men; Eldridge's brother-in-law, Henry Thompson; Frank Work, a Vanderbilt lieutenant; and two unknowns whom the papers identified as "J. Gould" and "Fisk," "Fiske," or "Fish."

The latter was of course Jim Fisk, the rollicking Green Mountain Boy whose business acumen Drew had quickly sized up when he negotiated the sale of Drew's steamboats on the sound four years before. Late in 1864 Fisk had returned to New York to have a crack at Wall Street. Opening a sumptuously furnished office, he had lavished good liquor and bad jokes on all comers, speculated haphazardly on margin, and within a few months had been cleaned out by the old hands. Packing a carpetbag for a quick return to Boston, where he hoped to raise more funds, he had reputedly told a friend, "I'll be back in Wall Street inside of twenty days. And if I don't make things squirm, I'll eat nothing but bone button soup till Judgment Day. Damn 'em—they'll learn to know Jim Fisk yet!"[2]

True to his word, he had scraped more money together in Boston and returned in less than a month. This time he renewed contact with Drew, who in 1865 arranged for him to work as a broker at Groesbeck's, and by 1866 had set him up with William Belden, another young broker at Groesbeck's, as the brokerage firm of Fisk & Belden, through which Drew then did much of his business. A greenhorn no longer, by now Fisk was flourishing, as evidenced by a shirtfront diamond, rings that flashed on his fingers, and his new home address at the fashionable Fifth Avenue Hotel. (His wife—a childhood sweetheart—was left to languish sumptuously in a new mansion in Boston, while her husband toiled and cavorted in Gotham.) Fisk's inclusion on the new Erie board probably resulted from substantial holdings of its stock, plus the right connections, including not only Uncle Daniel but the Boston men, with at least one of whom he had been associated both before and during the war. But no one—not the Boston men, not Drew, not Vanderbilt—suspected of what Jim Fisk was capable.

Sitting with Drew on the new five-man Erie executive committee was another newcomer: Jay Gould. The son of a farmer in Delaware County, New York, Gould at the age of fourteen had written a schoolboy essay entitled "Honesty Is the Best Policy," the irony of which no biographer of his has failed to comment on. By the age of twenty-three he had worked as a store clerk and professional surveyor, written and published a 450-page history of his home county, promoted a mousetrap, built a plank road in nearby Pennsylvania, and started a tannery there and helped found a bank. His early business associates, however, had found young Gould a slippery fellow to deal with. During the Panic of 1857 his partner Charles M. Leupp, a reputable New York City leather merchant, learned that Gould had misused Leupp's name and money in an attempt to corner the leather market and lost heavily. Apparently as a consequence of this, Leupp committed suicide.

Still solvent and ambitious, by 1860 Jay Gould had come to New York City, where he married the daughter of a wealthy grocer and during the war, with the help of his father-in-law's capital, bought control of two small ailing railroads, which he rejuvenated financially and sold to larger systems at a profit. Meanwhile he entered Wall Street, where he became a member of Smith, Martin & Company, which traded heavily in Erie and came to control much of its stock. At the approach of the 1867 election, having been recruited by Fisk, who found his name on a list of Erie shareholders, Gould helped Eldridge in canvassing for votes against Drew. This was Gould's first acquaintance with Fisk, with whom he soon became closely associated, although he and Fisk were opposites in manner and appearance. Hollow-chested, thin, and sallow-faced, Jay Gould—at thirty-one, a year Fisk's junior—was a small man with puny limbs, black clipped whiskers, and what one contemporary described as a "fatal" black eye—but for all that, a model husband and indulgent father, domestic, introverted, reticent, as soft-spoken and retiring as Fisk was blatant, gregarious, and assertive. Yet this modest, abstemious little man, fond of books and quiet, was an instinctive fighter and schemer, immensely ambitious, subtle of mind, and ruthless in method. No one who ever dealt with him forgot him.

Such was the new Erie board, a conglomeration of adventurers at cross-purposes who were about to enact a rich imbroglio of conflict, conspiracy, litigation, deceit, fraud, and farce, with Uncle Daniel smack in the center of it.

Meanwhile Brother Daniel Drew was tasting a rare fruition of beneficence in the establishment and formal opening of the Drew Theological Seminary. On March 13, 1867, the corporators and trustees had met at his Union Square mansion—doubtless in the same spacious parlors that had since witnessed the secret dickerings on the eve of the Erie election—at which time he had been unanimously elected president of the board of trustees, while his grandson Daniel Drew Chamberlain became the treasurer and his son William a trustee. President Drew then called to order the first meeting of the board, which elected John McClintock president of the seminary and approved a constitution and by-laws.

At all subsequent board meetings Daniel Drew, if he was present (and he usually was), officiated. It presents a piquant image, the thought of this colorful semiliterate presiding in his Sunday best over a meeting of distinguished Methodist clergy and educators, including Bishop Edmund S. Janes, the vice-president. Of course, he was on his best behavior: tactful, reserved, never assertive. Years later George R. Crooks remembered him as "one of the pleasantest figures in the New York Methodism of that period; reticent, no doubt, but loyal to his Church. . . . In all he did for this Seminary I never saw the slightest trace of vainglory. . . . Modest, kindly, and sensible, he . . . never for one moment assumed the manner of a dictator."[3] A model benefactor, it would seem, and prudent to a fault: during all his association with the school, no formal speech of any kind passed from his lips and no written communication from his hand, except checks and legal documents bearing the scrawl of his name.

Drew's tact was soon evidenced, for the Carmel site proposed by him was not favored by all the trustees and least of all by McClintock, who feared that life in that remote locality would prove the loneliest of cultural martyrdoms. Fortunately, when it was suggested to the founder that they seek an alternative site in New Jersey, he did not object. By June the trustees were considering "The Forest," a 230-acre estate at Madison, New Jersey, twenty-five miles due west of New York City and linked to it via Hoboken by the Morris and Essex Railroad. This property included an extensive oak woodland and a handsome Greek Revival mansion built in the 1830s by William Gibbons, whose father Thomas was the New Jersey steamboat operator, once the employer of Cornelius Vanderbilt, who had successfully fought the Fulton-Livingston monopoly all the way to the Supreme Court. The mansion seemed suitable for the seminary without alterations, and the present owner was willing to sell. In Drew's own time it was told how he called unexpectedly at the sumptuously furnished mansion and offered the astonished occupants a handsome sum for the estate, on condition that they pack up at once and depart, leaving behind everything but personal effects. The transaction was of course more mundane. For $140,000, on June 29 the property was conveyed to Drew, who made it immediately available to the seminary, to which he promised to deed the buildings plus one hundred acres of land.

On November 6, 1867, President McClintock staged a full-day formal opening of the seminary that assembled three hundred guests, including all nine bishops of the Methodist Episcopal church, four college presidents, eminent ministers and laymen from throughout the country, students and journalists, and an abundance of pious ladies. Dr. Joseph Cummings, the president of Wesleyan (to which, but three months before, Drew had donated a hundred thousand dollars), hailed Drew's noble illustration of "the Christian use of money," while Bishop Janes charged the founder, trustees, and faculty to make the seminary "the West Point of Methodism," training young men to urge God's sacramental host "onward and onward until all the cohorts of error are driven from the world."[4] After such an exhortation, what could President William H. Allen of Girard College do but repeat that the church needed the money of its wealthy men, and that he personally did not fear Mr. Drew as such, and so in closing added a negative to the famous line by Virgil: "*Non timeo Danaos dona ferentes*" (I do not fear the Greeks bearing gifts), which hopefully someone thought to translate for the founder.

Between the morning and the afternoon sessions, a collation was provided by Drew in Forest Hill Mansion, following which the guests had the opportunity to examine the mansion and grounds. The residence itself was an imposing Southern-style classical edifice fronted by a broad veranda with tall Corinthian columns, which now housed the school's lecture room, dining room, social room, and reading room, while the dormitory and refectory stood apart. Thanks to the beneficent donor, a fireproof library and four brick homes for professors were also to be built, costing an additional $25,000 and $84,000 respectively. Such generosity evoked unbounded praise for the founder. Yet the *Methodist* reported: "Of all the company present at Madison, on this opening day, the most modest and unassuming person was Mr. Drew himself. A lady who expressed a desire to see the founder of the seminary was told in our hearing that the most unobtrusive elderly gentleman she saw would be Mr. Drew. The description was perfectly exact."[5] And so, to the glory of its self-effacing founder, the Methodist West Point had been launched.

Daniel Drew's humble generosities were of little concern to Cornelius Vanderbilt, who in the fall and early winter of 1867, being preoccupied with acquiring control of the New York Central, counted on Drew and Frank Work to look after his interests in the Erie. Yet it must have disturbed the Commodore to learn that at an Erie board meeting on December 4, a committee including Eldridge, Drew, and Fisk had been named to initiate arrangements for a broad-gauge connection to Chicago, arrangements that would surely be detrimental to the Central. Equally ominous was a board resolution of the same date, authorizing stock issues in exchange for the securities of other railroads leased by the Erie. Perhaps Vanderbilt also got wind of Drew's loan to the Boston, Hartford and Erie Railroad of $1.5 million, taking B,H & E bonds as security—a loan that the Erie executive committee guaranteed on December 18. Seemingly, Drew and Eldridge had discovered a wealth of common interests.

Meanwhile, as agreed to before the election, Drew had taken charge of a pool that was meant to bull Erie by acquiring about nine million dollars of its stock. The chief participants were Drew, Vanderbilt, and four of Vanderbilt's lieutenants, including the Wall Street brokers Frank Work and Richard Schell. Throughout December, Erie fluctuated narrowly in the low seventies, but for all the pool's purchases never seemed able to advance. "I never seen sich a queer performance in my life," Uncle Daniel reportedly told the other pool members. "But keep on buyin', boys, for it's sartain to rise. Don't be skeered."[6] Reassured, the others redoubled their efforts. One of them, probably Richard Schell, decided to speculate on his own account as well and repeatedly borrowed large sums from Drew, who was happy to furnish them from the pool's money at interest. In January 1868 the market surged, with the

Vanderbilt stocks in the lead, yet Erie still languished in the seventies, dropping suddenly whenever it gained a few points. One evening following such a decline, Uncle Daniel was seen standing near the grand stairway of the Fifth Avenue Hotel, his face puckered with solicitude as he surveyed a throng of frustrated bulls. A prominent broker greeted him and asked, "Well, Mr. Drew, is Erie going down?" "Other folks think it is, though I can't give you any p'ints in it," said Drew, his gaze still fixed on the bulls.[7]

By now, however, the bulls were suspicious. The operator who had borrowed pool money from Drew instructed his brokers to investigate the source of the Erie shares that never failed to meet his demand. And where had those shares come from? Why, from the brokers of Daniel Drew! Outraged, the operator convened the pool at once and got the other members to appeal to Drew to run up Erie on his behalf. Drew, however, coolly announced that the pool neither had Erie nor wanted it; indeed, that he had sold out all its Erie at a profit and would now distribute the gains to the members. Thus the victim whom Drew had saddled with much of the pool's stock now received from him as profit a portion of the much larger sum that he had lost. Drew, of course, had been selling Erie all along.

Thereafter, each day brought further evidence of Drew's duplicity. Vanderbilt, elected president of the Central on December 11, expected to reach rate agreements with the Erie, but when he offered Erie one-third of the total profits, Erie's negotiators demanded one-half. The result was an impasse, with the looming prospect of yet another rate war, which as always was anathema to Vanderbilt. Then in February came worse news still. Drew's Erie committee was successfully completing negotiations with the Michigan Southern and Northern Indiana Railroad, so as to form a broad-gauge road running all the way from New York to Chicago. This road, it was said, would offer more comfortable passenger accommodations and a freight capacity fully fifty percent greater than that of the narrow-gauge Central, from which it was bound to steal business.

For Vanderbilt, this was the last straw. Having relented and let Drew back on the board, Uncle Daniel had repaid him by repeatedly working against Vanderbilt's interests in both the market and Erie's inner councils. And now Drew was stealing a march on the Central to give Erie—that mismanaged, debt-ridden joke of a railroad, which Vanderbilt had meant to bottle up in New York—the greatest prize of all, a through connection to Chicago and the West. The Commodore felt tricked, mocked, lied to, and defied. He was furious with the Erie and above all with Daniel Drew. It meant war, and it was going to be a war of giants.

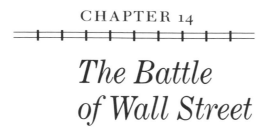

CHAPTER 14

The Battle
of Wall Street

One day when Cornelius Vanderbilt was driving his team at a leisurely pace along a road beside the Harlem Railroad tracks in upper Manhattan, with a friend sitting beside him, he saw an express train fast approaching. "Giddap!" he shouted to his sleek pair of trotters, launching them in a wild dash for a crossing that lay just ahead. Team and carriage whisked over the crossing with only seconds to spare, whereupon Vanderbilt waved cheerily to the astounded fireman, then turned to his friend and said: "There is not another man in New York who could do that!" "And you will never do it again with me in your wagon!" announced the ashen-faced friend.[1]

Such were the energy and daring of Cornelius Vanderbilt, who was in all ways an extraordinary man. Tall, thin, imposingly erect, his physiognomy strong-nosed and square-jawed, with a high forehead and gray hair turning strikingly white, he had the appearance and manner of a conqueror. Dressing simply but stylishly in black, although with the high collar and ample white neckcloth of another day, at seventy-four this aggressive worldling was still attractive to women. As unchurched and illiterate as ever, drinking, smoking, swearing, talking horse, he gave his mornings to business, his afternoons to fast trotters, and his evenings to whist-playing cronies. If he appeared at night in the parlors of the Fifth Avenue Hotel, where money kings and speculators congregated, the crowd parted spontaneously before him. On Harlem Lane, where every afternoon the city's horse fanciers raced their teams pell-mell while uttering unearthly whoops and screams, brokers and speculators refrained from passing him, both out of deference and in hopes of getting "points" in the market. Not that passing Cornele would be easy; he could do a mile in just over two minutes.

In business as in racing, the Commodore was a hard driver—aggressive and, if necessary, ruthless. Since negotiation and compromise had failed, he determined to get control of Erie by buying up its shares in the market. This was no simple matter, since at last report there were 251,058 shares of common and preferred, plus the stock pledged to Drew in 1866 and who knew what else besides. Only a man of inordinate ambition would have attempted it. "As trade now dominates the world," Charles Francis Adams observed, "and railways dominate trade, his object has been to make himself the virtual master of all by making himself absolute lord of the railways."[2]

Ironically, the chief obstacle to this ambition was a stooped and whiny-voiced old man, his face seamed with wrinkles, his fringe of gray chin whiskers as sparse and straggly as Vanderbilt's sideburns were ample; a loner attended by no army of friends or flunkeys, enhanced by no hint of the stately or heroic; negligent in dress, unobtrusive, circumspect; a pious churchgoer who shunned cards, whisky, sport, and profanity, and who while Vanderbilt was churning up the dust of Harlem Lane, was usually napping in the office of his broker. In all respects, then, Drew was a smaller man than the Commodore. But he was cunning, and it was this that Vanderbilt feared. The Commodore's first move, therefore, having formed a new pool to corner Erie in the market, would be to disarm Drew.

On February 17, 1868, Erie Director Frank Work applied to Judge George G. Barnard of the Supreme Court of New York, sitting in Manhattan, for an injunction against the board of directors of the Erie Railway Company and Daniel Drew. In his complaint Work charged that Drew had obtained the 58,000 shares in 1866 through a fraudulent transaction and that he should be made to account to the company for any resulting profits and be compelled to return the collateral. Vanderbilt's name appeared nowhere in the document (which was substantially the same complaint that he had threatened Drew with prior to the election), since the Commodore deemed it legally expedient to act through intermediaries. Work, however, was known to be his representative in Erie, nor was it any coincidence that he had selected Barnard to petition, since the judge, a dandified Tammany politician who frequented Delmonico's and the Astor House, was notoriously partial to wealthy litigants and above all to Cornelius Vanderbilt. The Vanderbilt party planned to neutralize the 58,000 shares by making Drew liable for their imminent return and to keep Drew from converting any more bonds into stock.

Predictably, Barnard issued a temporary injunction forbidding Drew and Erie to make any settlement of the 1866 loan, pending a judicial investigation, and he ordered Drew to appear in court. News of the injunction provoked much excitement on Wall Street, where Drew was said to be "in a fix" and about to be "sent to smithereens." The bulls began buying Erie with confidence.

Yet no sooner had they done so than they heard rumors that Erie was converting the bonds of the Buffalo, Bradford, and Pittsburgh Railroad into stock of the Erie Railway. Immediately, without even awaiting the outcome of the first injunction, Work on February 19 petitioned Judge Barnard again, charging that Erie's lease of the Buffalo, Bradford, and Pittsburgh was improper, and that Daniel Drew, by virtue of his speculations in Erie stock, was "guilty of gross misconduct and abuses of his trust," wherefore he asked that Drew be removed as director and treasurer. Compliantly, Barnard issued a second injunction, temporarily suspending Drew in both capacities and summoning him to court in this matter, too. Surely now, the bulls reasoned, it was safe to buy.

Targeted by two injunctions in three days, suspended from the Erie management, and threatened with prosecution, Uncle Daniel seemed remarkably chipper and blithe. He predicted that Erie, then selling in the mid-seventies, would go to 65 or 60, and cheerfully offered calls on it while the Vanderbilt pool kept buying. With the exception of Work, all the Erie directors had rallied to him and all seemed remarkably undaunted. To the bulls' puzzlement, Erie fluctuated in the seventies but refused to rise; rumors circulated that the Erie crowd were cooking something up. They were.

While New York State's General Railroad Act of 1850 prohibited railroad companies from increasing their capitalization by a direct issue of stock, it also permitted them to issue bonds so as to raise money for "completing, finishing, and operating the road," and furthermore to make such bonds convertible into the company's stock at par. This last provision was meant as an inducement to investors, who would be more inclined to buy a company's bonds if they could anticipate its stock rising above par, which would let them convert their bonds into stock for a profit. Whether or not this law applied to the Erie, whose capitalization was regulated by the New York State act of 1861 governing its reorganization, was an open question, and certainly the spirit if not the letter of the 1850 law required that the convertible bonds be issued to finance legitimate construction and not for the purpose of being immediately converted into stock. Such niceties, however, did not detain the guiding lights of Erie, who in the convertible-bond provision found an ingenious semilegal device for circumventing the prohibition of direct new issues of stock.

On February 18, the day following Barnard's first injunction and preceding the second one, President Eldridge called a special meeting of the board to consider the question of raising funds for new iron and construction and for liquidating demands on the treasury. These seemed to be valid albeit vaguely phrased matters that even Frank Work, who was present, could not object to, so they were duly referred to the executive committee. On the following day, even as Barnard was issuing his second injunction, the executive committee, comprising Eldridge, Drew, Gould, J.C. Bancroft Davis, and Henry Thompson, recommended to the board that it be authorized to borrow such sums as seemed necessary. The board, with Drew still sitting on it, granted this authority at once, and at Drew's suggestion—obviously, he knew of Barnard's impending proceedings—named an assistant treasurer to act in his place and under his directions. Immediately thereafter the executive committee convened and authorized ten million dollars' worth of new 7 percent convertible bonds, of which the treasurer was quickly instructed to sell up to half at not less than 72½, slightly less than Erie's price on the market. Pending this sale, the committee briefly adjourned.

Ten million dollars of new convertible bonds, or the equivalent of 100,000 new shares of stock, were to be fed, half now, half later, to the voracious Vanderbilt, so as to relieve him and his friends of some seven or eight million dollars! This was rascality raised to the level of grandeur, all the more so in that the proposed victim was the wealthiest, most powerful, and most arrogant man on the Street. Was it in Uncle Daniel's fertile mind that the scheme had been hatched? Certainly his 58,000 shares of 1866 constituted a worthy precedent, and he had grounds for revenge against Vanderbilt. Yet the vastness of the coup, the sheer epic daring of it, smacks of Jay Gould. But whosever inspiration it was, the whole executive committee embraced the scheme and made it their own. Not that the profits would go exclusively to Drew, since Fisk and Gould drafted an agreement that they made Drew sign, whereby he was to keep only half the proceeds, while half would be divided among Fisk, Gould, Thompson, and others. Yet Fisk was probably the only board member outside the executive committee who was in on the scheme.

Shortly after its adjournment on the afternoon of February 19, the executive committee reconvened. In the interim, Erie's treasurer sold $5 million of the new bonds at 72½ and at the same time, either just before or just after the sale, was struck by Barnard's second injunction, suspending him from office. In his absence, therefore, the committee ratified the sale of the bonds. In a strictly *pro forma* transaction, Drew sold the bonds to his broker Groesbeck, who within five minutes returned them to the company and received in exchange 50,000 shares of common stock. This new stock then went into Groesbeck's safe and sat there for ten days, while on the market Erie seesawed in the low seventies as the bulls bought every share of the old stock offered, amid a welter of rumors. In response to the two injunctions, on February 21 Drew appeared before Judge Barnard, flanked by three attorneys. After a preliminary skirmish of the lawyers, both suits were postponed to March 3. By Saturday, February 29, Erie stock had dropped below 70, depressed by rumors of a default on its bonds. At this point, the conspirators decided to spring their coup.

Stealthily, out of Groesbeck's safe came the 50,000 new shares of stock, to be distributed to three friendly brokerage houses that promptly fed them in turn to the Street. So deftly was it done that the Vanderbilt brokers seem not to have been aware at first that the great flood of stock engulfing them was emanating from a single source. They had standing orders to buy, so they bought, boldly, frantically, and waited for the stock to go up. All day on the twenty-ninth Erie seethed in the upper sixties, then on Monday morning, March 2, under the weight of stock offered, it sank to 65. "It'll git to 60 afore long," Drew reportedly predicted, "and I'm not afeard to venture that it'll go as low as 55 afore the day's over."[3] But the Vanderbilt brokers were resolute. In frenzied trading the price rallied to 67, and on the following day to 70, 72, 73, till by the day's end, at a cost of some three and a half million dollars, they had soaked up all 50,000 shares. Only the Commodore could have done it.

The delivery to their brokers' offices of quantities of fresh Erie certificates left the Vanderbilt camp alarmed and incredulous: even after two injunctions, the Old Bear was still not disarmed! Quickly lieutenants conferred, and lawyers were consulted. As a result, when the two suits came up before Barnard on March 3, Work thrust yet a third petition at the magistrate, who then granted a third injunction—a sweeping order restraining Erie's officers from issuing any stock whatsoever, from guaranteeing the bonds of other railroads, or from building a broad-gauge connection in the West, while at the same time enjoining Drew from all transactions in Erie until he returned the 58,000 shares pledged to him in 1866 and the 10,000 shares allegedly received by him in exchange for the Buffalo, Bradford, and Pittsburgh bonds. Now at last, the Vanderbilt party concluded, Drew and his confederates were bound by the full force and majesty of law. How could Drew possibly fulfill his numerous short contracts maturing on or about March 9? Commodore Vanderbilt must now achieve his fourth great corner, in Erie.

But Daniel Drew was no stranger to injunctions, and he and his counsel were well aware that New York State had not one Supreme Court justice but thirty-three, who in certain proceedings enjoyed identical powers applicable throughout the entire state. So if Vanderbilt had an obliging judge in Barnard, the Erie men could shop around for one of their own. Accordingly, on March 5 Fisk, Gould, and an Erie attorney hastened by rail to Binghamton, a good Erie town in Broome County, to petition Judge Ransom Balcom, who with a haste worthy of his colleague in New York issued the desired injunction. Frank Work, alleged to be a New York Central agent acting against the interests of the Erie, was suspended from the Erie board, and all parties involved were summoned to appear on March 7, prior to which the proceedings before Barnard were stayed. "This," remarked the *Herald*, "is diamond cutting diamond with a vengeance."[4] Noting the impasse, some observers registered incipient doubts about the arrangements of the state's judicial system.

Certainly that system's legal restraints were borne lightly by Drew and his colleagues, who thought them of no more consequence than the investigating committee that the state senate, taking note of the "Erie row," appointed on March 5. On March 3, however, Erie's executive committee had already authorized the sale of another $5 million of convertible bonds. Drew at once purchased these bonds at 72½, only to be smitten with Barnard's third injunction, barring him from any transactions in the company's stock. Since that same injunction was binding on his agents as well and prohibited the Erie board from issuing more stock, lesser spirits might have given up the project altogether. For the Erie inner circle, however, this meant only that the conversion of the second batch of bonds was rendered slightly more difficult.

Since the next hearings before Barnard were scheduled for Tuesday March 10 and many of Drew's short contracts matured on the ninth, the conspirators timed their coup for Monday, the ninth. First, lest Barnard name a receiver to take possession of the Erie treasury, President Eldridge was authorized on March 5 to draw a half million dollars for "legal and other needful expenses," which he sent for safekeeping to Boston. Then, over the weekend of March 7-8, the offices and homes of the Erie men and their agents fairly hummed with activity. While one team of lawyers and clerks prepared affidavits and petitions for injunctions, another team counseled the directors. At the request of the enjoined president, who said he needed them for transfers of existing stock, but was too unwell to sign them himself, Gen. Alexander S. Diven, the reputable but enjoined vice-president, spent Saturday night and Sunday at home, diligently signing hundreds of brand-new certificates. As he later assured the Senate investigating committee, he undertook this action in absolute good faith. (Throughout all his long career in Erie, this honored veteran of Antietam and Chancellorsville, with an iron gray moustache and whiskers and a martial look about him, would display invincible innocence.)

Meanwhile, on that same evening of Saturday March 7, stealthier hands were at work. Since Drew's broker, David Groesbeck, was likewise restrained by Barnard's injunction, some third party had to be found to buy the bonds and convert them. Accordingly, Groesbeck fetched from the Fifth Avenue Hotel one Martin F. Greene, a speculator who frequented his office, and took him to Drew's residence at 41 Union Square, where Drew explained that he wanted to sell Greene $5 million of convertible Erie bonds, holding him harmless for any loss. Since Greene seemed amenable, they and Jay Gould, who was waiting in the hall, then went together to the home of one of the Erie attorneys, so that the attorney and his staff could draw up the necessary papers. But when asked to sign a lengthy affidavit, Greene protested that it contained statements regarding Erie that he knew nothing of and despite Drew's urging backed out.

Undaunted by this flurry of integrity, Groesbeck then brought from a boarding house in Fourth Avenue another banker and broker of his acquaintance, Ossian D. Ashley, to whom Drew made the same proposition. Ashley too agreed, then likewise voiced a scruple. The affidavit stated that he had asked Erie to convert the bonds and been refused, which was false. This matter was resolved by having Ashley then and there request conversion of the bonds from Drew, who as treasurer (suspended, but no matter) refused because he must of course respect Barnard's injunction, whereupon Ashley signed the affidavit. It was now 11:00 P.M.; the purchaser departed.

As prearranged, on the morning of Monday March 9 Ashley appeared in Groesbeck's office and signed a note for the bonds. Groesbeck retained the bonds as security for the note, plus Ashley's authorization to Drew to dispose of the bonds whenever Drew thought it in Ashley's interest, a contingency that was realized at once. Although this straw man had signed away control of his property, he later testified that he considered this a *bona fide* sale, and while protected from loss, expected to receive any profits that might result. If true, this says little for his instincts as an operator or for his knowledge of Daniel Drew.

On that same Monday morning General Diven, the reputable enjoined vice-president, delivered the remaining books of new stock certificates to Horatio N. Otis, the enjoined secretary, in the company office at 187 West Street. Then at 10:00 A.M. a special meeting of the board minus Work and Drew was held, at which Diven read an executive committee report, carefully prepared for publication, that set forth the company's need for massive new construction and equipment, including the replacement of iron rails by steel (a project that the Erie management had discussed and tabled for years), to provide for which it announced the creation of $10 million of convertible bonds. This was the first official disclosure of the bonds, to further justify which the committee appended two confidential reports by Superintendent Hugh Riddle, dated March 3, stressing the ravages of a harsh winter on the road's iron rails, the condition of which caused Riddle anxiety for the safety of trains. The board did not question why, given the vast sums raised for improvements in previous years, the company's property should now be in such desperate straits. Instead, it approved the committee's report, which the Erie management then sent out for publication in the press.

Meanwhile, strange things were happening. On the president's instructions, prior to the board meeting Secretary Otis had added his signature to two books of the new stock certificates that Diven had signed and delivered, books containing 50,000 shares that, curiously enough, had already been made out to the brokerage firms of Fisk and Gould. Shortly after 11:00 A.M. Otis gave these books to the transfer clerk, for delivery to the company's transfer office at 11 Pine Street. Minutes later the clerk returned, dumbfounded, to announce that Director Fisk had suddenly appeared in the president's office, snatched the books away from him, and run off with them. Astonished, Otis searched immediately for Fisk, failed to find him, and when he reported the incident later to the president, was told, "That is all right." Thus, seemingly through no fault of the enjoined vice-president, secretary, transfer clerk, or anyone else—except, of course, the mysterious Fisk—certificates for 50,000 new shares of stock, all properly printed and signed, had been wrested from the company's control. Soon thereafter, quantities of fresh Erie certificates began turning up in Wall Street. Mr. Ashley's bonds, it seemed, had been sold and converted in the twinkling of an eye.

On that same busy Monday, the Vanderbilt camp petitioned the reliable Barnard once again, this time in the name of the Commodore's ally Richard Schell, obtaining an injunction (the fifth in the affair so far) that restrained the Erie board from meeting or transacting any business whatsoever, unless Frank Work was present and participating. Yet this maneuver, checkmating Judge Balcom's order issued March 5, was countered almost instantly in turn by the Erie conspirators' final finesse.

Bright and early Monday morning an Erie attorney visited the Brooklyn residence of Justice J.W. Gilbert, a respected but ailing magistrate who was in the habit of holding chambers in his home. Petitioned on behalf of bondholder Ashley to issue a writ ordering Erie to convert Ashley's bonds into stock, Gilbert refused, saying that the proper remedy was a mandatory injunction. That afternoon the attorney reappeared, accompanied by a second Erie attorney armed with a new summons, complaint, affidavits, and the draft of an injunction, with which they laid siege again to the magistrate. The new petition was in the name of Fisk's partner William Belden, who as an Erie stock and bondholder now launched a new action against Vanderbilt and his lieutenants. He charged them with having formed a combination to speculate in Erie, and with using the courts for this purpose, notably that of Justice George G. Barnard, who was himself now named as a defendant, accused of frequenting a Broad Street brokerage house involved in this nefarious operation.

Had Judge Gilbert reflected, he might have deduced quite correctly that the Erie forces had been spying on his fellow magistrate. Instead, after considerable persuasion he granted the injunction, although he insisted on modifying its text. What resulted was a marvelous instrument that restrained all parties to other suits from any acts in "furtherance of said conspiracy"; that ordered the Erie directors, with the exception of Work, to continue to discharge their duties; and that most specifically forbade the Erie directors to refuse to convert bonds into stock. Thus Barnard, who had countered Balcom, who had countered Barnard, was countered now by Gilbert, in whose defense one can only note that the poor man was ailing. Since whatever course it pursued, the Erie management must violate someone's injunction, it would of course select, in fact already had selected, the alternative that suited it.

And so, on that busy Monday morning, even as Ashley bought his bonds and Drew took charge of them, as the Erie board approved the bonds' creation, as the stock certificates vanished, and as Barnard and Gilbert were petitioned for injunctions, the conspirators unleashed the rest of their stock. On Saturday March 7 Erie had risen to 78½ in active trading. By now the "Erie Railway row," competing with President Andrew Johnson's impeachment in Washington, had begun to claim the attention of the papers, which billed the Vanderbilt-Drew struggle as a "battle of titans." Therefore on Monday March 9 all eyes were riveted on Erie.

At the urging of Frank Work and Richard Schell, who were with him in the pool, Vanderbilt had again given his brokers standing orders to sustain Erie in the market. Consequently, when the Stock Exchange's morning call began at 10:30, Erie had already been traded feverishly on the Open Board downstairs for half an hour at prices of from 79½ to 81. Now, in the vast upstairs hall, a dense throng of some two hundred top-hatted brokers waited as the vice-president in rapid order called out government bonds, state bonds, Pacific Mail, Canton, and New York Central, eliciting only a tepid response, then at last announced, "Erie!" What then ensued has been recounted by W. W. Fowler, a speculator of the day:

> For ten minutes bedlam seemed to have broken loose. Every operator and broker was on his feet in an instant, screaming and gesticulating. The different Vanderbilt brokers stood each in the center of a circle, wheeling as on a pivot from right to left, brandishing their arms and snatching at all the stock offered them. As the presiding officer's hammer fell and his hoarse voice thundered out, "That will do, gentlemen, I shall fine any other offer," Erie stood at 80. The crowd leaving the other stocks not yet called, poured out into the

street, where nothing was heard but Erie. Vanderbilt's brokers had orders to buy every share offered, and under their enormous purchases the price rose, by twelve o'clock, to 83.[5]

So the battle raged, with the two contending titans nowhere in sight nor even on the fringes of the fray, since like most big traders they directed their operations from headquarters somewhat removed. Vanderbilt used a little office at 2 West Fourth Street where early each morning, hidden from the press and public, he issued orders to an army of underlings, including his son, sons-in-law, vice-presidents, and attorneys, who in turn commanded clerks, brokers, secretaries, and runners. Drew was usually found in a back room at Groesbeck's in Broad Street, where the new ticker tape—Wall Street's first, installed in late December—let him follow the market with ease. On this particular morning, however, he went with Gould by carriage to the Erie office in West Street, so as to be close by when the board met at 10:00 A.M. He had contracted to sell Ashley's bonds to Fisk at 80, expecting Fisk to convert the bonds at once and dump the stock on the market, which would depress Erie and let him cover his shorts just in time. Now, however, he waited in vain to hear that Fisk had done so, and as he waited, he saw the price of Erie driven ever upward. With a fortune at stake, he became alarmed, then desperate; why was Fisk holding off? By late morning he could take it no longer: he sent a messenger to Groesbeck, telling him to cover his contracts at a loss. Yet no sooner had he done so, when word came that Fisk was throwing his stock on the market. Quickly Drew sent another messenger to countermand his order, but too late; Groesbeck had covered most of his shorts, buying the first of Fisk's stock at high prices. Drew had covered short contracts at 80 that he had made at 70, and so on that day took a heavy loss, although he had profits in Erie overall. Such was Fisk's little joke on his mentor, which amused Gould no end.

Meanwhile the 50,000 new shares of Erie hit the Street like an avalanche. As the Vanderbilt agents grasped at all the stock offered, unbelievable amounts changed hands. Then, shortly after noon, with Erie at 83, a rumor swept the Street that delivery was being made of hundreds of virgin pure Erie certificates dated only two days back. The discovery that new Erie stock—no one knew how much—was on the market struck panic in the hearts of the bulls. Instantly Vanderbilt's allies, Richard Schell and Frank Work among them, deserted him and dumped their Erie, whose price plummeted to 71½, while confusion and dismay gripped the Street.

What rich reserves of profanity escaped Cornelius Vanderbilt when he first learned that his millions were being spent on pristine bits of paper, history has not recorded. Immediately thereafter, however, one of his brokers asked if he should sell. "*Sell?*" Vanderbilt is said to have thundered, "You fool, *no*! Buy every share offered!"[6]

So ordering, he gave proof of the soundest judgment. His own prestige and fortune, as well as those of his friends, had been committed to Erie to the hilt; if he faltered now even for an instant, the incipient panic would demolish Erie and their combined resources with it, then spread to his other stocks and finally engulf the whole Street. Wrath and vengeance could wait; right now he had to sustain Erie in the market, even though it meant absorbing this entire new issue, as well as all the other Erie that his fainthearted friends—"skunks," he called them—had jettisoned in panic. His cash was gone; to do it, he would have to get loans. But his will did not crack, his brokers kept on buying, and Erie slowly recovered to close in the Long Room at 77¾. So ended one of the most hectic days in stock market history, a day of jackals when Drew and his allies cheated Vanderbilt, when Work and Schell deserted Vanderbilt, and Fisk hoodwinked Drew. In the end the panic had been stemmed, although at a cost to the Commodore of millions.

Tuesday March 10 was a busy day for all concerned. Although hard-pressed financially, Vanderbilt continued to support Erie in the market (the "skunks" were still deserting him), maintaining the price until it closed at 75½. Meanwhile, promptly delivered, those fresh certificates were piling up in his brokers' offices. Fisk, having unloaded the 50,000 shares between 79 and 80, out of the proceeds repaid Drew his original outlay for the bonds at 72½, but refused to pay Drew his profits in cash, pending a settlement regarding the division of the spoils. Secretary Otis was likewise busy, being summoned that day to testify before a closed meeting of the Senate committee investigating Erie, whose initial sessions in New York City coincided with Erie's convulsions in the market, and with the appearance in the press this day of the executive committee's report of March 9, announcing the $10 million of new convertible bonds and, by implication, the exact amount of new stock—100,000 shares—that had been foisted off on Vanderbilt.

The announcement of those $10 million of bonds was of more than casual interest to Justice Barnard, whose injunction banning new issues of Erie stock had been so brazenly flouted. On this same day, the original cases initiated by Frank Work were scheduled to be heard before the judge, who being involved in another case elsewhere had to postpone them to Wednesday. At this point Barnard was served with Judge Gilbert's injunction, whereby he himself became a defendant. Nor was the end in sight. Later that same day, upon complaint of John Bloodgood, a Vanderbilt broker who had bought some of Fisk's new stock, Judge Albert Cardozo of the Supreme Court in Manhattan issued still another injunction against Erie (the seventh in the war so far) reaffirming the earlier order by Barnard that enjoined the Erie board from acting without Frank Work. When the hearings resumed before Barnard on Wednesday the eleventh, both bench and bar were so hopelessly confused that Barnard declared a postponement until the fourteenth.

Meanwhile the Erie schemers, to tighten the screws further on the bulls, undertook still another ploy. By having their brokers call in their call loans and by withdrawing their deposits, which were especially large because of the recent sales of Erie, from the New York City banks, they took some $7 million out of circulation, creating a sudden money stringency that on March 10 sent rates for call loans soaring a full point to 7 percent. At the same time, Fisk and Groesbeck maneuvered to force the Tenth National Bank to withhold from circulation over $3 million that Fisk had deposited there and taken certified checks for, a stratagem that the bank president hotly protested, resenting being obliged to abet others in a lockup of greenbacks.

Intensified by these maneuverings, the pressure on the bulls was enormous. In absorbing Erie—Vanderbilt himself now had some 150,000 shares of it—they had exhausted their cash reserves. All had grievous losses and some were close to ruin. They dared not sell their Erie, lest they precipitate a panic, yet to support it in the market they needed credit just when credit was hardest to obtain. For several days feverish activity was noted in the Vanderbilt camp, the precise nature of which remained a closely guarded secret. There could be little doubt that the greatest reputation in Wall Street and the second largest fortune in America were in the throes of their worst crisis. That fortune amounted to tens of millions of dollars, but much of it was locked up in property at a time when the Commodore was desperate for cash. Many men would have broken under the strain, but with whispers of his ruin spreading, Vanderbilt gave orders to his agents in the morning, then each afternoon was seen driving his fast trotters on Harlem Lane, while in the evening he played whist with his cronies as usual.

To this rock of assurance the other bulls clung, and not in vain. After two or three days the Vanderbilt camp recovered its serenity: the Commodore was solvent, although no one quite knew how. At the time, rumors circulated of a multi-million-dollar mortgage of his railroads to a foreign banking house, but years later another story came out. At the height of the crisis Vanderbilt apparently sent Richard Schell to negotiate a loan from the leading New York bankers, who informed Schell that they would loan on Central but not on Erie. Schell, however, quickly confirmed that most of the banks held large amounts of Central as collateral. "Very well, gentlemen," he then announced, "if you don't lend the Commodore half a million on Erie at 50, and do it at once, he will put Central at 50 tomorrow and break half the houses on the Street. You know whether you will be among them."[7]

It was a desperate gambit, but it worked. Vanderbilt got his loan— surely far more than half a million—on Erie, which proved not wholly useless to him after all.

On the morning of Thursday March 12 Fisk and the executive committee were in the Erie offices in West Street. Certainly they knew the war was far from over. There were court proceedings to deal with (they had spies posted close by Judge Barnard's chambers), and a Senate investigating committee that would reconvene in Albany the next day, with several directors summoned to testify. As a precaution against attachments by the enemy, as well as to make money tight for the bulls, they had withdrawn all the company's money from the banks and contemplated sending it to safety in New Jersey. Yet they seem to have felt no imminent threat from Vanderbilt or Barnard, being doubtless carried away by sheer elation at having pulled off the biggest coup the Street had ever seen.

Suddenly an Erie spy dashed in to report that Barnard was at that very moment issuing processes of contempt against the lot of them, vowing to have them all in Ludlow Street Jail by night. Near panic gripped them. Not only would they themselves be seized—a prospect that Uncle Daniel, a distinguished churchman of seventy, found appalling—but the company's books and treasury, too, of which the last was absolutely essential for carrying on the war against Vanderbilt. Their one hope was to remove the company's records and assets, and themselves as well, to New Jersey as soon as humanly possible.

Shortly thereafter a police officer patrolling his beat in West Street was startled to see a group of well-dressed, respectable-looking men, accompanied by a platoon of clerks, issue from the Erie building in a wild stampede and rush headlong toward the docks nearby. With them they carried bundles of documents tied with red tape, account books, records, desks, drawers, and bales of money, while their pockets were stuffed with securities. Suspecting a gang of plunderers operating in broad daylight, the officer intervened, only to be assured that all was proper, that it was only the Erie executive committee effecting an impromptu change of locale. The flying squadron made off in hot haste, one of them—an elderly gentleman with a fringe of gray whiskers—in a hackney coach crammed with bales containing millions in greenbacks. Still suspicious, the officer followed the fugitives to the docks, where he saw them deposit themselves and their impedimenta aboard a ferry bound for New Jersey. Some time thereafter, this same mobile directorate, safe on the Jersey shore and breathing easier, entered Taylor's Hotel, a plain brick building in Exchange Place, hard by Erie's Long Dock property and depot in Jersey City, where after a conference with the manager they engaged a suite of rooms on the second floor for a stay of indefinite duration.

Once he put the Hudson between himself and Barnard's wrath and Vanderbilt's revenge, nothing could tempt Uncle Daniel to set foot again in New York. Fisk and Gould, however, wanted to wind up their affairs and therefore returned to the city, where by then deputy sheriffs were hunting for the Erie directors, calling at their homes, hotels, and clubs, and posting themselves at the docks. Eldridge and Thompson remained with Drew in Jersey City, where they knew nothing of the fate of the other directors, not even Fisk and Gould, until they returned that night soaked and bedraggled, with a tale to tell. Having decided on a last dinner at Delmonico's, they had been interrupted in mid-feast by word of their imminent arrest, which sent them scurrying by carriage to the docks, where to avoid the police they persuaded an officer of Drew's *St. John* to provide them with a small boat and two deckhands to row them over to New Jersey. Then, half way across, they got lost in a fog where they drifted about for an hour, being repeatedly all but run down and swamped by passing ferries, until they managed at last to clamber aboard one of them and so returned to New Jersey.

Reunited in their Jersey City haven, the fugitives—some drenched, some dry—settled into their strange new quarters, while word of their flight spread on both sides of the river, provoking stupefaction. It was the first time within living memory that a railroad had absconded. As for Uncle Daniel, not even the thought of Vanderbilt's $8 million lodged safely in a Jersey City bank could reassure him. He was shocked, breathless, dazed. Nothing like this had ever happened to him in his life!

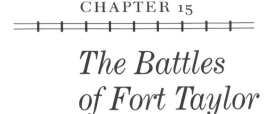

CHAPTER 15

The Battles
of Fort Taylor

"A stupendous fraud," cried the *Times* financial editor of the new Erie stock issue. The instigators, he insisted, must not escape "the public odium which is now being visited upon them, and the condign punishment in purse and reputation, by the Courts and Legislature, which assuredly awaits them."[1]

Yet it was not odium but curiosity that brought throngs of visitors swarming across the river to New Jersey, where the directors' dramatic flight had made them instant celebrities. Flocking in and around Taylor's Hotel in Jersey City were friends and acquaintances of the fugitives, journalists and would-be journalists, brokers, speculators, and Wall Street hangers-on, rubbing elbows with lawyers, messengers, perplexed Erie employees, and the idle curious. Besieged by visitors, the exiles quickly decided to restrict the admission of strangers to a select few, and those only if they came on business. The others were left to mill about outside, mingling with the local Jerseymen, the whole crowd oblivious of the presidential impeachment proceedings in Washington as they exchanged opinions on this most immediate of the crises of the day. "Ah," cried one gentleman overheard by a *Herald* reporter, "I often said that Drew was pluck to the backbone, and Vanderbilt has met his match. Take my word, my friends, Greek now meets Greek, and the man who now attempts to boss in Wall Street will find that two can play at that game."[2]

Among those admitted were reporters, who were invited first to the hotel's bar as Erie's guests, then directed upstairs to the second-floor reception room, where they found Drew, Eldridge, Fisk, Gould, and Thompson in the company of friends, fellow directors, and attorneys. Holding forth as chief host, public relations man, and master of the revels was Director James Fisk, Jr., rotund and jovial, who welcomed the press as "the great lever of public opinion," declaring that "those only who perform works of darkness shun the light."[3] Waving the journalists toward an array of bottles, goblets, and prime Havanas, he expounded the righteousness of Erie and the injustice of justice in New York, interspersing jokes and bad puns as he affirmed the exiles' determination to hold out in New Jersey if it took a month of Sundays.

As the visitors could see for themselves, the directors' suite was being set up as a functioning office, while freight agents and superintendents were being informed by telegraph of the closing of the New York headquarters and summoned to the hotel for instructions. Meanwhile couriers came and went, and there were secret whisperings in corridors and conferences behind the closed paneled doors of what was now called the directors' room. But in spite of Fisk's pronouncements, unanimity of opinion was lacking. A *World* reporter noted that if some directors were embittered against Vanderbilt, others in speaking of him remained polite and reticent, while still others, obviously not the Jersey City exiles, even voiced the opinion that "it is all nonsense to fight against Vanderbilt, as he is the smartest old man in the country and has energy enough to eat up all the rest of the directors."[4]

Thanks to Vanderbilt's money—those millions now safely deposited in a Jersey City bank—the siege, if long, would be a merry one; there was much evidence of daily wining and dining, with the Erie treasury footing the bill. Reporters were allowed even into the directors' special dining room, where a *Herald* man found the fugitives boisterously at table, joking about sieges and summonses to arms and reaffirming their watchword of No Surrender. When another journalist was admitted, Fisk interrupted the festivities to assert that the former rate agreement forced on Erie by Vanderbilt had kept one million barrels of flour and three million bushels of wheat out of the New York market, causing prices to soar. The Erie fight, he solemnly affirmed, was "in the interest of the poorer classes especially"[5]—novel perceptions for a champagne-tippling financier who habitually sported a gold-headed cane and a gleaming shirtfront diamond.

But where was Uncle Daniel, that exemplar of "pluck to the backbone"? Holding himself aloof from the revels, he sat huddled in a corner where he tried to nap, roused fitfully by the speeches and mirth of the banqueters, to which he responded with a few forced smiles, but still appeared peevish and depressed. Two days of visitors had worn him out; snatched away from home, church, and Wall Street, he felt insecure. Besides, as a dignified Methodist of seventy, how could he participate in these prolonged champagne banquets where hilarity abounded and grace was never said?

The banquets, moreover, were subject to sudden interruptions. On one occasion when the feast was in full swing, a messenger arrived and the exiles were summoned in a body from the table, where only Jay Gould lingered.

"Go bring Gould—hurry up, this is fearful!" exclaimed a voice in the corridor, within the hearing of the *World* reporter. "Tell him to leave his dinner. There is going to be a conference. Get him out!" "Why, what's the matter?" asked another individual, taking out a cigar. "Is it a flank movement of Schell's?" "Never mind, get him out. But stop! Gould is a family man. Sudden emotions are dangerous. Let him finish that quail. There is bloody work in there—he will need something to sustain him in the perils before us. I am awful afraid of Vanderbilt!"[6] And so Gould was left to finish his quail, before attending the fearful conference.

The reporter did not identify the speaker of these dramatic lines, yet who but Fisk could have postured so flamboyantly, especially within the hearing of the press? As for Uncle Daniel, mindful of spies, detectives, and process servers, that night he had a guard posted at his bedroom door and plugged the keyhole with cotton.

On Saturday March 14 the Erie litigation came up again before Judge Barnard in a courtroom crammed with learned counsel and spectators, no civil case having elicited such intense excitement in years. Although attachments had been issued against eight directors, all had eluded arrest except Diven, Erie's infinitely innocent vice-president, whose promise to appear in court had spared him a night in jail. William B. Skidmore and Frederick A. Lane now appeared voluntarily in court, as subsequently would J. C. Bancroft Davis, another Erie innocent who denied all knowledge of market speculations in the stock. These three gentlemen and Diven were all freed upon giving nominal bail of a hundred dollars, but for Fisk, Gould, Eldridge, and Thompson, Barnard decreed bail of a half million each. Contrary to the rumors that had reached him, no warrant had as yet been issued against Drew for contempt of court, probably because, having been suspended as director and treasurer, he could not be held legally responsible for the subsequent actions of the board. Even so, he had no intention of returning to New York, where other actions could be brought against him at any time, or a receiver named to relieve him of the Erie treasury. Besides, with accounts yet to be settled with his colleagues, he wanted to stick close to the money.

While these matters of bail were being settled, Erie counsel David Dudley Field—one of the most eminent lawyers of the day and a noted advocate of reform and codification of the law—protested against Barnard's hearing the case, since Barnard, as a result of the action brought by Fisk's partner Belden, was a party to it. The stylish Barnard, who while presiding over his courtroom whittled away on the bench at a stick of pine wood, replied that he was most definitely not involved in the case and that he would most certainly hear it, whereupon he proceeded to name George A. Osgood receiver of the proceeds from the sale of the 100,000 new shares of Erie. This was a futile gesture because with the money carried off to New Jersey, there was nothing for a receiver to receive, and it betokened the grossest partiality, since Osgood was Vanderbilt's son-in-law and broker and a personal friend of Barnard's to boot. "There is a day of reckoning coming," announced the indignant Field, "and there are parties who will have much to answer for."[7]

Meanwhile, consternation raged in Jersey City: there was a plot afoot to kidnap Daniel Drew! The first hint of this sinister enterprise came on the afternoon of March 16, when several parties of New York City "roughs"—hard-faced characters of the most undesirable nature—began arriving by the Pavonia ferry in New Jersey, until they numbered some forty or fifty in all. Proceeding in a straggly group to the nearby Erie depot, they asked for the freight contractor and when told by employees that he was not there inquired after Drew and the other directors. Summoned by one of his detectives, Inspector Hugh Masterson, chief of the Erie Railway police, now arrived on the scene and engaged the "b'hoys" in conversation. Having long been a New York City detective, he recognized among them such notorious individuals as Cusick, Jim Elliott, and other "man-chewing" toughs, from one of whom he learned that the raid had been organized in Cusick's ill-famed Eighth Ward gin mill, where $50,000 had been offered to anyone who could produce Drew, Fisk, or Eldridge on that side of the river, and a reduced sum for the others. Masterson quickly pointed out that none of the directors was in the immediate vicinity, and that he had forces on hand that outnumbered the "b'hoys" two to one. Dissuaded, the invaders had a drink in the depot and then withdrew, some returning at once by ferry to New York, although others first sauntered in the direction of Taylor's Hotel, as if to reconnoiter it.

Immediately, the wildest rumors ran through Jersey City, while at Taylor's Hotel the directors took alarm, especially Drew, whose person seemed to be the most particular target of the "grab." Never in all his seventy years had Uncle Daniel shown the slightest taste for physical encounter; the thought of now being seized upon by these Eighth Ward desperadoes appalled him. Would Cornelius Vanderbilt, his old friend and enemy of thirty-seven years, resort to violence? Drew knew him better than did any of the exiles—Vanderbilt, who had "wrastled" in his youth; who in his middle years, when physically attacked by a political opponent, took on his assailant, a champion pugilist, and beat him senseless; who, when his wife resisted moving back to Manhattan from her beloved Staten Island, had her locked up in an asylum until she changed her mind; and who quite recently justified forcing passengers to traipse through a midwinter snowstorm because the law was too slow for him. Would this titan of finance, wounded in purse and pride, stoop so low, play so foul? *Yes*, concluded Uncle Daniel. *Yes!*

Hurriedly, the directors summoned Police Chief Nathaniel R. Fowler, who required no explanations. He himself had been present at the depot in civilian clothing and, as a former dealer in the Washington Market, had recognized among the ruffians a number of ex-butchers turned sporting characters of whom he could believe the very worst. Indeed, New York was full of such elements, products of the seething underclass whose surfacing en masse in 1863 had produced the horror of the draft riots. It was quite believable that the hope of $50,000, or a half or a third or a tenth of it, would induce scores of them to risk limb, liberty, and life. The peril then was great, it being agreed by all that this daylight foray had been no more than a reconnaissance in force, that the desperadoes would return by night to undertake the "grab." Uncle Daniel trembled for his safety but was assured by Chief Fowler, backed up by Thomas Gaffney, president of the Jersey City Police Commissioners, that any such attempt would be foiled.

At the 9:00 P.M. roll call that evening, Chief Fowler alerted the entire city police force, instructing all men on duty that night to hasten to Taylor's Hotel should rockets be fired from the windows. Under his personal command, a detail of fifteen picked men armed with clubs and revolvers then marched to the hotel, entered quietly, and proceeded to the second floor, where James Fisk, Jr., who more than rose to the occasion, presented them to his anxious colleague, announcing, "Mr. Drew, these are the gentlemen that are going to take care of you," then added with a smile, "They look as though they can do it."[8] At this point Uncle Daniel himself managed a smile, thanked the officers (who saluted him smartly in return), and thereafter was heard to say that he didn't know much about fight, but knew a great deal about "No Surrender."

When he retired that night with cotton stuffed in the keyhole, the old gentleman took comfort not only from the presence of Jersey City's finest in an adjoining room, but also from a multitude of forces that Fisk had seen fit to deploy. There was a reinforcement of Erie detectives and other employees under the command of Inspector Masterson; a dozen couriers hastening back and forth between the Erie depot and New York; eleven Erie detectives at the depot and at ferry docks on both sides of the river; five others dispatched to areas in the city where toughs were known to congregate; three twelve-pounders mounted on the Long Dock, with the Hudson County artillery in reserve; and, patrolling the river nearby, four small boats manned by twenty-one men with Springfield rifles, which made Erie probably the first railroad in history to man a navy. But that night no rockets burst in the sky, no rifles crackled, no cannon boomed; the attackers desisted.

"A most ridiculous state of excitement," reported the *Times* the next day, attributing the whole affair to "the wildest and most absurd rumors." The *World* called the alarm the "stuff of romance"; the *Tribune* reported it straightfaced at first, then assumed a mock-heroic tone; the *Sun* declared the mere threat of violence to the directors "a burning shame"; while the *Herald*, usually so cynical, insisted, "There can be little doubt that a desperate attack was meditated."[9] On this assumption, the police guard continued day and night, reinforced by employees from the Erie depot and workshop organized into a corps of deputies, while Erie detectives maintained surveillance over the depot and ferry docks. Friends and business acquaintances continued to flock over from New York to urge "the old chancellor" (as the *Herald* now called Drew) to hold out, a message that scores of Erie workingmen also conveyed to him by letter. Bolstered by such support, even Daniel Drew could feel heroic.

Visiting the hotel, now christened Fort Taylor, on the eighteenth, the *Herald* reporter found the directors in the best of spirits: "The old chancellor seemed once more in Wall Street, vigorous as ever, thoroughly bent on business, and thereby allowing himself a few minutes to snatch a hasty meal. Mr. Eldridge, the president, was all smiles. Mr. Fisk, one would suppose, had just gained half a million in some gigantic speculation, while Mr. Gould swaggered about with the air of a conjuror who had just performed some extraordinary trick."[10] One reason for their jauntiness was the fact that they had just slashed their Buffalo fare to seven dollars, which was slightly more than half the fare on the Vanderbilt lines. Asked how long they could hold out, Fisk declared: "Why, sir, the question of duration is one that never troubles us; this is a public question, and we must not throw personal comforts in the balance. Six weeks, six months or six years are all equal to us in this sense. Just see and judge for yourself. We could not be more comfortable anywhere, while our hours of business are about the same as ever."[11]

Certainly Fisk's own routines were being maintained to a remarkable extent. Besides providing for feasts of quail and champagne, he had fetched over from New York his latest inamorata, Miss Helen Josephine Mansfield, a self-proclaimed actress whose delicate feet had yet to tread the boards. The previous November, when he had met her in an exclusive bordello, where she appeared strictly as a friend of the madam, Fisk had been quite smitten with this dark-haired, buxom beauty. He promptly paid her back rent, then set her up in a hotel suite and plied her with funds and attention. In honor of his new attachment, which promised to run fervent and deep, he had taken in hand the brushy red moustache that sprawled over his upper lip, waxing it to a rapier tip at the ends. Now, anticipating a lengthy stay in New Jersey, he installed her in some rooms of her own in the directors' suite.

Both good family men, Drew and Gould must have been incredulous. A fallen woman planted in their midst while they were engaged in the battle of their life, with reporters poking about daily? Surely Jimmy wouldn't let her stay! But he did, shrugging off their reaction with a wink. Fortunately she stuck to her rooms, and thanks to Fisk's liberality with liquor, the journalists confined themselves to veiled remarks about the home comforts with which the directors beguiled their weary hours. Uncle Daniel of course kept his distance, but his nostrils must have twitched at times from a hint of immoral perfumes. Worse still, since Josie herself later testified that during the day the directors sometimes used her rooms "as a sort of rendezvous," this pious seminary founder may on occasion have found himself lured into a harlot's boudoir for an impromptu council of war.[12] Never had it occurred to him that fleecing Vanderbilt of $8 million would bring him to such straits as these.

After a day or two of calm, the kidnap scare abated. In the company of the other directors, two or three times a day the old gentleman risked a walk through town. Then suddenly about noon of the nineteenth came alarming intelligence. A prominent member of the New York bar had advised the Erie counsel that the New York toughs were going to try to "copp" Drew again, the dread names of Cusick and Jim Elliott being invoked once more as the leaders. Instantly the directors informed Chief Fowler, who dispatched thirty-four men to occupy the corridors and reception room, while twenty specials were sworn in for night duty and some fifty Erie employees were rushed up as reinforcements. By 5:00 P.M. 125 men guarded Fort Taylor, while two companies of state militia were reported in readiness. Meanwhile the alarm spread like wildfire through the town, where several stores closed early while the nearby residents and even citizens of Hoboken and Hudson City turned out as armed volunteers. All day and night the tremulous Drew was sequestered and closely watched. The head of the stairs was guarded; reserves were stationed in the next room; and a special squad of six occupied the Speculative Director's bedroom, lest he be spirited out the window by stealth. But once again the marauders failed to show up.

Serious accounts of these events in certain New York City newspapers provoked the ridicule of the *Jersey City Daily Times*, which had already observed that Mr. Drew's protectors, both uniformed and otherwise, were not all strictly sober. The paper attributed the renewed invasion reports to local wags eager to play on Uncle Daniel's nerves and the credulity of big-city reporters. As for the support of the militia, the paper noted that on the nineteenth a militia company had been routinely drilling in Exchange Place near the hotel, which may have caused commuters in passing horsecars to spread rumors in outlying areas, where all kinds of would-be minutemen had armed themselves and come running to Taylor's Hotel. Concluded the *Daily Times*, "It was one of the biggest sells ever gotten up in this city."[13]

Yet again on the evening of the twenty-first came a report of New York toughs about to descend on New Jersey, with a consequent doubling of the police guard and renewed jitters for Drew, but no assault. This time even the *Herald* suggested that the old gentleman was being victimized by others, while the *Tribune* called the whole thing a fraud. Over the next few days Uncle Daniel quaked with apprehension while Fisk stalked martially about, puffing on his cigar, issuing orders, and vowing never to be taken alive. Bluecoats remained in evidence, backed up by Erie "detectives": seedy men in derbies, often tipsy, with big cigars planted in their teeth, who when off duty slouched and sprawled about in the hotel's former ladies' parlor, now the guard room. Gradually the excitement of these alarums and non-excursions diminished, although Chief Fowler assured a *World* reporter that he knew all the New York roughs and had his eye on them.

Was Vanderbilt really behind it? Then and later, the consensus said no. In the words of Charles Francis Adams: "A band of ruffians may have crossed the ferry, intending to kidnap Drew on speculation; but to suppose that the shrewd and energetic Commodore ever sent them to go gaping about a station, ignorant both of the person and the whereabouts of him they sought would be to impute to Vanderbilt at once a crime and a blunder. Such botching bears no trace of his clean handiwork."[14] If not Vanderbilt's handiwork, then whose? Surely Fisk's, as he had contacts in "sporting" circles, and by improvising these repeated crises could ascribe dark deeds to the Commodore and at the same time convince Drew, whose commitment to No Surrender was suspect, of the folly of seeking a truce with the foe. Besides, Fisk's appetite for farce was boundless, and a state of siege gave him the perfect stage to play soldier on.

Across the river, meanwhile, the litigation was proceeding with a momentum of its own. Through their attorneys, both Drew and Vanderbilt denied the charges brought against them. Repenting of his hasty action, Judge Gilbert vacated his injunction of the ninth, which hardly mattered, since the Erie counsel obtained two injunctions from Judge Thomas W. Clerke of the Appeals Court, the first restraining Barnard from all receivership proceedings in Erie and the second restraining the Vanderbilt side from any action whatsoever. Barnard, however, announced that he viewed this latest injunction as void, and proceeded with the Richard Schell suit against Erie. Over the following weeks, his courtroom featured hot exchanges between bench and bar and frequent glimpses into the corruptions of law and finance.

In Jersey City the Erie directors were now dealing vigorously with matters at hand. There were spoils to divide, a railroad to run, and Vanderbilt to outflank and outmaster. Regarding the spoils, Fisk and Gould forcefully reminded Drew of the paper that they had made him sign on February 19, whereby he promised to surrender half the profits that he had made on the bonds, to be divided among Fisk, Gould, and the others. As a result, Drew paid over the money. It was a new experience for Uncle Daniel to have smart partners who called him to account and even deceived him. In spite of Fisk's tricking him on March 9, the Speculative Director had ample gains from his Erie bond sales, short sales, and calls, but never again would he milk the Erie cow alone.

These matters were of course kept private. In public, the exiles carried on the fight against Vanderbilt, hanging their hopes on the passage of a bill that their allies had introduced in the state assembly at Albany on March 13 and that the Railroad Committee was now considering. This bill would legalize the new issue of convertible bonds, sanction Erie's guarantee of the Boston, Hartford, and Erie bonds, and block the consolidation of the Central and Erie in the hands of Vanderbilt. In other words, it would give the Erie directors everything they wanted and permit them to return to New York in triumph. But to get this bill through the legislature was no easy matter, since the Vanderbilt forces would fight it every step of the way. Erie, to be sure, had some $8 million of Vanderbilt money at its disposal, but its cause was not without embarrassments: Vanderbilt's proven ability for railroad management, versus Drew's for manipulation; the implicit confession of fraud in Erie's seeking legislation to legalize a bond issue that, if legal, should require no legislation; the current testimony before Senator Pierce's investigating committee by General Diven, Secretary Otis, and others—all professedly shocked by the events—affording vivid glimpses of how the bond issue had been perpetrated; the exiles' status as fugitives from justice; and their refusal, and that of certain nonexiled confederates as well, to appear before the Pierce committee at all.

Yet if the exiles' cause seemed somewhat compromised, their warnings against a Vanderbilt monopoly touched a tender nerve in Gotham. Although Vanderbilt ran his railroads with a ruthless efficiency, he was also a notorious rate-booster who abhorred competition. Clearly, control of Erie would give him a stranglehold on the commerce of New York and the West. By way of contrast, Erie had just slashed its passenger fares, so that even those outraged by its corruption had to think twice before advocating its reform by the Commodore. Pro-Vanderbilt to the core, the *Times* dismissed the "bugbear" of monopoly, but the *Sun*, the *Herald*, and the Jersey City papers pronounced it a very real threat. As early as March 12 the New York City Chamber of Commerce adopted a resolution in favor of Erie.

In all these maneuverings, the fugitives proved themselves deft fighters. To initiate the Albany legislation, they distributed antimonopolist petitions all along the road, which local residents signed and sent in a flood to Albany, while in Jersey City the directors themselves greeted reporters with scores of letters and telegrams, the gist of which was "no monopoly!" As for the fervent reformist sentiments of their adversaries, Gould on March 25 signed an affidavit, soon published in the press, revealing the partisan role of Caleb C. Norvell, the *Times* financial editor, in aiding the Vanderbilt camp, and the speculative activities in Erie of Vanderbilt and his allies, thus demolishing the *Times*'s pretense of objectivity and the Vanderbilt side's high moral pose. "The Vanderbilt party," concluded the *Herald*, "is as deep in the mire as the other side is in the mud."[15]

Vanderbilt was of course fighting back. He dispatched lobbyists to Albany, terminated an arrangement to share passengers with the People's Line, and had copies of the Erie superintendent's reports of March 3, stating the disastrous condition of the roadbed, distributed along the Erie line. Yet throughout the whole war he himself remained tight-lipped and aloof. Erie? What had he to do with the Erie? Why, he was running his railroads and racing his trotters as usual; reporters seeking information could talk to his lawyers. Besides distancing himself legally, this pose masked his chagrin: after all, he had been clipped for $8 million.

By way of contrast the Erie exiles, at Fisk's unflagging insistence, were wholly accessible to the press. Such exposure was a martyrdom for Drew, who longed for peace and privacy but was swept along by his colleagues as they gleefully indulged in whispered conferences, sent and received mysterious telegrams, and rushed back and forth between momentous councils of war. Then on March 19, while all eyes were fixed on the growing battle in Albany, a bill giving the Erie Railway Company (whose name was mentioned nowhere in the text) the full status of a New Jersey corporation was quietly passed by both houses of the New Jersey legislature and sent on to the governor's office to await his signature. That this important bill should have been slipped through the legislature so adroitly spoke volumes for the skill and prodigality of the Erie agents at work in Trenton.

Outflanked, the Vanderbilt camp belatedly rushed lobbyists to Trenton to dissuade Governor Marcus L. Ward from signing the bill and to urge the legislators to recover it from his office and kill it. The very next day, however, when in connection with some other legislation the Trenton lawmakers made an excursion en masse to Jersey City and dined at Taylor's Hotel, the directors entertained them lavishly. Many of the members, whom the press described as "in a state of high spiritual excitement," asked to pay their respects to Mr. Drew. Uncle Daniel, however, remained resolutely secluded in his room, having had his fill of inebriates, whether journalists, detectives, or legislators. It did not matter, however, since the prospect of luring this most generous of railroads to the Garden State was too tempting for all concerned. The bill remained in the hands of the governor, who signed it on March 30. Erie had now acquired a safe haven, so the guard at the hotel was dismissed, and the directors announced that Gould had bought a handsome residence in New Jersey, where he planned to establish himself with his family. The Erie Railway, it seemed, could do nicely without New York.

Yet the exiles had no desire to abandon New York and were fully aware that the issue would be decided at Albany, with the defeat or passage of the Erie bill before the assembly. For some weeks the Railroad Committee had been weighing Erie corruption against the threat of a Vanderbilt monopoly, even as the Pierce committee took testimony on Erie's recent issue of $10 million of remarkably convertible bonds. Still, few informed observers expected the matter to be settled on any basis other than money, given the high standards of venality prevailing in Albany, where susceptible legislators were routinely stalked through cloakrooms and corridors by a seedy legion of lobbyists flaunting diamond studs, big watch chains, ruddy noses, and cash. If even half the reports were true, votes from both parties on any measure could be bought in quantity.

One can well imagine the reaction in such circles to the first tidings of the Erie war. Veteran lobbyists who had left Albany in despair at an unprofitable season were reported packing their carpetbags for an immediate return, lured by wild rumors of "counsel fees," "retainers," and "hush money." Since a local paper estimated Vanderbilt's wealth at seventy million dollars and Drew's at only fifteen, the odds of course favored the Commodore, although Erie's agents were said to be prepared to spend lavishly—by one account, up to $2 million.

By March 25, when the assembly's Railroad Committee ended its hearings on the bill, nothing else was talked of in Albany. Many assemblymen had determined to bypass the lobbyists completely so as to "bag" all the money for themselves, deeming two or three thousand appropriate, although some held out for four. Vast was their indignation, then, upon learning that the Erie lobbyists were offering a paltry thousand dollars—five hundred down and five hundred upon passage of the bill. Worse still, when some of them tried to collect the five hundred down, they learned that the top Erie lobbyist—no doubt bribed by Vanderbilt—had vanished with the money. Not surprisingly, the Railroad Committee on March 27 unanimously reported the Erie bill adversely, whereupon the assembly adopted the report by a vote of 83 to 32. Score one for Vanderbilt.

But the fight was far from over. Determined that it too should share in the spoils, the senate had introduced a similar Erie bill of its own. The assembly vote, then, was simply a broad hint to the exiles that a more openhanded approach was in order. The hint became tangible in the person of Sen. Abner C. Mattoon of Oswego, a Republican, who made a special effort to get himself named to the five-man Pierce committee investigating Erie. When the committee came to New York to hold its first hearings on March 10, Mattoon dropped by the Erie office in West Street and introduced himself to Drew, Gould, Diven, and others. Diven later recalled Mattoon as saying that the committee's object was mercenary, but that he intended to assure fair play. Just why he felt the need to announce these noble sentiments to the directors, the very gentlemen whom his committee had been empowered to investigate, the senator did not make clear.

About the same time that he visited the Erie office, Mattoon called on Drew at his home and discussed the investigation, giving Drew the impression that he was out for money. Then, after the flight to New Jersey, the senator came to Jersey City and discussed the situation with Drew, Fisk, Eldridge, and Davis. According to Mattoon's later testimony, he was simply presenting himself as a friend of the railroad, mindful that his constituents in Oswego had benefited from an Erie branch that ran to their city. But Drew had a different recollection: "I think that Mattoon made use of this language to me at one time; that he, or no man, could go there [to Albany] and live on what their pay was; I said to him, 'I don't know; I have nothing to do with this matter at all, in any way or shape, and will not'; he intimated as if he would take money if it was offered to him, or anything like that."[16] Subsequently, the defeat of the Erie bill in the assembly prompted yet another visit to Jersey City by the senator on Saturday March 28, on which occasion, according to Gould's later account, the senator warned the directors that there were prejudices against them in Albany, prejudices that an Erie representative should come up personally to explain away.

The exiles took the hint. The battle in Albany could still be won, if waged more efficiently and more lavishly. One of their own number must brave Judge Barnard's wrath to take charge of their affairs at the capital. What was called for was energy, brazenness, cynicism, and a dearth of scruples. The choice fell on Jay Gould. But how could he avoid arrest? Erie's counsel, David Dudley Field, found the answer. By promising Sheriff James O'Brien of New York that Gould would appear before Barnard on April 4, he obtained an assurance that Gould would not be molested before then. This arrangement guaranteed Gould amost a full week of freedom, which was time enough, perhaps, to turn the tide of battle decisively.

On Sunday evening March 29, at Taylor's Hotel the press noted that the Erie directors were tight-lipped but jubilant. At last it leaked out that Director Gould had left suddenly for a secret destination, carrying a black traveling bag stuffed with two or three million dollars of Vanderbilt's money. Rumor had it that he was on his way to Ohio to let out the remaining contracts for building the connection to Chicago, but in point of fact he had taken the night boat to Albany. So began the final and climactic phase of the exiles' great struggle with Cornelius Vanderbilt. They knew the price of New Jersey. What was the price of New York?

CHAPTER 16

The Battle of Albany

Jay Gould had been in Albany less than two days, when Erie counsel David Dudley Field received a telegram:

> Albany, March 31, 1868.
> I am just arrested by the Sheriff—returnable Saturday. This is in violation of your agreement with the Sheriff. Bail, $500,000.
> Jay Gould.[1]

The exiles in Jersey City were dumbfounded. What had gone wrong?

Arriving by boat Monday morning March 30, Gould had promptly checked into Parlor 57 at the Delavan House, a well-appointed hotel frequented by lobbyists and politicians. Informed of his return to the Empire State, Vanderbilt's emissaries immediately wired their colleagues in New York. They in turn, ignorant or contemptuous of Erie's agreement with the sheriff, notified Judge Barnard, who at once ordered Gould's arrest for contempt of court. At 3:00 P.M. on Tuesday Gould was taken into custody at the Delavan House, but being amply funded, he had no difficulty in putting up the half million dollars of bail. These formalities seen to, he was free for the balance of the week, pending his appearance before Barnard on April 4. That very evening he made his way up State Street to the dome-topped capitol and appeared in the chamber of the assembly.

But more trouble was in store for Gould and Erie. No sooner had word spread that in Parlor 57 of the Delavan House free cigars and champagne were being lavishly dispensed, while from a nearby trunk (the black traveling bag had been marvelously metamorphosed) thousand-dollar bills were leaping forth into the eager palms of lawmakers and lobbyists—no sooner, in short, was the campaign gloriously under way, than Erie's cause was jolted from two different quarters simultaneously.

First, there was the Pierce committee. The Erie leaders, having been courted diligently by Senator Mattoon, assumed that his vote would guarantee a favorable report. When the committee met on March 31, two members signed one report and two another so that Mattoon could dictate which report, one critical of Erie, one not, should represent the majority opinion. Calling both reports "pretty strong," he declined to sign either and said he would like to sleep on it. Overnight, counterarguments from the Vanderbilt side must have reached him—by one report, $20,000 plus a thousand for his son, topping the $15,000 that he had already received from Erie. Therefore on April 1 Mattoon signed the unfavorable report. Thus the Pierce committee announced to the senate that Drew, Gould, Fisk, and Eldridge had violated law and morals in manipulating and overissuing Erie stock, while the minority report simply stated that no charges had been proven and offered an Erie bill similar to the one that the assembly had rejected.

Yet even as Erie suffered this defeat in the senate, high drama was unfolding in the assembly downstairs. On that same fateful first day of April Elijah M. K. Glenn of Wayne County, a quiet, white-bearded rural assemblyman, elderly and infirm, rose and in a voice quivering with emotion announced that the assembly's report and vote on the Erie bill had been bought, for which reason he charged "corruption deep, dark, and damning on a portion of this house." This accusation provoked a heated debate and calls for an investigation, while the press hailed in Glenn the determined righteousness of the martyred John Brown, whom he was said to resemble. Subsequently, however, the new hero, who was in the frailest health, gave only vague and rambling testimony before an investigating committee, which therefore exonerated a fellow assemblyman accused by him, though it held a minor lobbyist for grand jury action. Censured by a vote of his colleagues, Glenn resigned his seat in disgust and vanished into honest obscurity.

It was not Glenn who threatened to cramp Gould's style in Albany, but Justice Barnard, before whom the delinquent at last appeared on April 4, having returned from Albany in the custody of Sheriff O'Brien. Flanking the defendant in court were no less than seven Erie counsel, two of them ex-judges, who persuaded Barnard that he risked following improper procedures, whereupon the judge adjourned the case to April 8. The Erie counsel then had the sheriff served with a writ of *habeas corpus*, commanding him to produce his prisoner before Judge Barrett of the Court of Common Pleas, who put Gould in charge of James A. Oliver, an officer of his own court, in whose strict custody Gould was to remain until he appeared before Barrett. To observe this technicality, Gould induced Oliver to accompany him on a night train to Albany, where on arrival Gould announced that he was seriously ill, sought his room in the Delavan House, and sent for a doctor. On March 10 the baffled Oliver appeared in Barrett's court without his charge, explaining that Gould continued to plead illness, although able to walk to the capitol in a snowstorm and to entertain countless gentlemen in his quarters. Barrett's anger now matched Barnard's, but repeated summonses to the culprit were answered only by affidavits attesting to his illness in Albany, plus a charge that Oliver had become a spy there for Erie's enemies. In the end, the application for a *habeas corpus* was discharged and the prisoner returned to the custody of the sheriff, who had not laid eyes on him for days.

Meanwhile Gould had been expending vast amounts of energy and money to sway the lawmakers of Albany. Arrayed against him were an army of Vanderbilt agents headed by Vanderbilt's son-in-law Horace F. Clark. To counter their arguments and influence, this shy but guileful introvert held forth with remarkable aplomb in Parlor 57, greeting all comers with an openhandedness worthy of his partner Fisk. Under Gould's direction, Erie's largess poured forth not at a paltry five hundred dollars at a time, but in tens and hundreds of thousands, the total amount never to be known, although at the time estimates ranged from three hundred to eight hundred thousand dollars.

Where did the money go? According to Gould's later testimony, it went to counsel and agents for legitimate services in promoting the Erie bill in Albany. Still, he admitted telegraphing dozens of persons in districts served by the Erie, urging them to come to Albany and fight for the bill, for which efforts they were of course reimbursed. From all over the state, glowing reports of Erie's generosity precipitated a wild rush to the capital of hosts of would-be influence-peddlers, in dealing with whom, by his own account, the honest Gould displayed a naiveté that verged on delusion. Thus a Brooklyn harbor master with no known political connections received $5,000 (chiefly, Gould later insisted, to avoid trouble with the man and "smooth him over"), while the editor of the *Daily Advertiser* of Elmira, having already obtained over $60,000 from Director Henry Thompson in New York, became one of the chief Erie lobbyists in Albany, received still more money there (by one account, $100,000), then was paid by the other side to decamp.

These heroic initiatives the other Erie directors watched with interest from their exile in New Jersey, where visitors were fewer now and their life had become more routine. Their ranks were thinner, however, for Henry Thompson had been arrested upon appearing at the Astor House on March 21. Free now from kidnap threats, Uncle Daniel spent his time reading newspapers, conferring with friends and colleagues, or pacing up and down in the directors' suite, ruminating some new plan, exactly as he had done in Groesbeck's office in Broad Street, and in the taproom of the Bull's Head long before. Meanwhile Fisk, who was handling the daily business of the railroad, talked cheerfully with callers, his desk piled high with telegrams and letters, while the energetic Eldridge seemed always to be darting about, appearing one day in Trenton, another in Jersey City, and the following day no one knew where. Regarding events in Albany, they all professed to be immensely confident.

Drew, however, now found himself the target of keen personal shafts hurled by Horace Greeley, the crotchety crusading idealist whose *New York Tribune* was probably the most influential paper in the country. Although Greeley himself years before had subscribed five thousand dollars to Erie's construction, on which he claimed a forty percent loss, his financial editor had generally assailed the Erie management less savagely than had the *Times* and *Herald* and had even defended Drew's notorious loan of 1866. In the face of the latest Erie scandals, however, Greeley decided that the time for indulgence had passed. In a lengthy editorial that appeared on March 28, he rehearsed the "dark transactions" of Erie's recent history, then drew a telling contrast between the chief antagonists:

> We have said that, as between Drew and Vanderbilt, few people have any choice. But they do compare oddly, just now. Mr. Vanderbilt sits in his office in Fourth Street, buying Erie about as fast as his opponents print it, and preparing for the day . . . when he shall try, fairly and squarely, to make it a good property. . . . Mr. Drew is a fugitive from justice in hiding in New Jersey; seeking to arouse public sympathy by the concoction of Munchausenish tales of attempts to kidnap him; sending to Albany for whitewashing acts, and simultaneously sending to Trenton for acts to render him independent of Albany legislation; running from the process of Courts, and appealing to the same Courts to gag and bind his own stockholders . . . denouncing Commodore Vanderbilt as the great monopolist . . . and at the same time [here Greeley anticipated] sending private messengers to the same Commodore to beg for compromise on any terms.[2]

Greeley then repeated the familiar charge that every Erie director had enriched himself, but added a novel insight:

> As with the chiefs, so with the subordinates. Superintendents, conductors, station agents, and even brakemen, have saved small fortunes out of meager salaries. . . . When Mr. Drew was short of the stock, there was a sort of merit in making the passenger receipts as

light as possible; and in this particular we can quite understand how—as one of the "Jersey exiles" pathetically observed to a reporter—"the devotion of the Erie people to Mr. Drew is really touching."[3]

For these charges, however, there was no evidence.

Usually, the Speculative Director shrugged off adverse comment in the press, but this attack by the nation's foremost journalist stung. In reply, from Jersey City he sent the *Tribune* a statement dated April 2, in which he protested this "injurious discourse," defended his conduct as an officer of Erie, and regarding his status as a fugitive, declared: "I am in New Jersey, it is true, but whether the combination which has driven me from my home and business is an honorable one is precisely the question at issue. You seem to think it is; I hold it to be wicked and disgraceful."[4] The *Tribune* printed Drew's statement in full, but in an editorial of April 4 entitled "Mr. Daniel Drew," Greeley announced that he was declaring war on criminal railroad financiers and employees, and he invited Drew to answer ten questions on such delicate matters as Erie's finances and lack of dividends, the amount of his short transactions and resulting profits in the stock, and his 1866 loan "at most enormous usury," which questions, the editorial asserted, any honest businessman could answer. Then followed a pointed summons to the accused: "Will you come to the front?"[5]

Arraigned so sweepingly, Uncle Daniel had no intention of coming to the front. Nine days later another *Tribune* editorial bearing Drew's name as its title asked why he had "dried up" so suddenly. Reprinting the ten questions, it invited the legislature to get answers to them before altering the laws to oblige Mr. Drew. At this point, someone who signed himself "Alpha" sent the *Tribune* a lengthy and spirited defense of Drew, asserting that Drew had often been Erie's only friend in the past, and that his bearishness in the stock had done less harm than the mindless or self-interested bulling of it by newspapers like the *Tribune*, under whose influence the writer, as manager of an estate, had once bought the stock at 85, only to sell it at 37 a few months later.

Such arguments hardly made a dent on Greeley, who in any case had now shifted his scrutiny to the corruption in Albany, whose atmosphere, he declared in an editorial of April 11, was "mephitic and pestilential" and in need of some purifying thunderclaps. To help produce them, Greenley packed his worn carpetbag and hurried to the capital, where he cut an odd figure with his pinkish moon face fringed with whiskers, his baggy trousers and floppy wide-brimmed hat, as he shambled among the politicians and lobbyists.

Meanwhile, when not following events in Albany, Drew and the other Jersey City exiles had their gaze fixed on the courts of New York City, which daily offered to the public the rich entanglements of *The People* v. *the Erie Railway Company, etc.*; *Richard Schell and others* v. *the Same*; *John Bloodgood and others* v. *the Same*; *The Erie Railway Company and James Fisk, Jr.,* v. *Marshall B. Champlain, Attorney General, etc.*; *William Belden* v. *Cornelius Vanderbilt, etc.*; the contempt action against the Erie directors; the contempt action against Jay Gould; the *habeas corpus* action on behalf of Jay Gould; and diverse other proceedings, the exact relevance of which neither the public nor, one suspects, the bench and bar of New York ever quite grasped. The courtroom of Justice Barnard was especially favored with scenes of high and low drama. Attorneys traded barbs and insults; one lawyer all but came to blows with a witness; in a single session Fisk's partner Belden, for refusing to answer questions, was cited for contempt six times; while the judge himself, upon hearing his integrity impugned, threatened grand jury action one time, perjury charges another, and on other occasions orated, wept, or raged. To be sure, he had provocation. Erie spies had dogged his footsteps and one of them, straightfaced, had sworn to an affidavit accusing him of implication in the attempt to kidnap Drew; in retaliation, the judge hired spies of his own.

Far removed from the judicial carnival of Manhattan and the dynamic corruptions of Albany, the exiles now found their life in Jersey City tedious. Since a New York statute forbade arrests in civil suits on Sundays, they crossed the river once a week, Fisk and Mansfield to snatch at the delights of the metropolis, while Drew touched base at home. Yet during those twenty-four hours only were the exiles safe, since Barnard's wrath remained unallayed. Of the eight directors liable to arrest, only Fisk and Eldridge had not been served. Bored with New Jersey, in a fit of bravado Fisk appeared one night at the Manhattan Club on Fifth Avenue, the known resort of Vanderbilt and his cronies. Finding some Vanderbilt men on the premises, he greeted them blithely, but when one of them went for the police, he made a wild dash by carriage to the docks, where a waiting tugboat whisked him back to New Jersey.

Such escapades were not for Drew. Although no contempt proceedings before Barnard hung over him, he clung to the New Jersey haven, since as treasurer he felt especially vulnerable to the actions of a receiver, and his testimony on many matters was urgently desired in New York. But after weeks of exile, his endurance was wearing thin. For a man of his years and habits, it was not easy to be lodged cheek by jowl with the egregious Fisk and his fancy woman, the unconscionable Eldridge, and the scheming Gould. Repeatedly denounced by the press, he had been made the object of dire threats as well and shut up in his room, guarded from toughs by toughs. All around him there had been intemperance and profanity, coarse revels, even fornication. He longed for his quiet hearth, his family, and Wall Street. In his wavering mind, the talk of "no surrender" stirred ever fainter vibrations. Surely, if he and Cornele could sit down alone together face to face and talk, the whole thing could be ironed out.

Unknown to his Erie colleagues at the time, on Sunday March 29—soon after the kidnap threats and on the very eve of Gould's departure for Albany—Uncle Daniel utilized his Sabbath immunity to call on Vanderbilt at his home in New York. By one account, the meeting had been initiated by Vanderbilt, who to penetrate Fort Taylor's vigilant security had a detective posing as a commercial traveler take a room in the hotel. Finding Drew well guarded, the detective induced a waiter to smuggle a note to Drew at lunch, inviting him to a parley, an act that is said to have cost the waiter his job, although Vanderbilt got him a better one. But whosoever the initiative, the two antagonists met discreetly at 10 Washington Square. When the Commodore announced that Drew had been a damn fool to run off to Jersey City, Drew allowed as how he was "circumstanced in an ockerd light."[6] Vanderbilt presumably then ranted on a bit about how they had robbed him and he would not stand for it, while Drew interposed that perhaps they could work something out. Nothing was settled by the end of the interview, but the ice was broken. In time, however, word of the meeting reached Fisk and Eldridge, which put them on their guard.

In mid-April, even as three or four Erie suits were being heard simultaneously in New York, and as the senate was staging full-day debates on the Erie bill in Albany, came jolting news. Early on the morning of April 15 an eastbound Erie express, running to make up lost time in the rugged terrain around Carr's Rock, thirteen miles northwest of Port Jervis, New York, broke one of the weakened iron rails beneath it. As a result, the four rear coaches of the train jumped the track on a sharp curve and hurtled into a wild ravine fifty feet below. Many died instantly, and when a smashed sleeper burst into flames, many more burned to death trapped in the wreckage, their piercing screams adding a further note of terror to the scene. The final toll was forty dead and seventy-five injured.

The newspapers reacted at once with horror and outrage. The *World* decried the Erie directors for "weaving spiderwebs of financial intrigues" in Jersey City, instead of supervising their railroad. "Look at the mangled corpses at Port Jervis," the *Tribune* commanded both the warring railroad kings, "and answer upon your honor if you are not to a great degree responsible for the blood of these victims!"[7] Fresh in the editors' recollection were Superintendent Riddle's confidential reports of March 3, with their anxious mention of broken and worn-out rails, which the Erie management had publicized in order to demonstrate the need for the new issue of bonds. The Vanderbilt forces in Albany seized on the wreck as proof of Erie's corruption, while the Erie side reiterated their contention that the controversial new bonds were intended precisely to remedy the cause of the disaster with urgent work that the Vanderbilt injunctions had blocked.

Three days after the accident, with the horror still vivid in everybody's mind, the Erie bill came to a vote at last in the senate. The proposed act legalized the new issue of bonds, on condition that the proceeds be used to complete and operate the road, failure to do so being punishable by two to five years in prison. It also authorized Erie's guarantee of the bonds of connecting railroads, forbade any pooling of earnings between the Erie and the Central, and stipulated that no officer of the one should hold office in the other. Because of the bond provision, a *Tribune* editorial called the bill "a direct premium on rascality," and the *Times* financial editor insisted that the "insulting propostion" would surely be rejected in the end. Fisk told Josie Mansfield that his future was "either a Fisk palace in New York or a stone palace at Sing Sing"; if the latter, he urged her to take a cottage nearby, so that her presence would make his "rusty irons garlands of roses" and render the stones easier to crack.[8]

The chance of Jim Fisk's encountering rusty irons at Sing Sing decreased substantially on Saturday April 18, when the senate passed the Erie bill by a vote of 17 to 12. Among the ayes was the volatile Senator Mattoon, who had flipflopped once again.

That same day, however, the victorious Gould was not celebrating, but testifying before a senate committee headed by Sen. Matthew Hale, which in the wake of Assemblyman Glenn's charges had been appointed to investigate the alleged bribery of senators. Gould stated that he knew nothing of such practices; that he had spent money only for the legitimate services of counsel and lobbyists; that he had never speculated in Erie stock while a director; and that for his services to Erie in Albany he had not received one dollar, not even for expenses. Presumably he kept a straight face.

All eyes were now fixed on the assembly, where a desperate struggle was anticipated. Vanderbilt's Hudson River and Harlem lines had made a great point of extending the legislators' passes for two weeks beyond May 1 and, in anticipation of a vote in the assembly on Monday, ran a special train to Albany on Sunday evening April 19 to bring back the New York City members, who were especially inclined to Vanderbilt. On Monday morning, however, a report ran through the capital sowing panic in their hearts. At 9:00 A.M. both Jay Gould and the Vanderbilt lobbyists had received telegrams from New York announcing that some kind of compromise had been reached, or that the Commodore, having counted the votes, knew that he had lost. At any rate, Vanderbilt had withdrawn his opposition to the bill; not one more penny would he spend. Faces blanched at the news, voices gasped. By 10:00 A.M. the assemblymen were making a run on Parlor 57 of the Delavan House, where those who not long before had been holding out for five thousand dollars were now eager to settle for anything not under a hundred. But, with victory all but assured, Jay Gould had slammed Erie's coffers shut with a bang.

With this great overthrow of hope—this sudden blighting of the chance to sell oneself yet again, and exorbitantly, to one if not both sides—the members grew bitterly resentful. Reports had it that the Vanderbilt and Drew forces had reached an understanding at the Manhattan Club in New York the night before, so that even as they sped back to Albany on their special train, the assemblymen had been sold out. As their thwarted greed kindled into rage, it was Vanderbilt whom they vilified, since it was he who had abandoned the fight. Rushing to take up the bill, practically the same one they had rejected less than four weeks before, the assemblymen passed it 101 to 5. Then, to punish Vanderbilt, the members ransacked the docket and in rapid succession passed three bills deemed injurious to his railroads. No legislation was too sweeping, no curse too virulent, to vent their rage. Meanwhile the Erie bill went to Gov. Reuben E. Fenton, who signed it into law the next day.

So Erie won the great fight. Yet observers sensed that something was wrong: in the Vanderbilt camp they discerned not despair but quiet contentment, while in Jersey City there was turmoil, rage, and dismay. Fisk and Eldridge had just discovered that Uncle Daniel had vanished and with him the Erie treasury; he was going to hand it over to Vanderbilt!

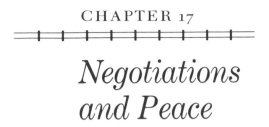

CHAPTER 17

Negotiations and Peace

The Speculative Director's desertion had been long a-building. Practically every Sunday in April, when he returned to New York to visit his family and church—and probably on other occasions as well, when he slipped off under cover of night and crossed by the Weehawken ferry to the north of Jersey City—Erie's treasurer called on Vanderbilt at his Washington Square residence. There, as so many times before, he plied the Commodore with guileful appeals and assurances, feeding him secrets from the Erie councils, urging compromise, and promising tearfully to mend his ways. Vanderbilt knew what Drew was up to, but he also knew that his chances at Albany were worsening, and that, as he himself put it, he could buy up the Erie Railway's outstanding stock, but he couldn't buy up its printing press. Moreover, the October election was a long way off, and prior to it there was no way he could get control of the railroad. So he was willing to treat with Drew in hopes of obtaining a settlement and, knowing Drew, of inducing him to desert his allies.

Meanwhile Drew's fellow exiles had become suspicious of his intermittent absences. On Sunday April 19—the day after the senate had passed the Erie bill and with the assembly's vote due the next morning—Drew went to the city again, but this time, so the story goes, Fisk had an Erie detective follow him to Vanderbilt's door. Already alarmed when their absent colleague failed to return that evening, shortly after midnight Fisk and Eldridge received the startling intelligence that Uncle Daniel was consorting with the enemy, and probably that he and Vanderbilt had reached some kind of agreement in New York. In genuine fear of an attack, they called on the police to guard both themselves and their money, which was lodged in a nearby bank. Obliging as ever, the local bluecoats turned out and stood guard all night. But Drew had either anticipated them or found a means of eluding their vigilance, for Fisk and Eldridge soon discovered that Erie was missing not only its treasurer but also its treasury. The loss was catastrophic.

Drew's removal of the Erie money to New York resulted from his Sabbath conference with Vanderbilt, to whom he confessed that he was heartily sick of his exile in New Jersey. Mindful that the greatest victory in Albany would still not permit him to set foot in his home state without fear of arrest, he wept, begged, and pleaded with the Commodore to allow him to return unmolested. In exchange, he promised to hand over the entire Erie treasury, which when once safe in the hands of the receiver—Vanderbilt's son-in-law, Osgood—would practically guarantee a Vanderbilt triumph in the war. Needless to say, the Commodore was amenable. With the arrangement all but completed, Drew returned to Jersey City to either allay the suspicions of his colleagues or persuade them to acquiesce in his *fait accompli*. He found them livid. Confronted by Fisk, who demanded to know what he had done with the money, he is said to have protested, "Why Jeems, ain't I treasurer of the company?" "That's all right, but we want to know what the treasurer has done with our money." "Well, it wasn't safe here, so I tuck it to York."

At this point Fisk sprang a little surprise of his own. Not only had the Erie treasury been deposited in New Jersey, but Drew's private funds had been placed there as well. Consequently, Fisk persuaded a local judge to attach those funds, pending the return of the treasury.

Uncle Daniel was stunned. He fell silent and paced back and forth, hands clasped behind his back, eyes down. For two minutes not a word was spoken, then he looked up with a winsome smile and said, "Well, Jeems, you are about as keen as you need to be. How kin we compromise this?"[1] In short order Drew returned the Erie money to New Jersey, following which Fisk removed the attachment on his funds.

Although Vanderbilt had been frustrated in his attempt to recover his money, he continued negotiations with Drew, hoping that through him he might persuade a majority of the Erie board to accept a settlement. But Fisk, Gould, and Eldridge now regarded Drew as a renegade. Henceforth they excluded him from their councils, monitored his telegrams and interviews, and hypothecated the Erie funds in Jersey City so that Drew could not withdraw them without their consent. Drew was now treasurer in name only. Erie's affairs, then, were in total disarray at the very moment when, surely by arrangement with Vanderbilt, the board of directors on April 22 managed to hold a long overdue formal meeting—the first since March 9—in New York. The Jersey exiles all crossed the river by ferry, but when eleven directors convened in the Erie office at 11:00 A.M. and then again at 5:00 P.M., neither Drew nor Eldridge was present. And when ten directors reconvened the following day at 3:00 P.M., Fisk and Gould were absent as well.

The absence of the Erie leaders betokened both dissension and confusion. Drew was at odds with his former allies and still technically suspended as director; moreover, even though he was working out a personal truce with the Commodore, it was not clear to what extent it might apply to his colleagues, especially since Vanderbilt did not necessarily speak for Judge Barnard. This was demonstrated when word came to the exiles in New Jersey that David Dudley Field had obtained a discharge of the contempt proceedings against them. Elated, Fisk crossed the river, dropped by his office to tidy up affairs, then hastened blithely to Judge Barnard's courtroom, where, bouncing himself down beside Field, he declared joyfully that at last he was "out of the hands of the Philistines." "Are you?" said Field, who quickly informed him that he had obtained no such discharge and that Barnard was as eager as ever to clap him in jail. Appalled, Fisk bolted, but the judge launched the police in pursuit. There followed another madcap race by carriage to the docks, where Fisk hailed a passing tug and urged the crew to "go like the devil for Jersey," promising them a fabulous reward. The police hailed a second tug, but too late, so that Fisk made it back to Jersey yet again.

With Erie's affairs in flux and an arrangement with Vanderbilt imminent, Drew had no time to attend the April 23 meeting—the first under a New Jersey charter—of the board of trustees of his seminary; instead, he sent his son. So it was that in the founder's absence the board accepted the new charter and elected officers. If the eminent Methodists present knew of the unflattering comments on their founder in the press, they gave no sign of it. They elected him president again, proposed that the school seal bear his likeness, and named the school's main building, the old Gibbons mansion, Mead Hall in honor of his wife. To be sure, one detail remained: Brother Drew had neglected to deed the grounds and buildings and to convey his endowment to the school. McClintock however announced that, in a recent interview, Mr. Drew had stated his anxiety to do so, "and only waited for the final consummation, for the difficulties now surrounding him to pass away." This was the only official note of Drew's predicament that the seminary ever took.[2]

April 23, the date of the seminary board meeting, was the last day and night that Drew was obliged to spend in the watchful company of his fellow exiles. On the twenty-fourth, word came at last from a Vanderbilt agent that he could resume residence in New York without fear of arrest, so immediately he packed his bags and departed. When he appeared on Broad Street in the afternoon, the market turned up sharply, reflecting the bulls' conviction that a truce between the railroad kings augured well. Scores of friends and acquaintances rushed up to welcome him back, while even those who had been outraged by his Erie misdeeds greeted him with courtesy and respect. After all, not just anyone could take on Vanderbilt and survive. Besides, he gave every indication of having fulfilled an American dream—to cheat big and get away with it.

Back in Jersey City, Fisk and Eldridge found themselves left in the shade. Both were New England men, long separated from their families. On the afternoon of April 25, therefore, they abandoned Fort Taylor for good, hired a tug to intercept a Rhode Island-bound steamboat, scrambled aboard, and set out for Boston. In the wake of their departure the bar earnings at Taylor's Hotel plummeted, while Jersey City settled back into a predictable and humdrum existence.

Thereafter, subtle hints from the courtrooms told the public that the railroad kings and their allies, or at least some of them, were engaged in prolonged secret parleys. In quick succession Drew's suspension as an Erie director was vacated, other motions were adjourned, and Gould's bail was reduced to a mere $10,000. Clearly, the whole affair was being let down gently, so that even the judicial vaudeville of Barnard's courtroom lapsed into a tedious decorum. From the Erie delinquents, however, Barnard still demanded some gesture of contrition, and this they declined to provide. From Boston, Eldridge sent an affidavit stating that his family were stricken with scarlet fever; Fisk also clung to the Hub, renewing acquaintance with his long-neglected wife; and Uncle Daniel, though subpoenaed to appear May 7, on that date was nowhere to be seen, and immediately afterward visited his family in Putnam County for a week. Fresh from his travails, he appeared to the home folks as a hero, the local paper noting that he looked remarkably well and possessed energy enough to tilt with Vanderbilt or any man.

Back in New York, the Merry Old Gentleman of Wall Street found himself served with an attachment at last, and therefore gave bail to guarantee his presence in court. Yet repeatedly he failed to appear, first, so he explained through his lawyer, because he had heard that the judge would take no more oral testimony; then because of a prior commitment as pallbearer; and finally because his lawyers argued that the proceedings were improper. That Barnard neither fumed nor ranted shows to what extent, with compromise in the air, he had huffed down by stages, until as Charles Francis Adams put it, "he roared as gently as any sucking dove, and finally he ceased to roar at all."[3]

By early June all the Erie exiles, by the grace of Vanderbilt and Barnard, were once again in New York. At a board meeting on June 11, the Erie executive committee announced that it was negotiating to end the litigation and hoped to do so with the consent of all leading stockholders.

This represented a victory for Drew, who by now had won Eldridge and Thompson over to the cause of compromise, so that a majority of the executive committee was behind him. The negotiations, however, stretched out over a period of weeks because many parties were involved, most of them at odds with one another and all clamoring to be richly satisfied. Fisk and Gould were still adamantly opposed to any settlement, and because of Drew's betrayal were determined to oust him as both treasurer and director. So weary of the affair was Uncle Daniel, that—on certain conditions—he was willing to go. As for Eldridge and his Boston clique, they too might be willing to bow out, if amply recompensed. All in all, then, a settlement seemed possible, if Fisk and Gould could be won over or got round.

Acting on the authority of an executive committee resolution of June 13, Eldridge pursued negotiations to resolve the litigation and settle Erie's accounts with Drew, accounts that over the previous four months included twenty thousand here and fifty there to Drew, Fisk, and Gould for "incidental" and "legal" expenses, as well as half a million to Eldridge. Meanwhile, in separate negotiations with Vanderbilt, Drew in late June agreed to relieve him of 50,000 shares of Erie at 80, when the stock was selling at 70, on condition that Vanderbilt hold another 50,000 shares and not sell them without consulting him. In this fashion, even though he would leave Erie now, the Speculative Director thought that, with Vanderbilt's help, he might regain control of the road before the next election in October.

But if Vanderbilt and Drew had any thoughts of concluding a private arrangement by themselves, they reckoned without Fisk. "Who is this Fisk?" Vanderbilt is said to have once asked a lieutenant, and when told he was "one of Drew's pets," announced: "Then we must kill him off. He's too sharp for a greenhorn, and too bold for an old hand. I don't know what to make of him."[4] Fisk of course had not been killed off and now, with Gould at his side, thrust himself into the negotiations. One day in late June the two of them sought out Vanderbilt at his home on Washington Square and were shown upstairs, where while Gould waited in a front room, Fisk was summoned into the bedroom by the Commodore. Fisk later recounted the episode in court with wit and bravura well calculated to keep the courtroom in stitches.

> Q. Did you call on Mr. Vanderbilt?
> Fisk. I think I did. (Laughter.)
> Q. Do you know that you did?
> Fisk. Most undoubtedly. (Laughter.) The recollection thereof is vivid and the memory green. (Laughter.)
> Q. What passed at the interview between you and Commodore Vanderbilt?

Fisk. Well, the Commodore received me with the most distinguished courtesy, and overwhelmed me with a perfect ambulance of good wishes for my health. When we sat down and got fairly quiet, we came plump up to the matter that was uppermost, and then we had it out. . . . He told me that several of the directors were trying to make a trade with him, and he would like to know who was the best man to trade with. "Why," said I, "if the trade is a good, honest one, you'd better trade with me." (Laughter.) Then he said that old man Drew was no better than a batter pudding (laughter), or words to that effect; that Eldridge was demoralized, and that our concern was without head or tail. (Laughter.) This wasn't overly complimentary; but, after thinking a minute, I said I thought so, too. (Laughter, in which the court was forced to join.) Then he became very earnest, and said he had got his bloodhounds on us, and would pursue us until we took that damned stock off his hands—he'd be damned if he would keep it. I was grieved to hear him swear so (laughter), but being obliged to say something, I remarked quietly that I'd be damned if we'd take it back (great laughter), and that we'd sell him stock jest as long as he'd stand up and take it. (Great laughter.) Well, when I made this observation, the Commodore mellowed down a little (laughter), and said he thought it would be a great deal better for us to get together and arrange this matter.[5]

According to Fisk, Vanderbilt then proposed that a deal be slipped through the Erie board, a notion that Fisk claimed to have virtuously rejected, being "dumbfounded, actually thunderstruck, to think that our directors, whom I had always esteemed as honorable men (great laughter), would have anything to do with such outrageous proceedings."[6]

Nothing was settled by this first interview between Vanderbilt and the two holdouts, so the latter were excluded from the ensuing negotiations. On the evening of July 2, Fisk and Gould had an appointment with Eldridge at the Fifth Avenue Hotel, but upon arriving failed to find him. Acting on a hunch, about 9:00 P.M. they went to the home of ex-Judge Edwards Pierrepont at 103 Fifth Avenue and asked the judge, an Erie counsel now representing Eldridge and the B, H & E, if Eldridge was there. After some hesitation, the judge said he was. Then, while Gould diverted Pierrepont in the hallway, Fisk burst into the drawing room and found Eldridge, Drew, Schell, and Work assembled there each with his attorney. Again, Fisk's account in court is a lively one:

I asked what was going on, and everybody seemed to wait for someone else to answer. (Laughter.) Being better acquainted with Drew than any of the rest of them, though perhaps having less confidence in him (laughter), I asked him what under heavens was up. He said they were arranging the suits. I told him they ought to adopt a very different manner of doing it than being there in the night—that no settlement could be made without requiring the money of the Corporation. He begun to picture his miseries to me, told me how he had suffered during his pilgrimage, saying he was worn and thrown away from his family, and wanted to settle matters up; that he had done everything he could, and saw no other way out either for himself or the Company. I told him I guessed he was more particular about himself than the Company, and he said, well, he was (laughter); that he was an old man and wanted to get out of the fight and his troubles; that he was much older in such affairs than we were—I was very glad to hear him say that (laughter)—and that it was no uncommon thing for great corporations to make arrangements of this sort. I told him if that was the case I thought our state prison ought to be enlarged. (Laughter.)[7]

Taking Fisk apart, Eldridge told him that the two sides were on the verge of a settlement, and that if he and Gould consented, the company would be free of litigation at last. Judge Pierrepont and the other counsel likewise strongly advised a settlement. After much argument, toward midnight Gould finally yielded. According to Fisk, Drew then came to him with tears in his eyes (Drew later denied it) and asked him to consent, and he consented, whereupon he and Gould signed whatever papers were handed them, after which they left in disgust.

What Fisk and Gould had signed were secret agreements to end the litigation, to recompense Schell and Work for their losses in Erie, and to pay a $25,000 fee to their lawyer. As a result, the various lawsuits initiated by the Vanderbilt camp were formally dropped the next day. There still remained, however, the little matter of pacifying the Commodore. Fisk and Gould took the charge in hand. Eager to oust Uncle Daniel once and for all, they had no intention of letting him arm himself to get back in. Vanderbilt had 100,000 shares he wanted to be rid of and he demanded compensation for his losses in the pool, the large amount of which he blamed on the "skunks" who had deserted him. Finally they agreed to take 50,000 shares at 70, to give him 625 guaranteed B,H & E bonds worth half a million, and to pay him a million-dollar bonus for his losses. In addition, he was to have two seats on the Erie board and give Erie a sixty-day call on the 50,000 shares he retained. "Boys," said Vanderbilt, when the terms had been agreed upon, "you are young, and if you carry out this settlement there will be peace and harmony between the roads."[8]

On July 10, while Vanderbilt awaited the results in his office, the Erie board met to vote on the settlement. Drew presented his accounts as treasurer, which were duly accepted and approved. He then submitted a written statement whereby, "for the sake of peace and quiet, at my advanced period of life,"[9] he offered to pay the company $540,000 in cash and to release it from repaying his loan of 1866, if the company would relinquish to him the stock he had received as collateral and release him from all claims involved in the seven different actions in which he had recently been named a defendant. He then resigned as treasurer and director and left the room, following which Gould was elected treasurer and Drew's proposal was formally accepted. After fifteen years, Uncle Daniel was out of Erie.

With Drew's accounts settled, President Eldridge submitted his report to the board, announcing the sums to be paid to Vanderbilt and his allies. Included in this remarkable document were two other items of note. First, the Erie company was to purchase outright of the Boston, Hartford and Erie Railroad 5,000 of its bonds for $4 million—one of the most financially unsound commitments imaginable, but necessary to give the Eldridge clique its slice of the pie. Second, the Erie was to pay $150,000 to its court-appointed nonreceiving receiver, who was now City Chamberlain Peter B. Sweeny, a payment without the slightest justification except that Sweeny was a powerful Tammany politician and a friend of Barnard, who ordered it. The board approved the president's report.

The cost of the settlement, then, was 50,000 shares of Erie bought from Vanderbilt at 70 costing $3.5 million; compensation to Vanderbilt for losses costing $1 million; compensation to Schell and Work for losses totaling $429,250; fees to Schell and Work's lawyer totaling $25,000; 5,000 B,H & E bonds at $800 each amounting to $4 million; and a payment to Receiver Sweeny of $150,000. The total was $9,104,250 plus sundry other debits. On the credit side stood only the $540,000 paid by Drew. Where were these $9 million to come from? Obviously, they would have to come from the treasury of the Erie Railway. So the more than $7 million realized from the controversial bond sale, plus other funds as well, went not to complete and operate the road—the lamentable condition of which had been dramatized by the Carr's Rock catastrophe—but to compensate stock market operators, attorneys, and politicos. By the provisions of the Erie bill passed in Albany, every director who approved this diversion of funds was liable for from two to five years' imprisonment. Although the terms of the settlement later came to light, no prosecution ever resulted.

The Erie settlement seemingly provided for everyone except Fisk and Gould. On July 30, 1868, however, Eldridge resigned as president of Erie and subsequently withdrew to his native New England, there to further promote his ten-times-mortgaged, ever projected, never completed railroad. Since Gould succeeded him as president, he and Fisk got the Erie, a bedraggled goose from which they still hoped to coax some golden eggs. With them in charge, Vanderbilt soon quietly unloaded his Erie stock on the market, nor did his two representatives ever assume their seats on the board. Having now lost one or two million dollars in Erie, he was heard to say, amid vibrant oaths, that he would "never have anything more to do with them blowers."[10] Nor did he, insofar as the decision rested with him.

So ended the Great Erie Railway Row of 1868, whereby the public had come to detect in Wall Street, railroads, courts, and legislatures the same rich taint of corruption. One matter remained: the injured dignity of Justice Barnard had finally to be satisfied. On June 30 he declared directors Eldridge, Thompson, Lane, Davis, Diven, and Skidmore guilty of mere technical contempt, for which he fined each of them ten dollars, while reserving judgment on the ever absent Fisk, Gould, and Drew. On July 25 Fisk and Gould appeared in court to be fined ten dollars each plus a clerk's fee of twelve and one-half cents. As for Uncle Daniel, there is no record of his ever having appeared, although in the opinion of Charles Francis Adams, writing in the *American Law Review* of October 1868, "Drew was guilty of as flagrant contempt of court, both directly and indirectly, as was ever committed." The Erie litigation absorbed the talents of at least thirty lawyers, among them the nation's most eminent, and a prodigious expenditure of time, money, red tape, and paper. Concluded Adams, "Not even a fly had been crushed."[11]

CHAPTER 18

The Greenback Lockup

During the summer of 1868 the Commodore and the Old Bear rested from the strain of battle. Following his habit of over twenty years, Vanderbilt, to escape the July and August heat in the city, went off to Saratoga to drink and play whist with his business friends, drive his fast trotters, and take in the races at the track. In August he was called back suddenly by the death of his wife Sophia, who had remained in the city. Married to him for nearly fifty-five years, Sophia had been worn out by childbearing and by the abrasive adventure of being helpmate to Cornelius Vanderbilt. Baffled by his expanding ambitions, she would have been quite content as the wife of a small-time shipowner on Staten Island; only now, through death, did she escape the enigma of his aspirations, the tyranny of his will.

Drew made use of his recovered leisure to attend a seminary board meeting at Madison on June 24, where at long last he deeded to the school one hundred acres of grounds and the buildings and delivered his bond for the promised endowment of $250,000, in thanks for which he received no less than nine congratulatory addresses from the board. No one seems to have quibbled at his failure to hand over the endowment in cash. Since the endowment was to be invested in interest-bearing securities, the trustees doubtless thought it appropriate to leave its investment to Brother Drew himself, whose grasp of financial matters was far more acute than their own. Thereafter, each year they would receive from him $17,500, representing 7 percent on their capital, which paid the professors' salaries and the other current expenses of the school.

These matters seen to, later in the summer Drew returned to Putnam County, where he deeded some land to his daughter, and on the farms now owned by his son found a sight to gladden his old drover's heart: fat bullocks sure to win top prizes at the county fair in September, including a pair of steers with an astonishing combined weight of 7,000 pounds that already were the talk of the township. Of course folks knew where Bill got the knack for it!

Meanwhile Fisk and Gould were far too busy to take any extended vacation. Gould had succeeded Drew as treasurer and Eldridge as president, while Fisk had become comptroller of accounts. They now dominated the executive committee and by not calling any board meetings prior to the October election ruled Erie without interference. Significantly, on July 30 they welcomed to the board the Hon. William Marcy Tweed, state senator and boss of Tammany. Henceforth, since Tammany controlled several judges, the Erie directors would not be running from the law but with it.

The first problem facing Fisk and Gould, with Erie's coffers empty, was how to raise a large amount of cash. Their solution was to sell the 50,000 shares repurchased from Vanderbilt, which they disposed of on the market in small amounts daily during July, while they circulated bullish rumors that kept the price near 70, a notable bit of market finesse. Yet one former bull refused to be duped: Vanderbilt, seeing Fisk and Gould in charge, liquidated his holdings. As for Drew, in early August he staged a surprise bear raid on the stock, then sold for a quick profit. Some Wall Streeters thought that he would now knock the stock down still further in order to buy large amounts of it and influence the coming election. Uncle Daniel's taste for peace and quiet, it seemed, had quickly evaporated.

But Erie's new masters had other plans. If it puzzled some observers that men who were out to control the October election were selling stock instead of buying it, an explanation was soon forthcoming. On August 19 the Erie transfer books were suddenly closed a full sixty days prior to the election, instead of only thirty days as prescribed by the company's by-laws. Clearly, the present managers were highly satisfied with the current disposition of the stock, little of which was held by Drew, whereas a lot of it, although sold by Fisk and Gould, was still registered in the name of their brokerage houses. Although they owned little of the stock, two months in advance of the election Fisk and Gould had determined its results. On October 13 their uncontested ticket won unanimously, and the Tammany alliance was confirmed by the formal election to the board of Boss Tweed and City Chamberlain Peter B. Sweeny.

The Erie election cleared the air a bit between Erie's new managers and Drew. Already, in late August, Drew's Erie Railway Steamboat Company and the railroad agreed to cancel their contract for connecting services, and Drew sold Erie his seven propellor-driven Lake Erie steamboats for $300,000 in promissory notes, thus severing his last business connection with the railroad. With their venerable colleague now out of Erie once and for all, Fisk and Gould quietly broached to him another little venture of their own, in which his millions could be put to good use. For Gould (surely the idea was his, it savors of his daring) had sinister designs upon that delicate behemoth, the United States economy.

Toward the third week in October, stocks were unsettled because of rumors of a new convertible bond issue by Erie, whose shares were now selling below 50, and because of fears of tight money. In New York, money was usually scarce in October because the banks of the South and the West called their deposits home to finance grain and cotton dealers' purchases of the new crops then being harvested. And this October money was even scarcer than usual because the Treasury Department, wishing to reduce the flood of paper money unleashed during the war, was selling gold in order to soak up vast amounts of it. So the financial markets of New York were especially vulnerable when suddenly they were jolted by disturbing rumors of what Wall Street dreaded most: a lockup of greenbacks. The "unprincipled stockjobbers" whom the *Herald* denounced as responsible were soon identified as the triumvirate in control of Erie—Gould, Fisk, and their fellow director Frederick A. Lane—and Daniel Drew.

A lockup of greenbacks had been tried a number of times in the past—by Drew, among others—sometimes with considerable short-term success. Since perhaps half the resources of the national banks of New York were regularly loaned out to stock and gold speculators, the prices on those markets were immediately sensitive to sudden changes in the supply of money. Consequently market operators, by suddenly making heavy withdrawals of greenbacks from the banks, could contract the money in circulation, making interest rates soar and causing the banks to call in loans, so that brokers and speculators had to dump heavy holdings on the market, depressing prices to the point where the operators, having sold short, could make a killing in the Street. Such operations incurred moral censure, but they were not illegal.

Assisting market operators in these exercises was the banks' liberal issuing of certified checks. Such checks were signed by a bank's cashier, guaranteeing that the check writer had ample funds on deposit to cover it. If these checks were withheld by the depositors, the banks were obliged to retain in their vaults sufficient sums to cover them. This money was thus withdrawn from circulation or "locked up." And if another bank's officers were in collusion with the operators, so that they made loans to them on these very same certified checks, the lockup could be even more severe. In the previous spring the Erie conspirators had withheld certified checks in order to lock up $7 million for three days and thus put further pressure on Vanderbilt, at the trivial cost to themselves of denunciations from the press and the Street.

Compared to what Gould now had in mind, however, that earlier lockup had been a schoolboy's exercise; it was time for a masterwork in panic. When Gould and Fisk broached the plan to him, Drew was impressed. Promising the pool $4 million, he immediately put in one, then joined them in shorting Erie heavily. As tight-money artists and panic makers, his young colleagues showed signs of genius.

The lockup was launched on October 20, when Gould's brokerage house obtained a large loan from one bank on collateral, then deposited these funds in three other banks, drew certified checks on the funds, and so withdrew from circulation about ten million dollars of greenbacks. Over the next few days more greenbacks were locked up; money rates rose from 7 to 12 percent; and certain bank managers, notably those of the Bank of the Commonwealth, where Gould's brokerage firm did its banking, fell under the suspicion of collusion. A storm of condemnation assailed the conspirators, who endured it with stoic dignity even as the U.S. Treasury, cleaving to the principle that speculator-induced crises were no concern of the government, continued to sell gold daily and thus abetted the lockup.

Accompanying the turmoil in the money market was the turmoil in Erie, whose depressed price caught the eye of purchasers in England. Unlike their American counterparts, English investors still believed in Erie as a vital link between New York and the West and therefore snapped it up at "bargain" prices. This buying panic now reached enormous proportions, as the price sagged to 43, then to 40. Meanwhile, reports persisted of fresh Erie certificates on the Street. As the rumors redoubled, on October 26 a three-man deputation from the Stock Exchange called on President Gould and asked him for clarification. Yes, he stated, since the settlement with Vanderbilt in July, the company—for the most legitimate reasons—had issued $10 million in convertible bonds, of which half had already been converted into stock and the other half would be soon. Should the company lay a third rail, he added, it would have to raise another $3 million by a further conversion of bonds into stock.

This quiet admission exploded like a bombshell on Wall Street. On top of the outrage of last March, another 100,000 shares of stock would be issued! Yet the quiet-voiced Gould had not even stated the half of it: in just four months his creative management had increased Erie's stock by not $10 million but $23 million. No wonder he and Fisk had consistently not bought Erie but sold it in the market!

Understatement though it was, the good round sum of $10 million was quite enough to stagger the Stock Exchange. Erie broke below 40 for the first time in over six years, as sell orders poured in by cable from London, where recent buyers were now stampeding to sell. As the lockup continued, other stocks weakened as well, trade was hampered, government bonds and commodities declined, and failures were feared. In all, some twelve to fifteen million dollars of greenbacks had now been withdrawn from circulation, but the banks dared not call in their loans, lest brokers dump stocks and precipitate a panic. The entire business community was shaken and demoralized.

And so was Daniel Drew. Although he had always considered a little panic now and then good for business—*his* business—this was something different. With everything headed for a smash, Uncle Daniel was "skeered" and wanted out. Just at this point the speculator Henry Keep, threatened with ruin by the decline in his own pet stock, Northwestern, came to Drew and pleaded for a loan of $2 million, offering to pay a steep rate of interest. The Old Bear reflected that this was money in the bank, without the risks of the lockup. So he held back the additional $3 million he had promised, took his profits in the market, unlocked his $1 million, and gave Keep the loan he asked for.

Gould and Fisk were furious. Because they needed his money, they had included Drew in their scheme in spite of his betrayal last spring. Now he had betrayed them again; they vowed revenge.

Meanwhile the stringency continued unrelieved, till on November 6 many brokers unloaded stocks for cash, inducing a four-hour panic on the market that caused a reputable house in Broad Street to fail. Only at this point, with a general collapse clearly threatening, did Secretary of the Treasury Hugh McCulloch deign to notice the strife. On November 7, just four days after Ulysses S. Grant had been elected president of the United States, McCulloch announced that, if necessary, he would reissue $50 million of greenbacks to relieve the stringency, whereupon loan rates fell again to 7 percent. Yet stocks still declined and the crisis was far from resolved.

This unsettled state of things—alarms, rumors, failures, and an impending panic—was meat to Daniel Drew. The whole market was shaky and Erie, with just a bit of a push, would plummet; he yearned to be in on the kill. And so, no sooner out of the market, he jumped back in. Over a period of days, while Erie was wavering in the upper thirties, he shorted it to the amount of 30,000 shares and sold calls for 40,000 more. He was planning to snatch a fortune from the bust.

For several days Erie declined slowly in the market, battered by the short sales of Drew and certain others, and above all by the heavy unloading of disillusioned English investors, who knew now what their "bargain" was worth. Then, on Friday November 13, panicky selling swept the market, plunging Erie to 35, which was just half of its price four months before. That evening, Uncle Daniel went to bed gloating.

On Saturday November 14 Erie opened on the Stock Exchange at 36⅝ and traded thereabouts until the exchange closed for the day at 1:00 P.M. Shortly thereafter, Wall Street was suddenly inundated with greenbacks that, after a lockup of twenty-five days, came pouring back into circulation, greedy for gold and Erie. Gold surged on the Gold Exchange, while in frenzied trading in the Long Room and outside on the street the price of Erie soared to 52¼, a recovery of close to seventeen points in one day! Brokers and traders were stunned, while the not so Merry Old Gentleman of Wall Street, short 70,000 Erie at an average price of 37, knew that he was trapped.

"However questionable these schemes may be," confessed the *Herald* a few days later, "their skill and success exhibit Napoleonic genius on the part of those who conceived them."[1] The genius was of course Gould who, having masterminded the money lockup, deemed the time ripe for a reversal of strategy and so engineered a corner in Erie. He and Fisk, noting the huge short interest in the stock, calculated that but little Erie remained on this side of the Atlantic and so covered their short contracts, unlocked their millions, and used them at once to corner Erie, hoping in the process to catch Drew and strip him of a fortune. At the same time they bought some six or eight million dollars of gold, convulsing that market as well until short sellers were paying as much as 1 percent a day to borrow gold. In switching from the bear to the bull side of the market, Gould had turned on a dime and launched two corners simultaneously. In committing deft financial mayhem with sangfroid, he had no peer.

That evening the dazed victims of these lightning maneuvers held an emergency meeting at the Fifth Avenue residence of Judge Edwards Pierrepont, whose hospitable parlor had housed the secret Erie negotiations during the previous July. Caught in the same net now were a curious assortment of fish, including Drew, the ex-partner of their common antagonists; Erie directors Henry Thompson and Frederick A. Lane, who like Drew had deserted Fisk and Gould and got caught on the bear side of the market; Frank Work and Richard Schell, who in taking another bite out of Erie found themselves bitten yet again; and the reputable German-born banker August Belmont, representing a host of English shareholders who, having been panicked into selling, had sold stock borrowed through their New York agents and so were technically short of the market pending the arrival of their certificates by ship in New York. Belmont, the American representative of the Rothschilds, must have been ill at ease in this carnival of thieves; whereas the others were simply out to save their own skins, he felt genuinely aggrieved for his customers.

All those at the meeting were desperate for Erie stock, and Erie stock was in fact on the way. From 50,000 to 200,000 shares sold by Belmont's customers were New York-bound on a ship due to arrive on the twenty-third. What was needed in the meantime, then, was legal action that would expose Gould's fraudulent management and persuade the courts to name an Erie receiver—a legal action that might also collapse Erie's price in the market. Such was the solution proposed by Work and Schell, with Drew in agreement. A complaint that had already been prepared was read now to the gathering, and Schell, with an eye to public opinion, persuaded the respectable Belmont to bring the suit in Belmont's name, while the others would remain in the background, with Work and Schell paying half the legal costs and Drew the other half. Only one more thing was required—an affidavit from Drew recounting the infamy of Erie, since nothing could be so detailed and damning as the confessions of an ex-insider. For Uncle Daniel this was a bit awkward, but in desperation he agreed. By the time the meeting broke up, the new allies felt vastly reassured. They planned to strike their blow the first thing Monday morning.

One fatal flaw marred the strategy of the cornered shorts: it hinged on Daniel Drew. No sooner had Drew agreed to the affidavit than he had second thoughts. To help the other shorts, he was about to smirch his own good name. Was there no other solution? He decided to try the personal appeal, which had worked well and often with Vanderbilt. And so, on the following Sabbath morning, instead of going to church he went to the Erie offices in West Street, where he found both Fisk and Gould. What then happened is told in detail through an affidavit sworn to by Fisk three days later and corroborated by Gould; Drew never either confirmed or contradicted it. Said Fisk:

> On Sunday morning, Nov. 15, 1868, Mr. Daniel Drew unexpectedly called upon me. He said he had come to make a clean breast of it, and to throw himself upon our mercy, that he was short of Erie stock 30,000 shares. I told him I knew that, and that was not half of it, for he was short in addition 40,000 calls. He complained bitterly of his position. He then entered into an explanation as to certain proceedings that he said were being got up by parties who were to attack us in the courts. He said he had been in the enemy's camp, and all that he cared about was to look out for number one, and if we were willing to help him he would make a clean breast of it. I told him that his disposition and his nature were so vacillating that I should not trust him, unless he made a clean breast of it to begin with. He finally, after much hesitation, said he would tell me. He said that Work, Schell, Lane, and Thompson were embarked in a

scheme with him. He refused to tell me in whose name the proceedings were to be instituted. Upon inquiring closely of him whether the case was taken up on its merits or as a mere stock operation, he admitted to me that it was to relieve those who were short of the stock. I presented the idea to him as to what the others would do, and he said that he could take the ringleaders with him if they were also provided for, and he would break up the whole scheme.

He begged and entreated me that I should go and bring Mr. Gould, saying that he knew if he could see Mr. Gould he could benefit his position, and would tell us who were to be the plaintiffs in the suit. I tried to convince him that this was one of his old tricks, and that he was the last man who should whine at any position he had put himself in with regard to the Erie. Finally I consented to go and get Mr. Gould, and did so. I was not present at the entire interview between Mr. Gould and Mr. Drew, but such portion of the conversation as I heard was of the same nature that Mr. Drew held with me. Also, he urged many arguments upon Mr. Gould and myself to induce us to help him with regard to the stock. He stated to us that it was within our power to protect ourselves, and urged us to issue more convertible bonds, saying no one could know anything about it; this Mr. Gould and I declined to accede to.

At this time he told us that a suit was to be brought in the name of August Belmont; that he was present at a meeting they had last night, and heard the papers read. We told him over and over again that we could not help him. He would not leave us, but insisted on remaining, and Mr. Gould and myself, unable to get rid of him in any other way, told him that we would meet him again at 10 o'clock that evening. We then parted.

Subsequently, about 11 o'clock, I found Mr. Drew waiting for us. At that time Mr. Gould was not present, and I again told Mr. Drew nothing could be done. He said:

"Then if you put this stock up I am a ruined man!"

He harped upon the fact that he was willing to pay a large amount of money for the use of 30,000 or 40,000 shares of stock for fifteen days, and offered me as high as three per cent., which would amount to nearly $100,000, for the use of it for fifteen days. Finding he could not induce me to accede to his wishes, he took another tack, saying there was a conspiracy against us, and they would ruin us if they could, and that they would have the stock down at all hazards; and that if I would not agree to anything with him, he would give his affidavit to the other side, having before this stated he would not give his affidavit if I came to his rescue. He said:

"You know during the whole of our other fights I objected to ever giving my affidavit, but I swear I will do you all the harm I can do you if you do not help me in this time of my great need!"

He also said: "You can loan me the stock," and repeating, "I will give you three per cent. for it. You have the power to issue more convertible bonds, and I will buy the bonds from you if you are caught, or I will buy the bonds of you with the understanding that I shall not pay for them unless you are caught."

I positively and unequivocally declined his proposition, as I had on each occasion. After talking in this strain for more than an hour, I adhering to my decision that nothing could be done, he, at about 1 o'clock Monday morning, said, "I will bid you good-night" and went away.[2]

Even taking into account Fisk's self-interest in relating the story, one is inclined to give full credit to this unique spectacle of the Old Bear at bay, profuse with treachery, sly, abject, cynical, pleading into the middle of the night, the whole scene replete with grim humor and irony that cannot have escaped his tormentors, and capped fittingly by the terse pathos of the old man's departure: "I will bid you good-night." One agrees with Charles Francis Adams, who thought the episode worthy of Dickens yet surpassing him. Fiction would be hard put to match it.

August Belmont's lawyers had no knowledge of this incident when they initiated proceedings Monday morning before Judge Josiah Sutherland, a reputable Supreme Court justice. Brought in the name of Belmont and his Wall Street partner Ernest B. Lucke, the complaint charged Gould, Fisk, and Lane with conniving to get control of the company, with issuing $26 million of illegal stock, and with misappropriating Erie funds for the lockup of greenbacks and other speculations and abuses. The petitioners asked the court to enjoin the defendants from any further acts as directors and to appoint a receiver.

Accompanying this complaint was the affidavit of Daniel Drew, including details about Erie's earlier issue of $10 million of convertible bonds; equally choice details about the secret Erie settlement with Vanderbilt; plus the added admission of his complicity in the recent lockup of greenbacks—an amazing self-indictment, formally sworn to, that gave the public its first solid knowledge of Erie's settlement with Vanderbilt, and discredited Drew all the more in that the motivation behind his confession was obviously cupidity, spite, and revenge.

In the face of such evidence, Judge Sutherland promptly issued an injunction restraining Gould and the other defendants from any further acts as directors. When word of this hit the Street, it perturbed both the gold and stock markets, causing Erie to fluctuate wildly before closing at 54. On the following day, Tuesday November 17, the gold corner collapsed when the U.S. Treasury resumed gold sales on government account. But Erie, still cornered, churned in the market, as the text of Belmont's complaint and Drew's affidavit became available to the public, prompting rumors that Gould and Fisk had decamped once again for New Jersey.

Nothing could have been further from the truth. On Wednesday the eighteenth came startling news that August Belmont's lawsuit had been forestalled by a prior legal action, that the enjoiners had been enjoined, that Erie could not receive a receiver because it already had one formally appointed by the court, and that the receiver's name was Jay Gould. Total confusion engulfed the Belmont party, Drew, Wall Street, the courts, and the press—just about everyone, in fact, but Gould and his associates, who had inflicted a stunning defeat on their foes.

Drew's Sabbath visit was surely responsible, since it had forewarned Gould. On Monday morning, November 16, only a few hours before the Belmont suit was initiated before Judge Sutherland, attorneys for Charles McIntosh, an Erie ferry agent and presumed stockholder, had appeared before Supreme Court Justice Barnard, no doubt catching that elegant magistrate either in bed or at breakfast. The petition presented in McIntosh's name declared that various persons had threatened to bring suit against the Erie Railway Company in order to depress the company's stock for purposes of speculation, to prevent which McIntosh, acting on behalf of all stockholders, asked to have such persons restrained from such actions, and to have a receiver appointed. After due consideration by Barnard—probably about one minute—an injunction was issued restraining all parties from bringing such suits against Erie or otherwise interfering with the actions of its officers, and naming Gould as the company's receiver, with full charge and custody of its funds.

In so doing, Barnard had more than maintained his reputation as one of the state's most exceptional justices, first, because he had received a petition that should have been directed to Judge Sutherland, and second, because his view of this new overissue of stock differed so markedly from his view of the overissue of the previous spring, which he had referred to as "counterfeit money." As a Tammany judge, Barnard was well aware of Boss Tweed's alliance with Erie, thanks to which the Erie managers felt no need to revisit the wilds of New Jersey.

When news of Barnard's injunction reached Wall Street in the early afternoon of Wednesday November 18, its immediate import was clear. There would be litigation—weeks, months of it—so that the Belmont suit could be of no immediate help to the bears. Consequently, Drew and his fellow victims rushed to cover their shorts as the bulls, competing for whatever Erie came into the Street, drove the stock up from 49 to 57½. On Thursday the nineteenth, even as the city was reading Fisk's sworn affidavit in the papers—his riposte to Drew, recounting the Old Bear's ordeal of the preceding Sunday—Uncle Daniel, his reputation shredded, was still bidding frantically for Erie, of which small amounts remained on the Street. Then came news that the obliging Barnard had granted receiver Gould authority to use Erie's treasury to repurchase and cancel 200,000 of the controversial new shares of Erie at any price below par, which was a marvelous help to the bulls. Against such weapons the bears were defenseless. Uncle Daniel would be bled of millions; only a miracle could save him.

And a miracle occurred. Suddenly, close to 2:00 P.M., with the stock hovering at 60 and the corner all but consummated, Wall Street was flooded with Erie. Out of the desk drawers, cash boxes, and safes of the small bankers, cigar vendors, tailors, and grocers of the city came an avalanche of ten-share certificates that by the clique's calculations were supposed to be in London but were not. These ten-share certificates, having never left home, were now brandished by a host of small investors who, long victimized by Wall Street, rushed to their brokers in order to capitalize on the high cash price of the stock. As the certificates poured in by the thousands, the Erie clique was obliged to bid for them frantically in order to deny them to Drew. This they had almost achieved when suddenly, alarmed by the amount of checks pouring in to be certified, their bank declined to certify more—a disaster, since the sellers were insisting on certified checks. Within five minutes Gould and his friends arranged to have their checks certified at another bank, but in that brief space of time Drew managed to cover his contracts at 57. At a cost, he had defeated the corner. Shortly thereafter, Erie collapsed to 42 in quiet trading.

As the dust settled, Drew could reckon his losses at about $1.4 million plus brokerage fees, which was hardly a victory, but not the total disaster that the Erie clique had hoped to inflict on him. Gould and Fisk, on the other hand, had been obliged to swallow vast quantities of Erie offered unexpectedly at high prices, plus further quantities about to arrive from England by ship, stock for which there was no market, since everyone was wary of it and Uncle Daniel talked it down further. As a result, the Erie kings were left sitting on their sheaves of certificates, with losses that some estimated as high as $3 million. If anyone had profits, for once it was the lucky outsiders on both sides of the ocean, although many of them, in selling, may simply have been cutting their losses.

The conspirators were denounced on every side, their critics feasting on the rich particulars provided in affidavits by the parties themselves. Preaching at his famous Plymouth Church in Brooklyn, the Rev. Henry Ward Beecher called Wall Street "the very sink of iniquity, the hot bed of corruption, and the magnet of ruin and desolation."[3] Meanwhile a petition to ban trading in Erie was gathering hosts of signatures at the Stock Exchange, while the press, suspicious of the state courts, appealed to the federal government for justice.

To those who had followed the earlier litigation in Erie, it was not surprising that the new round of Erie proceedings proved lengthy, costly, and futile, though not futile for Gould and Fisk. Newspaper readers avid of entertainment could read thereafter how Judge Sutherland had vacated Judge Barnard's order naming Gould receiver and had appointed a receiver of his own, who upon seeking access to Erie's halls was barred by a platoon of hired thugs; how the lords of Erie brought suit against Belmont, Lucke, Schell, Drew, and Work, alleging a conspiracy to manipulate Erie in the market; how they petitioned the U.S. District Court and got Gould named again as receiver; how more judges were drawn into the imbroglio, naming more receivers, vacating more orders, and reversing one another's actions; how on December 7 the Erie managers brought suit against Drew, alleging that as president of the Erie Railway Steamboat Company he had defrauded Erie; how on December 10 they brought suit against Vanderbilt to make him repay Erie the $4.5 million he had received in the Erie settlement in July; and how the whole ludicrous mishmash of actions fell at last into the judicial lap of Supreme Court Justice Albert Cardozo, another Tammany stalwart, who announced his decision, filling 110 pages of foolscap, on February 19, 1869. He decided that there were no grounds for appointing a receiver for Erie and that railroad directors were entitled to issue convertible bonds and convert them into stock at their pleasure, all of which brought things back to where they had been in the first place. Thereafter Gould and Fisk honored Justice Barnard by blazoning his name upon a new Erie locomotive in flaming gold. The litigation ultimately proved that Gould was cleverer than anyone and that the justices of the state and federal courts of New York were either naive, clumsy, stupid, or corrupt, bent as they seemed to be on confirming the judgment of Dickens's Mr. Bumble, to the effect that "the law is a ass."

For Uncle Daniel, 1868 had been the most eventful year of his life. It was the most controversial also and certainly the least consistent. He had betrayed the Vanderbilt camp by going short of Erie, and the Erie camp by treating with Vanderbilt; then the Erie camp by withdrawing from the lockup, and the Belmont camp by treating with the Erie camp. Worse still, this had all come to light. As a result, while editorialists denounced his recent confederates as scoundrels, they taxed him as a hypocrite as well.

"To such a disgusting degree of depravity do we see these stock operations carried," said the *Herald*, "that members of the church of high standing offer, when 'cornered,' to betray their brother 'pals,' and, in their forgetfulness of the morality to which they sanctimoniously listen every Sunday, state that 'all they care about is to look out for number one.'" Accordingly, the *Herald* proposed a new and more exact translation of the Bible in a special Wall Street edition, for the benefit of stock gamblers and thieves. It began: "1. Steal largely or not at all: for is it not preached in Gotham that he who steals largely and gives donations to the church shall enter the kingdom of heaven, while to him who confines his stealings to modest peculations shall be opened the doors of Sing Sing? 2. Steal largely! for in proportion to the magnitude of thy stealings shalt thou prosper and wax respectable throughout Gotham."[4]

For a long while Uncle Daniel was out of the market; it was definitely time to hunker down.

CHAPTER 19

Respite and Return

On May 19, 1869, with son and grandson present, Daniel Drew presided over the annual board meeting of the seminary at Madison, heard the yearly reports, was reelected president, and became a member of the school's finance committee. How pleasant it was, in this bucolic atmosphere, to be greeted with courtesy and esteem. Certainly the founder hoped that this recovered image of solid elderly citizen and philanthropist would efface the recent one of stockjobbing opportunist and gambler. "Stop speckerlatin'—don't tech Ayrie with no margin!"[1] he advised some Methodist brethren who, inspired by his own late example, had taken "points" and lost their margin in the market. This advice he himself followed as for two years, whether out of prudence and chagrin or from an access of piety, he remained a stranger to Wall Street.

For the Methodists, however, the revelations of his stockjobbing, some of them even from his own hand, must have been a grievous burden. The matter was not mentioned in public, but privately they had to acknowledge that Brother Drew was tied too much to money. Yet was he not the whitest in the black company of Wall Street? If he got money by questionable means, at least he found the noblest uses for it. And how often had they heard him at prayer meetings, his face streaked with tears, avow that he had served Mammon and forgotten God! What could they say to this anguished penitent whose sins were like a knife in his vitals, and whose money they needed? In the quiet of their hearts, they prayed for him.

Much of the summer of 1869 Drew spent on his farm in Carmel. When railroad fever hit the region because something called the New

York and Boston Railroad proposed to pass through the village of Carmel and so end its rustic isolation forever, Drew attended the town meeting in August to hear the promoters talk up their scheme, and thereafter he offered the road free transit across any of his lands. Meanwhile he was also giving close attention to the cattle on his farms, spurred on no doubt by his son Bill's success at the last county fair, nicely climaxed when Bill's two fattest steers appeared in New York City in February 1869 and the butcher who had bought them christened them "Commodore Vanderbilt" and "Daniel Drew" and paraded them through the streets in ribbons. At the fair of September 1869 the old man got the ten-dollar discretionary award for the best ten fat heifers, while his son and son-in-law got other cattle awards, his son's wife took half the flower prizes, and his grandson presided over the whole affair as president of the Agricultural Society.

But if Uncle Daniel had left Wall Street, Wall Street clung to him through exposé and litigation. How did it sit with his family, when he was summoned to testify before a state senate committee investigating charges of bribery relating to the Erie bill (of which bribery he pleaded total ignorance), and articles in *Fraser's Magasine* and the *North American Review* decried his Wall Street doings without any of the uneasy awe that they accorded Vanderbilt? His wife, to judge by her portrait, was a strong, stern woman whose mannish features and direct gaze bespoke character devoid of humor or grace. Not the easiest helpmate to go home to, one might think, yet when exiled in Jersey City Uncle Daniel yearned to do just that. For decades Roxanna, being wholly domestic, had given him the creaturely comforts of the hearth. Of his financial escapades, she probably grasped very little. His occasional absences, the coming and going of messengers, the sudden mysterious conferences with strangers in the downstairs parlors—all this was part of that baffling male world of business that made her husband what he was and provided her with silk dresses and a house on the square. To her, business was a consuming preoccupation from which, with luck, one reclaimed one's spouse for family dinners and holidays, formal Sabbath churchgoing, and a few precious weeks in the summer. As for her husband's reputation, he was president of the People's Line, a staunch Methodist, and the founder of a seminary. If anything else came to her ears, Daniel probably shrugged it off with a word or two: some folks would say just anything! Perhaps she nodded; it squared with her experience.

Like his mother, Bill lived at a remove from the Street and always thought of his father as honest. As for Drew's son-in-law the Reverend Clapp—a walrus-mustached moral heavyweight who was now Putnam County's most prominent minister—there is ample evidence that he walked the pastures talking "critters" with his father-in-law, but none at all that he ever got the old man down on his knees to pray for his soul. So when trouble came, it came from a different quarter: Drew's granddaughters took him to court.

The trouble stemmed from the will of his daughter Catherine's second husband, the long-deceased Robert W. Kelley. Under the terms of Kelley's will, his estate was to be divided equally between his wife Catherine and their five daughters and to be invested by the executors in income-bearing securities. Each child was to receive half her principal at age twenty-one and the other half at thirty-one, while the executors continued to invest the accruing income on her behalf. Of the three executors, however, one died and the other declined to serve, leaving Drew in control of the estate, which he had drawn on freely in the course of his Wall Street operations.

For years, no one questioned his management. Now, however, four of the granddaughters—refined young ladies who could speak French, sing, play the piano, and sketch a bit—had come of age and three had married, their husbands being affluent young gentlemen with a fondness for fine horses, hunting, and travel, but little inclination toward wartime military service or, except for one of them, work. Obviously, the continuation of this pleasant life depended in part on the girls' inheritance. The granddaughters may have pondered this themselves, or perhaps their husbands took time off from their fast trotters and quail-shooting to glance at the financial and editorial pages. At any rate, the sisters conceived doubts about their grandfather's execution of the trust. First Kathleen, one of the two unmarried sisters, requested a settlement and got it. Then, in May 1869, Georgiana, Josephine, and Louise brought suit against their grandfather as executor and trustee.

It must have hurt Uncle Daniel to the quick. Did the girls really think that their old Granddad would violate a sacred trust? God forbid! If he had used the estate's funds in his "speckilations" rather than investing them as prescribed by the will, it was only because he could do better with the principal himself. But if they wanted security and an income, why bless them, of course they should have it. To each granddaughter he offered a bond guaranteeing that he would pay $70,000 on demand, plus 7 percent interest in the meantime. This offer was accepted, the bonds were given, and the suit was dropped. Drew remained in control of the estate, while the granddaughters and their husbands, assured of steady income, came regularly from Putnam County to spend the winter on Union Square. In candid moments, Uncle Daniel might admit to having cut a few corners on Wall Street, but if there was anything he regarded as sacred, it was obligations to his family and church.

In his capacity as distinguished Methodist churchman and philanthropist, Drew now found himself drawn into closer social contact with the Commodore. In August 1869 America's foremost railroad king, then a widower of only one year, shocked his family and surprised the public by eloping to Canada with Miss Frank Crawford, an attractive thirty-year-old Southern gentlewoman to whom he was distantly related through his mother. Now established in the elegant brick mansion at 10 Washington Square, the new Mrs. Vanderbilt was determined not only to give her husband the youth and companionship he craved, while weaning him away from his clubs and card games, but also, ever so discreetly, to nudge him toward philanthropy and religion. She herself was a Methodist and among the Commodore's acquaintances must have quickly discerned the single one who, in sharp contrast to his hard-drinking, whist-playing cronies, stood out as a sterling example of Methodist benefaction and piety. However lacking in social graces, Drew was welcome in her home as a model and contributing influence toward the husband whom she hoped to remold.

Naturally, Drew was more than willing to help coax closer to the Mercy Seat this flourishing reprobate who had a settled antipathy for preachers. With great delicacy Frank Vanderbilt also managed to introduce her husband to her pastor, the Rev. Charles F. Deems, who became a frequent guest in the house and in time a good friend of the Commodore. Exercising the greatest tact, Deems, Mrs. Vanderbilt, and Drew conspired to interest the tightfisted Vanderbilt in Deems's project to establish a church of his own in the city, serving the needs of out-of-town visitors. By June 1870 they had brought the old man around. He gave Deems fifty thousand dollars with which the minister bought a vacant church in Mercer Street that he opened on October 2 of that year as the Church of the Strangers. Drew was one of the many prominent vice-presidents of its organizing committee. Thereafter, to the novelty of Cornelius Vanderbilt the founder of a church succeeded the near-miracle of Cornelius Vanderbilt a worshiper. On February 19, 1871, Drew and the Commodore appeared together in a pew in Deems's church, a sight so memorable that Deems recorded it in his private journal. To Uncle Daniel the event must have brought deep satisfaction; it was high time the old rat got religion.

Cornelius Vanderbilt's character and career were something that Drew could grasp and appreciate, but the doings of James Fisk, Jr., were quite another thing. What was Drew to think, when his one-time protégé exhibited himself to the public in a variety of exuberant guises? As Fisk the impresario he bought Pike's Opera House, refurbished it magnificently, and was now staging splashy musicals where scandalous female dancers raised their legs. As Fisk the self-styled admiral he was operating steamboats on Long Island Sound, strutting beside the gang-plank at departure time in a gold-buttoned blue naval uniform closely resembling that of an admiral of the United States Navy. And to top it off, Admiral and Impresario Fisk had moved the offices of the Erie Railway Company out of the business district and into the Opera House, where impressionable young male clerks risked encountering immoral women in tights. There, regally ensconced in his office, Fisk also assumed the guise of Prince Erie, the gaudy railroad magnate who reveled in Erie litigation and gave ebullient interviews to the press. No matter how he looked at Fisk's career, Uncle Daniel's business sense was baffled, his morality shocked.

Yet it was Drew who was out of step with the times, while his former pupil was leading the parade. To the very tips of his ring-studded fingers, Fisk embodied the Flash Age, that glittery postwar prolongation of the wartime boom of the North: an age of shirtfront diamonds and shiny equipages, of cancans and Offenbach, champagne and "fast" women; a time when the recent war's idealism, sacrifice, and suffering gave way to fun and frolic masking desperate greed and cynical corruption; an era when paunchy, shrewd Boss Tweed routinely rigged the local elections, and conspired with contractors to milk millions from the construction of a new county courthouse; when scheming men pushed on by venal women operated at every level of government, right up to the entourage of President Ulysses S. Grant.

Uncle Daniel, to be sure, had a genius for quiet conniving, but there was no flash in him, not even a glint. He was pious, homespun, reticent, and pastor-drab in his dress. On the *Drew* once, mistaking him for a crewman, a passenger asked, "Do you belong to the boat?" "No," he answered, "the boat belongs to me."[2] What could he be, then, but a perplexed onlooker in this circus of glint and corruption, whose ringmaster and chief performer was a rollicking exhibitionist whom bluebloods and moralists abhorred, but whom a host of friends applauded, and the masses admired shamelessly as yet another instance of the American dream come true?

Yet to be an onlooker and not a participant had its advantages. In September 1869 Fisk and Gould, who recently had twice hosted President Grant in New York, made a desperate attempt to corner gold. This daring operation almost succeeded, until on Friday September 24—known ever afterward as Black Friday—the treasury's sudden resumption of gold sales sent the price tumbling, while bulls and bears alike went bankrupt. Pursued through the streets by ruined speculators, Fisk and Gould had to take refuge behind the barricaded doors of the Opera House. To have been aloof from such hysteria, with its prolonged aftermath of lawsuits and a congressional investigation, Drew must have thanked Providence.

Not that he was free of his past. The Erie antagonists of 1868 were like a repertory company whom circumstances called on repeatedly to perform together in somewhat altered roles. Remarkably harmonious was the full-cast performance of November 10, 1869—a bare month and a half after the Black Friday convulsion—when Drew found himself seated on a bunting-bedecked platform in Hudson Street, along with Gould, Fisk, August Belmont, Horace Greeley, assorted admirals and ex-mayors, and a host of Vanderbilt lieutenants, to witness the unveiling of the massive pediment of the new Hudson River Railroad freight depot, dominated by a four-ton bronze statue of the Commodore, flanked by bas-reliefs portraying his career on land and sea with steamships and locomotives, Neptune, a sea monster and a boiler, birds, grapes, machinery, and cows. This was the city's half-million-dollar salute to its most dynamic citizen, whom Wall Streeters now referred to as Old Eighty Millions.

Just ten days later, however, the honored subject of that masterwork appeared in court to testify in the case of the *Erie Railway Company* v. *Cornelius Vanderbilt*, Fisk and Gould's suit to recover the $4.5 million given to the Commodore in the Erie settlement. Before a packed courtroom Vanderbilt insisted that he had nothing at all to do with the Erie litigation, that his dealings with Drew and Eldridge in July 1868 had been a purely private matter between them. Asked how much Erie stock he held at the time, he answered, "Them's are things I keep to myself."[3] From first to last he was tight-lipped and crusty, his lies stupendous, his oblivion invincible. The *Herald* advised the Erie lawyers to give up.

Nine days later it was the turn of Uncle Daniel, summoned as an unwilling witness by the plaintiff. Here at last, subjected to the rigors of the courtroom, was Erie's longtime evil genius, the guardian of its inmost secrets. Before a thronged courtroom presided over by Justice George G. Barnard, who welcomed him with a smile, Drew testified standing up at the request of Erie's attorney David Dudley Field, so that Field could look him straight in the eye. Drew met Field's gaze with his own and testified with remarkable composure, corroborating in every respect the testimony of Vanderbilt. But like the Commodore, he revealed tracts of oblivion, abysses of ignorance. When, over a year later, Drew was back on the stand again, interrogated by Erie attorneys, he demonstrated anew that in the art of gentle forgetfulness, sweet-tempered denial, and injured innocence, Uncle Daniel had no peer. Even Justice Barnard was baffled. Discovering no fraud in the settlement, he found for the defendant; Erie would not get the Commodore's millions. Fisk and Gould promptly appealed; the case dragged on for years.

In March 1870 Daniel and Roxanna celebrated their golden wedding anniversary. They had long anticipated it, especially since Christmas Eve of 1866, when they attended the golden wedding celebration of Thomas and Abigail Drew in Drewville. It had been the great hope of Daniel and Roxanna that, God willing, the two brothers and two sisters should be united again on the occasion of their own golden wedding.

And so they were. On the evening of Friday, March 4—the celebration was held one day early, lest it be prolonged past midnight and encroach on the Sabbath—the three spacious parlors of 41 Union Square, furnished tastefully with gilt furniture upholstered in silk, were adorned with flowers, while musicians provided soft music. Chatting amiably were family in abundance, Methodist clergymen and laity, steamboat captains, journalists, and financiers. Tactfully absent, although invited, were Messrs. Fisk and Gould, who instead sent lavish bouquets. Sitting apart on a sofa, looking hale and genial, the hosts received their guests, Roxanna wearing lavender silk and a point lace shawl, her brown hair but slightly tinged with gray. Compliments and congratulations were showered upon them, as well as costly gifts, of which the most impressive was that of the St. Paul's congregation: a silver flower stand filled with rare exotics, atop a golden urn from Tiffany's. Surrounded by four generations of family and a host of friends, Daniel was too moved to reply to the pastor's presentation. Then, after a fervent prayer, the guests partook of elegant refreshments from Delmonico's, following which they dispersed somewhat earlier than anticipated, having learned that John McClintock, the long ailing president of the seminary, had died that day at Madison.

The press was invited in force. Although saddened by the loss of his friend, Drew was able to read glowing accounts in all the papers except the *Times* the next day. One hundred and fifty guests had attended Vanderbilt's 1863 celebration; his had had three hundred.

The press accounts of the golden wedding presented Uncle Daniel as a gentleman of advanced years, surrounded by a loving family and friends and honored by his church. Certainly he had much to rejoice in: the affection of his family, a fine home, good health, an intact fortune, a prosperous steamboat line, a thriving seminary, other philanthropies, and farms in Putnam County that raised prize-winning stock—quite enough for a man of seventy-two who after a long business career could now relax serenely into the evening of life.

But if family, fortune, steamboats, good deeds, and fat cattle gave Uncle Daniel a range of satisfactions, not one of them gave him excitement. "I must have excitement," he had told his friend John Parker, "or I should die." He missed the risk and adventure of Wall Street; the sheer fun of secret combinations, of greenhorns and old hands flocking to him with offers, tips, schemes; the thrill of sending messengers racing to the exchanges with orders to buy or sell millions; the Street bleeding and the press agog because once again the Old Man had "taken a slice out 'em." Bored by tranquillity, sick of it, he itched for action. And so, after a two-year absence, he went back to Wall Street.

One of his first ventures was not a happy one. In January 1871 he opened a joint account with another prominent operator, Stephen V. White, to trade in the stock of Rock Island (the Chicago, Rock Island and Pacific Railroad), of which they went heavily short, only to find themselves all but cornered by a bull pool led by William S. Woodward, one of the boldest traders on the Street. Then, according to one account, on the evening of June 20, 1871, Drew received a surprise visit at his home from Woodward, who, being desperate for cash to consummate his corner, offered to let Drew off his short contracts and even share his profits with him, if Drew would lend him a quarter of a million dollars. With a benign smile, Drew agreed. Vastly relieved, Woodward left. "Wanted me to give him a rope for him to hang me with," Drew remarked to another Wall Street man who, sitting in the rear parlor, had overheard the entire conversation.[4]

The following morning Woodward went to Drew's brokerage house in Wall Street but discovered that the firm knew nothing of a loan. Desperate, he waited for word from Drew, but no word came. At last he realized that he had been doubly double-crossed—by Drew, who had no intention of helping him, and by his fellow pool members, who had been secretly unloading their stock on him. Woodward announced his suspension, Rock Island plummeted, and a dozen brokerage houses that had dealings with him failed. When Drew and White closed their joint account on June 26, they shared a loss of $102,000. But Woodward was wiped out; in time, he filed for bankruptcy.

That summer and fall Drew must have looked on with incredulity as the Erie Railway toiled in controversy and litigation under the management of Fisk and Gould. Drew himself made peace with the boys by an agreement of June 23, 1870, whereby he loaned the impoverished line $301,000 for a year, on condition that Erie drop all legal actions against him. Safe on the sidelines, he watched in serene disbelief as Erie hit new lows in the market, and angry English stockholders ripened fresh attempts to oust Fisk and Gould, paralleling a mounting campaign by reform-minded Gothamites, incensed by revelations of fraud in the construction of the new county courthouse, to overthrow Erie's ally, Boss Tweed.

Drew saw his former colleagues only rarely now but had no trouble following the spectacular career of Fisk, who after the president was the most reported-on man in the nation. It was now common knowledge that

Josie Mansfield, having milked Fisk for tens of thousands, had thrown him over for Ned Stokes, an elegant idler who conspired with her to blackmail Fisk by threatening to publish his letters. Then, in October 1871, just as Boss Tweed was arrested for fraud, Stokes and Mansfield brought several legal actions against Fisk that promised juicy revelations in court. It was too much for Gould, the embattled president of Erie. At his urging, on December 31, 1871, Fisk resigned as Erie's vice-president. To one of Uncle Daniel's morality, it must have seemed like a judgment. Rascality was no reason to oust a man, but a fancy woman was something else again.

It was just about this time that Fisk paid his last call on Drew. Having probably come on business, he was received by his host in a parlor of the Union Square mansion. A half century later, Drew's son William still remembered Fisk departing blithely down the front stoop to whichever of his six carriages awaited him. One wonders what guise the caller had assumed for the occasion: Admiral Fisk, in a blue nautical jacket with gold buttons; Colonel Fisk of the Ninth Regiment of the New York State National Guard, with gold braid and epaulettes, and a beaked cap topped by a plume; or just Prince Erie, tophatted, in a fancy suit with a low-cut vest displaying a cherry-sized diamond. Whatever his role and attire, he came to the sedately dressed Deacon flaunting jewels and gold, the Flash Age personified, an actor to the core.

A few days later he was dead, shot mortally in a downtown hotel by the enraged Stokes, whose shaky reputation had crumbled before the onslaught of Fisk's counsel in court. On January 8, 1872, Gotham gave him a full-fledged military funeral procession with a flag-draped coffin, and six colonels and a general in attendance—a spectacle not equaled since the death of Lincoln (a comparison that some thought obscene). To be sure, the Stock Exchange refused to lower its flag to half mast, and Erie stock surged on the market, but Fisk the rogue and clown was mourned sincerely by multitudes because he had made life fun. Uncle Daniel kept a distance from the funeral, but he too would miss this glad-handing punster, all snap and gumption, whom you could not stay mad at for long. Fisk was only thirty-six when he died.

With Tweed arrested and Fisk dead, the times were changing. As further proof, on March 11, 1872, a new Erie board of directors hostile to Gould was elected, and Gould himself, after legal and physical eva-sions and an overnight siege in the building, was ousted from the presi-dency and the premises. This was of great interest to Drew who, with Gould eliminated and Erie stock surging on the market, conceived a great urge to bear it. Accordingly, he sold Bischoffscheim & Gold-schmidt, an eminent London banking firm that was heavily interested in Erie, a contract to deliver 50,000 Erie at 55 before the end of the year, in a gamble in the grand style that at once became the talk of the Street.

Whether by luck or connivence Erie declined mysteriously that summer, letting Drew close out his contract in August for a profit of perhaps a third of a million. For Uncle Daniel, it was just like old times in "Ayrie."

In late June, Daniel and Roxanna went with their son and daughter-in-law to Long Branch, the fashionable coastal resort in New Jersey that had attained new popularity from the summer visits of President Grant. For a full month the Drews stayed at the Ocean House, where August Belmont and Leonard Jerome were among their fellow guests. It was not like Uncle Daniel to frequent a stylish resort. Probably his son Bill was responsible, arguing that money should be enjoyed, that if his father worked like a money king, he ought to play like a money king, too. Naturally the old man shunned the racier entertainments provided, but he and Roxanna attended a lavish masked ball at their hotel, where a large fountain bubbled with eau de cologne, and when they worshiped at the Methodist church nearby, found the president in the congregation. Meanwhile Bill was driving the finest private team at Long Branch, passing other noted trotters on the lanes. Well rested, by early August Drew had returned to the city, where he closed out his Erie contract at a profit, then left with his son and their wives for Saratoga: the Drews were living it up.

Back in New York in September, Drew found that Bischoffscheim & Goldschmidt, the new controlling power in Erie, had trapped the leading shorts in that stock: Gould and Henry N. Smith, Gould's longtime friend and partner, a dapper little man with a huge red mustache and ample red muttonchop whiskers. Delighted, the Old Bear at once became a bull, buying thousands of shares of Erie so as to squeeze the shorts all the more. On the nineteenth a *Herald* reporter found Drew in his cosy little basement back office at 51 Exchange Place and asked if he had helped corner Erie. "Well, I have a few sheers of Ayrie," said the old man, his eyes twinkling, twirling a cigar. "But I ain't in any pool nohow."[5] Little more would he say.

Thereafter Erie stock became so scarce that at one point the trapped shorts had to pay as much as 3 percent or six hundred dollars for the use of a hundred shares for one day. Drew remonstrated with one of his brokers: "Three percent is too much. The boys can't stand it, and it ain't right, nohow. Make it about one and a half for what sheers is wanted today. It'll suit the boys better'n any higher rate, and besides, they'll pay out their money freer, and they'll last a good deal longer. There's no sense in bein' so hard on sech good boys as Jay and Henry. Make it one and a half, sonny, until you hear from me again."[6]

Gould and Smith were well aware that this canny generosity was meant to stretch out their agony profitably. After a last desperate attempt at evasion, they settled with Drew, taking losses estimated at between eight hundred thousand and a million dollars. Some thought that Drew, in clipping these master manipulators so royally, had done a signal service to the nation.

At the end of September Drew was off inspecting the line of the Wabash Railroad, to whose board he had just been elected. When he got back, he found a new situation on the Street. Gould and Smith had had a sudden falling out, occasioned by Gould's covering his own short contracts but not Smith's one balmy Saturday when Smith had joined most of Wall Street at the races. Sticking close to his office, Gould received advance word from Washington that the U.S. Treasury had decided to relieve a stringency in money, which was bound to send the market soaring. As a result Gould switched to the bull side of the market and realized a handsome profit, while Smith took a sizable loss. Enraged, Smith vowed that he would so ruin Gould that in a year's time Gould would be roaming the city's streets with a hand organ and a monkey, while Gould announced that he would live to see Smith driving a dray wagon. One of Wall Street's great friendships had soured.

This in itself need not have concerned Uncle Daniel, but he learned as well that Gould and Smith were now playing opposite sides of the market, each bent on ruining the other. Aware that Gould was heavily long of the stock of the Chicago and Northwestern Railway, in early October Smith joined a clique of insiders in bearing the stock. Drew reflected. In the market, Gould had been a major enemy of his and Smith a minor one. Drew himself had often shorted "Nor'west," sometimes with delightful results, and the insiders were doing so now. Therefore he too went heavily short of the stock, for which Gould took his contracts and calls.

Over the following weeks, however, Northwestern went not down but up, surviving various bits of bad news and being buoyed with the rest of the market by the landslide reelection of Grant. Rumors circulated that the insiders had gone over to the bulls, following which, on November 20, as Drew and the other bears watched helplessly, the stock spurted twelve points to close at 95. That Gould had achieved a brilliant corner was confirmed when it reached 99 the next day, and then on Friday, November 22, soared in the afternoon without any sellers appearing. As it hit 112 on the ticker tape, brokers and speculators poured out of their offices and braved a pelting rain to the Stock Exchange, where jostling throngs watched as Northwestern continued its surge, to 130, to 150, even as reports circulated that Gould had been arrested. When the gong rang the closing hour of four, the stock closed at 200, having doubled in a single hour. Astonishment reigned, amid hysteria and fears of a panic.

It was quickly confirmed that Gould had been arrested just as he was launching the rise. The order was served on the complaint of President

Peter H. Watson of the Erie Railway Company, who brought suit to recover $10 million that Gould had allegedly misappropriated while president and treasurer of Erie. Watson's charges were based on an examination of the books of Smith, Gould, Martin & Company, which had just been delivered to him by Henry N. Smith, whose affidavit supported Watson's complaint. Since Horace F. Clark and Augustus Schell—two Vanderbilt men who had helped him in the corner—immediately posted the $1 million of bail, Gould was able to rush back and resume direction of the Northwestern corner within a scant half hour.

The arrest of Gould raised Wall Street's excitement to a fever pitch. Mere stockjobbing by the bears, insisted Gould, but President Watson— sincerely, no doubt, given his reputation for integrity—denied any knowledge of a corner; he had long wanted to bring action against Gould but had found grounds to do so only upon gaining access to Gould's old account books. Straightfaced, Smith insisted that the timing of the arrest was sheer coincidence and that his sole motive was to bring a criminal to justice. Uncle Daniel, although he admitted to prior knowledge of the arrest, denied being involved in any way, as perhaps he was not, although he hoped to take advantage of the coup.

On Saturday November 23, the drama's chief actors spent the day entrenched in their respective offices. Gould arrived at his brokers', Osborn & Chapin's in Broad Street, looking as imperturbable as ever, disappeared inside, and thereafter was seen by few, being wary of a second arrest. In his New Street office, Smith was conferring frenziedly with his lawyer and fellow bears in quest of legal loopholes. As for Uncle Daniel, he arrived early at his basement office in Exchange Place and remained secluded there, while the brokers and clerks in the front office settled up the first of his losses. All day a half dozen messengers shuttled between him and the exchange, while a private secretary came out of his office at intervals to check the ticker tape just outside the door. Occasionally the Old Bear himself would emerge with a rumpled, worn silk hat pushed back on his head, his trouser leg pulled up half way to his knee by a bootstrap, and a cigar between his teeth. Bending over the ticker tape, he would blow a clear space through the clouds of smoke, check the latest "Nor'west" quotation, then retreat back into his office. The tape gave only bad news—Northwestern was around 150—but whenever a fellow bear was ushered in to see him, he received him with unfailing good humor. Although he had no time for reporters, a *Herald* man caught him briefly as he hurried out later.

"Things have been lively?"

"Yes, kind o' that way."

"You were somewhat interested in Northwestern, weren't you, Mr. Drew?"

"Well, some people will have it so. Of course I was, in a certain way."

He clamped a cigar between his teeth, as if to keep from laughing or crying.

"But not to any extent, one way or the other?"

"Oh, the boys have had a little sport, you see, and I don't blame 'em, even if I had a few sheers." A peculiar grin crept over the old man's face.

"You had only a few?" said the reporter, but Uncle Daniel hurried away.[7]

Having put Northwestern to 200 on Friday, on Saturday Gould lowered it to 150 to let the small fry settle. Settle they did, waiting in line at Osborn & Chapin's to step into the private office and learn what terms they could get. Contracts were compromised at 150, or even less, if otherwise the victim might fail, since the subtle Gould wanted not a hecatomb of bankrupts, as on Black Friday, but juicy victims squirming on the hook. The bears submitted stoically, one of them boasting afterward that "the boys have stood up and been slaughtered like men." Several of them, their ordeal over, were lying prostrate on sofas in their offices.

But Uncle Daniel was not of a mind to be slaughtered, especially since, as one of the big fish in the net, he could hardly count on Gould's gracious mercy. He was short about 20,000 shares, of which he had covered half at the outset, using stock borrowed from the widow of the late Henry Keep. Even so, he faced an immense loss on the other half of his contracts, regarding which Gould now invited him to "step up to the captain's table and settle." It took a great deal of effort by the bulls to get Drew over to their office, but he put in an appearance at last. "There, boys," he said, brandishing his check, "there's the cash you've stolen from me. I hope it'll do you good."[8]

The check, however, was for a settlement at 125. Gould and his allies had no intention of letting the Deacon off so cheap, when the lesser shorts were being tenderly clipped at 150, so the old man went back to his basement. The evening before, talking to a *Times* reporter, Uncle Daniel had observed jokingly, "I hearn Nor'west's a-risin'." Now, as the stock closed at 230 on Saturday, someone remarked to him, "Northwestern is rising." "Risin'," he said, "*risin'?* It's *riz!*"[9]

On Sunday November 24, even as a *Herald* caption announced the "Agony of Daniel Drew," the Old Bear pondered and prayed. Perhaps his prayers had to do with "them air Nor'west sheers," although in the past he had been singularly unsuccessful in enlisting the Almighty's aid in his Wall Street operations. When trapped by Gould and Fisk in Erie exactly four years before, he is said to have taken a Christian brother's advice and had recourse to prayer, only to report to his adviser, "It's no use, brother—the market still goes up."[10] Aside from prayer, there was little left but blind hope.

On Monday morning the first quotations disabused him; the corner was as tight as ever. So he stepped over to Osborn & Chapin's and resumed negotiations with Gould. Gould, beaver-hatted as usual, was in a back room, sitting in an armchair before the fireplace, his feet on the marble mantel. Sitting down with this black-bearded, quiet little man, Drew found him disarmingly courteous and amiable as for a few minutes they chatted about "old times," but the moment they broached North-western, Gould became inexorable. Fixing Drew with his deepset, inky eyes, Gould informed him that he had received considerable instruction from him in a "financiering" way and often to his cost; nevertheless, he had always paid his losses like a man and now expected Drew to do the same. Drew then made another compromise offer, but Gould spurned it, so the Old Bear went back to his basement again.

Yet neither side was inclined to be adamant. Drew was tired of being "twisted," while Gould's sole aim was to extract all he could from him without the trouble and expense of litigation. So another meeting was arranged for eleven that night at Gould's residence at 578 Fifth Avenue, attended by Gould, Clark, Augustus Schell, Richard Schell, Drew, Drew's former broker David Groesbeck, and several others. The remaining holdout, Smith, was not present, having repeatedly told Gould to go to hell. After a protracted debate, with various terms proposed and rejected while Groesbeck acted as umpire and Uncle Daniel haggled and protested, an agreement was hammered out. He would settle at 125.

All Tuesday Drew and his various brokers were busy reckoning his debts and paying up; he lost at least $1 million. Interviewed at his home that evening by the *Tribune*, he frowned whenever Northwestern was mentioned but disclaimed any knowledge of a corner. He more than frowned, however, when on that and later occasions reporters informed him that President Watson of the Erie was thinking of having him arrested on the grounds of the stock issue of 1868.

"Arrest me!" he exclaimed to one reporter. "Why, how kin they arrest me? What have I done? Did I ever injure anybody? Who's goin' to arrest me? Why, I never heerd of sech a thing. What have I done? They can't arrest me. Mr. Watson, eh? Wal, they can't prove anything against me!"[11]

Meanwhile Henry Smith, having taken legal counsel, bought up all the Northwestern preferred stock that he could get and offered it in lieu of the common. Heated negotiations followed between the nervous little redheaded man and the quiet little black-bearded man, until Gould at last gave in, allowing Smith to settle at the preferred stock's price of 100. Immediately the common stock fell to 85 on the market and the great Northwestern corner was history. No one had gone bust, but the bulls had made two or three million dollars. Said one small operator, as the excitement subsided: "I should like to see Dan Drew, old Vanderbilt, little Hank Smith, and Jay Gould fight a quadrangular duel, and each one kill his man!"[12]

As a master operator, Jay Gould now reigned supreme. His alliance with Clark and Augustus Schell had led the newspapers to dub the bull clique in Northwestern the "Vanderbilt party," which irked the Commodore mightily. On November 26 he sent a statement to the papers protesting their linking of his name to Gould's in the corner. Since July 1868, he emphasized, he had had nothing to do with Gould and had urged the same course on all of his friends. Asked by a *Sun* reporter why he thought ill of Gould, Vanderbilt explained: "His face, sir; no man can have such a countenance as his, and still be honest." The Commodore, it turned out, believed quite literally that God Almighty had stamped each man's character on his face. Claiming to have read Gould like an open book the first time he saw him, he pronounced him "a damned villain."[13] Invited to comment, Gould remarked that the Commodore was in his dotage.

For Gould, to be sure, there remained that matter of the Erie suit to recover $10 million. Astutely, he opened negotiations with President Watson, convinced him that a compromise would be in Erie's interest, offered a settlement that the Erie board approved, and so turned their moral crusade for restitution into a mere business transaction between equals. Thereafter, Drew had little fear of arrest.

Bruised by his loss in Northwestern, Henry Smith retired from Wall Street to live on his stud farm near Trenton, where he devoted himself to breeding fast trotters. With him to the farm went the books of Smith, Gould, Martin & Company. One day in the spring of 1874, when there was talk of further litigation, some men appeared at the farm while only a hired man was on the premises, seized the books, and made off with them. The books were never heard of again.

Meanwhile Uncle Daniel remained in the market, but he steered clear of Gould. Twice now, each time in the wake of Grant's election to the presidency, Gould had relieved him of a million. Was this sinister little man his nemesis?

CHAPTER 20

Uncle Daniel Buys the Dream

In 1872, even while gambling millions in Erie and "Nor-'west," Daniel Drew sustained a remarkable interest in the quicksilver mines of California, the glorious future of the port of Baltimore, the fertile grainlands of Indiana and Illinois, and the vistas of the magnificent West. The names of these far-reaching ventures were Quicksilver, Canton, "Can'da Sethern," and "Waybosh." In nourishing them, his mind had embraced the continent.

Drew's interest in the Quicksilver Mining Company of New York became apparent on February 28, 1872, when he was elected to the board and promptly became the company's president. The company owned the New Almaden quicksilver mine in California, some sixty miles southeast of San Francisco, and in the 1860s had inspired high hopes based on the growing use of quicksilver in mining. Since then, alas, the price of quicksilver had dropped, earnings had plummeted, and the stock had been depressed on the market, becoming a volatile fancy shunned by serious investors. The company's new president, however, explained to all and sundry that the price of quicksilver had recovered dramatically, so that the company would soon pay off its mortgage bonds and start paying regular dividends. Impressed, even sharp Wall Street professionals bought the stock for a rise and sold puts in it, unaware that the mortgage was probably being paid off with borrowed money, and that as they were buying, Uncle Daniel was selling. Over a period of months Quicksilver stock rose, fell, rose, and fell again, but never quite went anywhere. So happy was the company's president with this performance that at the next election, in February 1873, he showed up with a majority interest and got himself reelected president. Not that he felt the slightest urge to visit the quicksilver mines in California. Why should he when right here on Wall Street Quicksilver had turned into a gold mine?

There were other gold mines, too. On March 12, 1872, Drew went to Baltimore in the company of Vanderbilt and department store magnate A. T. Stewart, two of the richest men in the country, to look over the property of the Canton Company of Baltimore. This real estate company had shared fully in the land boom of the 1830s, when unscrupulous Wall Street stockjobbers had hoisted its stock to an astronomical 300, until the Panic of 1837 and its aftermath had brought it crashing down. Since then it had been the most despised of fancies, but now, the company assured this visiting trio of millionaires, a new era was dawning for it. With the approaching completion of the eighteen-mile-long Union Railroad, linking up all railroads entering Baltimore and connecting them with tidewater on the Canton property, Baltimore would become the second if not the first port of the nation, luring to Canton's wharves the produce of a continent. Canton's present, then, was profitable and its future dazzling.

Drew and his companions inspected the Canton property and the railroad, and Drew, upon returning to New York, stepped up his purchases of stock. At the annual election on June 6, four New Yorkers joined the board: two Vanderbilt men, Drew, and Eugene N. Robinson, the young son of Drew's long dead partner Nelson Robinson, through whose Wall Street firm Drew did much of his trading. Thereafter, having acquired a majority interest in the stock, the Old Bear sang its praises. At his urging, in November 1872 the small Wall Street banking house of Biedermann & Company bought 18,600 shares at 100 for a rise to 150 or 200. Instead, the stock sold off, then plunged dramatically in the decline of September 1873. Ernst Biedermann later asserted that most of the stock had come to him from Drew through a blind, on which transaction he claimed a loss of $1 million. Whether or not Uncle Daniel believed in the Canton dream, he believed in the movements of its stock.

Quicksilver and Canton were Daniel Drew's little Eries, speculative toys that he manipulated more or less at will. Canada Southern, on the other hand, he viewed as a solid investment, a vision of transcontinental scope. Such visions were all the rage in the early 1870s, for with the completion of the Union Pacific and Central Pacific railroads in 1869, forming the first transcontinental line, Wall Street and the public anticipated vast new commerce with California and the upper Mississippi valley, causing a scramble among Eastern railroad men to secure connections with Chicago and the West. The great prize was snapped up by Vanderbilt, who, in acquiring control of the Lake Shore and Michigan

Southern Railroad in September 1869, pushed his New York Central through to Chicago.

If the Commodore was stretching his mind and schemes to national dimensions, Drew was inclined to do the same. In the spring of 1870 the experienced Canadian railroad promoter William A. Thomson came to New York City to interest Gotham's money men, Drew among them, in the Canada Southern Railway. This was a projected 229-mile line that would lie wholly in Ontario, Canada, linking Buffalo and Detroit by a road so direct and gradeless, said Thomson, that it must become the shortest, fastest route between those cities, in fact, between the Eastern seaboard and the great American West. Persuaded by Thomson's arguments, on May 23, 1870, Drew and six others signed a formal agreement to subscribe to $2 million of Canada Southern stock and reimburse Thomson for his promotional services and expenses. The names of the major subscribers constituted a roster of financial luminaries: Sidney Dillon, a director and future president of the newly completed Union Pacific; John F. Tracy, president of the Chicago, Rock Island and Pacific Railroad, and soon to become president of the Chicago and Northwestern Railroad, both lines linking Chicago to the West; William L. Scott, president of the Erie and Pittsburgh Railroad; Milton Courtright, a prominent civil engineer and railroad contractor, and a director of the Lake Shore, Rock Island, and Union Pacific lines; and Daniel Drew, whose name on Wall Street still ranked second only to Vanderbilt's. Drew saw in the venture a chance to let his Eastern capital, like Vanderbilt's, reach out toward the West, toward profits, glory, and empire.

Armed with Yankee commitments, promoter Thomson swung into action. Surveyors were hired, directors elected, and Milton Courtright chosen as president, while Director Drew served on the five-man executive and finance committee, and so become a power in the road. To be sure, when word circulated that a portion of the company's first-mortgage bonds would be offered to the American public, a skeptic who signed himself "Vindex" wrote a letter to the *Chicago Railway Review*, casting doubt on the Canada Southern's anticipated earnings, dividends, and connections. But in April 1872, when $5 million of the bonds were offered in New York, they were snapped up by small investors. Track laying began on May 1 and continued over the balance of the year. If the directors were especially jubilant, their sharing in the profits of the construction company, as later alleged, might have had something to do with it.

But this was just the beginning. Rather than depend on existing connections in Michigan, in 1871 the Canada Southern promoters organized a second company in the United States, called the Chicago and Canada Southern Railway, to link the Canada Southern to Chicago. Drew sat on this board, too. Then in 1872 the Canada Southern men acquired a controlling interest in the projected Michigan Midland and Canada Railroad in order to connect with other roads in Michigan, and, at the eastern end of their line, leased the little Erie and Niagara Railroad to assure connections there as well, which gave them four railroads to date.

But bigger things yet were on the anvil. From the outset the construction of the Canada Southern aroused great interest in the management of the Toledo, Wabash and Western Railway, an important line running southwest from Toledo, Ohio, across Indiana and Illinois to the Mississippi River. The Wabash boasted of traversing America's breadbasket and providing a gateway to the West, but it was desperate for a more effective eastern connection than the congested Lake Shore line now dominated by Vanderbilt, a connection that the Canada Southern promised to provide. Accordingly, President Azariah Boody of the Wabash was eager for a close collaboration. To link the two roads, therefore, the Canada Southern in 1872 organized a fifth railroad, the Toledo, Canada Southern and Detroit Railway, which would join Toledo to Detroit and both cities to the Canada Southern.

Uncle Daniel greeted the Canada Southern's tie-up with the Wabash enthusiastically, touting "Waybosh" stock with the same zeal that he had shown for Quicksilver and Canton. Indeed, on December 22, 1871, he had secretly formed a pool with ten others to operate in Wabash stock. Among his fellow pool members were Sidney Dillon of the Union Pacific, and three railroad presidents: Azariah Boody of the Wabash, Milton Courtright of the Canada Southern and the Chicago and Canada Southern, and Gen. John S. Casement of the Toledo, Canada Southern and Detroit. Besides speculative profits, however, these eminent gentlemen had their eye on the next Wabash election, thus precipitating a keen struggle with the Vanderbilt men of the Lake Shore line. As a result, on October 2, 1872, Drew and seven other Canada Southern men were elected to the Wabash board, supplanting the Lake Shore men as the dominant interest. Drew and his partners seriously intended to ally the two roads closely and perhaps even consolidate them by leasing one to the other. In the Canada Southern scheme of things, Wabash would be railroad number six.

But why stop at six? On Wall Street, by August 1872 far more was hinted at. In Uncle Daniel's fertile brain, it was said, a fabulous scheme had flowered. Not only would the Canada Southern hitch up with the Wabash, but across the Mississippi it would also get control of the Hannibal and St. Joseph Railroad, and beyond that something called the St. Joseph and Denver City, which connected with the Union Pacific. Linked to all of these (railroads seven, eight, and nine), the Canada Southern would acquire, besides the links already planned at Chicago, a second great connection to the West.

Here was continent-sized ambition, an empire-builder's dream. Had the Old Bear become a long-horned bull at last? Or were these reports mere gossip, or another ploy to manipulate the market? Probably there was something to the rumors—a tentative intention, if not a hardheaded scheme. Even for the Speculative Director, it was time to think transcontinentally. If Vanderbilt could get to Chicago; if Jay Cooke, America's foremost investment banker and propagandist, could project his 1800-mile Northern Pacific Railroad through a vast wilderness that he publicized as being rich, fertile, empty, and ripe for settlement; and if a host of like enthusiasts, teeming with vision and rapacity, could buy the dream of the West, why not Uncle Daniel as well? Holed up in his back office in Exchange Place, puffing his cigar, pacing and ruminating with one eye on the ticker tape, this sly old cheat bought the dream.

But 1873 was not a good year for dreams. The boldface ads for Cooke's Northern Pacific bonds, for the bonds of the Chicago and Canada Southern Railway, and for a host of other issues ran month after month in the newspapers, which was sure evidence that the bonds were not selling. Both at home and abroad there was a vague malaise in the air, a nascent climate of doubt and suspicion. The one transcontinental line already in operation was hardly a success. Debt-burdened and hastily built, the Central and the Union Pacific traversed vast empty spaces rich in Indians, bison, and rattlesnakes, none of which offered business to a railroad. Worse still, starting in January 1873, a Congressional investigation confirmed the colossal corruption engendered by the Crédit Mobilier of America, the Union Pacific's construction company, which had enriched insiders while systematically bribing Congressmen and government officials. Henceforth, all railroad promotions were suspect. Then in May 1873 a financial panic broke out in Europe, and as European capital contracted, the major source of funds for American railroad expansion dried up. With no help likely now from either the government or the public, many New York bankers and brokers had to dig deep into their own firm's pocket to sustain some pet railroad project to which they were heavily committed.

Surely no such difficulties marred the outlook of the Canada Southern line, with its board of millionaires. The last rail was laid on February 20, 1873, creating an almost straight-line route between the Niagara and Detroit rivers. Since neither of those rivers had been bridged as yet, the management delayed the road's opening until spring, when local trains began operating over part of the line. Admittedly, this was a far cry from a through express route between Buffalo and Chicago, but the first annual report, dated June 1, voiced confidence. At the road's western end there was a ferry that could accommodate whole trains at a time, while at the eastern end the International Bridge was supposed to be finished within the next sixty days. Of the whole system's projected 697 miles, 408 were now completed. However, because of the system's peculiar position, the report explained, no part could be opened until the main Canada Southern line and certain connections had been finished.

Four hundred miles of railroad had been constructed with scarcely a penny of earnings, at a projected cost of over $30 million; the International Bridge was still unfinished; and the bonds were not selling—did this not add up to trouble? Yet with only a little more work between Detroit and Toledo, and the opening of the International Bridge, through service could be initiated between Buffalo, Detroit, and Toledo, with connections to Chicago. It was no time, then, for discouragement. To meet the continuing drain of construction costs, the affluent Canada Southern directors endorsed the company's notes in large amounts. Since certain London investors had taken Canada Southern bonds in the past, the management still hoped to place large amounts with them in order to meet the company's notes as they fell due. The bonds would sell—they had to! Earnings were just around the corner.

No word of this was leaked to the public, who had every reason to believe that the Canada Southern's promoters could cope with any chance financial embarrassments. Drew alone could surely do so, even though last year he had taken a heavy loss in Northwestern. Surely he could do so, even though he was also loaded up with Quicksilver, Wabash, and Canton. And even though, as far back as the tail end of March 1873, there had been much puzzlement in Putnam County when work on his new Collegiate Institute at Carmel—a planned companion to the Female Seminary—had stopped, and the workers had suddenly packed up and left, no explanation given.

And surely there was no cause for alarm when, in that same month of March, President Boody of the Wabash brought suit against Drew and three others in the Wabash pool, the recent existence of which was thereby revealed, alleging that the charges of Drew's brokerage house in administering the pool had been excessive and that Drew and others had at the same time operated in the market on their own, as a consequence of which Boody demanded an accounting from all the defendants. The pool, it seemed, had ended up with a loss, while Uncle Daniel had netted a profit in the stock on his own. Perhaps the Wabash and the Canada Southern would not be linked so closely after all, since Boody could always rekindle the courtship by the Lake Shore line, whose management was as eager as ever to tie in with the Wabash. Had Uncle Daniel been "smart" just once too often?

On May 14 Drew and his son attended the annual meeting of the seminary board at Madison and, on the following day, the seminary's commencement. The worthy founder was reported by the *Christian Ad-*

vocate to be in quite feeble health; prayers were offered for him. Indeed, although he had been healthy all his life, at seventy-six Drew looked increasingly frail and was living in the shadow of mortality. He now rarely attended the Canada Southern board meetings in New York, and when the new executive and finance committee was named on July 8, for the first time he was not on it. Meanwhile his wife had suffered a stroke and was now partially paralyzed and confined to her bed, with little prospects of recovery. This was a fearful change in the long established patterns of his domestic life.

In July he went to Putnam County to stay with his son Bill in the Italian-villa-style mansion that, with his father's help, Bill had bought from Daniel Drew Chamberlain in 1867. But here too mortality stalked him. After a prolonged illness, his younger brother Thomas died at his residence in Drewville on July 31. A prosperous farmer and drover and more recently the trustee of a local bank, Uncle Thomas had been closely identified with the community all his life and was loved and respected by everyone. Daniel saw him buried near their parents in the old Clift Cemetery, now the Drew Cemetery, on the low knoll across the road from Bill's mansion, where Daniel meant to be buried himself. Then in mid-August Bill was off on a tour of the Adirondacks while his father, like many Wall Streeters, repaired again to Long Branch, where the Brewster paper reported that he stuck to his rooms at the Ocean House "like a burr to a sheep's back."[1] Apparently he was still not well.

By September Drew and most Wall Street men were back in the city. While he stayed quietly at home, the rest of them surveyed the business climate and were gratified by what they saw—busy factories, crowded shops, much construction, and a fine harvest. Yet this time of year always aroused uneasiness as money flowed to the West and the South, producing a stringency in New York—circumstances that once again spurred Gould to his most insidious and disruptive efforts. First, he launched a campaign to force up the price of gold, causing many to fear another Black Friday, and then, having reportedly sold out at the top, he began a new move to drive stocks down. His ruthlessness in finance, coupled with his aloofness—he was reticent and abstemious by nature, shunned parties and the sporting life, preferred books and botany—caused him to be hated and feared more than anyone. Black-bearded and secretive, with a lack of scruples unrelieved by Fisk's bonhomie, Vanderbilt's magnetism, or Drew's quaint rusticity, he had been christened "the Mephistopheles of Wall Street." Now, the whole financial community awaited his next move nervously. Suddenly a manipulation of Wabash stock depressed it from 70 to 66. For this, many held not Gould but Drew responsible, although the old man was ailing at home. More likely, the manipulator was Drew's broker, Kenyon Cox.

On Sunday September 7, vague bearish rumors brought many Wall

Streeters back early from a weekend at Long Branch, and on the next morning the New York Warehouse and Security Company, crippled by bad loans to railroads and railroad construction companies, announced its suspension. The stock market declined, then rallied, but a seed of doubt had been planted. Other Wall Street houses with heavy railroad commitments began scrutinizing them and calling in loans.

For several days the market remained skittish and vulnerable. On Wednesday, the tenth, rumors that the firm of Biedermann & Company was in difficulty caused Canton to plunge on the market. Uncle Daniel, who had long since unloaded much of his holdings on the firm, was said by some (wrongly, it would seem) to have inspired the sell-off. On the eleventh the *Herald* announced that "a sense of calamity, indescribable and perhaps superstitious, overhangs the street—a vague, intuitive expectation of something that is to be, but is not yet." Then, early in the exchange's morning session on Saturday September 13, came a startling announcement. Kenyon Cox & Company, Daniel Drew's brokerage house, which was considered one of the soundest on the Street, had suspended! Wall Street was stunned; prices plummeted.

The firm of Kenyon Cox & Company had been established in May 1870 by Kenyon Cox, whom Drew had long known as a member of another brokerage house allied with David Groesbeck & Company. Since Groesbeck was about to retire, from that time forth Drew gave Kenyon Cox the bulk of his Wall Street business and joined the firm as a special partner with limited liability, contributing $300,000. The firm and its partners were closely associated with Drew in his Canada Southern commitments and in his Wall Street operations. Consequently, news of its suspension provoked heated debates at the exchange as to whether Drew was now a special or a general partner. Special said some, which meant limited liability; not so said others who insisted—rightly, as it developed—that after the firm paid $300,000 on his Northwestern losses the previous November, Drew had become a general partner with full liability. The thought that, despite such liability, he had allowed the firm to fail, dismayed operators and fueled a panicky sell-off in which Wabash stock took the worst of the beating.

Shortly afterward Kenyon Cox himself appeared at the exchange, where he told friends that the suspension was probably temporary and in no way the result of speculation, but rather of the endorsement of Canada Southern notes. On Monday September 8, he said, a cable from London had informed the railroad that English investors declined to take any more of its bonds. An emergency meeting of the railroad's backers had elicited promises from them to each take a quota of the unsold bonds. However, some who were out of the city could not be reached in time, which meant that, unexpectedly, the endorsers of the company's notes would have to meet their obligations, totaling about two and a quarter million dollars. The Kenyon Cox partners could meet their immediate obligations, but not notes for a much larger sum due in thirty days, so in justice to the firm's creditors, Cox had suspended at once. He expressed the opinion that Canada Southern would soon meet its obligations, thus allowing Kenyon Cox & Company to resume. As for the firm's creditors, they would be paid in full.

Cox's statements allayed the excitement at the Stock Exchange, but rumors concerning Drew abounded: he wanted a panic, he feared a panic; he was manipulating the market or was a victim of it; he had let others come to grief, he had come to grief himself. Some believed that he was now heavily short of the Vanderbilt stocks; all were convinced that he was looking out for number one. This assumption was evidently shared by the Canada Southern board, for President Courtright told a reporter that in his opinion Drew could have prevented the failure. All over Wall Street, in the press thereafter, and at the Fifth Avenue Hotel on Sunday evening, Drew was denigrated while Cox and the other partners got sympathy. Yet Cox himself deplored these reports, stating repeatedly that Drew had in no way connived at the firm's suspension, that he had acted fairly throughout, and that if he had foreseen the crisis three weeks before, Drew would surely have saved the firm by converting some assets into cash.

While a police officer stood guard outside the firm's offices at 31 Wall Street, junior partners and clerks toiled feverishly at mounds of paper work, but Uncle Daniel was nowhere to be seen, nor had he been for some time. He was said to be ill or not ill, to be in Europe, at Saratoga, at Lake Mahopac. A reporter, however, found him at his Union Square residence, where in the briefest of interviews the old man confirmed that he was sick and refused to discuss the failure of the firm. Thereafter he remained tight-lipped, doubtless on the advice of his attorney.

In testimony three years later, Drew claimed that he had not known that the firm would fail until the night before, and he blamed the failure on Cox's speculations in Wabash. Yet one wonders if an old hand like Drew, even if distanced by illness, would have lost track of the firm's operations so completely. Certainly the crisis was abrupt and unforeseen, and in no sense, as some conjectured, a trick of Drew's to bring on a panic. The troubles of Kenyon Cox & Company and the Canada Southern were painfully real to him, for financially he was committed to the hilt. Perhaps, as one report at the time suggested, he refrained from rescuing the firm on the advice of his lawyer, so as to first learn the state of its affairs, an attitude that might have struck the other Canada Southern men as betrayal. In any event he had plenty to worry about: as a general partner with full liability, he was the only one of the four partners with assets enough to satisfy the creditors. That he of all people should find himself so vulnerable implies an uncharacteristic lapse of judgment, probably attributable to illness or age.

On Monday September 15, the rumors about Drew persisted, but no further failures were announced. Kenyon Cox & Company's customers, notified by telegram to take possesion of all stocks and bonds deposited with the firm, arrived in the city to find their securities intact, which encouraged hopes that the firm would resume. On Wednesday the seventeenth, the Canada Southern board held its first meeting since the Kenyon Cox failure in the company's offices at 13 William Street. In the absence of Drew and others, five directors discussed the company's financial situation, debated what the president would tell the stockholders at a meeting on the following day, and voted to get emergency loans from two Canadian banks for $55,000, a fraction of what the company needed. Meanwhile the stock market was reeling under a surprise assault by the bears, while distrust grew and rumors circulated to the effect that Gould was heading a bear clique, that the Western railroads were in trouble, and that a great failure was imminent.

With these reports hot in their ears, at 11:00 A.M. on Thursday the eighteenth, the Canada Southern stockholders convened at 13 William Street to be reassured by President Courtright, who stressed that the company's embarrassments were temporary. The stockholders received the report favorably, but adjourned to consider it at a later date. As they left the meeting, however, those who proceeded up William Street the two short blocks to Wall Street must have noticed at once excited crowds gathering up ahead, from whom they heard the most astonishing news: Jay Cooke & Company had suspended!

The collapse of America's foremost investment house was a financial thunderbolt. When it was announced late that morning at the Stock Exchange, a great roar went up and men gaped in disbelief and dismay. Jay Cooke, that giant of finance—he whose inspired efforts in the Civil War had saved the Union by selling millions' worth of government bonds not to the bankers but the people; no petty stockjobber or grasping profiteer, but a great, bold, hearty, open man, a faith-inducer, a visionary whose dreams were immense; a collaborator of the Barings and the Rothschilds, and a friend of presidents—this most successful and creative of bankers, his name an article of faith, had failed, being borne down by the interminable costs of pushing a railroad through the wilderness.

Immediately an avalanche of selling hit Wall Street, as on the Stock Exchange floor traders literally tore their hair and rushed about, collided, gesticulated, or stared dazedly. Banks tightened up on loans, money rates soared, and by afternoon two well-known brokerage houses—one of them Vanderbilt's old ally Richard Schell—had "gone up," compromised by a precipitate decline in Western Union. Hundreds more would follow, it was thought. One Canada Southern director, informed that afternoon, offered the bland hope that "the present feeling" would subside within a few days. Gould, however, was already spearheading a savage attack on the market, and Drew, when he heard of Cooke's failure at home, must have grasped instantly how all chances of a Kenyon Cox resumption had been blasted.

On Friday September 19, as a dark sky sent down a pelting rain, throngs flocked to Wall Street to crowd into their brokers' offices or stand outside under umbrellas in a thick black mud, their ranks packed solidly for blocks. At 10:00 A.M. the first click of the ticker tapes riveted everyone's attention in the offices, as the decline continued. Not even the resources of a Vanderbilt could keep his stocks from falling with the rest. Firm after firm failed; runs developed on banks. The banks were especially vulnerable, being seasonally short of cash and holding as collateral quantities of dubious railroad securities whose value was shrinking by the minute. Desperately they called in their loans, even as hard-pressed brokerage houses bombarded their customers with urgent margin calls that few were able to meet. Meanwhile news came of failures in Philadelphia and of business at a standstill in Baltimore. By the end of the day, the failures in New York were reckoned at 23, 25, or 30—nobody was sure of the count.

Housebound and ill, Drew was in a desperate position. His Wall Street firm was doomed, the Canada Southern directors were down on him, his brokers wanted margin, his creditors money, he was unwell, and to top it off, his own kin were after him again. Yes, at this very worst of times, his granddaughters Georgiana, Josephine, and Louise were clamoring for money. He had given them bonds guaranteeing payment of the $70,000 due each of them under the terms of their father's will, and up till now the arrangement had worked out nicely because he had had the use of the money, while the girls got their interest twice a year. Now, however, alarmed by the panic, the granddaughters feared lest their capital be lost. Joined by Antoinette—the baby of the family, married now and just come of age—they called on their grandfather to either produce the amounts due them or give them further security. Since money was nowhere to be had, Granddad talked to his lawyer. As a result, on Saturday September 20, he secured the granddaughters' claims against him with four mortgages, each for $70,000, on his property on Union Square. He could not keep the matter from his ailing wife, since she had to sign the mortgage papers, too. But the sacred trust was secure.

Little else was. On that same Saturday Augustus Schell's Union Trust Company, a firm tied to the Vanderbilt interest, suspended, proving that

even Vanderbilt houses could go bust. In all, four banks and eleven brokerage firms failed in New York that day, and more in Philadelphia, Albany, Chicago, and Toronto. While depositors made runs on banks, brokers at the Stock Exchange shouted themselves hoarse in hectic trading,
until the exchange's governing officer, in an act without precedent, declared it closed until further notice. At the time of the closing, Wabash
stock, having sold at 70 in early September, stood at 44; Canton, once
quoted at par, at 75; and Quicksilver common, worth 30 a week before,
at 24—prices ruinous to the Old Bear's tranquillity and credit. He was
being bled just like the bulls.

Could the panic be stopped? Not even Vanderbilt had the ready cash
needed to sustain the banks and restore confidence; the only hope was
the government. President Grant and Secretary of the Treasury William
A. Richardson arrived in New York Saturday evening and spent all Sunday conferring with leading merchants, financiers, and railroad men at
the Fifth Avenue Hotel. Closeted with the president, Vanderbilt urged
the government to place twenty to forty million greenbacks in selected
banks, but Grant and Richardson refused, convinced that they lacked
the authority. Instead, they proposed the conventional solution that the
U.S. Treasury buy government bonds in the open market in order to put
currency into circulation.

Uncle Daniel kept to his home, but that evening a *Sun* reporter
sought him out and wangled an interview. Yes, he had read reports in
the papers that he and Gould had profited from the panic and were con-
spiring to depress the market further. This was nonsense, of course, as
he himself had made no money at all in the panic, and had had no dealings with Gould for many years. The cause of all these failures? "All I
know about it is that it's a very bad affair for the country, and one it won't
recover from soon." On this note, he ushered the reporter to the door.[2]

During the week that followed, the treasury bought bonds to no
avail, the Stock Exchange remained closed, runs developed on savings
banks, and failures multiplied. With currency in short supply, business
was paralyzed nationwide, while distress was spreading. On the six-
teenth anniversary of the Fulton Street Prayer Meeting, initiated during
the dark days of 1857, the North Dutch Church was jammed.

Uncle Daniel had more to do than pray. It was obvious that Canada
Southern could not be bailed out, nor could Kenyon Cox & Company
resume. After a two-week grace period, the Kenyon Cox partners could
be forced into bankruptcy, which would put his assets at the mercy of the
creditors. So on Monday the twenty-second, he deeded his Union
Square mansion to his son for one hundred dollars, subject of course to
the four mortgages just executed, but took care not to have the new deed
recorded. Then two days later he sold Bill a thirty-seven-acre farm in

Carmel for a dollar. Likewise on the twenty-fourth, heeding the advice of the senior partner of Boyd, Vincent & Company, the brokerage house where he had his biggest account of the moment, Drew transferred that account—including numerous railroad bonds and his Quicksilver, Canton, and Canada Southern stock, valued in all at $2 million—from his own name to that of his son, who was apparently unaware of it at the time. In any event, the transfer was nominal only as the old man still had full control of the account.

By the end of the month the runs on banks had subsided, and the Stock Exchange reopened its doors, but this was of no help to Drew. While the hometown paper in Carmel was insisting that rumors of his difficulties were "all bosh," that he could stand a dozen failures like that of Kenyon Cox & Company, he himself knew better.[3] On October 11 he was served at home with a summons to answer a complaint by William L. Scott, a former Canada Southern director, who as a creditor of Kenyon Cox & Company was petitioning the U.S. District Court to declare Drew, Cox, and the two junior partners bankrupt and to seize their estates to satisfy their creditors. Scott, a prominent railroad and coal mine operator of Erie, Pennsylvania, was a Canada Southern and Wabash stockholder, and as such seems to have had it in for Uncle Daniel, especially upon learning of the four mortgages of September 20, which he saw as an attempt by Drew to defraud his creditors. Scott had therefore become the attorney for many of those creditors and a representative of the three railroads—the Canada Southern, Chicago and Canada Southern, and Toledo, Canada Southern and Detroit—whose notes the Kenyon Cox partners had endorsed. By legal means, he was out now to either extract a settlement from Drew or force him into bankruptcy.

For Uncle Daniel, this lawsuit put a cutting edge to things. Worse still, although he had only a two-fifths interest in the partnership, he would have to bear the brunt of the settlement. So while the market, depressed further by the news of the lawsuit, kept on going down, attorneys conferred, and Scott demanded a list of his assets. From memory, the old man dictated a list to a clerk and sent it on. When the case came up in federal court October 18, counsel on both sides agreed to a week's delay, as negotiations were in progress. Two more delays followed, then on November 8 it was announced that the case had been settled, and the proceedings were dropped. A week later the settlement was made public, and the world learned what it had cost Uncle Daniel to avoid bankruptcy.

The settlement had been effected by two documents signed on October 28. The first was an assignment by Drew's three partners to Scott of all the firm's real and personal estate, to be sold by Scott under stated circumstances in order to realize the creditors' claims. No creditor was to sue Drew for any claim against the firm for eighteen months, nor was the assignee to bring any action against him unless he defaulted in the attached guarantee. Sixty-one creditors signed the agreement.

Accompanying this assignment was a second document signed by Drew, whereby he promised to pay Scott any portion of the firm's debts over and above the amount realized under the assignment, up to half a million dollars, half of the sum to be paid in a year's time and the rest in eighteen months. As security for his half-million-dollar guarantee, Drew was to deliver to a trustee—David Dows, a New York broker and railroad man—assets evaluated at that amount, including eight mortgages that he held on the property of other individuals, 4,000 shares of Canton, and six mortgages that he now made on property of his own: 130 acres adjoining the seminary in New Jersey, one stock farm in Westchester County, and four in Putnam. Should Drew default on his guarantee, any or all of this property was to be sold by Dows at public auction, the proceeds to be delivered to Scott.

Before this complicated agreement could be implemented, the mortgages had to be signed not only by Drew but also by his bedridden wife. How much she grasped of it all is uncertain, but having recently signed four mortgages on her home, and now being asked to sign six more on every scrap of land remaining to her husband, she balked. Drew coaxed and argued, promising in compensation to give her legal possession of the house, its furnishings, and their horses and carriages, and so at last she made her mark. (Being partially paralyzed, she had reverted to her X.)

So the Old Bear bought himself a respite of from twelve to eighteen months. Meanwhile Stephen H. Alden, a dealer in puts and calls, was suing him for misrepresenting Quicksilver stock, demanding to be reimbursed for a market loss of $202,000. Then Ernst Biedermann and his partner brought a similar suit, charging that Drew had fraudulently unloaded Canton stock on Biedermann & Company, for which they demanded $1 million plus interest. To make matters worse, the *Tribune* played up both actions as a warning to investors, while the Boody suit over the pool in Wabash was continuing, and the Carmel paper reported in great detail the agreements with Scott, so that all the home folks knew of his predicament. Well, he must have reasoned, it's the sick heifer that the hounds will go for.

In the market, Wabash stock had recently touched below 35—just half its price in early September; Drew had long since been sold out by his brokers at a loss. At the Wabash election in Toledo on October 1, Kenyon Cox and the Canada Southern men had been reelected, but not Drew, while William L. Scott had joined the board. Gone forever was the grandiose dream of combining five or six or nine railroads in order to

forge a new route to the West. Both the Wabash and the Canada Southern were now fighting for their financial survival.

Throughout the fall and early winter the Canada Southern board held
a series of meetings in New York, but the Old Bear, who in any event
was still unwell, kept shy of them. As of December 1, Canada Southern
trains at last began operating over the International Bridge at Buffalo,
inaugurating through service between Buffalo and Detroit. But with
business shrinking in the wake of the panic, the company faced meager
earnings and the possibility of default on its bonds in January, so it was
readying a proposal for the bondholders. At a meeting on January 15,
1874, Milton Courtright stepped down as president and Drew resigned
from the board in absentia, while the inescapable Scott rejoined it. Although Drew clung for a while to his Canada Southern securities, in time
he sold them, too—for a loss, combined with the Wabash stock, of about
one million dollars. So ended his one great bullish venture, involving a
railroad on whose tracks he had probably never laid eyes.

The bubble had burst, and the Flash Age was dead. It was as dead as
Jim Fisk, who when his carriages had been auctioned off and his huge
debts paid, left his widow only a bare million; as dead as the prestige of
Boss Tweed, scapegoat for the sins of hundreds, who that same grim
November was convicted on 204 counts of an indictment and would finally die in prison; as dead as the thriving high times of Justice George
G. Barnard, who with two other Tammany magistrates had already been
impeached and allowed to resign. Gone were the easy old corruptions,
to be replaced by new ones; gone was a whole generation of dream merchants, con men, and connivers, swept away by the twin tides of ruin
and reform. Shackled with debts, Uncle Daniel faced a new, bleak age.
The country was in the throes of a depression. It would last six years.

CHAPTER 21

The Last
Great Caper

In December 1873 Wall Street heard that Daniel Drew was
again seriously ill, and then, that he was dying. To confirm the rumor,
the *Times* sent a reporter to interview Dr. Jared Linsly, Drew's personal
physician for nearly forty years. The report, said Dr. Linsly, was nonsense. His patient was improving steadily, could be up most of the day,
and would soon be riding out in his carriage. Contrary to rumor, Linsly
added, his patient's indisposition in no way resulted from the recent financial troubles.

So Uncle Daniel was seen again on Wall Street. Still, at seventy-six
his health was not what it had once been. Throughout 1874 he was intermittently ailing, which, combined with his losses in the panic, caused
him to lie low in the market. With himself often indisposed and his wife
an invalid, it might have been a somber household had not children and
grandchildren come for lengthy visits in the winter. That spring Bill's
wife Clara was there for her confinement, and on May 7 she gave birth
to a daughter, Catharine. This child was doubly welcome in that the
couple's firstborn, Daniel, had died there in infancy in February of the
previous year. Catharine was the Drew's ninth grandchild.

By late winter the old man was able to get out again. On February
25 he presided at the annual Quicksilver meeting, where he reported
the company's financial condition much improved. His son Bill joined
the board, and he himself was reelected president. In May, however, he
was ailing, so he sent his son in his place to attend the yearly meeting of
the seminary board at Madison on the twentieth. Of course they made
the old man president again. Meanwhile Roxanna, in spite of her bedridden state, likewise continued as president of the McClintock Associa-

240

tion, a Methodist ladies' organization providing financial aid to needy theology students. Moving Roxanna now was a problem, so that in late August, when they went to Putnam County as usual, their party of four made exclusive use of Cornelius Vanderbilt's private railway carriage, no doubt with a bed installed for the invalid.

The nation too was ailing, with multitudes prostrated by unemployment, poverty, and despair. Railroad construction had ceased, finances were in confusion, old managements were retiring, and new faces were coming in. In Boston on March 11, 1874, Jay Gould and several friends became directors of the troubled Union Pacific, while the indestructible Vanderbilt, having saved the Lake Shore line in the panic, was flinging himself with gusto into the rate wars that would preoccupy him for the rest of his life.

As a casualty of the panic, a "lame duck" in the parlance of Wall Street, Uncle Daniel had no share in these mighty doings. Although smarting from losses, he may have considered himself well out of it as his favorites of yesterday, Canada Southern and Wabash, foundered in debt and disarray. As for the two large holdings that remained to him, Quicksilver was prospering and Canton, thanks to the revenues of the Union Railroad, was weathering the storm. By spring, however, the quartet of granddaughters were back after him about that sacred trust. Since declining real estate values had eroded the security that the four mortgages on his home provided, they wanted that security increased. He could not refuse, but what did he have left to offer them? On June 12, 1874, he deposited with a trust company his 9,200 shares of stock in the New Jersey Steamboat Company, a controlling interest in the People's Line; his fortune was flaking away.

He could not let it happen. He had to get money—tens and hundreds of thousands—to settle the sacred trust, pay off his daughter (whom he also owed from the estate), give the seminary its quarter-million endowment, and save his farms from foreclosures. Besides, as his health improved, he yearned for action. Not just for a few little gambles like the puts in Canton that he sold in December and January, but millions at stake, the Street stood on its ear. He was going back big in the market.

When Drew returned to Wall Street in February 1875, the stock market had been stagnant for a year and a quarter. Going back as a bear, he sniffed out those companies that smelled ripe for receivership—Northwestern, Union Pacific, Western Union, and Wabash—all of which he shorted heavily. Wabash especially seemed vulnerable, having defaulted on its bonds and passed into receivership, so he sold vast quantities of calls in it, certain that its depressed price—it was selling around 11—would be whittled down to nothing.

On March 1, 1875, the stock market sprang to life as Pacific Mail soared three points and as Union Pacific and Western Union advanced a point and a half each. Wall Street was electrified, Drew was stunned, and Gould emerged as king of the bulls. On the very next day Gould, master already of the Union Pacific, gained control of the railroad's arch rival, the Pacific Mail Steamship Company, whose bitter competition with the railroad he vowed to transform into a lucrative harmony. This bold move sent Pacific Mail stock leaping ahead another two points. Thereafter, while solid investment issues like the Vanderbilt stocks languished, a select group of depressed fancies—Pacific Mail, Union Pacific, Western Union, Northwestern, and Erie—surged ahead. For the first time in months, Wall Street was an exciting place to be.

But was this advance to be trusted? Both Pacific Mail and Union Pacific had been tainted by scandal, while Erie had yet to recover from years of mismanagement. Indeed, could any market move spearheaded by the sinister Gould be more than a speculative ploy? Yes, insisted much of the press, asserting that the nation was on the verge of a spring recovery: once the severe winter receded, trade would pick up, railroad earnings rise, factories reopen, and unemployment drop. Especially fervent on the subject were the *Times* and *Tribune*, which certain competitors accused of complicity with Gould.

Fueled by hopes of recovery, the boom in the stock market was cheered by nearly everyone; to decry it seemed unpatriotic. Yet on Wall Street such perversity existed, and worse. On March 3 and 4 large amounts of gold were suddenly withdrawn from the market, so that the price surged to 115, while the rate for call loans—the loans that banks made to brokers—soared briefly and then fell back again, leaving the stock market feverish and unsettled. Clearly, someone was engineering a lockup of gold designed to reduce bank reserves so that the banks would have to call in their loans to brokers, forcing operators to sell heavily and depress the stock market. The chief culprits were identified as a prominent New York banker on the board of an important Western railroad and a venerable churchgoing speculator whose kindly advice to fellow operators had been known to speed them to ruin.

It was true: caught disastrously short of the market, Uncle Daniel had resolved to extricate himself by effecting a lockup of gold, and to this end formed a pool with Eugene N. Robinson, his chief broker, and with the financier Russell Sage. Robinson was a modest, cool young man still under thirty but already worth several million dollars, who on his own responsibility in 1873 sold out his customers' accounts before the panic and saved them from fearful losses. Sage was a well-known Wall Street speculator who had served in Congress in the 1850s and was now a bank officer and vice-president of the Chicago, Milwaukee and St. Paul Railroad, in whose stock he speculated much as Drew had once done in Erie.

He joined Drew because he also found himself caught short of the market in the sudden advance promoted by Gould, with whom he had a score to settle anyway, since Gould had ousted him as president of Pacific Mail.

What Drew and his allies had in mind was a medium-sized corner and panic, a lockup of just enough gold to make money tight, flatten the stock market, and extort high interest rates for gold, without keeping the gold price up so long as to bring vast hoards of it flowing to New York from elsewhere. The whole scheme was based on a set of minute calculations: how much gold had been sold short by speculators; how much of it importers and exporters needed for the demands of their business; and how much was available from California and abroad. Initially, the three allies agreed to buy $6 million of gold, with Drew and Robinson acting through a joint account established with Robinson's firm, while Sage operated independently.

On March 3 and 4 the three partners, having made further short sales of stock, suddenly called in all their loans. Meanwhile Sage's bank did the same, while Drew negotiated loans on his Canton and Quicksilver stock, and the partners bought their $6 million of gold, which they then borrowed on from Sage's bank and other lenders in order suddenly to make both gold and money scarce in the market. As a result, the price of gold in the Gold Room climbed at once to 115, while money rates and the loan rate for gold also surged.

But the manipulators had miscalculated. Much money lay idle in the uptown banks, so when the money rates on Wall Street rose, it flowed there to give brokers all the loans they needed, bringing the rates back down again. As for the higher loan rates for gold, since no speculators were short of gold at the time, importers who needed gold bore the full brunt of the squeeze, but even this proved temporary as gold came in promptly from Canada. Meanwhile stocks were just as buoyant as ever, on hopes of a reviving spring trade. So far, then, the squeeze was a fizzle. Russell Sage informed Drew that he would not buy any more gold.

Drew and Robinson shrugged off this faintheartedness and in a single day, March 7, bought $4 million more of gold. Thereafter, however, money still refused to get tight, while stocks kept on advancing. The conspirators had now acquired $11 million of gold, of which they held five off the market, while loaning out the remaining six in day-to-day loans in the Gold Room at varying rates determined by themselves. By March 16 gold was at 116½. With further hikes doubtless in the offing, the foreign exchange market was disrupted, importers were distressed, and trade impeded. When a *Times* reporter sought Drew out at Robinson, Chase & Company in Broad Street and questioned him point-blank, the old man responded at length:

My boy, I've really no interest in this thing. Some folks say I'm the leader of a pool, but I hain't anything to do with it. I almost never have any gold, and at the present time don't own a dollar of it. It's all folly; why don't they let me alone? I'm trying to run along pleasantly with everybody in the Street. But I can't. First the bulls charge me with being a bear, and then the bears say I'm a bull. They shouldn't orter. I'm only trying to make a few dollars in a quiet, easy way, and would like to do it without being bothered. Here's my brokers. They'll tell you I hain't anything to do with the thing—ask 'em—I won't keep them from telling the truth. They know all about me.[1]

Then on Friday the nineteenth, to the surprise of everyone, gold declined slightly on heavy sales in the Gold Room, mostly on the part of the clique. The other Gold Room brokers were mystified. Had the clique members broken ranks, or was this a "scoop" designed to lure traders into selling short, then raise the price and trap them? So secret were the pool's operations that even the shrewdest observers were baffled, and they remained so over the next few days as the price fell below 116. By now, there were whispers of a betrayal in the clique.

The whispers were true: Russell Sage had decided to get out. Finding gold and money still available, stocks buoyant, and himself being called unpleasant names, he wanted out, and accordingly had double-crossed his partners. From the nineteenth on, he had been selling gold in the Gold Room while secretly covering his shorts and going long of the stock market. When they discovered this, Drew and Robinson acted quickly to absorb Sage's $2 million of gold, maneuvering so adroitly that for two days no one was aware of their action. The partners' revised opinion of Sage they likewise kept to themselves. When a *Times* reporter saw Uncle Daniel in Robinson, Chase & Company's office on the nineteenth, he was unconcernedly reading a *Times* account of the spring freshets on the Delaware, where the breakup of an ice gorge had carried away some culverts on the Erie line. Removing his spectacles, the ex-director of Erie remarked, "This yere ice george's washed away all the culprits along the Ayrie road"—a comment that the *Times* thought too priceless not to publish.[2]

Having taken Sage's $2 million into their own joint account, Drew and Robinson continued to buy gold. But even as they called the tune in the Gold Room, Gould was having his way at the Stock Exchange, where day after day prices were surging on huge volume amid the wildest excitement. What was the good of putting gold to 116 or even 120, if one's short position in stocks became more perilous by the day and the hour?

At this point Eugene Robinson suddenly learned that his partner had deceived him regarding his position in the market. Perhaps Uncle Daniel too had been secretly dumping some gold, or perhaps Robinson had got wind of a lengthy conference between Drew and Gould in a broker's office on the morning of March 23, which had probably resulted in a compromise settlement of Drew's short position in Northwestern or some other stock. At any rate, Robinson confronted Drew at once, demanding that their joint account in gold be closed. Uncle Daniel remonstrated, calling him "sonny" and cajoling him as only he knew how, but Robinson remained adamant. So the joint account was closed with a profit, and Robinson transferred $11 million in gold to a new account that Drew opened for himself. Robinson wanted no more of the gold squeeze, but against his advice Drew persisted. So secret were these transactions that Wall Street never got word.

Even as the gold was transferred, stocks were spurting upward. On Holy Saturday, March 27, Union Pacific reached 61¼—a rise of over twenty points in a month. Gold was at 116, but who cared? Late that afternoon jubilant young speculators who had recently been lunching on a sandwich and a mug of beer, packed into Delmonico's on Fourteenth Street to dine sumptuously and sip fine wines, then scattered to the theaters, only to reassemble later at Delmonico's and other elegant establishments, celebrating well past midnight the resurrection not of Christ but of Wall Street. As for Uncle Daniel, whatever time he could subtract from his devotions on Easter Sunday he gave over to reflections on the market and the folly of trying to buck Gould and prosperity. Like it or not, the gold squeeze was a bust.

On Monday March 29, stocks opened strong, then fell back on news that gold had risen to 116¾. Meanwhile Drew's brokers withdrew another $5 million of gold from the market, boosting the loan rate for gold to 1 percent a day, or an astounding yearly rate of 365 percent. Immediately gold surged to 117, one brokerage firm failed, and after violent fluctuations stocks closed feverish and weak. Marshaling all his resources, Uncle Daniel had put gold up as far as he could; now it was time to slide out.

On Tuesday the thirtieth, Wall Street was more excited than at any time since the panic, as throughout the day prices rose and fell in a frenzied and mysterious confusion. Clearly something big was afoot, although no one quite knew what. In the Gold Room gold opened at 116⅞, then plummeted as vast quantities of it, some said a good $10 million, were sold out, mostly by the brokers of Daniel Drew. Was this the end of the squeeze or another "scoop" to trap the unwary? Some holders of Drew's puts in gold leaped at the chance to buy it cheap and sell it to him dear, but when they looked for him, he was nowhere to be found.

Yes, where was Ursa Major? Others were looking for him, too—holders of the calls in Wabash that he had sold so freely in February, when the company had passed into receivership. Lately the stock had surged on vague rumors of a new transcontinental connection, and many call holders had demanded the stock from Drew, who had honored every contract. Others, however, had held out for higher prices, then demanded delivery of the stock for the thirtieth. But now, when they flocked to Robinson, Chase & Company in Broad street, just across from the Stock Exchange, they were informed that Mr. Drew was taken ill at home and had given no instructions with regard to his contracts. Anxiety gripped the holders of the calls, many of whom were counting on the stock to fulfill obligations of their own. Suddenly Uncle Daniel's health was worth more than diamonds and pearls to them. But was he really sick, too sick to even forward instructions? It smelled fishy.

At this point Dickerson & Company, another firm with which Drew occasionally did business, received a telegram confirming that Drew was too ill to come to the Street and asking them to notify Robinson, Chase & Company, his regular brokers, that they should attend to his contracts. When news of this curiously roundabout way of sending instructions leaked out, it disconcerted the call holders. Then Robinson, Chase & Company announced that they would not recognize the authority of orders addressed to a third party. Only instructions addressed to them in Drew's own handwriting would do, they said, to obtain which they had dispatched a messenger uptown.

It was now close to 2:15 P.M., the deadline for settling the day's obligations. In panicky confusion the call holders rushed across the street to the exchange, spreading reports that Drew was either ill or faking it, that he had welshed on his contracts, and that he had ditched his partners in the gold pool and was up to all kinds of tricks. Stocks broke on the news, but Wabash soared to 18 on heavy volume as the call holders had the stock bought in for Drew's account. Hysteria also reigned in the Gold Room, where in the wake of Drew's massive unloading, gold closed at 115. The bears were jubilant and the bulls dismayed, until it occurred to the latter that Drew's defaulting on his contracts would put the call holders short of stocks, at which point the stock market rallied. Thanks to Uncle Daniel, the day had been a stunner.

Late in the afternoon Robinson, Chase & Company received a telegram from Drew, announcing that he would come down to the Street tomorrow and see to his contracts himself. Those bruised by the sudden selloff were cynical: of course he'll come, they said, now that the harm has been done. All that afternoon and evening the prime topic of conversation among Wall Streeters was Drew and his alleged ill health; never had the Old Bear been denounced so roundly. Yet a few noted that a sudden drop in the price of quicksilver in San Francisco could in itself have made a man of his years genuinely ill. Some also argued that if he "laid down" on his contracts, no one would ever buy his privileges again, to which others replied sourly that the whole affair must grieve him terribly, since he had always insisted that he "never did like to catch the boys nohow."[3] In everybody's mind loomed the question, would the old man show the next day?

At exactly 9:31 A.M. on Wednesday March 31, Daniel Drew stepped out of a carriage in Broad Street and entered the offices of Robinson, Chase & Company. Word spread fast. As the brokers arrived at their offices, their clerks passed on the news. By 10:00 A.M. the galleries of the Stock Exchange and the Gold Room were packed with visitors, while excited brokers assembled on the floor. At the exchange, a representative of Robinson, Chase & Company quietly informed the gathering crowd that Mr. Drew was down today and would honor all his engagements. Wall Street breathed a sigh of relief; stocks rose and gold declined in quiet trading. Meanwhile at 18 Broad Street a much-discussed old gentleman was receiving a stream of visitors, each with a contract in his hand.

Commenting on Uncle Daniel's return, the *Herald* pictured him as looking "fresh and rosy," and the *Sun*, as smiling benevolently, his eyes sparkling with their wonted brilliancy. The *Evening Post*, on the other hand, observed that it was not beyond reason that a man pushing eighty should be indisposed for a day and even neglect his obligations—especially obligations falling due at no fixed time —but only the *Daily Graphic* sent a reporter to see this maker and shaker of markets for himself. What he saw at 10:30 that morning, in an inner office at 18 Broad Street, was an old man sitting in a big leather-bottomed whitewood chair, clinging nervously to its arms, a low-crowned hat on his head, his face flushed and scowling, his body shrunken up within the wrinkles of his clothes. Eugene Robinson introduced the reporter to Drew.

As the old gentleman turned and tipped his head slightly he retreated into the further corner of his chair, as if on his guard, and kept his eyes warily fixed on his visitor.

"I called, Mr. Drew, to talk to you about the prospects in the Street today."

"The Street is all right," he replied quickly, and then added after a pause, as if it had just occurred to him, "and I'm all right."

"Mr. Drew, are you—"

Mr. Drew began to move slowly around in his chair, and Mr. Robinson came quickly to the rescue.

"Really, sir," said Mr. Robinson, "all there is to be said is that Mr. Drew was confined to his house yesterday, and without orders we could not attend to his engagements. Now that Mr. Drew has given us instructions, we are doing so."

"Yes," said Mr. Drew. "I'm all right."

But the reporter would not let it go at that.

"You saw, Mr. Drew, those statements in two of the morning papers against you?"

"No, I ain't seen no papers."

"Would you like to see them?" And the caller offered to produce the papers in question from his pocket.

Mr. Drew let go his hold on the left chair arm long enough to raise his thin hand in deprecation, while his face was contorted as if he had just taken a bitter medical potion. At this point a gentleman present suggested that the statements referred to were attacks inspired by Jay Gould.

"I s'pose so," said Mr. Drew, as he shook hands with his visitor. Three seconds later he was deep in the mysteries of the financial situation, whither he was accompanied by Mr. Robinson.[4]

The financial mysteries that claimed him were his contracts in Wabash and gold, settling which would cost him tens of thousands of dollars. Although the gold squeeze was at an end, the press would long remember him as a gambler who had obstructed the commerce of the nation, while much of Wall Street clung to its conviction that by settling one day late he had probably avoided far greater losses.

March had been a cruel month for Uncle Daniel; April and May would be crueler. When he closed out his once profitable gold account with Robinson, Chase & Company on April 26, it showed a loss of close to eighty thousand dollars. But a worse disaster awaited him in Wabash, where his vast short position had been only partially liquidated by his settlement of the calls in late March. In the bullish market of April, this vulnerable stock traded up to just above 16, threatening Drew with a huge loss if he settled his contracts now, but an even huger one if it continued to advance. His brokers—he had at least three or four—reflected that the old man's prestige was tattered, his credit shaky, his reputation for treachery unimpaired. They demanded more margin, but he had none to offer. Therefore, each acting on his own, they bought the stock in for him and settled his contracts at a loss. Soon afterward, in mid-May, Wabash sank below 10 on expectations of an ultimate foreclosure. So the Old Bear had been right after all: the company was rotten, the stock could only go down. But for him it was too late. His total losses in Wabash came to $1.2 million, a calamity from which he could not recover.

Lake Shore was next. In desperation—from March 29 on, just as he was getting out of gold—he switched to the bull side of the market, buying Lake Shore and selling puts in it at 70, in effect betting that Lake Shore would stay at or above this figure for months. This seemed safe since as a Vanderbilt stock it would presumably be supported by the Commodore. But in mid-May the business outlook darkened. Trade remained obstinately sluggish, while the great trunk lines fought their rate war more bitterly than ever, causing Erie to slip into receivership at last. Immediately public confidence in the railroads dwindled, stocks turned down, and Lake Shore plunged to 60, as word spread that Gould was attacking it.

Jay Gould attacking Lake Shore? The news stunned Drew and the bulls. Yes, that *enfant terrible* of the Street was now telling everyone that rail stocks were overpriced and shaky, that a revival of trade seemed unlikely, and that the panic had yet to play itself out. Needless to say, Mephistopheles had leaped nimbly to the bear side of the market and was reaping vast profits while the befuddled bulls were overwhelmed with losses. So much for the great boom in stocks and for the nation's long-awaited recovery.

But what was Vanderbilt doing? Some said that he had lost all interest in the market, others that he would trample the attacker yet, still others that not even he could sustain a stock against Gould.

"But where is Drew all this time?" a reporter asked some operators on May 28. "Oh, he has drawn out," was the answer. "Has he retired with a big pile, or is he crippled?" "You can bet the old man is badly hurt. Count him out."[5]

It was true that for this clash of titans, Uncle Daniel no longer qualified. Sold out by his brokers, he had lost in Lake Shore, too, in the amount of about four hundred thousand. Twice now in the spring of 1875, first as a bear and then as a bull, he had committed the costliest of errors by playing the opposite side of the market from Gould.

Little was left to him but Canton and Quicksilver. Eugene Robinson no longer held them, for after mutual recriminations—Robinson thought Drew wrongheaded and deceitful, while Drew blamed Robinson for selling out certain of his holdings—they agreed to a parting of the ways. On May 22 Robinson's firm delivered the old man's Quicksilver to Boyd, Vincent & Company, and his Canton and other securities to S.W. Boocock & Company, closing out the account. Meanwhile Robinson himself was off with other Wall Streeters on a tour of the Ozarks and the Kansas plains in a luxurious palace car as a guest, amid champagne feasts and euchre games, of the Atlantic and Pacific Railroad Company. But Uncle

Daniel stayed home to face the music, the death march of his last speculations. Three different brokerage houses now held his stocks as margin. He owed them all money, and the market, under the fierce poundings of Gould, was going down. One after another they sold him out. First the Canton stock went, for a loss of up to four hundred thousand, and then the Quicksilver—down sharply because the price of quicksilver had declined in California—for the last and greatest loss of all, his *coup de grâce* in the market.

March and April had been an unrelieved affliction for the Old Bear, and May an agony; in June he gave up the ghost. On June 3, at a special meeting of the Quicksilver board, he resigned as president and director, and his son as director; Vice-President A.B. Baylis, a Vanderbilt associate, succeeded him and promised a more active management. On June 10 his account with Boyd, Vincent & Company, still held in his son's name, was closed. His other accounts were closed as well, and his few remaining securities were delivered to him. Wall Streeters and journalists, being preoccupied with the rate wars of the railroad kings and the prestidigitations of Gould, hardly noticed, but for the first time in nearly forty years, Drew was completely out of the Street. It all happened so fast that it dazed him: he was wiped out.

CHAPTER 22

Bankruptcy

"**Y**ou must get out of this thing and not go into bank-ruptcy!" Drew's son Bill told him.[1] The old man agreed, vowing never to declare himself a bankrupt. Keeping his father solvent was now the ab-sorbing responsibility of William H. Drew. In the 1860s Drew's son had lived contentedly as a gentleman farmer in Putnam County, routinely seconding the old man on the seminary board but otherwise showing little interest in his affairs. Now, however, the young man rallied to his father with a great show of loyalty and support, as well as a surprising capacity for business. It was on Bill's energy, determination, and money that his father relied in his desperate efforts to prop up the tottering edifice of his fortune.

Their first concern was Scott, the financial nemesis who as assignee of Kenyon Cox & Company had disposed of the firm's assets to satisfy its creditors, but still demanded $295,000. Drew was liable for this entire sum, and since he failed to pay it within the period stipulated, Scott directed David Dows, the trustee, to sell Drew's mortgaged farms and certain other property at public auction. The sale was announced for June 24, 1875. But with real estate values depressed, Drew's son argued that the sale should at least be postponed, in hopes that prices would recover and the sale extinguish more of the debt. Accordingly, they in-tervened with Scott, promising to deliver more security. So the sale was put off, Drew handed over one hundred bonds of the Union and Titus-ville Railroad (a company already in receivership), and Scott agreed not to sell any more of Drew's property before January 7, 1876.

The sacred trusts claimed their attention as well. The semiannual

July interest on the granddaughters' estate and on the endowment promissory notes of the seminary and Wesleyan University were obligations on which the old man simply could not default. So he gave some of his little remaining Canton stock to Bill, who sold it and paid out the interest. But while he had given his daughter some bonds through Bill, he still owed her a third of what was due her under her second husband's will.

As for the nonsacred debts, what of them? What of the damages due Azariah Boody, following a court-ordered accounting of the transactions of the Wabash pool of 1872? Drew could only negotiate a settlement with Boody, signing four promissory notes on July 1, 1875, for a total of $20,000 plus 7 percent interest. And what of his puts and calls? On July 20 a Wall Street operator named David Van Emburg, holding a put of his for a thousand shares of Lake Shore at 70, tendered the stock and when he failed to find Drew on the Street, sold it for Drew's account and sued him for $9,375. This meant more litigation and another likely loss. Of the other privileges still out, some could be made due at the buyer's option to bring him further debts. In addition there were the architects' bills from the seminary and the female institute, certain old steamboat claims against him still in litigation, lawyers' fees, and his taxes. Bill could pay a little here, a little there, compromise this, and postpone that, but for how long?

At the same time there was a steamboat line to run. The old man had no time for it and had not seen a boat all year, relying for this as well on his son. In early March of 1875 William H. Drew had become vice-president and superintendent of the People's Line, in which capacity he closely supervised the annual refitting of the boats, including the introduction of steam heat in all the staterooms, at a cost of $115,000 in all. If Bill worked hard at the People's Line—he would kill himself, his father warned him—there was good reason, for the unsquelchable J.W. Hancox was up to his old tricks again. Ousted from the Troy run by the newly organized Citizens' Line, in 1874 Hancox had returned to the Hudson with the Merchants' Line, comprising but a single boat, the eleven-year-old *J.B. Schuyler*, skippered by his son Clement. One rainy night in Albany Clem Hancox flagged an approaching train to a halt, waved the passengers through the darkness to his boat, and made off with the whole trainload for New York before they realized they were not aboard the elegant *Dean Richmond*. On other occasions the *J.B. Schuyler* carried a band that struck up as it pulled alongside a rival, luring the rival's passengers to the rail, so that the other boat listed with one paddle wheel out of the water and lost speed, while the *J.B. Schuyler* raced ahead. To counter this stratagem, the People's Line at first lifted their boats' safety valves to create a screeching racket and then installed bands of their own. Finally in July 1875 the People's Line and the Citizens' Line bought Hancox off their routes, following which Hancox ran his vessel as an excursion boat for years. It was the last flare-up of old-time opposition on the river, but Daniel Drew was out of it.

One other incident marked William H. Drew's coming to the People's Line. In assuming the duties of vice-president, he replaced Capt. Alanson P. St. John, who, aged seventy-seven and suffering from ill health, had been forcibly retired by the board. St. John was one of the original founders of the People's Line, whose daily affairs he had run since Isaac Newton's death in 1858. Now, after over forty years his career was at an end; at times he seemed depressed. On the afternoon of April 23, 1875, he came from his home in New Jersey to inspect his favorite boat, the *St. John*, then undergoing repairs at the foot of Nineteenth Street. Chatting on the deck with the first mate, the retired skipper seemed in the best of health and spirits, following which he entered the steward's room alone. Five minutes later a shot rang out. Rushing inside the cabin, the workmen found the captain sprawled dead in an easy chair, a smoking revolver clasped in one hand, his features as composed as in sleep. The coroner's verdict was suicide "while laboring under temporary aberration of mind." Some attributed his depression to ill health, but others knew better: he could not live away from the river. For Daniel Drew it meant another old comrade gone. Who was left now but Vanderbilt?

Knowing that, thanks to Bill, the People's Line was maintaining its reputation on the river, brought the old man scant relief. His bedridden wife was dying, his own health was poor, his problems would not go away. In a time of depressed and still declining values, no security deposited by him ever seemed enough. The granddaughters tried to sell his steamboat stock, but nobody wanted it, so in November he handed over more stocks and bonds as a further guarantee of the $344,000 that he owed them. As for the Kenyon Cox & Company debts, having never received a penny from his partners, he was now out of devices to buy more time. On December 1 he signed an agreement permitting Scott and Dows to sell all the land and securities that he had given them; his long fight to save the farms had failed. Then in December two twelve-month puts in Canton were tendered by the holders, bringing him further losses; another would be tendered in January. Meanwhile he learned that the directors of the Canada Southern Railway, being desperate for money and unable to market more bonds, had acquiesced in the Commodore's acquisition of the road, so that another Drew egg ended in a Vanderbilt basket. If further irony were needed, he surely also heard of the recent dedication in Nashville of Vanderbilt University, a Methodist institution that the Commodore, newly beneficent under his wife's influence, endowed with a half million dollars.

It was a bleak New Year's. For the first time, he failed to pay the granddaughters their interest. And when Dr. John Fletcher Hurst, the president of Drew Theological Seminary, called on him at his home in December to pick up the check for the interest due on the endowment, Drew informed him that this was the last check he could give. Hurst looked Drew straight in the eye. "Mr. Drew, the report of such a failure as this will go around the world." "I know it," said Drew, "I have thought of it, but I can't help it."[2] And so the worst had come to pass. Or had it?

On January 27, 1876, Roxanna Drew died at the age of seventy-seven. Since she had long been an invalid without hope of recovery, her husband of fifty-five years must have seen her death as a release. On Sunday the thirtieth, a special train made up of the New York Central funeral car "Woodlawn" and the palace car "Duchess" took friends and family to Brewster, where a large throng attended the services at the local Methodist church, following which the cortege proceeded to the Drew Cemetery three miles south of town, where she was laid to rest with her husband's family. Throughout the ceremonies Daniel appeared quite feeble, walking to and from his carriage with difficulty, but at least he had buried her in style. Hers had been a quiet domestic existence, duly pious and charitable, completely conventional, almost unnotice-able. Her will, leaving her family gilt and turquoise vases, diamond rings, and silk and velvet dresses, was the will of a wealthy woman. Per-haps, in dying, she still thought of her husband as affluent.

On February 17 the seminary trustees met in special session in New York in the office of Judge E. L. Fancher, with Bishop Janes presiding in the founder's absence. Dr. Hurst recounted Drew's dismaying announce-ment of the previous December, and another trustee reported that he and Hurst had had a lengthy interview that very morning with Drew, who urged them to make other arrangements. Hurst produced Drew's promissory note of 1868 for $250,000 and the secretary read it to the board. It was payable on demand, but demanding, it appeared, would get them nothing. Their dilemma was vast.

Even though Drew's actual expenses to date on the seminary totaled $452,000, charity at first did not prevail. The board named a three-man committee "to take such proceedings, legal or otherwise, as in their judg-ment are judicious and necessary for the purpose of recovering the amount of the Note." The seminary's legal documents and papers were left with Judge Fancher, who was to inform Brother Drew of the board's action and confer with him. A resolution was framed for Fancher to pre-sent to the founder. It concluded: "Resolved: That we deeply sympathize with Mr. Drew in his present financial embarrassments, and thank him sincerely for what he has done for the cause of sound theological training in our Church, in founding the Seminary at Madison. And we at the same time express the ardent hope that he may still find it in his power to consummate all his arrangements for the establishment on a firm financial basis of the Institution that bears his name."[3] Clearly, the trustees were not about to let him off the hook. Moreover, Wesleyan University was surely in touch with them, since at a meeting of the executive committee of the university's board of trustees, held just four days later, a similar decision was made regarding Drew's promissory note for $100,000, which amount they determined to secure by "proceedings legal or otherwise."[4] Money, after all, was money.

Blow fell upon blow. His fortune was gone, his wife had died, and now men on whom he had showered beneficence were threatening to join the litigants already at his heels. His life had become a vicious round of lawsuits and mortgages, summonses and show-cause orders, fresh due bills and decade-old complaints. By late February his will caved in: he would declare bankruptcy.

On Saturday March 11, he and his attorney Alvin Burt filled out the petition in bankruptcy. In the total absence of account books and memoranda, the old man reached into his memory and fetched up a long list of debts and assets that were later confirmed as remarkably correct. As they completed page after page, to each he added his assenting scrawl, "D. Drew." The list of creditors was formidable. He owed the city $8,000 in property taxes; the granddaughters $344,000; Scott and the Kenyon Cox creditors $295,000; the seminary and the university $250,000 and $100,000 respectively; and various brokers, architects, and litigants some smaller sums, for a grand total in liabilities of $1,093,524.82. As his estate he listed his mortgaged real estate, the securities deposited in trust for his granddaughters, and other items, giving total assets of $746,459.46, which was a somewhat illusory figure, since it included unrealizable items like a claim against his Kenyon Cox partners for sums paid by him to discharge their debts.

Burt filed the petition in the clerk's office of the federal bankruptcy court that very afternoon. At the same time, he or a colleague saw to another little matter. Drew's sale to his son of his mortgaged Union Square residence in September 1873—part of his attempt to keep property from the Kenyon Cox creditors—had never been recorded, nor had the son's resale of the residence to his mother in January 1874. Accordingly, both deeds were now recorded at the county clerk's office, the more recent one "at the request of Roxanna Drew," who had been dead for a month and a half.

Word spread fast that one of Wall Street's most famous operators had filed for bankruptcy. When a *Times* reporter called, Drew estimated his total liabilities, optimistically, at about $600,000 and said that he hoped and believed his creditors could be satisfied. On Monday March 13, Drew's counsel attended a preliminary hearing held by Isaiah T. Williams, a register in bankruptcy, who formally declared Drew a bankrupt and issued a certificate of protection freeing the old man from his creditors' importunings at last.

"Not a very brilliant end to thirty years of stock-jobbing," remarked a Monday editorial in the *Times*. A *Sun* reporter interviewed the bankrupt, who chatted affably of his misfortunes, insisting that his assets would satisfy his creditors. Less rosy were the predictions on Wall Street, where the long-expected bankruptcy provoked not even a flurry in the market, scant sympathy, but much gossip. Brokers marveled not that the old man had failed, but rather that, being a speculator, he had kept his money as long as he had.

When the bankrupt's schedule appeared in the papers, much comment greeted the entries under "Wearing Apparel and Ornaments of the Person" and "Books": one gold watch and chain, valued at $150; one sealskin coat, valued at $150; ordinary wearing apparel, valued at $100; and one Bible, several hymn books, and other family books, amounting to $130—all items that he asked to have exempted. The sealskin coat was famous, for Eugene Robinson had given it to him amid much hilarity at the time of their operations in gold. As for the books listed—the elegantly bound family Bible, with its elaborate genealogical record, and the hymnals from his pew at St. Paul's, with his name gilt-lettered on the covers—they were noted mirthfully by Wall Streeters, who had never taken his piety seriously. Those who were among his creditors, however, noted tartly that his property was mortgaged to the hilt.

So the dread step had been taken, and his embarrassments were proclaimed to the world. Yet he maintained a calm and even cheerful countenance, seemed resigned, and talked freely. To a *Tribune* man he said: "I had been wonderfully blessed in moneymaking. I got to be a millionaire afore I know'd it, hardly. I was always pretty lucky till lately, and I didn't think I could ever lose very extensively. I was ambitious to make a great fortune like Vanderbilt and I tried every way I knew, but got caught at last. Besides that, I liked the excitement of making money and giving it away. I've given a good deal of money away and am glad of it. So much has been saved, anyhow."[5] Of course, he acknowledged, he should have made good on his philanthropies years before and left his children rich for life. But he added that his son was tolerably well off, his daughter had money from her second husband, and the granddaughters were amply secured.

Admirable composure, it would seem. His career of decades had been a huge and exciting game of chance, until luck failed him and he "got caught at last." No empire shattered, no great dream broken, only the solitary ruin of a gambler now resigned to his fate. One yearns for a hint of tragedy, a stabbing sense of futility, the bite of irony or regret.

Of course they were there, but well hidden. Not that bankruptcy brought shame in America. Forty years before, Tocqueville had noted that in a nation encouraging speculative boldness, failure was inevitably common and not thought to stigmatize the bankrupt. This attitude still prevailed in the depression-ridden 1870s, when respected businessmen failed by the thousands. But for Daniel Drew, having been a millionaire for over a quarter of a century, now ailing and feeble and too old to make a fresh start, bankruptcy was the final scorecard of failure. He had emulated giants like Vanderbilt and had gloried in fighting new money kings like Gould. But Vanderbilt had amassed a railroad empire in the East, and Gould was amassing a railroad empire in the West, whereas he had overstayed his luck and his judgment and lost his millions, thus compromising his church, his family, and himself. By every standard of the times, and above all by his own, he had failed utterly; in his own private thoughts, he was crushed.

Coming to comfort him in this time of desolation was his old friend the Rev. John Parker, who even more than his pastors, had served as his spiritual adviser over the years, time and again kneeling with him in private prayer, fortifying his troubled soul against the inroads of business. As the minister of various Methodist churches in New York and Brooklyn, Parker had acquired a reputation as a forceful preacher and an inspired singer who in noble causes could beg, sing, or argue money from the most parsimonious of gatherings. Drew had given generously to his causes and now, when the old man's giving was over, Parker hastened to his aid.

"Brother Drew," he asked, "you believe that God answers prayer?"

"Yes, I do," said Drew.

"And you believe that the Lord hears and answers the prayers of his children?"

"Yes, I do."

"I have heard you say a good many times on your knees, 'O Lord, whatever happens to me, save my soul.' Now then, perhaps this is the only way that God could answer your prayers. It may be that he could not have got you to heaven with fifteen millions of dollars, but he can without."

The old man thought a minute, then looked up and said, "That is so. That is all right."[6]

To comfort his friend in his troubles, Parker wrote a hymn that he must have sung to the old man often, his rich baritone voice sweet on the higher notes and strong on the lower ones, vibrant and compelling.

His Care

God holds the key of all unknown,
    And I am glad;
If other hands should hold the key,
Or if He trusted it to me,
    I might be sad.

The very dimness of my sight
    Makes me secure,
For groping in my misty way
I feel His hand, I hear Him say,
    "My help is sure."

Enough; this covers all my want,
    And so I rest;
For what I cannot, He can see,
And in His care I sure shall be
    Forever blest.[7]

Groping in his misty way, the bankrupt was comforted; perhaps he had been ruined to be saved. Was it not even possible that, unconsciously, this compulsive stock gambler had contrived to slough off his dirty millions, so as to face God clean? But the old man was not given to introspection; if the thought occurred to him, he did not dwell on it.

His ordeal was far from over. Pending his examination before the register in bankruptcy—an examination that his creditors had vowed to make ruthlessly probing—those creditors held a preliminary meeting on April 6 to pick an assignee. Drew was on hand, flanked by attorneys, while Judge Fancher, representing the two Methodist institutions, rubbed elbows with a crowd of Wall Street speculators and their lawyers. No agreement as to an assignee was reached, but at a second meeting on April 12 they finally settled on Isaac H. Bailey, a commissioner of the Department of Public Charities and Correction.

Meanwhile Wesleyan was soliciting contributions from its alumni throughout the country, but in the midst of a depression many could not respond, and some even questioned the soundness of the university's financial management. President Hurst of the seminary had broken the bad news of Drew's insolvency to a dismayed faculty and student body at a meeting in the campus chapel, and was now appealing to trustees, bishops, clergy, and laymen for support. The faculty had taken a one-third cut in pay, and at the annual board meeting on April 20, which the founder did not attend, Hurst thanked the banker Andrew V. Stout, a fellow worshiper of Drew's at St. Paul's, for a gift of forty thousand dollars, which he hoped would be an incentive to others. Noting the seminary's predicament, the *Sun* commented: "The gold is bright, the greenbacks are crisp, the buildings are strong, the glebe is fertile, though it all came from the mire of the Street. But is it not a little strange that the theological plant has grown in such a soil?"[8]

On April 29 Drew was served with a summons at his home. The four granddaughters had initiated foreclosure proceedings on the house. Since his children too could be considered to have an interest in the property, Drew's son and daughter-in-law were served at the same time, while his daughter and the Reverend Clapp were served in Carmel two days later, so that the whole family was caught up in his calamity. Then, a month later, the same four plaintiffs petitioned the State Supreme Court to have their grandfather removed as trustee of their father's estate, their published complaint exposing to all the world the old man's lamentable mismanagement. He denied nothing and opposed neither proceeding.

Throughout May, Uncle Daniel was heartsick and just plain sick. Summoned to an examination at Register Williams's office on the eleventh, he was in no condition to go. Dr. Linsly and another physician informed the court that their patient had been confined to his bed. Then again on the twenty-third Linsly sent word that Drew had been prostrated by a severe attack of diarrhea, and again the case was adjourned.

Linsly, who was now attending the old man daily, informed him regularly of the condition of another of his patients, Vanderbilt, whose health was at last deteriorating and who had been confined to his house since April. Although Drew's ailment was scarcely noticed, the infirmity of America's greatest multimillionaire provoked widespread interest and prompted daily bulletins in the newspapers. On May 10, when a report of the Commodore's approaching end sent Lake Shore plunging on the market, and a *Herald* reporter called at 10 Washington Square to verify Vanderbilt's condition, the subject of interest bellowed down the stairs that his slight disorder had all but passed and that if he could lay hands on the rumor mongers, he had strength aplenty to "knock all the lies for hereafter out of them, thereby causing the biggest job for undertakers that both Wall and Broad Streets have afforded for a very great number of years!"[9] And when Vanderbilt heard that Drew, three years his junior, was also ill, he exclaimed: "Aha! Breakin' down so young? Well, Dan'l Drew never did have any constitution!"[10]

Gradually Drew's condition improved, and Dr. Linsly could no longer have the examination postponed. The creditors were clamoring for it, the Wall Streeters among them being inclined to view the illness as a dodge, convinced as they were that only one year before, when his Wabash calls had come due, Uncle Daniel had played sick for a day to minimize his losses. But his ailments were real. When the examination took place at 10:00 A.M. on June 1, it was in the old man's bedroom at his residence, the only ones admitted being Register Williams and his stenographer; Simon H. Stern, the attorney for the assignee; Drew's own attorney, Alvin Burt; and Dr. Linsly. The bankrupt received them lying in his bed, bolstered up and very feeble. As the representative of the creditors, Stern put a series of questions to him that he answered under oath, with great effort, in a whisper that was scarcely audible.

Prior to filing for bankruptcy, where had Mr. Drew done business? He answered that he had done none at all in over a year's time. Prior to that, where did he have his office? He replied that he had none, except in the offices of his brokers. Who worked for him? No one. Who looked over the statements that his brokers sent to him? No one; he trusted to their honesty. Where were those statements now? He didn't know. Did he have any checkbooks? No, he never used them, except for a small personal account long ago.

And so, through questioning, the picture emerged of a peculiar old man who had had no office, no clerk or bookkeeper, no checkbooks, no personal records, and who in buying and selling securities worth millions had always kept his accounts in his head. As the questions continued, the invalid grew weaker and weaker, his replies so faint as to be almost inaudible, and great tears began rolling down his cheeks. Finally, after almost three-quarters of an hour, Dr. Linsly protested that his patient was too exhausted to continue. As the old man lay back wearily on his pillow and closed his eyes, the register adjourned to the following day.

After putting seventy-three questions to the bankrupt, the creditors had learned little but the eccentric business practices of the gentleman in question, practices that left no written records for them to scrutinize. The examination was by no means concluded, but when the register and attorneys called at 41 Union Square over the next few days, they were invariably told at the door that the master was too ill to see anyone, or that the doctor said he could not be examined. Then on June 8, when they arrived to resume proceedings at 10:00 A.M., a maid informed them that Mr. Drew was not at home. Register Williams's suggestion that the old gentleman might be hiding in the house provoked a vehement denial, but there was no clarification as to where he might have gone. Only by pressing the matter further did they learn, first, that Drew had been driven off in a closed carriage last seen turning into Fourth Avenue, and then, that he had been taken to Vanderbilt's new Grand Central Depot to be put on a train to "Put County." In short, he had given them the slip.

To the ailing old man, enfeebled and harassed, it must have seemed the only way out. Even in the sanctuary of his sick room, they were hounding him with their questions, nor would that sanctuary be his much longer, since on May 25 the court ordered that his mortgaged residence be sold at public auction. With his health and his world a shambles, Putnam County had never looked so good. Getting there, however, would be an ordeal. So his son went up ahead to prepare things, having first arranged for the Central's Harlem line to put the palace car "Duchess"—the very one that had brought mourners to his mother's funeral—at his father's disposal with a bed. Then on the morning of the eighth, helped down the steep stoop by a young Irish servant and J. Fowler Frost, a former Brewster merchant who was now the proprietor of a hotel nearby, the invalid left his home of nineteen years forever, fled to the station, and caught the 10:35 express. Two hours later he rose from his bed to get off at Croton Falls, where his two companions assisted him to a waiting carriage and thence to his son's farm three miles away. There at last the fugitive could rest.

His repose did not last long, however, because of course they examined him again. They came on June 20, Register Williams, his stenographer, and the attorneys. Improved but still ailing, the old man again received them lying in his bed, giving evidence without rising. At the start he volunteered a statement that summarized his losses, including a million in the "Nor'west" corner, then another million in "Waybosh 'n' Can'da Sethern" ("an almighty loss"), then millions more in "Waybosh" again, and Lake Shore, Canton, and Quicksilver. It was a piteous catalogue of ill luck, bad judgment, and the arbitrary actions of his brokers, who he insisted had closed out his contracts even when they had ample margin. He complained, he lamented, his mind at times skipped erratically, losing the thread and then recovering it, his answers to Stern's questions sometimes precise, sometimes maddeningly vague. His brokers' memorandums? Probably he had torn them up. Did those brokers now have any property of his? "Not without they chiseled me out of it." The value of the steamboat stock? "There's no buyers for it; nobody wants it."[11]

Whether it was right or wrong of him to declare bankruptcy the old man could not say, but remorse gnawed at him. "It is a wonderful thing for one to think of sometimes; I can't get rid of it. To think where I was and ought to have stopped, and didn't. If I had done right by my children—that is the awful thing."[12] And again, remembering how he had never paid his daughter a third of what was due her: "That was the worst thing about my misfortune—that I didn't do right when I could have done it. People think I have got some great—I don't know what. I know I ain't. I tell you I ain't. It seems like a dream to me."[13]

Even as he testified, in New York his Union Square property was offered on the auction block. Over the previous two weeks the gilt-framed family portraits on the walls had come down, the furniture had been removed, and the house stripped; horses and carriages had already been sold. Although the square had long since ceased to be a fashionable residential area, the property had great potential value commercially. Only four years before, Drew was said to have rejected an offer for it of $300,000. Now, however, with the real estate market depressed, no such sum could be expected, so the four granddaughters elected to acquire it at a low price themselves and rent out the floors. They paid $112,000, which did not extinguish even one-half of their grandfather's debt to them.

So it was that the elegant brownstone that the wealthy Suydam family had long ago built and then lost through financial reverses; the house where Nelson Robinson had lived in his heady days of success, only to be carried paralyzed up the steep front steps to die there; the handsome mansion where Daniel Drew had hosted the very grandchildren now bidding for it, and received clergy, celebrated his golden wedding, founded a seminary, and hatched Wall Street schemes and betrayals—that house and the stables behind it were now sold and given over to commerce, thereafter to shelter a real estate agency, an art school, and a drugstore. If the dazed old man up in "Put" thought about it, he must have mused again, "It seems like a dream to me." At seventy-nine years of age, after decades of striving and getting, he was no wealthier than he had been at nineteen.

CHAPTER 23

The Oldest Man on the Street

Throughout the summer and fall of 1876, Daniel Drew remained a convalescent in the country, slowly regaining his strength and recovering his equilibrium. Once he was able to get downstairs, he could sit on the porticoed front veranda and enjoy a fine view of the grounds, with trees and shrubs and well-trimmed, sweeping lawns. On the farm were hothouses where Bill grew grapes highly prized by the fruit dealers of New York City; stables with fine horses; cows that produced milk for the Borden plant in Brewster; and what the old man understood best— steers from the West that his son was fattening for the New York City market, where they would fetch high prices and yield top-grade beef that only Delmonico's and other fancy restaurateurs could afford. To see his son, who was otherwise busy with the People's Line, devoting weekends and holidays to personally inspecting the livestock must have pleased the old ex-drover immensely; this, at least, he had been able to give the boy.

By late August the old man was occasionally riding into Brewster for a shave at Stephen Wood's barber shop. News of his improved condition prompted the *Brewster Standard* to send a young reporter out to the farm to interview him. Arriving in mid-afternoon, the young man was received in a kindly manner by Drew who, having just finished lunch, waved him to a chair on the veranda. Dressed in a rusty black suit and carpet slippers, the old gentleman had a careworn look. His young visitor remained courteous and deferential, letting his host chat cheerily throughout. Yes, he was improving; this must be the healthiest place in the country. In time, though, perhaps he would go back to New York.

263

He was born near here, of course, knew everyone, or rather their children, for his old friends had died.

Asked if he had seen Vanderbilt since the Commodore himself had fallen ill, Drew replied: "No, I ain't, and I regret it very much. If it was possible for me to travel to New York, I'd go and see him at once; but I can't do it, and I'm afeared that when I'm able, it'll be too late." Having discussed the Commodore's condition with Dr. Linsly, he had no hope of his friend's recovery. His admiration for the Commodore was unbounded: "He's a wonderful man—the most wonderful, I think, in the world. What an intellect he has! And what vitality! I've known him, I believe, for fifty years."

Asked about the country's depressed condition, the recent bankrupt expounded: "What do I think is the cause of all this? Well, sir, we ain't got far to search for the cause. We've all been traveling a great deal too fast. That's it. We've been embarking in enterprises without counting the cost. Thousands of miles of railroad have been built that shouldn't have been thought of for years to come, and millions of dollars have been borrowed from European capitalists to pay for them. We're swamped with debt and ain't got any credit." But he admitted that he had no solution.

Queried about the coming election, he said that Gov. Samuel J. Tilden, whom he had known for years, would make an excellent president, although that Republican from Ohio—what d'you call him—would no doubt run very well. Although he usually voted Republican, he was still open-minded, but probably would not vote at all, not having resided there long enough to register.[1]

So ended the interview. The young reporter started back to town, leaving the convalescent to snooze on the veranda.

While Daniel Drew played rusticating sage in Southeast, his name was still before the public in New York. Attorney Stern, acting on behalf of the creditors, had concluded that he could get no more information out of the bankrupt himself, and so summoned Eugene Robinson, Drew's chief broker during the time of his great losses, to be examined in the presence of the register. Stern now entertained the notion that his brokers might have victimized Uncle Daniel. After Robinson's testimony, however, and the examination of five cartloads of books containing Drew's twelve different accounts with the firm, Stern and the register concluded that Drew's millions had been truly and properly lost and so terminated the proceedings. For years, though, certain Wall Street creditors were teased by the suspicion that Uncle Daniel had somehow stashed away a fortune. The legend of Daniel Drew's hidden wealth eventually survived the man himself by decades, but no such wealth was ever found.

October in Putnam County brought a good apple crop, which meant cheap cider. Chestnuts and walnuts were being gathered, corn was being husked, and by the end of the month wild geese were seen flying south. As the year waned, the convalescent improved, although his fortunes did not. On September 21 his four mortgaged farms were auctioned off in the town hall at Brewster (his son got two of them); on the twenty-second, his 130 acres adjoining the seminary at Madison were sold; and on October 14, the court formally removed him as the trustee of his granddaughters' estate.

On November 17, 1876—just ten days after Gov. Rutherford B. Hayes of Ohio was elected president in a highly controversial election— Uncle Daniel appeared in the Supreme Court in Brooklyn, to be on hand for the case of *White* v. *Drew*. The suit had been brought by the Wall Street operator Stephen V. White, who claimed that Drew owed him $41,400 from a call in Union Pacific, whereas Drew asserted that White owed him $51,000 from their joint account in Rock Island. Many Wall Streeters turned out to get their first look in months at the bankrupt and found a seemingly hale old gentleman, slightly stooped, wearing a big ulster over a somber black suit relieved by a white neckerchief, who sat quietly in the courtroom, legs crossed, scrunched down inside his coat's high collar, watched by all but apparently indifferent to everything around him. When he testified on the twenty-first, however, his testimony was not the highlight of the day. That came when Kenyon Cox took the stand as a defense witness, to give testimony regarding the old man's reputation on the Street. Pressed in cross-examination, Cox tried to avoid answering, then finally spat it out: "I suppose that in Wall Street his character does not stand A Number One." "I don't know what A Number One means," remarked the judge. "Maybe the jury does." "His reputation," Cox explained, "is rather bad. I have known him over twenty years, was his partner from 1870, and before that was his confidential clerk."[2]

Cox then returned to his seat beside Drew, who having glared throughout the testimony, immediately took him to task. Fortunately for Drew, soon afterward ex-Judge Freeman J. Fithian waxed eloquent on his behalf in an exchange with the plaintiff's counsel: "I want to show that no man has a character in Wall Street. The men who do business there are all right uptown, where they build churches, hire pews, do charitable things; but in the Street each man is at the mercy of every other man's malignity. I take deep interest in the attempt, sir, to impeach this gentleman, who has dwelt so long in the community, and whom now, on the brink of the grave, our adversaries wish to thrust entirely under by imposing the burden of an impeachment."[3] As his attorney spoke, Uncle Daniel showed considerable emotion. Thereafter other brokers testified, some speaking well of him, some not. In the end it was one man's word against another's, which might have augured ill for the defendant, but the jury was unable to agree.

By December, the Commodore was close to the end. Bedridden for months, he had fought pain, disease, and death just as he had fought Daniel Drew and a hundred others on the water, and Daniel Drew and a thousand others on the land: boldly, obstinately, irascibly. His bladder inflamed, his inner organs diseased, his digestion almost paralyzed, this supreme artist of go-ahead clung tenaciously to the shreds of life still left in him, forcing himself in a wheelchair to the window to view his favorite horses brought into view—magnificent thoroughbreds that he would never again drive impetuously through the dust of Harlem Lane. Newspapers issued daily bulletins on his health, and journalists rented quarters in the neighborhood in order to maintain a round-the-clock vigil near his residence. Meanwhile, twisted with pain, the old man spat out the tea his nurses gave him; hurled hot water bottles at his doctors and called them "Grannies," then broke into tears and begged their forgiveness; and thundered profanities at Wall Streeters who he heard were trading on reports of his death. Although he kept at a distance the aged daughters whom he had never loved and his second son whom he scorned, he summoned the Rev. Charles Deems and said to him with tears in his eyes: "Doctor, I sent for you to tell you how I love you."[4]

Love and piety flowered in his stern heart at last, their seed sown in him in childhood by his mother and now carefully nurtured by Deems and his wife. As the old man sank slowly, rallied, then sank again, his splendid organism crumbling, his features wasted, he achieved a Christian dying. On January 3, 1877, he bade farewell to those he most loved, joined in falteringly as they sang his favorite hymns, asked Deems to pray, then said: "That's a good prayer. I shall never give up trust in Jesus. How could I let that go?"[5] These were his last words; on the morning of the fourth he settled back, closed his eyes quietly, breathed one last rasping breath, and expired.

That this most profane of men—a stranger to churches, his life characterized by total selfishness and total ruthlessness (although softened through pain and love at the end)—should have died a Christian, must have struck Drew as a vindication, a wonder, and a glory. On the morning of January 7, when the host of notables invited by the family assembled in the downstairs parlors of the residence on Washington

Square, Drew was among them, his improved health now making trips to the city feasible. The Commodore was laid out in a massive silver-mounted casket in the hallway, clothed in a dress black suit with a low-cut vest revealing the silver studs of his shirtfront. But when Drew viewed the remains of this man whom he had so admired and so cheated, surely he was shocked. Instead of the ruddy-faced, strong-featured Vanderbilt, strikingly handsome, whom he remembered, he found a shrunken, emanciated wraith with pallid skin, hollow cheeks, and jutting cheekbones, the once brilliant eyes now closed and sunken under shaggy brows. Yet for all that, the massive forehead and firmly set mouth suggested a sternness worthy of the Commodore.

When the lid was screwed down and the casket carried out, Drew and the other mourners followed through the slippery, slush-covered streets to the Church of the Strangers two blocks away. Then, after a simple service, he joined the cortege of over a hundred carriages down Broadway to the Battery, where a waiting ferry boat embarked the coffin for Staten Island. Like most of the mourners, Drew turned back at the dock, his fragile health compromised already by the chill air of a January thaw.

It was the end of a lifetime of rivalry, of a friendship of forty-six years seasoned with esteem, sentiment, guile, and betrayal, as one frail old man paid his last respects to the shrunken ghost of another—a feeble bankrupt bidding farewell to the man whom he had emulated most in the world and who had died worth a hundred million. Opposites in many ways—the one blunt, physical, profane, rocklike in his strength and fixity; the other serpentine and cunning, abstemious and inclined to piety—they had been shaped of the same rough clay: poor, uneducated, practical, determined to achieve and acquire. What was Daniel Drew now, without the Commodore's shadow to walk in?

The year 1877 passed quietly as Drew lived with his son and daughter-in-law—the "young folks," as he called them—in rustic tranquillity. In March he retired at last—he had held the office nineteen years—as president of the People's Line, being succeeded by his son. When the seminary board held its annual meeting in Madison on May 16, he attended with his son and grandson, both of whom offered on-the-spot contributions to help make up the $5,000 deficit from the previous year's operations.

Strenuous fund-raising efforts had gone a long way toward saving the seminary, and as it acquired a far broader and surer base of support, pious observers discerned in the crisis the hand and wisdom of God. Such reflections may have prompted the board, on this first visit of the founder since his bankruptcy, to pass a resolution releasing him from his note and to approve another resolution proposed by President Hurst: "Resolved, that we are glad to be favored with the presence of our Venerable Founder Daniel Drew at this annual meeting and direct this special minute to be recorded, appreciative thereof."[6] At the commencement on the following day, he appeared on the platform with other dignitaries and when his name was mentioned, hearty applause broke out. At least the Methodists forgave.

Wesleyan University had likewise released its benefactor from its claim upon him, and when he returned to Madison for the seminary's tenth anniversary on October 25—Founder's Day, as some now called it—his appearance again produced an enthusiastic response. At a board meeting in the chapel afterward, the trustees concurred in Prof. William Wells's eloquent congratulations to Drew on having attained his eightieth year and on "the joy of knowing that, whatever else else might be evanescent, his monument here at Madison is a thing of joy forever."[7] Methodists and others were well aware that whatever the old gentleman had kept for himself had been lost, whereas all that he had given away had endured; he himself was the first to agree.

Absolved by the Methodists, freed from his creditors, the bankrupt might have spent his remaining years peacefully and obscurely in the country. His grandchildren were living in and about Drewville contentedly, the husbands raising trotters for trotting meets and fairs, depleting the local quail in the hunting season, and planting maples and elms; for a change they and their wives visited the White Mountains, spent a season in Paris or a year in Switzerland. The old man's daughter Catherine still resided in Carmel village, her husband the Reverend Clapp prepared as always to sermonize on man's justification before God, or lecture on yellow fever or the immoral condition of the French. Even Daniel's grandson—Daniel Drew Chamberlain, who had known Wall Street in the giddy days of the war—had retired without regret, living happily near Carmel as a gentleman farmer, raising prize oxen, distributing awards at the female seminary, and promoting Sunday school. Surely then in Putnam County, surrounded by his family, Uncle Daniel should have found the good life possible.

But he yearned for New York. For one who had known such men as Vanderbilt, A.T. Stewart, Tilden, and Fisk, and had made and lost millions habitually, "Old Put" could never be enough. In this quiet, healthy corner of the country, where the biggest news was a plague of potato bugs in Drewville, the Methodist ladies' annual strawberry festival in June, or the theft of some melons from a granddaughter's garden, the old man viewed a few weeks or even months as a vacation, but years as an imprisonment. Even bankrupt, he had to get back to the city.

This was not difficult. His son was now fully involved with the

People's Line and not wholly indifferent to the contacts that his father could still provide on Wall Street. So in November 1877 Bill and his family moved for the winter to the city, where they took up residence at the Hotel Bristol. Thereafter, quietly and discreetly, Uncle Daniel was seen again on the Street. Penniless, he remained on the sidelines, but at least he could chat and reminisce. On one occasion, talking with the broker Henry Clews, who had failed in the panic but resumed, Drew explained why he had left "Old Put": "I was troubled with visitors, some of 'em well on to one hundred years old. Some of 'em said I bought cattle from 'em when I was young, on credit, and they wanted their bills. I kept no books, and how was I to know I owed 'em for them critters? It was dull outen thar, and yer never can tell till the next day how sheers is gone."[8]

A picturesque has-been, Uncle Daniel was by no means forgotten in the city. Whenever he appeared in court, press and public took notice. In February 1878 he testified in a suit brought by his son against a broker named John N. Harriman, who in 1870 had given the old man a note for $8,000. Drew had since sold the note to his son, and his son was demanding payment. Called to the stand, Uncle Daniel advanced with a surprisingly elastic step, wearing his famous sealskin coat. Testifying in a feeble voice, he stated that he had sold the note to his son for $3,500.

"Did you sell this note because you needed money?" "Yes, sir." "What did you want money for—for stock operations?" "No, sir." "What for, then?" "For family expenses." The courtroom roared with laughter, but the court made a judgment for his son.[9]

Then on March 8, 1878, Drew appeared as a witness in the most celebrated trial of the moment, the Vanderbilt will case, in which one of the Commodore's daughters challenged the will in which the old man left the bulk of his estate to his eldest son, William. The court testimony afforded piquant glimpses of the aged Commodore as a cranky invalid, as a credulous believer in clairvoyance and magnetic healing, and even—allegedly—as a septuagenarian Romeo. To all this, however, Drew's testimony added little. Asked about a conversation that he was said to have had twenty years before with the Commodore, on the subject of Vanderbilt's disinherited second son Cornelius Jr., he recalled nothing. But the real news of Uncle Daniel's appearance in court was his springy step, agile movement, and flourishing look. In contrast to the lean and wrinkled old man in shabby clothes of his prosperous days, the *World* noted that "he was accurately dressed in black broadcloth and a white tie, and his expanded waistcoat betokened that at eighty-four [really eighty] he is getting—fat!"[10] Bankruptcy, it seemed, had done wonders for him.

Drew might have agreed. His friend John Parker's argument that perhaps God could not get him to heaven with fifteen million dollars but could get him there without had weighed mightily. Often now he remarked that his money-getting career was behind him, that he longed for rest. Never obsessed with the trappings of wealth, he was heard to say: "How much better this is than the old way. I can step into the street-car, go to church or prayer meeting; I have no trouble to bring out a carriage, or keep a coachman waiting for me."[11] Having applied for a pension as a War of 1812 veteran back when he still had his millions, he lined up regularly at the pension agent's office with the other old men to get his eight dollars a month, which was his only income, apart from the bounty of his son.

As always, he was seen regularly in his pew at St. Paul's, unless his health detained him, and appeared as well at the prayer meetings and love feasts, his fellow worshipers marveling at the look of supreme peace that had settled over the furrows of his face. Among the Methodists his bankruptcy was deemed a personal benefit since it had wrenched him from Mammon. John Parker was firmly convinced that his elderly friend had been relieved of the cares of the world, that being ruled again by his mother's early training he had returned with a tender heart to God. Certainly he spent long hours reading the Bible, praying privately, and singing the Methodist hymns. And what he had discovered for himself, he tried to impart to others. A leading Wall Street man who had business with him later recalled: "I met Mr. Drew and transacted my business, when he said: 'I have something to say to you. You can't live always. You can't take your money with you.' Then he exhorted me in the most feeling manner, and got me down on my knees and prayed for me. No man ever talked to me about my soul as did Daniel Drew. If there is a Christian on the earth, it is Daniel Drew."[12] A saint, then, at the end of his life, one who, having had everything and lost it, fought through to Christian resignation, to peace.

Almost. For the serene old gentleman who was seen praying in his pew on the Sabbath or chatting about town with friends in the parlors of first-class hotels, still hobnobbed with brokers and at times was seen on the Street. And if he himself was too old to make a fortune there, his son was not. After all, since Bill had proved himself a chip off the old block in the managing of cattle and steamboats, why not on Wall Street too?

Perhaps with this in mind, in November 1878 William H. Drew resigned as president of the New Jersey Steamboat Company, being succeeded by William W. Everett, the husband of Daniel's granddaughter Georgiana. The change may not have been wholly amicable, since by means of it the last vestige of Daniel's influence was eliminated, putting the company wholly in the hands of the granddaughters and their husbands, who then controlled it for a quarter of a century. The following

March a report circulated that new opposition to the People's Line was being organized by William H. Drew and J.W. Hancox, but the former promptly and unequivocally denied it.

No longer a steamboat manager, by May 1879 Bill had become a broker with Lawrence Brothers & Company at 31 Broad Street. At the same time he leased a brownstone at 3 East Forty-second Street—an uptown location where fashionable residences and hotels were now appearing in the vicinity of Grand Central Depot, whose proximity made commuting to and from the country easier. Thereafter Daniel was often seen dining and chatting with Darius Lawrence, through whom the old gentleman began executing small transactions in the market.

And so, trivially, using modest sums provided by his son, the tearful hymn-singing penitent found his way back to Wall Street. There he was considered a "dead duck," differentiated from the mob of pathetic hangers-on chiefly by his picturesque status as the oldest man on the Street. He was approaching eighty-two, but his gray eyes had not lost their fire, occasionally glinting with the joy of a small "killing" that would give him pocket money. Yet better days might be at hand. William H. Vanderbilt, now a portly plutocrat whose fortune increased by millions every year, remembered the old man with affection as his Wall Street employer of forty years before. He was said to give Uncle Daniel "points" in the market and to intend to provide the old gentleman with the means for another start in life. If at least half Daniel's hopes were fixed on such a prospect instead of the hereafter, he could not help it: stock gambling was in his blood and his bone.

He missed the seminary board meetings in the spring and fall of 1878, but in September of that year—discreetly, no doubt, lest his creditors get wind of it—he gave the school fifteen hundred dollars. Then on May 14, 1879, he again attended the annual meeting at Madison and on the following day appeared on the platform at commencement. Of a proposed new endowment of $300,000, some $248,000 had been pledged, almost the equivalent of the lost quarter million. "The hour of extreme peril is tided over," announced the *Advocate*, "the Drew must and will live."[13] And with it, presumably, his name.

Summer came and Daniel returned to the Clift farm with the "young folks" and their daughter. In the time he could spare from Wall Street, Bill was still living grandly as a country gentleman, giving a gold piece to each employee at Christmas, tending his superb hothouse grapes, and on the evening of July Fourth entertaining guests with a brilliant display of fireworks at the house. But in his own way, the old man could also play the squire. He had long patronized Stephen Wood's barbershop in Brewster, located on a second floor to which a staircase without a railing gave access. In early August, just after his eighty-second birthday, he provided the stairs with a handsome black-walnut railing installed at his own expense, which was promptly reported in the paper. Not that this was pure altruism, since he needed it to get up the stairs.

On August 14 Daniel accompanied his son's family to Long Branch, where they spent the balance of the month. By September they returned to New York, Bill and his father remaining in the city while the rest of the family went back for a while to the farm. On Sunday the fourteenth, the old man appeared as usual in his pew at St. Paul's, where many fellow worshipers commented on the restfulness that showed in his face. Was it spiritual repose or just a good vacation?

The following Thursday, September 18, Daniel dined at 6:00 P.M. with Darius Lawrence at the Grand Union Hotel, where the two often had dinner together and spent the evening sitting outside in front of the hotel. On this occasion the old gentleman ate heartily and seemed in good spirits and health. After dinner the two men returned to 3 East Forty-second Street, where they chatted pleasantly until 9:00 P.M., when Lawrence said that it was time for him to leave. At this point Drew complained of not feeling well and, since his son was absent from the house, asked Lawrence to stay for a time. Lawrence agreed, remaining in the next room while the old man retired. About 10:15 P.M. Drew entered the room and said he felt worse, whereupon Lawrence sent at once for Drew's physician. "I've got a severe pain here on my heart," the old man told Lawrence, "just as my mother had the moment before she died." [14]

No sooner had he spoken when his head slumped forward on his chest. Lawrence sprang toward him, and he fell dead in the younger man's arms. Shortly afterward, when another doctor arrived from next door and examined him, he found the cause of death to be not heart failure, as originally thought, but cerebral apoplexy. The son was informed; the news went out. On the death certificate, the doctor gave the deceased's occupation as broker.

And so Daniel Drew died, his last thoughts on his mother before expiring in the arms of Wall Street. It was a death as sudden, brief, and easy as the Commodore's had been protracted and agonizing. Having long known and said the worst about him, the New York dailies hailed the passing of an American original who was, as the *Tribune* put it, worthy of Hogarth, although they might more aptly have said a Yankee Dickens. The *Albany Argus* insisted that "speculation and sanctification do not go well together," but the *Advocate* observed that Mr. Drew's piety, like certain rivers of the West, having been long sunken in the desert of his scheming, had surfaced at the end to make his last days "green and gladsome." [15]

On September 23 the plain rosewood casket was conveyed to Grand Central Depot, where a special three-coach train was waiting. About one hundred mourners boarded it, including close friends and relatives; trustees and representatives from the Drew Theological Seminary, Wesleyan University, St. Paul's Church, Troy University, and the Concord Biblical Institute; and lawyers, butchers, brokers, circus and steamboat men, and prominent Methodist laymen and ladies. In Brewster the post office and all the village stores were closed, and the bell of the Methodist church was tolling. From the station, a cortege of carriages proceeded to the white-steepled church, where the local mourners waited: more friends and relatives, faculty and students from the Drew Female Seminary at Carmel, most of Brewster, and a host of farmers who had ridden in over the hills and down the valleys from twenty-five or thirty miles away.

In the crowded church—decorated sparingly with flowers owing to the deceased's expressed desire for simplicity—six clergymen officiated, of whom three gave addresses. By far the most moving testimony was that of John Parker, who spoke feelingly of the unceasing war in his departed brother's heart between business and piety and of his love for his mother. After the service, the mile-long cortege drove to the Drew Cemetery where, among cedars and flower beds, the coffin was deposited in a brick tomb beside the grave of Roxanna, near the tombstones of Drew's parents and his long-deceased infant daughter Josephine. Lamented by those whom he had loved and benefited, enriched and wronged, Daniel Drew slept with his own.

Epilogue

Daniel Drew's will, made on December 2, 1873—after the Kenyon Cox failure and the assignment of his property to Scott, but before his bankruptcy—left half his estate to his son and half to his daughter. His son as executor inventoried the estate, which included 500 shares capital stock, Baldy Sour Mining Company, at $50, amounting to $250; 1,250 shares capital stock, Sweetwater Mining Company, at $50, amounting to $625; $148.22 in cash; and one lot wearing apparel, valued at $50; amounting to a total of $1,073.22. Since there was no market for the stock or the apparel, Drew's estate came to $148.22.

Humans perish but litigation endures. In 1886 certain of Drew's creditors got Isaac H. Bailey, his assignee in bankruptcy, to bring suit against Drew's son and grandson, to demand from them an accounting of certain securities that Drew had allegedly given them in fraud of his creditors. After a prolonged sifting of the old man's tangled finances, the court dismissed the complaints in 1891, fully twelve years after Daniel Drew's death.

William H. Drew returned to Putnam County, where he lived most of his life as a gentleman farmer. In 1900 he sold the Clift farm, by then known with varied spellings as Drewsclift, but continued to reside in the vicinity until his death in 1912.

Drewsclift was purchased in 1906 by the wealthy New York City contractor Patrick Ryan (1853-1925), who transformed the mansion into a massive stone castle with a round tower, in which form it survives today. In 1930 the property was acquired by Victoria Dreyfus, wife of the millionaire music publisher Max Dreyfus (1874-1964), who renamed it Madrey Farm. Since Victoria's death in 1976, some of the estate has been sold, but the mansion still awaits a new owner.

Drew's daughter Catherine died in 1883, and her husband the Reverend Clapp in 1889. Most of the married grandchildren lived in the Drewville vicinity until early in this century, when the area became a New York City reservoir.

The floating palaces of the People's Line continued to ply between New York and Albany under the management of William W. Everett until 1902, when control of the New Jersey Steamboat Company passed to Charles Wyman Morse, who subsequently absorbed it into a company of his own.

Jay Gould persisted in his brilliant career of corporate takeovers and stock manipulations, specializing in Western railroads. The most hated man in America, he appeared in public always accompanied by bodyguards, but spent his private hours quietly with his family in seclusion, raising exotic plants and reading. He died of consumption in 1892.

Today Daniel Drew's name has been forgotten, and the Drew Cemetery in Putnam County lies abandoned and overgrown. The Drew Theological Seminary, however, survives as Drew University, where on the walls of Mead Hall hang portraits of Daniel and Roxanna donated by their son—surely the very ones that once hung in the parlor at 41 Union Square.

The legend of Daniel Drew's hidden treasure survived well into the twentieth century. In 1972, when a grandson of the only daughter of William H. Drew visited an abandoned farm near Port Elizabeth, New Jersey, where his grandmother, estranged from her family, had spent the last years of her life, he found the property pitted with excavations. For years, people from all over the county had been digging there for buried wealth.

What are we to make of this man, the legend of whose phantom wealth all but survived his own name? Certainly both apologists and critics of laissez-faire capitalism can arm themselves with facts from his career. As drover, innkeeper, and steamboat operator he was able simultaneously to pursue his own interests and significantly benefit society, while as a Wall Street speculator he showed to what infamy untrammeled self-interest can lead. As a financial miscreant he differed from the other money kings of his time primarily in one respect: unlike them, he was also conspicuous as a prayerful Methodist and on this count, both then and ever since, has been labeled a hypocrite.

Daniel Drew, however, was not really a hypocrite, for his bouts of tearful repentance were sincere as far as they went. The anguish that he felt was essentially that which, long before setting foot on Wall Street, he had experienced at the age of fourteen. His was the agony of a sinner who fears the wrath of his God. Only insofar as it distracted him from religion did his business career fuel such agony. At the end of his life, ruined, he felt keen remorse for having failed his family and his church, but none at all, it would seem, for having duped others, helped mismanage Erie, or on more than one occasion disrupted the nation's commerce. His mind was compartmentalized, and the fervors of religion rarely infiltrated the arena of finance. What he lacked was pervasive moral perception. A consistent sense of responsibility to shareholders, the business community, and the public was simply beyond his grasp.

In being innocent of such responsibility, Drew did not differ markedly from Fisk, Gould, and Vanderbilt. Yet such were the range of his experience and the contradictions of his character that Drew provides a far richer study than do they. Drew knew, and poignantly, not only triumph but loss. And while any human life, if scrutinized, yields a nest of paradoxes, few yield as many as Drew's. Daniel Drew was a hard-headed man of business driven by two deep passions—religion and speculation; a brilliant money manager who through his own fault died penniless; a masterful Wall Street tactician who could rarely conceive, and never adhere to, a long-range strategy; a natural actor who, having fooled others all his life, ended up fooling himself; a conniver who routinely betrayed allies in finance, yet remained unfailingly loyal to his church; a remorse-stricken penitent who on Wall Street disclaimed the slightest responsibility to others; one who in cheating big always found time to cheat small; a canny old man who at heart remained a little boy out for fun and excitement, viewing his multimillion-dollar manipulations essentially as one big game. He was not necessarily better than his severest critics have depicted him, but far subtler and more complex.

What should such a life mean to us? Drew's character and career offer a thick, savory slice of America. This book pleads not for Uncle Daniel himself, but for a better memory and understanding of him. If we know him in his full gamut and true complexity, neither masking his faults nor belittling his virtues, we better know our nation and ourselves. In our own less heady and more sophisticated age, deeds and misdeeds are veiled in corporate anonymity. Yet philanthropy and rascality still flourish and, as in Drew's case, have been known to proceed hand in hand. Go-ahead and "smartness" are not dead, albeit refashioned to suit the style of the times. With changed and proliferating rules, the money game continues, and Wall Street still exists. It behooves us, then, to take another look at the life of this shrewd old man, with its rich texture of color, excitement, humor, arresting paradoxes, biting irony, high drama, and farce, although in the end it inspires a feeling of waste. What final comment should be made on the career of this exponent of aggressive self-interest who, after decades of getting and doing, from this world's experience had only his mother's memory and two worthless mining stocks to clutch? Perhaps he himself summarized it best: "It seems like a dream to me."

Bouck White's
"Book of Daniel Drew":
An Enduring Fake

Bouck White's *Book of Daniel Drew*, published by Double-day, Page & Company, went on sale in New York on Monday, April 11, 1910, heralded one day earlier by a brief announcement in the *New York Times* book section, and an account of its contents covering almost a full page in the magazine section. This edition contained a three-page editor's note in which Bouck White quoted in part an article from the *New York Tribune* of February 8, 1905, announcing that a grandniece of Daniel Drew had discovered his diary in an old trunk shipped to her in New York "from the Drew estate in Carmel" and that she meant to have it published.

The manuscript in question, White explained in the note, had been "in the most jumbled and helter-skelter form imaginable,"[1] obliging him as editor to organize and supplement it for the sake of coherence and clarity, and to correct Drew's grammar and spelling throughout. Although he put his supplements in the first person and anticipated some errors of detail in his editing, White emphasized that "in the drift and temper of the work as a whole, I pledged myself to absolute adherence to the originals."[2] White signed the note "Bouck White, Head Resident's Study, Trinity Neighborhood House, New York City," thus implying that he was Head Resident of the settlement house of Holy Trinity Episcopal Church in Brooklyn—a further guarantee, perhaps, of his editorial integrity.

Thus presented as the edited and amplified diary of Daniel Drew, the book certainly received more attention than it would have as a mere biography or historical novel. Here, seemingly from the hand of the subject himself, was a revealing portrait of an unscrupulous robber baron—

greedy, selfish, cunning, and on occasion cruel; a "boiler-plated" rascal who "didn't care a hill of beans for the speech of people" and admitted that "business slobbers a fellow up," but insisted that a man could still be decent in his private life, since "straight trees can have crooked roots"; a despicable hymn-singing hypocrite who stated candidly that the church was not "skittish" about a businessman's ethics, and who viewed his gifts to religion as a good investment like paying taxes, since "God keeps a full set of books"[3]—all in all, the most self-damning portrait conceivable of the capitalist, and one that for decades to come would cement Drew's image as a treacherous, pietistic villain.

Even so, from the outset most reviewers questioned the propriety of White's casting his own contributions in the form of a first-person narrative, thus masking their extent. The *Christian Advocate* reviewer, writing before any controversy had erupted, also noted that White's book chiefly recapitulated newspaper accounts from Drew's own time, rather than adducing new facts, while the *Times* review on May 7 dismissed the whole work as spurious and no adequate basis on which to judge Drew's career (a view restated vigorously by a *Times* editorial of November 1, 1914, after White had achieved notoriety).

The most telling criticism of all, however, came in an interview with William H. Drew, Daniel Drew's surviving only son, which appeared in the *New York World* of April 25, 1910. William H. Drew emphatically denounced the book as a fraud, declaring that his father had left no diary or other papers—as his father's executor, he should know better than anyone—and furthermore that his father could scarcely write, and that what he wrote no one could read. Moreover, he said, there was no grandniece in the city, and if he was surprised at the accuracy of certain of the book's information, such as the "D-O-A-R-E" story and the steers named "Daniel Drew" and "Commodore Vanderbilt," other facts were manifestly false, such as his father's boorish speech at the golden wedding, and his erecting a great granite cross in the Drew Cemetery—a cross that William H. Drew himself had put up four years after his father's death and for which he still had the receipt! The son said that for several years the family had been receiving mysterious requests for genealogical data, requests that they had never complied with and whose meaning was clear only now. Upon hearing of the book's imminent publication, he had gone to New York to see Frank N. Doubleday in person and obtain a copy of it. When he protested the falseness of its contents, Doubleday had agreed to delay placing the book on the market until Drew put his objections in writing. On second thought, however, Drew consulted a lawyer instead and was now planning a criminal suit to prevent the book's distribution.

Invited by the press to comment, a Doubleday representative insisted that "of course every word and every fact in the book was carefully gone over by us before it was printed, and we are sure of everything in it."[4] White likewise maintained that the diary had been discovered in 1905 by a grandniece, Margaret Drew, who was an actress, and that the family would not sue because it was too aware of the book's truth to challenge it. The Methodist church, he declared, could not assist in America's civic and social redemption as long as her leading divinity school bore the name of a man "reputed to have been well-nigh the wickedest in business malpractice"; however ignorant the Methodists were of Drew's ill deeds, the world was not and viewed a "Drew" theological seminary as a joke.[5]

White put the seminary on the spot. As soon as they got wind of the book, the seminary authorities had queried the family as to the diary's authenticity and received William H. Drew's strenuous denial. When interviewed by a *Brooklyn Daily Eagle* reporter on April 27, President Henry Anson Buttz insisted that some of the book's statements (he declined to say which) were false, and stressed that, in fairness to both Drew and the seminary, verification should be demanded. Although no official word of it was given to the press, the seminary authorities were embarrassed by the mounting controversy and eager to forestall it, since if an aroused public opinion obliged them to change the institution's name (as some of them secretly longed to), this might provoke costly legal complications regarding Drew's original donation, which had been given on condition that the seminary bear his name. Indeed, would the seminary not be morally obliged to renounce the original quarter-million-dollar endowment, something that it was in no financial position to do?

White required nothing less of the seminary. Interviewed almost daily, he declared that "the Methodists have canonized a man whose deeds are a stench in the nostrils of honest men," and that he, as self-appointed devil's advocate, had undertaken to force them to "decanonize" Drew by changing the seminary's name and restoring the original donation not to the family, who had no right to it, but to the shareholders of the still troubled Erie Railway! Such a deed, he said, "would stand as a lighthouse, whose rays would pierce the spiritual and moral darkness that is now covering our country, and reach to the uttermost parts of these United States."[6]

William H. Drew saw things differently. "This book is a libel pure and simple," he announced on April 28 when, accompanied by his lawyer, he handed a copy of it to New York District Attorney Charles S. Whitman, entering a complaint of criminal libel against the author and publisher—an unusual action in that it alleged offense to a man not living.[7] Whitman gave the copy, with its objectionable passages marked by Drew, to an assistant district attorney for investigation.

A week later, however, Whitman announced that no suit for libel was likely, since William H. Drew had declined to swear formally to a complaint specifying the passages alleged to be libelous. Lacking such a complaint, Whitman was unwilling to proceed, being of the opinion that Drew had decided to drop the action. White at once declared himself vindicated, and since William H. Drew made no further statement and the seminary was not inclined to take the matter up, the controversy subsided.

Why did William H. Drew abandon the legal action that he had initiated with such determination? Prior to his death in 1912, he gave no public explanation. His descendants today have no knowledge of the matter, nor is there any mention of it in the minutes of the seminary's board of trustees. Certainly it was not because, as White asserted, Drew knew the truth of the book's statements about his father. Perhaps the seminary authorities and other Methodists convinced him that a public controversy would do irreparable harm to the seminary, but this is pure conjecture. His abandonment of the lawsuit remains an unresolved mystery, all the more so in that it let White, his father's alleged libeler, claim victory without ever having produced the manuscript of the diary or the grandniece who had supposedly discovered it.

Who was Bouck White, and how did he come to write the *Book of Daniel Drew?*

Born Charles Browning White on October 20, 1874, he was the son of a Methodist dry-goods merchant in the small village of Middleburg in Schoharie County, in the Catskill Mountains to the west of Albany, New York. Having grown up in Middleburg and attended Harvard, from which he graduated in 1896, he felt a call to the ministry and after studying at Union Theological Seminary in New York, was ordained a Congregational minister. From college on he went by the name of Bouck White ("Bouck" being his mother's maiden name), which he adopted legally in 1907. After four years as pastor of a Congregational church in Clayton, New York, he came to Brooklyn to serve as a social worker—but not the Head Resident—of the settlement house of Holy Trinity Church, whose pastor was a friend of his. In 1903 he published his first work, *Quo Vaditis? A Call to the Old Moralities*, which was an immature denunciation of the sins and vices of the day, including profit-motivated imperialism, the cure for which he saw in a vague brotherhood of all men with God.

Thereafter, a first-hand experience of the slums of New York turned him into a radical Socialist, in which capacity he undertook his second work, the *Book of Daniel Drew*, whose subject aroused his enmity as an arch robber-baron capitalist who seemingly compounded his sins by affecting, at least on the Sabbath, a colorful brand of old-fashioned piety. White was equally outraged by Drew the capitalist and Drew the hypocrite, both of whom he determined to expose and castigate with words planted in Drew's own mouth.

Decades later, when queried by the young historian Irvin G. Wyllie about the supposed Drew diary, White admitted that it had never existed, and a lifelong friend of White's informed Wyllie that White had acquired information for the book by visiting Drew's former haunts to interview old-timers who had known him. Doubleday, Page & Company, then, was either White's dupe or his accomplice. At the very least the firm, contrary to its public statements, failed utterly to verify the authenticity of the manuscript submitted to it. Nor was the April 1910 edition the first; in January another edition had been printed without any preliminary editor's note at all, a gross deception that seems to have been reconsidered by the publisher out of last-minute scruples or prudence, or perhaps because of William H. Drew's intervention.

And what of the grandniece Margaret Drew, who had supposedly discovered the diary in 1905? Although no grandniece, a Margaret Drew indeed existed. She was an attractive, young, round-faced actress who in 1905 had been playing in an English farce, *Mrs. Temple's Telegram*, and who after further appearances in New York went on the road and in time headed a stock company touring Montana and Washington. Her connection with White remains a mystery, but the article planted in the *Tribune* of February 8, 1905, probably served the double purpose of giving a young actress some free publicity and of documenting a radical reformer's future claim that he had only edited, not written, the alleged diary of Daniel Drew.

Even without White's later testimony, a close inspection of the *Book of Daniel Drew* reveals it as a fraud, since countless passages can be traced to printed sources available to White at the time. From E.H. Mott's *Between the Ocean and the Lakes: The Story of Erie* (1899) White derives much information on the Erie Railway, while he relies on John H. Morrison's *History of American Steam Navigation* (1903) for steamboat data, including the J.W. Hancox ad that he cites on pp. 105-6 and the *Alida* ad on pp. 108-9 (from Morrison, pp. 61-62 and 88). Henry Clews's *Twenty-eight Years in Wall Street* (1887), or the augmented edition of 1908, supply the stock-watering story (White, pp. 43-60); Vanderbilt's getting word to Drew at Taylor's Hotel (pp. 266-67); Drew's tricking the young Wall Street speculators in Oshkosh stock (pp. 401-2); and the spurious story of Drew taking refuge in bed with a liquor bottle (p. 422).[8]

The story of Drew's meeting his steamboat captain in the bar is taken from D.L. Buckman, *Old Steamboat Days on the Hudson River* (1909), pp. 62-63, while the 1831 and 1852 sections of Charles H. Haswell's *Reminiscences of an Octogenarian of the City of New York* (1896) inspired White's account of how Drew cheated the Hudson River Steamboat Association (White, pp. 99-100); how Boss Tweed lost money in Erie—an unverified story (pp. 164, 325); and how Drew unloaded Erie stock on a young lawyer (pp. 321-23). From W.W. Fowler's *Ten Years in Wall Street* (1870), or the augmented 1880 edition of it, comes the supposed Wall Street saying "Daniel says 'up'—Erie goes up" (White, p. 154); the description of Groesbeck's office in the 1860s (pp. 416-17); and other Wall Street lore.[9] Still more details were culled from the New York dailies' obituaries and other articles, from the *Methodist* and the *Christian Advocate*, the New York City *Directory*, and William Pelletreau's *History of Putnam County, New York* (1886). Much of the description of the golden wedding on pp. 350-51 was lifted almost intact from the florid, cliché-ridden account in the *Herald* of March 5, 1870.

White's *Book of Daniel Drew*, then, is a pastiche of printed sources, fleshed out with further details amassed on "field trips" to Putnam County, Drew Theological Seminary, Wall Street, and probably even the old Bull's Head Tavern (demolished in 1906). Not that his attempts at research preserved him from errors, for the book abounds in them. White makes Drew the younger, not the elder brother (pp. 10, 15, 37)—a mistake induced by certain obituaries and the tombstone itself of Thomas Drew; he names the Peter Lorillard family and not the butchers' association as the owners of the Bull's Head when Drew was there (p. 62), and has the Buck's Horn Tavern still standing (p. 68), although it was demolished in 1826; he mentions the *General Jackson* explosion (p. 95) without explaining how it triggered popular resentment against Jacob Vanderbilt, thus following Drew's own incomplete account in the McClintock article of 1859, which was drawn on by the obituaries; he presents Drew's partner Robert Kelley as an experienced and well-to-do drover when he joined Drew's Wall Street firm (p. 118), whereas Kelley was only nineteen; he has Drew build the Union Square mansion himself (p. 155), whereas Drew bought it from Nelson Robinson's estate; he has Vanderbilt on hand at the secret meeting at Judge Pierrepont's that helped resolve the Erie litigation of 1868 (pp. 272-78), when it is certain that Vanderbilt never attended it; he makes Isaac Newton die of thin-skinned overreaction to a steamboat disaster during the Civil War (p. 311), whereas that tough-grained gentleman actually died in 1858; he has Fisk on hand when Drew received his sealskin coat (pp. 418-19), when Fisk was in fact already dead; and so on. No allowance for mere editorial lapses by White could explain the innumerable errors of detail to be found on nearly every page of the book, which must be spurious from beginning to end.

Worse still, White's antipathy to his subject led him to deliberately distort his material. Thus he has Drew launch himself as a drover by engaging in an illicit trade in bob calves (pp. 19-20), for which there is no authority. He creates the story of the cheating of Henry Astor (pp. 43-60), and recasts the California Parker story in order to make Drew a coldhearted villain (pp. 190-97). In adapting the steamboat *Alida* ad from Morrison, p. 88, he substitutes the name of the *Drew* for the *Troy* as the *Alida*'s rival (pp. 108-9), thus replacing one vessel with another built twenty years later! More outrageous still, he has Drew state that the Erie was a prosperous line until he forced himself on the board (pp. 142-43), whereas Mott's history of the road—a source well known to White—says the opposite on nearly every page. So convinced was White of Drew's utter villainy, that he felt justified in bending the facts as he chose.

How is it, then, that this deliberately deceitful text, so fraught with errors and malice, has endured over the decades, resurrected in a variety of editions (some with the editor's note, some without) that scholars have used with caution but never with scorn—finally even inspiring an unmemorable 1937 RKO movie focused not on Drew but on Fisk, as well as a 1943 German translation meant to fuel Nazi propaganda's denunciation of American capitalism? For one thing, it has been the only full-length book on Drew; no other substantial source was available. And if even the most vigilant scholars have given it the benefit of a doubt, one must credit White's remarkable success in re-creating the idiom of his subject.

Himself born and raised in rural New York, White deftly fashioned a rustic speech of short, simple sentences rich in homespun imagery that closely approximated the language of the real Daniel Drew. It is hard not to hear an old ex-drover speaking when the Drew of the narrative tells of a Bull's Head customer getting "mad as a Durham bull," boasts that "I had the sow by the ear," tells how Erie stock "dropped like a dead heifer," and to justify his insider speculations, insists that "when you own a cow, you own her milk also."[10] Vivid, concrete images permeate the book, lending it color and charm, and on occasion rise almost to the level of poetry: "To speckilate in Wall Street when you are no longer an insider, is like buying cows by candlelight" (p. 423). Shrewdly, White sensed that for all his piety Uncle Daniel was not a Bible spouter but a cattle man whose speech was concrete and savory. The Daniel Drew that he conveys is a caricature, but the idiom that he speaks rings true. It is a pity that in this, his most readable and least dated work, White squandered his creative powers on a hoax.

Bouck White's subsequent career was a chain of violent explosions followed by a long quiescence. In 1911 Doubleday, Page & Company published his next book, *The Call of the Carpenter*, which presents Christ as a working-class labor organizer preaching social revolution against Roman imperialism, so unorthodox a view that the Congregational church expelled him. In 1913 he was arrested while assisting some

striking garment workers in Brooklyn whom he claimed had been men-
aced by thugs. Then in the following year he moved to Manhattan and
established the Church of the Social Revolution, whose membership of
agnostic socialists and anarchists he led in weekly parades behind a blaz-
ing red banner and to whom he preached sermons less Christian than
revolutionary in spirit. In 1914 he was jailed for six months for disrupting
services at John D. Rockefeller's Baptist church on Fifth Avenue, while
in 1916 he served thirty days for burning the American flag in a public
gesture of internationalism. Thereafter he was expelled by the Socialist
Party for indiscipline, and when the United States entered World War I
he reversed himself and urged pacifists to support the struggle. By 1919
he was advocating the reorganization of society through a world federa-
tion of small city-states, to further which he proposed that New York City
secede and become an independent municipal republic.

After a decade of provocative gestures and strident rhetoric, White
had failed to change the world in the slightest. Going to Paris in 1921,
he married a young French girl and brought her back to the United
Stated to live with him in a shack in the Catskill Mountains. Fast weary-
ing of rustic simplicity and her husband's politics, she initiated a sensa-
tional divorce suit in the course of which White's neighbors, scandalized
by his radicalism, dragged him from his shack one night to tar and
feather him. Thereafter, mindful of the example of Christ, a carpenter
who had worked with his hands, White went back to Europe to study
pottery-making techniques. Returning in 1932, he bought a small plot of
land in the Helderberg Mountains west of Albany, where with his own
hands he built a curious limestone castle and lived in it with two Swedish
assistants, making pottery.

Thirteen years he spent on the mountain, becoming the legendary
"Hermit of the Helderbergs": a bronzed, healthy, balding recluse who
claimed descent (quite falsely) from the Iroquois and subsisted by selling
pottery to visitors. He hoped to die there in his cliffside retreat, from
which on clear days he could see a hundred miles in three directions,
but in 1946 illness forced him to leave his mountain for a home for aged
men near Albany, after which he paid only rare visits to the site. He died
in the home on January 7, 1951, aged seventy-six. In accordance with his
last wishes, his body was cremated and the ashes scattered in a cleft near
his castle.

Notes

The following abbreviations have been used:

> *ARJ American Railroad Journal*, New York, N.Y.
> *BS Brewster Standard*, Brewster, N.Y.
> *CA Christian Advocate*, New York, N.Y.
> *PCC Putnam County Courier*, Carmel, N.Y.

Unless otherwise indicated, other newspapers cited were published in New York City.

Prologue

1. William W. Fowler, *Ten Years in Wall Street; or, Revelations of Inside Life and Experience on 'Change* (Hartford, Conn., 1870), p. 443.

CHAPTER 1. *Beginnings*

1. Mrs. Alvin Behr, historian of the township of Kent, has discovered the stone foundations of another old house lying a short distance to the north and east of the Northrup house, usually submerged by the waters of a reservoir but on occasion visible from the present Nichols Road. In her opinion, these foundations mark the true site of the Gilbert Drew homestead.
2. In 1812 the southern part of Dutchess County was organized as the new county of Putnam, with the small village of Carmel as its county seat.
3. *Tribune*, 19 Sept. 1879.

CHAPTER 2. *Circus and Drover Days*

1. William S. Pelletreau, *History of Putnam County, New York* (1886; reprint, Brewster, N.Y.: Landmarks Preservation Committee of Southeast Museum, 1975), p. 690n.

CHAPTER 3. *King of the Bull's Head Tavern*

1. Presumably from Drew + Clift, but certain later variants of the name, such as Drewcliff, Drewscliffe, and others, may indicate awareness of the family's alleged

descent from a knightly family of Drew living at a place called Drewscliff in Devonshire.
2. *Tribune*, 19 Sept. 1879.
3. On the night of June 2, 1841, a fire destroyed most of the Bull's Head Tavern and its adjacent buildings, with a great loss of animals as well. The brick wall fronting Third Avenue survived, however, and the hotel was rebuilt. In 1848 the cattle market moved north to Forty-fourth Street, and the Bull's Head became the center of the horse market. It survived into this century as a working men's hotel and was demolished in 1906.

CHAPTER 4. *Into Steamboating*

1. *Commercial Advertiser*, 20 June 1831.
2. Rev. J. McClintock, "Daniel Drew, Esquire, of New York," *Ladies Repository* 19 (Sept. 1859), p. 515.
3. Frances Trollope, *Domestic Manners of the Americans* (Gloucester, Mass.: Peter Smith, 1974), p. 352.
4. Charles Dickens, *American Notes and Pictures from Italy* (London: Oxford Univ. Press, 1957), p. 246.
5. *The Diary of Philip Hone* (New York: Dodd, Mead, 1927), pp. 138-39.
6. McClintock, "Daniel Drew, Esquire," p. 514.

CHAPTER 5. *Top Dog on the River*

1. The length recorded in the official Custom House enrollment of a vessel differed from the overall length announced (and often exaggerated) by the owner. The tonnage of the enrollment represented a cubic measurement, not the vessel's weight.
2. *Tribune*, 12 Oct. 1846.
3. *Evening Post*, 27 Dec. 1849.

CHAPTER 6. *Wall Street*

1. *Tribune*, 19 Sept. 1879.
2. From George G. Foster's anonymously published *New York in Slices: By an Experienced Carver* (New York, 1849), p. 116.
3. McClintock, "Daniel Drew, Esquire," p. 516.
4. CA, 2 Oct. 1879.
5. Ibid.
6. Bishop William Lawrence, "The Relation of Wealth to Morals," in *The World's Work* 1 (Jan. 1901), pp. 286, 290.

CHAPTER 7. *Enter the Iron Horse*

1. McClintock, "Daniel Drew, Esquire," p. 515.
2. *The Diary of George Templeton Strong*, vol. 2, eds. Allen Nevins and Milton H. Thomas (New York: Macmillan, 1952), p. 17.
3. *ARJ*, 21 May 1853.
4. *Evening Mail*, 14 Nov. 1867.

CHAPTER 8. *The Best Friend a Railroad Ever Had*

1. E. H. Mott, *Between the Ocean and the Lakes: The Story of Erie* (New York: Ticker Publishing Co., 1908), p. 105.
2. *Evening Mail*, 15 Nov. 1867.
3. Strong, *Diary*, vol. 2, pp. 355–56.
4. McClintock, "Daniel Drew, Esquire," p. 516.
5. Robert Sobel, *Panic on Wall Street* (London: Macmillan, 1968), p. 108.

CHAPTER 9. *Wartime*

1. *Herald,* 5 Dec. 1859.
2. McClintock, "Daniel Drew, Esquire," p. 517.
3. F. B. Carpenter, *Six Months at the White House with Abraham Lincoln* (New York, 1866), p. 84.
4. W. A. Croffut, *The Vanderbilts and the Story of Their Fortune* (Chicago and New York, 1886), p. 72.
5. Croffut, *Vanderbilts,* pp. 77-78.
6. Fowler, *Ten Years in Wall Street,* p. 351.
7. Croffut, *Vanderbilts,* p. 79.
8. Richard B. Kimball, "The Career of a Great Speculator," in *Frank Leslie's Popular Monthly,* Dec. 1879, p. 646.
9. Fowler, *Ten Years in Wall Street,* p. 356.
10. Fowler, *Ten Years in Wall Street,* p. 406.
11. Croffut, *Vanderbilts,* p. 79.

CHAPTER 10. *The Virtuoso of Erie*

1. David Lear Buckman, *Old Steamboat Days on the Hudson River,* rev. ed. (New York: Grafton Press, 1909), pp. 62-63.
2. *ARJ,* 2 Feb. 1861.
3. *Evening Mail,* 15 Nov. 1867.
4. Fowler, *Ten Years in Wall Street,* pp. 438-39.
5. Charles H. Haswell, *Reminiscences of an Octogenarian of the City of New York (1816 to 1860)* (New York: Harper & Brothers, 1896), p. 485.
6. Fowler, *Ten Years in Wall Street,* pp. 217-18.
7. Fowler, *Ten Years in Wall Street,* p. 124.

CHAPTER 11. *A Seminary, an Injunction, and a Loan*

1. Bouck White, *Book of Daniel Drew* (1910; reprint, Larchmont, N.Y.: American Research Council, 1965), p. 310. White is confirmed by William H. Drew in the *World,* 25 Apr. 1910.
2. *CA,* 2 Oct. 1879.
3. Ibid.
4. Ibid.
5. Ibid.
6. William A. Croffut, *An American Procession, 1855-1914: A Personal Chronicle of Famous Men* (Boston: Little, Brown, and Co., 1931), p. 278.
7. Matthew H. Smith, *Sunshine and Shadow in New York* (Hartford, 1868), pp. 525-26.
8. From McClintock's address at the seminary's opening, reported in the *Methodist,* 16 Nov. 1867.
9. *Methodist,* 3 Feb. 1866.
10. *CA,* 2 Oct. 1879.
11. Fowler, *Ten Years in Wall Street,* p. 472.
12. *Tribune,* 7 Apr. 1866.
13. *Herald,* 30 May 1866.
14. *Herald,* 4 June 1866; *Commercial Advertiser,* quoted in the *Times* of June 3 and 5, 1866.
15. Fowler, *Ten Years in Wall Street,* p. 468.

CHAPTER 12. *Uncle Daniel's Little Railroads*

1. *World,* 26 Apr. 1867.
2. *PCC,* 26 Nov. 1864.
3. *Times,* 9 Aug. 1864.

4. Croffut, *Vanderbilts*, p. 81.
5. *Documents of the Assembly of the State of New York*, 90th sess., 1867, vol. 2, p. 207.
6. Ibid., p. 202.
7. *Albany Evening Journal*, 24 Sept. 1867.
8. The coup de grâce to the Athens branch came on the night of June 18, 1876, when a conflagration destroyed the entire terminal, following which most of the rails were taken up and the White Elephant became only a memory.

CHAPTER 13. *The Great Erie War: Preliminaries*

1. *Tribune*, 6 Mar. 1871, quoting testimony before a New York State Assembly investigating committee in March 1869.
2. R. W. McAlpine, *The Life and Times of Col. James Fisk, Jr.* (New York, 1872), p. 46.
3. Rev. George R. Crooks, "Historical Review of the Twenty-Five Years," in *Proceedings of the Celebration of the Twenty-fifth Anniversary of the Founding of Drew Theological Seminary, October 26, 1892* (New York, 1892), pp. 20-21.
4. *Methodist*, 16 Nov. 1867.
5. Ibid.
6. McAlpine, *Fisk*, p. 60.
7. Fowler, *Ten Years in Wall Street*, p. 496.

CHAPTER 14. *The Battle of Wall Street*

1. Matthew Hale Smith, *Twenty Years among the Bulls and Bears of Wall Street* (Hartford, 1870), p. 125.
2. Charles Francis Adams, Jr., "A Chapter of Erie," in Charles Francis Adams, Jr. and Henry Adams, *Chapters of Erie* (1871; reprint, Ithaca, N.Y.: Cornell University Press, 1968), p. 10.
3. McAlpine, *Fisk*, p. 75.
4. *Herald*, 6 Mar. 1868.
5. Fowler, *Ten Years in Wall Street*, p. 500.
6. Anon., *A Life of James Fisk, Jr.* (New York, 1871), p. 85.
7. Croffut, *Vanderbilts*, p. 91.

CHAPTER 15. *The Battles of Fort Taylor*

1. *Times*, 14 Mar. 1868.
2. *Herald*, 15 Mar. 1868.
3. Ibid.
4. *World*, 14 Mar. 1868.
5. *Herald*, 15 Mar. 1868.
6. *World*, 14 Mar. 1868.
7. *Times*, 15 Mar. 1868.
8. *Sun*, 18 Mar. 1868.
9. *Times, Tribune*, and *Herald*, 17 Mar.; *World*, 18 Mar.; *Sun*, 20 Mar. 1868.
10. *Herald*, 19 Mar. 1868.
11. Ibid.
12. W. A. Swanberg, *Jim Fisk: The Career of an Improbable Rascal* (New York: Scribner's, 1959), p. 258. Mansfield testified in a libel suit that she brought against Fisk.
13. *Jersey City Daily Times*, 20 Mar. 1868.
14. Adams, *Chapters of Erie*, p. 43.
15. *Herald*, 28 Mar. 1868.
16. *Documents of the Senate of the State of New York*, 92nd sess., 1869, p. 109.

CHAPTER 16. *The Battle of Albany*

1. Mott, *Between the Ocean and the Lakes*, p. 152.
2. Editorial, *Tribune*, 28 Mar. 1868.
3. Ibid.
4. *Tribune*, 3 Apr. 1868.
5. Editorial, *Tribune*, 4 Apr. 1868.
6. Croffut, *Vanderbilts*, p. 95.
7. *World* and *Tribune*, 16 Apr. 1868.
8. Swanberg, *Jim Fisk*, p. 59.

CHAPTER 17. *Negotiations and Peace*

1. McAlpine, *Fisk*, p. 124.
2. Minutes, Board of Trustees, Drew Theological Seminary, 23 Apr. 1868.
3. Adams, *Chapters of Erie*, p. 41.
4. McAlpine, *Fisk*, p. 486.
5. McAlpine, *Fisk*, pp. 184-86. This is Fisk's testimony of March 17 and 18, 1870, reported also in the New York City dailies of March 18 and 19.
6. McAlpine, *Fisk*, p. 186.
7. McAlpine, *Fisk*, pp. 188-89.
8. McAlpine, *Fisk*, p. 192.
9. Board of Directors Minutes, Erie Railway Company, 10 July 1868.
10. Croffut, *Vanderbilts*, p. 97.
11. Charles Francis Adams, "The Erie Railway Row," *American Law Review*, Oct. 1868, pp. 85, 84.

CHAPTER 18. *The Greenback Lockup*

1. *Herald*, 19 Nov. 1868.
2. *Times*, 19 Nov. 1868. The text has been edited slightly for the sake of readability.
3. *Herald*, 23 Nov. 1868.
4. *Herald*, 22 Nov. 1868.

CHAPTER 19. *Respite and Return*

1. *Tribune*, 19 Sept. 1879.
2. *PCC*, 4 Mar. 1871.
3. *Herald*, 21 Nov. 1869.
4. Edward C. Stedman, ed., *The New York Stock Exchange* (1905, reprint, New York: Greenwood Press, 1969), p. 243.
5. *Herald*, 20 Sept. 1872.
6. *Tribune*, 26 Sept. 1872.
7. *Herald*, 24 Nov. 1872.
8. Ibid.
9. *Times*, 24 Nov. 1872.
10. Henry Clews, *Twenty-eight Years in Wall Street* (New York, 1887), p. 143.
11. *Sun*, 27 Nov. 1872.
12. *Sun*, 26 Nov. 1872.
13. *Sun*, 27 Nov. 1872.

CHAPTER 20. *Uncle Daniel Buys the Dream*

1. *BS*, 23 Aug. 1873.
2. Quoted in *Frank Leslie's Illustrated Newspaper*, 4 Oct. 1873.
3. *PCC*, 18 Oct. 1873.

CHAPTER 21. *The Last Great Caper*

1. *Times*, 18 Mar. 1875.
2. *Times*, 20 Mar. 1875.

3. *Sun*, 31 Mar. 1875.
4. *Daily Graphic*, 31 Mar. 1875.
5. *Daily Graphic*, 28 May 1875.

CHAPTER 22. *Bankruptcy*

1. Bankruptcy file, Drew's testimony of 20 June 1876.
2. Albert Osborn, *John Fletcher Hurst: A Biography* (New York: Eaton & Mains, 1905), p. 204.
3. Minutes, Board of Trustees, Drew Theological Seminary, 17 Feb. 1876.
4. Minutes of the Executive Committee, Board of Trustees, Wesleyan University, 21 Feb. 1876.
5. *Tribune*, 19 Sept. 1879. The interview seems not to have been published at the time of Drew's bankruptcy.
6. *CA*, 2 Oct. 1879.
7. *CA*, 18 Sept. 1911. The complete hymn includes five stanzas.
8. *Sun*, 7 Apr. 1876.
9. *Herald*, 11 May 1876.
10. *World*, 9 Mar. 1878.
11. Bankruptcy file, testimony of 20 June 1876.
12. Ibid.
13. *Tribune*, 23 June 1876.

CHAPTER 23. *The Oldest Man on the Street*

1. *BS*, 1 Sept. 1876.
2. *Sun*, 22 Nov. 1876.
3. Ibid.
4. *Autobiography of Charles Force Deems, D.D., LL.D., Pastor of the Church of the Strangers, New York City, and President of the American Institute of Christian Philosophy, and Memoir by His Sons, Rev. Edw. M. Deems, A.M., Ph.D., and Francis M. Deems, M.D., Ph.D.* (New York, 1897), p. 268.
5. Ibid., p. 271.
6. Minutes, Board of Trustees, Drew Theological Seminary, 16 May 1877.
7. *CA*, 8 Nov. 1877.
8. Clews, *Twenty-eight Years*, p. 152.
9. *Herald*, 5 Feb. 1878.
10. *World*, 9 Mar. 1878.
11. *CA*, 25 Sept. 1879.
12. *CA*, 25 Sept. 1879.
13. *CA*, 22 May 1879.
14. *Sun*, 19 Sept. 1879.
15. *Albany Argus*, 20 Sept. 1879; *CA*, 25 Sept. 1879.

Appendix. *White's "Book of Daniel Drew"*

1. White, *Book of Daniel Drew*, p. xii.
2. Ibid., p. xiii.
3. Ibid., pp. 6, 128, 390, 306-7, 188-89.
4. *World*, 26 Apr. 1910.
5. *Brooklyn Daily Eagle*, 25 Apr. 1910.
6. *Brooklyn Daily Eagle*, 29 Apr. 1910.
7. *World*, 29 Apr. 1910.
8. Clews, *Twenty-eight Years*, pp. 121, 134-35, 122-23, 155.
9. Fowler, *Ten Years in Wall Street*, pp. 142, 214-15.
10. White, *Book of Daniel Drew*, pp. 63, 152, 231, 221.

Bibliography

Preliminary Note

The only full-length book on Daniel Drew is Bouck White's *Book of Daniel Drew* (1910; reprint, Larchmont, N.Y.: American Research Council, 1965), hereafter cited as White. This is a fraudulent fictional narration that purports to be Drew's edited autobiography (see Appendix).

Useful contemporary biographical sketches include Rev. J. McClintock, D.D., "Daniel Drew, Esquire, of New York," in the *Ladies Repository* 19 (Sept. 1859), pp. 513-17, cited hereafter as McClintock, which, based on information from Drew, is the best account of the early part of his career; an unsigned sketch in the *New York Evening Mail* of November 14 and 15, 1867; the obituaries in the New York City dailies of September 19, 1879; and Richard B. Kimball, "The Career of a Great Speculator," in *Frank Leslie's Popular Monthly*, 8 (Dec. 1879), pp. 641-49, 652.

No manuscript in Drew's handwriting survives, except his signature on documents. Being semiliterate, he almost never wrote letters, and the few that he did write were illegible.

The following abbreviations have been used throughout:

ARJ American Railroad Journal, New York, N.Y.
BS Brewster Standard, Brewster, N.Y.
CA Christian Advocate, New York, N.Y.
DAB Dictionary of American Biography
PCC Putnam County Courier, Carmel, N.Y.

Unless otherwise indicated, other newspapers cited were published in New York City.

CHAPTER 1. *Beginnings*

Genealogical information on Gilbert Drew can be found in Ella Drew, *The Drews of Sussex County, New Jersey* (undated); Dr. A. E. Tepper, "Supplement to *The Drews of Sussex County, New Jersey*, by Ella Drew," (1966), a typed manuscript deposited with the New Hampshire Historical Society at Concord, N.H.; Ralph D. Phillips, "Drew Family of Putnam County, N.Y.," (undated), a typed manuscript deposited with the New York Public Library; and Ralph D. Phillips, "Gilbert Drew, His Wives and Children," *New York Genealogical and Biographical Record* 101 (1970): 82-86. Ella Drew tries to link Gilbert to certain Drews who settled in Massachusetts and New Hampshire in the seventeenth century, and through them to the Drews of Devonshire in England. The Tepper paper corrects certain of her errors, and after a prolonged investigation concludes that the date and place of birth and the parentage of Gilbert Sr. remain unknown. The Phillips articles are useful, but the one printed in 1970 has many errors regarding Daniel Drew and his children.

Further genealogical information on the Putnam County Drews and their relations is found in Barbara Smith Buys, *Old Gravestones of Putnam County, New York* (Baltimore: Gateway Press, 1975).

The story of Catherine Muckelworth's adoption by the Lawrence family appears in the Ralph D. Phillips manuscript cited above. Although the writer has not been able to confirm this story, it seems plausible and explains why Catherine used two surnames.

The standard source for early Putnam County history is William S. Pelletreau, *History of Putnam County, New York* (1886; reprint, Brewster, N.Y.: Landmarks Preservation Committee of Southeast Museum, 1975), cited hereafter as Pelletreau.

For the spirit of early Methodism, see William W. Sweet, *Religion on the American Frontier, 1783-1840*, volume 4, *The Methodists: A Collection of Source Materials* (New York: Cooper Square Publishers, 1964); the same author's *Story of Religion in America* (New York: Harper & Row, 1950); and Charles A. Johnson, *The Frontier Camp Meeting* (Dallas: Southern Methodist Univ. Press, 1955). Although especially concerned with the frontier, these books are also relevant for Methodism in the East. The coming of Methodism to Putnam County is best treated in a brief paper by the Rev. W. C. Smith, "Introduction of Methodism into Putnam County, New York," *Brewster Standard*, 5 Aug. 1932; Daniel Drew is mentioned specifically.

Gilbert Drew's will is on file at the Dutchess County Surrogate's Court in Poughkeepsie, N.Y.

Information about Daniel and Thomas Drew's service in the War of 1812 comes from their pension, bounty land warrant application, and military records in the National Archives in Washington, D.C.; and from their claims for compensation on file with the Bureau of War Records maintained by the Division of Military and Naval Affairs in Albany, N.Y. Background information is provided by R. S. Guernsey, *New York City and Vicinity during the War of 1812-15* (New York, 1895).

CHAPTER 2. *Circus and Drover Days*

There is no book wholly devoted to the Eastern drover. For the drover's trade viewed in a larger perspective, see Clarence H. Danhof, *Change in Agriculture: The Northern United States, 1820-1870* (Cambridge, Mass.: Harvard Univ. Press, 1969); and Percy W. Bidwell and John I. Falconer, *History of Agriculture in the Northern United States, 1620-1860* (New York: Peter Smith, 1941). There is a good treatment of drovers and highway life in New York State in Alexander C. Flick, ed., *History of the State of New York*, vol. 5 (New York: Columbia Univ. Press, 1934), chap. 8, "The Turnpike Era," by Oliver W. Holmes. For details specific to Putnam County, see "Putnam County History: 'Work Shop,'" papers produced at the first to third workshops organized by Horace E. Hillery, Putnam County historian, 1954-57, vol. 2 passim.

The early American circus is treated in Isaac J. Greenwood, *The Circus: Its Origin and Growth Prior to 1835* (New York, 1898); Earl Chapin May, *The Circus from Rome to Ringling* (New York: Duffield and Green, 1932); R.W.G. Vail, *Random Notes on the History of the Early American Circus* (Barre, Mass.: Barre Gazette, 1956); and George L. Chindahl, *A History of the Circus in America* (Caldwell, Idaho: Caxton Printers, 1959). Drew's circus experience and the conversion that ended it are related briefly in the *Herald* obituary.

For the old Bull's Head, see Thomas F. De Voe, *The Market Book* (New York, 1862), which discusses the butchers and old markets of New York in charming detail; also Alvin F. Harlow, *Old Bowery Days* (New York and London: D. Appleton, 1931).

There are somewhat different versions of the lightning incident. The one in McClintock is followed here because his article is the earliest, and he probably got the story straight from Drew.

For Henry Astor, see De Voe, *The Market Book*, and Harlow, *Old Bowery Days*, as well as brief mentions in Arthur D. Howden Smith, *John Jacob Astor* (Philadelphia: Lippincott, 1929). White tells the stock-watering story on pp. 42-60. Drew's honesty as a drover is mentioned in the *Times* and *Herald* obituaries. Pelletreau attributes the term "water stock" (*sic*) to Drew (p. 690n). Perhaps the first to attribute the practice itself to Drew as a drover, although without mention of Henry Astor, was the banker Henry Clews in *Twenty-eight Years in Wall Street* (New York, 1887), p. 121—a work that White certainly knew. Drew's son William H. Drew discounts the story in an interview in the *World*, 25 Apr. 1910.

McClintock states that Drew came to the Bull's Head in 1829, but Drew's name does not appear in the tavern license cash book for 1829-30, which is preserved in the Municipal Archives of New York City. Since he sold his Putnam County farm on April 1, 1830, he probably took over at the Bull's Head on May 1, the traditional date for new leases.

CHAPTER 3. *King of the Bull's Head Tavern*

For Mrs. Trollope's comments on America, prompted by her visit of 1827-31, see Frances Trollope, *Domestic Manners of the Americans* (Gloucester, Mass.: Peter Smith, 1974), passim. The growth of New York City's commerce is studied in depth by Robert Greenhalgh Albion, *The Rise of New York Port: 1815-1860* (New York: Scribner's, 1939).

The best source for the Bull's Head under Daniel Drew is C. C. Buel, "At the Old Bull's Head," *Scribner's Monthly* 17 (1879), an article that preceded Drew's death and draws on old-timers' recollections. Other details come from a short article in the *Tribune* of October 11, 1894, and from the New York City dailies of June 3, 1841, reporting the fire at the Bull's Head on the day preceding.

There are no detailed descriptions of market day at the Bull's Head, but it would not have differed appreciably from the later New York City market described briefly in "The Cattle Trade of New York," in *The Plough, the Loom, and the Anvil* 1 (1848); or from the 1840 Brighton market, its New England equivalent, described in Nathaniel Hawthorne's *American Note Books*. White's treatment of the Bull's Head (pp. 61–77) is rich in detail that may derive from valid sources or from a visit to the building shortly before its demolition in 1906; but it is rich in errors, too.

The Ohio cattle trade has been well researched, notably by Paul C. Henlein, *Cattle Kingdom in the Ohio Valley: 1783-1860* (Lexington: Univ. of Kentucky Press, 1959). See also the invaluable recollections of William Renick in *Memoirs, Correspondence and Reminiscences* (Circleville, Ohio, 1880); I. F. King, "The Coming and Going of Ohio Droving," *Ohio Archaeological and Historical Quar-*

terly 17 (1908); Robert L. Jones, "The Beef Cattle Industry in Ohio Prior to the Civil War, pt. 2," *Ohio Historical Quarterly*, July 1955.

For the trans-Allegheny trails, see above all the firsthand recollections of John S. Orr, "The Three Mountain Road," *The Kittochtinny Historical Society Papers* 5 (1908); also Minnie Dubbs Millbrook, "Three Mountain Cattle Trail," *The Westerners. New York Posse. Brand Book*, vol. 5, no. 2 (1958); and Harry S. Drago, *Great American Cattle Trails* (New York: Dodd, Mead, 1965). Philip D. Jordan, *The National Road* (Gloucester, Mass.: Peter Smith, 1966) provides a good over-all picture of life on the Western roads.

Drew's own trans-Allegheny drives are related briefly in the McClintock article and the obituaries (especially the *Herald* and the *Tribune*). Henlein places Drew's first trans-Allegheny drive in 1818 or 1819 (*Cattle Kingdom*, p. 115), but in this he is surely mistaken. White's account (pp. 77-86) is imaginative, but because it accepts Drew's claim to have made the first drive over the mountains, he describes the circumstances as unduly primitive and desolate; by the time of Drew's drive, inns existed along most of the way and pasture was generally available.

CHAPTER 4. *Into Steamboating*

Basic sources for Hudson River steamboating include John H. Morrison, *History of American Steam Navigation* (New York: W. F. Sametz, 1903); David Lear Buckman, *Old Steamboat Days on the Hudson River*, rev. ed. (New York: Grafton Press, 1909); Fred Erving Dayton, *Steamboat Days* (New York: Frederick A. Stokes, 1925); Robert Greenhalgh Albion, *The Rise of New York Port: 1815-1860* (New York: Scribner's, 1939), chap. 8; Carl D. Lane, *American Paddle Boats* (New York: Coward-McCann, 1943); and Frank Donovan, *River Boats of America* (New York: Thomas Y. Crowell, 1966). Although its focus is not on Drew's People's Line, Donald C. Ringwald's *Hudson River Day Line* (Berkeley, Calif.: Howell-North Books, 1965) has useful information, including illustrations and a bibliography.

Further information on individual vessels can be obtained from Erik Heyl, *Early American Steamers*, 6 vols. (Buffalo, N.Y.: the author, 1953-69), which contains some errors; the veteran marine engineer George W. Murdock's articles in the scrapbooks of the Murdock Collection at the New York Historical Society in New York City; and the successive certificates of enrollment originally filed for each vessel in the various federal custom houses, and now available at the National Archives in Washington, D.C.

The *General Jackson* explosion and its aftermath were reported in the *Evening Post* of June 8 and 14, and the *Commercial Advertiser* of June 8-10, 15, and 20, 1831. Brief accounts of the *Water Witch*, sometimes mutually contradictory in details, are found in McClintock; the *Herald* obituary, 19 Sept. 1879; the Murdock Collection; and Charles H. Haswell, *Reminiscences of an Octogenarian of the City of New York (1816 to 1860)* (New York: Harper & Brothers, 1896). Cornelius Vanderbilt's later version of the story, included in a biographical sketch of him in *Harper's Weekly* (5 Mar. 1859), has Cornelius heroically confront the unreasoning fury of the public and gradually win out against a monopoly charging a higher fare. Drew's own 1859 account in McClintock naturally gives no hint of a betrayal, nor does it describe the public's fury against Jacob Vanderbilt, with whom Drew by then had business dealings. The account presented here attempts to reconcile all these sources with the aid of contemporary newspapers and the certificates of enrollment.

Wheaton J. Lane, *Commodore Vanderbilt: An Epic of the Steam Age* (New York: Knopf, 1942) provides an excellent account of Cornelius Vanderbilt's business career. It can be supplemented by the interviews with Vanderbilt's contemporaries in the *Herald* of January 7, 1877.

The account of the origin of both Vanderbilt's and Drew's People's Line is based mostly on contemporary newspapers. Who owned the *Westchester* in 1835 cannot be stated with certainty, since no copy of the relevant certificate of enrollment survives. The story of Drew's cheating the Hudson River Steamboat Association of $8,000 is told by Haswell, *Reminiscences*, pp. 257-58.

CHAPTER 5. *Top Dog on the River*

For Isaac Newton, see *DAB* and the obituaries in the *Evening Post* and *Albany Evening Journal* of November 23; the *Tribune* and *Herald* of November 24; and the *Albany Argus* of November 25, 1858. The *De Witt Clinton's* ramming of the *Napoleon* is recounted in New York and Albany papers of June 15-17, 1840, and in the Murdock Collection's article on the *Napoleon*.

Information concerning the organization and history of the People's Line Association can be found in the original case files of *George Monteath* v. *Isaac Newton, Daniel Drew, and others*, preserved in the County Clerk's Office in Albany, N.Y. Included in the files are the text of the company's articles of association and other relevant documents.

The palace steamboat and the taste that created it are well treated in Russell Lynes, *The Tastemakers* (New York: Harper & Brothers, 1954), chap. 6. The *Hendrik Hudson* is mentioned in the *Evening Post* and *Tribune* of October 8, 1845; the *Isaac Newton*, in the *Herald* of October 9, the *Post* of October 10, and the *Tribune* of October 12, 1846; and the *New World*, in the *Herald* of June 11 and 12, the *Tribune* of June 14, and the *Evening Post* of June 13, 1849. The *New World's* record passenger load is reported in the *Albany Evening Journal* of September 5, 1850.

For a brief account of George Monteath, see Joel Munsell, *The Annals of Albany*, vol. 8 (Albany: J. Munsell, 1857), p. 332. The records of his case against the People's Line Association are preserved in Albany as stated above. Except for announcements and accounts of the sale, the New York and Albany papers seem scarcely to have mentioned the affair. The terms of Drew's settlement with Van Santvoord are recorded in the ledger of the Hudson River Steamboat Company (1845-69), preserved as part of the Hudson River Day Line Collection at the New York Historical Society.

CHAPTER 6. *Wall Street*

General histories of Wall Street include Robert Sobel, *The Big Board: A History of the New York Stock Market* (New York: Free Press, 1965); Edward C. Stedman, ed., *The New York Stock Exchange* (1905; reprint, New York: Greenwood Press, 1969); Henry Wysham Lanier, *A Century of Banking in New York: 1822–1922* (New York: George H. Doran, 1922); Francis Eames, *The New York Stock Exchange* (1894; reprint, New York: Greenwood Press, 1968). For a general study of New York City during this period, see Edward K. Spann, *The New Metropolis: New York City, 1840-1857* (New York: Columbia Univ. Press, 1981).

Drew's first Wall Street partnership is mentioned by McClintock and the *Evening Post* of September 19, 1879. Nelson Robinson's career is mentioned in *PCC*, 29 Mar. 1856, and in William Armstrong's anonymously published *Stocks and Stock-Jobbing in Wall-Street, with Sketches of the Brokers, and Fancy Stocks . . . By a Reformed Stock Gambler* (New York, 1848), which is also a useful source generally for Wall Street in the 1840s. For Jacob Little, see especially his obituary in the *Herald* of March 29, 1865.

Drew's 1841 conversion is described by McClintock; his feeling for his mother and his tearful public penitence are related in the funeral addresses of John Parker and Cyrus D. Foss in *CA*, 2 Oct. 1879. The Mulberry Street Church's history is related in Samuel A. Seaman, *Annals of New York Methodism* (New York, 1892); the old church records are now in the possession of the Saint Paul and Saint Andrew Methodist Church of New York.

Drew's interest in the New Jersey Steam Navigation Company and the Stonington line is recounted briefly by McClintock; Lane's *Commodore Vanderbilt*, chap. 4; and Morrison, *History of American Steam Navigation*, chap. 5. See also the steamboat ads of the day; *Annual Reports of the New York, Providence & Boston R.R. Co., 1833 to 1874* (Westerly, R.I., 1874); and Edward Chase Kirkland, *Men, Cities and Transportation: A Study in New England History, 1820–1900*, vol. 1 (Cambridge, Mass.: Harvard Univ. Press, 1948).

Drew's illness of circa 1851 is mentioned by him in *BS*, 1 Sept. 1876, and by his pastor of the time, Randolph Sinks Foster, who is quoted in Charles Fremont Sitterly, *The Building of Drew University* (New York: Methodist Book Concern, 1938), pp. 46-47. Foster's statement, made many years afterward, dates the illness somewhat later, but Drew's own account places it about 1851, when Foster was indeed his pastor.

CHAPTER 7. *Enter the Iron Horse*

The story of the Hudson River Railroad is told in chapters 9 and 10 of Edward Hungerford, *Men and Iron: The History of the New York Central* (New York: Thomas Y. Crowell, 1938). The effect of the railroad on Hudson River steamboating is discussed in Morrison, *American Steam Navigation*, pp. 156, 160, 165. For James Boorman, see *DAB* and the *Times* of January 26, 1866. John F. Stover, *Iron Road to the West: American Railroads in the 1850s* (New York: Columbia Univ. Press, 1978) surveys the burgeoning rail network of that decade, but errs in stating (p. 176) that the Hudson River steamboats of that period encountered no serious competition from the railroad.

For the accident on the *New World* and its aftermath, see Morrison, *American Steam Navigation*, pp. 113-16; the *Herald* of July 2, 1853; and the *Albany Daily Argus* of July 4, 1853.

The People's Line alliance with the New York Central is mentioned in Hungerford, *Men and Iron*, chap. 10, and in Edward Harold Mott, *Between the Ocean and the Lakes: The Story of Erie* (New York: Ticker Publishing, 1908), p. 123.

The act incorporating the New Jersey Steamboat Company is found in the *Acts of the Seventy-eighth Legislature of the State of New Jersey* (Mount Holly, N.J., 1854), pp. 166-69.

The renovated *New World* is described in the *Albany Journal* of September 7, 1855; its profits are reported in Joel Munsell, *The Annals of Albany*, vol. 10, p. 415.

For Drew's involvement in Lake Champlain steamboating, see The Champlain Transportation Company, *The Steamboats of Lake Champlain: 1809 to 1930*, Major Ogden J. Ross, ed. (n.p.: Press of the Delaware and Hudson Railroad, 1930), chaps. 6 and 7. A ticket for the Jenny Lind package deal appears as an illustration on p. 82 of Frank Donovan, *River Boats of America* (New York: Thomas Y. Crowell, 1966).

Drew and his daughter in Putnam County and the annual county fairs are reported in *PCC* of the 1850s. Drew's cattle raising is mentioned in the *Tribune* Cattle Market Report of November 20 and 27, 1856, and November 4, 1858, and in McClintock.

CHAPTER 8. *The Best Friend a Railroad Ever Had*

The standard history of the Erie Railroad is E.H. Mott, *Between the Ocean and the Lakes: The Story of Erie*, which reprints many primary sources in part or full and includes invaluable appendices. For the Erie crisis of 1854, see also the *Herald* and *Tribune* of late August and early September 1854, and *ARJ* of September 30, 1854.

There are obituaries of Nelson Robinson in the *Times* of March 25, 1856, and *PCC* of March 29, 1856. He is mentioned also in James K. Medbery, *Men and Mysteries of Wall Street* (1870; reprint, Wells, Vt.: Fraser Publishing, 1968), pp. 312-13, and in the sketch of Drew in the *Evening Mail* of November 15, 1867.

For the Panic of 1857 and what led to it, see chapter 3 of Robert Sobel, *Panic on Wall Street: A History of America's Financial Disasters* (New York: Macmillan, 1969) for a descriptive account, and George W. Van Vleck, *The Panic of 1857: An Analytical Study* (New York: AMS Press, 1967), for an analysis. Erie's issue of 5,000 shares of new stock is reported in the *Herald* of March 30, 1857.

The events of October 13, 1857, on Wall Street are recounted in the *Herald*, *Times*, and *Tribune* of October 14, and in Strong's diary entry for October 13. The painting in question is "Wall Street, half past 2 o'clock, October 13, 1857," by James H. Cafferty and Charles G. Rosenberg, which hangs in the Museum of the City of New York, and is reproduced on p. 263 of John A. Kouwenhoven, *The Columbia Historical Portrait of New York* (New York: Doubleday, 1953); a few figures are identified in the Museum's *Bulletin* of May 1940, pp. 68-72. Clews's comments on the Panic and Wall Street appear in chapter 1 of *Twenty-eight Years in Wall Street*.

CHAPTER 9. *Wartime*

Details of the Prince of Wales's visit are reported in various issues of the *Times*, *Herald*, *Post*, and *World*, and the *Albany Evening Journal* and *Atlas and Argus*, of October 15-18, 1860. The story of Drew's son standing in for the Prince of Wales was communicated to the author by Drew's great-grand-daughter, Mrs. Dorothy Illingworth Pearsall.

For the wartime boom in the North, see Allan Nevins, *The War for the Union* (New York: Scribner's, 1959-71), vols. 2 and 3; and Emerson David Fite, *Social and Industrial Conditions in the North during the Civil War* (1910; reprint, New York: Frederick Ungar Publishing, 1963). Vessels bought or chartered by the Quartermaster's Department in the Civil War are listed in 40th Congress, 2d Sess., House of Representatives, Ex. Doc. 337.

Wall Street in the Civil War is described in Robert Sobel's *The Big Board*, *Panic on Wall Street*, and *The Curbstone Brokers: The Origins of the American Stock Exchange* (New York: Macmillan, 1970). Interesting pictorial material is found in Leonard Louis Levinson, *Wall Street: A Pictorial History* (New York: Ziff-Davis Publishing, 1961).

Invaluable details concerning wartime Wall Street are provided by the memoirs of the time: W.W. Fowler, *Ten Years in Wall Street*; James K. Medbery, *Men and Mysteries of Wall Street*; Henry Clews, *Twenty-eight Years in Wall Street*; and Matthew Hale Smith, *Twenty Years among the Bulls and Bears of Wall Street* (Hartford, 1870); all these works contain firsthand impressions of Drew.

The two Harlem Corners are recounted most accurately in Wheaton J. Lane, *Commodore Vanderbilt*, chap. 9, and Edward C. Stedman, ed., *The New York Stock Exchange*, chap. 12. Also useful, although not without errors, are W.A. Croffut, *The Vanderbilts and the Story of Their Fortune* (New York, 1886), chap. 9 and p. 18, and, among the Wall Street memoirs just cited, Fowler, chapts. 11 and 21; Medbery, pp. 92-93, 162-63; and Clews, pp. 110-16, 128, 349.

For relevant contemporary newspaper accounts of the Second Harlem Corner, see the *Herald* of March 10, 16, April 20, 27, 30, May 15, and June 3, 1864; the *Times* of March 16 and April 22, 1864, and January 5, 1877; and the *Tribune* of March 24, April 23, 26, 29, 30, and May 17-19, 1864. Later sources often confuse the two Harlem Corners, or speak of them as if there had been only one.

CHAPTER 10. *The Virtuoso of Erie*

For contemporary accounts of the *St. John*, see the *Daily News* of February 16 and March 15; the *Evening Post* of March 14; and the *Tribune* and *World* of March 15, 1864. The *Dean Richmond* is described in the *Times* and *World* of July 28, 1865.

Drew's 1864 income was published in a list in the *Herald* of January 15, 1865. His settlement of the *Dean Richmond* claims is recounted in Matthew Hale Smith, *Twenty Years among the Bulls and Bears of Wall Street*, chap. 7. Information on the New Jersey Steam Navigation Company liquidation comes from Morrison, *American Steam Navigation*, pp. 291-94, and from law reports in the *Tribune* of December 12, 1874, and March 30, 1875, and the *Times* and *Tribune* of January 12, 1876.

Jim Fisk's meeting with Drew is related in the anonymous *A Life of James Fisk, Jr.* (New York, 1871), chap. 3, and R.W. McAlpine, *The Life and Times of Col. James Fisk, Jr.* (New York, 1872), chap. 6. In this and other regards, both accounts contain errors—especially the second, which is semifictional, with much obviously invented dialogue. Certain errors from these sources and Fisk's obituaries are repeated in W.A. Swanberg, *Jim Fisk: The Career of an Improbable Rascal* (New York: Scribner's, 1959), which even so is an excellent and most readable biography.

The reorganization of the New York and Erie Railroad Company as the Erie Railway Company is recounted in E.H. Mott, *The Story of Erie*, chap. 13; for critical comments on those involved, see *ARJ*, October 22 and 29, 1859.

Drew's 1860 coup in Erie stock is mentioned in the *Herald* of September 19, 1879, and Fowler, *Ten Years in Wall Street*, pp. 142-43. For the Erie Railway Steamboat Company, see the Articles of Association and other documents on file with the Department of State in Albany; *ARJ*, August 9, 1862; and the *Times* of December 8, 1868.

Drew's stock market operations of 1864-65 are recounted in Fowler, *Ten Years in Wall Street*, chapts. 28 and 31; James K. Medbery, *Men and Mysteries of Wall Street*, pp. 105-6; and the newspapers of the day, of which the following issues are especially useful: the *Herald* of May 22, July 29, August 2, 18, 21, 24, 25, 28, September 4, 11, 25, and October 2, 1865; the *Times* of January 22, March 22, April 9, July 12, 27, August 25, and September 3, 1865; and the *Tribune* of January 6, 25, July 27, and September 5, 1865.

For Leonard Jerome, see the *Times* of March 5, 1891, and Smith, *Twenty Years*, chap. 17 (an account not without inaccuracies). White's "Daniel says 'up'" saying (p. 154) was prompted by Fowler, *Ten Years in Wall Street*, p. 142.

The Uncle Daniel stories cited in the text are from Charles Haswell, *Reminiscences of an Octogenarian*, p. 485; Henry Clews, *Twenty-eight Years in Wall Street*, pp. 125-26; Fowler, *Ten Years in Wall Street*, pp. 217-18, 483-84; and Medbery, *Men and Mysteries of Wall Street*, pp. 83-86. The California Parker story appears in White, pp. 190-97; Clews, pp. 155-56; and Fowler, pp. 252-53, 261.

CHAPTER 11. *A Seminary, an Injunction, and a Loan*

Testimony regarding Drew's piety and fervor appears in *CA*, October 2, 1879, which also includes the Rev. John Parker's reminiscences of Drew.

The founding of Drew Theological Seminary is best told by John T. Cunningham, *University in the Forest: The Story of Drew University* (n.p.: Afton Publishing, 1972). Useful firsthand testimony is provided by Cunningham's sources: Rev. George R. Crooks, "Historical Review of the Twenty-five Years," *Proceedings of the Celebration of the Twenty-fifth Anniversary of the Founding of Drew Theological Seminary, October 26, 1892* (New York, 1892); Ezra Squier Tipple, ed., *Drew Theological Seminary, 1867-1917: A Review of the First Half Century* (New York: Methodist Book Concern, 1917); and Charles Fremont Sitterly, *The Building of Drew University* (New York: Methodist Book Concern, 1938).

The corner in Old Southern is described in Fowler, *Ten Years in Wall Street*, chap. 30, and in the *Times*, *Herald*, and *Tribune* of April 5-9 and the *Times* of April 15, 1866.

Drew's operations in Erie in 1866-67, including his loan to the company, are reported in the *Herald* of May 29-31, June 1-5, and July 10 and 12, 1866; in the *Tribune* of May 31 and June 1, 1866; and in the *Times* of May 29-31, June 1-9, 16, and 29, July 11, 12, 18, and 27, and October 8-10, 1866, and January 26, 1867. Further details are provided by the minutes of the Erie board and executive committee; the *Times* of March 12, 1868, which prints Drew's affidavit of March 9; and the Pierce committee reports in *Documents of the Senate of the State of New York*, 91st sess., 1868, Doc. 67.

For William H. Marston and his operations in Erie, see Fowler, *Ten Years in Wall Street*, p. 468 and chap. 31; James K. Medbery, *Men and Mysteries of Wall Street*, pp. 190-91; and Marston's testimony in *White* v. *Drew*, reported in the *Herald* of November 23, 1876. White's anecdote, which calls Marston "Marsden," appears on pp. 354-58.

The erroneous impression that Drew pulled off a spectacular coup in Erie in May 1866 seems to have originated with James K. Medbery's article "The Great Erie Imbroglio," *Atlantic Monthly*, July 1868, and Charles Francis Adams, Jr.'s 1869 article "A Chapter of Erie," reprinted in Charles Francis Adams, Jr. and Henry Adams, *Chapters of Erie* (1871; reprint, Ithaca, N.Y.: Cornell Univ. Press, 1968). Adams's account (pp. 6-7) was accepted by E. H. Mott in chapter 14 of his history of Erie, *Between the Ocean and the Lakes*, which furthermore makes Vanderbilt a victim of Drew's 1866 operation (a circumstance verified by no contemporary source); sanctioned by Mott, this version of the story has been told ever since.

CHAPTER 12. *Uncle Daniel's Little Railroads*

The steamboat *Drew* is described in the *Albany Evening Journal* of April 24, the *Albany Argus* of April 25, and the *Times*, *Tribune*, and *World* of April 26, 1867.

Drew's connection with the Port Jervis church is recounted in information made available to the author by the Church History Committee of the Drew United Methodist Church of Port Jervis, N.Y. For Drew and his family in Putnam County, see Pelletreau and *PCC* of the 1860s. The construction of the Italian-villa-style mansion that William H. Drew later called Drewscliff has usually been attributed to Drew, but he seems never to have used the Clift farm as a residence.

Information on the various railroads mentioned is found in Henry V. Poor's *History of the Railroads and Canals of the United States of America* (New York, 1860); his *Manual of the Railroads of the United States, for 1868-69* (New York, 1868); and *ARJ*.

An account of the Adirondack Company appears in Jim Shaughnessy, *Delaware & Hudson* (Berkeley, Calif.: Howell-North Books, 1967), chap. 6; and Harold K. Hochschild, *Doctor Durant and His Iron Horse* (Blue Mountain Lake, N.Y.: Adirondack Museum, 1961).

Information on the Buffalo, Bradford and Pittsburgh Railroad is found in Mott, *Between the Ocean and the Lakes*, pp. 142, 145, 148; in the testimony of J.C. Bancroft Davis and James M. Cross in *Documents of the Senate of the State of New York*, 91st sess., 1868, Doc. 67; and the testimony of Joseph W. Guppy in *Report of the Special Committee on Railroads* (Albany, 1880), 3, 2462-63.

For the Saratoga and Hudson River Railroad, see the Articles of Association filed with the Department of State in Albany; the board minutes of the New York Central Railroad for 1866 and 1867; the *Times* of March 19 and May 31, 1866, and July 20, 1867; *ARJ*, July 13 and 20, 1867; the *Albany Argus* and *Albany Evening Journal* of March-September 1867, passim; and the testimony of Horace F. Clark and Cornelius Vanderbilt in *Documents of the Assembly of the State of New York*, 90th sess., 1867, Doc. 19. Vanderbilt's reported backing of Hancox's Troy line is mentioned in Morrison, *American Steam Navigation*, pp. 132-33.

Vanderbilt's acquisition and management of the Harlem, Hudson River, and New York Central Railroads is recounted in Wheaton J. Lane, *Commodore Vanderbilt*, chapts. 9 and 10.

CHAPTER 13. *The Great Erie War: Preliminaries*

For the Erie election of October 1867 and the events leading up to it, see E.H. Mott, *Between the Ocean and the Lakes*, chap. 14; Charles Francis Adams, Jr., "A Chapter of Erie"; Lane, *Commodore Vanderbilt*, chap. 11; and the New York City dailies of October 8-10, 1867. Additional details are provided by Vice-president Diven's testimony before the Pierce committee, printed in the *Tribune* of March 26, 1868; and by Jay Gould's not altogether disinterested affidavit of March 25, 1868, also printed in the *Tribune* of March 26, 1868. The Boston, Hartford and Erie Railroad is described in the *Times* of June 10, 1867.

For Jim Fisk, see the works mentioned in chapter 10. Jay Gould's business career is best covered by Julius Grodinsky, *Jay Gould: His Business Career, 1867-1892* (Philadelphia: Univ. of Philadelphia Press, 1957), which can be supplemented by Edwin P. Hoyt. *The Goulds: A Social History* (New York: Weybright and Talley, 1969). Richard O'Connor's *Gould's Millions* (Garden City, N.Y.: Doubleday, 1962) is less scholarly than Grodinsky; earlier biographies add little. A biographical sketch of Gould in Mott, *Between the Ocean and the Lakes*, pp. 466-69, views Gould positively. Further details are provided by his loyal associate G.P. Morosini's "Reminiscences of Jay Gould" (1893), a manuscript at the New York Historical Society.

The organization and opening of Drew Theological Seminary is related in the works cited in chapter 11 and the minutes of the board of trustees. An account of the opening ceremonies is given in the *Methodist* of November 16, 1867.

For the growing antagonism between Drew and Vanderbilt in Erie, see accounts in Mott, Adams, and Lane. Drew's Erie pool is also mentioned in Fowler, *Ten Years in Wall Street*, chap. 32, and in Gould's affidavit of March 25, 1868.

CHAPTER 14. *The Battle of Wall Street*

The later Vanderbilt is described in Lane, *Commodore Vanderbilt*; Edwin P. Hoyt, *Commodore Vanderbilt* (Chicago: Reilly & Lee, 1962); and Smith, *Twenty Years*.

For the Erie War of 1868 see Adams's "A Chapter of Erie" (the basic account, despite small inaccuracies); Mott, *Between the Oceans and the Lakes*, chap. 15 and appendices; Lane, chap. 11; W. A. Croffut, *The Vanderbilts and the Story of Their Fortune*, chap. 10; James K. Medbery, "The Great Erie Imbroglio," *Atlantic Monthly*, July 1868; the books on Fisk and Gould cited earlier; Fowler, *Ten Years in Wall Street*, chap. 32; the minutes of the Erie board and executive committee meetings; and the newspapers of the day, of which the *Herald*, *Times*, *Tribune*, and *World* are especially useful.

The innumerable injunctions are discussed in Charles Francis Adams, Jr.'s unsigned article, "The Erie Railroad Row," *American Law Review*, 3 (October 1868), pp. 41-86. Details of the new Erie convertible bond issue and its conversion into stock were revealed in testimony before the Senate's Pierce committee and the New York City courts, reported in the newspapers of March-May 1868, and in Drew's affidavit published in the *Herald* of November 18, 1868. For the full text of the Senate committee report, see *Documents of the Senate of the State of New York*, 91st sess., 1868, Doc. 67.

Fisk's tricking Drew into covering his shorts at a loss is told by Gould in his testimony in *The Erie Railway* v. *Cornelius Vanderbilt*, reported in the New York City papers of March 17, 1870. The flight of the Erie directors to New Jersey is recounted in Adams, pp. 29-30; Fowler, p. 502; the *Herald* of March 14 and 17, the *Tribune* of March 14, and *Harper's Weekly* of April 11, 1868.

CHAPTER 15. *The Battles of Fort Taylor*

For the Erie war generally, see the sources cited in chapter 14. For the directors in Jersey City and the kidnap threats, see the *Times* of March 14, 17, and 20; the *Herald* of March 15, 17 22, 27, and April 1; the *Tribune* of March 16-21 and 24; the *World* of March 14, 17, 20, 21, 26, and 27; the *Sun* of March 18 and 20; and *Harper's Weekly* of April 11, 1868. Additional information is found in the Jersey City papers of the same period: the *Evening Journal*, *American Standard*, and *Daily Times*.

The New Jersey Erie bill is mentioned in the New York City Dailies of March 20–31, 1868. The text of the bill appears in *Acts of the Ninety-Second Legislature of the State of New Jersey*, 1868, p. 550.

For the lobbying in Albany, see the *Times* of March 27, and the *Herald* of March 21, 23, and 28, 1868. Senator Mattoon's overtures to Erie are recorded in the testimony of Drew, Gould, Diven, and Mattoon himself before the Hale investigating committee, printed in *Documents of the Senate of the State of New York*, 92nd sess., 1869, Doc. 52.

CHAPTER 16. *The Battle of Albany*

For Jay Gould in Albany, see especially the *Herald* of April 15, 20, and 21, 1868. Elijah M. K. Glenn's accusations and the resulting assembly investigation are reported in the New York City papers of April 2-16, 1868, as well as in Adams and Mott. Details of the bribery in Albany are revealed in the Hale committee report: *Documents of the Senate*, 1869, Doc. 52. The work of the Pierce and

Hale committees is well covered in Mott's Appendix, "Under the Legislative Probe," pp. 447-51.

The *Tribune*'s campaign against Drew is found in the issues of March 28 and April 3, 4, and 13, 1868. "Alpha"'s defense of Drew was published anonymously as Alpha, *The Erie Question* (n.p.: the author, undated).

The story of Vanderbilt's getting a message to Drew in Jersey City through a waiter is told by Henry Clews, *Twenty-eight Years in Wall Street*, pp. 134-35.

CHAPTER 17. *Negotiations and Peace*

Drew's taking the Erie money to New York is recounted by Gould and Fisk in their testimony in *The Erie Railway* v. *Cornelius Vanderbilt*, reported in the New York City papers of March 17 and 18, 1870; Drew denied it. A fuller account appears in R.W. McAlpine, *The Life and Times of Col. James Fisk, Jr.*, chap. 17, which surely adds fictional touches. The immediate reaction of Drew's colleagues in Jersey City is described in the April 30 issue of the *American Standard* of Jersey City.

Fisk's flight from Barnard's courtroom is reported in the *Tribune* of April 27 and the *Jersey City Daily Times* of April 30, 1868; the latter presumably misdates it.

Details of the Erie negotiations with Vanderbilt appear in the testimony of Vanderbilt, Drew, Gould, and Fisk in *The Erie Railway* v. *Cornelius Vanderbilt*, reported in the papers of November 21 and 30, 1869, and March 16-19, 1870.

CHAPTER 18. *The Greenback Lockup*

Gould and Fisk's operations in Erie of July-November 1868 and the lockup of greenbacks are treated by Adams, "A Chapter of Erie"; Mott, *Between the Ocean and the Lakes*, chap. 16; Julius Grodinsky, *Jay Gould*, chap. 3; and chap. 7 of the anonymous *A Life of James Fisk, Jr.* (1871). See also the New York dailies, especially the *Times* and *Herald*, of October-November 1868.

Fisk's affidavit recounting Drew's Sunday visit to the Erie offices appeared in the *Times* of November 19, 1868, and was corroborated by a briefer affidavit by Gould published in the *Times* of December 1. August Belmont's complaint and the accompanying affidavit by Drew appeared in the New York papers of November 18. Other details are found in the complaints of two Erie suits against Schell, Drew, and others published in the *Times* of November 25, 1868.

Two versions exist of the end of the Erie corner on November 19, 1868: the *Herald* of November 20 and 23 says that Drew capitulated and settled his contracts with the Erie clique, while the story of the ten-share certificates is told by Adams, by *A Life of James Fisk, Jr.*, and by Henry Clews's *Twenty-eight Years in Wall Street*, pp. 144-45, with some confirmation in the *Times* of November 20; the weight of the evidence favors the second version.

CHAPTER 19. *Respite and Return*

For the Methodists on Drew's Wall Street career, see especially *CA*, September 25, 1879.

William H. Drew's fat steers are mentioned in the *Tribune* of February 18 and March 2, the *Times* and *Sun* of February 19, and *Harper's Weekly* of March 6, 1869.

Information on the 1869 suit against Drew by his granddaughters is found in the file of *Louise R. Edey and others* v. *Daniel Drew and others* in the Hall of Records, New York City.

For Drew's relationship with the Vanderbilts and Charles F. Deems, see Lane, chap. 14, and the *Autobiography of Charles Force Deems . . . and Mem-*

oir by His Sons (New York, 1897), chap. 7.

For Fisk's career, see W.A. Swanberg, *Jim Fisk: The Career of an Improbable Rascal* (New York: Scribner's, 1959). The Vanderbilt bronze is described in Lane, pp. 226–27, and in the New York dailies of November 10 and 11, 1869. Vanderbilt's testimony in *The Erie Railway Company* v. *Cornelius Vanderbilt* appeared in the New York dailies on November 21, 1869; Drew's, on November 30, 1869 (the *Sun's* account is especially descriptive) and March 28, 1871; Fisk and Gould's, on March 16-18, 1870.

The Drew's golden wedding was reported in the New York dailies of March 5 and the *Methodist* of March 12, 1870. White's version, which has Drew make a rather boorish speech (pp. 351-52), was belied by Drew's son in the *World* of April 25, 1910.

William S. Woodward's failure in the Rock Island corner is reported in the New York dailies of June 22-24, 1871. Drew's treachery is not mentioned in the dailies, but is recounted by Edmund C. Stedman in *The New York Stock Exchange*, pp. 239-44. Drew's losses in Rock Island came to light in litigation between him and Stephen V. White reported in the *Brooklyn Eagle* of November 17, 1876.

Drew's contract for 50,000 Erie is reported in the papers of March 28 and 29, and August 6 and 7, 1872. The Drews at Long Branch are mentioned in the *Evening Mail* of July 6, 13, 22, 24, and 25, 1872. Drew's market operations of September 1872 are reported in the New York dailies. The quarrel between Smith and Gould is reported in the *Herald* of October 16 and November 23, 1872. For the corner in Northwestern, see the *Herald*, *Times*, *Tribune*, *Sun*, and *World* of late October and November 1872.

CHAPTER 20. *Uncle Daniel Buys the Dream*

For the Quicksilver Mining Company, see the annual reports of 1864 and 1869; *ARJ*, 1870-73; and the *Herald* of February 29, 1872, and the *Tribune* of April 19 and June 19, 1872, and February 28, 1873. Drew's manipulation of the stock is revealed in a suit brought against him by Stephen H. Alden, a Wall Street operator, reported in the *Tribune* of November 15, 1873.

For the Canton Company of Baltimore, see the company's own history, *Canton Days: The First Hundred Years or So* (Baltimore: Canton Company of Baltimore, 1928); the annual reports of 1872-75; *ARJ*, 1870-73; and the *Baltimore Sun* of March 14 and 15, and June 21 and 22, 1872. Drew's duping of Biedermann & Company is asserted in Biedermann's suit against Drew and the sellers, reported in the *Tribune* of November 24, 1873.

Information on the Canada Southern and connecting lines is found in the board minutes and the documents book of the Canada Southern Railway Company, now in the custody of the Consolidated Rail Corporation (Conrail). See also Poor's *Manual of the Railroads* and *ARJ* for 1871-76 (both are indexed). A critical view of the whole enterprise is found in the *Daily Graphic* of May 10, 1875, quoted from the *Pall Mall Gazette* of London. See also the Wabash annual reports for 1872 and 1873, and the Canada Southern report of June 1873. Details of the Wabash pool were revealed in Azariah Boody's suit against Drew, reported most fully in the *Tribune* and *World* of November 13, 1874, and the *World* of January 6, 1875. The fight for control of the Wabash is mentioned in the *Herald* of July 22 and October 3, 1872; Drew's scheme to consolidate five railroads, in the *Tribune* of August 5, 1872.

For the Panic of 1873, see especially Robert Sobel, *Panic on Wall Street*, chap. 5, and Edward C. Stedman, *The New York Stock Exchange*, chap. 19. The failure of Kenyon Cox & Company is reported in the *Herald*, *Times*, *Tribune*,

World, Evening Mail, Journal of Commerce, and *Commercial Advertiser* of September 1873; other details are provided by Drew's testimony of June 20, 1876, before the examiner in bankruptcy, included in his bankruptcy file at the Federal Archives and Records Center at Bayonne, N.J.

Information on Drew's assignment of his securities to his son is contained in the file of *Isaac H. Bailey, assignee, v. William H. Drew*, an 1891 lawsuit to recover assets for Drew's creditors from his son; the records are on file at the Hall of Records, New York City.

William L. Scott's suit to force Drew into bankruptcy was reported in the New York City papers of October 14-18, 1873; the file of the case is at the Federal Archives at Bayonne, N.J. The case's settlement is reported in detail in the *Tribune* and *Sun* of November 17, and *PCC* of November 22, 1873; more information is found in Drew's bankruptcy file.

The Alden and Biedermann suits against Drew are reported in the *Tribune* of November 15 and 24, 1873.

CHAPTER 21. *The Last Great Caper*

Drew's illnesses, real and rumored, are mentioned in the *Times* of December 28, 1873; *PCC* of January 3, 1874; and the *Times* and *Tribune* of February 28, 1874.

Drew's operations in gold are reported in all the New York dailies of March and early April 1875, although he is rarely mentioned by name. More information is provided by Eugene N. Robinson's testimony of July 17 and 19 and September 1, 1876, before the examiner in bankruptcy, included in Drew's bankruptcy file. For Russell Sage, see *DAB* and Grodinsky, *Jay Gould*, chap. 7.

The chief source for Drew's final stock market losses in the spring of 1875 is his own somewhat erratic testimony of June 20, 1876, before the examiner in bankruptcy, supplemented by Robinson's testimony; there is little specific confirmation in the newspapers. One of Drew's puts in Wabash occasioned a lawsuit reported in the *Times* of September 28, 1875.

CHAPTER 22. *Bankruptcy*

Information on Drew's financial problems and bankruptcy comes primarily from his bankruptcy file, but also from the New York City dailies of the time.

For William H. Drew and the People's Line, see *BS* of March 5, 1875, and September 10, 1909, and the *Times* of March 12, 1875. Hancox's opposition is recounted in the Murdock Collection article on the *J.B. Schuyler*. St. John's suicide is reported in the *Herald* and *Times* of April 24, 1875.

Roxanna Drew's will is filed in New York City. Interviews with Drew at the time of his bankruptcy appear in the *Times* of March 13 and the *Sun* of March 14, 1876, and the *Tribune* of September 19, 1879.

For Drew and John Parker, see Parker's address at Drew's funeral in *CA*, October 2, 1879, and Parker's obituary in *CA*, September 28, 1911.

The granddaughters' actions to foreclose on Drew's residence and remove him as trustee are filed in the New York City Hall of Records as *Georgianna Everett, etc. v. Daniel Drew, etc.* and *Louise R. Edey, etc. v. Daniel Drew, etc.*; they were also reported in the newspapers. Drew's flight from the city is recounted in the *Sun, Herald*, and *BS* of June 9, 1876.

CHAPTER 23. *The Oldest Man on the Street*

The Drew interview appeared in *BS* of September 1, 1876. *White v. Drew* was reported in the *Brooklyn Eagle* of November 17, the *Sun* of November 22, and the *Herald* of November 22 and 23, 1876.

For Vanderbilt's death, see Lane, *Commodore Vanderbilt*, chap. 15; Edwin

P. Hoyt, *Commodore Vanderbilt,* chap. 11; Charles F. Deems's *Autobiography,* chapts. 10 and 11; and the newspapers of the time.

Drew's later relations with Drew Theological Seminary are recorded in the seminary board minutes, *CA,* and the *Methodist.* Other information on his last years comes from *PCC* and *BS,* passim, and from *CA* of September 25 and October 2, 1879. His court appearances are reported in the *Herald* of February 5 and the *Sun* and *World* of March 9, 1878.

For William H. Drew and the People's Line, see *PCC* of November 30, 1878, and March 3 and 29, 1879; and the *Times* of March 13, 1879.

The circumstances of Drew's death and funeral are related in the New York dailies of September 19, 20, and 24; *BS* of September 19 and 26; *PCC* of September 27; and *CA* of October 2, 1879.

Epilogue

Daniel Drew's will is on file at the Putnam County Surrogate's Court in Carmel, New York. The suits by Isaac H. Bailey against William H. Drew and Daniel D. Chamberlain are on file at the New York City Hall of Records.

For the story of people digging to find Drew's buried treasure, I am indebted to Daniel Drew's great-great-grandson, Drew Illingworth Pearsall.

Appendix

As elsewhere, all citations from the *Book of Daniel Drew* are from the American Research Council edition of 1965, which reproduces the April 1910 edition's three-page editor's note and its main text of forty chapters on 423 pages, ending with the interrupted verse of a hymn. Certain other editions omit the editor's note and end with the complete stanza of the hymn.

White has been the subject of two masters dissertations, to both of which the author is indebted: Hugh Donald Rank, "Bouck White: A Survey of His Life and Writings," Notre Dame 1956; and Mary Elizabeth Kenton, "Soul on the Open Road: Bouck White: The Life of an American Social Agitator," Wright State University 1978. Both Rank and Kenton brand the *Book of Daniel Drew* a fake. See also F. E. Schultz, "Bouck White, Hermit of the Helderbergs," *York State Tradition,* 17, no. 2 (Spring 1963), pp. 9-13; and the obituary in the *Times* of January 9, 1951.

The controversy between Bouck White and William H. Drew is reported in the *World* of April 25, 26, 29, and 30; the *Tribune* and *Herald* of April 29; and the *Brooklyn Daily Eagle* of April 25-29 and May 7, 1910.

Irvin G. Wyllie's information about the *Book of Daniel Drew* is cited in the Kenton dissertation, p. x. There is a file on the actress Margaret Drew in the Robinson Locke Collection of Dramatic Scrapbooks, series 2, at the Lincoln Center branch of the New York Public Library.

The RKO movie based on the *Book of Daniel Drew* was entitled "The Toast of New York" (1937). The German translation is *Daniel Drew: Aus dem Tagebuch eines amerikanischen Börsemannes* (Berlin: Verlag Dr. Von Arnim, 1943).

Not all the readers of White's book have been fooled by it. Typed on the flyleaf in a donated copy of an edition published without the editor's note by George H. Doran, which the author found in the New York Public Library, is the following comment: "The author of this book, pretending to write the autobiography of Daniel Drew, has unwarrantably made Daniel Drew a partisan against himself. . . . The author has dragged a dead man from his grave and thrust the pen in his defenceless hand—an inexcusable and grewsome thing to do. Daniel Drew—no matter what kind of man he was—would have written a very different book from this. G.H.B."

Index

Adams, Charles Francis, 153, 173, 191, 196, 205
Adirondack Co., 135–36
Albany, N.Y.: steamboat navigation to, 39; steamboat men from, in People's Line, 48, 52–56; joined to New York by Hudson River Railroad, 70–72; citizens oppose Athens line, 140–41. *See also* New York legislature, People's Line; steamboats
Albany, 33
Alden, Stephen H., 238
Alida, 285
Armenia, 93
Armstrong, William, 62
Ashley, Ossian D., 158
Astor, Henry, 20–22, 28, 30
Astor, John Jacob, 20, 63
Athens, N.Y., 137–41, 290 n. 12.8
Atlantic and Pacific Railroad, 249

Bailey, Hackaliah, 14, 33, 34, 37, 39
Bailey, Isaac H., 258, 274
Balcom, Ransom, 157
Baldy Sour Mining Co., 274
Barnard, George G.: grants injunctions against Erie, 153–57, 159; named as defendant by Erie, 159–60, 162–63; orders Erie board arrested, 164; presides over Erie litigation, 168–69, 173, 183–84, 191, 195, 196, 206–7; has Gould arrested, 179, 180; tries to

arrest Fisk, 190; Erie locomotive named for, 208; presides over Erie's suit against Vanderbilt, 215; impeached, 239
Barrett (judge), 180, 181
Baylis, A.B., 250
Beach, Moses Yale, 62
Beecher, Henry Ward, 207
Belden, William, 147, 159, 168, 184
Belle, 48
Bellona, 33
Belmont, August, 202–3, 204, 205, 206, 208, 215, 219
Bennett, James Gordon, 44, 84
Berdell, Robert H., 112, 128, 129, 130, 144, 145, 146
Biedermann, Ernst, 226, 238
Biedermann of Co., 226, 232, 238
Bischoffscheim & Goldschmidt, 218, 219
Bleecker Street (New York City), 31, 63, 68
Bloodgood, John, 162
Boody, Azariah, 228, 230, 238, 252
Book of Daniel Drew: published, 2, 279–80, 283; sources, 283–84; errors and distortions, 284–85; movie of, 285, 307; German edition, 285, 307; convincing rustic speech in, 285. *See also* White, Bouck
Boorman, James, 70–71, 74
Boston, Mass., 65–67, 70

309

Judeo-Christian Perspectives on Psychology

HUMAN NATURE, MOTIVATION, AND CHANGE

EDITED BY

William R. Miller
and Harold D. Delaney

AMERICAN PSYCHOLOGICAL ASSOCIATION
WASHINGTON, DC

Published by
American Psychological Association
750 First Street, NE
Washington, DC 20002
www.apa.org

To order
APA Order Department
P.O. Box 92984
Washington, DC 20090-2984
Tel: (800) 374-2721; Direct: (202) 336-5510
Fax: (202) 336-5502; TDD/TTY: (202) 336-6123
Online: www.apa.org/books/
E-mail: order@apa.org

In the U.K., Europe, Africa, and the Middle East, copies may be ordered from
American Psychological Association
3 Henrietta Street
Covent Garden, London
WC2E 8LU England

Typeset in Goudy by Stephen McDougal, Mechanicsville, MD

Printer: United Book Press, Inc., Baltimore, MD
Cover Designer: Berg Design, Albany, NY
Technical/Production Editor: Tiffany L. Klaff

The opinions and statements published are the responsibility of the authors, and such opinions and statements do not necessarily represent the policies of the American Psychological Association.

Library of Congress Cataloging-in-Publication Data

Judeo-Christian perspectives on psychology : human nature, motivation, and change /
edited by William R. Miller and Harold D. Delaney.
　　p. cm.
　Includes bibliographical references and indexes.
　ISBN 1-59147-161-3
　1. Psychology and religion. 2. Judaism and psychology. 3. Christianity—Psychology.
I. Miller, William R. II. Delaney, Harold D.

　BF51.J83 2004
　261.5'15—dc22　　　　　　　　　　　　　　　　　　　　　2004009504

British Library Cataloguing-in-Publication Data
A CIP record is available from the British Library.

Printed in the United States of America
First Edition

In memory of David B. Larson, MD, untimely departed,
whose life profoundly advanced scientific discourse on religion,
spirituality, and health.

—William R. Miller

In gratitude to Dennis F. Kinlaw, Alan E. Moulton, and
David A. Seamands, mentors and models of
Judeo-Christian perspectives.

—Harold D. Delaney

CONTENTS

CONTRIBUTORS

Pew Psychology Panel Members and Primary Chapter Authors

Roy F. Baumeister, PhD, is a social psychologist and Francis Eppes Professor of Psychology at Florida State University. His 15 books include *Meanings of Life* (1991), *Your Own Worst Enemy: Understanding the Paradox of Self-Defeating Behavior* (1993), *Losing Control* (1994), *Evil: Inside Human Violence and Cruelty* (1997), *The Social Dimension of Sex* (2000), and *The Cultural Animal: Human Nature, Meaning, and Social Life* (2005). His recent grants include *Ego Depletion Patterns and Self-Control Failure* and *Destructive Effects of Social Rejection* (National Institute of Mental Health) and *Humility, Egotism, Forgiveness, and the Victim Role* (Templeton Foundation). His recent research spans consciousness, free choice, guilt, forgiveness, self-control, narcissism, the need to belong, self-esteem, love, meaning, and identity.

Thomas H. Bien, PhD, is a clinical psychologist in private practice in Albuquerque, New Mexico, who also holds a master's degree in theology from Princeton Theological Seminary. He is a former United Methodist pastor and has also had a long-standing interest in Asian spirituality. His psychology background includes research in the field of addictive behaviors as well as extensive clinical practice. His current work emphasizes the integration of spirituality and psychology, especially the Buddhist practice of mindfulness. Together with his wife, Beverly, he has written two books, *Mindful Recovery: A Spiritual Path to Healing From Addiction*, and *Holding the Center Within: The Healing Way of Mindfulness Meditation*.

Stephanie Brown, PhD, is a clinical psychologist and Director of the Addictions Institute in Menlo Park, California. She founded (in 1977) and served as the first director of the Stanford Alcohol Clinic at Stanford University.

She is best known for her published work on psychotherapy and family therapy for alcoholism and on the process of recovery. Her books include *Treating Alcoholism* (1995) and *The Alcoholic Family in Recovery: A Developmental Model* (1999). She serves on the Council of Fellows of the California Association of Drug and Alcohol Counselors and was selected to deliver the 2000 Norman Zinberg Memorial Lecture at Harvard University.

Harold D. Delaney, PhD, is Professor of Psychology in the Department of Psychology at the University of New Mexico. He was a Fulbright Senior Lecturer in Budapest, Hungary for the 1991–1992 academic year. He received a Templeton Foundation Science and Religion course award for his interdisciplinary undergraduate honors course on the relationship between scientific psychology and Christian theism. A specialist in research methodology, his best-known work is a graduate text titled *Designing Experiments and Analyzing Data: A Model Comparison Perspective* (2nd ed., 2004), coauthored with Scott Maxwell of the University of Notre Dame. Currently he is pursuing research on spiritual formation as part of the Spiritual Transformation Scientific Research Program.

Carlo C. DiClemente, PhD, is Professor and Chair of the Department of Psychology at the University of Maryland, Baltimore County. His development with Professor James Prochaska of a transtheoretical model of change has had broad international impact on both research and practice in psychology. His research has been funded by five National Institutes of Health institutes, and he is a recipient of the Distinguished Contribution Award from the American Psychological Association Division 50 (Addictions). He began his career as Assistant Pastor in the Catholic Diocese of Wilmington, Delaware.

C. Stephen Evans, PhD, is currently University Professor of Philosophy at Baylor University, having recently moved from Calvin College where he was Professor of Philosophy and also served as Dean for Research and Scholarship. He is particularly well-known as a Kierkegaard scholar, and his 14 books include *Preserving the Person: A Look at the Human Sciences* (1994), *Wisdom and Humanness in Psychology: Prospects for a Christian Approach* (1996), *Faith Beyond Reason* (1998), and *The Historical Christ and the Jesus of Faith* (1996), which won the Best Christian Scholarly Book of 1996 award from the Institute for Advanced Christian Studies. He has also been the recipient of a three-year grant as a Pew Evangelical Senior Scholar and two National Endowment for the Humanities fellowships for college teachers.

Stanton L. Jones, PhD, is Professor of Psychology and Provost and Dean of the Graduate School at Wheaton College. His writings have focused on the interface of psychology and religion, and on issues of sex education. His books include *Modern Psychotherapies: A Comprehensive Christian Appraisal* (1991), and *Psychology and Christianity: Four Views* (2000). His work has been recognized by a Templeton Prize for Scholarship in Science and Religion and a fellowship from the Pew Evangelical Scholars Program.

Jared D. Kass, PhD, is Professor of Counseling and Psychology in the Graduate School of Arts and Social Sciences at Lesley University in Cambridge, Massachusetts. He holds a Contemplative Practice Fellowship from the American Council of Learned Societies and is Coordinator of the Boston Clergy and Religious Leaders Group for Interfaith Dialogue. He has served as an associate of the Higher Education Center for Alcohol and Other Drug Prevention and was a colleague and collaborator with the late Carl R. Rogers. He is author of the *Spirituality and Resilience Assessment Packet* and is currently writing a book entitled *Contemplative Practice in University Life.*

Martin L. Maehr, PhD, MDiv, is Professor of Education and Psychology at the University of Michigan and a fellow of both the American Psychological Association and the American Psychological Society. Throughout his career he has studied achievement motivation and its relationship to cultural diversity, with particular emphasis on how schools can have an impact on motivation. He has served as Director of the Combined Program in Education and Psychology at the University of Michigan and of the Institute for Research on Human Development at the University of Illinois.

Brenda A. Miller, PhD, is currently with the Pacific Institute on Research and Evaluation's Prevention Research Center of Berkeley, California. She recently moved from the University of Buffalo where she was the Janet P. Wattles Endowed Professor in the School of Social Work and directed the Center for Research on Urban Social Work Practice. Her research interests and extensive publications span women's health, family violence, substance abuse, and family-based prevention. Her recent grants focused on *Family-Based Prevention for Children of Alcoholics* and *Mother's Alcohol Problems and Children's Victimization.* She has served on grant review panels for the National Institutes of Health and is an associate senior research scientist with the Research Institute on Addictions in Buffalo, New York, where she previously served as Deputy Director and Acting Director.

William R. Miller, PhD, is Distinguished Professor of Psychology and Psychiatry at the University of New Mexico. He is the recipient of a number of international awards for his clinical research on the effectiveness of treatments for substance use disorders. His 40 books include *Practical Psychology for Pastors* (1995), *Integrating Spirituality Into Treatment* (1999), and *Quantum Change: When Sudden Insights and Epiphanies Transform Ordinary Lives* (2001). He is a fellow of both the American Psychological Association and the American Psychological Society.

Kenneth I. Pargament, PhD, is Professor of Psychology in clinical psychology at Bowling Green State University in Ohio, as well as Adjunct Professor of Psychology at the School of Theology and Religious Studies at Boston University. A fellow of both the American Psychological Association and the American Psychological Society, his research has focused on religious coping and forgiveness. He received the William James Award for excellence in research in the psychology of religion from the American Psychological Association Division 36 (Psychology of Religion), and was later elected as its president. He is author of *The Psychology of Religion and Coping: Theory, Research, Practice* (1997) and recently published (with Michael McCullough & Carl Thoresen) *Forgiveness: Theory, Research, and Practice*.

Carl E. Thoresen, PhD, Professor of Education and Psychology at Stanford University, is a prolific pioneer in the study of behavioral self-control. He has participated in many studies of coronary-prone behavior, chronic stress, and cancer and heart disease prevention, with a recent focus on spiritual and philosophical issues in overall health and well-being. His clinical research lies at the interface of humanistic psychology, cognitive–behavioral therapy, and spirituality. He recently edited a special "Spirituality and Health" issue of the *Journal of Health Psychology* and published (with Michael McCullough & Kenneth I. Pargament) *Forgiveness: Theory, Research, and Practice*. He is a fellow of the American Association for the Advancement of Science, and the American Psychological Association.

Everett L. Worthington Jr., PhD, is Professor and Chair of the Department of Psychology at Virginia Commonwealth University in Richmond. He is involved in both basic and intervention research on forgiveness and reconciliation, with related research interests in marital relationships and religious values. He is the founding editor of the journal *Marriage and Family: A Christian Journal* and serves as Executive Director of A Campaign for Forgiveness Research (www.forgiving.org). He has published 18 books, 7 of which are in foreign translations.

Additional Contributors

Gene G. Ano, MA, is a doctoral student in clinical psychology at Bowling Green State University in Ohio. He was a two-year member of the National Institute of Mental Health Career Opportunities in Research scholarship program at California State University, Long Beach. He won a first and second place award in separate research competitions for his work on religious coping. His professional and research interests include Christian counseling, the integration of psychology and theology, religious coping, spiritual struggles, and ecumenically based psychospiritual interventions.

Jack W. Berry, PhD, is Director of Research for the Marriage Assessment, Treatment, and Enrichment Center at Virginia Commonwealth University in Richmond. His academic specialty areas are in personality and individual differences, evolutionary psychology, and objective psychological measurement. His most recent research includes studies of the disposition to forgive and its relationship to physical and mental health, forgiveness, cortisol stress responses in happy and unhappy relationships, and the classical moral virtues and altruism considered from an evolutionary perspective. In collaboration with the Jane Goodall Institute, he is also currently conducting research on personality and psychopathology among chimpanzees.

Alex H. S. Harris, PhD, is currently a postdoctoral fellow in Health Services Research at the Veterans Affairs Palo Alto Health Care System. He recently served as Guest Associate Editor of a special "Spirituality and Health" issue of the *Journal of Health Psychology* and has coauthored chapters in several recent books, including *Forgiveness: Theory, Research, and Practice* (McCullough, Pargament, & Thoresen, Eds.), *Faith and Health* (Plante & Sherman, Eds.), and *Counseling Psychology and Optimal Human Functioning* (Walsh, Ed.). Current research interests include forgiveness, physical activity as treatment for mental disorders, and clinical decision making.

Heather R. Hostler, MA, is currently pursuing a doctorate in psychology at Wheaton College. Her research interests include the developmental challenges of midlife, sexual orientation and spiritual development, and how religion and coping affect well-being.

Susan Lennox, JD, is a doctoral student in psychology at the Fielding Institute in Santa Barbara, California. A lawyer and former organizational consultant to corporations, she is now investigating the process of transformative learning.

Gina M. Magyar, MA, is a doctoral student in clinical psychology at Bowling Green State University in Ohio. She received her bachelor's degree in psychology and history from the University of Michigan. She is completing her predoctoral internship in health psychology at the University of Wisconsin Hospital and Clinics in Madison. Her research and clinical interests include studies focused on the impact of the loss and violation of what individuals perceive as sacred, integrating spirituality into psychotherapy with adults suffering from trauma, and the interface between spirituality and health psychology.

Nichole A. Murray-Swank, PhD, is an assistant professor in the Department of Pastoral Counseling at Loyola College in Maryland. She obtained her doctorate in clinical psychology from Bowling Green State University in

Ohio. Her primary research and clinical interests are in the areas of trauma, sexuality, and the integration of spirituality into counseling.

Doug Oman, PhD, is Assistant Adjunct Professor in the School of Public Health at the University of California, Berkeley. His research involves theoretical, observational, and experimental studies of spirituality, religion, and health, including epidemiologic studies of religious involvement and mortality, the application of social cognitive theory to religion and spirituality, and studies of effects on health professionals from receiving training in a comprehensive nonsectarian spiritual toolkit.

ACKNOWLEDGMENTS

We are delighted that this book is being published by the American Psychological Association (APA), and we are grateful for the substantial support we received from APA throughout its preparation. The book was considerably strengthened by the initial APA peer reviews, which were coordinated by development editor Vanessa Downing, and in particular by the insightful comments of the referees. We also gratefully acknowledge that the work of the psychology panel that led to this volume was supported by a grant from the Pew Charitable Trusts, through a subcontract from the University of Notre Dame. We especially wish to recognize Notre Dame Provost Nathan Hatch, whose vision led to the overall multidisciplinary Pew project on the nature of the human person, of which the psychology panel was just one part. In addition to us, the members of this stimulating psychology panel were

Roy F. Baumeister, PhD	Florida State University
Stephanie Brown, PhD	Addictions Institute, Menlo Park, CA
Carlo C. DiClemente, PhD	University of Maryland, Baltimore County
C. Stephen Evans, PhD	Baylor University
George S. Howard, PhD	University of Notre Dame
Stanton L. Jones, PhD	Wheaton College
Jared D. Kass, PhD	Lesley University
Martin L. Maehr, PhD	University of Michigan
Brenda A. Miller, PhD	University of Buffalo
Kenneth I. Pargament, PhD	Bowling Green State University
Carl E. Thoresen, PhD	Stanford University
Everett L. Worthington Jr., PhD	Virginia Commonwealth University

The following individuals also participated by invitation in at least one of the panel's two meetings:

Eric G. Bing, MD, PhD   Drew University of Medicine and Sciences
Candace M. Fleming, PhD   University of Colorado Health Sciences
                                         Center
Jennifer Hettema, BS   University of New Mexico
Stacey Langfitt Hendrickson, BS   University of New Mexico
Vanessa Lopez-Viets, PhD   University of New Mexico
Francisco P. Sanchez, PhD   VA Medical Center, Albuquerque
Scott T. Walters, PhD   University of New Mexico
Paula L. Wilbourne, MS   University of New Mexico

What a pleasure and privilege it has been for us to work with this group of talented colleagues through a creative and emergent process on such a rich topic. We thank them all for their many contributions throughout the panel's work, and ultimately for the quality of this book.

Judeo-Christian Perspectives on Psychology

INTRODUCTION

A conventional account of the history of psychology is that it began as a discipline in the experimental laboratories of Wundt and Titchener. To be sure, in psychology, as in the field of medicine, the application of scientific method to the study of human beings was a breakthrough that has led to many important discoveries.

However, psychology did not spring fully formed from the mind of Wilhelm Wundt. It was rooted in and continuous with millennia of philosophical and theological thought regarding the nature of human beings. Historically, the *psyche* was the soul, the very essence of an individual. Over the course of the 20th century, however, the psyche, the subject matter of the discipline of psychology, came to be more narrowly defined, first as mind and then as behavior or even neural activity. The lens through which many psychologists viewed humanity shrank, fostered further by specialization to focus on one part of behavior or its biological substrates, to the point that William James might not recognize the American discipline that he is credited with fathering.

Something else occurred in psychology over the course of the 20th century. It became, by far, one of the least religious disciplines in the United States. More than most other professions or scientific disciplines, more than academics in general, far more than the general population, psychologists disavowed religious affiliation, belief, and practice. In matters of spirituality and religion, psychologists drew progressively further away from the people we study and serve. Within clinical psychology in particular, substantial antipathy toward religion was often evident. Influential historical figures (e.g., Sigmund Freud and Albert Ellis) expressed vituperative disdain for religion. Others such as Gordon Allport and Carl Jung gave prominent attention to spirituality and religion in their theories of personality. The modal response of psychologists to religion in research, practice, and training, however, became one of silence and neglect.

Is this a historical coincidence? We think not. The personal histories of major 20th-century figures in the development of psychology are seldom devoid of religion; rather, they often include substantial levels of spiritual struggle, followed by breaking away from a religious tradition that they found unacceptably restrictive. Carl Rogers, for example, trained at Union Theological Seminary but later distanced himself from his Protestant roots. His Judeo-Christian theological heritage, however, is everywhere apparent in his theory of personality and treatment, a parallelism that he willingly explored in dialogues with theologians including Martin Buber and Paul Tillich. Indeed, with regard to an understanding of human nature, Rogers clearly had far more in common with such Jewish and Christian theologians than he did with Sigmund Freud or B. F. Skinner. It is our experience that such spiritual struggle and rejection of formal religion is common among psychologists.

Such disavowal of religion might be attributed to scientific skepticism. As in other sciences, psychologists are trained in critical thinking: to evaluate and test beliefs and assumptions rather than accepting them on faith. Yet psychologists are far less religious than our colleagues in the physical sciences such as chemistry, physics, and astronomy. Perhaps because our subject matter is people, psychologists have clung to a peculiar causal determinism about human nature that contradicts everyday experience, basic shared cultural assumptions, and even our own data.

Yet something is changing. During the last decade of the 20th century, psychology began to show signs of greater openness to, and even reconciliation with, its spiritual roots. The American Psychological Association began publishing a series of volumes (including this one) on the interface of psychology with spirituality and religion. Positive psychology arose, affirming secular values and areas of study that overlap substantially with traditional interests and values of major world religions. Radical behaviorists began writing about acceptance. There has been an upsurge in both public and scientific interest in the relationship of spirituality, religion, and health. This change is reflected in continuing education, conferences, and requests for proposals for research funding. The emergence of evolutionary psychology has revived interest in and sparked dialogue regarding human nature. It is as though the discipline itself is undergoing the kind of spiritual struggle that its members previously experienced. Having thoroughly distanced itself from its roots, psychology now seems to be emerging into a mature exploration of spirituality.

THE PROJECT THAT LED TO THIS BOOK

It is also happening in other disciplines. This volume is the result and final report of a scholarly process initiated by the Pew Charitable Trusts. Pew issued a challenge to eight academic disciplines: Assemble a panel of senior scholars to identify the dominant models within your discipline, comparing and contrasting them with historic Christian perspectives regarding human nature. The identified disciplines were economics, history, law, literature, philosophy, political science, psychology, and sociology. Within economics, for example, the current dominant model is that human nature is driven by rational self-interest. The disciplinary panels worked independently, although some broad parallels emerged. The guiding paradigms of the disciplines were not judged to be incorrect but rather incomplete portrayals of humanity. Usually this had to do with strong focus on one particular aspect of human nature to the exclusion (or at least de-emphasis) of others.

Within the discipline of psychology, the currently dominant models are unambiguously reductionistic. Scientific focus is on the "determinants" of animal and human behavior, with an implication that if one could but know the full range of learning history, neural, and contextual factors, individual behavior would be totally predictable.

We hasten to affirm that reductionistic approaches do not guide all of psychology. The historic humanistic–existential "third force" in psychology arose in response to and rejection of the philosophical determinism inherent in both psychoanalysis and behaviorism. Phenomenological approaches have been and continue to be important in the development of the discipline of psychology. The spiritual and religious side of human nature has been explored by many psychologists and psychiatrists, including Gordon Allport, Ralph Hood, William James, Carl Jung, Gerald May, Karl Menninger, O. H. Mowrer, and M. Scott Peck. The psychology of religion and spirituality is an enduring specialty, represented by Division 36 of the American Psychological Association, as is transpersonal psychology. None of these perspectives, however, can be construed as dominant models of the discipline.

The psychology panel chose to compare regnant psychological models with Judeo-Christian conceptions of human nature rather than focusing on Christianity alone. The term *Judeo-Christian* is meant to encompass the perspectives of both Judaism and Christianity as historic and living world religions. It recognizes the origins and continuity of Christianity with Judaism, but the term is not meant to subsume either faith within the other. Much of what is discussed in this book could apply to Islam as well, the third major monotheistic faith that arose from the same Abrahamic roots, or to other world religions. However, by virtue of its authorship, this book draws primarily on Jewish and Christian perspectives.

THE PSYCHOLOGY PANEL'S PROCESS

Consistent with guidelines provided by the Pew Charitable Trusts, we selected as panel members well-established senior psychologists (as well as a philosopher of psychology) with strong scholarly credentials who themselves identified with varying spiritual and religious perspectives. By self-identification, the chapter authors represented Protestant, Catholic, Jewish, Buddhist, and secular nontheist traditions.

Within a broad overall theme of "Personhood, Human Motivation, and Change," the panel focused its initial meeting on five broad issues: (a) the role of human identity, volition, and personal agency; (b) the role of values in human motivation and change; (c) scientifically testable hypotheses from Judeo-Christian teachings; (d) what behavioral science has to offer to religious people; and (e) transformational change. The first meeting was convened in May 2001 in Santa Fe, New Mexico. As an organizing structure for the two-day meeting, the panel was presented with a series of 17 questions to stimulate discussion. For each, panel members took individual time to write personal responses before discussion began—a method of "nominal group brainstorming" that tends to generate far more ideas than group discussion alone. All written responses to these questions were transcribed and distributed to the panel after the meeting to further stimulate thinking. The starting stimulus questions were the following:

- What do you see as missing from modern scientific psychology? What more should we be doing? What puzzles should we be thinking about or studying that currently receive too little attention?
- Whereas disciplines such as philosophy and political science have encountered the shortcomings of and moved past logical positivism and behaviorism, it seems that psychology has been slower to do so. If you agree that this is so, why might this be true of our discipline?
- In what ways (if at all) do your own faith perspectives influence how you think about psychology and human nature, the phenomena you choose to study, and how you study them?
- The scientific utility of methodological reductionism is easily defended but gets readily confused with philosophical ("nothing but") reductionism. Reductionistic perspectives in psychology have led to the clarification of many scientifically replicable influences on human behavior—for example, "laws" of learning and conditioning, neurotransmitters, systematic pro-

cesses and biases of memory and cognition, genetic influences, and so on. If you perceive other aspects of the human person that govern what we do and who we are—for example, executive agency and volition, values—how do these fit together with the mechanistic processes that most scientific psychologists now study?

- In what ways have religion and religious perspectives shaped the lives and work of prominent figures in the history of psychology? Which five people in the history of the discipline would you say were most importantly influenced (positively or negatively) by religion and religious thinking?
- Human persons include children. How do developmental perspectives inform the issues that we are addressing?
- What is the self? Is it epiphenomenal or essential? How is it related to the concepts of soul and consciousness? How is it related to reducible phenomena such as language, neurophysiology, learning and memory, and so on?
- Evangelical Christians in particular sometimes respond to the word "humanistic" with revulsion. Yet it seems that within psychology, a Judeo-Christian understanding of the human person lies closest to what has been called the "third force" in our discipline, exemplified by psychologists such as Carl Rogers, Abraham Maslow, and Roberto Assagioli. Humanistic psychologists have often been as adamant in disavowing religious roots of their theories. Why is that?
- What are the origins and current status in psychology of the concept of "values"? What role do values play in the guidance of human behavior? How are values related to behavioral economics and choice theories? What factors influence value-behavior consistency?
- What are alternatives to a "God of the gaps" way of thinking—to using the transcendent to fill in for whatever it is that cannot be explained by reductionistic determinants?
- What are your own perspectives on the issue of human agency and free will versus automaticity of behavior and determinism?
- What are some of the starting, fundamental premises of a Judeo-Christian perspective about the nature of the human person?
- What are some chief concerns within a Judeo-Christian perspective that would point us to particular processes or phenomena that should be high priority for psychologists to study—particularly those that may be understudied at present?
- Which aspects of spirituality or religiousness are most likely to influence directly (for better or worse) physical and psychological health?

- Does it make sense to hypothesize effects of the *absence of* religiousness as well as its presence?
- How might a psychologist go about defining and studying sin or evil?
- What do your own life and work have to do with all of this?

By the end of the first meeting, discussion of these questions led toward the identification of a set of topics on which to focus the project and their assignment to particular panel members who would prepare a scholarly paper for presentation at the second panel meeting in Santa Fe a year later. All papers were distributed to the full panel in advance of its second meeting with the expectation that every panel member would read and comment on each paper. At the meeting, each paper was briefly summarized by its author and was then critiqued by the group. Each author left the second and final meeting of the panel with written critiques and edits from colleagues as well as notes from the panel discussion as guidelines for revision. The two of us served as second-round editors for the revised papers, in all cases requesting further changes before they were sent to the publisher. The American Psychological Association then provided two additional rounds of editorial and peer review requiring further revisions, during which process one author withdrew and was replaced.

The result is the volume that you hold in your hands. Each chapter has benefited from critique by at least 16 senior colleagues across four rounds of review. This two-year process also led to a book with higher levels of consistency, focus, integration, and cross-referencing than one often finds in edited volumes. This commentary on the discipline of psychology from various faith perspectives parallels a similar volume edited by Doniger (1962) four decades ago, whose contributors included Carl Rogers, Karen Horney, Paul Tillich, James McCord, and Karl Menninger. It is our hope that the current volume will help stimulate an increasing dialogue between psychology and faith perspectives in the decades to come.

REFERENCE

Doniger, S. (Ed.). (1962). *The nature of man in theological and psychological perspective.* New York: Harper.

I

FOUNDATIONS
AND CONTEXT

1

WHAT IS HUMAN NATURE? REFLECTIONS FROM JUDEO-CHRISTIAN PERSPECTIVES

WILLIAM R. MILLER

It is said that during the 20th century, psychology lost first its soul and then its mind. Not long after William James (1902) published *Varieties of Religious Experience: A Study in Human Nature*, the discipline of psychology began to distance itself from the spiritual side of humanity. Human behavior came to be viewed merely as the product of lawful principles of learning and conditioning. Human consciousness, thought, intention, and values were dismissed as mentalistic epiphenomena. By 1925, J. B. Watson was boasting, in what has subsequently been termed *naïve behaviorism*, that he could take any normal infant and, given complete control of the environment, turn the child into whatever kind of person he might choose. Neuroscience added a new layer of biological reductionism in psychology, describing consciousness as a by-product of neural activity and behavior as the sequela of genetics, evolution, and brain chemistry. A recent wave of interest in automaticity reflects this view of willful choice as illusory, with human nature and behavior determined by factors of which people are largely unaware (Bargh & Ferguson, 2000). In sum, if one could but know all of the biological, learning, and environmental antecedents, it would then be possible to predict (and

11

perhaps control) all of human behavior. In chapter 2, Harold D. Delaney and Carlo C. DiClemente trace in more detail some of these aspects of psychology's history.

Few would deny that human nature and behavior are influenced by lawful processes. People are significantly shaped and limited by their biological nature. Research continues to trace the degree of heritability of various traits and vulnerabilities. Principles of learning, memory, and cognition are well understood and can be applied effectively in spheres of influence as diverse as teaching, psychotherapy, advertising, and parenting. Changes in brain chemistry produced by pharmacotherapies have been effective aids in the treatment of schizophrenia, bipolar disorder, depression, and alcoholism. Predictable parts of the brain light up with electric activity in association with specific behaviors, cognitions, emotions, and spiritual experiences.

It is at a more basic point that scientific psychology has departed historically from the view of most world religions, and indeed from what most people would regard to be common sense. That point is the assumption that people are merely the sum of these lawful principles, that human behavior is entirely determined by our biology, genes, unconscious processes, environment, and learning history, perhaps with a small random error term. It is the view that human nature can be reduced to such components and fully understood in these terms. Such reductionism is not shared by the world's great religions, in courts of law, nor in the self-understanding of most people including, I suspect, most psychologists.

Perhaps reductionism is just a useful scientific convention, a lens through which to view human behavior in a quest to determine how much of the variance can be accounted for by lawful principles. From the perspective of world religions and common sense, such research may be of interest, but it disregards many of the most important and defining aspects of human nature. Few people would hope that one day human behavior will be so well understood that it can be completely predicted and controlled. That dream is the nightmare of Orwell's *1984* (1992) and Huxley's *Brave New World* (1998).

A WORD ABOUT WORDS

Before proceeding further, it will be useful to consider the much-debated meaning of the terms *spirituality* and *religion*. At the beginning of the 20th century, as in the writings of William James, these terms seem to have been roughly interchangeable. In the subsequent century, however, they have become differentiated, and they are now used differently in common language. People can and do meaningfully describe themselves as "spiritual but not religious" (Fuller, 2001).

Particularly from a psychological perspective, *spirituality* (like personality or health) can be understood as an attribute of the individual. It is a latent construct with multiple dimensions (e.g., behavior, belief, motivation, and subjective experience) pertaining to humanity's search for the sacred, for that which transcends material existence. As with multitrait representations of personality, every individual can be located somewhere along these vectors in multidimensional space (Fetzer Institute and National Institute on Aging Working Group, 1999; Gorsuch & Miller, 1999). From this perspective, it makes no sense to classify people as spiritual versus not spiritual, any more than one would characterize individuals as having or not having a personality. Neither is spirituality (or personality) something that people have to varying degrees, in that it is not a single variable. One may have higher or lower levels of introversion, but not of personality. Similarly, one may have higher or lower levels of faith in God, but not of spirituality. Finally, although personality, spirituality, and health can be used to describe individuals, these terms can also be applied to characterize smaller (e.g., a family) or larger groups (e.g., a nation).

Religion, as used here, describes a social entity. Whereas spirituality is notoriously difficult to delimit, religions are defined by their boundaries. There are group members and nonmembers, prescribed and proscribed behaviors, characteristic beliefs. Spirituality is a central concern of religions, but not the only concern. A religion can also involve important social, political, and economic goals. The term *religiousness* is used here to describe the extent to which an individual is identified and involved with religion. In this sense, religiousness (e.g., involvement with a particular religion) could have beneficial or detrimental effects on one's spirituality.

These linguistic distinctions evolved through a series of panels of health scientists wrestling with definitions of spirituality and religion (Larson, Swyers, & McCullough, 1998; Miller & Thoresen, 2003; National Institute on Alcohol Abuse and Alcoholism, 1999) and are clearly debatable. For purposes of this chapter and book, we have used them as conventions: Spirituality is multidimensional and describes attributes of the individual; religion is a social entity with defined boundaries; religiousness is the individual's degree and type of involvement in religion.

PSYCHOLOGY'S GREATEST TABOO

For thousands of years and in virtually every culture, basic assumptions about the nature of reality and humanity have been both shaped and reflected by religion. The most basic assumption of religion is that there is a spiritual as well as a physical dimension to reality and human nature. To Jews and Christians, this spiritual aspect is understood primarily as a relation between each human person and a single divine being, and as central to human nature. More than 90% of Americans continue to profess belief in God, and many describe their religion as central to their lives, the very core of what gives them meaning and guides their actions (Gallup, 1985, 1995). There is substantial empirical evidence for a positive relationship of religiousness to physical and mental health (Koenig, 1998; Koenig, McCullough, & Larson, 2000; Larson et al., 1998; Levin, 1994).

It seems odd, then, that so little attention has been devoted to spirituality and religion in mainstream psychological research and practice. Clinical psychologists ask their clients about the most intimate details of almost any other aspect of their lives yet frequently shy away from exploring their religion and spirituality. The large array of psychometrically sound instruments for assessing religiousness (Hill & Hood, 1999) remain unknown and unused by most practicing and research psychologists. Spirituality and religion are conspicuously absent in most psychology textbooks and in undergraduate and graduate curricula. Spirituality has been psychology's clearest taboo, an enormous blind spot in the realm of human experience.

In fairness, there are significant sectors of psychology that have never lost interest in spirituality. Certainly, spiritual aspects of human nature have been of keen interest within Jungian circles. The psychology of religion remains an active specialty area, albeit somewhat isolated from mainstream scientific and clinical psychology. The "third force" within psychology arose in counterpoint to the deterministic emphasis in both psychoanalysis and behaviorism. This perspective is usually referred to as *humanistic*, a term sometimes viewed as antithetical to religion. In fact, a humanistic understanding of the person as expressed by Abraham Maslow and Carl Rogers shares a great deal with (and indeed was importantly influenced by) religious perspectives. Rogers engaged in fascinating dialogues with Martin Buber (Anderson & Cissna, 1977) and Paul Tillich (Tillich & Rogers, 1966), and participated four decades ago in a volume rather similar to this one on *The Nature of Man in Theological and Psychological Perspective* (Doniger, 1962).

Psychology's more general aversion to religion (or at least to spirituality) appears to be lifting. Paralleling a public resurgence of interest in religion and spirituality, psychology is also experiencing a renewal of attention to these issues that so fascinated James (1902). For the first time in its history, the American Psychological Association has published a series of books on the interface of psychology with religion and spirituality (Miller, 1999; Richards & Bergin, 1997; Shafranske, 1996). The National Institutes of Health have begun to request applications for and fund research on spirituality and health (e.g., National Institute on Alcohol Abuse and Alcoholism, 1999). Conferences on spirituality and health draw large audiences. What may be newest in these cultural changes is an increased willingness to listen to and learn from what religion has to offer to psychology.

DARE WE DEVELOP A THEISTIC PSYCHOLOGY?

The discipline of psychology arose during the 19th century from roots in philosophy and theology. Throughout most of the 20th century, consideration of God or religion was largely missing from mainstream psychological theories, research, and therapies. Even the third force in psychology, although manifesting holistic and humanistic values, largely ignored theistic faiths. Instead, scientific psychology focused primarily on reductionistic explanations of human action as solely the product of physical, unconscious, and environmental causes.

When I began my graduate training in clinical psychology in 1969, I quickly learned that religion, much less God, was an improper and impolite topic for open discussion. This was communicated through silence, jokes, readings, and the complete absence of spiritual and religious material in coursework, supervision, and scientific meetings. The message seemed to be that, "If you must believe such things, for heaven's sake keep it to yourself." We could and did discuss virtually everything else about human nature, but this was a black hole.

In 1986, George Howard asked in a book title, *Dare We Develop a Human Science?* that includes personal volition and agency. If anything, the field moved farther away from such consideration and toward automaticity in the subsequent decade (Bargh & Chartrand, 1999; Kirsch & Lynn, 1999). Whether or not psychologists themselves share a theistic understanding of reality, it is reasonable to ask how psychology and human nature might be different when viewed from a theistic perspective and how such a view might inform the science of human behavior. The monotheistic religions of Islam, Judaism, and Christianity continue to guide the self-understanding, values, and perceptions of large portions of the population of the Americas and the Western world. To exclude this from consideration is to constrain understanding of human nature and motivation.

This is neither a call for psychologists to embrace theism, nor to abandon scientific method as a means for advancing knowledge of human nature. Instead, my urging is to attend to special issues, variables, and research agendas that are raised when one considers humanity from this perspective, using the best clinical and scientific approaches at our disposal. (Just how this might be done is suggested in the chapters that follow, with the implications being summarized in the two concluding chapters in Part V.) Disciplinary allegiance to secularism has long blinded psychology to phenomena that are of natural interest in understanding human behavior and has encouraged psychologists to divorce their science from the insights and priorities of a theistic perspective, even when it is a perspective that they share.

Imagine, then, a theistic psychology, one that begins with a Judeo-Christian *anthropology* or set of fundamental presuppositions about human nature. The starting assumptions regarding human nature are surely no more strange or unscientific than those of psychoanalysis, behaviorism, or existential psychology. A theistic psychology would not constrain scientific method or place certain topics off limits for investigation. To the contrary, it would lift mainstream psychology's century-long taboo against studying spiritual topics. A Judeo-Christian view of human nature is a valid anthropology for guiding the work of psychologists (Hoekema, 1986). It would also bring into focus new areas of consciousness and concern for the discipline of psychology in a manner paralleling the contributions of feminist and humanistic perspectives. Psychological science may also have much to contribute to Judeo-Christian spirituality.

WHAT DOES IT MEAN TO BE HUMAN?

The basic challenge and question that gave rise to this book was of how the dominant models within psychology compare and contrast with Judeo-Christian views of the human person. As a starting point, this section outlines some basic and essential elements of a Judeo-Christian view of human nature. From that beginning, one can then ask how a psychological perspective (and the research or clinical practice that follows from it) might be different if informed by and viewed through this understanding of the human person.

A Theistic Understanding of Human Nature

I find quite useful the German noun *Menschenbild*—one's fundamental understanding (picture) of the nature of the human person. It is the person-level parallel to a more familiar term within psychology, *Weltanschauung*—one's world view or broader understanding of reality.

What, then, are the basic components of a theistic *Menschenbild* such as that held by Jews and Christians? I suggest eight tenets as fundamental to a theistic understanding of human nature. Some of these are unique to a theistic viewpoint, whereas others are not. On a great many other points, of course, there is a pluralistic range of belief among people of faith.

1. *Reality of Spirit.* First and most basic is the assertion that there is more to life than the material world, that there is also an unseen spiritual dimension of reality to which humans are meaningfully related. That relationship is, in fact, central to a Judeo-Christian understanding of human nature (Hoekema, 1986; Pannenberg, 1970). Within monotheistic thought, the essence of this realm of spirit is God, an ultimate higher power and authority who created and continues to relate to humanity. The reality of God, of spirit, is affirmed whether one understands the human person to be a physi-

cal object or as dualistic in nature, having both a physical body and a separable spirit with which it is united (Brown, Murphy, & Malony, 1998).

2. *Not God*. It follows from this that humans are not God (Kurtz, 1979), not the ultimate arbiters of morality. Rather, there is a natural law, an absolute standard of good and evil against which human nature and behavior can be evaluated. Truth exists independent of our conceptions of it, as does a set of ultimate values and virtues that are not dependent on human judgment (see chap. 8). (One need not be a theist, of course, to affirm absolute standards for what is good; both Plato and the Buddha asserted the transcendent nature of goodness.) The essence of this second component of a theistic *Menschenbild* is that there is a higher standard, an ideal, an intended nature for human beings that exists apart from context and human thought. Although there are differences of interpretation on specific points, some broad qualities of virtue are clear in Jewish and Christian thought, such as honesty, humility, forgiveness, fidelity in marriage, acting with justice toward the poor and oppressed, and selfless love, all of which are defined as virtues within other world religions as well (Templeton, 1997).

3. *Sin*. If there are absolute standards of virtue and right behavior, then it is surely the human condition to fall short, even when diligently seeking to adhere to them. In Jewish and Christian scripture, this is termed *sin*, which is variously described in metaphors drawn from legal (e.g., guilt, trespasses), interpersonal (e.g., defiance, rebellion), economic (e.g., debts, enslavement), and medical (e.g., sickness) contexts. Human nature includes the potential for both good and evil; openness to God and to the needs of others is in constant tension with self-centeredness (Pannenberg, 1970). In both Jewish and Christian scripture, sin is not limited to actions but extends to one's thoughts and motives (Hoekema, 1986). Religious traditions and practices can be understood, in part, as means for recognizing, addressing, and surpassing the human propensity for falling short of our intended nature.

4. *Agency*. This further implies that human nature involves a choice in the tension between virtue and its opposite (Hoekema, 1986). Behavior is purposive, influenced by choices—a fact that seems subjectively self-evident. People are willing, choosing, deciding agents of their own thought and actions (see chap. 3). With this choice comes responsibility (within certain limits) for the outcomes of one's actions. This assumption underlies all Western criminal justice systems. This is not to say that behavior is totally volitional. Certainly there are constraints and influences on behavior, and the volitional control of behavior is a matter of degree and effort (Howard, 1986; Miller & Brown, 1991). Theistic religions clearly recognize determinants of behavior other than will. Rather, the implication in theistic religion (as in secular law) is that human beings can and should consciously override influences favoring improper (sinful, illegal) behavior—a parallel to current psychological distinctions of automatic versus controlled processing. Although "a very small fragment of [human] existence is constituted by the remnants

of instinctive behavior," people ultimately decide the purposes to which they will commit their time on earth (Pannenberg, 1970, p. 54). Pannenberg characterized human nature (in contrast to the closed-system instinctual base of animal behavior) as "unending movement into the open," with a great deal of freedom to choose different responses. This view stands, of course, in stark contrast to the deterministic anthropology of B. F. Skinner (1972).

5. *Spiritual Health.* Prior to the emergence of psychology and the writings of William James, there had already been thousands of years of reflection on spiritual health and care. As with wellness of mind and body, optimal spiritual health is not automatic but can be promoted and maintained through certain forms of vigilance and practice. Among these are the traditional spiritual disciplines of prayer, fasting, meditation, service to others, and the study of sacred writings (Foster, 1998; see chap. 11, this volume). It is also noteworthy that within Judeo-Christian perspectives, spiritual wellness is intimately related to mental and physical health. Spirituality is not the isolated domain of specialists, comparable to a dentist's care of one's teeth (Merton, 1960). Psychologists who are interested in the whole person should rightly be concerned with the spiritual side of human nature as well.

6. *Relational Responsibility.* Jewish teachings in particular take personal agency and accountability a step further, to a shared responsibility for the condition and actions of one's community (see chap. 4). One is responsible not only for one's own sin or health but also for accepting and tolerating sin (e.g., injustice) in one's community or nation. *Shalom* is not merely personal peace of mind but the communal state of ordered peace and justice that God intends. This same communal consciousness appears in first-century Christianity, wherein believers pooled their possessions to ensure that no one was in want of basic needs.

7. *Hope.* The human condition might appear quite bleak if this were the extent of it, and humanity were left pulling itself up by the bootstraps. In Jewish and Christian thought, however, humankind is not struggling alone. There is, to come full circle, the spiritual realm beyond material reality to which people can turn for help. People exist in relation to that which is greater than and transcends material existence—a source of guidance, comfort, hope, and aid for those who seek it. There is a radical openness in Judeo-Christian views of reality and humanity, a conscious expectation that God will do and is doing something new.

8. *Transformation.* This in turn widens the human potential for change. People are redeemable. There is hope for change beyond the step-by-step approximations of learning and will, beyond self-reliance, beyond what appear to be insurmountable limitations and obstacles. Transformation can occur suddenly, dramatically, unexpectedly (Miller & C'de Baca, 2001; see chap. 9, this volume). Radical personal transformation is ever possible and lies at the heart of scriptural stories in both Judaism (e.g., Moses) and Christianity (e.g., Paul).

Whatever a psychologist's own location within the multidimensional space of spirituality, any understanding of human nature is incomplete if it does not take spirituality into account. The fact that many people experience reality in this way is vital to understanding their motivations, values, self-concept, choices, and actions. The prized professional concept of "cultural competence" surely must include substantive appreciation of religion as a major, even defining influence within a culture. It is impossible, for example, to understand the individual or collective experience of living in African American, Islamic, or Mormon communities without taking into account the central role of religion.

Special Concerns: Values and Research Agenda

How people (including psychologists) spend their time reflects what they value. Matters of the heart, of special concern, influence a practitioner's choice of clients with whom to work or the scientist's choice of topics to study. What might be the special concerns to which one would be drawn if viewing human nature through Judeo-Christian lenses? How might the eight basic assumptions just outlined inform the topics that are particularly worthy of study?

1. *Reality of Spirit.* Once one assumes the reality of God and that humans bear the *imago Dei* (i.e., human nature reflects God's nature), the spiritual aspect of human nature becomes a matter of interest in psychological practice and research. A vital concern in theistic religions, as in 12-step programs such as Alcoholics Anonymous, is one's conscious and intentional contact with God. Prayer and meditation are the most universal forms of human endeavor for this purpose and the ones most often studied in research (Benson & Klipper, 1990; Dossey, 1995; Poloma & Gallup, 1991). More than 90% of Americans report that they pray at least occasionally (Gallup Organization, 1993). Less studied are other spiritual disciplines intended to foster conscious contact with God, such as fasting, singing or chanting, and rituals. One emerging avenue for such study is through noninvasive neuroscience imaging technology to better understand the human capacity for consciousness of God (e.g., d'Aquili & Newburg, 1999). For example, areas of neural activity associated with self-reported God consciousness can be studied in relation to specific spiritual practices. The extent and strength of God consciousness could in turn be related to aspects of personality, social adjustment, or health. The broad effects of long-term practice of spiritual disciplines likewise remain to be clarified (see chap. 11). Although faithful practice of contemplative prayer and meditation is associated with deep calming and peacefulness, it is also reported by mystics to lead at times to deeply disturbing anxiety and depression in a "dark night of the soul" (St. John of the Cross, 1959).

2. *Not God.* If one assumes the presence of absolute virtues and standards of goodness that are independent of human context and judgment, then psychological consultation and research can be directed toward helping the human person approach these ultimate goals. It is a common concern among people of faith to conform their lives to virtues that they desire, but from which they are drawn away by behavioral influences that are well understood by psychologists. Here emerges the difference between personality and character. Personality has been the subject of myriad studies examining the ways in which individuals are distributed across continuous or categorical variables, without necessarily judging one disposition to be more desirable than another. Introversion and extroversion, for example, represent opposite poles of a dimension along which humans vary, and although cultures or subcultures may differentially value these traits, both are considered psychologically normal. The multidimensional construct of character, conversely, includes an absolute judgment that one end of the spectrum is the proper, intended, desirable state of human beings. It makes sense to speak of a person as having good character, less so to say that he or she is of good personality. Personality comprises traits; character comprises virtues. Such distinction is disquieting to a moral relativist, of course, but the perception of character is clearly inherent in natural language and is a component of public discourse. It is the everyday substance of biography, drama, and eulogy.

The exposition of character raises the natural question of which factors promote the development and maintenance of character or contribute to its impairment or demise. Much is known from psychological research about the genesis of introversion or neuroticism; much less about the origins of virtues such as generosity or honesty. Psychologists could certainly advance knowledge of what constitutes and promotes specific virtues such as humility, integrity, wisdom, and nonviolence.

3. *Sin.* Virtuous behavior also has its opposite, which is described as vice in common parlance and as sin within Jewish and Christian traditions. Discussion of sin and evil has not been entirely absent in psychological and psychiatric discourse. Menninger (1973) titled one influential treatise *Whatever Happened to Sin?* Peck (1983) devoted his second popular book, *People of the Lie,* to an exploration of the psychology of evil.

Sin is behavior that is inherently undesirable from a spiritual perspective, although it may be associated with powerful immediate positive reinforcement. A central concern in theistic religions is the avoidance of sinful behavior. Whether or not psychologists share a person's religious perspectives regarding the moral nature of character and sin, they know much about self-control and what influences behavior. The overriding of immediate reinforcement (temptation) in favor of achieving longer term goals is a familiar scenario for psychologists (Baumeister, 2003; Baumeister, Heatherton, & Tice, 1994), particularly those who work with addiction, a clear example of the misplaced priorities that scriptures define as idolatry. Psychological research and perspectives can also be useful in understanding factors that promote or exacerbate specific sins or vices such as violence, lying, self-centeredness, adultery, covetousness, and enslavement to material possessions.

4. *Agency*. If humans are willing, choosing, deciding agents, then it is important to understand how such executive control interacts with and overrides other determinants of behavior. Miller and Brown (1991) described volitional control as one source of influence on behavior, with the proportion of variance controllable by willful effort varying across specific behaviors, individuals, and time. Some behaviors are highly subject to volitional regulation, whereas others are relatively impervious to willful control. Some that are ordinarily outside volitional influence can be brought under conscious control with experience, as through biofeedback training of physiological functions. Behavioral self-control training involves teaching principles of learning to then be applied in regulating one's own behavior (Hester, 2003; Thoresen & Mahoney, 1974).

Too often, psychological research has focused on reducing human behavior to mechanistic determinants, ignoring or dismissing executive control (Howard, 1986). A Judeo-Christian understanding of the human person, implicit in law and manifest in commonsense public self-perception, assumes that agentive control is not illusory. Rather, choice is a significant determinant of action and is in a sense the most distinctly human aspect of behavioral control. Instead of dismissing or minimizing human agency, a psychologist who shares this perspective would be vitally concerned to understand and facilitate the willful control of behavior.

5. *Spiritual Health*. Health is itself a complex and elusive concept, comprising multiple dimensions of well-being (Miller & Thoresen, 1999). Medical checkups are designed to evaluate vital signs and markers of crucial aspects of physical health. Comprehensive personality assessment similarly surveys multiple dimensions of mental status.

From a theistic or other holistic perspective, spiritual health becomes a third important dimension, and a comprehensive appraisal of the human person would encompass body, mind, and spirit. Substantial advances have been made in psychometric validation of instruments for assessing spirituality and religion (Gorsuch & Miller, 1999; Hill & Hood, 1999). Pruyser (1976) outlined an approach for assessing spiritual health specifically from the perspective of Christian theology. Others have developed and validated measures for assessing general spiritual well-being (Paloutzian & Ellison, 1991) and styles of spiritual coping (Pargament, 1997). Fowler (1995) described a system for understanding and assessing faith development, and others have proposed measures of spiritual maturity (Hill & Hood, 1999). A multidimensional inventory of spiritual and religious scales has been published by the Fetzer Institute in collaboration with the National Institute on Aging (1999).

With such a wealth of instrumentation already available, research is feasible to study spiritual health measures as independent, predictor, mediator, moderator, or dependent variables. For example, spiritual health and character measures may be correlated with mental and physical health indices, both concurrently and as predictors in longitudinal studies. A large literature points to salutary relationships between religiousness and health (Koenig et al., 2000), but the underlying reasons for these relationships need to be clarified. Similarly, little is known about the positive or negative impact of various forms of psychotherapy or pharmacotherapy on spiritual health outcomes as dependent variables.

6. *Relational Responsibility*. The concept of relational responsibility for the behavior and welfare of one's larger community points to certain concerns that would be given high priority for research within a theistic perspective. Jewish and Christian scriptures both reflect preferential concern for the plight of the poor and oppressed, populations that are often underrepresented among research participants. Processes that promote peacemaking and harmonious relationships within a community are of urgent concern. Pertinent here is research on factors promoting behaviors that enhance social harmony: forgiveness, cooperation, voluntarism, charitable giving, selfless love, and altruism (e.g., Myers, 1992; Post, Underwood, Schloss, & Hurlbut, 2002).

Relational responsibility extends to religious communities themselves. Clearly great harm has been done at times in the name of religion, both at an individual or local level (as in mass suicides within a cult) and on a broader societal or international scale (as exemplified by the Crusades, historic violence in Northern Ireland and the Middle East, and the September 11, 2001, attacks on New York and Washington). What factors contribute to such misappropriations of religion? How can religious communities guard against doing harm to individuals and against communal dangers that lead toward more widespread harm? What kinds of harm are inflicted on individuals by "toxic religion," and how can such wounds be healed? Answers to such questions require not only analysis of but meaningful dialogue with religion.

7. *Hope*. Most healers recognize the mysterious power of hope, but research is at an early stage to understand the phenomenon itself and how it affects human welfare (Snyder 1994; Yahne & Miller, 1999). Those who believe in God manifest a particular form of hope that may or may not resemble other forms such as optimism or evidence-based prediction. The hope for divine intervention particularly inspires the widespread practice of petitionary or intercessory prayer (Poloma & Gallup, 1991). Although there has been more research on the impact of such prayer than most scientists realize (Dossey, 1995; Matthews, 1998), studies of prayer's effects on human health outcomes have less often been published in peer-reviewed scientific journals. Some clinical trials have reported significant benevolent effects of double-blind intercessory prayer for others by strangers (McCullough, 1995), and some have not (e.g., Walker, Tonnigan, Miller, Comer, & Kahlich, 1997).

Also of import is the effect of various types of prayer, including petitionary prayer, on one's own physical, mental, and spiritual health or on that of loved ones (McCullough & Larson, 1999; Poloma & Gallup, 1991). Within the 12-step programs, surrendering self-control and asking for God's help are seen as vital steps toward recovery (Alcoholics Anonymous, 1976). Psychologists have studied the coping value of such letting go (Baugh, 1988; Cole & Pargament, 1999) and acceptance (Hayes, Jacobson, Follette, & Dougher, 1994); less understood are the specific effects of asking for divine intervention.

8. *Transformation.* Psychologists typically study small changes, such as the step-by-step approximations of a learning curve. Psychotherapy is usually understood to yield gradual change, in relatively small steps over a span of weeks, months, or years. With addictive behaviors, the normal course is not abrupt recovery, but approximations over time with reversals back to prior behavior (Brownell, Marlatt, Lichtenstein, & Wilson, 1986; Westerberg, Miller, Harris, & Tonigan, 1998).

It has long been recognized, however, that dramatic and sweeping transformation of a person can happen abruptly, in the course of a few minutes or hours, yielding highly stable changes. James (1902) described such events and speculated on factors that may predispose people to such sudden transformation. Members of Alcoholics Anonymous (1976), including its co-founder Bill W., have reported sudden and permanent release from well-established addiction, including the absence of any craving or desire to return. Theologians have described processes by which such conversions or transformations occur (Loder, 1981; Rambo, 1993), and psychologists have published occasional case reports documenting them (e.g., Barlow, Abel, & Blanchard, 1977). More recently, Miller and C'de Baca (2001) synthesized 55 such narratives to describe a phenomenon of "quantum change" with two subtypes: sudden insights and mystical epiphanies. Autobiography and biography are also replete with examples of abruptly transformed minds and hearts.

For people of faith, such events are less surprising. Scripture contains a salient example of the sudden dramatic transformation of Saul, who, on the road to Damascus in the midst of arresting and persecuting early Christians, became one of the church's most ardent and eloquent proponents as the renamed apostle Paul. Such about-face conversions may be understood by believers as literal acts of God. Among the 55 quantum changes studied by Miller and C'de Baca (2001), the most common immediate antecedent was an ardent prayer for God's help, often the person's first prayer ever, or in many years. If such dramatic and permanent change can occur within a matter of minutes, surely it should be of interest to psychologists, whether theistic or not.

ONWARD

A central purpose of this book is to explore the interface of psychology with Judeo-Christian anthropology. This chapter and the next provide a conceptual and historical context for considering this unaccustomed juxtaposition of perspectives.[1]

Part II then takes up three fundamental aspects of selfhood that overlap psychology and Judeo-Christian spirituality. The first of these is agency and volition, an essential component in Jewish and Christian understandings of human nature. Roy F. Baumeister (chap. 3), a secular social psychologist, describes this much-discussed and well-studied issue from the perspective of the psychology of self-regulation. In chapter 4, the Christian philosopher C. Stephen Evans contrasts individualistic concepts of self with relational understandings of human nature. Drawing particularly on the writings of Søren Kierkegaard, he constructs an anthropology that embraces self in relation both to others and to God. Then in chapter 5, Thomas H. Bien, a former pastor whose current work (Bien & Bien, 2002) involves the integration of Buddhist mindfulness with Western psychology and spirituality, explores the importance of narrative in Judeo-Christian religion and in the psychology of self. Stories, he maintains, form a core of identity for individuals, groups, and religions.

Part III takes up issues of motivation at the interface of psychology with Judeo-Christian anthropology. Human sexuality provides a fruitful dimension within which to consider the dialogue of religious and psychological perspectives. In chapter 6, Stanton L. Jones, a Christian clinical psychologist and university provost, and Heather R. Hostler discuss philosophical contrasts and commonalities in these perspectives on sexuality. Martin L. Maehr (chap. 7), a social psychologist whose research focuses on motivation, extends his prior work to more broadly consider the role of meaning and values in motivating human behavior. Finally, Everett L. Worthington Jr., a Christian clinical psychologist and department chair, and Jack W. Berry explore the parallels of what psychologists call moral development with classic character concepts of virtues and vices.

This provides a bridge to the five chapters of Part IV, where the focus is on change and transformation within a longitudinal perspective. In chapter 9, psychotherapists Stephanie Brown and William R. Miller explicate the phenomenon of spiritual transformation and take beginning steps toward a model for understanding how they occur. Jared D. Kass, a Jewish psychologist of religion whose interests took shape while working with Carl Rogers on the Person-Centered Approach Project, considers with Susan Lennox in chapter 10 how facilitating spiritual development may provide a broad foundation for the formation of prosocial and health behavior. Carl E. Thoresen, Doug Oman, and Alex H. S. Harris (chap. 11) review the rapidly growing literature on the relationship of spiritual–religious practices to health outcomes,

---

[1]The authors cite a number of translations of biblical material. In addition to the citations of chapter and verse, the particular translation quoted is often included in the parenthetical citation as designated by the following abbreviations: King James Version (KJV); Revised Standard Version (RSV); New International Version (NIV); and New American Bible (NAB).

and Brenda A. Miller (chap. 12) discusses how spirituality and religiousness are transmitted across generations. Concluding Part IV, Kenneth I. Pargament, a Jewish clinical psychologist of religion, with Nichole A. Murray-Swank, Gina M. Magyar, and Gene G. Ano discuss the common developmental phenomenon of spiritual struggles, their consequences, and ways to help people move through them (chap. 13).

In our concluding Part V, Carlo C. DiClemente and Harold D. Delaney draw together some implications of Judeo-Christian perspectives for the science and practice of psychology. Finally, in chapter 15, we offer our own reflections from the three years of collaboration that led to this volume.

The quest to understand the nature of the human person did not begin with psychology, nor did the desire to improve the human condition. The vision of psychology as a means for promoting human welfare (G. Miller, 1969) is a desire shared not only with other sciences but also with the humanities and with world religions. There are differences in approach, to be sure, but there are also many opportunities for shared vision and action. True collaboration involves being willing to step into another's frame of reference and understand assumptions, perceptions, needs, and priorities from the other's perspective. Until recently, religious perspectives have been oddly absent and unwelcome in mainstream psychology's understanding of human nature. Perhaps in the decades ahead, it will become clearer just how much we have been missing.

REFERENCES

Alcoholics Anonymous. (1976). *Alcoholics Anonymous* (3rd ed.). New York: AlcoholicsAnonymous World Services.

Anderson, R., & Cissna, K. N. (1977). *The Martin Buber Carl Rogers dialogue: A new transcript with commentary*. Albany: State University of New York Press.

Bargh, J. A., & Chartrand, T. L. (1999). The unbearable automaticity of being. *American Psychologist, 54*, 462–479.

Bargh, J. A., & Ferguson, M. J. (2000). Beyond behaviorism: On the automaticity of higher mental processes. *Psychological Bulletin, 126*, 925–945.

Barlow, D. H., Abel, G. G., & Blanchard, E. G. (1977). Gender identity change in a transsexual: An exorcism. *Archives of Sexual Behavior, 6*, 387–395.

Baugh, J. R. (1988). Gaining control by giving up control: Strategies for coping with powerlessness. In W. R. Miller & J. E. Martin (Eds.), *Behavior therapy and religion: Integrating spiritual and behavioral approaches to change* (pp. 125–138). Newbury Park, CA: Sage.

Baumeister, R. F. (2003). Ego depletion and self-regulation failure: A resource model of self-control. *Alcoholism: Clinical and Experimental Research, 27*, 281–284.

Baumeister, R. F., Heatherton, T. F., & Tice, D. M. (1994). *Losing control: How and why people fail at self-regulation*. New York: Academic Press.

Benson, H., & Klipper, M. Z. (1990). *The relaxation response*. New York: Avon Books.

Bien, T., & Bien, B. (2002). *Mindful recovery: A spiritual path to healing from addiction*. New York: Wiley.

Brown, W. S., Murphy, N. C., & Malony, H. N. (Eds.). (1998). *Whatever happened to the soul? Scientific and theological portraits of human nature*. Minneapolis, MN: Fortress Press.

Brownell, K. D., Marlatt, G. A., Lichtenstein, E., & Wilson, G. T. (1986). Understanding and preventing relapse. *American Psychologist, 41*, 765–782.

Cole, B. S., & Pargament, K. I. (1999). Spiritual surrender: A paradoxical path to control. In W. R. Miller (Ed.), *Integrating spirituality into treatment: Resources for practitioners* (pp. 179–198). Washington, DC: American Psychological Association.

d'Aquili, E., & Newberg, A. B. (1999). *The mystical mind: Probing the biology of religious experience*. Minneapolis, MN: Fortress Press.

Doniger, S. (Ed.). (1962). *The nature of man in theological and psychological perspective*. New York: Harper.

Dossey, L. (1995). *Healing words: The power of prayer and the practice of medicine*. San Francisco: Harper.

Fetzer Institute and National Institute on Aging Working Group. (1999). *Multidimensional measurement of religiousness/spirituality for use in health research*. Kalamazoo, MI: Fetzer Institute.

Foster, R. J. (1998). *Celebration of discipline: The path to spiritual growth*. San Francisco: HarperCollins.

Fowler, J. (1995). *Stages of faith: The psychology of human development and the quest for meaning*. San Francisco: HarperCollins.

Fuller, R. C. (2001). *Spiritual, but not religious: Understanding unchurched America*. New York: Oxford University Press.

Gallup, G. (1985). *Religion in America, 50 years: 1935–1985*. Princeton, NJ: Princeton Religious Research Center.

Gallup, G. (1995). *The Gallup Poll: Public opinion 1995*. Wilmington, DE: Scholarly Reserves.

Gallup Organization. (1993). *GO LIFE survey on prayer*. Princeton, NJ: Author.

Gorsuch, R. L., & Miller, W. R. (1999). Measuring spirituality. In W. R. Miller (Ed.), *Integrating spirituality into treatment: Resources for practitioners* (pp. 47–64). Washington, DC: American Psychological Association.

Hayes, S. C., Jacobson, N. S., Follette, V. M., & Dougher, M. J. (Eds.). (1994). *Acceptance and change*. Reno, NV: Context Press.

Hester, R. K. (2003). Behavioral self-control training. In R. K. Hester & W. R. Miller (Eds.), *Handbook of alcoholism treatment approaches: Effective alternatives* (3rd ed., pp. 152–164). Boston: Allyn & Bacon.

Hill, P. C., & Hood, R. W. (1999). *Measures of religious behavior.* Birmingham, AL: Religious Education Press.

Hoekema, A. A. (1986). *Created in God's image.* Grand Rapids, MI: Eerdmans.

Howard, G. (1986). *Dare we develop a human science?* Notre Dame, IN: Academic Publications.

Huxley, A. (1998). *Brave new world.* New York: Harper Perennial.

James, W. (1902). *The varieties of religious experience: A study in human nature.* Cambridge, MA: Harvard University Press.

Kirsch, I., & Lynn, S. J. (1999). Automaticity in clinical psychology. *American Psychologist, 54,* 504–515.

Koenig, H. G. (Ed.). (1998). *Handbook of religion and mental health.* San Diego, CA: Academic Press.

Koenig, H. G., McCullough, M. E., & Larson, D. B. (2000). *Handbook of religion and health.* New York: Oxford University Press.

Kurtz, E. (1979). *Not God: A history of Alcoholics Anonymous.* Center City, MN: Hazelden.

Larson, D. B., Swyers, J. P., & McCullough, M. E. (Eds.). (1998). *Scientific research on spirituality and health: A consensus report.* Rockville, MD: National Institute for Healthcare Research.

Levin, J. S. (1994). Religion and health: Is there an association, is it valid, and is it causal? *Social Science in Medicine, 38,* 1475–1482.

Loder, J. E. (1981). *The transforming moment: Understanding convictional experiences.* New York: HarperCollins.

Matthews, D. A. (1998). *The faith factor: Proof of the healing power of prayer.* New York: Penguin Books.

McCullough, M. E. (1995). Prayer and health: Conceptual issues, research review, and research agenda. *Journal of Psychology and Theology, 23,* 15–29.

McCullough, M. E., & Larson, D. B. (1999). Prayer. In W. R. Miller (Ed.), *Integrating spirituality into treatment: Resources for practitioners* (pp. 85–110). Washington, DC: American Psychological Association.

Menninger, K. (1973). *Whatever happened to sin?* New York: Dutton.

Merton, T. (1960). *Spiritual direction and meditation.* Collegeville, MN: Liturgical Press.

Miller, G. A. (1969). Psychology as a means of promoting human welfare. *American Psychologist, 24,* 1063–1075.

Miller, W. R. (Ed.). (1999). *Integrating spirituality into treatment: Resources for practitioners.* Washington, DC: American Psychological Association.

Miller, W. R., & Brown, J. M. (1991). Self-regulation as a conceptual basis for the prevention and treatment of addictive behaviours. In N. Heather, W. R. Miller, & J. Greeley (Eds.), *Self-control and the addictive behaviours* (pp. 3–79). Sydney, Australia: Maxwell Macmillan.

Miller, W. R., & C'de Baca, J. (2001). *Quantum change: When sudden insights and epiphanies transform ordinary lives.* New York: Guilford Press.

Miller, W. R., & Thoresen, C. E. (1999). Spirituality and health. In W. R. Miller (Ed.), *Integrating spirituality into treatment: Resources for practitioners* (pp. 3–18). Washington, DC: American Psychological Association.

Miller, W. R., & Thoresen, C. E. (2003). Spirituality, religion, and health: An emerging research field. *American Psychologist, 58,* 24–35.

Myers, D. G. (1992). *The pursuit of happiness.* New York: Avon Books.

National Institute on Alcohol Abuse and Alcoholism. (1999). *Conference summary: Studying spirituality and alcohol.* Bethesda, MD: Author.

Orwell, G. (1992). *1984.* New York: Knopf.

Paloutzian, R. F., & Ellison, C. W. (1991). *Manual for the spiritual well-being scale.* Nyack, NY: Life Advances.

Pannenberg, W. (1970). *What is man? Contemporary anthropology in theological perspective.* Philadelphia: Fortress Press.

Pargament, K. (1997). *The psychology of religion and coping: Theory, research, practice.* New York: Guilford Press.

Peck, M. S. (1983). *People of the lie: The hope for healing human evil.* New York: Simon & Schuster.

Poloma, M. M., & Gallup, G. H., Jr. (1991). *Varieties of prayer: A survey report.* Philadelphia: Trinity Press International.

Post, S. G., Underwood, L. G., Schloss, J. P., & Hurlbut, W. B. (Eds.). (2002). *Altruism and altruistic love: Science, philosophy, and religion in dialogue.* Oxford, England: Oxford University Press.

Pruyser, P. W. (1976). *The minister as diagnostician: Personal problems in pastoral perspective.* Philadelphia: Westminster John Knox.

Rambo, L. R. (1993). *Understanding religious conversion.* New Haven, CT: Yale University Press.

Richards, P. S., & Bergin, A. E. (1997). *A spiritual strategy for counseling and psychotherapy.* Washington, DC: American Psychological Association.

Shafranske, E. P. (Ed.). (1996). *Religion and the clinical practice of psychology.* Washington, DC: American Psychological Association.

Skinner, B. F. (1972). *Beyond freedom and dignity.* New York: Knopf.

Snyder, C. R. (1994). *Psychology of hope.* New York: Free Press.

St. John of the Cross. (1959). *Dark night of the soul.* New York: Image Books.

Templeton, J. M. (1997). *Worldwide laws of life: 200 eternal spiritual principles.* Philadelphia: Templeton Foundation Press.

Thoresen, C. E., & Mahoney, M. J. (1974). *Behavioral self-control.* New York: Holt, Rinehart & Winston.

Tillich, P., & Rogers, C. (1966). *Paul Tillich & Carl Rogers: A dialogue* (transcript). San Diego, CA: San Diego State College Radio.

Walker, S. R., Tonigan, J. S., Miller, W. R., Comer, S., & Kahlich, L. (1997). Intercessory prayer in the treatment of alcohol dependence: A pilot investigation. *Alternative Therapies, 3*(6), 79–86.

Watson, J. B. (1925). *Behaviorism*. New York: People's Institute.

Westerberg, V. S., Miller, W. R., Harris, R. J., & Tonigan, J. S. (1998). The topography of relapse in clinical samples. *Addictive Behaviors, 23*, 325–337.

Yahne, C. E., & Miller, W. R. (1999). Evoking hope. In W. R. Miller (Ed.), *Integrating spirituality into treatment: Resources for practitioners* (pp. 217–233). Washington, DC: American Psychological Association.

2

PSYCHOLOGY'S ROOTS: A BRIEF HISTORY OF THE INFLUENCE OF JUDEO-CHRISTIAN PERSPECTIVES

HAROLD D. DELANEY AND CARLO C. DiCLEMENTE

Throughout most of the 20th century, the idea of taking Judeo Chris tian teaching seriously within psychology was generally considered taboo (cf. Jones, 1994). This was perhaps particularly true with regard to religious ideas of sin, guilt, or repentance as relevant to psychological health. As Donald Campbell observed in his 1975 American Psychological Association (APA) presidential address, "present day psychology and psychiatry in all their major forms are more hostile to the inhibitory messages of traditional religious moralizing than is scientifically justified" (1975, p. 1103). This has not always been the case, and need not be in the 21st century (cf. chap. 3, this volume). Indeed, the psychological ramifications of Judeo-Christian beliefs about morality and what it means to be human have been considered by great thinkers for centuries and lie at the heart of our shared cultural heritage in the West. Thomas Cahill (1998) has recently called attention to the fact

The authors gratefully acknowledge the numerous helpful suggestions of Hendrika Vande Kemp. The chapter was greatly improved by reviews and feedback from Pew panel members, the APA referees and editors, and Nancy Delaney and Monica Stump.

that how we view ourselves is a gift of this long tradition of "ethical mono-theism without which our ideas of equality and personalism are unlikely ever to have come into being" (p. 250). It is the purpose of this chapter to set the rediscovery of religious and spiritual aspects of individuals that has emerged in behavioral research over the past 25 years in the context of the panoramic sweep of centuries of Judeo-Christian thought about the human person and to show the relevance of that thought for the emergence and development of the discipline of psychology. By highlighting the views of important Jewish and Christian thinkers on psychological issues and their influence on the development of psychology, we hope to lay the foundation for this volume's attempt to foster a more fruitful dialogue between current psychology and religion. Obviously, only the tallest peaks can be noted in our survey. Al-though other themes emerge as well, we see that the issues of greatest impor-tance historically include several of those introduced by Miller in the previ-ous chapter, such as (a) *agency*, and the problem of human freedom; (b) values derived from a transcendent source rather than from sources that are *not* God; (c) *sin*, as a reason for experiencing guilt and lack of spiritual well-being; and (d) *transformation*, or how meaningful change occurs.

THE PATRISTIC AND SCHOLASTIC ERAS

Although any history of psychology begins, as does the history of most academic disciplines, with a respectful nod to the Greeks, our discipline is perhaps unusual in the sense that "the emergence of Christianity must be counted as an occurrence whose importance to Psychology is matched, if at all, only by the Hellenic epoch" (Robinson, 1981, p. 111). Given the Jewish context from which Christianity emerged, one must broaden the question suggested by Robinson's assertion, asking, "Why the great importance of Judeo-Christian perspectives for the history of psychology?" A comparison with Hellenic views provides a helpful starting point for developing an answer. The naturalistic perspective on human behavior had been established in Democritus's atomism, in the primitive evolutionary speculations of Anaximander and Empedocles, and, most importantly, in Aristotle's detailed analyses of learning and memory processes. The Greek legacy also included reflective analyses of the problem of human conduct, with the Platonic view providing the rationalist solution that the problem is essentially one of knowl-edge or discerning what is right. Against this backdrop, the Judeo-Christian perspective, although endorsing the significance of both the natural created order and a transcendent realm, provided a sharp contrast in its analysis of human behavior. The focus in the early Christian era shifted to the intense struggles of individuals with their internal conflicts. Behavior was seen as often not rationally governed even when one knows what is right and at some level wants to pursue it. The elements of a depth psychology that profoundly grappled with sexuality, ambivalence, the unconscious, and guilt were crystallized in the writings of Augustine, a paramount figure not only in Christian thought but also in Western intellectual history more generally (Johnson, 1998).

Augustine (354–430)

Augustine's personal history, which powerfully informed his many intellectual contributions, illustrates many of the themes of this volume such as volition, motivation, virtue, and transformational change. Although now revered by Protestants (some view the Reformation as an Augustinian revival) and regarded as a saint by Roman Catholics, Augustine was something of a prodigal as an adolescent and went through a prolonged period of searching before his conversion to Christianity at age 32. The details of his life are vividly recounted in the autobiographical *Confessions* (Augustine, 400/1952), which he wrote so that "whosoever reads this may think out of what depths we are to cry unto Thee" (pp. 9–10). Thus, we learn of him stealing pears as a bit of juvenile mischief and of his struggles with the consequences of indulging his sexual desires outside of marriage over a 15-year period. Despite the fact that reading Cicero as a teen gave him a deep thirst for immortal wisdom (400/1952, p. 14), Augustine reported that his mind, like his sexual life, was impure and misguided (p. 25), with the result that he spent over a decade as an inquirer with the Manichean sect. Eventually at age 29, Augustine decided that the answers he received to his questions even from the most eminent spokesman for the Manichees were unsatisfactory, and certainly less compelling than the eloquent discourses of Ambrose, the outstanding bishop of Milan whom Augustine encountered while teaching rhetoric there. As opposed to the Manichean system, which mocked his credulity "by a promise of certain knowledge," the Christianity of Ambrose more honestly asked for certain things to be taken on faith or on a scriptural basis (400/1952, pp. 36–37). At age 32, Augustine was still struggling with the sort of halfhearted willing that had prompted him to pray a dozen years earlier, "Give me chastity and continency, only not yet" (400/1952, p. 57). Although convinced of the truth of Christianity, he found that his inner self was still a house divided against itself, held back by old habits and indulgences. Finally came the famous conversion scene in the garden in which Augustine heard a voice telling him to "take up and read" and opened a Bible to Romans 13:13: "not in orgies and drunkenness, not in sexual immorality and debauchery, not in dissension and jealousy. Rather, clothe yourselves with the Lord Jesus Christ, and do not think about how to gratify the desires of the sinful nature." Becoming a Christian, Augustine returned to his home in northern Africa and devoted the rest of his life as a celibate to the service of the church, spending 35 years as bishop of Hippo and writing various commentaries and doctrinal treatises, culminating in the *City of God* (427/1952).

The single descriptor most often attached to Augustine's thought is Neoplatonist (cf. Leahey, 2000, p. 95). Although in basic agreement with Platonic thought on the existence of a transcendent realm and the inadequacy of the senses for discovering unchanging truths, Augustine's thought, informed increasingly over time by his Christian worldview, departed from Platonic thought in major respects (Robinson, 1981, p. 120). Most fundamentally, Augustine was thoroughly *theocentric*; thus, his reflections about human nature generally, and his own struggles were in the context of God as the creator and center of life (Johnson, 1998). So thoroughly did this inform his perspective that even his autobiography included over 800 paraphrases or quotations of Scripture. In terms of his epistemology, Augustine relied largely on an interior sense or awareness of truth and right and responsibility (Clark, 1965; Robinson, 1981, p. 121). Thus, the focus was on reason led by faith and illuminated by revelation, both scriptural and personal. A profound difference in the way human nature was viewed resulted from this shift away from Platonic philosophy toward the interior realm of motives and conflict seen by an omniscient deity to whom one is personally accountable. As Daniel Robinson put it, "Where the Republic was the enlargement allowing a clearer view of human nature, the Christian was the miniature in whom God's reality could be established. This shift in emphasis provided early Christian scholarship with a decidedly psychological cast" (Robinson, 1981, p. 123).

In particular, whereas Plato had asserted the need for reason to rule over the passions, Augustine's focus was on the passionate side of human nature that Plato condemned. Indeed, in positing that the basic human motive was the desire for happiness, Augustine (400/1952, VI, 16) agreed to some extent with Epicurus. Augustine came to realize, however, that seeking happiness in pleasures or things was to pursue an unreal happiness, concluding instead, "And this is the happy life, to rejoice to Thee, of Thee, for Thee; this is it, and there is no other" (400/1952, X, 22). Reflecting on how he arrived at this point, Augustine saw God's mercy in the fact that God was always "flavoring all my unlawful pleasures with bitter discontent" (II, 4, as quoted by Woollcott, 1966, p. 278). Most prominent for Augustine both before and after his conversion were his struggles with sexual temptations and with guilt feelings both for his sexual indulgence before his conversion and for the sexuality of his dream life subsequently. So we see that personal morality is at the core of Augustinian psychology, with one's accountability, in his view, extending even to one's thought life while asleep. Whereas for Plato, virtuous action was the natural consequence of knowledge of the good, Augustine's experience (cf. 400/1952, X, 28) often was more like that of Paul described in Romans: "For what I do is not the good I want to do; no, the evil I do not want to do—this I keep on doing" (Rom. 7:19).

The Augustinian legacy to psychology includes not only the first depth psychology to focus in a sustained, intensely personal way on such internal conflicts (e.g., 400/1952, VIII, 8–12) but also the prominent role of sexuality, the value of dreams in revealing unresolved issues, and the cathartic release resulting from candidly facing one's ambivalent feelings. In these emphases, it is obvious that Augustine anticipated much of what would later be given to the modern world in the form of Freudian psychoanalysis, although of course Augustine and Freud's views of God and faith were diametrically opposed. Given the fact that so many of Freud's valid insights were Augustinian, it is unfortunate and ironic that much of the scant attention given to Augustine's thought by 20th-century psychologists was a deconstruction of his ideas from the point of view of a thoroughgoing Freudian cynicism regarding religion (e.g., Bakan, 1965; Woollcott, 1966).

A final area in which the Christian view represented a major departure from the Platonic was an outgrowth of the belief that all are bearers of *imago Dei*. Thus, the Greek idea of certain people as natural slaves was replaced with an egalitarian view derived from the doctrine that all people are created in God's image, an idea as foreign to the aristocratic Greeks' hereditarian views as it is foreign to some modern eugenic theories. The egalitarian doctrine, however, made more pressing the problem of the varying degrees of virtue observed in different individuals. Augustine's solution to this problem, and to the problem of evil more generally, was to regard people as possessing free will or being morally responsible agents: "Free-will was the cause of our doing ill, and . . . I knew as well that I had a will as that I lived" (400/1952, VII, 3). This freedom operated within limits, however. Because our actions are sometimes limited by our circumstances, intent becomes even more important than action (Robinson, 1981, p. 128). Further, human will is not sufficient for attaining the salvation that instead depends on God's grace: "Our wills have just so much power as God willed and foreknew that they would have" (427/1952, V, 9; cf. Piper's [2000] discussion of Augustine's controversy with Pelagius).

When Augustine died on August 28, 430, the Vandals were at the gates of Hippo, and the fall of the Roman Empire was well underway. Yet his depth of thought, "the very reverse of the thin objectivity that plagues so many of our modern psychological studies" (Clark, 1965, p. 148), set the standard for Christian intellectual life, such as it was, for the next eight centuries until the scholarship in the universities emerging from the cathedral schools of Europe took on a more systematic form, reaching its pinnacle in "the angelic doctor," Thomas Aquinas.

Aquinas (1225–1274)

Although secular moderns may feel some connection with Francis of Assisi (1182–1226) because of his poetry or his love of nature and might regard him as the more deserving successor to Augustine in Christian influences on psychology, it is more difficult to find ready appreciation for that other Italian friar, Thomas Aquinas. The "Dumb Ox" was the epithet given him by his classmates who thought the fat, slow, and retiring Thomas a dunce. Today, his masterwork, *Summa Theologica* (1273/1952), with its hundreds of questions and thousands of objections and replies to objections, holds about as much attraction for the typical psychology student as thousands of pages of mathematical proofs of obscure theorems. Yet if the task of the Patristic era was the formation of orthodoxy and the task of the Scholastic era was to build a set of principles on the foundation of Christian belief, then there is no question that Aquinas was the master builder. Like the majestic Gothic cathedrals that were constructed from Paris to Canterbury, the *Summa Theologica* is a towering intellectual monument, constructed by one who had a vision for how the work of many who went before could be tied together. Although stimulated in part by the rediscovery of Aristotle through the Arabic translations of his works, Aristotle to him was not the final authority: "St. Thomas did not reconcile Christ to Aristotle; he reconciled Aristotle to Christ" (Chesterton, 1933, p. 14). Indeed, he was willing to draw on Platonic, Augustinian, Jewish, and Arabian sources in the belief that "all knowledge and all truth, whatever its source, is capable of harmonious adjustment" (Brennan, 1945, p. 62).

Among these sources was *The Guide for the Perplexed*, written by the greatest Rabbinic authority of his era, Moses ben Maimon, or Maimonides (1135–1204). Reared in Saracen Spain and educated by Arabic masters, Maimonides used arguments from Aristotle such as the unmoved mover[1] to provide philosophical support for conclusions such as God's existence. Maimonides's view of humans' free will—as necessary for moral accountability yet present in varying degrees in different individuals and different circumstances—was especially similar to the nuanced view of Aquinas (Schimmel, 1997, pp. 224ff.; cf. Schimmel, 2000). (Maimonides's contributions are discussed in greater detail in chap. 10, this volume.)

Although some of the topics of *Summa Theologica* are strictly doctrinal (e.g., the discussion of angels or the Trinity), the longest portions include treatises on man, on habits, and on virtues. The most important question for psychology in Aquinas's view was the relation of soul to body. His position is typically explained as agreeing with Aristotle that the soul is united to the body as its principle of operation, or as form is to matter, but it is certainly legitimate to argue that in opposing a more Platonic dualism Aquinas was adopting a more thoroughly Christian view. As Chesterton (1933) suggested, "A Christian *means* a man who believes that deity or sanctity has attached to matter or entered the world of the senses. . . . [St. Thomas] wanted the body, and all its senses, because he believed, rightly or wrongly, that it was a Chris-

---

[1]Aristotle's philosophy centered around "becoming," and in his *Physics* (trans. 1952, Book VII) he argues that the beginning of motion, or the origin of its becoming, must ultimately be in a mover that is unmoved and eternal. This conclusion solved the problem of infinite regress involved in the repeated attribution of motion to something that is merely an instrument of motion and that itself was caused to move by something else.

tian thing" (pp. 32–33). Thus, in arguing for the validity of knowledge gained from the senses, as opposed to a pure rationalism, Aquinas was paving the way for an empirical science.

Having given legitimacy to the senses, the problem remained as to how one derives knowledge of universal truths. Aquinas's answer was that although experience gives us knowledge of particulars, reason comprehends the universals. In particular, what he termed the *agens intellectus*, or agent-intellect, was the rational faculty that is able to abstract the underlying form from the attributes of objects: "The senses can respond only to the matter and not to the principle . . . but the principles themselves are of course immaterial. The psychology of knowledge, then, is a *cognitive psychology*, not an empirical psychology" (Robinson, 1981, pp. 152–153). Furthermore, "the abstraction is no lie" (e.g., Aquinas, 1273/1952 [I,Q7,A3], p. 32). That is, by God's grace, the principles inherent in the material world are discovered, not invented, by the mind.

With regard to the will, Aquinas agreed with Augustine up to a point regarding the freedom of the will (cf. Chesterton, 1933, p. 29). In contrast to Augustine, however, for Aquinas the will was subordinate to intellect (Watson, 1963, pp. 118–119). The will was thought to naturally desire happiness and the enjoyment of the good but could choose among only those options apprehended by the intellect: "Knowledge precedes the acts of the appetites. . . . The roots of freedom, therefore, are in our intellectual apprehensions" (Brennan, 1945, pp. 73–74). Similarly, failure to use one's moral freedom properly, which can result from failing to perceive one's duty or failing to act once perceived, meant that "in either case, the sin is a departure from the rule of reason" (Robinson, 1981, p. 154).

A final contribution of Aquinas is perhaps the most important for those who would approach scholarly work from a Judeo-Christian perspective, namely, the relation of faith and reason. Having identified a legitimate role for reason in arriving at truth, Aquinas toward the end of his life was confronted with Western disciples of Averroës, such as Siger of Brabant, who endorsed a doctrine of two truths (cf. Evans, 1996, p. 11; Watson, 1963, p. 144ff.). The Averroists argued that certain positions in Aristotle, such as the belief that matter has existed eternally, should be accepted even though directly contradicting the teaching of the church on creation because there were two truths: the truth of the material world and the truth of the supernatural world. As Chesterton (1933, p. 102ff.) tells the story, this was the one time in Aquinas's life, other than when his brothers had a prostitute attempt to seduce him, that the man who epitomized patience was roused to anger. His thunderous reply was that there is one truth, and that although there may be different paths to truth, there ultimately can be no contradiction. Although acknowledging that some truths belong only to faith because they cannot be known by reason, such as the mystery of the Trinity, and other truths are concerned with reason alone (e.g., geometric proofs), there are many truths that are common to both reason and revelation. Because the "author of the revealed mysteries of faith is also the author of the first principles of natural knowledge," there can be no ultimate contradiction. That does not mean that in the short run there may not be apparent contradiction, either because of misinterpretation of Scripture (e.g., in thinking a geocentric view is a necessary teaching) or because of scientific "facts" really being scientific fictions (e.g., "those who lectured us about determinism in psychology are already talking about indeterminism in matter"; Chesterton, 1933, p. 106). Aquinas nonetheless paved the way for an experimental science with full confidence that the church has nothing to fear from empirically discovered truths. As Bacon was to advise, it is impossible "to be too well studied in the book of God's word, or in the book of God's works" (Bacon, 1605/1952, p. 4).

RENAISSANCE AND ENLIGHTENMENT THINKERS

Space does not permit a development of the psychological views of the scholars of the Renaissance and Enlightenment periods. Suffice it to say that the Christian worldview was dominant:

> The most significant event of the Renaissance, Copernicus' theory of the earth's revolution, was judged by its author as no more than a footnote to God's great design. The same may be said of Kepler's assessment of his theory and Newton's of his. It is equally true of Galileo and of Locke and Descartes, of Leibniz. . . . The greatest scholars in philosophy and science, even through much of the nineteenth century, labored under the light of Christian faith. . . . The skeptics trained their doubts on man, not on God; on Aristotle, not the Nazarene. (Robinson, 1981, p. 294)

The extent to which this view informed such scholars' systems of thought is worth noting. Although most psychology students know Locke's role in founding the British empiricism out of which modern psychology grew, few appreciate the fact that the truths gained through the senses were less compelling for Locke than demonstrative knowledge. And the foremost truth that reason demonstrates, something that is known with certainty according to Locke, is that an eternal, omnipotent Being exists. His argument in part was that "man knows that he himself exists" with an intuitive certainty and that such a being cannot have come from nothing, "therefore something must have existed from eternity" (Locke, 1690/1952, bk. IV, chap. 2 and 10). Although all recognize his *tabula rasa* principle, few realize that Locke devoted considerable attention in the opening book of his *Essay* to explaining why, although the idea of God is not innate, it nonetheless is known to be true by "wise men of all nations" (Locke, 1690/1952, bk. I, chap. 3, sec. 16).

Similarly, Descartes is widely known for his dualistic interactionism, and students can dutifully recite "*Cogito ergo sum*" and perhaps explain how

Descartes's doubting led to his concluding his own existence indubitable. Although some may even recognize his standing at the forefront of the modern rationalist tradition and hence his contribution to the rationalist legacy to psychology that includes theories of cognitive development and language, many may not appreciate that his doubts led him just as indubitably to the conclusion that an ultimate cause, God, must exist (Descartes, 1641/1952, med. III, p. 81ff.). The same conclusion was reached by many early figures who wrote extensively about psychology in the United States, such as Thomas Upham, James McCosh, Noah Porter, and Laurens P. Hickok (Roback, 1952; Spilka, 1987), although they are overlooked in histories of psychology that restrict their attention in the United States to experimentalists (e.g., Boring, 1950).

MID-17TH- TO MID-19TH-CENTURY DEVELOPMENTS

Early American Psychology

The first half century of higher education in America after the founding of Harvard in 1636 consisted of one option, the study of Puritan theology and a curriculum organized in the medieval model (Marsden, 1994). Psychological doctrine was essentially that of the Scholastics (Fay, 1939), with bachelor's candidates in "physics" (or natural science) often defending psychological theses such as "The functioning of the soul depends on the body" or "The will contains nothing that was not previously in the intellect" (Roback, 1952, p. 14ff.). The medieval psychology being taught had been unaffected by the rapid developments in Europe throughout the 17th century but then "perished in the early eighteenth century, however, when America's first great philosopher, Jonathan Edwards (1703–1758), read Locke" (Leahey, 2000, p. 337; cf. Marsden, 2003, p. 60ff.).

Jonathan Edwards (1703–1758)

With his father, a pastor and Harvard graduate, supervising his early education, Jonathan Edwards met the admission requirements for Yale, which included being "expert in Latin and Greek authors" (Anderson, 1980, p. 5), at a young age, matriculating just before his 13th birthday in 1716. While Edwards was an undergraduate, the education possible at Yale was dramatically altered by the arrival of copies of Locke's *Essay Concerning Human Understanding* (1690/1952) and of Newton's *Principia Mathematica* (1687/1952) and *Optics* (1706/1952). Edwards was strongly influenced by Locke's empiricism and his associationist perspective on the human mind. He became an enthusiastic student of scientific works during his undergraduate and graduate days at Yale and maintained an interest in scientific issues, especially physics.[2] Edwards was appointed to the faculty of Yale in 1724 but after two years accepted a pastoral position in Northhampton, Massachusetts, and served as chief pastor there from 1729 till 1750. The revival movements that began in this church contributed to the Great Awakening and provided occasions for his observing intense religious experiences such as dramatic conversions. His most important works for psychology include A *Treatise Concerning Religious Affections* (1746/1959), *Freedom of the Will* (1754/1969), written during the years when Edwards was serving as a missionary to Native Americans, and a series of articles on "The Mind" that was published posthumously (1829/1980). In 1758, Edwards succeeded his son-in-law Aaron Burr as president of Princeton (then the College of New Jersey) but died one month later.

Edwards's psychology was more similar than earlier Christian writers to the predominant view of modern psychology in his determinism. He arrived at his denial of the freedom of the will as a result of following to its logical conclusion the standard scholastic division of the faculties of the mind into just two basic faculties: reason or understanding, and inclination or desire (Edwards, 1746/1959, pp. 96ff.; Fay, 1939, pp. 43ff., 180; Smith, 1959, p. 13). A person necessarily wills what he most desires; in brief, "he is free to do what he pleases, but he is not free to please what he pleases" (Fay, 1939, p. 45). Thus, in this determinism, Edwards sides with Hobbes and Spinoza, or for that matter with Freud and Skinner, as opposed to Augustine, Aquinas, and Locke, with the exception that Edwards traces the responsibility for the motive or desire back to the will of God (cf. Roback, 1952, p. 25). Nonetheless, like the ancient Stoics, Edwards placed great emphasis on how one responded to one's fate, exhorting a humble submission to God's will.

Virtually ignored, even in the psychology of religion itself (Roback, 1952, p. 29; Wulff, 1996), are Edwards's contributions to psychology of religion, despite the fact that they are "perhaps the best in this country before William James's *The Varieties of Religious Experience*" (Kaufman & Frankena, 1969, p. xi). Obviously as a result of the revival in his parish, Edwards's attention was drawn to the "psychology of the awakening soul" (Fay, 1939, p. 183). After his threatening sermons elicited great emotionality in the listeners, Edwards adopted the detached attitude of the scientist in attempting to chart successive stages in the transformation from great distress and conviction of one's sins to conversion and great emotional release. Critics of course fault Edwards for being more concerned with the hearers' acknowl-

---

[2]For example, Edwards grasped the emerging scientific conception of the universe as a vast system of constantly moving, interrelated parts and foresaw the amazing implications for the incredible fine-tuning required at its origin. He recorded in a notebook on natural science begun while a graduate student (Marsden, 2003, p. 67) that he aspired eventually to write fully about "how the motion, rest and direction of the least atom has an influence on the motion of every body in the universe," taking "notice of the great wisdom that is necessary in order thus to dispose every atom at first, as that they should go for the best" (quoted in Marsden, 2003, p. 70).

edgment of their sinfulness before a holy God than with the resulting psychological distress (Roback, 1952, p. 30). Others deride the inconsistency apparent in denying the freedom of the will while going about "calling upon men everywhere to use their wills in forsaking their sins" (Brown, 1955, p. 19). One could also critique the demand characteristic in the message that the religion God requires is not a lukewarm assent but a "fervent, vigorous engagedness of the heart" and if "our wills and inclinations be not strongly exercised, we are nothing" (Edwards, 1746/1959, p. 99). Edwards recognized such could be feigned, but concluded that "much affection" does not prove a man "has any true religion: but if he has no affection, it proves that he has no true religion" (Edwards, 1746/1959, p. 121). A major part of Edwards's intellectual project was to defend the importance of religious affections such as love, joy, and zeal and also to provide guidance in distinguishing between mere emotionalism and true distinguishing signs of God's gracious activity in an individual's life.

Thomas Upham (1799–1872)

An explicitly Christian influence on psychology might be said to have reached its apex in terms of the American academic mainstream in Thomas Upham, Bowdoin College professor of mental and moral philosophy (1825–1868) and "author of the best psychological textbook in English prior to William James" (Roback, 1952, p. 48). So popular was Upham's *Mental Philosophy* that it went through 57 editions over a 73-year period (1826–1899; Salter, 1986, p. 12). Among his 16 other books was the first treatise on abnormal psychology, as well as several on religious figures and themes. Complementing the practical observations of pioneering psychiatrist Benjamin Rush (1745–1813) in the previous century, Upham was the leading academic popularizer of a conception of mental faculties offered in part as a response to Edwards's bipartite account. In particular, Upham restored the will to psychology by developing a tripartite division of mental phenomena into intellectual, sentient, and voluntary (Fay, 1939, p. 93ff.). Intellect subsumed sensation and perception, attention, habit, association, and memory as well as reasoning; sensibilities included natural emotions and desires, such as appetites, propensities, and affections, and also moral emotions, such as a feeling of obligation. The last division of the mind, the will, allowed for volition as a basic component of human nature. This positing of a will free to choose between desires and obligations reflects Upham's own spiritual journey from a Calvinistic background to the Wesleyan holiness perspective,[3] similar to

---

[3]The Methodist revivalism spurred by John Wesley that became a dominant force in 18th-century England also spread rapidly in the United States, contributing to the Second Great Awakening in the years around 1800. Wesleyan theology departed from Calvinism not only in emphasizing the role of human will in accepting God's grace but also in emphasizing the pursuit of holiness and sanctification subsequent to salvation (Cairns, 1954).

that of Asa Mahan, president of Oberlin (Salter, 1986, e.g., pp. 28, 62). In terms of the emergence of psychology as a separate academic discipline, Upham may be said to have supplied the necessary transitional stage between the "speculative philosophy of Jonathan Edwards and the empirical psychology of William James" (Salter, 1986, p. 6). Like James in drawing on a broad range of sources and intellectual traditions, Upham also anticipated many of the ideas of modern psychologists, for example, the James–Lange theory of emotions, introversion and extroversion, rationalizations, and moral development (Fay, 1939; cf. Roback, 1952). Perhaps most important, however, was that Upham's was a sort of *positive* psychology. In one sense the viewpoint, like his tripartite system, was almost Platonic: There are fundamental, transcendent laws, and living in harmony with them is the key to mental and spiritual health (Salter, 1986, p. 183). Building on Edwards's logic that God's purpose in creation was to extend and communicate happiness to created beings (Marsden, 2003, p. 460ff.), Upham stressed a pursuit of happiness as a legitimate end of creatures of a benevolent God (Salter, 1986, p. 31). The intellectual foundation for a healthy as opposed to sick kind of religiosity (cf. James, 1902/1985) was thus laid. Upham's contributions were supplemented by those of many others such as James McCosh (1811–1894) of Princeton, who offered similar analyses of human nature steeped in Scottish commonsense realism and Protestant theology and who provided the soil out of which the discipline of psychology emerged in the United States (Spilka, 1987).

Søren Kierkegaard (1813–1855)

Clearly the most important European thinker to address psychological themes from an explicitly Christian perspective in the 200 years prior to the emergence of psychology as a separate academic discipline was the Danish writer Søren Kierkegaard. Although considered by many psychologists as the father of existentialist philosophy or as a thinker similar to Nietzsche (cf. Hergenhahn, 2001, p. 190), Kierkegaard explicitly considered himself a psychologist (Evans, 1990, p. 25) and saw his central mission as using psychology as an aid to the reintroduction of true Christianity into "the monstrous illusion we call Christendom" (Kierkegaard, 1859/1962, pp. 5–6). Although like Nietzsche and modern existentialists Kierkegaard was concerned with the individual's will and authentic existence, on many other points he would be diametrically opposed. It is true that Kierkegaard's psychology was a depth psychology focused on anxiety, self-deception, and despair, but the attempt to use one's freedom to become autonomous and arbitrarily create one's essence by one's choices, as Sartre would have it, is for Kierkegaard the definition of sin—a prideful attempt to break away from the self God wants you to become (Evans, 1990, p. 57; see chap. 4, this volume, for more on Kierkegaard's view of the self). Similarly, rather than values being created by the arbitrary decisions of an autonomous individual, there are moral demands to lead an ethical life that one may recognize or fail to recognize. Although trying to satisfy these ethical demands is a higher stage of personal moral development than simply living for pleasure (the aesthetic stage), it is not the highest stage. Rather, acknowledging one's own need for grace and making the leap of faith to avail oneself of the provision for one's sin constitute true selfhood as God intended (cf. Evans, 1990).

Much of Kierkegaard's writing is difficult, either because of the complexity of individual passages or because of the different points of view adopted by the author; for example, Kierkegaard wrote under a variety of pseudonyms that represented persons at different stages of moral development. (A brief overview of his major works is provided by Evans, 1990, p. 130ff.) A shorter work more transparently in line with the theme of transformation and spiritual development addressed in Part IV of this volume is Kierkegaard's *Purity of Heart is to Will One Thing* (1847/1966). Here Kierkegaard speaks straightforwardly, if severely, about the self-deceptions that can so easily seduce one into double-mindedness or trying to have the world and God both. Those who would like to see what a penetrating Christian psychology might look like can find no clearer historical example than Kierkegaard.

FOUNDING OF PSYCHOLOGY AS A DISCIPLINE

The psychophysics that Gustav Fechner developed, following his insight in 1850 about how changes in sensations might be related to changes in stimulus intensity, were arguably driven by a religious motive to defend consciousness (cf. Vande Kemp, 2002). Although he did not solve the mind–body problem as he hoped, he gave psychology a reliable empirical base decades before Wilhelm Wundt. In the United States as well, the first fruits of an experimental approach were studies in psychophysics carried out by Charles S. Peirce (1839–1914). Peirce was part of the Metaphysical Club of young Harvard graduates including Oliver Wendell Holmes and William James. Their conclusions about philosophy in the age of Darwin led to sea changes in American philosophy and greatly affected the form that the discipline of psychology was to assume in the United States. Peirce's pragmatic philosophy was that truth pertains to the "scientific method of settling opinions" (cf. Maxwell & Delaney, 2004, p. 20). Thus, true beliefs are beliefs that work, in the sense of producing habits of action that reflect reality (Leahey, 2000, p. 340). The popularizing of this pragmatic philosophy fell not to Peirce but to the gifted writer who was to become "America's psychologist," William James.

William James (1842–1910)

Widely read and traveled, James turned to psychology for a time after joining the Harvard faculty in physiology. After abandoning early ambitions as a painter, James received training as a physician, like several other founding psychologists of the era. Although he found the pursuit of philosophy more pleasant than laboratory work, his dabbling in psychology was sufficient to have him regarded by many as the greatest American psychologist. Despite being attracted to the working hypothesis that psychology should be approached as a physical science, "James's loyalty to the hypothesis sustains first embarrassment and then abandonment" (Robinson, 1981, p. 373). As his reclusive friend Peirce wrote, "The materialistic doctrine seems to me quite as repugnant to scientific logic as to common sense; since it requires us to suppose that a certain kind of mechanism will feel, which would be a hypothesis absolutely irreducible to reason" (quoted in Robinson, 1981, p. 374). Never one to think, as Santayana said of James, that any important question was finally settled, James was less direct but kept raising the issue of whether the essence of human nature should not be regarded as spiritual rather than material. For example, in his landmark text *The Principles of Psychology*, James argued that the "spiritual me" is the basis of the self, commenting on its nature as follows:

> The very core and nucleus of our self, as we know it, the very sanctuary of our life, is the sense of activity which certain inner states possess. This sense of activity is often held to be a direct revelation of the living substance of our Soul. Whether this be so or not is an ulterior question. (1890, p. 181)

In terms of his own life and view of himself, James carried with him throughout his professional life the insight that pulled him out of the depression and intellectual crisis he became mired in after contemplating the implications of materialistic physiology and philosophy. As he wrote in his diary, "Yesterday was a crisis in my life . . . I . . . see no reason why . . . free will . . . need be . . . an illusion. At any rate, I will assume for the present—until next year—that it is no illusion. My first act of free will shall be to believe in free will." James eventually concluded not only that his experiment of believing in free will worked for him but also that it was absolutely essential to the idea of moral responsibility (James, 1884/1956). Furthermore, this suggested that the narrow objectivism of science was shallow and inadequate for many aspects of persons (1902/1985, Lecture XX).

The descriptive approach taken by James in his classic *Varieties of Religious Experience* illustrated how one might incorporate personal testimonies and case studies as a means of documenting the powerful role played by religion in individuals' lives. Despite his "inability to accept either popular Christianity or scholastic theism" (p. 521), in the conclusion of *Varieties* when he states his own "overbeliefs," James is willing to affirm the reality of a mystical or supernatural realm, for example, "I will call this higher part of the universe by the name of God. We and God have business with each other; and in opening ourselves to his influence our deepest destiny is fulfilled . . . God is real since he produces real effects" (pp. 516–517). In his affirmation that "in the faith-state and in the prayer-state . . . higher energies filter in" (p. 519), James takes a position similar to that held by psychologist Daniel Robinson and Nobel Laureate John Eccles when they describe their dualistic theory of "the liaison brain" (Eccles & Robinson, 1984). James cites as examples accounts of prophecy or supernatural guidance. He also presents arguments against medical materialism (the dogma that identification of the psychophysiological correlates of a religious phenomenon serves to invalidate it) and bemoans the bias in science against recognizing religion: "and this antipathy to religion finds an echo within the very science of religion itself" (p. 490). One seems to hear just such an echo in the impact on the science of religion made by the founder of the APA, G. Stanley Hall.

G. Stanley Hall (1844–1924)

After a brief stint at Union Theological Seminary, it became apparent that Hall was not cut out for a pastoral role, nor was he sufficiently orthodox in his beliefs to enter the clergy. Instead he went to Harvard to study under James, where he became the first person in the United States to obtain a doctorate in psychology in 1878. During multiple trips to Europe, Hall became enamored with the Germans' higher criticism, Helmholtz's materialism, and, perhaps most important, with Haeckel's soon discredited ideas regarding ontogeny recapitulating phylogeny (Hall, 1923b; Vande Kemp, 1992). Hall's genetic psychology was based on the fundamental premise that individual psychic development repeats the entire history of the race. This premise informed his approach both to developmental psychology and to religious psychology, with the latter being a preoccupation throughout his career. While president at Clark University, Hall offered a course on religious psychology or the psychology of Jesus annually for nearly 20 years. More than a third of the 150 theses and dissertations that Hall chaired at Clark University were on religious psychology, with many being published in the *Journal of Religious Psychology*, which he founded (Vande Kemp, 1992). Hall saw the reinterpretation of Jesus as "one of the great tasks" of psychology, but his application of his genetic model to Jesus (Hall, 1923a) was not well received, being critiqued not only on theological grounds but also for its "sloppy and superficial scholarship" more generally (Vande Kemp, 1992, p. 294). Somewhat like Freud, Hall developed a sexual theory of conversion and became "obsessed with digging out the pathological implications of Christianity," being determined to wage "eternal warfare upon orthodoxies" (Vande Kemp, 1992, p. 295). Hall (1923b) thought "the Positivists had pretty much made out their case" and that the "theological stage" of societies characterized by belief in a personal deity was a primitive stage that should be abandoned (p. 222). It is not surprising that the Clark School of Religious Psychology that he spawned, out of which came some of the most prominent psychologists of religion of the 20th century (e.g., James Leuba and Edwin Starbuck), frequently viewed faith as a pathological object to be deconstructed (Hood, Spilka, Hunsberger, & Gorsuch, 1996, pp. 18, 215, 229, 411; Meadow & Kahoe, 1984, p. 11; Paloutzian, 1996, p. 39ff.; Wulff, 1996, p. 48).

DEMISE AND RETURN OF RELIGION IN PSYCHOLOGY

The three decades after the founding of the APA in Hall's office in 1892 were characterized by rapid growth of the field and an increasing preoccupation with being scientific. Although short-lived within philosophy of science per se, the philosophy of logical positivism, which asserted that the only meaningful statements were those that could be empirically verified, was embraced uncritically by American psychology (Maxwell & Delaney, 2004, p. 10ff.). A deterministic positivism seemed the perfect rebuttal to those who claimed psychology was incapable of becoming a science because of its subjective subject matter and fit well with Watson's naïve behaviorism. Given that "psychologists were stationed at the periphery of science, and therefore they were the most threatened by challenges to the boundary" (Coon, 1992, p. 150), spirituality and religion were rejected along with introspective methods and cognition generally in favor of animal learning and conditioning studies. By 1920, Watsonian behaviorism was dominant, and the long era of attempts to build a positivistic psychology had begun.

Despite notable exceptions such as Jung and Allport, religion was marginalized in mainstream academic psychology for much of the 20th century. Concerted efforts in opposition to this were maintained only in certain sectarian contexts, particularly in Roman Catholic institutions up through midcentury (Misiak & Staudt, 1954). Strong condemnations of the pansexualism of Freudian theory as well as concern that psychoanalytic treatments would subvert religious belief and practice came from Bishop Fulton Sheen in New York and Pope Pius XII in Rome. Concerns about liberalism and "modernism," and how both psychiatry and psychology were connected to these morally problematic positions, fueled the controversy. The integration of psychology into Catholic thought and practice has nonetheless been fairly extensive for several reasons. First, the academic philosophical tradition, especially that of Thomas Aquinas, provided a gateway for Catholic philosophers and theologians to examine the emerging science and practice of psychology with a critical but rather accepting view. Second, the academically oriented mission of some religious orders, particularly the Jesuits, encouraged clergy and others to obtain degrees in fields other than theology. These leaders then began to develop psychology programs in Catholic universities in which they could educate and examine current knowledge in the context of the extensive academic traditions of these institutions. Third, the fact that clergy and others in religious service as well as laypersons were active in the study and practice of psychiatry and psychology provided a significant force for integration and alliances between psychology and the views of the Catholic tradition (Gillespie, 2001; Vande Kemp, 1996).

Among the different initiatives growing out of the alliances between psychology and the Catholic tradition was Edward Pace's founding of one of the nation's first experimental psychology laboratories at the Catholic University of America in 1892. Strong departments of psychology were developed at St. Louis University, Loyola in Chicago, and Fordham in New York. A number of organizations attempted to represent both Catholicism and psychology, like the Catholic Psychiatric Association and the American Catholic Psychological Association, created in 1949 and then transformed by Father William Bier and Virginia Staudt Sexton into Division 36 of the APA (originally Psychologists Interested in Religious Issues, now titled Psychology of Religion). In addition to those just named, large numbers of psychologists and psychiatrists have labored in their writings and practice to create dialogue and an alliance between the psychological and the spiritual, and between psychotherapy and religious practice (Leo Bartmeier, Thomas Verner Moore, Annette Walters, Gregory Zilboorg, Charles Curran, Adrian Van Kaam, Henri Nouwen, and many others). Although historical tensions (cf. Roback, 1952) continue to exist and the perspective of scientific and clinical psychology clashes with some teaching and practice for Catholics as it does for evangelical Protestants (e.g., Vitz, 1977), there continues to be significant dialogue between psychology and the Catholic tradition.

The better known modern psychologists with interests in religion have come from Protestant or Jewish backgrounds. Their contributions are welcomed by most people of faith as an acknowledgment of the importance of religion, even though these psychologists have typically viewed their projects either as more of a rejection than as an outgrowth of orthodox belief or at least as an attempt to approach religion from the perspective of psychology rather than vice versa. Thus Carl Jung wrote that modern man realizes the Christian church has "failed to stand the baptism by fire—the test of reality" (1933, p. 200) in a volume whose preface says it is addressed to those "who have outgrown the Church as exemplified in Christianity" (1933, p. viii). On the one hand, his detailed analyses of Christian doctrines (e.g. the Trinity, incarnation, resurrection) as psychological symbols can be seen as suggesting that he views such doctrines as being a key to understanding the psychic life (cf. Fuller, 1994). On the other hand, even though Jung claimed to limit himself to analysis of the microcosm of the psychic world (1969, p. 278ff.), in fact some have argued that he purported to know that divine figures such as Christ do "*not* exist outside the psyche" (Fuller, 1994, p. 111).

Gordon Allport's (1950) classic book on the role of religion in the individual personality perhaps comes closer to achieving his goal, similar to Jung's, of adopting a neutral stance regarding the content of religious beliefs: "My approach is psychological, some would call it naturalistic. I make no assumptions and no denials regarding the claims of revealed religion. Writing as a scientist I am not entitled to do either" (p. xi). Such strict detachment was not typical of the humanistic psychologists like Carl Rogers, who may have attended Union Theological Seminary but who was explicit in the rejection of the Christian beliefs of his parents and who concluded he could not enter any field where he "would be required to believe in some specified religious doctrine" (1961, pp. 7–8). This certainly is not to say that being reared under some of these religious doctrines might not have prepared Rogers for embracing certain concepts like "unconditional positive regard," but only that he did not posit such ideas as flowing from an explicit religious perspective.

Perhaps the prominent 20th-century psychologist whose theoretical perspective seemed most open to the sacred was Jewish psychologist Abraham Maslow. In his early work, he saw his humanistic psychology as offering an alternative to the more narrow perspectives of scientific psychology that he described as being used in the service of a "desacralized, and desanctified *Weltanschauung*" (1966, p. 139). The now well-known alternative Maslow offered was a view of people as attempting to satisfy a hierarchy of needs. The self-actualization at the top of this hierarchy was characterized in part by mystic or peak experiences, described in ways similar to how some might characterize intense religious experiences. It was clear, however, that Maslow saw values as something to be derived from psychology rather than from religion (e.g., Maslow, 1959, p. 119ff.), that the God he could accept was an impersonal part of nature, not transcendent (Fuller, 1994, p. 178), and the transpersonal psychology he proposed toward the end of his life was explicitly offered as a religion-surrogate (cf. Hergenhahn, 2001, p. 523).

Despite the interest or background in religion on the part of a few, religion through most of the 20th century received scant attention within psychology; as Allport (1950) noted midcentury, "The subject of religion appears to have gone into hiding" (p. 1). For example, a recent systematic review of seven journals published by the APA between 1991 and 1994 revealed that less than 3% of quantitative studies included a religious or spiritual variable. In the few articles that did include a religious variable, more than 75% of the time the religious variable consisted of only a single question, and less than 30% of the time was any previously published religious research cited (Weaver et al., 1998). In part, this may be due to the underrepresentation of people of faith within the field of psychology. Whereas 95% of the general public affirm a belief in God, only 43% of APA members do. Furthermore, psychologists indicate a lower level of religious involvement than do other groups of mental health professionals such as psychiatrists, social workers, or marriage and family therapists (Weaver et al., 1998).

In recent decades, medicine has led the way in the recognition of religion as a positive force (e.g., Koenig, McCullough, & Larson, 2001). Although some publications had been emerging from doctoral programs in psychology in Protestant institutions such as Wheaton (e.g., Jones & Butman,

1991), Fuller Theological Seminary (e.g., Malony, 1988), or Rosemead (cf. its *Journal of Psychology and Theology*), it is only in the last 10 years that mainstream psychology has begun to manifest the kind of open, constructive relationship with religion called for in Jones's (1994) seminal article. Evidence of this includes APA's publication of volumes such as those edited by Shafranske (1996) and Miller (1999). It is hoped that the current volume will help foster this dialogue by offering Judeo-Christian perspectives on contemporary psychology.

CONCLUSION

We have seen from Augustine up through Upham and Kierkegaard several agreed-on components of a psychology appropriate for beings bearing the *imago Dei*. The role of the will in choosing between desires and obligations and as necessary for the authentic selfhood God intended is clear and is developed further in Part II of this book. The existence of transcendent values with which we can be in harmony or discord is another component of Judeo-Christian perspective on the person, and is addressed in Part III. The traps of the "unlawful pleasures" that Augustine struggled with are part of the need for persons to change and develop spiritually, which are themes addressed in Part IV.

Given the thousands of published sources at the interface between psychology and theology (cf. Vande Kemp, 1984), this chapter could only highlight a few of the most important contributions. In closing, we mention some valuable sources providing alternative perspectives on this history. Forty years ago, Paul Tillich, Karl Menninger, Karen Horney, and Carl Rogers contributed to a volume similar to the current one (Doniger, 1962). Among the most helpful recent histories of this relationship are chapters that are written from an evangelical Christian perspective (Johnson & Jones, 2000); cite relationships to more general cultural trends (Kurtz, 1999); review the development of relevant professional societies, journals, and textbooks (Vande Kemp, 1996); or focus on the history of psychiatry (Thielman, 1998). Some of the most noteworthy book-length treatments are a philosopher's call for a development of a distinctively Christian psychology (Evans, 1996), a social psychologist's evaluation of the status of the person in psychology (Van Leeuwen, 1985), an analysis of the evolving relationship between Roman Catholicism and psychology (Gillespie, 2001), and a compendium of examples of Christian psychology (Roberts & Talbot, 1997). Similar prominent examples from outside the United States include a volume by a former president of the International Neurospsychological Symposium (Jeeves, 1997), one coauthored by a former president of the British Psychological Society (Watts & Williams, 1988), and one summarizing an international symposium held in the Netherlands (Verhagen & Glas, 1996).

REFERENCES

Allport, G. W. (1950). *The individual and his religion*. London: Macmillan.

Anderson, W. E. (1980). Editor's introduction. In W. E. Anderson (Ed.), *Jonathan Edwards: Scientific and philosophical writings* (pp. 1–143). New Haven, CT: Yale University Press.

Augustine. (1952). *Confessions*. In R. M. Hutchins & M. J. Adler (Eds.), *Great books of the Western world: Vol. 18. Augustine* (pp. 1–125). Chicago: Encyclopaedia Britannica. (Original work written 397–400)

Augustine. (1952). *City of God*. In R. M. Hutchins & M. J. Adler (Eds.), *Great books of the Western world: Vol. 18. Augustine* (pp. 127–618). Chicago: Encyclopaedia Britannica. (Original work written 413–427)

Aquinas, T. (1952). *Summa theologica*. In R. M. Hutchins & M. J. Adler (Eds.), *Great books of the Western world: Vols. 19–20. Thomas Aquinas*. Chicago: Encyclopaedia Britannica. (Original work written 1273)

Aristotle. (1952). *Physics*. In R. M. Hutchins & M. J. Adler (Eds.), *Great books of the Western world: Vol. 8. Aristotle* (pp. 257–355). Chicago: Encyclopaedia Britannica. (Original work written ca. 440 B.C.)

Bacon, F. (1952). *Advancement of learning*. In R. M. Hutchins & M. J. Adler (Eds.), *Great books of the Western world: Vol. 30. Francis Bacon* (pp. 1–101). Chicago: Encyclopaedia Britannica. (Original work published 1605)

Bakan, D. (1965). Some thoughts on reading Augustine's *Confessions*. *Journal for the Scientific Study of Religion, 5*, 149–152.

Boring, E. G. (1950). *A history of experimental psychology* (2nd ed.). New York: Appleton-Century-Crofts.

Brennan, R. E. (1945). *History of psychology from the standpoint of a Thomist*. New York: Macmillan.

Brown, C. R. (1955). Jonathan Edwards. *Encyclopaedia Britannica* (Vol. 8, pp. 18–20). Chicago: Encyclopaedia Britannica.

Cahill, T. (1998). *The gifts of the Jews: How a tribe of desert nomads changed the way everyone thinks and feels*. New York: Nan A. Talese/Anchor Books.

Cairns, E. E. (1954). *Christianity through the centuries: A history of the Christian church*. Grand Rapids, MI: Zondervan.

Campbell, D. T. (1975). On the conflicts between biological and social evolution and between psychology and moral tradition. *American Psychologist, 30*, 1103–1126.

Chesterton, G. K. (1933). *St. Thomas Aquinas*. New York: Sheed & Ward.

Clark, W. H. (1965). Depth and rationality in Augustine's *Confessions*. *Journal for the Scientific Study of Religion, 5*, 144–148.

Coon, D. J. (1992). Testing the limits of sense and science: American experimental psychologists combat spiritualism, 1880–1920. *American Psychologist, 47*, 143–151.

Descartes, R. (1952). *Meditations on first philosophy*. In R. M. Hutchins & M. J. Adler (Eds.), *Great books of the Western world: Vol. 31. Descartes/Spinoza* (pp. 69–103). Chicago: Encyclopaedia Britannica. (Original work published 1641)

Doniger, S. (Ed.). (1962). *The nature of man in theological and psychological perspective*. New York: Harper & Brothers.

Eccles, J., & Robinson, D. (1984). *The wonder of being human: Our brain and our mind*. New York: Macmillan.

Edwards, J. (1959). *A treatise concerning religious affections*. In J. E. Smith (Ed.), *Works of Jonathan Edwards* (Vol. 2, pp. 91–461). New Haven, CT: Yale University Press. (Original work published 1746)

Edwards, J. (1969). *Freedom of the will*. New York: Bobbs-Merrill. (Original work published 1754)

Edwards, J. (1980). The mind. In W. E. Anderson (Ed.), *Jonathan Edwards: Scientific and philosophical writings* (pp. 311–398). New Haven, CT: Yale University Press. (Original work published 1829)

Evans, C. S. (1990). *Søren Kierkegaard's Christian psychology*. Vancouver, Canada: Regent College.

Evans, C. S. (1996). *Wisdom and humanness in psychology: Prospects for a Christian approach*. Vancouver, Canada: Regent College.

Fay, J. W. (1939). *American psychology before William James*. New Brunswick, NJ: Rutgers University Press.

Fuller, A. R. (1994). *Psychology and religion: Eight points of view* (3rd ed.). London: Rowman & Littlefield.

Gillespie, C. K. (2001). *Psychology and American Catholicism: From confession to therapy?* New York: Crossroads.

Hall, G. S. (1923a). *Jesus, the Christ, in the light of psychology*. London: Allen & Unwin.

Hall, G. S. (1923b). *Life and confessions of a psychologist*. New York: Appleton.

Hergenhahn, B. R. (2001). *An introduction to the history of psychology*. Belmont, CA: Wadsworth/Thomson Learning.

Hood, R. W., Jr., Spilka, B., Hunsberger, B., & Gorsuch, R. (1996). *The psychology of religion: An empirical approach* (2nd ed.). New York: Guilford Press.

James, W. (1956). *The will to believe and other essays in popular philosophy and human immortality*. New York: Dover. (Original work published 1884)

James, W. (1890). *The principles of psychology*. New York: Henry Holt.

James, W. (1985). *The varieties of religious experience*. Cambridge, MA: Harvard University Press. (Original work published 1902)

Jeeves, M. A. (1997). *Human nature at the millennium: Reflections on the integration of psychology and Christianity*. Grand Rapids, MI: Baker.

Johnson, E. L. (1998). Some contributions of Augustine to a Christian psychology. *Journal of Psychology and Christianity, 17*, 293–305.

Johnson, E. L., & Jones, S. L. (2000). A history of Christians in psychology. In E. L. Johnson & S. L. Jones (Eds.), *Psychology and Christianity: Four views* (pp. 11–53). Downers Grove, IL: InterVarsity Press.

Jones, S. L. (1994). A constructive relationship for religion with the science and profession of psychology. *American Psychologist, 49,* 184–199.

Jones, S. L., & Butman, R. (1991). *Modern psychotherapies: A comprehensive Christian appraisal.* Downers Grove, IL: InterVarsity.

Jung, C. G. (1933). *Modern man in search of a soul.* New York: Harcout, Brace & World.

Jung, C. G. (1969). *The structure and dynamics of the psyche.* Princeton, NJ: Princeton University Press.

Kaufman, A. S., & Frankena, W. K. (Eds.). (1969). *Jonathan Edwards: Freedom of the will.* New York: Bobbs-Merrill.

Kierkegaard, S. (1966). *Purity of heart is to will one thing.* London: Collins. (Original work published 1847)

Kierkegaard, S. (1962). *The point of view for my work as an author.* New York: Harper & Row. (Original work published 1859)

Koenig, H. G., McCullough, M. E., & Larson, D. B. (2001). *Handbook of religion and health.* Oxford, England: Oxford University Press.

Kurtz, E. (1999). The historical context. In W. R. Miller (Ed.), *Integrating spirituality into treatment: Resources for practitioners* (pp. 19–46). Washington, DC: American Psychological Association.

Leahey, T. H. (2000). *A history of psychology: Main currents in psychological thought.* Upper Saddle River, NJ: Prentice Hall.

Locke, J. (1952). An essay concerning human understanding. In R. M. Hutchins & M. J. Adler (Eds.), *Great books of the Western world* (Vol. 35, pp. 83–295). Chicago: Encyclopaedia Britannica. (Original work published 1690)

Malony, H. N. (1988). The clinical assessment of optimal religious functioning. *Review of Religious Research, 30,* 3–17.

Marsden, G. M. (1994). *The soul of the American university.* New York: Oxford University Press.

Marsden, G. M. (2003). *Jonathan Edwards: A life.* New Haven, CT: Yale University Press.

Maslow, A. H. (1966). *The psychology of science: A reconnaissance.* South Bend, IN: Gateway Editions.

Maslow, A. H. (Ed.). (1959). *New knowledge in human values.* Chicago: Henry Regnery.

Maxwell, S. E., & Delaney, H. D. (2004). *Designing experiments and analyzing data: A model comparison perspective* (2nd ed.). Mahwah, NJ: Erlbaum.

Meadow, M. J., & Kahoe, R. D. (1984). *Psychology of religion: Religion in individual lives.* New York: Harper & Row.

Miller, W. R. (Ed.). (1999). *Integrating spirituality into treatment: Resources for practitioners.* Washington, DC: American Psychological Association.

Misiak, H., & Staudt, V. M. (1954). *Catholics in psychology: A historical survey.* New York: McGraw-Hill.

Newton, I. (1952). Mathematical principles of natural philosophy. In. R. M. Hutchins & M. J. Adler (Eds.), *Great books of the Western world* (Vol. 34, pp. 1–372). Chicago: Encyclopaedia Britannica. (Original work published 1687)

Newton, I. (1952). Optics. In. R. M. Hutchins & M. J. Adler (Eds.), *Great books of the Western world* (Vol. 34, pp. 373–544). Chicago: Encyclopaedia Britannica. (Original work published 1706)

Paloutzian, R. F. (1996). *Invitation to the psychology of religion* (2nd ed.). Boston: Allyn & Bacon.

Piper, J. (2000). *The legacy of sovereign joy*. Wheaton, IL: Crossway.

Roback, A. A. (1952). *History of American psychology*. New York: Library.

Roberts, R. C., & Talbot, M. R. (Eds.). (1997). *Limning the psyche: Explorations in Christian psychology*. Grand Rapids, MI: Eerdmans.

Robinson, D. N. (1981). *An intellectual history of psychology*. New York: Macmillan.

Rogers, C. R. (1961). *On becoming a person*. Boston: Houghton Mifflin.

Salter, D. L. (1986). *Spirit and intellect: Thomas Upham's holiness theology*. Metuchen, NJ: Scarecrow Press.

Schimmel, S. (1997). *The seven deadly sins: Jewish, Christian and classical reflections on human psychology*. New York: Oxford University Press.

Schimmel, S. (2000). Vices, virtues and sources of human strength in historical perspective. *Journal of Social and Clinical Psychology, 19,* 137–150.

Shafranske, E. P. (Ed.). (1996). *Religion and the clinical practice of psychology*. Washington, DC: American Psychological Association.

Smith, J. E. (Ed.). (1959). *Works of Jonathan Edwards* (Vol. 2). New Haven, CT: Yale University Press.

Spilka, B. (1987). Religion and science in early American psychology. *Journal of Psychology and Theology, 15,* 3–9.

Thielman, S. B. (1998). Reflections on the role of religion in the history of psychiatry. In H. G. Koenig (Ed.), *Handbook of religion and mental health* (pp. 3–20). San Diego, CA: Academic Press.

Vande Kemp, H. (with Malony, H. N.). (1984). *Psychology and theology in Western thought, 1672–1965: A historical and annotated bibliography*. Millwood, NY: Kraus International.

Vande Kemp, H. (1992). G. Stanley Hall and the Clark school of religious psychology. *American Psychologist, 47,* 290–298.

Vande Kemp, H. (1996). Historical perspective: Religion and clinical psychology in America. In E. P. Shafranske (Ed.), *Religion and the clinical practice of psychology* (pp. 71–112). Washington, DC: American Psychological Association.

Vande Kemp, H. (2002). *Great psychologists as "unknown" psychologists of religion*. Unpublished manuscript, Fuller Theological Seminary Graduate School of Psychology, Padadena, CA.

Van Leeuwen, M. S. (1985). *The person in psychology: A contemporary Christian appraisal*. Grand Rapids, MI: Eerdmans.

Verhagen, P. J., & Glas, G. (1996). *Psyche and faith—Beyond professionalism: Proceedings of the first international symposium of the Christian Association of Psychiatrists, Psychologists and Psychotherapists in the Netherlands*. Zoetermeer, The Netherlands: Uitgeverij Boekencentrum.

Vitz, P. C. (1977). *Psychology as religion: The cult of self-worship*. Grand Rapids, MI: Eerdmans.

Watson, R. I. (1963). *The great psychologists from Aristotle to Freud*. Philadelphia: Lippincott.

Watts, F., & Williams, M. (1988). *The psychology of religious knowing*. New York: Cambridge University Press.

Weaver, A. J., Kline, A. E., Samford, J. A., Lucas, L. A., Larson, D. B., & Gorsuch, R. L. (1998). Is religion taboo in psychology? A systematic analysis of research on religion in seven major American Psychological Association journals: 1991–1994. *Journal of Psychology and Christianity, 17, 220–232.*

Woollcott, P., Jr. (1966). Some considerations of creativity and religious experience in St. Augustine of Hippo. *Journal for the Scientific Study of Religion, 5, 273–283.*

Wulff, D. M. (1996). The psychology of religion: An overview. In E. P. Shafranske (Ed.), *Religion and the clinical practice of psychology* (pp. 43–70). Washington, DC: American Psychological Association.

Wulff, D. M. (2001). *Psychology of religion: Classic and contemporary views*. New York: Wiley.

II

THE NATURE OF THE
HUMAN PERSON

3

SELF AND VOLITION

ROY F. BAUMEISTER

One of the most basic and central beliefs in the Judeo-Christian view of human nature is that people are free to make important choices. The opening pages of the Bible tell of the fateful choice of Adam and Eve to eat from the tree of knowledge of good and evil, initiating the moral decisions that all humans must face. The Christian concept of sin assumes that people know right from wrong and are able to choose either one. In many (although not all) versions of Christian theology, salvation and redemption depend at least in part on what choices the individual makes. This assumption of freedom is hardly limited to Christian theology; modern laws likewise assume that people are free to make choices, evaluate alleged crimes on the basis of how freely the person chose to perform the illegal act, and assign the harshest punishments to those who had ample opportunity to do what is right but chose to act badly.

Modern psychology has also been fascinated with issues of choice and volition, although many research psychologists are squeamish about the notion of free will, presumably because it flies in the face of the deterministic positivism that many psychologists still embrace as crucial to a scientific approach to understanding. To be sure, there are also some research psychologists as well as a large number of clinical and counseling psychologists who believe that humans can be free to act as they choose. Despite this squeamishness, choice and control have been studied extensively. Stress is vastly reduced when people have the ability to exert some control over events (e.g., Glass, Singer, & Friedman, 1969). People seek to maintain their freedom of action and respond assertively, sometimes even aggressively, when their freedoms are taken away or threatened (Brehm, 1966). People accept responsibility for their own behavior and seek to maintain consistent identities much more extensively when they have choice than when they do not. Repeated experiences of loss of control can produce pathological, destructive reactions, such as learned helplessness (Seligman, 1975). Concepts of addiction have some reduced control and reduced volition at their core, which in turn implies that psychologists recognize differing degrees of volitional control over one's behavior (Miller & Brown, 1991). To put that another way: The concept of addiction implies a loss of control, and so the control had to be there in the first place to be lost.

This chapter considers volition in the context of what psychology has recently learned about the self and how that can be related to a Judeo-Christian perspective. It begins by examining the role of volition in the context of the nature of the self overall. Questions of freedom and consciousness are then addressed, because these are central to the problem of volition. Self-regulation is discussed as a crucial form of volition, and recent findings are presented to show how self-regulation operates. The possibility of strengthening self-regulation, thereby increasing the self's freedom of volition, is considered. These findings permit the question of freedom to be considered again. The chapter closes with a brief consideration of some of the main implications.

WHAT IS THE SELF?

In attempting to review and integrate the vast amount of research done by psychologists on the self, Baumeister (1998) concluded that several basic features of selfhood are universal and form the basis for the self. The self starts with the body, but it soon develops far beyond that. Three essential phenomena define and delineate the self.

The first of these is reflexive consciousness. Human beings are able to be aware of their environment, but they are also able to turn this awareness around to focus on its source. They thus become self-aware, and they can develop this awareness of self into a body of knowledge about their individual selves (the self-concept). Without self-knowledge and self-awareness, the very notion of self would be incomprehensible. In the Judeo-Christian tradition, reflexive consciousness was one of the defining traits of humanity. When Adam and Eve disobeyed God and ate from the Tree of Knowledge, which would result in their expulsion from paradise, they realized their nakedness and shame and attempted to hide.

The second is interpersonal being. Human beings have a powerful and fundamental "need to belong," in the sense that they are deeply motivated to form and maintain at least a minimum number of close interpersonal relationships (Baumeister & Leary, 1995). The self is an important tool for accomplishing this. People will fashion and alter the self so as to enhance their appeal to others and increase their chances for social acceptance. Like other religions, Judaism and Christianity place heavy emphasis on family and community.

The third phenomenal aspect of self is the executive function. This is clearly the one that is most relevant to this chapter's theme of volition because it encompasses choice, control, and initiative, as well as self-regulation. Christian thinking has evolved over the centuries to place increasing emphasis on individual freedom and choice: The most momentous choices made while acting as a free agent during one's life on earth are those that impact one's eternal fate.

Taken together, these three dimensions provide a reasonably comprehensive and usable blueprint for understanding the self. For present purposes, the key point is that volition is relevant to the least well-understood aspect of the self, namely, the executive function. The processes by which the self makes choices and decisions, initiates and controls action, and regulates its own responses constitute a vital key to understanding human selfhood overall.

PSYCHOLOGY AND FREEDOM

Most thinkers in the Judeo-Christian tradition share the assumption of free will, and that assumption runs contrary to the beliefs in determinism that are espoused by many research psychologists. Determinism is the belief that all events (including all human actions) are fully caused by prior events. Nothing else was possible other than what actually happens—in other words, the possible and the actual are identical in the long run. With full knowledge of circumstances and correct psychological principles, psychologists could predict all human behavior with 100% accuracy, or at least that is what strict determinists believe.

In my view, the belief in determinism requires a leap of faith that is at least as large as what is necessary to support belief in God. The faith in determinism is contrary to everyday experience, insofar as people have the experience of making choices in which more than one outcome is genuinely possible. (Determinists must believe that humans are mistaken when they think that more than one option is possible for them to choose.) The faith in determinism is also contrary to psychological data, which have almost invariably fallen far short of 100% accuracy in predicting human behavior and which almost unanimously show causality as a matter of changing the odds that some behavior will occur. In other words, psychological data depict causality as probabilistic, not deterministic. Last, the doctrine of determinism is almost by definition unproven and unprovable.

Thus, determinism is hardly a proven fact, but rather an article of faith. Psychologists who find that some individual's behavior fails to conform to their predictions despite circumstances that correspond well to established causal principles end up having to assert that the strict antecedent causes must be there although they do not know what they are. In this, the exercise of faith is hardly distinguishable from that of a religious person who accepts some terrible, seemingly inexplicable misfortune by saying that God must have his reasons for allowing this to happen, even if the individual cannot begin to guess what those might be.

Given the present state of knowledge, it seems most precise and appropriate to postulate a limited degree of human freedom (see also Bandura, 1989; Miller & Brown, 1991). Human behavior is undeniably affected by antecedent and material causes, but people may also be correct in believing that they have some degree of freedom to make choices. This view avoids the extremes of determinism, which insist that free choice is always an illusion. It also avoids the extremes of belief in freedom, such as Sartre's (1943/1956) famous assertion that people are "condemned to be free."

FREEDOM AND CONSCIOUSNESS

A careful consideration of Sartre's (1943/1956) overstated case for human freedom can reveal how freedom and antecedent causality can coexist. Sartre's arguments repeatedly boil down to saying that a person could always have done something differently. In one passage, he describes a hiker who sits down from exhaustion and says, "I can't take another step." Sartre insists, quite plausibly, that the hiker could probably have taken another five steps, just as he might have quit five steps earlier (e.g., if an appealing place to sit had appeared right there). Sartre's comment is that the decision to stop at that particular spot reflects free choice because the person could have done differently, although the person was undoubtedly quite tired.

Implicit in Sartre's arguments, however, is that the person could have made a conscious decision to respond differently. Consciousness thus emerges as vital to freedom of action. Without conscious intervention, the body grew tired at a certain rate and stopped walking at a certain point.

My view is that the function of consciousness is to override the causal processes that would otherwise determine behavior. Sartre's hiker does expend his energy and grow tired, and his body finds a place to rest. He could consciously override this hankering to rest and force himself to walk a bit farther. Unless he does that, however, his stopping place could be predicted with potentially very high accuracy. If his conscious mind overrides that process, however, then it becomes much harder to predict where he will stop.

The view of consciousness as an override function that frees the individual from the rule of inner, causal processes does not even require one to accept a full or radical version of free will. Consciousness can accomplish a kind of limited freedom from particular causes, thereby making behavior somewhat less predictable, even if the diehard determinist insists that some other hidden causes must be lurking to determine the eventual outcome.

To be sure, this view differs from the usual psychological approach to consciousness, which generally emphasizes its role in perception. But control of behavior is arguably an important function of consciousness. It would, after all, be useful and adaptive to be able to override and alter one's responses, and consciousness might well have provided this.

The simplest form of behavior mechanism would be automatic reflexes that are innately prepared. These would involve highly specific responses to well-defined stimuli or events. Undoubtedly human evolutionary history included some of these primitive response patterns, and some human responses such as hunger or sexual arousal can at least sometimes follow these rules. Basic human impulses can certainly set off behaviors.

A somewhat more complex mechanism for behavior control would involve emotion. Many emotions contain clear tendencies to perform certain kinds of action (e.g., Frijda, 1986), and it is likely that the emotion system evolved to provide this kind of action control.

Motivated impulses and emotions tend to be based in the evolutionarily oldest parts of the brain, far toward the back. In contrast, the self's functions of conscious control appear to be based in the newer (frontal and prefrontal) parts of the brain. This raises the possibility that the self emerged later in human evolution, as a new way of controlling behavior. In an important sense, the self replaced emotion and impulse as the direct controller of behavior. But emotion and impulse can probably still control behavior if the self does not intervene.

I do not want to give the impression that I think emotion has become obsolete in human psychology. This is actually a fairly common view, although not stated quite so baldly. In novels and movies—most famously Stanley Kubrick's film *2001: A Space Odyssey,* and in *Star Trek*'s characters of Mr. Spock and Data, emotion is presented as an impediment to reasoning, and often more advanced creatures (robots or, in the case of Mr. Spock, characters from another planet where there is no emotion) are presented as able to reason and calculate better than human beings precisely because their thought processes are not perturbed by emotional silliness. In contrast, Damasio (1994) has presented fairly convincing studies of brain-damaged individuals who lack emotional responses, and these people are typically quite impaired in their ability to function in a community. Emotion thus is still helpful in human functioning, but perhaps its method of operation has changed. Instead of directly causing behavior, as it originally may have evolved to do, emotion now operates by pushing and pulling the mental apparatus around, so that people notice what is important and adjust their behavior so as to function more effectively. More precisely, emotion operates by directing attention to important issues and problems, so that the thinking apparatus can be used to solve problems and bring about desired outcomes.

Thus, consciousness functions to allow the self to override some responses. Natural responses and learned ones follow established principles of behavior to produce predictable outcomes—unless a conscious act enables the self to override them and prevent those responses. Such moments enable people to form the concept of free will, because they see that they are not behaving in a robotlike, prescribed, preset fashion.

Regardless of whether one accepts the notion of totally free will, conscious behavior can be recognized as less rigidly determined and less predictable than other (nonconscious) behavior. The role of insight in psychotherapy suggests that making something conscious can free the person from maladaptive, neurotic styles of response. In laboratory studies, when people become conscious of some pattern of behavior or some aspect of their own responses, their behavior becomes less predictable.

VOLITION AND SELF-REGULATION

The Judeo-Christian view of human nature emphasizes that people are able to know the difference between right and wrong and are able to choose to act one way or the other. God has so ordered the universe that people who act properly (including both morally virtuous action and proper worship) can anticipate an eternal reward in heaven, whereas those who choose to act otherwise are destined for eternal punishment. Such an ordering would make no sense if people's actions were caused entirely by events outside their control. In practice, Christian writings and speakers have exhorted people to behave in the ways that are good, which again presumes that people can choose. Judeo-Christian thought also emphasizes that people have desires and impulses that are sinful and that ought therefore to be overcome. One purpose of human freedom is therefore to ensure that sinful impulses do not inevitably result in sinful actions.

How does the self manage to override and alter its responses? Past writings have suggested several possible answers (for review, see Baumeister, Heatherton, & Tice, 1994). One is based on the traditional concept of "willpower." According to this view, people have a certain quantity of strength or energy that can be used to counter strong desires and impulses.

Another possible theory would regard volition and self-regulation as essentially cognitive processes. In this view, the self contains knowledge about itself and the world, and so when a certain response of the self is not suited to the current situation, the self can recognize this, compute the desired response, and simply initiate the substitution. According to this view, self-regulation operates much like a computer software program.

The third possibility is that self-regulation is a kind of skill. Developmental psychologists are fond of discussing how children acquire skills as they grow up, and the ability to alter one's responses would be such a skill.

My colleagues and I spent several years trying to test these theories against each other. One sphere in which they make contrary predictions encompasses what happens when people must perform two consecutive (but otherwise unrelated) acts of self-regulation. Is the second act affected by the fact that the person just performed the first, and if so, how?

The willpower theory says that self-regulation depends on expending some kind of energy resource, and if some of that resource was already expended in the first act of self-regulation, there would be less left over for the second act; so self-control would be impaired on the second task. In contrast, the cognitive theory regards self-regulation as depending on a kind of master program, and if the first act of self-regulation has loaded the program into active functioning, the second act would be facilitated. In an important sense, the person would already be in a self-controlling mode, and so it should be easier to exert further self-control. Cognitive patterns of this sort have been well established in the research literature on priming (Bargh, Bond, Lombardi, & Tota, 1986; Higgins & King, 1981; Srull & Wyer, 1979, 1980). The third and final theory would predict no change in the second self-control performance as a result of the first, because skill does not change rapidly. Skill level is essentially the same from one trial to the next (although over the long run, accumulated practice does increase skill).

A long series of experiments was conducted to see how people would fare at self-control depending on whether they had or had not already just performed a different act of self-control. Over and over, we found support for the willpower theory rather than the cognitive or skill theory. Thus, people who initially tried to control their emotions while watching an upsetting film showed decrements in physical stamina, compared with people who had watched the same upsetting film without trying to control their emotions (Muraven, Tice, & Baumeister, 1998). The implication is that trying to regulate their emotions used up some resource that was no longer available to help them continue the physical exertion (squeezing a handgrip exerciser) longer. Likewise, people who had to try to suppress a certain thought (of a white bear) subsequently gave up faster on an unsolvable anagram task (Muraven et al., 1998), compared with people who did not try to suppress a thought.

Perhaps the most vivid demonstration from this series of studies involved resisting temptation (Baumeister, Bratslavsky, Muraven, & Tice, 1998). Hungry students were brought individually into a lab room that was filled with the delicious aroma of freshly baked chocolate chip cookies and were seated at a table that contained a plate of these cookies and chocolate candies. Also on the table was a bowl of radishes. In the crucial condition, the experimenter told the student, "You've been assigned to the radish condition" and went on to explain that the task would be to eat as many radishes as possible, and only radishes, for the next five minutes. They were left alone to maximize the temptation to eat some of the chocolates or cookies. In contrast, one control group was told to eat the chocolates and cookies, and in another control group there was no food at all.

Next, all food was cleared away, and each participant was given a set of puzzles to solve. These required tracing a figure without retracing any line and without lifting one's pencil from the paper. Several were rigged to be unsolvable. This procedure has been used in stress research (e.g., Glass & Singer, 1972) to see how fast people will give up on a difficult challenge. We found that the people who had resisted temptation gave up significantly faster than people in the control condition. Thus, resisting temptation used up some crucial resource that was then no longer available to help them keep persisting and trying in the face of failure. Again, these results supported the willpower theory and contradicted the other two.

Thus, the human being's ability to alter the person's own responses and change the way the person thinks, feels, and acts depends on a crucial resource that seems to operate like an energy or strength. This resource appears to be quite limited in quantity, so that even a single act of self-control in a laboratory setting is enough to deplete it, with measurable effects. Furthermore, the same resource seems to be used for a broad range of very different acts of self-regulation. We have found the effects of depleting this resource to carry over across widely varying spheres of response, including controlling emotions, controlling thoughts, impulse control and resisting temptation, and controlling performance.

Crucially, this same resource appears to be involved in choice and decision making. That is, making choices and decisions depletes the same resource, resulting in discernible impairments of self-control. In several studies, we found that people who made either one (somewhat) momentous choice or a long series of relatively minor choices showed the same patterns of impaired self-control as we had earlier observed after initial acts of self-control (Baumeister et al., 1998; Vohs et al., 2004). Taking responsibility, exerting control, and making difficult decisions—in other words, the full range of acts of volition—seem to depend on the same limited resource (willpower, if you prefer) as is used in self-control.

The view of self-control as a limited resource can be interpreted in various ways, including a spiritually agnostic evolutionary argument, but it fits well with the Judeo-Christian worldview. Apparently, God (or whatever forces designed the human psyche) gave us enough power to do the right thing with some effort—but did not make us so that we would inevitably, automatically do the right thing. Human choice takes place amid the competing pulls of virtue and sin. Choosing virtue over sin is difficult and strenuous, even for those who desire to live virtuously.

STRENGTHENING THE MORAL MUSCLE

Thus far we have seen that the self's ability to make choices and regulate its behavior depends on a resource that resembles a muscle in crucial respects. That is, it operates like a kind of strength or energy resource, insofar as it becomes tired after use. Elsewhere we have argued that self-control can be understood as the psyche's "moral muscle" because it is useful for resisting temptation and performing other feats of moral choice (Baumeister & Exline, 1999, 2000). Indeed, self-control can be considered as underlying human virtue generally. The seven deadly sins of medieval Christian theology, for example, can all be conceptualized as failures of self-control. This is obvious for cases such as greed, sloth, and anger, and the only one that is difficult to fit into the formula is pride. Yet pride, too, is something that puts the self ahead of others and often must be deliberately restrained by acts of self-regulation. As one sign, alcohol intoxication reduces self-control generally and causes people to indulge the impulses that they have been restraining, and alcohol intoxication causes people to become more boastful and confident (see Banaji & Steele, 1989; Steele & Southwick, 1985).

For centuries, wise men and women have recommended efforts to build character so as to increase the capacity for virtue. From the perspective of self-regulation theory, the essence of these practices is to exercise the moral muscle so as to increase its strength. Thus, spiritual novices may engage in a variety of exercises that revolve around self-regulation. Meditation involves exerting control over the mind and attention, as the person tries to maintain a specific focus. Desires for material comfort must be thwarted as the novice accepts discomfort and in some cases pain, and of course greedy desires for wealth or material objects are deliberately checked. The novice may have to regulate behavior to fit externally imposed schedules and the overall discipline of spiritual humility.

Recent field studies have begun to provide empirical evidence to support the idea that self-control can be strengthened by exercise. In one study, participants were randomly assigned to perform any of several exercises in self-regulation, such as keeping track of all their foods, regulating their negative emotions, or improving their posture. The posture exercise is of particular interest because it resembles the sort of character-building exercise that has been used in various settings to make children learn how to discipline their own behavior so as to conform to external standards. After two weeks of such exercises, participants were found to exhibit improved self-control in a laboratory test when compared with people in the control condition who had not performed the exercises. Moreover, the more people had exercised, the greater their improvement in self-control (Muraven, Baumeister, & Tice, 1999).

In another study, participants were given an assortment of exercises that involved minor adjustments to everyday behavior. These included saying "Yes" instead of the colloquial "Yeah," trying to speak in complete sentences rather than phrases, and performing certain everyday tasks (such as brushing teeth) with the nondominant hand. Again, these tasks involved seemingly minor or even arbitrary exercises with little intrinsic value—but they required the person to exercise self-control. Again, the people who performed these were found to improve on laboratory tests of self-control, including in this case the Stroop color–word task (Oaten & Cheng, 2001). These findings indicate that self-control can be improved through exercise, just as a muscle grows stronger from exercise. They fit the "willpower" theory of volition.

CONSERVATION AND REPLENISHMENT

A further aspect of the muscle model of willpower is that people may seek to conserve their strength as it begins to become depleted. For example, athletes do not typically exert their muscles at full capacity until these muscles are utterly exhausted. Rather, athletes may exert themselves to the fullest at first, but as soon as they start to become tired, they begin to conserve their strength by expending effort judiciously. A tennis player might run after every ball at first, but as tiredness begins, he or she may refrain from trying for shots that seem out of reach, so as to conserve strength for the more promising opportunities.

Muraven (1998) found that people manage their self-control resources in the same way. First, he showed that when volition begins to decline, people are actually conserving rather than being utterly exhausted. He managed to counteract the effects of depletion by offering some people a large cash incentive to perform better on a second task, and in that case they were able to perform well. Thus, the effect of the initial depletion was not so much to exhaust the self's resources to the point of being incapable of volition; rather, the person simply conserved the remaining resources in case an important occasion arose, and when one did (signified by the experimenter's offer of a substantial amount of money), the person was able to find the resources to respond.

In another study, Muraven (1998) showed the conservation effect by telling some participants that they would need to exert self-control in the near future (ostensibly on a third task that was promised). The amount of impairment they showed on the second task (after having their resources depleted on the first) was affected by whether they had a reason to conserve for the third. People who expected the demanding third task were more likely to conserve resources on the second task. Specifically, the second task required people to hold their hands in ice water for as long as they could, and so those who expected the third task gave up faster on the ice water task.

Muscles also replenish their strength through rest and possibly through other means. We have begun to explore how the self replenishes its capacity for volition. Rest is certainly one means, and indeed there is some evidence that systematic relaxation akin to meditation can help restore the self's willpower (Smith, 2002). Other studies have suggested that a dose of positive emotion, especially humor, seems to have some restorative powers. When this positive emotion was interspersed between an initial task designed to deplete the self and a second self-regulation task, people's performance on the second task was much less impaired than in no-emotion (or negative affect) conditions.

WHAT CONSTITUTES FREEDOM?

The debate about free will has taken an odd turn. Psychologists have gradually come to embrace an idea of free will as involving behavior that is utterly free from external or antecedent causes. Yet as Kant (1787/1956) pointed out, we understand most events in terms of causality. Therefore, even if free action did exist in this extreme sense, we would not be able to explain it or understand it, given how our minds think. Freedom of action thus becomes something that by definition could not be explained or understood, especially in the scientific and causal terms favored by psychologists.

This tension is not unique to psychology and its philosophical roots. Christian theology has likewise grappled with the question of how humans might be free to choose as-yet-undetermined courses of action whereas God presumably knows everything including what each person will eventually choose to do. The Calvinist view that each person is predestined to choose freely exactly what he or she will eventually do (so that all the person's choices are already laid out at birth although in some sense they are freely made as the person moves through life) is not unlike many modern attempts in psychological theory to reconcile the experience of free choice with a deterministic faith that everything that happens is fully caused by previous events.

Perhaps the inability to conceptualize total freedom is itself somehow proof that it cannot exist. Then again, perhaps that merely reflects a shortcoming in our ability to understand. Our mental model of the world may not perfectly match the reality of the world. This would hardly be the only case. Some paradoxes of physics, such as that light is both a particle and a wave, are inimical to human conceptual understanding.

In a different work, Kant (1797/1967) offered a way of thinking about freedom that does not require exemption from all causality. By his account, action is free if it is guided by reason, in particular, if it is based on moral principles that he believed were innate in the mind. (Philosophical experts say that Kant actually waffled a bit as to whether using reason was sufficient to entail freedom, as opposed to there being a free choice to use reason in the first place.) Unfree action was simply responding to external circumstances. People can be manipulated by their environments, or they can resist those external influences and instead use their reason to select the proper form of behavior. To be sure, not all inner processes constituted freedom in Kant's view; yielding to all impulses and appetites, even if they originate from inside the self, would not qualify as freedom.

It could be profitable for psychology to use Kant's concept of freedom, even if it means embracing only a partial or limited view of freedom (as opposed to the radical but incomprehensible notion of utter freedom from all causality). People certainly can resist some external influences and temptations, and they can instead use their reasoning capacity to choose to behave in a better way. (Indeed, they can even counteract the effects of alcohol to an extent by compensating in other ways; Williams, Goldman, & Williams, 1981.) There is an important difference between simply yielding to all influences or temptations and acting instead in a more reasonable, thoughtful manner. In fact, that difference may be in practical terms the most important aspect of freedom. Moreover, it does capture what would be distinctively human about volition: Animals with smaller brains, little or no language, and inability to represent (mentally) alternative courses of action would be essentially unable to accomplish it. This limited definition of freedom is thus what is, in fact, special about human behavior.

IMPLICATIONS

The view of volition that is expressed in this chapter holds that the self can free its actions from being determined by particular influences, especially those of which it is aware. Regardless of whether one embraces the idea of a totally free will, which can initiate action that is utterly independent of all antecedent causes, there is certainly an important distinction between having one's actions dictated by immediate external stimuli and being able to act in a different manner, such as pursuing distal goals rather than reacting to immediate influences. Moreover, that distinction is crucial for the human capacity to grow, change, adapt, and create the immensely diverse spectrum of human action.

If people can act in such a free, enlightened manner, why do they not always do so? The answer I have proposed is that it is difficult and effortful to liberate one's behavior from simply responding to immediate situational influences. Choice, self-regulation, and other forms of volition all depend on a very limited resource that operates like a strength or energy. It becomes depleted when it is used. Moreover, that same limited resource is used for a broad variety of volitional acts. Because of this, it is sensible, even vital, for the self to preserve the resource.

Hence, most of life has to be lived according to routine, habit, automatic responses, and other efficient forms of action. People can free their will from the ordinary flow of here-and-now determination, but there is a substantial cost to doing so. It is moreover a cost that people can afford only on an occasional basis.

Ultimately, is this not the sense of free will that is implicit in the Judeo-Christian scriptural tradition? Freedom is within reach, but not all human actions can attain to this high ideal. Thus, in my view, both current scientific findings and religious traditions can agree that human action can be free, at least in a limited sense, and at least sometimes.

This approach can inform clinical practice as well as theory. Miller and Brown (1991) elaborated how volition in general, and self-regulation in particular, can be used to address the problem of addiction. They noted how popular conceptions of addiction suggest that the external substances possess immense powers such that anyone who is briefly exposed to them will become a helplessly addicted slave to ineluctable cravings. In contrast, the actual evidence indicates that many people can use even the most addictive substances without becoming addicted, and moreover many people who addictively abuse substances at times are found at other times to use them in controlled, moderate ways.

The key, according to Miller and Brown (1991), is that self-control waxes and wanes in accordance with a broad variety of internal and external circumstances. People who have problems with self-regulation are more prone to become addicted in the first place. Moreover, events that undermine self-regulation make for greater abuse and addiction, whereas when self-regulation becomes stronger the person becomes better able to manage substance use and resist its temptations. The implications for therapy may thus include exercises to strengthen the self's powers of volition, as well as helping people plan their lives so that their resources are not depleted when they face the temptation to resume their addictive behaviors.

Thus, self-regulation is an important form of volition. Both psychological theory and practice can benefit from an enhanced understanding of how the self regulates itself and, more broadly, how it uses the limited range of freedom of action that the forces of creation have bestowed on the human psyche.

The Judeo-Christian view of human nature has generally emphasized that people are free agents who bear responsibility for their actions because they can genuinely choose to act either well or badly. Some traditions in research psychology have resisted this view and insisted instead that people's actions are fully determined products of their genetic inclinations and environmental experiences. Perhaps the most notable of these was the Skinnerian insistence that human behavior is simply a result of environmental conditioning. Those views have been jettisoned as inadequate to encompass the range and diversity of human action. My prediction is that current theories that deny human freedom will likewise be found to be wanting and that very denial of freedom will be an important cause of their eclipse. Psychologists would be better off accepting the view (whether from Judeo-Christian sources or others) that people can in fact be free to make choices and do sometimes (although not always) use that freedom.

I close by noting that those psychologists who deny the existence of human freedom may do significant harm. A recent study by Vohs and Schooler (2003) sought to manipulate people's beliefs in free will by having some of them read an essay arguing that freedom is an illusion and all action is fully determined. The participants who read that essay went on to cheat significantly more on a test, compared with people in the control condition who read an article that had nothing to do with free will. The Judeo-Christian tradition has long emphasized human freedom in part as a way to promote socially responsible, virtuous action, and now laboratory data have confirmed the wisdom of that approach: People who are led to reject the idea of free will become more prone to act in selfish, immoral ways that can harm others.

Put another way, the Judeo-Christian view of human freedom is not just an idle theological opinion but rather a form of social influence that can promote socially desirable behavior. Psychologists should be aware that rejecting that doctrine can harm society. From where I sit, nothing in the current research journals is compelling enough to justify taking that step.

REFERENCES

Banaji, M. R., & Steele, C. M. (1989). Alcohol and self-evaluation: Is a social cognition approach beneficial? *Social Cognition, 7,* 137–151.

Bandura, A. (1989). Human agency in social cognitive theory. *American Psychologist, 44,* 1175–1184.

Bargh, J. A., Bond, R. N., Lombardi, W. J., & Tota, M. E. (1986). The additive nature of chronic and temporary sources of construct accessibility. *Journal of Personality and Social Psychology, 50,* 869–878.

Baumeister, R. F. (1998). The self. In D. T. Gilbert, S. T. Fiske, & G. Lindzey (Eds.), *Handbook of social psychology* (4th ed., pp. 680–740). New York: McGraw-Hill.

Baumeister, R. F., Bratslavsky, E., Muraven, M., & Tice, D. M. (1998). Ego depletion: Is the active self a limited resource? *Journal of Personality and Social Psychology, 74,* 1252–1265.

Baumeister, R. F., & Exline, J. J. (1999). Virtue, personality, and social relations: Self-control as the moral muscle. *Journal of Personality, 67,* 1165–1194.

Baumeister, R. F., & Exline, J. J. (2000). Self-control, morality, and human strength. *Journal of Social and Clinical Psychology, 19,* 29–42.

Baumeister, R. F., Heatherton, T. F., & Tice, D. M. (1994). *Losing control: How and why people fail at self-regulation*. San Diego, CA: Academic Press.

Baumeister, R. F., & Leary, M. R. (1995). The need to belong: Desire for interpersonal attachments as a fundamental human motivation. *Psychological Bulletin, 117*, 497–529.

Brehm, J. W. (1966). *A theory of psychological reactance*. New York: Academic Press.

Damasio, A. R. (1994). *Descartes' error: Emotion, reason, and the human brain*. New York: Avon Books.

Frijda, N. H. (1986). *The emotions*. Cambridge, England: Cambridge University Press.

Glass, D. C., & Singer, J. E. (1972). *Urban stress: Experiments on noise and social stressors*. New York: Academic Press.

Glass, D. C., Singer, J. E., & Friedman, L. N. (1969). Psychic cost of adaptation to an environmental stressor. *Journal of Personality and Social Psychology, 12*, 200–210.

Higgins, E. T., & King, G. A. (1981). Accessibility of social constructs: Information processing consequences of individual and contextual variability. In N. Cantor & J. Kihlstrom (Eds.), *Personality, cognition, and social interaction* (pp. 69–121). Hillsdale, NJ: Erlbaum.

Kant, I. (1956). *Kritik der reinen Vernunft* [Critique of pure reason]. Frankfurt, Germany: Felix Meiner Verlag. (Original work published 1787)

Kant, I. (1967). *Kritik der praktischen Vernunft* [Critique of practical reason]. Hamburg, Germany: Felix Meiner Verlag. (Original work published 1797)

Miller, W. R., & Brown, J. M. (1991). Self-regulation as a conceptual basis for the prevention of addictive behaviours. In N. Heather, W. R. Miller, & J. Greeley (Eds.), *Self-control and the addictive behaviours* (pp. 3–79). Sydney, Australia: Maxwell Macmillan.

Muraven, M. (1998). *Mechanisms of self-control failure: Motivation and limited resources*. Unpublished doctoral dissertation, Case Western Reserve University, Cleveland, OH.

Muraven, M., Baumeister, R. F., & Tice, D. M. (1999). Longitudinal improvement of self-regulation through practice: Building self-control through repeated exercise. *Journal of Social Psychology, 139*, 446–457.

Muraven, M., Tice, D. M., & Baumeister, R. F. (1998). Self-control as limited resource: Regulatory depletion patterns. *Journal of Personality and Social Psychology, 74*, 774–789.

Oaten, C. M., & Cheng, K. (2001). *Strengthening the regulatory muscle: The longitudinal benefits of exercising self-control*. Unpublished master's thesis, Macquarrie University, Sydney, Australia.

Sartre, J.-P. (1956). *Being and nothingness* (H. E. Barnes, Trans.). Secaucus, NJ: Citadel Press. (Original work published 1943)

Seligman, M. E. P. (1975). *Helplessness: On depression, development, and death*. San Francisco: Freeman.

Smith, R. W. (2002). *Effects of relaxation on self-regulatory depletion.* Unpublished doctoral dissertation, Case Western Reserve University, Cleveland, OH.

Srull, T. K., & Wyer, R. S., Jr. (1979). The role of category accessibility in the interpretation of information about persons: Some determinants and implications. *Journal of Personality and Social Psychology, 37,* 1660–1672.

Srull, T. K., & Wyer, R. S., Jr. (1980). Category accessibility and social perception: Some implications for the study of person memory and interpersonal judgment. *Journal of Personality and Social Psychology, 38,* 841–856.

Steele, C. M., & Southwick, L. (1985). Alcohol and social behavior I: The psychology of drunken excess. *Journal of Personality and Social Psychology, 48,* 18–34.

Vohs, K. D., Baumeister, R. F., Twenge, J. M., Schmeichel, B. J., Tice, D. M., & Crocker, J. (2004). *Self-regulatory resources are depleted by decision making—but also by accomodating to unchosen alternatives.* Manuscript submitted for publication.

Vohs, K. D., & Schooler, J. (2003). [Free will beliefs and antisocial behavior]. Unpublished raw data, University of British Columbia, Vancouver.

Williams, R. M., Goldman, M. S., & Williams, D. L. (1981). Expectancy and pharmacological effects of alcohol on human cognitive and motor performance: The compensation for alcohol effect. *Journal of Abnormal Psychology, 90,* 267–270.

4

THE RELATIONAL SELF:
PSYCHOLOGICAL AND
THEOLOGICAL PERSPECTIVES

C. STEPHEN EVANS

The social character of the human self has been recognized from ancient times. When Aristotle affirmed that "man is a political animal" (c. 330 B.C./1968, 1253a[1]), he really meant that human beings were essentially social creatures. Most philosophers—ancient, medieval, and modern—have agreed with this judgment, which has been, as we see, powerfully confirmed by contemporary empirical psychology.

The social character of the human self is equally prominent in the Judeo-Christian tradition. The creation account in Genesis 2 puts it simply and elegantly: "It is not good for the man to be alone." The biblical narrative of God's interaction with human beings puts great emphasis on families and community. God's purpose is not merely to have a relationship with individual human selves but to form a "people," a covenant community.

In this chapter, I try to see how psychological findings about the relatedness of the self mesh with a theological perspective on that same relatedness. I begin with a review of some of the major psychological findings, al-

---

[1]The numbers refer to the pagination of the Bekken edition of the Greek text of Aristotle, the standard way to refer to Aristotle in English, since this pagination is reproduced in the margins of all scholarly English editions, thus enabling the reader to find the passage regardless of the translation used.

though this review is sharply limited, both because of space and because I am, as a philosopher, writing outside my field. I then look at the social character of the self through the eyes of Christian theology. My perspective on that rich tradition here is, of course, a particular and historically situated one, but I try to approach the issues in an ecumenical spirit that does not trade too heavily on beliefs that divide the various branches of the Christian faith. I write from a Christian perspective because, as a Christian, I necessarily reflect my own tradition, and it is also the tradition I know best. I believe, however, that much of what I have to say could be affirmed from a Jewish perspective as well.

I use the 19th-century Danish philosopher–theologian Søren Kierkegaard as a representative Christian thinker. Kierkegaard is an especially good choice, I believe, for several reasons. First of all, he has a reputation as an arch-individualist, the "father of existentialism," who dedicated many of his books to "the individual" and considered this to be "his category" (1859/1998). If the social character of the self turns out to be an important and prominent theme in Kierkegaard's thought, then this is powerful evidence of how deeply central human relatedness is to the Christian tradition. Second, Kierkegaard shows an unusual degree of interest and sensitivity to psychology and psychological issues, although of course he wrote before the birth of contemporary empirical psychology. Still, his interest in psychological questions facilitates the recognition of connections between contemporary findings and his own theologically charged perspective.

My thesis is not merely the weak claim that psychological findings and theological perspectives are consistent and coherent with each other, although that is certainly true. Rather, I argue for a stronger and more interesting claim: If we take seriously a theological perspective on human beings, this gives us an important context in which to understand and interpret the psychological findings about human relatedness. Specifically, I argue that if we believe that human beings were created by God and intended by God to have a relation to God, this allows us to understand how the self can be fundamentally relational and yet possess a limited, although real, capacity to transcend human social relations. If the self is completely a product of relations with others, then one might wonder how it is possible for the self to have any real independence of those others. I argue that a theological perspective allows us to understand how it is possible for human selves to possess what we might call relative autonomy without denying that humans are thoroughly relational.

WHAT KIND OF AN ENTITY IS A SELF?

Contemporary psychologists have had much to say about selfhood, but much of it deals with the self in relation to some other concept. Thus, research has focused on such topics as self-concept, self-awareness, self-esteem, self-regulation, self-presentation, and many more hyphenated concepts. Psychologists have been more comfortable with these concepts than the pure concept of the self, probably because they have agreed with philosophers David Hume (1739/1890) and Immanuel Kant (1789/1965) that the self cannot be directly observed, at least not "by itself." As Baumeister has argued in his excellent review article on the self in *The Handbook of Social Psychology*, "The self is not perceived, but some activity of the self is perceived, and one can learn about the self from that" (1998, p. 683).[2] If one combines this point with a positivist-inspired suspicion of entities that cannot be directly observed, something that I believe remains as a kind of suppressed tendency even in the postbehaviorist world of cognitivized psychology, then one can easily understand why the self is frequently studied in this hyphenated form. Research on these topics has, of course, turned out to be highly useful and enlightening.

Baumeister concludes from the fact that the self cannot be directly observed that the self "that transcends situations is therefore always a construction, which is to say a product of abstraction, inference, and deduction, rather than something known directly," and he seems to understand this claim that the self is a construction as implying that the self is not a "real entity" (p. 684). I believe that this claim, which I may have misunderstood, is questionable for two reasons.

First, from the claim that we can never observe the self apart from some activity that the self is performing, it does not follow that the self cannot be directly observed. All that follows is that the self cannot be observed alone. Suppose it is true that I can never observe myself without observing myself as active in some way; I observe myself observing the world, acting in the world, responding emotionally to situations. Just because the self in this case is observed by observing what it is doing, it does not follow that there is no direct observation of the self. Observations of many (perhaps most) entities are observations of those entities in the context of what those entities do. Perhaps it is correct to say that we never observe the whole of the self when we observe its activities. Our experience of ourselves is always provisional and partial, a snapshot rather than a comprehensive vision. This does not mean, however, that we do not observe the self at all.

Baumeister's claim seems questionable for a second reason as well. Even if we agree with him that we cannot directly observe the self, it does not follow that the self we observe is merely a "construct, the result of cognitive processes, rather than a real entity that exists in the world." Baumeister seems to infer this from the claim that the self that we get to know is the product of "abstraction, inference, and deduction." This seems to confuse the concept

---

[2]Much of what follows was learned from this article, and I wish to express my gratitude to Baumeister for his help.

of the self that we humans develop with the reality to which this concept is intended to refer. Perhaps it is right to say that our *concept* of the self is a "construction," and even that the concept of the self is a theoretical concept, one developed for the sake of interaction with the world, as Higgins (1996) has argued. We may go even further and agree with Epstein (1973) that we ought to speak of a "self-theory" rather than a self-concept because our self-understanding consists in a complex web of beliefs. Such a "theory" about the self is clearly a human construction. It does not follow from this that the self to which such a theory or concept refers is not a real entity. Black holes are not directly observable, and the theory that postulates their existence is clearly a human construction, but most scientists would not doubt the independent reality of black holes. It is true that the self is a complex object, and it is likely that it is never completely captured by our theoretical constructions. This does not mean, however, that our concept of selfhood does not refer to a real entity and at least sometimes discloses some real features of that entity.

Baumeister himself really recognizes this point earlier in his chapter, when he criticizes the confusion in social psychology between the ideas of *self* and *self-concept* "as if the two terms were interchangeable" (1998, p. 681). Baumeister argues this is a fallacy because "if the self were only a concept, how could it make decisions or carry on relationships to people?" (1998, p. 681). The same logic implies that the self is not merely a theoretical construction, however, for such a construction is equally incapable of actions and relations. We should therefore generalize the point he makes about self-concept and extend it to all of our concepts of the self: "A self-concept is an idea about something; the entity to which the self-concept refers is the self" (1998, p. 681).

I think that Baumeister is right, however, when he says that it is not an accident that such confusions occur. The reason for this, I think, is that the self is a unique type of entity, an entity whose being is partially constituted by how it conceives of itself. A self is not merely a biological organism with a particular history, although it is certainly that, but a self-conscious being whose actions both form the self and also reflect the self's conception of itself. We are, in the words of philosopher Charles Taylor (1985), "self-interpreting animals," or in the formulation of Martin Heidegger (1927/1962), entities whose being in part consists in raising questions about the meaning of their existence. Thus, although a human self is not identical with its conception of itself, it is partly shaped by that conception. In this case, the reality of the self is not completely independent of how it conceives of that reality; a change in self-understanding implies there has been some change in the self.

Baumeister's review helpfully groups research about the self into three categories that reflect what he terms the "three important roots of selfhood" (cf. chap. 3, this volume). These are, respectively, the "experience of reflexive consciousness," the "interpersonal aspect of selfhood," and what Baumeister terms the "executive function, the agent, the controller, the origin." I think he is right to focus on these three categories, for they are all fundamental to our sense of what it is to be a self. A self is, on one hand, what we are aware of when we consciously attend to our own mental life. As we see, however, that mental life is in turn unintelligible apart from a pattern of relations with other selves that shape our identity. Finally, we experience this self that we know when we attend to our own mental life, which is in turn shaped by its relation to others, as an agent, as a source of actions for which we sometimes have responsibility. Baumeister treats these three aspects separately, claiming that an understanding of how they are interrelated is "at least several decades away." I would argue that even this prediction may be optimistic; even some materialist philosophers believe that the self may turn out to be essentially mysterious in ways that bar full and complete human understanding (McGinn, 1999). Nevertheless, it is important to see that these three "roots" of selfhood are all attempting to unpack dimensions of the same entity. We may not fully understand the self, but there is no great difficulty in conceiving it as an entity that has some awareness of itself, is shaped by relations to other selves, and has a capacity for action. Because my theme is the social character of the self, it is the second of these three dimensions of selfhood that will be my primary focus in this chapter.

THE SHIFT TOWARD A SOCIAL VIEW OF THE SELF

Although it is always risky for an outsider to make such a judgment, it appears to me that recent decades in psychology have seen a pronounced trend toward a deeper understanding of the self as a social being. Of course, behaviorist approaches to human behavior neglected the self altogether and emphasized how human behavior is shaped by environmental contingencies, some of which were, of course, social in nature. On such a view, the "self" almost disappeared, or appeared only as a passive product of outside conditioning. Approaches that emphasized innate individual differences such as those of "temperament" naturally put more emphasis on what is "internal" to the individual but did not necessarily locate those inner variables in a recognizable self. Cognitive theories that see human behavior as mediated by inner mental processing naturally see the self as more important, an active shaper of the environment and not simply a passive product of it. Such views, however, still tend to see the self as a distinct, more or less autonomous entity, interacting with its environment. Recent research suggests, in many ways, that the nature and identity of the self is often profoundly shaped by its social relations.

For example, even self-awareness seems to involve relations to others. Much of self-awareness involves invoking a standard to which the self is being compared (Duval & Wicklund, 1972). Even a person's perception of such things as his or her height or weight tends to be colored by a comparison to ideal standards. No one is "fat" or "thin" except with reference to some standard or "ideal" weight. Two kinds of standards are emphasized by researchers such as Harter (1987) and Higgins and Parsons (1983). One type seems more social in character and has to do with an individual's performance relative to the expectations or evaluations of others. Another kind of standard is more individual and has to do with an individual's success relative to intrinsic goals.

Even the more individual type of standard clearly has a social dimension, however. According to social learning theory, children by and large develop ideals from models they have observed, including parents, of course, but also peers and even characters portrayed in the media (Bandura & Walters, 1963). In some ways, then, all the standards involved in self-awareness have a social character that colors our knowledge of ourselves. As philosophers such as Hegel (1807/1977) had already recognized some time ago, we perceive ourselves partly by perceiving how others perceive us. This does not mean that our perception of ourselves is usually in agreement with how others actually perceive us; rather, the connection is between self-perception and how we believe others perceive us (Shrauger & Schoeneman, 1979). The negative side of this truth is dramatically (and somewhat painfully) portrayed in J. P. Sartre's (1949) play *No Exit*, in which three deceased characters are confined to a room in Hell. Each of the three craves from one of the other two recognition of some quality the person wants to see him- or herself as possessing; without that recognition from the other none of them can see themselves as they wish. Each person becomes another's torturer, and "Hell is other people."

Not only is it the case that self-knowledge has a social dimension, however. The motivation for self-knowledge usually has a social character to it as well. Baumeister (1998) says that there are three main motives to obtain self-knowledge: People want accurate information about themselves, favorable information about themselves (whether accurate or not), and information that is consistent with and confirms their existing beliefs about their self. It is somewhat surprising that research by Sedikides (1993) shows that the desire for accurate information is the weakest of the three, and the desire for favorable information from others is by far the strongest. This suggests that people appear to need to see themselves in a favorable light, and to do so they need to perceive other people as perceiving them favorably, even if this benefit is gained at the cost of accuracy.

It is not too surprising, then, that people's views about themselves are not generally all that accurate. The great majority of people see themselves as above average in many respects. For example, people see themselves as more ethical and less prejudiced than their peers (Lamm & Myers, 1978). In one study, 90% of adults believed themselves to be better than average drivers (Svenson, 1981). A College Board survey of high school seniors found that 0% rated themselves as below average in ability to get along with others, whereas 25% rated themselves as being in the top 1% in this respect (College Board, cited in Baumeister, 1998; Myers, 1980). People involved in cooperative activities consistently tend to take credit for successes and blame others for failures; students who do well on an exam usually say the exam was fair, whereas those who do poorly tend to blame the exam (Myers, 1980). It seems that humans have a chronic tendency to make themselves look good in their own eyes by comparing themselves favorably with others. It is interesting, however, that even self-deception seems linked to interpersonal relations. One of the most effective techniques for convincing oneself that some view is true is to attempt to convince others (Haight, 1980). Unfavorable information about oneself is often ignored or forgotten if it is not public, but if other people know about it, this seems to give the information a reality that makes it hard for the self to ignore (Baumeister & Cairns, 1992).

Self-knowledge is not the only type of knowledge that is strongly linked to social relations. There is strong evidence that people's beliefs about all kinds of things are strongly influenced by others. This is dramatically illustrated in the phenomenon of brainwashing. A common feature of more successful attempts to transform a person's views in a comprehensive manner is that they require that the person be separated from all of the person's previous acquaintances. When prisoners undergo indoctrination during the day but then return to their fellow prisoners in the evening, the brainwashing is ineffective (Baumeister, 1986). Brainwashing clearly represents an extreme and unusual situation, but it is hardly surprising to learn that people tend to think like those with whom they associate.

The previous findings represent pretty well-established and well-known conclusions of social psychology. Recently, however, psychologists have made discoveries that imply there is a social dimension even to what may appear to be intrapsychic processes. One of the most studied aspects of selfhood is self-esteem. There is a puzzle concerning self-esteem in that "it does not have strong pragmatic or material consequences, and yet people go to great lengths to preserve and protect it" (Baumeister, 1998, p. 696). It does not seem rational that people would work so hard to get something that seems not to be worth very much. A plausible part of the answer to this puzzle is found in the work of Leary, Tambor, Terdal, and Downs (1995), who theorize that self-esteem is a *sociometer*, an internal measure of how successful a person is at being accepted and included by others. People avoid low self-esteem for the same reason that people carefully avoid allowing a gas gauge on an automobile to register "E." The position of the gauge is not important in itself, but because it is a measure of something else that is important. Perhaps this is only one of the reasons people value self-esteem, but the theory does fit nicely with the strong evidence that people have a pervasive "need to form and maintain interpersonal connections" (Baumeister & Leary, 1995). It is also supported by evidence that some of the behavioral differences between people with high and low self-esteem only manifest themselves in public, interpersonal settings (Baumeister, Hutton, & Tice, 1989). The "sociometer" theory thus takes what might on the surface appear to be a purely intrapsychic phenomenon and implies that it actually has a social dimension.

This result is analogous to the conclusions that resulted from the debate concerning "cognitive dissonance." It has long been recognized that people have a tendency to make their inner beliefs consistent with their actions, and it seems natural to explain this by an inner cognitive mechanism that seeks to reduce inconsistency. Baumeister (1982) and other researchers have provided strong evidence that some of the changes in people explained by social psychologists in terms of intrapsychic, cognitive processes only occurred when the agents involved were being observed by others. This suggests, for example, that people who change their attitudes after taking some public action for a position do so not only to make their own beliefs consistent with their actions but also to address a concern with how others perceive them. To explain the changes, one must consider what psychologists term "self-presentational factors."

A similar result can be seen with respect to "biased scanning" theories of inner change, as developed by Fazio, Effrein, and Falender (1981). People who are asked loaded questions seem to undergo significant shifts in their self-concept when questioned later. Biased scanning theory explains this as a result of a scanning mechanism in which the recent behavior is prominent in memory and this gives a biased picture to the self of its own behavior. Tice (1992), however, recognized that the results could be partly explained by the interpersonal dimensions of the experiment, rather than simply by an internal cognitive process. She developed procedures to separate out the interpersonal dimension from a biased memory scan, for example, by having some questions answered privately and anonymously. The results were that the changes in self-concept only occurred when another person was interacting with the participant. I do not believe such findings should lead us to question the reality and importance of the self. Rather, they should lead us to question whether intrapsychic and interpersonal processes can be sharply distinguished. If the "inner self" and social relations constantly and reciprocally influence each other, then it is unhelpful to think of them as completely independent factors. The "inner self" is not an entity distinct from its social relations, but an entity whose identity is profoundly shaped by those relations.

So far I have mostly focused on the self's knowledge, particularly knowledge of itself. There is good reason, however, to think that other aspects of the self are equally shaped by interpersonal factors. There is solid evidence that the only reliable objective predictor of happiness is social connectedness, which is a much stronger factor than such things as wealth, health, education, and place of residence (Baumeister 1991; Myers, 1992, 2000a, 2000b). Even an emotion such as guilt, which might appear to be a private, inner phenomenon, seems closely linked to interpersonal relations. A literature review (Baumeister, Stillwell, & Heatherton, 1994) strongly supports the view that guilt is linked to a "need to belong" and is linked to the breaking of relationships. The same action can produce vastly different levels of guilt if the relationship between two people is different. In a case of "survivor guilt," the person who feels guilty has performed no morally bad act toward anyone else. Yet even in this case, Tice and Baumeister (2001) plausibly link the sense of guilt to the person's sense of having received inequitable benefits in relation to others.

What Baumeister calls the executive function of the self can also be seen to have a social dimension. A crucial aspect of the self's agency lies in the notion of self-control or self-regulation. Without such an ability, morality would be impossible, and it is arguable that without morality, social life, or at least the distinctive kind of social life that humans seem to have, would not exist. Twenge, Catanese, and Baumeister (2003) obtained strong evidence that a person's ability to control him- or herself is strongly linked to whether a person feels accepted or rejected by others. Almost everyone who has had an undergraduate psychology course is familiar with the famous experiment of Stanley Milgram (1965) on obedience, in which most people involved in a psychological experiment were willing to administer painful electrical shocks to people when they were instructed to do so by an authoritative figure. Clearly, in this case, people were willing to act in ways contrary to their convictions because of the pressure of the social situation.

Of course, a great deal more evidence of this sort could be cited and many more issues discussed, but what has been said seems sufficient to support the claim that contemporary psychology, in recovering the inner self, is also increasingly seeing that the identity of that self is strongly tied to relationships to others. It is true that "no man is an island." The interpersonal dimension of the self seen in empirical psychology stands in strong contrast to some of the thinking about the self found in popular culture and even what might be termed "pop psychology," which often speaks of "finding yourself," as if the self were a completely autonomous, fully existing entity. Such talk can be a flimsy rationalization for breaking relationships and failing to fulfill obligations, which are seen as somehow "not true to my real self."

THEOLOGICAL PERSPECTIVES ON HUMAN RELATEDNESS

The Judeo-Christian tradition is fully consistent with these empirical findings about the way in which the human self gets defined and constituted by its relationships. Like contemporary psychologists, the biblical tradition does not see the human self as merely a passive recipient of influences but as an active shaper and participant in its own development. The self that is active in this way is never a self that can be understood in isolation from others, however. The Bible consistently portrays people as members of families and communities that are important to their identities.

One important clue to the importance of relatedness in the biblical tradition can be found in the way sexuality is viewed. Genesis 1:27 (NIV) says, "So God created man in his own image, in the image of God he created him; male and female he created them." In the Hebrew Bible, couplets such as these last two lines commonly use a poetic technique known as Hebrew parallelism, in which the second line restates the content of the first line in a poetically interesting way. It has been argued that this is what is occurring in this passage in Genesis (Bird, 1995). If this is correct, then the passage is not merely saying that both men and women are created in the image of God, significant as that would be in the ancient world, in which many cultures placed a low value on women. Rather, the passage is saying that in some way the image of God itself can be seen in the fact that God created human beings as male and female. In that case, the image of God itself is something that humans only possess relationally. Men and women were created for relationship with each other, and this relationality itself reflects the nature of the God who made them.

Some Christian theologians take this to be a hint of the Christian doctrine of the Trinity, the claim that God, while being one God, is nevertheless three persons. The Trinity is admittedly a deeply mysterious doctrine. Yet however little we may understand it, it seems to imply that God's very being is intrinsically relational (O'Collins, 1999). Even apart from creation, God can be thought of as embodying some of the characteristics of a community; each member of the Trinity enjoys perfect love and communion from the other two. Perhaps in creating human beings as male and female, intended for relationship, God was indeed placing in human beings something of God's own relational nature.[3]

It is true that there is an individualistic element in Christian theology because each individual has a relation to God, and God, as a righteous judge, holds individuals responsible for their actions, as well as communities. Yet this individualism should not obscure the equally important social character of humans. The fundamental importance of human sociality can be seen in the fact that God's redemptive activity is fundamentally oriented toward the creation of a people, a community. In the Hebrew Bible (Christian Old Testament) the Jewish people are selected by God so as to convey a crucial message to the whole of humankind. Most contemporary Christians, while not rejecting the idea of the Jews as God's chosen people in a "supercessionist" fashion, believe that God has created in the Church a new people of God, a people to be drawn from every tribe and nation, crossing barriers of language and race. The final picture of human redemption says much about the Chris-

---

[3]It is true, of course, that Christian and Jewish theologians have traditionally used male pronouns to refer to God, and Christians in particular have imaged God as Father. These theologians have usually been clear that God himself is not male, however, and that the image of Father is intended to say something about the relationship between God and his creation and not to assign God a gender.

tian vision: Paradise is pictured through such social symbols as the new Jerusalem, the City of God, and a heavenly banquet, in which food and drink are shared and enjoyed by a community.

KIERKEGAARD ON HUMAN RELATIONALITY

In this section of the chapter, I show, with the help of Søren Kierkegaard, how a theological perspective on the self illuminates its relational character. Specifically, I argue that a theological account of the self helps us understand how human selves can be thoroughly relational and yet sometimes transcend, in a relative and partial way, the social influences that have shaped them and continue to do so.

Kierkegaard's account of selfhood in *The Sickness Unto Death* seems initially obscure: "But what is the self? The self is a relation that relates itself to itself" (Kierkegaard, 1849/1980, p. 13). This is hardly transparent prose, but it certainly seems to imply that the self, even considered intrapsychically, is complex and relational in character. We might compare Kierkegaard here with William James's famous distinction between the "I" and the "me." At least part of what Kierkegaard means to say here is that to be a self is to have a reflexive awareness, in which the activity of awareness is distinguished from the object of awareness. We might think of the "I" as the self that is aware and the "me" as the object of the awareness. Kierkegaard wants to say that the self is not exhausted by either of these alone but consists in a relation between the two.

Kierkegaard's account of the self does not stop with this intrapsychic description but immediately goes on to define the self in terms of its relations to what is outside the self: "Such a relation that relates itself to itself, a self, must either have established itself or have been established by another" (1849/1980, p. 13). A self that established itself would be a self that is completely autonomous and independent, similar to God. If a self does not possess this godlike power, if it is in some way dependent on something outside itself, then it carries out its task of relating itself to itself only by carrying out another task: that of relating to what is outside itself. Kierkegaard says that human beings are clearly finite selves of this second kind: "The human self is such a derived, established relation, a relation that relates itself to itself and in relating itself to itself relates itself to another" (pp. 13–14). In effect, Kierkegaard is saying that for human beings the identity of the self is always grounded in a relation to something outside the self. We might compare this with the common view of contemporary psychologists that self-awareness involves reference to some kind of ideal or standard, which is socially derived.

Throughout *The Sickness Unto Death*, Kierkegaard attempts to look at various ways humans fail to be a self, a state of being Kierkegaard calls despair and which often manifests itself in an emotion of conscious despair, although it is also possible for humans to fail to be aware of this condition. The failure to be a self, however, must always be seen against the backdrop of an ideal, healthy self, a self that is in proper relationship to that ideal that defines it: "The formula that describes the state of the self when despair is completely rooted out is this: in relating itself to itself and in willing to be itself, the self rests transparently in the power that established it" (1849/1980, p. 14).

What is this "power?" The language is suggestive of that used in Alcoholics Anonymous, which speaks of a "higher power," and I believe that there is a significant parallel. In both cases, it is tempting to identify this power with God. Metaphysically, this identification would be correct for Kierkegaard; to him, it is literally true that God created the self and is ultimately responsible for its being. (This is, of course, consistent with there being a natural, scientific story to be told about how the human self came to be.) We can also say that for Kierkegaard the identification is correct, psychologically, as an ideal. God has created humans in such a way that they need a relation to God to be all they were intended to be. Yet although God is the metaphysical "power" that established the self, and ideally is the self's psychological ground as well, Kierkegaard recognizes that from a psychological point of view, the self can ground itself in various kinds of "higher powers." He says that God, who created the relation that constitutes the self, "releases it from his hand, as it were" (1849/1980, p. 16). That is, God has given to humans a degree of freedom in the shaping of their own identity. To realize fully God's intentions in creating them, humans need a relation to God. Because humans are free, however, they often ground their identity in what is less than God (the essence of idolatry), and the result of this misuse of freedom is that humans exhibit a variety of pathologies. Some of Kierkegaard's ideas here would suggest interesting lines of empirical research.

For example, Kierkegaard describes what he terms the despair of finitude and the despair of infinitude (1849/1980, pp. 29–35). The despair of infinitude is a condition in which a self has an inability to come to terms with its own finitude and accept its own creaturely status. Such a self is detached from actuality and lives in possibilities that are not linked in a concrete way to the actual self with a history. The despair of finitude is the opposite state, in which the self sees itself in a deterministic way purely as a product or victim of forces over which it has no control. In both cases, the therapy prescribed includes the development of a correct relation to God.

To see how this is so is to see the humanizing possibility inherent in a God-relation for Kierkegaard. When I see myself as God's creature, I am protected against both these kinds of despair. On the one hand, I am not tempted to see myself as God, but I am fully aware of my creaturely status. I was born male or female, in a particular place and time, in a particular social setting, with a body and biologically grounded nature not of my own making.

Any possibilities that are authentically mine must be grounded in those concrete, limiting realities.

That I am a creature of God, however, a creature made in God's image to be a self, implies that I am not merely a product of impersonal factors. God is the God for whom all things are possible, and to be endowed by God with self-consciousness is to be endowed with possibilities. For Kierkegaard, each person has what we might call a *vocation* or *calling* from God; each person has been created by God to become a particular individual. (We can here see how Kierkegaard gets his reputation as an "individualist.") This vocation can be seen as the telos or end-form of a human being, the ideal self that will develop if all goes well. One can see parallels here with the work of psychologists such as Rogers (1961) and Maslow (1968), who also see humans as having an ideal self that can be actualized, although there are significant differences between the content of the ends envisioned. Each one of us needs the courage to seek to become that person, which may require us to defy social stereotypes and expectations of various kinds. This call to become "an individual before God" is by no means a call to eccentricity, much less a call to ignore other people. Rather, for Kierkegaard (1847/1995), God's fundamental call is to love God and to love one's neighbor as oneself, the fundamental message of both the Jewish and Christian revelations.

Kierkegaard's "individualism" is by no means rooted in the view that humans are isolated, autonomous individuals. He is only too aware of the power of social conformism to prevent people from hearing and following their calling. It is only too easy to ignore the call to love the neighbor by attending to what "the others" say or by doing as "everyone" does (1849/1980, pp. 33–35). These aspects of Kierkegaard's thought have virtually become clichés in contemporary culture; we all know about the numbing effects of social conformism. It is important to recognize, however, that for Kierkegaard (1846/1978), the chief impact of this "leveling" effect is to dampen people's capacity for what we might call ethical heroism. The individual who takes seriously the call to love the neighbor faces a "double danger" according to Kierkegaard (1847/1995, pp. 76–82). On the one hand, this person faces the danger of selfishness. To truly love the neighbor as myself, I must put aside the human tendency to make myself the center of the universe. The person who successfully makes progress in this area faces a second danger or temptation. Other people will be made uncomfortable by his or her example. The person who seriously loves the neighbor must not expect social rewards or approval, but rather should not be surprised if other people try to persuade him or her not to strive so high. If this persuasion is resisted, the individual may be bitterly resented. This is particularly true if the one who loves the neighbor reaches across social barriers to love "the other" who is marginalized in a society.

Kierkegaard has often been criticized for putting too much emphasis on a "vertical" relationship to God in the formation of the self and not enough emphasis on the "horizontal" relation to other humans. I believe this criticism misses the mark for two reasons. First of all, God is not to be thought of as a finite person who competes for love with other finite persons. It is not true that if a person loves God more, then that person will necessarily have less love for other persons. At least this will not be true if the person's understanding of God and love for God is authentic. Kierkegaard puts the point across with a vivid financial metaphor:

> If you want to show that your life is intended to serve God, then let it serve people, yet continually with the thought of God. God does not have a share in existence in such a way he asks for his share for himself; he asks for everything, but as you bring it to him you immediately receive, if I may put it this way, a notice designating where it should be forwarded, because God does not ask for anything for himself, although he asks for everything from you. (1847/1995, p. 161)[4]

The second reason this criticism is misplaced is that it misunderstands the reason for Kierkegaard's emphasis on the God-relationship. Kierkegaard stresses the relation to God not because he thinks that relations to other human persons are unimportant, but because he is all too aware of how powerful and important such influences are. Humans are by nature relational creatures, and they cannot form an identity that is completely "autonomous" and "independent." The God-relation has for him a liberating aspect. A human self does not lose its relational character by a God-relation but rather, through the call of God, gains some power to transcend in part the identity one gains from finite relations:

> And what infinite reality the self gains by being conscious of existing before God, by becoming a human self whose criterion is God! A cattleman who (if this were possible) is a self directly before his cattle is a very low self, and, similarly, a master who is a self directly before his slaves is actually no self—for in both cases a criterion is lacking. The child who previously has had only his parents as a criterion becomes a self as an adult by getting the state as a criterion, but what an infinite accent falls on the self by having God as the criterion! (1849/1980, p. 79)

Here Kierkegaard briefly indicates various defective ways of becoming a self. In speaking of the cattleman or the slave owner, he indicts those who gain their sense of self through a sense of superiority to others. It is pathological to gain one's identity through the domination or oppression of others. In more "normal" development, he says that the child gains a "criterion" or standard from the parents, which is later generalized to "the state" or society more broadly. Yet to gain some critical distance on one's own society, to truly be able to be "an individual," a person needs some standard or "crite-

---

[4] I have slightly modified the Hong translation here. The Hongs translate the Danish "skal besørges" literally (and awkwardly in English) as "delivered further," but the English dynamic equivalent is clear: "forwarded."

rion" higher than that of society. For Kierkegaard, the call of God to the individual can perform this liberating function.

Individuals such as Socrates and Jesus (today we might add Gandhi) cannot be fully explained, according to Kierkegaard, as a product of their society. It is not possible for an individual simply to invent a new critical perspective, however. The self is always defined by its "criterion," a criterion that is also its "goal and measure." For Kierkegaard, such a criterion is developed through a social relationship. If God is a real person, then the relation to God is a transcendent one that can give humans a critical perspective on the social practices and customs that generally define the self. Kierkegaard then emphasizes the task of living as an individual "before God"—not because human relationships are not important, but because they are so important that without the God-relation genuine individuality cannot develop. Even our individuality, then, reflects our relational character.

To summarize, Kierkegaard agrees with contemporary psychology that the self is a profoundly relational being, whose identity is intertwined with the relationships of the self to others, particularly those others who provide a "criterion" of selfhood. His view goes beyond the perspective of scientific psychology, however, in holding out the possibility of a real relation to God that offers the possibility of transcending the social forces that have produced the self.

Such a claim about the importance of the God-relation raises many important questions, especially to secular-minded academics. In the remaining section of this chapter, I raise and briefly answer some of the more pressing concerns a critic might have, concerns that might raise legitimate questions about the value of further research in this area. My purposes are twofold. First and foremost, I suggest some possible questions that could point toward lines of research. Second, in connection with this, I try to answer some of the critical questions that might be thought to make such research dubious. For the sake of clarity, I adopt a straightforward question-and-answer format.

CRITICAL QUESTIONS

1. *How do people become aware of the call of God?* For Kierkegaard, there is no one way in which this happens. For many people, the call of God is heard through a revelation from God. For Judaism, the Hebrew Bible constitutes such a revelation, and for Christians the historical figure of Jesus of Nazareth and the Christian Bible constitute such a revelation. Other major religions will, of course, have their own beliefs about what constitutes a special revelation from God. Kierkegaard also says that "to have a conscience is to have a God-relation," which implies that a more general revelation from God is given through human moral experience. Obviously, Kierkegaard is aware that conscience is formed in a human context and that there is there-

fore a good deal of relativity in our moral judgments. In and through that humanly formed conscience we sometimes become aware of what is truly good and truly evil, what is truly right and what is truly wrong, and when this occurs, we do hear the call of God.

Some interesting cross-cultural research has already been done by sociologist Rodney Stark on the impact of theistic belief on the way people make moral decisions, showing that people with a belief in God are less likely to engage in various forms of questionable behavior (Stark, 2003). Psychologists could build on this work, perhaps studying the way various spiritual practices, such as Bible reading, prayer, and meditation might affect moral behavior and the sense of "calling" that many people have.

2. Does Kierkegaard's view imply that a person must believe in God to be an authentic individual? If so, one might think that his view must be wrong because it seems evident that there are people who live authentically and care for their neighbors who do not believe in God, and also that some people who do believe in God do not truly love their neighbors. Kierkegaard's answer is that it is not simply propositional belief that God exists that is important. It is possible for people to have a relation to God and a kind of awareness of God's reality without realizing that it is God whom they are encountering. Because the conscience is the vehicle for a God-relation (see previous question), whenever people do, in and through their socially formed moral convictions, gain a genuine sense of true, absolute moral obligations, then they have an awareness of God's reality, although they may not be aware that it is God with whom they are dealing. Conversely, people may affirm in a propositional way that God exists without true awareness of God's character and the nature of God's call or without responding to that call in a proper manner.

Here the directions for research between religion and moral behavior run in both directions. One could study whether people who are altruistically inclined are more open to religious thinking than people who are more egoistic. Research could also be done as to whether religiously committed people (defined in a suitably complex way to reflect the idea of a sense of calling from God) are more likely to be altruistic.

3. Does not such a view justify the actions of a David Koresh or an Osama Bin Laden? It is certainly true that many evil actions are done in the name of God. Human beings are rarely able to do evil in a knowing, self-conscious way, which is itself testimony to the power of conscience. Rather, to do evil, humans generally first convince themselves that what they wish to do is good, either through self-deception or by succumbing to what we might call socially induced illusions. Hence, we should expect that humans will appeal to whatever is believed to be the highest and best to justify their actions. Often, although not always, that highest ideal will be religious in character. (It is worth noting, however, that Stalin killed millions in the name of a future ideal that was officially atheistic.)

It is important to distinguish two types of cases. Type 1 cases are cases in which people mistakenly believe God has called them to do what is evil. Within this class, we might distinguish culpable cases involving self-deception from cases in which individuals may have been socialized or even brainwashed to believe in the goodness of what they are doing. If God's call is an objective reality, this does not mean that humans cannot be mistaken about its character, as they are about many other things. Given our finitude and ethical shortcomings, I see no way we can completely prevent this kind of failure.

There might seem to be a second class of possible cases. What if God actually did call an individual to perform some horrible act? Would that make the act right? There are deep philosophical and theological issues in this neighborhood, and a full treatment would be extensive.[5] The following is merely a sketch of what I think should be said on the issue.

Why should humans be willing to follow the call of God? Kierkegaard's answer to this question does not appeal to God's power or to God's ability to reward and punish. Rather, his view is solidly rooted in the view that obligations are grounded in social relationships. I have an obligation to respect and care for parents who have loved and cared for me, precisely because of the relationship and history I have with them. I have an obligation to love my wife and be faithful to her because of the promises we have made to each other and our shared history. In a similar way, Kierkegaard argues that our obligation to obey God is grounded in the specific relationship we have with God, a relationship that is historical, beginning with our birth and continuing beyond our death. Just as the obligations romantic lovers have to each other are rooted in their history with each other, grounded in the promises they have made and the loving actions they have performed, so our duties to God are rooted in our history with God, a history that precedes any obligations created by human actions: "But that eternal love-history has begun much earlier; it began with your beginning, when you came into existence out of nothing, and just as surely as you do not become nothing, it does not end at a grave" (1847/1995, pp. 149–150). My obligations to God stem from the fact that God has created me and intends me to have a life of eternal happiness.

It is crucial that the God who has done this is a good God, a loving God. A God who is cruel or evil simply would have no claim on my allegiance. If this is correct, then we can be confident that God would not ask any human to commit an act that is genuinely evil. Furthermore, a being who asked us to do evil would forfeit any claim to our obedience; such a being would show himself (or herself) not to be the true God. Of course, this

---

[5]See chapter 12 of Robert Adams, *Finite and Infinite Goods* (Oxford, England: Oxford University Press, 1999), and chapter 13 of my own *Kierkegaard's Ethic of Love: Divine Commands and Moral Obligations* (Oxford, England: Oxford University Press, 2004) for fuller treatments of this issue.

does not mean that God cannot ask humans to do what may go counter to the social practices of a particular culture. God might inspire an individual to see that the sacrifice of children is wrong or that the burning of widows is wrong, even if this goes contrary to what has previously been believed in a particular society.

To conclude with the "payoff" from these reflections, research could be done on people who have a religious sense of calling to see whether there are significant differences between people in this category who perform evil actions (such as a David Koresh) and those who perform such actions as risking their own lives to protect the innocent. It would be helpful to know whether these two groups of people have significantly different conceptions of God and how each understands the notion of calling.

4. *Is the call of God only heard by a few exceptional individuals, or is it something relevant to ordinary people's lives?* The impact of the call of God is most evident in the lives of notable individuals such as Moses, Socrates, Jesus, St. Francis, and Gandhi. This is particularly the case for individuals who are the bearers of revelation, those who have had mystical experiences or special visions that are authentic. This does not mean that ordinary individuals cannot hear the call of God, however. I claimed (in answer to Question 1) that the call of God can often be heard in the voice of conscience, and this provides one way whereby ordinary individuals can discern the call of God.

It is also important to recognize that it is not just exceptional individuals who receive revelations from God. Rather, individuals such as Moses and Jesus receive revelations that they in turn pass on to others. Many Jews believe that the call of God can be heard in the Law of Moses. Christians believe that the call of God can be seen in the life, death, and resurrection of Jesus of Nazareth. Such revelations become embodied in the life of a historical community and are passed down to others. Thus, for many it is by participation in a community that the call of God is heard, and revelations are offered to many and not just the exceptional individual.

Research in this area could focus on the ways in which people gain a sense of calling from God and the prevalence of spiritual transformation on the part of people who have such a calling.

If there is a criticism to be made of Kierkegaard in his view of the relatedness in the human self, I would say that it is located here. Kierkegaard is sensitive to the ways in which human social relations can obscure and dim the voice of God by pressuring individuals to conform to social norms. He does not, however, emphasize the ways in which a human community can become a positive vehicle for hearing the call of God.[6] The call of God to the individual does not come only to people while they are alone, but can also come through the witness of a community that has preserved the revelation

---

[6]Here Kierkegaard could be complemented by the Jewish thinker Martin Buber (1970), who has written eloquently on how God can be found in relation to others.

of God. Even if that community often fails fully to realize the implications of the revelation they have transmitted, they can still be a vehicle for human selves to hear the call of God to become themselves. And the selves we are called to become—before God—are never isolated selves, but finally selves in community, that community that Christians call the kingdom of God.

REFERENCES

Aristotle. (1968). *Politics*. In R. McKeon (Ed.), *The basic writings of Aristotle*. New York: Random House. (Original work written c. 330 B.C.)

Bandura, A., & Walters, R. H. (1963). *Social learning and personality development*. New York: Holt, Rinehart & Winston.

Baumeister, R. F. (1982). A self-presentational view of social phenomena. *Psychological Bulletin, 91*, 3–26.

Baumeister, R. F. (1986). *Identity: Cultural change and the struggle for self*. New York: Oxford University Press.

Baumeister, R. F. (1991). *Meanings of life*. New York: Guilford Press.

Baumeister, R. F. (1998). The self. In D. Gilbert, S. Fiske, & G. Lindzey (Eds.), *Handbook of social psychology* (Vol. 1, pp. 680–740). Boston: McGraw-Hill.

Baumeister, R. F., & Cairns, K. J. (1992). Repression and self-presentation: When audiences interfere with self-deceptive strategies. *Journal of Personality and Social Psychology, 62*, 851–862.

Baumeister, R. F., Hutton, D. G., & Tice, D. M. (1989). Cognitive processes during deliberate self-presentation: How self-presenters alter and misinterpret the behavior of their interaction partners. *Journal of Experimental Social Psychology, 25*, 59–78.

Baumeister, R. F., & Leary, M. R. (1995). The need to belong: Desire for interpersonal attachments as a fundamental human motivation. *Psychological Bulletin, 117*, 497–529.

Baumeister, R. F., Stillwell, A. M., & Heatherton, T. F. (1994). Guilt: An interpersonal approach. *Psychological Bulletin, 115*, 243–267.

Bird, P. A. (1995). Sexual differentiation and divine image in the Genesis creation texts. In K. E. Borresen (Ed.), *Image of God and gender models in Judeo-Christian tradition* (pp. 5–28). Minneapolis, MN: Fortress Press.

Buber, M. (1970). *I and thou* (W. Kausmann, Trans.). New York: Scribner.

Duval, S., & Wicklund, R. A. (1972). *A theory of objective self-awareness*. New York: Academic Press.

Epstein, S. (1973). The self-concept revisited: Or a theory of a theory. *American Psychologist, 28*, 404–416.

Fazio, R. H., Effrein, E. A., & Falender, V. J. (1981). Self-perceptions following social interactions. *Journal of Personality and Social Psychology, 41*, 232–242.

Haight, M. R. (1980). *A study of self-deception*. Atlantic Highlands, NJ: Humanities Press.

Harter, S. (1987). The determinants and mediational role of global self-worth in children. In N. Eisenberg (Ed.), *Contemporary topics in developmental psychology* (pp. 219–242). New York: Wiley.

Hegel, G. W. F. (1977). *Phenomenology of spirit* (A. V. Miller, Trans.). New York: Oxford University Press. (Original work published 1807)

Heidegger, M. (1962). *Being and time* (J. MacQuarrie & E. Robinson,Trans.). New York: Harper & Row. (Original work published 1927)

Higgins, E. T. (1996). The "self-digest": Self-knowledge serving self-regulatory functions. *Journal of Personality and Social Psychology, 71*, 1062–1083.

Higgins, E. T., & Parsons, J. E. (1983). Social cognition and the social life of the child: Stages as subcultures. In E. T. Higgins, D. N. Ruble, & W. W. Hartup (Eds.), *Social cognition and social development* (pp. 15–62). New York: Cambridge University Press.

Hume, D. (1890). *A treatise of human nature.* Oxford, England: Clarendon Press. (Original work published 1739)

Kant, I. (1965). *Critique of pure reason* (N. K. Smith, Trans.). New York: St. Martin's Press. (Original work published 1789)

Kierkegaard, S. (1978). *Two ages* (H. V. Hong & E. H. Hong, Trans. and Eds.). Princeton, NJ: Princeton University Press. (Original work published 1846)

Kierkegaard, S. (1995). *Works of love: Some Christian reflections in the forms of discourses* (H. V. Hong & E. H. Hong, Trans. and Eds.). Princeton, NJ: Princeton University Press. (Original work published 1847)

Kierkegaard, S. (1980). *The sickness unto death* (H. V. Hong & E. H. Hong, Trans. and Eds.). Princeton, NJ: Princeton University Press. (Original work published 1849)

Kierkegaard, S. (1998). *The point of view for my work as an author* (H. V. Hong & E. H. Hong, Trans. and Eds.). Princeton, NJ: Princeton University Press. (Original work published 1859)

Lamm, H., & Myers, D. G. (1978). Group-induced polarization of attitudes and behavior. In L. Berkowitz (Ed.), *Advances in experimental social psychology* (Vol. 2, 145–195). New York: Academic Press.

Leary, M. R., Tambor, E. S., Terdal, S. K., & Downs, D. L. (1995). Self-esteem as an interpersonal monitor: The sociometer hypothesis. *Journal of Personality and Social Psychology, 68*, 518–530.

Maslow, A. H. (1968). *Toward a psychology of being* (2nd ed.). New York: Van Nostrand Reinhold.

McGinn, C. (1999). *The mysterious flame: Conscious minds in a material world.* New York: Basic Books.

Milgram, S. (1965). Some conditions of obedience and disobedience to authority. *Human Relations, 18*, 57–75.

Myers, D. (1980). *The inflated self: Human illusions and the biblical call to hope.* New York: Seabury Press.

Myers, D. (1992). *The pursuit of happiness.* New York: Morrow.

Myers, D. (2000a). The funds, friends, and faith of happy people. *American Psychologist, 55*, 56–67.

Myers, D. (2000b). Money and misery. In *The American paradox: Spiritual hunger in an age of plenty* (pp. 126–160). New Haven, CT: Yale University Press.

O'Collins, G. (1999). *The tripersonal God: Understanding and interpreting the trinity.* New York: Paulist Press.

Rogers, C. R. (1961). *On becoming a person.* New York: Houghton Mifflin.

Sartre, J. P. (1949). *No exit and three other plays.* New York: Vintage Books.

Sedikides, C. (1993). Assessment, enhancement, and verification determinants of the self-evaluation process. *Journal of Personality and Social Psychology, 65*, 317–338.

Shrauger, J. S., & Schoeneman, T. J. (1979). Symbolic interactionist view of self-concept: Through the looking glass darkly. *Psychological Bulletin, 86*, 549–573.

Stark, R. (2003). *For the glory of God: How monotheism led to reformation, witch-hunts, and the end of slavery.* Princeton, NJ: Princeton University Press.

Svenson, O. (1981). Are we all less risky and more skillful than our fellow drivers? *Acta Psychologica, 47*, 143–148.

Taylor, C. (1985). Self-interpreting animals. In *Human agency and language* (pp. 45–76). Cambridge, England: Cambridge University Press.

Tice, D. M. (1992). Self-presentation and self-concept change: The looking glass self is also a magnifying glass. *Journal of Personality and Social Psychology, 63*, 135–151.

Tice, D. M., & Baumeister, R. F. (2001). The primacy of the interpersonal self. In C. Sedikides & M. Brewer (Eds.), *Individual self, relational self, collective self: Partners, opposed, or ambiguous* (pp. 71–88). Philadelphia: Psychology Press.

Twenge, J. M., Catanese, K. R., & Baumeister, R. F. (2002). Social exclusion causes self-defeating behavior. *Journal of Personality and Social Psychology, 83*, 606–615.

5

STORY AND NARRATIVE

THOMAS H. BIEN

Now let us recite the story of Pesah as we find it in the Torah and in the writings of the Rabbis.

Once we were slaves unto Pharaoh in Egypt, but the Lord, our God, brought us forth with a strong hand and an outstretched arm.

—*The New Haggadah*, 1978

As a young child I asked an older person why the sky was blue. I received an answer of a scientific nature regarding dust particles and reflected light. I remember how this explanation affected me. Although I could not have begun to express the feeling at the time, it was one of vague disappointment. Somehow, that was not what I was really asking. It was not the kind of answer I was looking for.

The creation story in the first chapter of Genesis, the first book of the Bible, provides a different kind of answer about why the sky is blue. There we learn that God created heaven and earth. The account in Genesis is not a *creatio ex nihilo*, the appearance of matter out of nothing, but rather a story of bringing forth the basic conditions necessary for life out of a formless, chaotic void.[1] To accomplish this, God had to separate the water from the dry

---

[1]*Editors' Note:* The traditional Judeo-Christian view of creation is that God spoke the universe into existence out of nothing (Ross, 1988; Wenham, 1987). Despite the simplicity of the assertion in the opening verse, "In the beginning God created," there has been "a complex and protracted debate about the correct interpretation" (Wenham, 1987, p. 11) of the first three verses of Genesis. At issue is whether verse 1 describes a first act of creation and verses 2 and 3 describe subsequent phases of creation (the traditional view) or whether verse 1 is to be viewed as subordinate to verse 2's main clause, "the earth was without form and void." Helpful summaries of the major views are provided by Ross (1988, p. 718ff.) and Wenham (1987, p. 11ff.). Also, for brief discussions of alternative views of the literary genre of Genesis, see Cassuto (1972, pp. 1–19), Ross (1988, pp. 50–64), or Waltke (2001, pp. 73–78).

land, both horizontally and vertically. That is, on the horizontal plane, the seas had to be separated from the land masses, and on the vertical plane, the water above had to be separated from the land and water below by what the biblical author calls a firmament. Picture, if you will, a solid dome over a flat-disc earth, which keeps the water above from pouring down on us, maintaining the necessary conditions for life against the forces of primordial chaos. Because water is blue and the sky is also blue, and because sometimes water pours down on us from the sky, therefore, self-evidently, the sky must be water! Once, in the account of Noah, God allowed the forces of chaos to temporarily regain their aboriginal dominance, releasing water in life-destroying excess. God subsequently promised never to do this again, however, giving the rainbow as testimony.

If you consider the information at hand to ancient people, it would be difficult to create a more compelling explanation. As science, it is naïve. Most of us would agree there is no firmament holding back a body of water in the sky. Yet to view the creation story in Genesis as science misses the point. The writer of Genesis is not interested in providing a scientific account but wants us to know that the world does not exist by accident and that we do not exist by accident, that our life is made possible by the creator God. From the biblical writer's viewpoint, this is a species of truth far more important than an account of dust particles. In Genesis, we enter the realm of the *mythopoetic*, by which I do not mean something untrue but something that tells of deeper truth or ultimate truth, an account going beyond dry fact to satisfy the imagination, to feed the heart.

It is not necessary to have to choose between these two kinds of accounts, the scientific and the biblical. These are stories told for different purposes. If one's purpose is naturalistic explanation, there is no question which account suits the purpose better: The scientific account wins. But if one's purpose is to understand ultimate truth, to feed the heart as well as the mind, there is also no question which account better fits the bill. For that purpose, Genesis is by far the more satisfying.

In this chapter, I discuss story as a fundamental aspect of being human. Story can connect us with others and help create harmony and balance between the competing needs of the self. I show that in Jewish and Christian practice, this connecting aspect of story is tapped through retelling and ritual. Beyond this, some stories connect us with the transcendent. I also show how story and narrative are relevant to clinical practice, considering their relevance to reframing some commonly used clinical concepts in narrative terms, rewriting negative life stories, connecting with life purpose, using Jewish and Christian narrative themes in therapy, assessing a client's view of God, and a note about going beyond story. Finally, I make concrete recommendations concerning what psychologists can learn from story as it is used in Jewish and Christian tradition.

STORY IN HUMAN LIFE

The Human Being as Homo Narrator

In the early part of the 20th century, interest in narrative within the field of psychology was substantial (Polkinghorne, 1988). A narrative approach to understanding human nature, however, conflicted with the stringent tenets of observability, prediction, and control required by positivism and behaviorism as they increasingly dominated the middle third of the century. Since the advent of the cognitive revolution, there has been a revival of interest in narrative in psychology (Bruner, 1986, 1990, 2002; de Rivera & Sarbin, 1998; Hermans & Hermans-Jansen, 1995; Sarbin, 1986; Shafer, 1983; Spence, 1982). None of this interest taps specifically into the place that story and narrative have within the Judeo-Christian tradition.

In this chapter, I use the words *story* and *narrative* interchangeably to indicate sequential events related to each other in a way that produces a whole, whether fictional or nonfictional. Whatever the precise definition, the creation of stories is so fundamentally human that the case could be made to consider human beings not so much as *homo sapiens* but as *homo narrator*—as storytellers. Hermans and Hermans-Jansen (1995) described human beings as *motivated* storytellers. For these authors, the primary motivations in stories or narratives about the self are self-enhancement on the one hand, and connection and unity on the other. In other words, stories are always told for a certain purpose. The purpose at times may be simply to entertain. Whatever the purpose, there are no adequate criteria for evaluating a good story unless the purpose of its telling is considered.

Once we understand the purpose of a story, we hold the key to unlocking the text. The purpose of the author of the gospel of John does not conceal his motivation in recounting the ministry of Jesus. Acknowledging the incompleteness of his account and that Christ did many things besides those of which he wrote, he stated, "but these are written that you may believe that Jesus is the Christ" (John 20:31). For this purpose, his work is admirable. It may not, however, emphasize the kind of facts that a modern scientist or historian would most like to know.

There is abundant evidence that human beings are storytellers by nature. Ask someone about their life, and you will hear a story of victory and defeat, heroism and cowardice, loyalty and betrayal, joy and grief, struggle and peace. Even during sleep, the brain makes stories. In the activation-synthesis model Hobson (1988) suggested that dreams result from random firings of the pons organized by the brain into meaningful patterns. These patterns often take the form of a story. Jung's (1974) analysis showed complete dreams to have a narrative structure that includes four elements: exposition (setting), development of the plot, peripeteia (culmination of the plot in some decisive fashion), and lysis (solution or result). Indeed, these same four elements could be used as well to describe any narrative, not just dreams.

If telling stories is an essentially human activity and at the heart of how we understand the world, then our narrative capacity may even provide a key for understanding the scientific enterprise, in both how it is the same as and how it differs from our capacity for narrative. A psychological meaning of Genesis is that the world is constantly being created out of chaos. That is, the human brain is continually at work selecting which elements of experience to attend to and which to ignore. It could not possibly be otherwise. The flood of sensory input is immense and can only be sampled. Indeed, in telling a story about ourselves, even with no intention to prevaricate, there is often an underlying sense that our tale is not completely true in a hard-nosed, factual sense because we may be aware of selecting certain elements, enhancing some and eliminating others to suit the structure and purpose of our narrative. Thus, the great German writer Johann Wolfgang von Goethe called his autobiography *Dichtung und Wahrheit* (Poetry and Truth), acknowledging that the autobiographical task is never simply truth telling but is also a poetic, interpretive enterprise.

Although Bruner (1986) contrasted narrative thinking with logico-mathematical thinking, they are far from distant relations. Scientists carefully select which data they will concern themselves with and which they will deem irrelevant. This choice is guided by certain generally agreed-on principles. In the positivist tradition, the relevant data must be observable, repeatable, and so on. Furthermore, the selection of what to investigate is guided by assumptions of feasibility, such that, generally speaking, the outcomes of a new surgical technique may seem prima facie a more scientific enterprise than does the investigation of extrasensory perception. Yet once we understand that science is itself a kind of storytelling—broadly considered, a world-creating endeavor through a process of selection—there are two wonderful results: First, we as scientists can reexamine our assumptions and avoid tunnel vision. Second, we can be open to story, in the usual sense, as an important way, if not the primary way, of human knowing.

A narrative understanding provides psychology with a useful counterpoint to the bias favoring the *nomothetic* over the *idiographic*. If we understand all ways of knowing as world-creating processes, selecting information out of chaos to give it sense, meaning, and form, there is no particular reason to favor one of these broad classes of methodology over another. Instead, it depends on our *purpose*. Similarly, we might reexamine our reflexive discounting of "anecdotal" evidence, seeing it more as a particular type of evidence rather than evidence of an inherently inferior form. As I hinted previously, certain areas of inquiry may be reevaluated, such as the effects of prayer and religious faith, if, in fact, the essence of science is to transcend personal bias.

Connecting Self and Other

A shorthand summary of the psychological ills of our time might be found in the terms *fragmentation* and *alienation* (Bien & Bien, 2003). By *fragmentation*, I mean a split within us along any dimension. This may be, in psychoanalytic terms, a split between the needs of id and superego, or, more generally, a split between competing needs such as our need for self-enhancement in conflict with our need for connection; or yet again a split between competing roles (note that this is a dramatic term), as when we experience a tension between our desire to be a good parent and our desire to fulfill time-consuming career aspirations. By *alienation*, I intend a lack of connectedness. This can include a lack of felt connection between ourselves and the social world, between ourselves and the world of nature, between ourselves and the past or future, and between ourselves and the realm of meaning. These two difficulties may arguably account for the bulk of common psychological ills, both depressive and anxiety spectrum disorders.

In my view, clinical psychology excels primarily, although not exclusively, in providing help with problems of fragmentation. Many of our clinical interventions help the individual find a balance between competing needs of the self. Although there is some emphasis in clinical practice on the need for connection, overall we have less to say about that. Because it seems clear enough that social support inoculates against a variety of ills (e.g., Baron et al., 1990; Berkman & Syme, 1979; Jemmott et al., 1990), we may recommend that clients seek to create this in their lives. Clinicians may also teach assertiveness and social skills. This scarcely touches the kind of connectedness available through religious and spiritual teaching, however.

One way that religions in general, and the Judeo-Christian tradition in particular, provide help with alienation is by connecting people with stories larger than themselves. In the Judeo-Christian tradition, I experience myself not only as a nonfragmented, relatively harmonious whole, and not only as connected to my family history, but also as connected to a much larger story—the story of the Jewish people or the story of Christ—more generally, the story of God's salvific work in history. This connects me in the present time both with my faith community and with the community that existed before me and that will exist after me, what Christians call the "communion of saints."

Telling the Story in Ritual

Over the centuries, the Judeo-Christian tradition has developed its own powerful technology of change and healing, and much of this revolves around the telling of the story. The simplest of these is the reading and contemplating of the story itself, in Scripture, in rabbinical literature such as the Talmud, in the Apocrypha, and in the lives of the saints. All Jewish and Christian traditions include this aspect. To a more variable degree, Jews and Christians have also developed *rituals* that symbolically reenact the story to appropriate it personally. Through ritual, I come to see the story not just as involving people long ago and far away, but as *my own* story, a story of which I am very much a part. Theologians call this *anamnesis*, a remembering of the story in a way that forges a sense of personal connection.

The classic examples of anamnesis are the Passover ritual for the Jew and Holy Communion or the Eucharist for the Christian. The *Haggadah*, a text used for the ritual reenactment of Passover, is itself a study in how to tell a story in a way that helps the reader appropriate it as one's own. Special foods are eaten, many of which are given symbolic interpretations. Why do we eat unleavened bread (matzo) at Passover? In the *Haggadah*, we learn that we eat it in remembrance of the haste with which we had to leave Egypt, having no time to let the loaves rise. Why do we eat bitter herbs? We do this to remember the bitterness of slavery. Children are involved in answering special questions and in a special game of hide and seek with a piece of matzo called the *afikomen*. Everyone is given the opportunity to share the leadership and to be actively involved in the process. Familiar songs are sung, triggering comforting associations going back to childhood. Informal family history and legend are recounted. Every sense modality is engaged to create involvement and help participants see themselves as belonging to this larger story. The strength of this ritual may be a significant part of how the Jewish people survived the Diaspora and centuries of persecution. For to participate in the Seder is to know who you are and to know your connection to the larger story of God's salvific work in the history of the Jewish people.

The most nearly comparable rite for Christians, growing directly out of the Passover tradition, is the Eucharist (meaning thanksgiving) or Communion (highlighting connection). The Eucharist recalls the last night Jesus spent with his disciples, an event which all four canonical gospels connect with Passover. Here the meaning of the Passover meal called the Seder is reinterpreted to involve an ongoing connection between the Christian and Christ. The exact nature of this connection is interpreted differently, ranging from pure anamnesis to the traditional Roman Catholic doctrine of *transubstantiation*, meaning that the bread and wine are literally transformed into the body and blood of Christ. (This is believed to occur when the priest says *Hoc est corpus meum*, "this is my body," which is the origin of the expression, hocus pocus.) The point in all traditions is that Christ is truly present and available to the participant in this ritual. As in the Seder, so also in the Eucharist special words are read, special music is sung, special food is eaten, and in some cases special smells (incense) are used as well, making it a full-spectrum sensory experience. Christians who participate deeply in this ritual *know* themselves to be a part of the Christian story, in a way going beyond intellectual knowing.

Connecting With the Transcendent

From the perspective of faith, these stories and their ritual enactments do more than just connect the participant with a tradition and a past, present, and future community. They also directly connect the participant with the transcendent. This is an aspect of overcoming alienation through connectedness that psychology cannot—and perhaps should not—attempt to duplicate. This does not mean it cannot be explored, as the tradition of William James (1902/1985) shows. Jewish tradition generally does not try to describe God directly (Fromm, 1966) because God, as the ultimate reality, is ultimately ineffable, and to a large extent Christians have continued this tradition. Instead, the answer to what God is like is most often given in narrative form. We were slaves in Egypt, and God led us into freedom. We were lost until found by Christ.

THERAPEUTIC USES OF NARRATIVE

Reframing Clinical Concepts as Narrative Structures

Two examples of clinical concepts that can be reenvisioned through a narrative understanding are *irrational beliefs* (Beck, 1976; Burns, 1980; Ellis & Dryden, 1987) and *schemas* (Young & Klesko, 1993). Irrational beliefs in the realm of cognitive therapy are understood as errors in logic. The problem is that the client is in some way thinking incorrectly or irrationally. The solution, therefore, is to teach the client to think differently (i.e., more rationally), which will result in the client also feeling and behaving differently.

This is clearly a *homo sapiens* model of human beings. Human beings are seen as logicians, in this case, faulty ones. Although this kind of treatment has been found effective, its effectiveness might be extended if the model more fully incorporated not only the logical reasoning faculty of human beings but also their storytelling capacity. An irrational belief such as, "I must always be liked by everyone" can then be understood not just as faulty logic but as a crystallized, frozen story. The job of the clinician becomes, then, not so much a matter of arguing against this as poor logic (although of course this can be included as well) as it is of unpacking the story. The clinician then can help the client understand where this story came from, what its origins are, and how this story continues to unfold in daily life. In its crystallized, concentrated form, the story is unassailable. But once one comes to see that this is a storied view, a way of selecting and editing past experience, it becomes open to revision.

Schemas are even more directly related to narrative. An abandonment schema, for example, is quite clearly a story that runs something like, "People I depend on always leave me in the end." By unpacking the account of how this story began, it can become more fluid, more capable of reorganization. Viewing schemas and irrational beliefs as narrative elements more than logical ones may provide a helpfully different perspective.

Rewriting Negative Stories

Every clinician is aware of the power of negative story as well. Clients who say they are losers are also telling a story about themselves. They are preselecting certain kinds of experience and information that fit this crystallized narrative, and rejecting those that do not fit. Such stories also come to function as self-fulfilling prophecies. Believing oneself to be a loser, one comes to act as such, and therein perpetuates the very narrative theme one wants to change. Perhaps also, as Hermans and Hermans-Jansen suggested (1995), such negative themes serve a protective function: Believing myself to be a loser, I have a measure of protection from future disappointment because I do not expect anything better.

Negative stories can involve negative connectedness as well as negative identity. That is to say, I may evaluate myself in a negative way, but I may also evaluate my family or my faith community in a negative light. Psychologists can expand their work not only by rewriting story themes involving negative self-identity but also by helping clients revise negative connectedness elements in stories. In fact, the kind of story developed in therapy may initially increase the importance of self-identity at the expense of connectedness, in effect telling clients not to be so hard on themselves because their parents and other important people were ultimately to blame. Although this may be legitimate as a phase of retelling a client's story, if it stops there, only building identity at the expense of connection, the clinician has merely assisted in reassigning blame and may have created as many problems as were solved. False memory syndrome is just one of the more extreme examples of this problem.

There is a realism in the Judeo-Christian tradition about negative connectedness. In the book of Exodus (34:7) it is written that, although God is gracious and merciful, the iniquity of the fathers will be visited upon the children to the third and fourth generations. As a statement of justice, of course, this is problematic. But as a statement of psychological truth, it is unfortunately all too valid. Problems that parents carry unresolved may indeed be passed on to children and grandchildren. The narrative strategy for the psychotherapist in this situation may involve helping people see themselves as transitional persons, a form of the hero (Campbell, 1949), doing the necessary work of change and growth so that the problem is not reenacted by future generations.

A different kind of problem that clients may demonstrate is an addiction to drama. This is a hallmark of many personality disorders (Lester, 2002). People with borderline personality disorder, for example, may seem more interested in perpetuating a self-destructive drama than they are in solving their problems in living. Perhaps it will make sense to help such individuals connect with a different kind of story, substituting calmer, more growth-enhancing themes for their destructive soap opera themes. If human beings are storytellers, it may be more plausible to substitute positive stories than to attempt to deprive a person of story through logical argument. Research and treatment in the area of personality disorders may find this a fruitful realm for further investigation.

Teleological Perspective: Finding Life Purpose

Stories and narratives convey a sense of motion, of movement toward some resolution rather than stasis. They are novels rather than poems, motion pictures rather than still photographs. The Judeo-Christian story moves toward shalom or peace, toward the Kingdom of God, toward salvation and healing. Clinicians can use this quality of story to help clients envision what their current difficulties may be moving them toward. After empathically listening to the narrative of what the present difficulties are and how they came to be, at some point one can pose questions such as, "Where might this be leading?" or "What kind of qualities would the resolution of these difficulties require you to bring forth in yourself?" As a clinician, I have found these questions quite useful. Even when they do not generate an immediate answer, one can witness a shift in the client's perspective on the problem as they begin to view it—perhaps for the first time—as potentially leading somewhere and containing positive possibilities.

USING CLASSIC JUDEO-CHRISTIAN THEMES IN PSYCHOTHERAPY

The major themes of Judeo-Christian narrative are not the exclusive property of Jews and Christians but reflect themes that are universally human. More than that, even with people outside this tradition, these themes are omnipresent in Western culture, structuring the way we see life and the nature of the questions we raise. In a psychotherapy context with individuals who identify with Jewish or Christian tradition, these themes are directly applicable. The religiously sensitive therapist may be able to help clients sort out where such themes are being used in an unhealthy way and redirect the client toward alternate strands of the tradition that may be more helpful. Even with those outside these traditions, the same themes may present themselves in nonreligious guise. Being alert to this possibility may still be advantageous, although the themes will require nonreligious framing. For this reason, the exploration of such themes and their relationship to health and pathology is no minor issue. Following are some themes worth considering.

Slavery and Freedom

As shown in the epigraph at the beginning of this chapter, this is a major theme in Jewish tradition. Although we still hear occasional news reports of slavery or slaverylike conditions, these forms are generally unlike the institutionalized version of slavery in times past. Yet even apart from literal slavery, human beings continue to be enslaved by oppressive forces. The Judeo-Christian narrative insists that God desires our freedom, and this includes freedom from oppressive social forces as well as freedom from the internal oppression of anxiety, depression, self-doubt, or an addictive process.

An important part of freedom is not just freedom *from*, however, but freedom *to*. Freedom ultimately involves moving toward shalom or the Kingdom of God—toward a state of positive fulfillment, well-being, and peace. This theme is consistent with the growing emphasis on positive psychology (e.g., Seligman, 2002).

Idolatry and Monotheism

The types of idolatry that bind us today have little to do with idols and the original concerns of the Jewish people. "Our fearsome gods," wrote Carl Jung (1953), "have only changed their names: they now rhyme with ism." In addition to being trapped by our ideology, we are trapped by anything occupying a position of unmerited centrality. Materialism, nationalism, hedonism, conservatism or liberalism, and so on, when pushed to fanatical extremes, can all too readily supply tragic examples of the devastation that occurs when something other than God lies at the center of human life. In the Judeo-Christian view, it is only by giving God this central place that we can be prevented from succumbing to these fearsome modern-day idols. This theme may apply to people outside of the Judeo-Christian faith just as well in the sense that, unless one has some higher, self-transcending purpose or ideal, life lacks a center of meaning and may be vulnerable to imbalance. Both in clinical work and in research, it may be important to track what is central in people's lives, and the extent to which what they say is central may be in tension with how they invest their time and energy. The extent to which there is such a discrepancy may correlate with problems of alienation and fragmentation.

Lost and Found

Jesus' own teaching was often in the form of parables, and of these, one of his favorite themes was that of lost and found. Parables following this theme include the parables of the lost coin, the lost sheep, and the lost son.

A related theme occurs in the light that has lost its shine (because it is hidden), and the salt that has lost its taste.

From developmental psychology, it is clear that the importance given this theme is not accidental. It may explain why, for example, children delight in playing peek-a-boo. Young children can find fun in the endless repetition of the process of being found, over and over again. Some of the games of older children involve this theme as well, hide-and-seek being one example.

Many of the stories clients tell can be traced along these thematic lines. Clients feel lost and seek direction and purpose, suggesting the importance of metaphors such as finding one's way or path in clinical practice. Clients want to be found, to be seen behind their masks, to be valued for who they really are and not just seen as a case or a disorder.

Life and Death

To be alive is different from simply existing. When Moses proclaims to the people, "See, I have set before you this day life and good, death and evil" (Deut. 30:15), or when Jesus declares that he came so his followers might have life (John 10:10), both are talking about a quality of life that is meaningful, connected, and full of shalom. Such fullness of life is established, in the Judeo-Christian view, only by making God central. The idols to which we cling bring anxiety, disconnection, fragmentation, death. Paradoxically, placing God at the center can even produce life out of apparent death. The story of Abraham is replete with the theme of letting go of the old life to find a new life with God in the land of promise. In the Christian gospels, resurrection is necessarily preceded by crucifixion. By letting go of our own life, our clinging to a narrow existence, we are born into a new quality of life. Similarly, the client struggling to make a significant life change is often involved in a frightening process of letting go of the old (death) and moving toward the new (life). In the classroom, students presented with new ways of understanding the world can also go through a kind of death and rebirth, as is certainly the case with seminary students who are exposed, perhaps for the first time, to the historical-critical method of interpreting the Bible, or with psychology students as they learn to challenge cultural assumptions about human beings and their behavior.

For people with a meaningful connection to their Jewish or Christian faith, it may be possible to discuss what they are clinging to and whether they experience this as truly life enhancing, or death dealing. The theme of death and resurrection is a universal one, found in many cultures (Campbell, 1988), and we can therefore expect it to operate in those who do not identify with Judaism or Christianity as well as in those who do. What are the central values to which people cling? What is the result—life or death? Placing drug use at the center of our lives leads in one kind of direction; placing service to others at the center leads in another.

Sin and Grace

These themes are discussed elsewhere in this volume. Let me just add in this context that the deep theological meaning of Sin (capital S) is often obscured by the focus on sins. In other words, Sin is a theological way of describing alienation from the Divine Ground of our being. It is a state of disconnection and fragmentation. This is a much more profound concept than rule violations, although there is of course some connection between the two. Psychotherapy clients with neurotic guilt may benefit from focusing more on the larger theme of overcoming alienation rather than rule violation.

Grace, conversely, concerns the receiving of unmerited aid or blessing. All of us exist to some extent in a state of alienation and fragmentation. Yet all of us have also encountered help along the way, sometimes when least expected. Clinicians should be alert for opportunities to help clients note moments of grace, whether theologically conceived or not. Moments of quantum change (Miller & C'de Baca, 2001) are only the most dramatic of these. This theme suggests the healing power of gratitude and is fertile soil for psychological exploration.

Incarnation

Much Christian thinking has emphasized sin and redemption and God's payment of the unpayable debt, themes contained in the writings of such early Christian thinkers as Paul, Augustine, and Anselm. These terms have become tainted for many people to such a degree that they have become difficult to hear. An equally valid strand of Christian tradition, however, is incarnational theology. In essence, what incarnational theology does is answer the question, where is God?

Elie Wiesel is a well-known Jewish teacher and Holocaust survivor. In the moving story of his experiences in a Nazi concentration camp (Wiesel, 1960), he described the senseless and tragic hanging of a beautiful youth. The other prisoners were forced to parade past the victim and his two similarly executed companions. Horribly, Wiesel recounted that because the young boy was so slight, it took a long time for the weight of his body to kill him. When Wiesel walked past, the boy was still alive. Someone among the prisoners cried out, "Where is God?" Wiesel wrote that a voice within him answered, "Where is he? Here He is—He is hanging here on the gallows." Both the Jewish and the Christian answers are ultimately that God is right there, hanging from that cruel gallows. God is most present where suffering is greatest.

In Christian theology and reflection, incarnational theology means in essence that God encounters humanity in Christ, who was, as the intellectually torturous creedal affirmations of the early church councils affirm, fully human as well as fully divine. In other words, it is this very human life of ours wherein we meet the sacred. We meet God in our work, in our families, in our struggles, in our joys. We meet God on the freeway, in the airport, with the rude receptionist, in the morning shower. An incarnational understanding of ascetism emphasizes that meeting the difficulties of our own lives with faith and courage is sufficient without imposing artificial discipline. Incarnational theology is a supreme affirmation of our humanity. It relates to the theme of humanity's creation in the image of God and represents a rich contact point between humanism and Western religious tradition.

A People of the Lord or *the* People of the Lord

Psychotherapy and psychological research are not value-free (Bergin & Garfield, 1994). In accord with Richards and Bergin's (1997) recommendation to make values explicit, I would like to mention one that I think is vital in today's historical context and to propose that one element of a healthy religion and spirituality concerns how individuals of one tradition view individuals of other traditions or of no tradition. The birth of the Judeo-Christian tradition was essentially a *tribal* affair. What functioned adequately in such a historical context may not always function adequately in a context that is increasingly *global*. In Jewish tradition, there is an underlying tension between being *a* people of the Lord and *the* people of the Lord, a dilemma that Christians inherited and continued. Yet the central texts of both Jewish and Christian traditions bespeak a God of love, which means far more than just tolerating or putting up with people who view things differently. In a post-September 11 world, it is crucial to establish an understanding that goes beyond a sense of safe superiority to true openness and learning from other traditions. The belief in the unquestionable superiority of one's own creed already contains the seed of violence. Terrorism, whether in the form of the modern Islamic martyr or the medieval Christian crusader, is arguably the ultimate consequence of an unquestioning belief in the superiority of one's own religious (and sometimes nonreligious) viewpoint.

THE CLIENT'S VIEW OF GOD

To understand a complex narrative requires a consideration of central principles. The Jewish and Christian scriptures are complex and diverse, spanning the gamut from the existentialism of the writer of Ecclesiastes to the bare-bones historical accounts of Chronicles, to profound statements of faith and love. It is impossible to approach this material and give equal weight to all parts. Deuteronomy, for example, enjoins the people of Israel to a jihad against the people already dwelling in the Promised Land, saying, "you must utterly destroy them." (Deut. 7:2). The Psalmist (137:9) gleefully writes of the enemies of God, "Happy shall he be who takes your little ones and dashes them against the rock!" Most theologians understand that these and other passages must be understood in light of their *Sitz im Leben*, the historical and cultural context of the faith community in which they originated. They also must be seen in terms of their accord with central interpretive principles. For Christian and Jew alike, God is above all a God of love and grace.

One way to assess the health of an individual's faith is to listen for that person's central principles. A commonsense and testable hypothesis is that those whose emphasis is on love and grace may be more emotionally healthy than those who give centrality to anger, vengeance, or judgment. The life narrative of the individual person may connect with their faith tradition in unhealthy as well as healthy ways. For example, depressed, highly self-critical people may readily accept themselves as sinners but find difficulty connecting to God's grace. Such individuals confuse a theological reality (Sin) with a psychological one (e.g., depression or low self-esteem) and may need help to reconnect to central themes of God's self-giving love and grace.

BEYOND STORY

As shown here, story or narrative does not have exclusively positive potentialities but negative ones as well. Those who adopt a central hermeneutic for their own lives of abandonment (lost rather than found), for example, are writing a negative story, attending more to life events that confirm this point of view and largely ignoring experiences that disconfirm it.

Less recognizable, however, is that even positive stories may function in undesirable ways. Individuals who see themselves in a self-aggrandizing way are constructing life narratives that do not generate much internal distress (fragmentation) but that may nonetheless be problematic in other ways, such as in their connection with others (alienation).

Understanding the storied nature of human beings reveals that we are always constructing stories, selecting some and ignoring other aspects of our experience, and trying to place the selected information into a sequential and coherent whole. The test of an adequate story from a psychological perspective may be its functionality rather than its reliability in terms of ultimate truth. Yet most world religions have a name for that which goes beyond such selective knowing to a kind of ultimate knowing. Hindus call it *moksha* and Buddhists *nirvana*. This is referred to in Judeo-Christian tradition as the Kingdom of Heaven, or as Paul expressed it, the "peace beyond understanding" (Philippians 4:7). In this realm, we no longer see in a mirror dimly (I Corinthians 13:12) but know fully in a way beyond normal knowing. Those who have experienced this state of being, such as the Jewish and Christian mystics, describe it in a way that contains enough regularity across individual descriptions to obviate casual dismissal. Indeed, Miller and C'de Baca (2001) made an excellent return to this kind of exploration, restoring a tradition in psychology going back to its origins as a separate discipline (James, 1902/1985).

RECOMMENDATIONS FOR PSYCHOLOGISTS

Familiarity with Judeo-Christian narrative and the recognition of the centrality of this aspect of our humanity can be helpful to psychologists in a number of ways.

1. In general, if we are storytelling beings, we can learn much about human psychology through increased research in the area of narrative. Existing research may be just the beginning.
2. Before the stranglehold of positivism on psychological inquiry, there was a flourishing interest in narrative (Polkinghorne, 1988). Some of this work may be worth reconsideration. To give just one example, psychologists might reconsider Murray's (1938) work on the Thematic Apperception Test. Methods currently in use are of obvious value, but without supplementation through other forms of inquiry, the current methods are limited and may even represent a kind of "methodolatry."
3. Schemas and irrational cognitions might be reframed as crystallized, concentrated story elements. Reexamination of current approaches such as cognitive therapy, schema therapy, or interpersonal therapy from the perspective of story might provide fruitful new avenues for understanding human beings when seen in the context of narrative.
4. People trained in the human sciences and familiar with research have acquired the capacity to examine statistical data and their attendant tests of significance and make meaning out of them. It is easy for us to forget that these numbers do not always tell a meaningful story to people outside our own discipline. Many psychotherapists have probably been in the situation of citing a research finding to a client only to have it be rejected by a client's anecdotal experience. Likewise, in teaching psychology, we encounter the student who challenges our nomothetic and probabilistic statements with their own individual experience, as when, for example, a teacher says children of an alcoholic parent are at greater risk than others for alcoholism, and the student replies, "That can't be true.

My friend's father is an alcoholic, but my friend doesn't even drink."

When we present our information to a world not educated in our methodology, it may help to remember that anecdotal evidence in the form of a narrative may often be more persuasive to the nonscientist than the best experimental evidence. When psychologists write self-help books or summarize information for the general public or testify in a court or before a senate committee, we would do well to remember that people are moved by stories. Rather than abandoning our numerical data, we should instead remember to supplement it by telling the human story behind the data.

5. Because psychologists are also human beings (*contra opinionem omnium*), perhaps it would be useful for us as well to include stories in our research reports. In reports of clinical findings, for example, one could include a brief narrative of a typical case, as well as those that are atypically positive or negative in outcome, using the narrative format to explore what went wrong and what went right and to generate new hypotheses. I would like to see a time when this became as standard a practice as tests of statistical significance.

6. Relegitimizing the study of narrative puts psychology in direct touch with other human sciences and humanities and can help overcome the compartmentalism into which our field and others have fallen. Dialogue with anthropologists, mythologists, philologists, historians, and others becomes possible again. Not the least of these others would be theologians, many of whom know little about post-Freudian psychology and about whose valuable work many psychologists know little. This contact and interplay might be extremely fertile ground for all involved.

7. There are almost too many possibilities to mention for psychological investigation and clinical reflection, such as, What is the relationship between the deep appropriation of a faith tradition as one's own and psychological well-being or pathology? What factors determine whether people successfully appropriate this material in such a way? Are there specific narrative themes within the tradition that are positively or negatively correlated with psychological health? Under what conditions might the same narrative themes correlate positively or negatively with health or well-being? How are the themes of the Judeo-Christian cultural worldview implicitly present in our operating assumptions as researchers or clinicians and in our research participants and clients?

EPILOGUE

There is an old hymn called, "I Love to Tell the Story." It is a Victorian-era piece, full of syrup and sentiment. I can still hear my mother's thin, sweet voice singing it at the kitchen sink when I was a child. I can hear, too, the sound of a large Methodist congregation singing it with full-throated organ accompaniment. Yet if the hymn is sentimental, in a sense that is exactly the point. Stories are full of feeling, cognitive and emotive at the same time. Indeed, human life itself is always both, and the separation of thought and emotion is only a convenient abstraction. Our stories, which contain both, are always part of us, and part of what it means to be human. Perhaps the most essential part.

REFERENCES

Baron, R. S., Cutrona, C. E., Hicklin, D., Russel, D. W., & Lubaroff, D. M. (1990). Social support and immune function among spouses of cancer patients. *Journal of Personality and Social Psychology, 59,* 344–352.

Beck, A. T. (1976). *Cognitive therapy and the emotional disorders.* New York: International Universities Press.

Bergin, A. E., & Garfield, S. L. (Eds.). (1994). *Handbook of psychotherapy and behavior change* (4th ed.). New York: Wiley.

Berkman, L., & Syme, S. L. (1979). Social networks, host resistance, and mortality: A nine-year follow up study of Alameda County residents. *American Journal of Epidemiology, 109,* 186–204.

Bien, T. H., & Bien, B. (2003). *Finding the center within: The healing way of mindfulness meditation.* New York: Wiley.

Bruner, J. (1986). *Actual minds, possible worlds.* Cambridge, MA: Harvard University Press.

Bruner, J. (1990). *Acts of meaning.* Cambridge, MA: Harvard University Press.

Bruner, J. (2002). *Making stories: Law, literature, and life.* New York: Farrar, Straus & Giroux.

Burns, D. B. (1980). *Feeling good: The new mood therapy.* New York: Avon Books.

Campbell, J. (1949). *The hero with a thousand faces.* New York: Pantheon Books.

Campbell, J. (with Moyers, B.). (1988). *The meaning of myth.* New York: Doubleday.

Cassuto, U. (1972). *From Adam to Noah: A commentary on the book of Genesis.* Jerusalem: Hebrew University.

de Rivera, J., & Sarbin, T. R. (Eds.). (1998). *Believed-in imaginings: The narrative construction of reality.* Washington, DC: American Psychological Association.

Ellis, A., & Dryden, W. (1987). *The practice of rational emotive therapy.* New York: Springer Publishing Company.

Fromm, E. (1966). *You shall be as gods: A radical interpretation of the Old Testament and its tradition.* New York: Holt.

Hermans, H. J. M., & Hermans-Jansen, E. (1995). *Self-narratives: The construction of meaning in psychotherapy.* New York: Guilford Press.

Hobson, J. A. (1988). *The dreaming brain.* New York: Basic Books.

James, W. R. (1985). *The varieties of religious experience.* Cambridge, MA: Harvard University Press. (Original work published 1902)

Jemmott, J. B., III, Hellman, C., McClelland, D. C., Locke, S. E., Kraus, L. J., Williams, R. M., & Valeri, C. R. (1990). Motivational syndromes associated with natural killer cell activity. *Journal of Behavioral Medicine, 13,* 53–73.

Jung, C. G. (1953). *Two essays on analytical psychology.* Princeton, NJ: Bollingen.

Jung, C. G. (1974). *Dreams.* Princeton, NJ: Bollingen.

Lester, G. (2002, December). *Personality disorders in social work and health care.* Presentation, Albuquerque, NM.

Miller, W. R., & C'de Baca, J. (2001). *Quantum change.* New York: Guilford Press.

Murray, H. A. (1938). *Explorations in personality.* New York: Oxford University Press.

Polkinghorne, D. E. (1988). *Narrative knowing and the human sciences.* Albany: State University of New York Press.

Richards, P. S., & Bergin, A. E. (1997). *A spiritual strategy for counseling and psychotherapy.* Washington, DC: American Psychological Association.

Ross, A. P. (1988). *Creation and blessing: A guide to the study and exposition of the book of Genesis.* Grand Rapids, MI: Baker.

Sarbin, T. R. (Ed.). (1986). *Narrative psychology: The storied nature of human conduct.* New York: Praeger Publishers.

Seligman, M. E. P. (2002). *Authentic happiness: Using the new positive psychology to realize your potential for lasting fulfillment.* New York: Free Press.

Shafer, R. (1983). *The analytic attitude.* New York: Basic Books.

Spence, D. P. (1982). *Narrative truth and historical truth: Meaning and interpretation in psychoanalysis.* New York: Norton.

Waltke, B. K. (2001). *Genesis: A commentary.* Grand Rapids, MI: Zondervan.

Wenham, G. J. (1987). *Word biblical commentary, Vol. 1: Genesis 1–15.* Waco, TX: Word.

Wiesel, E. (1960). *Night.* New York: Bantam Books.

Young, J. E., & Klesko, J. S. (1993). *Reinventing your life: How to break free from negative life patterns.* New York: Dutton.

III

MOTIVATION, VIRTUES, AND VALUES

6

THE ROLE OF SEXUALITY IN PERSONHOOD: AN INTEGRATIVE EXPLORATION

STANTON L. JONES AND HEATHER R. HOSTLER

The premise of this chapter is that psychological science and practice can be (and, to some extent, have been) enriched through a sustained dialogue with religion about the nature of the human condition. This chapter presents reflections about one aspect of the human condition, our sexuality, as a case study of just such a dialogue.

Those who would argue that no such dialogue is possible would do so on the presumption that the respective natures of psychology (as a science) and of the religions (as something distinctly other than science) would make such a dialogue meaningless or that, on putatively historical grounds, the relationship between science and religion has been one of "warfare" and that science only prospers as it distances itself from religion. The latter argument has been thoroughly refuted by such outstanding work in the history of science as that of Brooke (1991) and Lindberg (1992; Lindberg & Numbers, 1986) showing that science and religion, generally, have not been "at war" and that religious belief and practice have served in certain cases to facilitate the progress of science.

Regarding the former argument, we have suggested that a sophisticated understanding of the nature of science and of the religions establishes the possibility for such a meaningful dialogue even while respecting the distinctive identities of science and religion (Jones, 1994, 2000). One key component of such a justification would include recognition of the cognitively meaningful, propositional (or declarative) dimension of religious belief. It is, in fact, a distortion to treat the religions as noncognitive phenomena of an exclusively intuitive or experiential nature that make no claims about reality. Nevertheless, such declarative aspects of religious belief, as we see here, can be complex, inconsistent, and vague, not unlike those of psychological paradigms.

A second key to justifying the legitimacy of this dialogue involves the recognition that a variety of metaphysical statements or commitments (Mahrer, 2000; O'Donohue, 1989) shape the practice of science. Two recent articles have provided support for the claim that such metaphysical statements, including religious beliefs, often are a factor in the shaping of the conceptualizations of the subject matter on which psychological research and practice are built. Sampson (2000) focused directly on the "role of religion in setting the terms" of the entire discipline of psychology for the conceptualization of a fundamental dimension of personhood, namely, whether we adopt a "collectivist or an individualistic understanding of the person–other relationship" (p. 1425). Contrary to the standard account contrasting supposed Western Judeo-Christian individualism with Eastern Buddhist collectivism, Sampson contrasted Protestant Christian individualism with Judaic-Rabbinic collectivism. He discussed the tendency for psychologists to underestimate the impact of religion on culture, arguing that key assumptions that shape our research programs are influenced by religious conceptions and convictions. Specifically, "the very choice of the individual as the central object of psychological study and the key to unlocking the mysteries of human nature is supported by a set of assumptions that are derived in great measure from a particular configuration of religious beliefs and values, primarily Christian" (Sampson, 2000, p. 1426).

Although we support the broad contours of his argument, we disagree with two aspects of Sampson's analysis. First, we would question whether Protestant Christianity per se really is the source of the type of individualism of which he writes. Instead, we would postulate that the religious roots of this pervasive individualism were in the 19th-century deistic–rationalistic–modernistic (and hence individualistic) amalgam that Ingraffia (1995) called "ontotheology" and against which the founders of postmodern theory—Nietzsche, Heidegger, and Derrida (who all mistakenly called this ontotheology "Christianity")—were in reaction. This ontotheology was profoundly non-Christian or sub-Christian in nature. Second, we would thus quibble with the contention that psychology "is a field in which the underlying conception of human nature and the understanding of the nature of the individual, its primary object of study, have been significantly affected by the same nexus of Protestant Christian values and beliefs" (Sampson, 2000, p. 1426). We would argue instead that psychology has been much more profoundly affected by this deistic–rationalistic–modernistic ontotheology than by Protestantism. Although profoundly agreeing that religious beliefs have been influential in shaping the terms of psychology's engagement with this issue, we disagree with Sampson's analysis of which types of beliefs have had this influence.

A second example is Redding (2001), who made the provocative suggestion that political ideology can function in much the same way as religion (as we, Sampson, and others have argued) in shaping the ways we conceive of problems in our discipline. Redding suggests that background assumptions of a political nature (and his argument works for religion as well) shape what we simply assume versus what we deem as requiring explanation, what we construe as a legitimate question and a legitimate answer to that question and what we deem to be methodology suitable for providing a valid answer:

> how one defines a problem goes a long way in determining the proposed solution. . . . sociopolitical biases influence the questions asked, the research methods selected, the interpretation of research results, the peer review process, judgments about research quality, and decisions about whether to use the research in policy advocacy. (Redding, 2001, p. 206)

Redding argues that only by expanding the ideological vision, the array of ideological background assumptions stimulating psychological research and application can the field truly serve the public well and embody liberal learning.

With Redding, Sampson, and philosopher of science Mary Midgley, we would argue that we

> have a choice of what myths, what visions we will use to help us understand the physical world [i.e., the subject matter of science]. We do not have a choice of understanding it without using any myths or visions at all. Again, we have a real choice between becoming aware of these myths and ignoring them. If we ignore them, we travel blindly inside myths and visions which are largely provided by other people. This makes it much harder to know where we are going. (Midgley, 1992, p. 13)

Even so, as psychologists we must recognize that the success of any such dialogue about the beliefs that are guiding our psychological work will be measured by the empirical fecundity of the dialogue, by the capacity of the dialogue to generate theoretical approaches that will in turn generate novel and significant hypotheses regarding measurable phenomena that yet in turn yield empirically powerful findings in comparison to competing explanatory systems. Meehl (1993), chafing about those he regards as "obscurantists" who minimize the importance of scientific accountability to data by appealing to philosopher of science Thomas Kuhn on the theory-ladenness of data, said

"[No] quotes from Kuhn can avoid the task of *proving* what one claims to have observed, and in a way that does not require the skeptic to accept one's theory, *that being what is in dispute*" (p. 710). We concur with Meehl: Dialogue that never results in empirically fertile inquiry is dialogue that ultimately fails to engage the field. The point of the dialogue is to give religious traditions and resources the chance to explicitly shape the framework of metaphysical assumptions that in turn shape how we do our research and on what topics, and how it is interpreted and applied. The jury is yet out on whether this dialogue will indeed be recognized as productive by the field.

We proceed with this dialogue by briefly discussing how psychology has conceptualized sexuality, then explore several religious conceptualizations about sexuality, and conclude with reflections on enrichment of psychology from this dialogue.

REFLECTIONS ON THE CONCEPTUALIZATION
OF SEXUALITY IN PSYCHOLOGY

Modern scientific psychology, deeply influenced at the level of its metaphysical assumptions by rationalistic modernism, has often treated sexuality simplistically and with a sense of detachment and embarrassment. The earliest paradigm of scientific psychology, Wundt's introspective psychology (which evolved into structuralism) perfectly exemplified disembodied rationalistic modernism both in its embrace of a methodology for the acquisition of knowledge (the introspection experiment) and in its choice of subject matter (human consciousness). By focusing on consciousness, the "mind" is abstracted from embodied existence and the "higher" faculties celebrated, with the necessary result being a lack of attention to sexuality.

Behaviorism de-emphasized or denied the uniqueness of human faculties such as consciousness, emphasizing the continuity of the seemingly unique and complex human capacities across species lines and with more basic learned human behavior patterns. Unique human capacities such as consciousness or language were viewed as simply more complex, compounded variants of the same capacities manifested by nonhuman species and as continuous with more simple foundational capacities for the acquisition of learned behavior. In the process of reducing complex behavior to simpler learning processes, complex patterns of behavior became disconnected from networks of meaning that are only possible in a nonreductive analysis. Sexuality appeared in behavioristic accounts of human personality through the basic capacity of the organism to experience pleasure in sexual stimulation. Skinner, reflecting a commonly shared understanding of the origins of such pleasure in the evolutionarily derived imperative to reproduce, saw the pursuit of sexual pleasure as grounded in some sort of survival motive. Still, behaviorism never had the paradigmatic resources to develop anything more than an ultimately trivial understanding of sexuality as the ground for primary reinforcement.

Would humanistic psychology offer a more fully orbed vision of sexuality? Certainly by focusing on the experiencing individual, humanistic psychology opened the possibility for a deepened subjective understanding of sexuality, but certain key factors limited this approach's strengths in dealing with sexuality. First, the approach de-emphasizes embodiment. Maslow's famous hierarchy of needs put the biological needs in the basement, the foundation, seemingly following Wundt in relegating biologically linked phenomena to the status of lesser interest in favor of the elevated, unembodied, distinctly and uniquely human capacities for meaning making. Furthermore, the approach must be seen as individualistic in orientation, and such a perspective fundamentally impedes a complex relational understanding of sexuality.

Evolutionary psychology, an influential contemporary paradigm, represents a return to understanding sexuality as central to human character. The basic argument of the approach is that all significant extant behavior must be understood as grounded finally in psychological processes that exist now because they once served to abet the reproductive success of the behaving organism (Buss, 1994). All behavior is presumed to be rooted in the foundational motive of projecting one's genes into the next generation because, just as physical structures that aided genetic propagation would have been passed on to subsequent generations through natural selection, so also would psychological and behavioral patterns that aided genetic propagation. In a real sense in this view, the final "meaning" of any pattern of behavior must be its contribution to reproduction. Hence, the place to start in any analysis of behavior must be the contribution of the target behavior to reproductive success. This paradigm has been directed toward the understanding of sex differences generally, and of behavior related to mating and reproduction in particular, but also to a diverse array of behavioral patterns.

Numerous concerns and criticisms have been directed at this approach. Eagly and Wood (1999) contrasted this approach both conceptually and empirically with a social structuralist account to explain psychological sex differences. Noting that both accounts saw behavior as functionally responsive to current environmental conditions, they nevertheless "differ radically in their analysis of the nature and timing of the adjustments that are most important" (p. 408). The former approach, in particular, sees all behavior including stable sex differences as grounded in evolutionary adaptations to ancient environments, with those adaptations determining contemporary behavior. The impact of these adaptations is hence seen as fixed, essentially rooted in the past, and as universal. Eagly and Wood, in contrast, described the social structuralist view as one that attributes psychological sex differences to the adjustments men and women must make because they "tend to occupy different social roles" (p. 408), and thus these behavioral differences would ultimately be rooted largely in the present and would not be universal. They found that this social structuralist view accounted for the data they reviewed as well as the evolutionary approach. We would agree with Eagly and Wood's expressed concern that the evolutionary approach may narrow the attention of psychologists to how behavior abets reproductive fitness. Going beyond their critique, we are concerned that this approach pushes a reductive tendency grounded in a narrowly materialistic set of metaphysical assumptions. We will return to a discussion later of how, from a religious perspective, consideration of reproductive fitness as one of several sexual ground motives in a nonreductive framework might be configured.

The only major approach that manifests what in our view would constitute a sustained and deep engagement with and understanding of sexuality is the psychoanalytic approach of Freud. Freud's psychology is often understood today as influenced by the simplistic associative neuropsychology of his day, by the best contemporary technology of his day (hydraulics, an enduring metaphor in his thought), by the evolutionary thought of Darwin, by the provocative and mysterious practice of hypnosis (and the speculative explanations of its effectiveness), and by his Jewish roots, especially perhaps by the mystical Kabalistic tradition of Jewish spirituality. It is particularly striking that sexual motivation for Freud was not merely basic, but was also all-pervasive in its influence. Libido was the source of the most fundamental psychic energy that pervaded all of human experience. Human psychological experience was thoroughly embodied. Criticisms of this view are legion. We do not advocate for it, but it does embody certain patterns of thinking about sexuality that we find appealing, including a full embrace of embodiment, an understanding of sexuality as a fundamental human motivation, and a complex vision of human life as conflicted. The most fundamental problem with the Freudian vision of sexuality is perhaps its biological reductionism, a tendency resulting in a privileging of a primitive and also negative understanding of sexual motivation. Browning (1987) provided a thoughtful analysis of Freud's vision of personality in religious perspective. He suggested that Freud's embrace of sexuality as the motivational core of the person may have been a product in part of his religious heritage. Browning argued that Judaism (and by extension Christianity) has "very positive views of nature [i.e., embodiment] and instinctuality" (p. 45). Freud's view, however, was significantly less positive, viewing the id, for instance, as what Browning called a "seething, formless 'cauldron'" (p. 45). With such a coarsened view of nature and instinctuality, Freud was forced to regard the distinctly human aspects of the person as imposed "from the outside of human nature, that is, from parental prohibitions, the superego, and finally, for those fortunate enough to be analyzed, from analytic insight" (p. 45). Thus, any civilized human capacity—the capacity to love and be loved, to be faithful or to be altruistic—becomes alien to the core of the person.

> In Freud's view, people are motivated by their drives arising from their bodies and demanding satisfaction. . . . Unrestrained sexual . . . impulses

are incompatible with social life; our needs for instinctual gratification and social relationships coexist uneasily. (Harding, 2001, p. 9)

This conclusion sits uneasily with most.

Contemporary psychodynamic traditions, not surprisingly then, are less reductionistic and more relationally holistic than Freud's views. They generalize the libidinal into the broader need for relatedness and thus considerably broaden that which is considered "sexual."

> The key claim is that the relevant framework for considering these issues is that sexuality is inside the symbolic order, not purely an expression of instinctual needs. Biological determinants are not wholly cast aside, but the rigidity of their determining role is greatly reduced. . . . It is now commonplace that sexuality has a history, that is, it is inside the contingency of culture, not merely fixed and innate in a stereotyped way. (Young, 2001, p. 23)

REFLECTIONS ON THE CONCEPTUALIZATION OF SEXUALITY IN TWO RELIGIOUS TRADITIONS

To advance the dialogue between psychology and religion, we here briefly explore the very different approaches to sexuality of Buddhism and Christianity, the former briefly and the latter more extensively.[1] By contrasting these two disparate views, we heighten the potential distinctive conceptual contributions of each.

Buddhism

The Sanskrit word *Buddha* means the awakened or enlightened one. Buddhism is, fundamentally, the pursuit of enlightenment as understood within a distinctive view of reality. Reality as commonly experienced (for instance, in our sensory experience of our bodies and of the physical world) is presumed to be "appearance" (a complex concept indicating that experienced reality is neither the final nor most important aspect of reality), and it is precisely the bondage of the individual to experienced reality that must be broken through the discipline of renunciation (Kamilar, 2002). Buddhists believe in reincarnation governed by karma, whereby past choices create a momentum of lived reality that transcends multiple lives. The enlightened individual achieves, whether within one life span or across several, release

---

[1]We would like to acknowledge, as we approach this brief description of Buddhism, that we have rarely encountered any description of our own faith system of Christianity written by a nonadherent that we regarded as adequate. It is hence intimidating to embark on that very task with another faith system.

from the suffering of this temporal world through acceptance of the inevitable dimension of suffering in this life and cessation from striving and inordinate desire through the embrace of the "Eightfold Path" taught by the Buddha. Renunciation, particularly of demands for how our lives must be, is central. To experience enlightenment, we "have to give up, to surrender, to recognize that we will not have our way in the world of impermanence. What must be renounced are the hopes and dreams for permanence, ease, and security that drive conventional lifestyles" (Gross, 2000, p. 97).

It is difficult to specify "the" Buddhist view of sexuality because differing traditions or styles of Buddhism have emerged with differing views of sexuality (Kamilar, 2002). The three principal types of Buddhism, in rough chronological order of their appearance, are individualistic or monastic (*Hinayana*), messianic or universal (*Mahayana*), and apocalyptic (*Vajrayana*). The Hinayana or monastic style emphasizes renunciation, meditation, and the concept of impermanence. The ultimate goal is to achieve liberation for oneself. Before one can be of use to others, it is necessary to cultivate a clear state of mind. However, the Mahayana or messianic path entails accomplishing liberation for the sake of others. The *bodhisattva* (traveler) on this journey, postpones his or her own liberation to work to relieve the suffering of all other beings. The goal is to develop *bodhichitta*, an awakened heart. Both of these older styles of Buddhism consistently view all expression of sexuality as an impediment to further spiritual progress; the body and its desires are one focus of renunciation. This stance is consistent with a view of physical, experienced reality as only appearance and seductive. The Buddhist monastic tradition is an ascetic one that in its infancy adopted lifelong celibacy for those seeking true enlightenment. Celibacy is an aid to attaining spiritual and psychological transformation—the freedom, detachment, and tranquility called enlightenment (Gross, 2000). The majority of Buddhist lay followers were and are not expected, however, to be sexually abstinent but to adhere to a system of sexual ethics that mirrors the taboos and concerns of premodern Indian society (forbidding, for instance, adultery[2]). This view is preserved today, reflecting a deep respect for the past as it informs present behavioral norms (Cabezon, 1992). There can be no question that the less rigorous, nonascetic path is viewed as likely to produce only limited enlightenment and hence to be of less value in this tradition.

The most recent variant is different. Vajrayana (meaning diamond of indestructible vehicle) Buddhism is currently practiced in Tibet and is be-

---

[2]The Dalai Lama recently stated in a magazine interview that the Buddhist view of sexual ethics is that "Genitals were created for reproduction between the masculine and the feminine and that anything that deviates from that is not acceptable from the Buddhist point of view," including, per his listing, oral and anal sexual intercourse, male and female homosexual conduct, and masturbation. (This interview, reported in French and translated for me by a colleague, was written for the magazine *Dimanche*, December 30, 2000, and was retrieved June 2, 2002 at www.dimanche.ch/article2.asp?IaD=1528. The Web site is no longer active, however, the text of the interview can be found at www.geocities.com/hearland_sg/According2.htm)

coming increasingly popular in the West. From approximately 500 to 1000 A.D., this apocalyptic style spread throughout the Buddhist world. In the Vajrayana Buddhist texts called *tantras*, the virtues of wisdom and compassion are personified as female and male, and the two are painted and sculpted in sexual embrace (usually called the *yab-yum icon*). This icon is a focus of contemplative and meditative practices, including visualizing oneself as the pair joined in embrace. Sexuality, in this approach, rather than being a private and somewhat embarrassing or guilt-ridden indulgence, is understood to function as a symbol of a profound religious truth and as an exercise for developing one's enlightenment. One of the most profound implications of the use of the human sexual relationship to symbolize ultimate reality is that of equal gender status. The male and female are joyous, equally cooperative partners. This open celebration of sexuality as a sacred, transformative encounter between divine partners challenges the notion that nonprocreative sex is deficient. This symbolism also permits the possibility of spiritual (or *dharmic*) ecstasy between women and men. Such relationships are not necessarily conventional domestic or romantic arrangements, but provide mutual support while striving for spiritual discipline. Sexuality is an element within, but not the basis of, such relationships (Gross, 2000). Hence it is only within this approach that sexual expression can be so celebrated as to be termed "Tantric Exotericism" (Cabezon, 1992, p. 210).

There is thus no one monolithic Buddhist understanding of sexuality. In two of the great traditions, sexuality seems best understood as a seductive diversion from true enlightenment. In the third tradition, sexuality is both a symbol of enlightenment and a method of obtaining that enlightenment. Two conclusions bear emphasizing, however: First, the ontology underlying Buddhism remains constant across all three traditions; that is, the teaching that the physical world (and human sexuality in particular) is ultimately an appearance only and hence the proper target of renunciation. Second, it then becomes clear that the primary difference between Vajrayana Buddhism in its view of sexuality and that of the older styles is the symbolic (as opposed to substantive) function that sexual action serves as the practitioner strives to develop enlightenment. In other words, in the Vajrayana approach, sexuality is not really good in itself, but rather good as a symbol of and a practice that can put one in touch with some deeper spiritual truth.

Christianity

If Buddhism emphasizes the human person striving for enlightenment, Christianity proclaims the loving God who reveals himself and his will to a rebellious humanity and who intrudes in history in an unexpected way to break down the human-erected barriers between God and humanity. God entered history decisively by becoming human in the fully human and yet fully divine person of Jesus Christ. After living a perfect life and teaching his ways, Jesus was crucified. His death functioned as a sacrificial offering to pay the death penalty for all human rebellion against God, and by rising from the dead to new life, he forever conquered death and offers new life to all who believe in him and give their lives to him. But what about sexuality? As with Buddhism, one cannot speak about a monolithic view of sexuality in the Christian tradition. Grounded in the complex, multiauthorial Hebrew and Christian scriptures, innumerable commentators have spoken to this issue from myriad cultural and pastoral contexts over two millennia. These commentators have always been in dialogue with their cultures, as attested by the contrast between the sensualism of the Corinthian church (see 1 and 2 Corinthians) and the neo-Platonic dualism regarding sexuality that emerged in the Greek church within several generations of the first apostles (and which still flavors aspects of Roman Catholic teaching about sexuality). No utterly unanimous voice can be identified in this broad conversation within the Christian church (see a brief review of exemplary cases in Jones & Hostler, 2002), but this does not mean that a dominant voice cannot be identified, and it is there we turn. (The following is loosely dependent on such sources as Barnhouse & Holmes, 1976; General Synod, 1991; Grenz, 1990; Kelsey & Kelsey, 1996; Smedes, 1994.)

Many think of moral prohibitions when they think of a Christian view of sexuality. That system of ethics is imbedded in a deeper understanding of human sexuality, one that starts with a view of physical reality. In contrast to the Buddhist view, Jews and Christians view physical existence as a good creation of a benevolent God. God spoke the physical world into existence out of nothing. That God did not make the world out of his own divine essence or some other type of preexisting divine "stuff" prevents any move to regard the physical world as worthy of our worship, whereas God's own repeated declaration that the creation is "good" prevents any diminishing of the goodness of physical existence and establishes a basis for regarding the created world with the reverence due to the handiwork of the Creator.

Human existence as embodied persons is an aspect of this good (but not divine) physicality. We are more than bodies, being made "in the image of God"[3] (Genesis 1:27) including the spiritual and soulish aspects of our persons, but we are nevertheless "living beings," bodies "formed . . . from the dust of the ground" into which has been breathed "the breath of life" (Genesis 2:7). The goodness of bodily existence is supported and grounded not only in the doctrine of creation as just discussed, but in two additional key theological themes of traditional Christianity as well. The doctrine of the incarnation is central to Christianity and is perhaps its most stark contrast with Judaism (as well as the other Abrahamic faith, Islam). Christians believe that God (God the Son, the second person of the Trinitarian God) became fully human as the man Jesus. Clearly, bodily existence must not be

---

[3]All biblical quotes are from the New International Version.

intrinsically evil or incompatible with the perfect good if God can assume human life. This teaching would attest that the bedrock of Christian theology is incarnate, embodied love. The other great theological theme is that of the resurrection of the body. Christians believe that the final state of redeemed humanity will be as resurrected and perfected bodies and that we will, in that state, enjoy God forever. Christians have thus, throughout most of history, held views of their own existences as fundamentally embodied (in a positive way as opposed to the negative view of embodiment from Buddhism). Bynum (1995), for example, documents that consideration of the physical body was central to reflections about identity and personhood, and about the very nature of the soul, for a huge swath of church history.

This embodiment, although not reducible to sexuality, certainly grounds sexuality. Unlike other creation stories in surrounding Mesopotamian and Hellenistic cultures, the Genesis narrative about creation declares God's creation of a gendered people to have been by divine intent, with *both* sexes declared to have been made in the "image of God" (Genesis 1:27) and both the male and female together declared "very good" (Genesis 1:31). This was a radically egalitarian declaration in the context of the ancient world.

We are given clear indications of a relational conceptualization of human character, a relationality grounded in part (but perhaps not reducible to) our sexuality. The first man, as the story unfolds in Genesis 2 before the creation of the first woman, living in a state of perfection himself in the perfect environment and in the context of a perfect relationship with God, is judged incomplete by his Creator. "It is not good for the man to be alone," God says (Genesis 2:18), and God then creates the suitable partner for the man. The man himself recognizes the profound complementarity of this new creation, and God declares that because of this reality, "a man will leave his father and mother and be united to his wife, and they will become one flesh" (Genesis 2:24). This union of husband and wife is tied to passionate love and deep communion in a number of places in the Scriptures (the Song of Songs; Proverbs 5:18–19), although the patriarchal society of the time with its arranged marriages did not always exalt this potentiality.

The declaration that the two "will become one flesh," explicitly tied to sexual union in intercourse in other parts of the Christian scriptures, is the foundational teaching of the Christian tradition anchoring its view of marriage. Other meanings besides one-flesh union are attached to full sexual intimacy: (a) the prospect of bearing children is voiced as a blessing on the first couple (Genesis 1:28) and on other subsequent persons in Scripture; (b) Scripture itself extols the physical pleasures of sexual union (Proverbs 5) and links eroticism explicitly with romantic love and intimacy in the Song of Songs; and (c) the Christian apostle Paul even gives stern admonition to married couples that fulfillment of sexual need is a legitimate function that each spousal partner should provide for the other (and again, does so in a remarkably egalitarian fashion; 1 Corinthians 7:1–6). Despite these other meanings, however, it is the inevitability that sexual intercourse will unite a woman and man in a one-flesh unity—some sort of transindividual reality— that anchors the prohibition on adultery and of all sexual union outside of marriage (what is commonly called sexual immorality; 1 Corinthians 6:12–17) and against divorce in the teachings of Jesus (Matthew 19:1–10). Sexual intercourse thus is seen as having a determinate or fixed meaning regardless of the intentions of the participants in the act; both the Corinthian man and the prostitute with whom he is consorting mean their encounter to be a pleasurable, casual, and transient one, but Paul asserts that the meaning and function of the act is nonetheless one of the establishment of a one-flesh union.

In the context of marriage, the teaching of the Christian Scriptures is unequivocal that sexual intercourse is a created good that should serve the wholly positive purposes in marriage of one-flesh union, but also reproduction, pleasure, and need gratification (e.g., Hebrews 13:4, 1 Timothy 4:1–5). Sexual union is foundational to marriage, but marriage in turn serves crucial purposes, one of which might be termed iconic. An icon (most common in the various Orthodox traditions of Christianity) is a tangible object that serves as a "window" to the transcendent. The Scriptures present marriage as an instantiation of spiritual truth, an earthly model or icon of the relationship of the risen Jesus Christ to his "Bride" the church[4] (Ephesians 5:25–33). Marriages are formed by sexual union, but also by the public exchange of vows of fidelity. Engaging in sexual union with one's spouse, whether with great awkwardness at its novelty or with the emotional transparency that comes with time, functions to continually renew and reaffirm the covenant between God, husband, and wife.

In discussing evolutionary psychology, we mentioned earlier how, from a religious perspective, consideration of reproductive fitness as one of several sexual ground motives in a nonreductive framework might be configured. From the foregoing, we would deduce that a deep motive to reproduce would not be alien to a biblical view of human nature. What would be alien is a failure to condition that motive by placing it alongside other less reductive sexual motives, such as the desire for relatedness in marriage and family, for pleasure, and for intimacy, and alongside other nonsexual motivations such as to work productively or to be in relationship with God.

In discussing Freud, we commended his view of humanity as conflicted because of its resonance with Christian teaching. God provided moral boundaries for our sexuality because of our human proclivity to rebel against God and to behave in ways utterly contrary to his will for our lives (i.e., sin). Humanity is seen, in Christian theology, as retaining our creational goodness as a foundational reality, but we are also seen as "totally depraved." The

---

[4]This iconic function of sexuality could be argued to be somewhat similar to the symbolizing function of sexuality in Vajrayana Buddhism.

concept of total depravity may be the most frequently misunderstood of the major doctrines of the church. It does not assert that we are "as evil at every moment and in every way as it is possible to be" (a clear impossibility because we can all always imagine how to behave yet more badly than we currently are behaving), the doctrine instead means that there is no aspect of our human existence that does not reflect our brokenness and rebellion against God. This reality has not eradicated the primal good of human character, but it conditions all of human experience. Our sexual longings, for example, are grounded in our good capacities for union and love and pleasure but are tainted with such evil tendencies as selfishness, sensuality (the disconnection of physical appetites from the transcendent purposes to which they are connected), or subjugation or violence flowing from inclinations toward broken and evil domination of the other. Hence, we experience a deep conflictedness in our sexuality (as in all our experience) wherein we know the potential and realized good of our sexual natures, but never experience that good distilled and pure, disconnected from our sinfulness.

It is for this reason that explicit moral boundaries are placed on sexual behavior. The core moral prohibition of the Hebrew and Christian scriptures is found in the Ten Commandments: "You shall not commit adultery" (Exodus 20:14). Full sexual intimacy was to be reserved for one relationship, that of heterosexual marriage. All of the subsidiary moral prohibitions were extensions of and supportive of this core restriction: Rape was forbidden (e.g., Deuteronomy 22:25–27), as was incest (e.g., Leviticus 18:6 and surrounding), homosexual intercourse (e.g., Leviticus 18:22; 20:13; see Gagnon, 2001, on the extension of these commands into the New Testament), and sexual intercourse with animals (e.g., Leviticus 18:23; 20:15–16). In Matthew 5:27–30, Jesus added lust as an additional moral prohibition, broadening the explicit moral concerns of the faith from behavioral acts to thought acts. Despite these moral boundaries, adherents of the Christian faith (including leaders charged and entrusted to be exemplars of wholeness and integrity) manifest their brokenness in failing to live by these constraints. At the worst, adherents and leaders do not just "fail to live up to these standards," but manifest the most heinous enslavement to sexual brokenness, as exemplified in the tragic crisis current at the moment of this writing of sexual abuse of children and adolescents by priests of the Roman Catholic Church (and of other branches of Christianity). Equally, Christians themselves have often reduced their understanding of sexuality to these prohibitions alone, resulting in a repressive and negative approach to sexuality of the type that would produce the (likely unrepresentative) negative stereotypes many psychologists summon up from clinical experience when they think of religion and sexuality.

In Christian perspective, what role does sexuality play in the broad understanding of personhood? Is the sexual a more "primitive" aspect of the person? Is the reproductive urge the base motivation of all life forms including humans? In many ways, sexuality (embodiment, gender differentiation, relational capacities and needs, and the special function of sexual intercourse) pervades and conditions the whole of human existence, and a deep understanding of human nature would be impossible without careful consideration of our sexual nature. Still, the sexual dimension cannot stand alone without being contextualized by other irreducible human characteristics no more or less foundational to the person than the sexual. With our sexual nature, we might also ask what role overt sexual gratification plays in personal happiness and well-being, as well as in relational happiness and well-being. Is sex essential to happiness or wholeness? Historically, Christian theology has answered that our sexual natures can be accepted and actualized without overt genital intimacy; this possibility and pattern is attested to both by the moral constraints placed on sexual intimacy and by the lived models of celibate individuals (foremost in the person of Jesus) who nevertheless lived fully actualized human lives. To experience the fullness of human life, denial of the specific physical, sexual needs of the self for the sake of living faithfully with and to God can be as or more essential than gratification of those physical needs, even as such choices create pressing practical and developmental challenges for the person to meet.

CONCLUDING REFLECTIONS ON "A FRUITFUL DIALOGUE"

In deciding whether a dialogue with religion could enrich psychological theory, research, and practice, we note that religious thought will rarely contribute unequivocal, immediately quantifiable, testable hypotheses. As McClay (1997, p. 235) said,

> Christian perspective will not necessarily generate a specific or uniform agenda. Christianity is not an ideology, and it almost never leads its adherents to identical positions on questions of policy or politics. But it will profoundly shape the way questions are posed.

In shaping how questions are posed, however, a religious vision can generate, by extrapolation, hypotheses that can inspire research programs. The following reflections on how to pose better psychological questions will reflect only a Christian perspective.

Given the Christian view of sexuality and of human nature, any number of empirical findings in the field are unsurprising even if not tightly predicted by this view. Contrary to the received wisdom that cohabitating relationships facilitate preparation for marriage and better judgments about marital compatibility, empirical studies of cohabitation consistently suggest that cohabitation is associated with higher postmarriage divorce rates, higher rates of extramarital affairs, and less sexual satisfaction in marriage. Furthermore, an immense literature attests to the quality-of-life benefits of traditional marriage and of two-parent family arrangements (summarized in Waite & Gallagher, 2000). Religious faith has rarely been measured in psychological studies of marriage, but interesting results have emerged when it has, perhaps none more interesting than the Greeley (1991) report on a Gallup study of marriage sponsored by *Psychology Today*. This report indicated that a powerful predictor of a good marriage was whether couples pray together regularly, that joint prayer was highly correlated with sexual satisfaction, and that the couple able to pray together and enjoy good sex together was the least likely to divorce. Mahoney et al. (1999) summarized other research linking greater religiousness to marital satisfaction and adjustment, and in an elegant and innovative study found "better marital functioning to be generally associated with more joint religious activities between couples as well as greater perceptions of marriage having spiritual characteristics and significance" (p. 333). If humans were intended in their creational state for a monogamous and permanent union sustained by sexual intimacy, then the strong relationship of religiousness, sexual fidelity, and relational stability and quality is to be expected and deserves much more extensive empirical exploration.

Furthermore, the connection of the quality of sexual experience to general relationship quality could have been anticipated in the development of sex therapy. One of us, Jones, was trained in sex therapy at a time when the field was dominated by simplistic and reductionistic training exercises that were deemed capable of erasing all sexual performance problems (leading to one memorable charge that sex therapy was really the application of "massage parlor technology;" Bailey, 1978). In those early years of sex therapy, psychodynamic therapists dismissed the field as dealing at the physical symptomatic level only, and as hence doomed to produce no enduring change. Those psychodynamic therapists sought to produce change in sexual symptoms via depth individual and couple therapy alone. Since that time, simplistic sex therapy techniques in isolation have been found useful in some cases but are now presented in combination with psychotherapeutic approaches suitable for relational intervention (Leiblum & Rosen, 2000). This balanced openness to both relational intervention (where sexual problems are deemed symptomatic) and to direct intervention in sexual behavior patterns or even the biological substrate of sexuality is consistent with the complex understanding of sexuality in this view. A Christian view of sexuality, marriage, and human relatedness would give latitude for some functional autonomy of the physical and biological without allowing for reductionism of the sexual to the physical or of utter independence of the physical from the relational. So, for example, acquisition of skills facilitative of orgasmic experience can play a legitimate role in enhancing sexual pleasure, but it is to be further expected that sexual technique would be only one determinant of sexual pleasure and satisfaction, and that sexual pleasure and satisfaction in turn will be only one of many complex determinants of full marital intimacy.

Finally, the complex Christian understandings of (a) the relationality of humanity; (b) the understanding of sexual union as creating a unity of persons that transcends individuality in expanding circles of marital union, nuclear families, extended families, and communities of faith; and (c) the intricate interdependence of our embodied existences with those aspects of our personhood that are not reducible to our embodiment, together can serve to stretch our understandings of human psychology. They can contribute to the other arguments for transcending the individualism of American psychology (e.g., Sampson, 2000), help to refocus us on incorporation of marital and familial connections as essential to a full understanding of the person, contribute to the integration of biological and irreducibly nonphysical aspects of personhood, and expand the complex array of human motives understood to be operative in common human life.

REFERENCES

Bailey, K. G. (1978). Psychotherapy or massage parlor technology? Comments on the Zeiss, Rosen, and Zeiss treatment procedure. *Journal of Consulting and Clinical Psychology, 46,* 1502–1506.

Barnhouse, R. T., & Holmes, U. T., III. (Eds.). (1976). *Male and female: Christian approaches to sexuality.* New York: Seabury Press.

Brooke, J. H. (1991). *Science and religion: Some historical perspectives.* Cambridge, England: Cambridge University Press.

Browning, D. (1987). *Religious thought and the modern psychologies.* Philadelphia: Fortress.

Buss, D. (1994). *The evolution of desire.* New York: Basic Books.

Bynum, C. W. (1995). *The resurrection of the body in Western Christianity, 200–1336.* New York: Columbia University Press.

Cabezon, J. I. (Ed.). (1992). *Buddhism, sexuality, and gender.* New York: State University of New York Press.

Eagly, A. H., & Wood, W. (1999). The origins of sex differences in human behavior: Evolved dispositions versus social roles. *American Psychologist, 54,* 408–423.

Gagnon, R. A. J. (2001). The Bible and homosexual practice: Theology, analogies and genes. *Theology Matters, 7,* 1–13.

General Synod of the Church of England. (1991). *Issues in human sexuality: A statement by the House of Bishops; General Synod of the Church of England.* Harrisburg, PA: Morehouse.

Greeley, A. (1991). *Faithful attraction: Discovering intimacy, love and fidelity in American marriage.* New York: Tor.

Grenz, S. (1990). *Sexual ethics: A biblical perspective.* Dallas, TX: Word.

Gross, R. M. (2000). *Soaring and settling.* New York: Continuum.

Harding, C. (2001). Introduction: Making sense of sexuality. In C. Harding (Ed.), *Sexuality: Psychoanalytic perspectives* (pp. 1–17). New York: Brunner-Routledge.

Ingraffia, B. D. (1995). *Postmodern theory and biblical theology*. Cambridge, England: Cambridge University Press.

Jones, S. (1994). A constructive relationship for religion with the science and profession of psychology: Perhaps the boldest model yet. *American Psychologist, 49,* 184–199.

Jones, S. (2000). Religion and psychology: Theories and methods. In A. Kazdin (Ed.), *Encyclopedia of psychology* (Vol. 7, pp. 38–42). Washington, DC: American Psychological Association; and New York: Oxford University Press.

Jones, S., & Hostler, H. (2002). Sexual script theory: An integrative exploration of the possibilities and limits of sexual self-definition. *Journal of Psychology and Theology, 30,* 120–130.

Kamilar, S. (2002). A Buddhist psychology. In R. P. Olson (Ed.), *Religious theories of personality and psychotherapy: East meets West* (pp. 85–140). New York: Haworth Press.

Kelsey, M. T., & Kelsey, B. (1996). *The sacrament of sexuality: The spirituality and psychology of sex*. Warwick, NY: Amity House.

Leiblum, S. R., & Rosen, R. C. (2000). *Principles and practice of sex therapy*. New York: Guilford Press.

Lindberg, D. C. (1992). *The beginnings of Western science: The European scientific tradition in philosophical, religious, and institutional context, 600 B.C. to A.D. 1450.* Chicago: University of Chicago Press.

Lindberg, D. C., & Numbers, R. L. (Eds.). (1986). *God and nature: Historical essays on the encounter between Christianity and science*. Berkeley: University of California Press.

Mahoney, A., Pargament, K. I., Jewell, T., Swank, A. B., Scott, E., Emery, E., & Rye, M. (1999). Marriage and the spiritual realm: The role of proximal and distal religious constructs in marital functioning. *Journal of Family Psychology, 13,* 321–338.

Mahrer, A. R. (2000). Philosophy of science and the foundations of psychotherapy. *American Psychologist, 55,* 1117–1125.

McClay, W. M. (1997). Filling the hollow core: Religious faith and the postmodern university. In G. Wolfe (Ed.), *The new religious humanists: A reader* (pp. 231–246). New York: Free Press.

Meehl, P. E. (1993). Philosophy of science: Help or hindrance? *Psychological Reports, 72,* 707–733.

Midgley, M. (1992). *Science as salvation: A modern myth and its meaning*. London: Routledge.

O'Donohue, W. (1989). The (even) bolder model: The clinical psychologist as metaphysician–scientist–practitioner. *American Psychologist, 44,* 1460–1468.

Redding, R. E. (2001). Sociopolitical diversity in psychology: The case for pluralism. *American Psychologist, 56,* 205–215.

Sampson, E. E. (2000). Reinterpreting individualism and collectivism: Their religious roots and monologic versus dialogic person–other relationship. *American Psychologist, 55,* 1425–1432.

Smedes, L. (1994). *Sex for Christians* (Rev. ed.). Grand Rapids, MI: Eerdmans.

Waite, L. J., & Gallagher, M. (2000). *The case for marriage*. New York: Broadway.

Young, R. M. (2001). Locating and relocating psychoanalytic ideas of sexuality. In C. Harding (Ed.), *Sexuality: Psychoanalytic perspectives* (pp. 18–34). New York: Brunner-Routledge.

7

THE MEANING THAT RELIGION OFFERS AND THE MOTIVATION THAT MAY RESULT

MARTIN L. MAEHR

A number of years ago, I attended the funeral of an aunt and stayed on for a social gathering that followed. A cousin and I struck up a conversation. Concluding a career as a minister in a large East Coast congregation, he exhibited all the social and verbal skills that one might expect of someone in this role. Inevitably, he got around to the question, "What is your area of research?" I replied, "Motivation" and quickly rambled into a cursory description of my latest project. After less than two sentences, he interrupted, "Motivation? I don't need that—I've got my religion!" Slipping back into his more diplomatic self, he changed the topic to inquire about my family. I smiled and mentally crossed him off my Christmas card list.

Different thoughts prevailed as I made the long drive home, however. I had confronted skeptical attitudes toward psychology before. I also was well aware of misgivings that some clergy held vis-à-vis the nature of human nature portrayed by representatives of my profession (cf. Doniger, 1962; Evans, 1989; Meehl, 1958; Myers, 1978). Yet what struck me most was that my cousin had made a valid point. Religion demonstrably has been, and remains, a powerful motivational force in the lives of many people. Reflecting on that, I also realized that those who study motivation arguably pay slim attention to the possible role that spiritual beliefs and membership in religious communities play in framing thoughts, actions, feelings, and emotions. In addition, in the past when social scientists considered religion, the focus was often on the bizarre or the diabolic. Even in this instance, I was tempted to introduce the consideration of the motivational effects of religion by referring to the tragedy of September 11, 2001, and the continuing rash of suicide bombings conducted in the name of Allah. Of course, there are examples aplenty of believers moved to heroic as well as commonplace acts of charity, service, and sacrifice that stand as profound evidence of how faith commitments play a significant, positive, and productive role in the world. My cousin's challenge, an invitation from the editors, and perhaps also a faith commitment, *motivated* me to write this chapter.

RELEVANT RESEARCH AND PERSPECTIVES

At first glance, the current psychological literature hardly reflects major interest in or concern with religion as a motivational factor per se. For example, an electronic PsycINFO search identified a thousand articles and books dealing with the topic of "religion and psychology" that appeared in press in 2000 and 2001. Remarkably, only one of those was a report of empirical research in a major journal focusing on basic social psychological processes—and that article (Cohen & Rozin, 2001), interesting as it was, was not concerned with motivation! Later searches revealed multiple new studies but reflected no major change in this state of affairs.

Casting a broader net, however, I eventually identified programs of research not specifically listed under "motivation" that might figure prominently in the understanding of how religion affects motivation. As primary examples, the recent work on *goals* (e.g., Baumeister, 1991; Emmons, 1999; Emmons & Paloutzian, 2003) and the large and still growing literature on *self* and *identity* (e.g., Baumeister, 1998) should figure significantly into how religion may affect motivation. Likewise, concerns with *belonging* (e.g., Baumeister & Leary, 1995) as well as culture and community provide new bases for reconsidering religion as a motivational force of significance.

Of equal if not greater importance is the stimulation that is prompted by the recent work on spirituality, religion, mental health, and well-being. There is little question but that this literature has prompted a reconsideration of the importance of religion—not only as a healing force but also as a significant perspective for understanding the nature of human nature. Chapters in this volume attest to this, as do recent articles in widely disseminated psychological journals (e.g., Hill & Pargament, 2003; Miller & Thoresen, 2003; Powell, Shahabi, & Thoresen, 2003; Seeman, Dubin, & Seeman, 2003).

The strength of the associations between religious commitments and spirituality to human health also prompt questions as to the mediating role that motivation and other basic psychological processes play in the causal chain. How is it that religious beliefs are instrumental in creating or encouraging health? Is it possible, at least in part, that religious and spiritual beliefs lead individuals to invest in different endeavors and invest their personal resources of time, energy, and competence in ways that happen to contribute to, rather than undermine, health? If so, motivational processes would be significantly implicated.

In this chapter, then, the impact of religion on the motivational processes that direct thoughts, feelings, and actions is examined.

A FOUNDATION ON WHICH TO BUILD

Given that minimal attention is currently being given to religion as an important motivational force, it is ironic that the contemporary approach in the study of motivation arguably emerged from a reconsideration of Max Weber's "The Protestant Ethic and the Spirit of Capitalism" (McClelland, 1961; Weber, 1930). So, perhaps by not attending to religion as a motivational force, we have lost something important—not only for the understanding of the influences of religion but also for theorizing about the nature, origins, and effects of human motivation.

Although one may reject various features of Weber's argument, question the quality of the data on which it is based, and doubt the implication that "Protestantism" has exclusive or special ownership of this ethic, Weber was arguably making an important point about religion and its influences—on motivation, in particular. Fortunately for the study of motivation and possibly also for understanding the impact of religion on motivation, almost a half century ago an emerging leader in the field, David McClelland, rediscovered Weber's work and sensed its implications for understanding the sociocultural origins of motivation. McClelland called special attention to several facets of Weber's work, including especially how ideology was embedded in and perhaps created the culture that framed individual achievement orientations. Thus, the good citizens of Holland in the time of which Weber wrote accepted the necessity of acting in a certain way, carefully using their personal resources as a "gift from God" and energetically endeavoring to store up more resources in response to an expectation to "make the most of one's gifts." Perhaps in some cases individuals also experienced some "reinforcement" for doing so by hazarding the thought that God had blessed them, even to the extent of indicating their membership among "the elect." It did not hurt that their beliefs simultaneously inhibited the squandering of personal resources on "pleasures of the flesh." Perhaps most of all, however, there was the overriding sense of a calling to do one's best in God's world.

McClelland, a clergyman's son, saw in this not merely an ideological perspective, but a system of beliefs, values, norms, and expectations that framed cultures, creating certain kinds of institutions, roles, laws, and especially ways of rearing children. Specifically, McClelland hypothesized that it was the ways in which children were reared, taught about what to expect in life, how to act, what to be and do, that this "protestant ethic" was not only retained but passed along. In addition, McClelland stretched this a bit to indicate that children were taught not only to "use their gifts" but also, specifically, to "challenge" themselves.

It is not altogether clear how this extension comes out of the "Protestant ethic," but it did become an important feature of McClelland's construction of an "achievement culture," leading to venturesomeness, accepting challenges, defining attainable but difficult to reach goals, or *achievement motivation*. Then, in one of the most ambitious cross-cultural studies of motivation ever, he went about studying cross-cultural variation in effects of stress on achievement motivation, and its influence on economic activity.

In this seminal study, McClelland focused specifically on how achievement emphases in school settings would culminate in an achieving society several decades later—when the children could be presumed to be significant contributors to the economy (McClelland, 1961). By any standard, this project was truly a massive undertaking, and the results were impressive. Across 33 diverse societies around the world, there tended to be a significant correlation between a standardized index of "achievement-oriented" child-rearing practices and economic productivity 25 years later, at a time when the children could be expected to have an impact on a country's economy. Although this particular study did not give primary attention to other cultural factors, McClelland and his colleagues certainly did recognize broader dimensions of achievement and analyzed multiple cultural origins of achievement motivation, including religion (e.g., McClelland, 1985).

McClelland's emphasis was typically placed on how child rearing in different cultures had various effects on an enduring personality trait to aspire, to invest one's personal and capital resources wisely, and to use "one's gifts" fully. Yet others have concluded that the continuing cultural context in which individuals live, work, act, and interact throughout their lives is also likely to be an important determinant. The bottom line, however, is that religious beliefs—as they engender values, strong feelings about what is worth doing and why—were pointed up as critical features not just of the "moral life," but at the very heart of human thought, feelings, and actions. Although some of McClelland's early work leaned heavily on Freud in defining the dynamics of action, his later work took account of the more recent developments of cognitive theory (McClelland, 1985; McClelland, Koestner, & Weinberger, 1989). Yet the stress remained on the role of acquired affective dispositions that prompted venturesomeness, the pursuit of challenge and, more broadly, an "entrepreneurial spirit." Individuals were presumably socialized to *feel* positively about challenge and moderate risk taking. They were emotionally disposed to "venturesomeness."

As an aside, it is noteworthy that the work of Weber, as extended by McClelland, stands as an early and notable example of religion shaping motivation in what might be understood as a "positive way." The Weber–McClelland achievement-oriented person was not Mr. Scrooge; rather, he (in an earlier era) or she (increasingly today) was best seen as an entrepreneur, an explorer, someone who sought and accepted challenges. Possibly, he or she might be seen as one striving to actualize his or her potential (cf. Rogers, 1961). Of course, entrepreneurship can lead to bad as well as good actions, but that is not the essence of entrepreneurship as set forth in the Weber–McClelland tradition.

Achievement, however, and almost every other human endeavor, involves not only "approach" but also "avoidance" behavioral patterns. Although ultimately incorporated into McClelland's work, it was particularly stressed by his student and collaborator, J. W. Atkinson (1957) and remains an important feature of motivational research (e.g., Elliot, 1999). Weber's capitalists were prudent folk, which means that they kept track of themselves and avoided evil and foolish entanglements. Currently, it would likely be said that they exhibited an optimum level of self-regulation in avoiding "foolish pleasures," "sins of the flesh," and, above all, "squandering" their resources. Today, self-regulation remains an important area of study within the broad domain of achievement theory as well as within the health professions and psychology, generally. As Baumeister points out in chapter 3 of this volume, religion not only has been deeply concerned about such issues but also provides a perspective as well as an incentive for resisting temptation, eschewing evil, and doing good, anticipating contemporary motivation theory.

In any event, it is difficult to ignore the fact that McClelland's reconsideration of this work opened up new perspectives on human motivation. In systematically linking culture to motivation, achievement, and productivity, he also prepared the way for considering how various organizational or group contexts may be viewed as reflecting a culture that affects motivation and achievement as well as other important variables. Multiple studies of group and organizational cultures have been conducted (e.g., Maehr & Braskamp, 1986; Maehr & Midgley, 1996; Schein, 1985) with implications for religious communal life, which have only been minimally pursued. Indeed, it may be specifically noted that considering religious communities as cultures may be a useful approach for studying religious practices, thoughts, feelings, and motivational processes. Also, as McClelland implies, because this influence begins in childhood, studying religion and its effects exclusively with adults may miss the important, formative role that religion and "religious cultures" likely hold.

Although the work of Weber and McClelland was foundational, it was not the final word. In certain respects, it has limited specific value in current studies of religion and motivation. Nevertheless, it has prompted research that has extended and provided a basis for rethinking the role of religion as a motivational factor. It was in effect the work of Atkinson that provided the transition to a framework that would prove particularly useful for considering religion and motivation within the emerging social science context. Atkinson reconsidered motivation in terms of an emerging perspective within the social sciences: choice and decision theory.

Choice and decision theory, then and now, essentially consists of multiple components. First, there is the outcome of action taken, direction of that action in the first instance—but, in later work on motivation, also the degree and quality of the action taken. For example, is the person deeply invested, and for how long? Does the investment reflect "deep processing" leading to new and novel solutions (cf. Amabile & Hennessey, 1992; Csikszentmihalyi, 1996)? Parenthetically, the application of a decision theory model in the study of motivation emphasizes that motivation is, in the first instance, an inference essentially derived from observations of behavioral patterns, variation in their nature, direction, and quality. These observations of changes in direction, intensity, and quality of engagement in a particular activity prompt motivation inferences. Therewith, attention is called to the behavioral basis for making motivational inferences.

This choice and decision theory perspective has influenced the definition and study of motivation in several ways. First, it has called attention to specific behavioral indicators of motivation, specific choices made, persistence in these choices, as well as the depth and degree of investment. More broadly, these could be viewed as "personal investments" of time, talent, and treasure that persons make in various endeavors for short and long periods (Maehr & Braskamp, 1986). These "investments" of valued personal resources are the most direct and empirical evidence of motivation.

What was equally important, however, was that choice and decision theory led to a focus on a different set of causes than did the previous theories of motivation which centered on "needs," "instincts," or "drives." Briefly, decision theory is concerned with three essential causes. First, there is an awareness of more or less acceptable behavior options. Second, there is the recognition of an individual's sense of ability to pursue these options successfully. Finally, there is an assumption that these options vary in value to the individuals (Allport, 1955; Eccles, 1983).

Perhaps the most important recent development is the emergence of "purpose" as a, if not the, major motivational variable. Of course, researchers in the area of personality and social psychology have exhibited a longstanding interest in goals or purposes (e.g., Emmons, 1999). Recent consideration of purpose in the study of work, learning, and achievement, however, has yielded important new perspectives that may also have wider application. In particular, they may suggest a useful perspective for studying faith life, especially in groups, organizations, communities, and sociocultural context. This study might also have practical implications not only for understanding religious phenomena but also for enhancing religious practices.

What is perhaps different and important about the renewed emphasis on goals, largely emerging within achievement theory, is that it has produced specific suggestions that have implications for practice in the world of work, school, and possibly also for the practice of religion. Although the term *achievement goal theory* may make it seem irrelevant to the realm of religion, I suggest that it is not. The term here is used initially to recognize the research tradition from which much current research on goals has emerged and within which they continue to play a major role.

Essentially, work stemming from achievement goal theory has revolved around four primary goals. As described in greater detail elsewhere (e.g., Maehr & Braskamp, 1986), each goal contributes to motivation, but in different ways and with different results. For example, extrinsic goals motivate primarily if and as extrinsic rewards continue to be received. When the purpose is to obtain *extrinsic rewards*, people tend to invest time and effort if and as extrinsic rewards are made available and obtained. In the case of *social solidarity* goals, social acceptance and approval are important. Holding *ego* goals tends to enhance self-awareness which may enhance or undermine motivation depending on how one feels about oneself. Finally, those persons holding *task* goals tend to put the focus on the activity to be done and the role of self is minimized.

These goals are treated as both "trait" and "state" variables. That is, considerable research has been conducted on how individuals differ in their goal orientations across time, place, and circumstances, and other research has focused on the oftentimes situated nature of these goals. Apparently, goals can be "primed," or made more or less salient by what is happening in a particular context. For example, in some contexts it is not productive to put the focus on "who you are and what you can do," when venturing forth to learn a new skill. Thus, when the stress on ability is emphasized too soon or too much, those who—rightly or wrongly—feel least competent will avoid engagement. Similarly, the exclusive concern with social solidarity may diminish achievement if the ultimate goal is simply to please others. When extrinsic rewards are salient, they and not, let us say, the task itself or fellow workers may take precedent.

Why might this be of importance in the study and practice of religion? First, one of the preeminent functions of religious organizations is to teach; a primary goal of those who belong to such groups is to learn, develop, and grow. This is certainly the case within the Judeo-Christian tradition in which terms such as *teaching*, *learning*, and *spiritual growth* are salient in the sacred writings, as well as in the gathering of the committed throughout history. It is not surprising, then, that religious leaders and organizations do well to consider what kind of purposes are or should be reflected in the venues and undertakings that comprise temple and church activities. Arguably, learning, development, and growth-related purposes should be preeminent.

Research (Midgley, 2002) indicates that learning, especially in the early stages, is likely to be especially facilitated by mastery goal contexts. First, these goals reduce the focus on self, on who one is, and on what one can do. The emphasis is, instead, on intrinsic reasons for doing and being. Also, mastery goals are less likely to encourage interpersonal competition and social exclusion and more likely to encourage help seeking and giving (e.g., Karabenick, 2003; Ryan, Gheen, & Midgley, 1998). Even when the focus is on achievement and on doing one's best, mastery goals tend to complement social solidarity goals by making personal growth, not interpersonal competition, the focus. Although this may relate most readily to schools and other instructional activities conducted under the aegis of a religious group, it likely has implications far beyond this.

Somewhat less attention has been given to a third variable in a decision model: Choices to act are made between perceived options. The work on "subjective culture" (e.g., Triandis, 1972) as well as "possible selves" (Markus & Kitayama, 1991; Markus & Nurius, 1986) illustrates and underscores how the sociocultural matrix in which a person lives, moves, and has being prescribes, proscribes, or actually promotes action alternatives. Religion is arguably a major contributor to the definition of roles and norms, possible and ideal selves. It therefore likely contributes significantly to choice options that are salient to those who are adherents.

The roles that we play, the norms to which we conform, the options that we perceive as possible, allowable, and worthy are established by and set within a community or multiple communities. These communities are often created around belief systems, and although individuals play special and important roles, these roles are enacted within the community. Certainly, within the Judeo-Christian traditions, the concept of belonging to and participating in a faith community is a major factor. For example, the God of the Hebrew Bible and the prophets who represent God repeatedly address a "people." The concept of a "faith community" was retained within the Christian tradition. As reflected in the epistle traditionally attributed to the Apostle Peter, "Once you were no people; now you are God's people" (1 Peter 2:10 RSV).

Although books on the psychology of religion sometimes use titles such as *The Individual and His Religion* or *Religion and the Individual* (e.g., Allport, 1950; Batson, Schoenrade, & Ventis, 1993), these reflect a more recent concern with religion, especially as viewed in the Western world. What is more reflective of religious practice and belief within the Judeo-Christian tradition is an emphasis on membership and participation in a community. Regularly, the prophet or apostle frames a call for "right behavior" in terms of identity, for example, "people of God." As stated in that manner, identity, special responsibility, or a "calling" is stressed as the basis for a moral, just, or benevolent response. More generally, within the Judeo-Christian tradition, right thought, feeling, and action is regularly framed by an awareness of who you are, by your place before God, rather than relying on a catalogue of "do's and don'ts." Parallel to that, comfort, hope, promise, and well-being come with one's identity as a member of a community. Moreover, church and synagogue as well as other organizations have their own cultures—ways of being, thinking, and feeling. Particularly important are the "behavioral options" that they promote or discourage. Certainly in the study of religious life within the Judeo-Christian tradition, it is particularly valuable to consider also the culture that is presented and promoted by local congregations.

In summary, motivational processes, as viewed from a decision theory framework, involve the consideration of purpose, concept of self, and identity as these evolve from or are situated within a sociocultural context that presents acceptable and unacceptable options for thinking, acting, and feeling. This viewpoint suggests that the study of religion should, importantly, focus on congregations of the faithful: the place and importance of the congregation in the individual's life, the nature of the interpersonal interactions that occur, and the outcomes that seem to result. Although the study of the "individual and his or her religion" certainly has its place, the study of the individual as a member of a congregation or religious group dare not be ignored.

CONCLUSION

After some initial misgivings, it occurs to me that my cousin was essentially right. Religion can be and often is a significant motivational factor. It likely has whatever effects it has, however, as it influences certain basic psychological processes that are well-known and often studied by psychologists: the concept of *self*, the framing of *purpose* and purposiveness, and the responsiveness to *social expectations*, norms, and interpersonal influences—including those defined and promoted and sustained by gatherings to worship, pray, seek help, find, and give comfort—within religious communities. Work in the social sciences reminds us of an established perspective of the Judeo-Christian tradition: The person is not an island, although we sometimes study him or her in that way. Persons decide, choose, and act within a sociocultural framework that can and often does include a religious community or at least one that recognizes and shares assumptions about identity, purpose, meaning, and worth. If this perspective is valid, then perhaps more research ought to be focused on religion and spirituality as part of a sociocultural matrix in which the individual lives, moves, and has being. The study of religious congregations and schools is one place to begin. Some notable work has paved the way, and I cite one example not often cited in the current literature on religion and spirituality. Religious schools are not only a fitting but also an accessible venue for considering the sociocultural matrix that faith communities provide. In this regard, Peshkin's (e.g., 1986) ethnographic studies of church-sponsored schools might be a fitting place to begin. The ever-increasing body of literature in psychology dealing with help seeking, help giving, inclusion, and exclusion within school and other social contexts provides a complementary extension of this endeavor.

There is also point and purpose in considering other outcomes stemming from life in religious communities, however, including religious schools in particular: variables such as creativity, (Amabile, 1996; Csikszentmihalyi, 1996) health, and well-being (e.g., Myers, 2000). And yes, also achievement. "Protestants" no longer have any special claim on achievement, if indeed they ever did. In this regard, an important study on the effectiveness of parochial (Roman Catholic) schools was conducted by Bryk, Lee, and Holland (1993). A major conclusion was that these schools were especially effective in serving children of minority-group backgrounds, those often at risk for school failure in public school. Bryk et al. attributed this finding to the focused curriculum, not to the "spiritual context" that was not really studied. Possibly, however, considering whether spiritual beliefs are related to investments in learning and achievement is not a bad idea. After all, such a relationship, noted in an earlier era (Weber, 1930), laid a basis for the present concern with religion, motivation, and achievement.

Perhaps the current promotion of faith-based organizations as purveyors of social services may be fitting and profitable venues for careful and systematic examination of whether and how *The Meaning That Religion Offers* may serve to motivate.

REFERENCES

Allport, G. W. (1950). *The individual and his religion: A psychological interpretation.* New York: Macmillan.

Allport, G. W. (1955). *Becoming: Basic considerations for a psychology of personality.* New Haven, CT: Yale University Press.

Amabile, T. M. (1996). *Creativity in context.* Boulder, CO: Westview Press; and HarperCollins, New York.

Amabile, T. M., & Hennessey, B. A. (1992). The motivation for creativity in children. In A. K. Boggiano & T. S. Pittman (Eds.), *Achievement and motivation: A social-developmental perspective* (pp. 54–74). New York: Cambridge University Press.

Atkinson, J. W. (1957). Motivational determinants of risk-taking behavior. *Psychological Review, 64,* 359–372.

Batson, C. D., Schoenrade, P., & Ventis, W. L. (1993). *Religion and the individual: A social-psychological perspective*. New York: Oxford University Press.

Baumeister, R. F. (1991). *Meanings of life*. New York: Guilford Press.

Baumeister, R. F. (1998). The self. In D. T. Gilbert, S. T. Fiske, & G. Lindzey (Eds.), *Handbook of social psychology* (4th ed., Vol. 1, pp. 680–740). New York: McGraw-Hill; and Oxford University Press.

Baumeister, R. F., & Leary, M. R. (1995). The need to belong: Desire for interpersonal attachments as a fundamental human motivation. *Psychological Bulletin, 117*, 497–529.

Bryk, A. S., Lee, V. E., & Holland, P. B. (1993). *Catholic schools and the common good*. Cambridge, MA: Harvard University Press.

Cohen, A. B., & Rozin, P. (2001). Religion and the morality of mentality. *Journal of Personality and Social Psychology, 81*, 697–710.

Csikszentmihalyi, M. (1996). *Creativity: Flow and the psychology of discovery and invention*. New York: HarperCollins.

Doniger, S. E. (1962). *The nature of man*. New York: Harper.

Eccles, J. (1983). Expectancies, values, and academic behaviors. In J. T. Spence (Ed.), *Achievement and achievement motives* (pp. 75–146). San Francisco: Freeman.

Elliot, A. J. (1997). Integrating the "classic" and "contemporary" approaches to achievement motivation: A hierarchical model of approach and avoidance achievement motivation. In M. L. Maehr & P. R. Pintrich (Eds.), *Advances in motivation and achievement* (Vol. 10, pp. 143–179). Greenwich, CT: JAI Press.

Elliot, A. J. (1999). Approach and avoidance motivation and achievement goals. *Educational Psychologist, 34*, 169–189.

Emmons, R. A. (1999). *The psychology of ultimate concerns: Motivation and spirituality in personality*. New York: Guilford Press.

Emmons, R. A., & Paloutzian, R. F. (2003). The psychology of religion. *Annual Review of Psychology, 54*, 377–402.

Evans, C. S. (1989). *Wisdom and humanness in psychology: Prospects for a Christian approach*. Grand Rapids, MI: Baker Book House.

Hill, P. C., & Pargament, K. I. (2003). Advances in the conceptualization and measurement of religion and spirituality: Implications for physical and mental health research. *American Psychologist, 58*, 64–74.

Karabenick, S. A. (2003). Seeking help in large college classes: A person-centered approach. *Contemporary Educational Psychology, 28*, 37–58.

Maehr, M. L., & Braskamp, L. A. (1986). *The motivation factor: A theory of personal investment*. Lexington, MA: Heath.

Maehr, M. L., & Midgley, C. (1996). *Transforming school cultures*. Boulder, CO: Westview Press.

Markus, H. R., & Kitayama, S. (1991). Culture and the self: Implications for cognition, emotion, and motivation. *Psychological Review, 98*, 224–253.

Markus, H., & Nurius, P. (1986). Possible selves. *American Psychologist, 41*, 954–969.

McClelland, D. C. (1961). *The achieving society*. Princeton, NJ: Van Nostrand.

McClelland, D. C. (1985). *Human motivation*. Chicago: Scott Foresman.

McClelland, D. C., Koestner, R., & Weinberger, J. (1989). How do self-attributed and implicit motives differ? *Psychological Review, 96*, 690–702.

Meehl, P. (1958). *What then is man?* St. Louis, MO: Concordia.

Midgley, C. (2002). *Goals, goal structures, and patterns of adaptive learning*. Mahwah, NJ: Erlbaum.

Miller, W. R., & Thoresen, C. E. (2003). Spirituality, religion, and health: An emerging research field. *American Psychologist, 58*, 24–35.

Myers, D. G. (1978). *The human puzzle: Psychological research and Christian belief*. San Francisco: Harper & Row.

Myers, D. G. (2000). *The American paradox: Spiritual hunger in an age of plenty*. New Haven, CT: Yale University Press.

Peshkin, A. (1986). *God's choice: The total world of a fundamentalist Christian school*. Chicago: University of Chicago Press.

Powell, L. H., Shahabi, L., & Thoresen, C. E. (2003). Religion and spirituality: Linkages to physical health. *American Psychologist, 58*, 36–52.

Rogers, C. R. (1961). *On becoming a person*. Boston: Houghton Mifflin.

Ryan, A. M., Gheen, M. H., & Midgley, C. (1998). Why do some students avoid asking for help? An examination of the interplay among students' academic efficacy, teachers' social-emotional role, and the classroom goal structure. *Journal of Educational Psychology, 90*, 528–535.

Schein, E. H. (1985). *Organizational culture and leadership*. San Francisco: Jossey-Bass.

Seeman, T. E., Dubin, L. F., & Seeman, M. (2003). Religiosity/spirituality and health: A critical review of the evidence for biological pathways. *American Psychologist, 58*, 53–63.

Triandis, H. C. (1972). *The analysis of subjective culture*. New York: Wiley-Interscience.

Weber, M. (1930). *The Protestant ethic and the spirit of capitalism*. New York: Scribner.

8

VIRTUES, VICES, AND CHARACTER EDUCATION

EVERETT L. WORTHINGTON JR. AND JACK W. BERRY

Purity of soul cannot be lost without consent.

—Karl Barth

The central question addressed in this chapter is this: If psychologists took a Judeo-Christian religious worldview seriously, how would that affect research and practice regarding character development, virtues, and vices? This central question invites several discussions around further questions. (a) Is there a single Judeo-Christian worldview? (b) How do secular, Jewish, and Christian approaches to virtues and vices interact? (c) What can Judaism and Christianity add to secular psychology's understanding of virtues, vices, and character education? and (d) Can integration of the psychological and theological fields take place in this domain?

EXAMINING DIFFERENCES IN JUDEO-CHRISTIAN WORLDVIEWS

Although Jews and Christians share the Hebrew scriptures, they interpret them differently. Within each of the three major varieties of Judaism—

We gratefully acknowledge support for portions of the research on which this chapter is based from the Fetzer Institute (Grant 1653.3 to Jack W. Berry, principal investigator [PI], Everett L. Worthington Jr. Co-PI) and the John Templeton Foundation (Grant 239 to Everett L. Worthington Jr., PI). We also thank the editors and panelists for their feedback, and especially Harold Delaney for suggesting clever names for the clusters of virtues. We also acknowledge Rabbi Jack Spiro, who provided valuable background information about Jewish perspectives.

145

Orthodox, Conservative, and Reformed—there are multiple variants. Christianity is even more fragmented. There are three major varieties—Roman Catholic, Orthodox (Greek, Russian, and other), and Protestant (e.g., mainline, evangelical, and fundamentalist). Across Christian traditions there are differences in theology, with liberal–conservative being just one of several dimensions of difference. There are hundreds of variations of Christianity with many understandings of virtue and vice. There is no unitary "Christian worldview," "Jewish worldview," or secular worldview. Despite some commonalties, there certainly is no single Judeo-Christian worldview.

Virtue has been understood classically to be a character trait that predisposes a person toward doing or being what is good, right, or excellent and avoiding *vice* (which is bad, wrong, or evil).

This view, shared by ancient Greeks, Jews, and Christians, assumed that the good existed objectively and absolutely (as did evil) and that it was not generally equivalent to what one naturally wanted to do. For example, if I want to eat dessert and do so, my act is not virtuous. A virtuous person would aspire eventually to desire what was good, right, or excellent, however—regardless of whether it was easy or difficult, costly or not, required or did not require effort. Greeks, Jews, and Christians and people within those traditions often disagreed about precisely what was virtue or vice, but they agreed that virtue and vice truly existed.

After Kant, people began to understand virtue as character that is acquired with effort and requires effort to practice. Thus, if a woman does a kind act because she wants to or because she gets rewarded for it or feels good afterward, it is not considered a virtue. If a person does not rob because he was conditioned not to rob, that, too, is not virtue. In this way of understanding, virtue thus requires effort to acquire and practice. Both absolute-good and effort-based understandings of virtue exist today.

Virtue and vice are not always seen as moral. For instance, the virtue of honesty is a moral virtue that involves telling truth and eschewing lying. But creativity might also be seen as a virtue, although whether one strives to manifest the creative or whether one seeks to avoid being humdrum or mundane is not a moral decision.

Many lists of virtues and vices exist, including a recent list developed in positive psychology (http://www.psych.upenn.edu/seligman/taxonomy.htm). The virtues or vices on each list tend to be reflections of which historical legacy the author has followed. Let us examine, in broadbrush strokes, the major historical paths to understanding virtue, vice, and educating in character.

Here we examine secular, Jewish, and Christian approaches to virtue, vice, and character education, identifying three themes: (a) the primacy of either reason or passion, (b) the role of relationships, and (c) whether the primary responsibility for an individual's acting virtuously and avoiding vice rests with the person (i.e., self-control) or with the Divine (i.e., control by God; see also chap. 9, this volume).

GREEK, ROMAN, AND MODERN SECULAR PHILOSOPHY AND PSYCHOLOGY

Secular Philosophy on Passion Versus Reason, Relationships, and Self-Control

Three broad philosophical movements have produced legacies that continue to shape modern psychological approaches to virtue, vice, and character education: (a) classical Greek and Roman virtue ethics; (b) the Enlightenment quest for universal, formal (rule-based) grounds for moral action; and (c) Romantic and postmodern alternatives to the Enlightenment.

In classical antiquity, Greek and Roman philosophers viewed ethics as a matter of developing qualities of character that lead to the good life. Plato held that there were three levels of the soul. The appetites involve the natural body appetites for food, sex, sleep, and so on. The spirit includes passion for honor, desire for glory, anger, and the other emotions. At the top level, the intellect could be engaged in rational thought and decision making and could control the lower passions. In the healthy soul, the intellect controls the spirit and the appetites in such a way that it guides the person toward nobility and virtuous life. For Aristotle, too, virtue was a public matter, and character education was educating for rational self-control of the passions. Roman Stoic philosophers, such as Epictetus and Seneca, advocated detachment from the world. They recommended pure reason to promote self-control and virtue. Despite differences in details, ancient Greek and Rome philosophers saw human reason at the center of virtuous living within society. The virtues formed a unity, and all were rooted in human effort toward self-control.

The classical Greek and Roman view of the supremacy of reason, revived with the Renaissance, lasted for centuries. With the Enlightenment, however, under the influence of Kant and the Utilitarians, virtue-based ethics were replaced (or given a secondary status) by rational, rule-based ethics. Objective duty and moral rules, universally applicable to all rational humans and independent of any particular community, were the guiding principles of ethics.

With the rise of Romanticism, the Enlightenment assumption of objective and universal moral rules came under attack. Instead, intuition, creativity, exoticism, and a trust in the goodness of human passions came to dominate ethical thought. Himmelfarb (1994) argued that modernism oriented society away from an interest in virtue to an interest in values. She saw values as (a) separate from each other and from virtue and (b) fundamentally subjective. Today, postmodern philosophy continues the rejection of absolute truth, promoting a radical relativism of values and a focus on historically contingent communities of knowledge and ethics.

Secular Philosophy Manifested in Modern Psychology

Traces of these broad secular philosophies can be found in modern psychological theories touching on moral development and behavior. Freud's structural theory bears similarities to Plato's three levels of soul, and the ego (reason) is given primacy over the appetitive and emotional aspects of personality. Baumeister's (1997) approach to evil (vice) and human strengths (virtue), like that of classical antiquity, places self-control at the center of moral behavior. We discuss Baumeister's theory in more detail later.

Like many Enlightenment theories, recent behavioral theories of moral action emphasize the acquisition of moral rules and disregard concepts of virtuous character development. Likewise, Kohlberg (Puka, 1994), who is explicitly Kantian in his ethical framework, treats the stages of moral development from a strictly formal, reasoning-based standpoint.

Finally, humanistic psychology, multiculturalism, and narrative psychology all show the influence of Romanticism and its postmodern offshoots. This is especially manifested in the promotion of intuitive and relativistic values. Postmodern philosophy, which denies the possibility of universal moral principles, has provided an umbrella under which contradicting theories can take shelter. It has made respectable conversations between religion and psychology (Jones, 1994). It has also allowed psychologists to consider virtues and vices again, but with a difference from classical approaches to virtue and vice (Sandage & Hill, 2001). Virtues are considered within the recently coalescing field of positive psychology (Seligman & Csikszentmihalyi, 2000). Unlike classical Greek and Roman ethical theory, modern psychological theories do not emphasize the unity of the virtues. Each positive trait and action is viewed as independent of others and has its own literature.

In Table 8.1, we have analyzed some psychological review articles and books on virtues. These sources represent a convenience sample selected because the authors were experts in their area (or books were edited volumes of chapters by experts). As a gross measure of the insulation of the virtues from each other, we have analyzed each bibliography. We tallied the number of references (a) totally, (b) to the specific virtue under examination, (c) to one or more of the other virtues within Table 8.1, (d) to other virtues not listed in Table 8.1, (e) to religion, (f) to self-control, and (g) to any other source. We calculated the fraction of articles citing the focal virtue (i.e., mean of [b] divided by [a] for each article). The mean is .18. This suggests that *sources emphasize the focal virtues*. However, the mean fraction of references to all nine *other* virtues tabulated in Table 8.1 (mean of [c] divided by

TABLE 8.1
Content Analysis of References Within Bibliographies in 10 Reviews of Research on Virtues

Virtue	Reference	Total (a)	This virtue (b)	Nine other virtues tabulated (c)	Virtues not listed in this table (d)	Religion (e)	Self-control (f)	Other (g)
					Number of references			
Hope	Snyder (1994)	899	69	7	6	1	18	798
Gratitude	McCullough, Kilpatrick, Emmons, and Larson (2001)	141	19	9	1	2	0	110
Forgiveness	McCullough, Pargament, and Thoresen (2000)	708	240	9	5	47	4	403
Spirituality	Emmons (2000)	403	22	6	1	85	5	284
Wisdom	Brown (2001)	606	37	4	1	27	0	537
Love	Levin (2000)	85	39	4	0	7	0	35
Self-control	Baumeister and Exline (2000)	20	8	1	1	1	N/A[a]	9
Humility	Tangney (2000)	43	7	4	2	0	0	30
Altruism	Post et al. (2002)	989	78	48	67	70	7	719

[a]See column b.

[a]) for each article was only .03. *This suggests a substantial separation of the literatures* of virtues from each other. The mean proportion of references to religion (i.e., mean of [e] divided by [a] for each article) is .06. *This suggests that virtues are being largely separated from religion.*

Secular Philosophy Manifested in the Psychology of Character Education

Many constituencies are interested in character development. Parents (e.g., see Bornstein, 1995); public, private, and home schools (Devin, 1999); and churches and synagogues support *intentional* character education. Unintentional character education by peers (Harris, 1998; see chap. 12, this volume) and the media (Danish & Donahue, 1996) is also powerful.

Most modern, secular psychological models of character development could be described as Enlightenment models. For example, (a) Kohlberg's (Puka, 1994) model of the development of moral reasoning (for a review, see Jaffee & Hyde, 2000), (b) Enright's (1994) model of reasoning about forgiveness, (c) Salovey's emotional intelligence (Salovey & Mayer, 1989–1990), and (d) Fowler's (1981) model of the development of faith (for a review, see Worthington, 1989) are based on individual psychology, and all emphasize rule-based reasoning and rational problem solving. Unlike classical virtue ethics and most religious approaches to ethics, these models neglect broader issues of character development and do not take into account the relational nature of humans in showing how character develops.

A Secular–Psychological Approach to Virtue and Vice

Baumeister (1997) has studied evil from a social–psychological point of view. We examine this theory in some detail because it has affinities with classical virtue ethics and could provide a secular, scientific basis for character education unlike the Enlightenment models. Baumeister has described his method saying, "I sought to build a theory based on all the facts and findings I could gather, so I have not made a systematic effort to cover what theorists have had to say about evil. . . . I hope that staying scrupulously attentive and faithful to the mass of factual evidence would yield the most correct conclusions possible" (p. vii).

Baumeister analyzes evil from the perpetrator's viewpoint. Generally, we conceptualize evil from the point of view of the victim, bystander, or society. Victims perceive evil to be motivated typically by the perpetrator's pleasure or by desire to create chaos and disruption. From the point of view of perpetrators, however, most violence occurs because persecutors feel attacked or their esteem is threatened. Usually, both sides involved in a violent episode feel provoked (Baumeister, 1997). People focus on the other side's aggressive or harmful actions to justify their victim status and legitimate retaliatory violence. Because of guilt, most people who commit evil acts must perform some cognitive manipulation to allow themselves to harm another person. Typically, they think about their own justification to act evilly or they construe the situation as presenting a problem that requires a mechanical solution. Conflict, warfare, and evil acts against others are part of in-group/out-group differences. Acts of self-protection are seen as justified against the evil "them."

Throughout history, all seem capable of evil. In fact, Baumeister suggests that it might be easier to explain why people do evil than why they do not do evil. Yet society has forces that pull for good; social relations are smoother and survival more likely if people act pro-socially. He suggests that humans do not perpetrate more evil than they do because self-control restrains evil (see also chap. 3, this volume). When people's self-control is weakened through stress, tiredness, social conditions that disinhibit aggression, or cognitive justifications supporting and encouraging aggression, then people indulge their evil motives. Baumeister has studied self-control extensively (Baumeister & Exline, 2000). Because self-control can be learned and increased through practice, this virtue could play an important part in character education. We critique this position later.

JUDAISM

Fundamental Beliefs

Judaism is generally viewed as both a religion and a sociopolitical community (Silver, 1957). Most Jews, regardless of their tradition, believe that humans are born with the capacity to choose good and evil. The central focus of Judaism is placed on living by the Torah—living a Godly life and knowing God (see chap. 10, this volume). One central characteristic of Judaism is *teshuvah*, which means return to the path of God (Dorff, 1998), for all people stray into sin at times. Through Hebrew history, God revealed the way humans can live. When Jews stray from the path, the Torah describes how to return. Initially, the Torah (literally, laws for righteous behavior) described the path to God. New voices appeared in the form of the prophets and other biblical writers who interpreted the Torah in light of their circumstances, and the writings were collected in the Hebrew scriptures. When the writing of those scriptures ceased (about 400 B.C.), there was still a need to interpret how the Torah could be applied in many of the vexing new situations that Jews faced (collected as the *Mishnah*, which were pithy sayings that collected the wisdom of the rabbis into a single volume). In the Jewish tradition, rabbis stated truths succinctly. Rabbis often wrote explanatory material to flesh out the sayings. These explanations are known as *midrash*, which consist of written explanations and sermons. As Jews were dispersed worldwide, after 70 A.D., many experts wrote letters explaining the intent of the Torah and Mishnah into (then) contemporary settings. This collection is known as the *Talmud*, which describes, in a massive volume, the various laws and interpretations that help people return to the path of God and live as Jews in favor with God.

It is not enough to know the Torah and choose rationally. In *Pirke Avot*—Ethics of the Fathers—a Mishna Tactate, if it comes to a choice between study of the Torah without good deeds or doing good deeds without studying the Torah, good deeds come first. Steinberg (1947) writes, "In its eyes, moral excellence stands higher than intellectual, the merciful and just heart above the head no matter how informed and discerning. . . . And while the heroes of Judaism are good before they are wise, they are usually wise as well as good" (p. 66).

Jewish Views of Virtue and Vice

In spite of the diversity within Judaism, on the essentials most traditions agree—namely, (a) people have the capacity for good and evil, (b) choosing the good is a central concern, (c) reason is the key characteristic by which Jews can live a righteous life (i.e., choosing to live by the Torah and other sacred writings) instead of choosing evil and can return to the path if they stray from it, and (d) Jews are a sociopolitical community (Schimmel, 1997; Silver, 1957; Steinsaltz, 1980). For Jews, then, virtue and vice are choices. Virtues that become character traits or dispositions are formed by practicing Godly choices. For most Jews, the master virtues are (a) living a Godly life, (b) reason and logical decision making, and (c) self-control to follow through on rational decisions as virtuous means to achieve a Godly life.

CHRISTIANITY

A Classical Christian Worldview and Its Modern Manifestation

Christianity inherited from Judaism its notions of sin and repentance. Beginning with Augustine, Christians began to engage with classical thought over the nature of virtue. For Christians, the telos of humanity is a loving, obedient, "yielding" relationship with God. Because virtue cannot be considered apart from this relationship, Christians have not placed autonomous reason or self-control at the center of their understanding of virtue. According to Aquinas, reason cannot control the passions (although certainly Aquinas held reason in particularly high regard); rather, the passions themselves must be transformed. It is the passionate love of God, which replaces evil passions, that should guide Christians' lives. Christianity emphasizes virtues that were either unknown to or considered less important to classical philosophy, such as faith, hope, charity, and humility. Our purpose is not to provide a historical account of development of Christian thought (see chap. 2, this volume), so we do not go into details. Suffice it to say that in the Middle Ages, many articulations of Christian virtues were developed.

In early Christianity, the church sought to transmit Christian virtues by educating youth and adults in the life of Jesus Christ. The Christian model of virtue is Christ. A primary educational strategy for Christians has always been the imitation of Christ and of saintly members of the Christian community. Christian virtue is therefore transmitted by a community of believers with a particular narrative.

SHARED AND UNIQUE VARIANCE BETWEEN JUDAISM AND CHRISTIANITY

People Have the Capacity for Virtue and Vice

Both Judaism (see Silver, 1957) and Christianity understand people to have the capacity for good and evil. Christians see the capacity for good and evil as arising in three steps. First, humans were created in God's image, *imago Dei*, and retain that image. As such, humans are fundamentally relational, meaning making (i.e., rational), morally motivated, creative, and volitional. Second, humans became sinful (i.e., fallen). Christians see a fundamental moral gap between God and humans that is due to human choice of willful disobedience. Evil is thus inherent in humans along with good. Third, Christians see Jesus' substitutionary death as restoring the capacity for good to the extent that people allow Jesus to work through them. Christians have a "new self," which is understood differently across Christian traditions.

People Are Relational

Jews and Christians also agree that people are primarily relational (see chap. 4 and chap. 10, this volume). People are thus not able to live virtuously apart from community. For Jews, the relationship between God and people is primary. From Adam and Eve to God's call of Abraham and God's creation of a covenant people of Israel (Abraham's grandchild), the relationship between God and Israel has continued to this day. For Jews, religion also involves relations within the community of Israelites. Much of Jewish law is aimed at how people relate to each other within the Jewish community and how Jews can relate to people outside the Jewish community. Relationship is at the heart of Judaism.

For Christians, the doctrine of the Trinity suggests that relationship preexisted humanity, that is, the three persons of the Trinity related with each other before time began. Relationships between God and humans, within Israel, and within the church, then, were a natural outgrowth of the relational nature of a triune God. In Christianity, the relational nature of people is also rooted in Jesus' commands that all of the law and the prophets are summarized in two commands: to love God with all one's heart, soul, and might (Deut. 6:5; Matt. 22:37) and love the neighbor as the self (Lev. 19:18; Matt. 19:19; Matt. 22:39). These commands define the Christian as having a life mission that is relational at its center and thus pursuing virtue and experiencing consequences of vice in social community.

People Are Not in Perfect Relationship With God

Humans' capacity for evil creates problems for their relationship with God. Both Jews and Christians sense their relational, meaningful, moral, creative, and volitional imperfections. Because people were created to be in relationship with God, the central problem of human existence is how reconciliation with God is believed to occur.

In Judaism, God is the initiator. God spared Adam and Eve, saved Noah, called Abraham, called Moses, established the Davidic kingdom, and restored Jews from captivity in Babylon and Media Persia. Christianity also sees God as the initiator of reconciliation, drawing on the Hebrew accounts but seeing many of those historical events as foreshadowing the incarnation of Jesus of Nazareth—God who became a man to die a substitutionary death for humans who accept God's reconciliative efforts.

Jews and Christians respond to God's offer of reconciliation differently. For Jews (see Applebaum, 1959; Silver, 1957), the key is the reasoned, volitional pursuit of a Godly life through following the Torah and return to the path of God when sin occurs. Jews are most concerned with what people do, with bringing behavior into conscious conformity with moral and ethical precepts, and with implications of those precepts. Christians are most concerned with responding to God's reconciliative initiative in gratitude by accepting God's forgiveness on the basis of Jesus' act. Gratitude might be the fundamental Christian emotion that motivates love (and thus virtuous behavior) in response to God's gift.

Reason Versus Passion

Without trying to overgeneralize about Judaism and Christianity and with a clear belief that we are talking about main effects, we would put forth some hypotheses that are fundamentally empirical questions. We tentatively hypothesize the following. Jews place reason in higher regard than do most Christians. For Jews, reason is the way people make responsible choices and exert self-control. Thus, for Jews, character virtues are built and vices decreased as a consequence of attempting to stay on the path to God. For most

Christian traditions, reason is necessary but not sufficient for salvation (see 1 John). Virtues are built and vices decreased in gratitude and love in response to Jesus' substitutionary death for humans as the Triune God is allowed to control one's will.

An Important Caveat

Let us be clear about what we are and are not hypothesizing. First, by hypothesizing that Jews might emphasize reason more than Christians, we are not suggesting that Christians lack or are deficient in reason. Nor are we arguing that Jews lack or are deficient in gratitude. We are hypothesizing that there are group differences in relative importance placed on achieving specific virtues and perhaps avoiding specific vices. Certainly, patterns contrary to these hypotheses will be found in subgroups within each religion, congregations, and individuals.

Second, we are not arguing that patterns of virtues and vices will mirror precisely the patterns suggested by antiquity. Over time, people's understandings of what is virtue and vice have evolved. Our hypotheses concern current practices, not strict conformity to particular philosophies or theologies from history.

Third, Judaism and Christianity may share more points of similarity than points of divergence. Rokeach (1973) suggested that there were two types of values—*terminal* values, which specify desired end states, and *instrumental* values, which specify pathways to reaching the end states. Using this schema as an explanatory tool (even realizing that empirical cross-cultural research by Schwartz and Sagiv [1995] has not supported Rokeach's schema), we might suggest the following. On terminal goals, Jews and Christians seem to share a primary virtue of knowing God and differ from psychology, whose desired virtue of understanding people is relatively higher. On instrumental values, however, Jews and secular psychologists might elevate reason and self-control higher than Christians, whereas Christians might elevate yieldedness to God's control relatively higher than Jews and secular psychologists.

WHAT CAN JUDAISM AND CHRISTIANITY ADD TO SECULAR PSYCHOLOGY'S APPROACH TO VIRTUES? SIX POTENTIAL ADDITIONS

If we took Jewish and Christian worldviews seriously, at least six additions to secular approaches to virtues would be possible.

1. Religious perspectives could contribute to better understanding of highly religious people.
2. Religious perspectives could critique secular psychological approaches to virtue (for a critique of secular psychotherapies, see Jones & Butman, 1991).

3. Theorizing about a virtue from a religious perspective could provide testable hypotheses (Roberts, 2001).
4. Theological approaches could be critiqued by secular approaches, which could improve the theological approach.
5. The interaction and integration of religious and psychological perspectives could suggest interrelationships not present in either.
6. Theologically tailored approaches to virtue (and avoidance of vice) could provide applied information using presuppositions and concepts that subgroups of religious people could use.

Religious Perspectives Can Help Understand Religious People

First, Christian theology can help understand people whose major motivation is not self-control but is yieldedness to God. Almost all current psychological theories treat self-control as a major (if not *the* major) virtue. Yet more people throughout the world embrace Christianity than any other religion (Park, 2003), which might suggest that our major psychological theories might be deficient at explaining virtue and vice for a substantial plurality of people.

Second, in our multicultural postmodern world, religion orders and organizes virtues. Christianity prescribes virtues related to love, gratitude, humility, mercy, fidelity, and forgiveness. Judaism prescribes virtues related to good deeds; Torah prescribes virtues related to consistent living, rationality, self-control, communal loyalty, and achievement. As can be seen from the tally we presented in Table 8.1, psychology treats virtues as fundamentally independent of each other. Psychology might be enriched by treating virtues in religion-congruent clusters instead of as independent.

Third, whereas psychology has been reluctant to make moral judgments, both Judaism and Christianity clearly prescribe morality, providing guidance for their adherents. Whether religious people choose to behave virtuously or not, choices are clearer for religious people than for those who are secular. Religious considerations can help psychologists understand people whose behavior is guided by religious morality.

Fourth, both Judaism and Christianity emphasize relationships more so than most secular psychology. Holding a relational view of humans would focus psychology's attention differently. Most virtues and vices have been understood to reside within individuals. True, individuals who act virtuously affect other people; individuals who indulge in vice affect others also. In most classical (and even many Christian) versions of the development of virtue and vice, the process is thought primarily to be individual. If, however, we see virtue as being the product of a community interaction in which people are exposed, intentionally or unintentionally, to different interlocking communities that promote an ideal of virtuous behavior, then we see virtue as being an interaction between individual capabilities and the strength of impact of different communities. Integrating Jewish and Christian emphases on relationships can help understand those communities.

Religious Perspectives Can Critique Secular Models

Earlier we described Baumeister's theories of virtue and vice based on his explicit attempt to rely solely on scientific data. Christians might offer two basic critiques. They would disagree with Baumeister's conclusion and his method.

Self-Control Is Not the Master Virtue

Baumeister and Exline (2000) claim that self-control is the master virtue. Christian theologians emphasize that self-control should be seen as a fruit of God's action in one's life rather than something akin to a master virtue (Roberts, 1993). Christians should yield actively to God. Yielding is the master virtue, which produces control by the "new self." Attempting to achieve moral control is experienced by each of us as a battle among our passions. Passions motivating virtue push us in one direction. Passions motivating vice push us in the opposite direction. One set of passions will reign supreme at any moment. Can effortful self-control win the battle for virtue? A Christian view of self-control finds the self to be *inadequate* to win the struggle for virtue on its own. Paul writes,

> I do not do what I want, but I do the very thing that I hate. . . . For I know that nothing good dwells within me, that is, in my flesh. I can will what is right, but I cannot do it. For I do not do the good I want, but the evil I do not want is what I do. (Rom. 7:15b, 18–19, RSV)

Paul concludes that people cannot through effortful self-control control vice and promote virtue. He concludes, "Who will deliver me from this body of death? Thanks be to God through Jesus Christ our Lord!" (Rom. 7:24b–25a, RSV)

Even development of one's natural virtues cannot produce the master virtue of loving God. Oswald Chambers (1935/1963) has written a popular devotional guide for Christians. In his December 9 entry, he writes,

> It is the things that are right and noble and good from the natural standpoint that keep us back from God's best. . . . It is the good that hates the best, and the higher up you get in the scale of natural virtues, the more intense the opposition to Jesus Christ.

Baumeister's Method Is Influenced by His Experience

Baumeister's conclusion that self-control is the master virtue arises in part because he follows a post-Enlightenment legacy but also because he studied evil. He concluded that self-control restrains a person's inherent evil impulses. Imagine, however, that Baumeister had spent 10 years studying love instead of evil. Certainly self-control is important in avoiding temptations and maintaining commitment to a loved one, but few people would cite self-control as the *master virtue* behind the development of love. One finds it more difficult to create feelings of love through self-control than to restrain negative impulses through self-control.

Christianity would argue that this illustrates a problem in studying human nature strictly psychologically. The data that a psychologist might use presumably describe phenomena, but the theories that one develops depend on *which* observations one makes. Which observations are considered data depend on subjective choices, however, such as Baumeister's study of restraint of evil and the role of self-control in doing so. In effect, psychology is trying to arrive at truths about aspects of human nature on the basis of a moving reference point.

In contrast, religious frameworks claim to have universal truth. Humility is necessary because one cannot know whether one's interpretations of religious truth are correct. Yet sacred writings and interpretations change less frequently than do scientific findings. Thus, science is maneuverable, like a powerboat; religion is more stable, like an ocean liner.

Religious Perspectives Can Propose Testable Models

Roberts (2001) has articulated a Christian psychology based on New Testament Pauline writings without reference to psychology (i.e., the religious complement to Baumeister's writing on evil). Paul places the new (redeemed) self in opposition to the old (fallen) self. The *sarx* (the flesh; Rom. 7:5; Gal. 5:16–17) is used in the same way as other words, such as *somates hamartais* (body of sin; Rom. 6:6), *soma tes sarkos* (body of flesh; Col. 2:11), *polaios anthropos* (old self; Rom. 6:6, Col. 3:9), or *soma* (body; Rom. 8:13). Roberts catalogues the virtues arising from the new self and the vices arising from the old self. A Pauline view of virtue and vice goes back to Roman 7 (quoted earlier), in which Paul confesses his inability to control himself and states that Jesus is his deliverer.

A Pauline view of virtues and vices asks what is God's versus what is the person's part in acting virtuously? Roberts suggests that a person can (a) actively yield to the will of God, (b) walk in the newness of life, (c) put off the practice of vices, (d) put on behavior that is characteristic of Christ, (e) put to death the ways of death, and (f) imitate Paul, as Paul imitates Christ. Meanwhile God works internally in the believer. In the Pauline view of virtue and vice, there is a balance between what God does through God the Father's sovereign acts, Jesus' example, and the Holy Spirit's intervention within the person.

Roberts suggests that Christians are transformed people and have wills that ought to be conformed out of gratitude to the character expected by a virtuous God. This provides a testable hypothesis that committed Christians should have high intercorrelations among the range of virtues. This is in contrast to the fragmentation of virtues shown in Table 8.1 and perhaps manifested in nonreligious people in a postmodern environment. It is important that the data are expected to have substantial variance. Few Christians (perhaps none, see Rom. 7) can embody complete yieldedness to God. Yet group differences among highly committed Christians, less committed Christians, and nonbelievers are hypothesized.

Secular Perspectives Can Critique Religious Models

Roberts is a philosopher–theologian, not a psychologist. He uses mainly philosophical and theological methods to uncover truth. Psychology is based on the *scientific method*. A psychologist could critique Roberts's model by operationalizing the constructs, setting up tests of key premises, and measuring outcomes. By treating Roberts's model as a scientific model, it could be evaluated according to the standards of science (e.g., accumulated findings from a *body* of literature, parsimony of theory, elegance of theory, ability to explain the important questions, etc.). Second, the body of the science from which a psychologist draws will be broad and deep. It will include experimental and clinical theories. When Roberts attempts to integrate psychological findings, he uses only clinical psychology, not experimental psychology (Roberts, 1993). Aspects of behavior not commented on in the Bible could be examined to expand Roberts's model. Scientists could ask, "Are there findings from experimental psychology that contribute to a psychology of virtues, vices, and character education?"

The Integration of Secular and Religious Perspectives Can Suggest Relationships Not Present in Either

In previous writing (Worthington, Berry, & Parrott, 2001), we classified virtues into two types: conscientiousness-based virtues (e.g., conscientiousness, honesty, accountability, scrupulousness, self-control, and the like) and warmth-based virtues (e.g. gratitude, forgiveness, love, caring, and the like). We attempted to bring together the classical virtues based on intellect and rationality with the virtues stemming from Romanticism, modernity, and postmodernity that are more guided by positive emotions. We hypothesized that some religions might promote more of one type of virtue than might other religions. We believe that in doctrine, most major religions value both conscientiousness-based and warmth-based virtues but in practice might emphasize one type more than the other. For example, Islam and Judaism might be found to promote mostly conscientiousness-based virtues, whereas

Christianity might be found to promote mostly warmth-based virtues. We suggest that denominations within each religion might differ in their relative emphasis of types of virtues (e.g., Southern Baptists might be found to be more conscientiousness-based and Lutherans more warmth-based), just as congregations within denominations might differ and individuals within congregations might differ. In applying such generalizations, researchers and clinicians thus must be wary of stereotyping or attributing more importance to the "main effects" of such generalizations. Nevertheless, studying the two types of virtues within and outside of religious traditions (more or less finely focused) might permit questions to be asked that would not have been otherwise addressed.

Since suggesting our original two classes of virtues (Worthington et al., 2001), we have created a more extensive listing of virtues and hypothesized three classes of virtues—warmth-based virtues, conscientiousness-based virtues (renamed works-based virtues), and wisdom-based virtues (e.g., wisdom, knowledge). Roughly, these are weighted toward affect, behavior, and cognition, respectively. We hypothesize that religions that emphasize warmth will have longtime adherents and committed new adherents who will manifest warmth-based virtues. Similar reasoning would maintain for works-based and wisdom-based religions.

Religions Can Provide Applied Methods to Help People Become More Virtuous

Schimmel (1997) suggested that classical sources of wisdom and the faith traditions could provide information on helping people live better. Both philosophy and religion can help people cultivate reason and self-control and thus live more virtuously. Pastoral and devotional literatures have reflected the wisdom of billions of adherents to different faiths over the centuries. Although religious practices do not yield data in the sense of controlled and precise measurements, they have withstood the test of time. Therefore, religion and classical philosophy could supply ideas for clinical practice and for academic clinical psychology (see chap. 11, this volume; chap. 3, this volume).

To date, some investigations of the use of ecclesiastical techniques (e.g., prayer, meditation, Scripture reading) as adjuncts to psychotherapy have been conducted (for reviews, see chap. 11, this volume; Worthington, Kurusu, McCullough, & Sandage, 1996; Worthington & Sandage, 2002). Typically, these religious techniques have been treated as tools to enhance self-control of dysfunctional behavior. Only recently have psychologists promoted use of classical religion toward inherently religious (not psychological) ends (see Hall & McMinn, 2000, 2001). Such an emphasis on Christian "yielding" or acceptance rather than on self-control is more in line with traditional Christianity than are previous investigations of ecclesiastical techniques in therapy.

Another Caution

Whereas we hope our position is clear from the development of this chapter, we believe (on the basis of comments from reviewers of this chapter) that it is prudent to emphasize our main thesis again. First, religions have articulated belief systems that will tend to result in religious people embracing specific clusters of virtues more than secularists. Secularists, too, share common virtues (because *culture* is a vehicle to convey values and virtues and to censure vices), but more variance is anticipated (relative to religious groups) because belief systems are not as codified as with religious systems. Second, religions are expected to differ in the *relative* degree to which they embrace specific virtues. Third, there will be common variance because religious systems exist within cultural contexts.

CAN INTEGRATION OF PSYCHOLOGY AND THEOLOGY TAKE PLACE?

Realistically, religion may make only limited inroads in influencing secular–psychological research. It is more likely to influence secular–psychological practice. Integration of religion and psychology can take place at many levels (Worthington, 1994). It can occur, for example, at the level of intellectual disciplines. This would involve creating a conceptual melding of a theology with a conception of psychology as a scientific or practice-oriented discipline. Perhaps more useful, however, is whether individuals can integrate religion into their research or practice or vice versa.

Researchers tend to focus their research on specific topics and methods, and they rarely stray from the straight and narrow. Integration in individual research usually amounts to adding measures of religion or spirituality as moderators on outcome variables. The incorporation of religious issues seems most likely in areas of (a) moral and spiritual development, (b) positive psychology, (c) family and relationships, and (d) religion and health (including mental health). Spirituality has been targeted for federal funding recently, which also could lead researchers into its study—often as an add-on variable.

Clinicians are likely to be more open to what a religious and spiritual perspective might offer them than are experimental or clinical researchers. Most people in the United States profess a belief in God (Gallup, 2000), and most of those are Jews or Christians (although religious and spiritual diversity has increased within the last 25 years because of increasing multiculturalism and immigration). Thus, clinicians daily face clients who have religious and spiritual issues. Clinicians can offer the best counsel or referral if they understand more about their clients' personal spirituality and their clients' religious beliefs and values. This has led to a number of books on religion and spirituality published by the American Psychological Association (Miller, 1999; Richards & Bergin, 1997, 2000; Shafranske, 1996).

In conclusion, there are potential benefits to psychology in taking Jewish and Christian worldviews seriously. We hope that this chapter has made clear, for those concerned with the intersection of the religious and psychological realms in either research or practice, some of the many points of contact and mutual enrichment that can emerge in the area of virtues, vices, and character education.

REFERENCES

Applebaum, M. M. (1959). *What everyone should know about Judaism: Answers to the questions most frequently asked about Judaism*. New York: Philosophical Library.

Baumeister, R. F. (1997). *Evil: Inside human violence and cruelty*. New York: Freeman.

Baumeister, R. F., & Exline, J. J. (2000). Self-control, morality, and human strength. *Journal of Social and Clinical Psychology, 19*, 29–42.

Bornstein, M. (1995). *Handbook of parenting* (Vol. 1). Mahwah, NJ: Erlbaum.

Brown, W. S. (Ed.). (2001). *Understanding wisdom: Sources, science, and society*. Philadelphia: Templeton Foundation Press.

Chambers, O. (1963). *My utmost for his highest*. Toronto, Canada: McClelland and Stewart. (Original work published 1935)

Danish, S. J., & Donahue, T. (1996). Understanding the media's influence on the development of antisocial and prosocial behavior. In R. L. Hampton & P. Jenkins (Eds.), *Preventing violence in America: Issues in children's and families' lives* (Vol. 4, pp. 133–155). Thousand Oaks, CA: Sage.

Devin, T. T. (1999). *Life goals as a framework for character education*. New York: International Educational Foundation.

Dorff, E. N. (1998). The elements of forgiveness: A Jewish approach. In E. L. Worthington Jr. (Ed.), *Dimensions of forgiveness: Psychological research and theological perspectives* (pp. 29–55). Philadelphia: Templeton Foundation Press.

Emmons, R. A. (2000). *The psychology of ultimate concerns: Motivation and spirituality in personality*. New York: Guilford Press.

Enright, R. D. (1994). The moral development of forgiveness. In B. Puka (Ed.), *Reaching out: Caring, altruism, and prosocial behavior. Moral development: A compendium* (Vol. 7, pp. 219–248). New York: Garland Publishing.

Fowler, J. W. (1981). *Stages of faith: The psychology of human development and the quest for meaning*. San Francisco: Harper & Row.

Gallup Organization. (2000, March). *The future of religion in the 21st century*. Philadelphia: Templeton Foundation.

Hall, T. W., & McMinn, M. R. (Eds.). (2000). Christian spirituality: Theoretical and empirical perspectives? Part 1 [Special issue]. *Journal of Psychology and Theology, 28*.

Hall, T. W., & McMinn, M. R. (Eds.). (2001). Christian spirituality: Theoretical and empirical perspectives? Part 2 [Special issue]. *Journal of Psychology and Theology, 29.*

Harris, J. (1998). *The nurture assumption: Why children turn out the way they do.* New York: Free Press.

Himmelfarb, G. (1994). *The demoralization of society: From Victorian virtues to modern values.* New York: First Vintage Books.

Jaffee, S., & Hyde, J. S. (2000). Gender differences in moral orientation: A meta-analysis. *Psychological Bulletin, 126,* 703–726.

Jones, S. L. (1994). A constructive relationship for religion with the science and profession of psychology: Perhaps the boldest model yet. *American Psychologist, 49,* 184–199.

Jones, S. L., & Butman, R. E. (1991). *Modern psychotherapies: A comprehensive Christian appraisal.* Downers Grove, IL: InterVarsity Press.

Levin, J. (2000). A prolegomenon to an epidemiology of love: Theory, measurement, and health outcomes. *Journal of Social and Clinical Psychology, 19,* 117–136.

McCullough, M. E., Kilpatrick, S. D., Emmons, R. A., & Larson, D. B. (2001). Is gratitude a moral affect? *Psychological Bulletin, 127,* 249–266.

McCullough, M. E., Pargament, K. I., & Thoresen, C. (2000). *Forgiveness: Theory, research, and practice.* New York: Guilford Press.

Miller, M. R. (Ed.). (1999). *Integrating spirituality into treatment: Resources for practitioners.* Washington, DC: American Psychological Association.

Park, K. (2003). *World almanac and book of facts.* New York: World Almanac Books.

Post, S. G., Underwood, L. G., Schloss, J. P., & Hurlbut, W. B. (2002). *Altruism and altruistic love.* Oxford, England: Oxford University Press.

Puka, B. (Ed.). (1994). *Moral development: A compendium: Vol. 3. Kohlberg's original study of moral development.* New York: Garland Publishing.

Richards, P. S., & Bergin, A. E. (1997). *A spiritual strategy for counseling and psychotherapy.* Washington, DC: American Psychological Association.

Richards, P. S., & Bergin, A. E. (Eds.). (2000). *Handbook of psychotherapy and religious diversity.* Washington, DC: American Psychological Association.

Roberts, R. C. (1993). *Taking the world to heart: Self and other in an age of therapies.* Grand Rapids, MI: Eerdmans.

Roberts, R. C. (2001). Outline of Pauline psychotherapy. In M. R. McMinn & T. R. Phillips (Eds.), *Care for the soul: Exploring the intersection of psychology and theology* (pp.134–163). Downers Grove, IL: InterVarsity Press.

Rokeach, M. (1973). *The nature of human values.* New York: Free Press.

Salovey, P., & Mayer, J. D. (1989–1990). Emotional intelligence. *Imagination, Cognition, and Personality, 9,* 185–211.

Sandage, S. J., & Hill, P. C. (2001). The virtues of positive psychology: The rapprochement and challenges of an affirmative postmodern response. *Journal for the Theory of Social Behaviour, 31*, 241–260.

Schimmel, S. (1997). *The seven deadly sins*. Oxford, England: Oxford University Press.

Schwartz, S. H., & Sagiv, L. (1995). Identifying culture-specifics in the content and structure of values. *Journal of Cross-Cultural Psychology, 26*, 92–116.

Seligman, M. E. P., & Csikszentmihalyi, M. (2000). Positive psychology: An introduction. *American Psychologist, 55*, 5–14.

Shafranske, E. P. (Ed.). (1996). *Religion and the clinical practice of psychology*. Washington, DC: American Psychological Association.

Silver, A. H. (1957). *Where Judaism differed: An inquiry into the distinctiveness of Judaism*. New York: Macmillan.

Snyder, C. R. (1994). *The psychology of hope*. New York: Free Press.

Steinberg, M. (1947). *Basic Judaism*. New York: Harcourt Brace.

Steinsaltz, A. (1980). *The thirteen petalled rose* (Y. Hanegbi, Trans.). New York: Basic Books.

Tangney, J. P. (2000). Humility: Theoretical perspectives, empirical findings and directions for future research. *Journal of Social and Clinical Psychology, 19*, 70–82.

Worthington, E. L., Jr. (1989). Religious faith across the life span: Implications for counseling and research. *Counseling Psychologist, 17*, 555–612.

Worthington, E. L., Jr. (1994). A blueprint for interdisciplinary integration. *Journal of Psychology and Theology, 22*, 79–86.

Worthington, E. L., Jr., Berry, J. W., & Parrott, L., III. (2001). Unforgiveness, forgiveness, religion, and health. In T. G. Plante & A. Sherman (Eds.), *Faith and health: Psychological perspectives* (pp. 107–138). New York: Guilford Press.

Worthington, E. L., Jr., Kurusu, T., McCullough, M. E., & Sandage, S. J. (1996). Empirical research on religion and psychotherapeutic processes and outcomes: A ten-year review and research prospectus. *Psychological Bulletin, 119*, 448–487.

Worthington, E. L., Jr., & Sandage, S. J. (2002). Religion and spirituality in psychotherapy. In J. C. Norcross (Ed.), *Psychotherapy relationships that work* (pp. 383–399). New York: Oxford University Press.

IV

TRANSFORMATION, CHANGE, AND DEVELOPMENT

9

TRANSFORMATIONAL CHANGE

STEPHANIE BROWN AND WILLIAM R. MILLER

Change has been the subject of research and debate for many years, with questions encompassing the kinds, properties, processes, and causes of change. Psychologists have usually studied small incremental changes, like the successive approximations of a learning curve. Sometimes, however, human change happens on a grander scale, altering not only behavior but also the individual's fundamental identity or personality. *Transformation* is change that is radical in scope, whether it occurs suddenly or gradually.

The potential for transformation of self, usually but not always in a positive direction, is central to a Judeo-Christian understanding of human nature. Vibrant examples of sudden, mystical, permanent, and radical change are found in both Jewish (Moses) and Christian scriptures (Paul). In religious contexts, such transformational change is often termed *conversion* (although the same term is sometimes used to describe a shift in religious or denominational affiliation). Transformational change occurs, however, both within and outside religious contexts, with similar characteristics (Miller & C'de Baca, 2001). Conversion experiences fascinated early psychologists, including William James (1902) and G. Stanley Hall (1904), and remain a subject of substantial psychological research (Spilka, Hood, Hunsberger, & Gorsuch, 2003).

Conversion is often differentiated into passive versus active types. In the passive type, the person has little sense of being a causal agent and may experience being acted on by forces beyond the self. This was the case for both Moses and Paul, and in theological terms such experiences are often understood as the product of divine intervention. Perhaps more common are turnabout transformations (*metanoia* in Greek) in which the person takes a more volitional and decisional role, and which in Judeo-Christian language is usually described as repentance. Both psychologically and theologically, however, the distinction is not so sharp. James (1902) understood transformational changes, whether sudden or gradual, instigated or uninvited, as a process of integration with one's "higher self," or in theistic terms of conscious contact with God (Barnard, 1997). Other scholars describe transformation as a culmination of a person's deep search for significance (Pargament, 1997), meaning (Fowler, 1993), and knowing (Loder, 1989). In Judeo-Christian thought, volitional acts of repentance are not readily separated from the graceful acts of God.

Radical change is not unknown in psychology. Watzlawick, Weakland, and Fisch (1974) differentiated first- and second-order change, and Piaget (1970) defined two interactive change processes in cognitive development. Case studies of unexplained, sudden transformations have been reported by psychologists (e.g., Barlow, Abel, & Blanchard, 1977). Yet psychology has lacked a unifying theory, or even consensus terminology for transformation. Consequently, what has been a central and familiar concept in religion is seldom found in the index of psychology textbooks.

The purpose of this chapter is to define and describe transformational human change from the perspectives of both religion and psychology. First, we ask "What is it?" considering natural language definitions of change and transformation. Next, we outline common properties that comprise a transformational experience and describe how change occurs as a multileveled interaction between process and structure within a developmental frame. We then describe a developmental process of transformational change, including antecedents, a radical shift in deep belief and focus of attachment that accompanies and completes a transition, and finally, the resolution or completed transformational change that includes movement from a two-dimensional to a three-dimensional frame of time and space.

Concepts of self and self-and-other, as systems, are organizing constructs for theories of transformational change. Elements of conflict, human searching, power, will, surrender, acceptance of human limits, and recognition of "other" are all central features of religious and psychological perspectives. We seek here to bridge contemporary religious and psychological views, drawing particularly on the example of Alcoholics Anonymous (AA), a peer support organization with roots in both psychology and religion (Alcoholics Anonymous, 1976).

DEFINITIONS OF CHANGE AND TRANSFORMATION

Webster's Third New International Dictionary (1981) defined change as small change: "to make different in some particular, but short of conversion into something else." In contrast, definitions of transformation involve conversion: "to change completely or essentially in composition or structure" (Webster's, 1981). Transformation is radical discontinuity, sometimes occurring suddenly, at least in appearance (Bien, 2004). It is a shift, not of approximation, but to something different, such as ice to water (Miller & C'de Baca, 2001); it is a shift in form, as well as in content and process.

Transformational change can be an event, a process, and a result. It can be slow and cumulative or rapid and abrupt. As an event, it is a radical rupture: the moment of the shift from ice to water, or the moment of clarity that forever changes one's perceptions and experience of self. Many Christians identify a moment of *metanoia* (turnabout) at which they were "saved." Many in AA similarly recall a turning point that changed them forever, the moment of deep awareness of having lost control of drinking and a subsequent "spiritual awakening" (Forcehimes, 2004). Even when there is a transformational event, it is a developmental process of change, before, during, and after (Brown, 1985, 1993).

CHARACTERISTICS OF TRANSFORMATIONAL CHANGE

Various lists of characteristics of transformation have been compiled, but across conceptions two properties are relatively consistent. Transformational change is a discontinuous shift that is radical in scope. Often, but not always, it is also a permanent change.

Discontinuity

Theorists define *discontinuity* as a distinguishing feature of transformational change. James (1902) differentiated the incremental "educational variety" of change from transformation (conversion). Koestler (1967) defined a perceptual and linguistic process of "bisociation" to describe the radical change that occurs in the "perception of a situation or event in two habitually incompatible contexts that requires an abrupt transfer to different rules or logic." These frames of reference converge, usually with surprising suddenness, to compose a meaningful unity. Bateson (1971) described transformation as an opening within the self rather than a closure.

Transformations also occur at larger system levels. Philosopher Thomas Kuhn (1962) described the limitations of "development-by-accumulation" or incremental change. Scientific revolutions, he asserted, have been characterized by surprising discovery that leads to an unexpected shift in baseline theory, or paradigm. "Each of them necessitated the community's rejection of one time-honored scientific theory in favor of another incompatible with it. Each produced a consequent shift in the problems available for scientific scrutiny and in the standards by which the profession determined what should count as an admissible problem or as a legitimate problem-solution" (p. 6). Scientific revolutions involve a transformation in worldview. "Led by a new paradigm, scientists adopt new instruments and look in new places. Even more important, during revolutions scientists see new and different things when looking with familiar instruments in places they have looked before," a "switch in visual gestalt." "What were ducks in the scientist's world before the revolution are rabbits afterwards" (p. 111).

Discontinuity also characterizes religious thought regarding transformation. Theologian James Loder (1989) described a "logic of transformation" similar to innate grammar. Change cannot be determined while inside the bounds of a particular system. A break occurs, like that of a radical perceptual shift between figure and ground, resulting in an entirely new perception (gestalt). This is a structural change, the self-level equivalent of Kuhn's paradigm shift. Transformation "occurs whenever, within a given frame of reference or experience, hidden orders of coherence and meaning emerge to alter axioms of a given frame and reorder its elements accordingly" (Loder, p. 4). Premises are transposed, leading to "systemic interconnectedness."

Convictional knowing is also a discontinuous transformational event. At the center is a nonrational intrusion of a convicting insight. Like the "aha" when puzzle pieces come together, insight comes like the reversal of figure and ground. Miller and C'de Baca (2001) described this as "the insightful type" of quantum change.

Radical Change

Transformation involves a change in essential structure. Milton Rokeach (1973) characterized it as the sudden reorganization of personality, including the reorganization of reality experience. Carl Jung, an early observer of AA, described these radical changes for alcoholics:

> They appear to be in the nature of huge emotional displacements and rearrangements. Ideas, emotions, and attitudes which were once the guiding forces of the lives of these [people] are suddenly cast to one side, and a completely new set of conceptions and motives begin to dominate them. (Alcoholics Anonymous, 1976, p. 27)

The idea of a quantum leap into the unknown is central to existential thought. Yalom (1980) described an ultimate vacuum within the human psyche, and the individual's defensive efforts to ward off knowing or experiencing this void. Anxiety about death—the ultimate void—is central to the human condition. Yalom also saw paradox as central to transformational change. The individual leaps into the void, the space of unknowing, as the route to finding "knowing" and the internal peace that accompanies it.

These rapid turnabouts are different from the usual incremental changes that characterize people's lives. Quantum change is a "vivid, surprising, benevolent, and enduring personal transformation" involving a "shift in perception and the realization of a new reality" at a deep level (Miller & C'de Baca, 2001, p. 40).

Permanence and Movement

Less clear is the permanence of transformation. A circular definition is that impermanent change was not "true" transformation. Some psychological theories depict oscillation between alternating, stable states (Apter, 1982; Bateson, 1971; Watzlawick et al., 1974), a perspective consistent with at least some strands of Judeo-Christian thought wherein conversion is not irreversible. Indeed, *apostasy*—the loss of a prior faith perspective—is a longstanding subject of study and can occur gradually or abruptly (Spilka et al., 2003). Both Jewish and Christian scripture provide examples of individuals and communities falling out of (and back into) harmony with God.

Of interest, however, is the fact that these large, radical, and sometimes sudden transformations often are permanent. Convictional transformations that were lifelong, although not without internal struggles, are amply illustrated in both Jewish and Christian scriptures. Furthermore, some people who had transformational experiences report knowing at the time that they had passed through a one-way door through which there was no going back. Most "quantum changers" nevertheless describe an ongoing process of opening and evolving, set in motion but not completed by the initial transforming event (Miller & C'de Baca, 2001).

Issues of permanence and movement are key to understanding the process of change for members of AA (Brown, 1985). The acceptance of loss of control of one's drinking as permanent rather than temporary is an early step in transformation within AA, relinquishing a hope to return to drinking and self-control. In this process, many people do move forward and backward, with oscillation between drinking and abstinence, until they achieve stable long-term sobriety. Here, then, is a picture of oscillation that eventually leads to permanent positive change.

Many early philosophers believed in forward movement toward an ideal, although Plato regarded all movement or change to be a degeneration from an original, perfect state (Popper, 1966). Theorists of the "third force" human potential movement in psychology, such as Abraham Maslow and Carl Rogers, endorsed a view of human nature as naturally moving in a positive, growthful direction. Theories of religious development or maturation similarly define transformational change as an expansion, always a move toward higher levels of consciousness and integration with the sacred (Pargament, 1997). Movement for people in AA involves an expansion in consciousness, with an increasingly deeper and wider capacity to know and experience reality, of self and other, without permanent regression to limiting defenses (Brown, 1985).

Yet there is at least anecdotal evidence of transformations that in most structural respects mirror positive quantum changes yet leave the person in what most would agree to be a worse state (Miller & C'de Baca, 2001; Nowinski, 2004). Psychodynamic and developmental theorists highlight physical and emotional trauma or unresolved internal conflict as precursors of a transformational change that moves backward, reducing consciousness, breadth of thought and action. This negative direction of change requires an increase in defenses and a reduction in adaptive function. The individual is locked into an internalized state of repetitions and defensive efforts to control symptoms (Herman, 1992; van der Kolk, 1987). Psychodynamic theorists might argue further that an individual can move out of one closed system of severe conflict into another, via the creation of a delusion. The individual shifts the locus of an internal conflict to an external source, determining, for example, that there is a persecutor who must be kept at bay. This shift from internal to external may reorient the internal world at the level of a transformational change, as conflict is quieted and directed outward. Many would not consider such formation of a delusion to be a move toward health or greater expansion in consciousness, even though the deluded individual is in a sense "resolving" the conflict and "escaping" from a closed system.

A DEVELOPMENTAL PROCESS OF
TRANSFORMATIONAL CHANGE

Development and Change

The idea of development as a process of forward movement and maturation is ancient. Hegel described a "world of flux" that is in a state of emergent and creative evolution. Each of its stages contains the previous ones, from which it originates, and each stage supersedes all previous stages, approaching nearer and nearer to perfection. The general law of development is thus one of forward progression (Popper, 1966).

Development is a key construct in world religions as well (Fowler, 1995). Through both incremental change and transformation, individuals and humanity are meant to move progressively toward a state of perfection. The concept of *perfect* bears a bit of exegesis here. In modern usage, the term implies an immaculate and error-free state. Viewed in this way, the charge to "be perfect, even as God is perfect" (NIV, Matt. 5:48) sounds impossible. The Greek verb *teleo*, derivations of which are translated as "perfect," has rather different connotations. *Telios* is the finished, completed, mature result of development. The acorn is perfected in the oak tree. It is the same root as the dying word of Jesus: "It is finished."

The idea of development also became an early cornerstone of psychological theories of human behavior, with the influence of Darwinian evolution on Freud and other stage theorists. Developmental theory evolved to include a distinction between process (movement) and structure, the "interrelation of parts as dominated by the general character of the whole" (Webster's, 1981). Both religious and psychological theorists define process as continuous movement within a certain "character of the whole," whereas a change in structure is discontinuous and radically alters the whole. Process involves motion, and structure involves the form or the container. Psychologist Althea Horner (1990) further defined structure as the "psychological self," including somatic experience, affect, impulse, perception, and thought. She noted that the mental structures of self and object representations develop in a manner similar to Piaget's (1936/1952) theory of the interaction between process and structure in cognitive development.

Piaget (1954/1968, 1970) saw an innate developmental potential for humans to move in their thinking from the concrete to the abstract. He outlined two kinds of normal, interactive processes of change in cognitive growth that form the structures for people to fulfill this potential naturally. The first involves continuous movement in thinking, a logical, incremental process of incorporating information into an existing cognitive frame, without a change in that frame, which he called *assimilation*. The second involves a radical shift in cognitive frame, or structure, which he called *accommodation*. These integrated processes together move the individual from early sensory-motor levels of cognition to concrete operational, to formal abstract capacities as a child matures. Piaget's theory illustrates how processes of stability and conservation (no change, or incremental change) and transformation are interactive.

Change theorists Watzlawick et al. (1974) defined a model of change that similarly reconciles "the strange interdependence of opposites." They distinguished between first-order change, which is continuous within a given system in which opposites are not a concern, and second-order change that is discontinuous, radical, and involves a resolution of conflictual opposites. With first-order change, the structure remains unchanged, similar to Piaget's assimilation. Second-order, transformational change always involves a next higher developmental level, a move that entails a shift, jump, or discontinuity that provides a way out of the current system, changes that same system, and lays the foundation for a new system. They also suggested that second-order change is usually viewed by the person as

> something uncontrollable, even incomprehensible, a quantum jump, a sudden illumination which unpredictably comes at the end of a long,

often frustrating mental and emotional labor, sometimes in a dream, sometimes almost as an act of grace in the theological sense. (p. 23)

It is a new way of thinking that cannot be familiar or understandable within the logic of what would be a continuous first-order change.

This is similar to Loder (1989), Kuhn (1962), Koestler (1967), and Rokeach (1973) who all noted that factors seemingly remote, even in space and time, may generate coherent insight and new understanding, what then becomes a new gestalt and perceptual reality. Most of the quantum changers interviewed by Miller and C'de Baca (2001) experienced it as coming from outside the self, rather than being self-initiated or controlled. The transformed individual finds, or is found by, meaning that occurs outside of personal control, outside of the person's closed system of meaning (Fowler, 1993). It is "clearly a transcendental phenomenon. It is something to be found rather than to be given, discovered rather than invented" (Frankl, 1984, p. 62).

A Self-System

The interaction between process and structure within a developmental frame is central to systems theory. *Cybernetics* is the interaction between continuous movement within the same frame or structure and radical discontinuous movement that changes the structure of the system. These processes work to establish and maintain a dynamic equilibrium within the self (Bateson, 1971).

A self-system is open or closed according to freedom of movement to grow from lower to higher levels. A closed system is locked into a competitive, polarized struggle of opposite premises, with no opportunity to resolve the conflict. An open system has opportunity for growth because the premises of the system are complementary rather than opposing. Parts of a whole can coexist and together promote growth that is greater than the separate parts. The internal shift from an oppositional to a complementary view of self and world can be a radical psychological and spiritual change. Such a shift operates within the 12 steps of AA, to move from drinking to abstinence and the maintenance of sobriety (Bateson, 1971). The individual acknowledges loss of control and seeks help to deal with this new reality.

Cybernetics theory accents the necessity of structural change (i.e., a shift from a competitive to a complementary frame) in the self-system to achieve a transformation. The system that is locked in a status quo is closed. Movement to resolve the conflict simply reinforces it and narrows the scope of the system. The resolution of a blocked system involves paradox: The recognition that the dichotomy of the conflicted system cannot be willfully changed except by reaching outside the boundaries of that system. In essence, it must involve a recognition of "other." The shift in internal structures of thought involves a rupture and discontinuity in the current system.

In AA, one accepts loss of control and invokes a higher power (often God), outside the self, for help.

Transformation—as an event, a process, or a result—is developmental. A conflict or discontent occurs for an individual within that person's first-order process and self-system. The conflict leads to an arrest in natural movement, which can become the status quo, or the conflict can be a preparation for radical change, which often involves a crisis, moment of clarity, or turning point. This crisis sets in motion a shift in structure, which moves the individual from a two-dimensional, closed self-system to a three-dimensional, open frame, from an individual related only to self to an individual related to self and other. The new structure provides a different way of seeing and interpreting the self and world that forms the foundation for new growth and development. This is quite descriptive of the shift in perspectives reported spontaneously by quantum changers (Miller & C'de Baca, 2001).

Preparation for Transformation

If transformation is a developmental process, then in some sense one should be able to "see it coming," at least in retrospect. Certain antecedents can set the stage for a radical, discontinuous change, but they are often clear only in hindsight, and they do not automatically lead to transformation. The time preceding transformation can involve both preparedness for change and a state of arrested movement. Most developmental theories of change suggest that the roots of change lie within these preceding stages, so that preparation, conscious and unconscious, is inherent to the process. Loder (1989) suggested that

> there is an innate structure in human nature that responds to transformation wherever it appears, even in pagan mythic systems. One may be personally well-prepared for an existential transformation by having suffered irreversible losses for which transformational narratives suggest an undoing. (p. 152)

About half of Miller and C'de Baca's (2001) storytellers reported having been unhappy, often desperately so, prior to the surprising event that preceded their quantum change. Some "hit bottom," whereas others held a victim identity related to experienced traumatic events. Some felt trapped, with no way out, whereas others felt locked in aimless wandering with no sense of purpose. The most common precipitating event for transformation in this group was prayer.

Scholars of human change in both religion and psychology have posited that the heart of transformation involves a change in self, and that what is changed is a self in conflict. Preparation for transformation may involve conscious spiritual "seeking" (Pargament, 1997). A spiritual seeker is unsatisfied with the status quo and aware of a sense of insufficiency, actively pursuing resolution through attachment to, and incorporation of, the sacred. From a psychological viewpoint, preparation for transformation suggests elements of discontent such as conflict, deficits, or arrests in development. It is noteworthy, however, that about half of the quantum changers interviewed by Miller and C'de Baca remembered no conscious distress prior to their experience, which seemed to come uninvited "out of the blue."

Putting together the pieces considered thus far, in a state of preparedness for transformation or conversion, the individual encounters some conflict or limitation that cannot be changed by will (Soper, 1951). The awareness of limitation creates a crisis or turning point that can set a transformation process into motion. Familiar ways of being and responding do not work to resolve the crisis, and in some sense the individual must reach outside the current self for help.

Acceptance

Often in American psychology in general, and clinical psychology in particular, emphasis has been placed on control. Implicitly, the individual is the agent of willful change and self-control. Clinical interventions are often directed at strengthening self-regulation in an effort to gain or regain control. The same approach is not unknown in pastoral counseling as well. American psychology has been criticized as fixated on control and on the power and independence of the individual (Pargament, 1997; Worthington & Berry, chap. 8, this volume).

Judeo-Christian views of human nature suggest some alternatives. The self can be construed not as an autonomous entity but as self-in-relation, and yet more than the sum of its relations (see Evans, chap. 4, this volume). Both Jewish and Christian anthropology understand the person in horizontal relation to the larger community and in vertical relationship to God. Denial of and separation from those relational ties is a quintessential characteristic of sin.

This view of self clashes, of course, with the American cultural ideal of development as moving from dependence to independence. Commenting on the cultural relativism of the concept of dependence, Neki (1976) contrasted U.S. obsession with independence and the developmental norms of more communal cultures, including his native India. The alternative norm, he suggested, is to develop from dependence to dependability, and then with aging to cycle naturally back toward dependence. In a culture in which there are only dependent and independent individuals, who is dependable? Neki's relational anthropology viewed dependence as a natural developmental process rather than a state to be escaped as quickly as possible in adolescence and then shunned as shameful throughout the rest of life.

In this context, transformation can be understood as a developmental process, moving from a closed (self-sufficiency) to a more open system. A first step in this direction is recognition and acceptance of limitation of the self, which can come as a "hitting bottom" crisis or may emerge gradually over time. The limited and incomplete nature of self is taken for granted in religion, wherein the individual exists in conscious relatedness to (and dependence on) other people and to what Jung (1953) called the "higher other." Willingness to "surrender" and be subject to that higher other is fundamental to religion (Rambo, 1993).

There is a balance here between empowerment to shape that which can be influenced, and acceptance of that which is beyond personal control and limitations. The most familiar expression of this balance is Reinhold Niebuhr's (1943) prayer penned during World War II: "God grant us grace to accept with serenity the things that cannot be changed, courage to change the things which should be changed, and the wisdom to distinguish the one from the other." In slightly modified form, Niebuhr's petition continues to be recited worldwide as the "serenity prayer" of AA. Although psychology has heavily emphasized control, there has been growing recognition of the complementary therapeutic value of acceptance, forgiveness, and letting go (Cole & Pargament, 1999; Hayes, Jacobson, Follette, & Dougher, 1994; Sanderson & Linehan, 1999; Worthington, 2000).

Transformation of the Self

If transformation involves a radical change in self, what sort of change is it? In one sense it involves a loss of self, at least of the self-sufficient, self-centered, self-directed, closed-system self. There is a shift from belief in self-power to connectedness with that which is greater than the old self, with an "other." It is a change from self-alone to self-with-other. In spiritual language, that other is the Sacred, the Holy, or God. This shift from a closed to an open system constitutes a discontinuous, transformative change in figure and ground. It also frees the person from a denial of human limitation that keeps him or her locked in a constant struggle for control. It is a paradox: Giving up control (letting go, surrender) paves the way for greater mastery in life. "For when I am weak, then I am strong" (2 Cor. 12:10b, NIV).

The loss of self involved in transformation can be understood more fully as an expansion or opening of self to include (not control) the other. The process of transformational change affirms both the limited self and the "other," to whom an attachment is made and power granted. The individual, in this interactional process, then internalizes the power of the "other" to achieve a more complete self. Religious and psychological theorists describe the process of change following transformation as one of "indwelling" (Loder, 1989) or "internalizing" (Brown, 1985; Pargament, 1997) the other as part of the self (or self as part of the larger other). This is the key to what makes a change transformational: the acceptance of a limited self with power vested in a higher other. It moves the individual from a two-dimensional to a three-dimensional frame. It shifts the individual from an unresolvable, dichotomous inner conflict to a complementary, relational sense of self, a move that resolves the conflict. "Whoever finds his life will lose it, and whoever loses his life for my sake will find it" (Matt. 10:39, NIV).

Judeo-Christian religion departs from psychology, of course, in affirming the reality of the spiritual "other" as God, experienced as a real presence. As a science, psychology can neither confirm nor disconfirm this leap of faith.

Transformation also opens the self to ongoing change toward wholeness. As in Piaget's (1954/1968, 1970) developmental psychology, change occurs as part of a natural progression, moving toward a more complete whole. The third force humanistic movement in psychology similarly views psychotherapy not as a route to a cure, but rather as a method to help individuals resolve conflict and move past obstacles in a way that frees their capacity for continued expansive growth and fulfillment of natural potential within a new, open system. There are apparent and direct parallels to what we are describing as transformation.

It must be acknowledged, however, that many, perhaps most transformational changes seem to occur naturally or spontaneously, without the guidance of a psychotherapist or other expert. The quantum changers described by Miller and C'de Baca (2001) reported precisely this kind of opening and expansion of self—a realization of intimate connectedness to all of humankind or creation. They also experienced their transformation as unfinished—an open and continuing process that was set in motion at a memorable turning point. Their turning point experiences often included encounter with an unknown "other" presence.

Finally, transformation of the self seems to include a radical change in priorities. As Jung observed (Alcoholics Anonymous, 1976), values that had guided the person before are often turned upside down (Miller & C'de Baca, 2001). The transformed person "seeks to give up the 'old love objects,' and the life built around them. In their place, the convert looks for another organizing force, a new 'center of loyalty' " (Pratt, 1946). There is a change in what Tillich (1951) termed the person's "ground of being" and "ultimate concern." A new sense of purpose and direction emerges, similar to the change in structure described by Piaget and by Watzlawick et al. (1974).

THE EXAMPLE OF ALCOHOLICS ANONYMOUS

The fellowship of AA (1976) provides a fascinating context within which to study the process of transformation. Its 12 steps describe a program explicitly intended to lead to spiritual transformation, and AA makes claims and promises that are in some ways more specific (and therefore empirically testable) than those of world religions.

The concept of transformation, of radical change in the self, is central to AA's understanding of recovery from alcoholism. It is a mirror opposite of "take-control" approaches, and in this way the designation of AA as a "self-help" program is mistaken. The imperfection of human beings and the fundamental limitations of self-control represent a cornerstone belief in AA (Kurtz & Ketcham, 1994). Early members of AA recounted their experiences of absolute deflation and surrender from their prior efforts to will a change.

The first step of AA, then, involves recognition of personal limitation, described as "powerlessness." This discontinuous shift in self-conception opens a search for help outside the self. In AA, this involves the recognition and acceptance of an "other," a "higher power" greater than the self. Like many spiritual insights, it is a paradox: to find wholeness through an acknowledgment of limitation (Kurtz, 1979). The third step, in essence a prayer, involves asking the other for help. Put succinctly, these early steps might be summarized as (a) I can't. (b) God can. (c) Please do. The conversion reflected in these first three steps is only a beginning and unfolds into an entire "program" for living that places the self in relation and submission to the other.

The struggle of the alcoholic with alcohol represents, within AA, a microcosm of the larger struggle of human nature. A faulty belief in the power of self is the central dynamic of addiction, with the relinquishment of that belief the paradoxical core of recovery. The alcoholic is cornered by the tension of a double bind: needing more alcohol but denying that need or explaining it as something else. Tension breaks and reality wins with the deep acceptance of having lost control (an acceptance of a limited self) of one's drinking. This surrender forms the foundation for transformation (Tiebout, 1944). Bateson (1971) applied cybernetic theory to alcoholism, emphasizing the critical significance of defeat, or "hitting bottom" in AA terms. Surrender "is the first spiritual experience. The myth of self-power is broken by the demonstration of greater power" (p. 3).

But surrender to what? Within AA, belief in an other, a higher power is necessary to facilitate and maintain the shift in personal view. A relinquishment of a belief in self-control paradoxically enables the individual to place the self *in relation* to others on an equal level. Power is vested in something greater than the self and also greater than any other person. Only with the shift to a complementary frame can the struggle for power be transformed. The alcoholic acknowledges lack of power over self, turns the source of control "over" to an abstract, external, "higher power" that the individual defines, and then, through the process of recovery, reclaims and internalizes. Recovery as described in AA is thus a radical process of second-order change.

Brown (1985), following Bateson and Tiebout, described recovery for members of AA as a developmental event, process, and result, proceeding in stages, each with defined tasks. The individual "hits bottom," accepts loss of control, experiences the death of the old (drinking) self, and separates from alcohol. A process of new growth is set in motion by asking for help, which is a recognition of "other."

The transformation resolves the conflict of control, freeing energy and attention for new development. Acknowledgment of loss of control provides coherence and clarity, and it sets in motion a new search for meaning. At the center is the experience of convictional knowing. The individual "knows" the deepest truth: I am an alcoholic. There is a direct parallel here to the Judeo-Christian confession of sin, recognition of oneself as imperfect, limited, flawed. In AA, this knowledge provides a foundation for new development of the self that involves active reconstruction of the past and new construction in the present. The individual creates a narrative, a new story about the self that incorporates the truth of human limits. The self-system is open and expanding from an ego-centered self-view to a view of self in relation to other, similar to religious theory. "Through an act of yielding, the self becomes part of a new world. The ego is lifted up. The individual moves from an exclusive self-preoccupation to an identification with something larger" (Loder, 1989).

Structural change occurs in the transfer of the belief in self-control to a belief in a higher power. This moves the individual from a first-order effort to regain self-power to an investment of power outside the self, a second-order transformational change. In the ongoing process of development, the individual internalizes and incorporates this belief in something greater so that the self is permanently changed. Although people may oscillate, in the long-term process they strengthen their belief in, and commitment to, a "higher other." They are then changed by this belief as it operates as a new ordering principle for their ongoing growth. The individual has a transformation and is then transformed by engaging in a process of recovery.

CONCLUSION

Transformational change is a real phenomenon, a multileveled event, process, and result, characterized by properties of radical, discontinuous movement and structural change within a developmental frame. Transformation involves preparation, both conscious and unconscious, followed by turning points that lead to, or follow, a rupture in the current frame. This discontinuity moves the individual from a two-dimensional internal framework to a three-dimensional plane that involves a recognition and incorporation of "other." A paradigm of transformation is central to AA that, like Judeo-Christian theology, recognizes the essential limits of self, with ultimate unlimited power vested in a higher "other." The move from a focus on self to a belief in, and incorporation of, the power of "other" constitutes the foundation for radical, transformational change.

REFERENCES

Alcoholics Anonymous. (1976). *Alcoholics Anonymous* (3rd ed.). New York: Alcoholics Anonymous World Services.

Apter, M. J. (1982). *The experience of motivation: The theory of psychological reversals.* London: Academic Press.

Barlow, D. H., Abel, G. G., & Blanchard, E. G. (1977). Gender identity change in a transsexual: An exorcism. *Archives of Sexual Behavior, 6,* 387–395.

Barnard, G. W. (1997). *Exploring unseen worlds: William James and the philosophy of mysticism.* Albany: State University of New York Press.

Bateson, G. (1971). The cybernetics of self: A theory of alcoholism. *Psychiatry, 34*(1), 1–18.

Bien, T. H. (2004). Quantum change and psychotherapy. *Journal of Clinical Psychology, 60,* 493–502.

Brown, S. (1985). *Treating the alcoholic: A developmental model of recovery.* New York: Wiley.

Brown, S. (1993). Therapeutic processes in Alcoholics Anonymous. In B. McCrady & W. Miller (Eds.), *Research on Alcoholics Anonymous* (pp. 137–152). New Brunswick, NJ: Rutgers Center of Alcohol Studies.

Cole, B. S., & Pargament, K. I. (1999). Spiritual surrender: A paradoxical path to control. In W. R. Miller (Ed.), *Integrating spirituality into treatment* (pp. 179–198). Washington, DC: American Psychological Association.

Forcehimes, A. A. (2004). *De profundis:* Spiritual transformation in Alcoholics Anonymous. *Journal of Clinical Psychology, 60,* 503–518.

Fowler, J. (1993). Alcoholics Anonymous and faith development. In B. McCrady & W. Miller (Eds.), *Research on Alcoholics Anonymous* (pp. 113–135). New Brunswick, NJ: Rutgers Center of Alcohol Studies.

Fowler, J. (1995). *Stages of faith: The psychology of human development and the quest for meaning.* San Francisco: HarperCollins.

Frankl, V. (1984). *The will to meaning: Foundations and applications of logotherapy.* New York: Vintage Books.

Hall, G. S. (1904). *Adolescence: Its psychology and relations to physiology, anthropology, sociology, sex, crime, religion, and education.* New York: Appleton.

Hayes, S. C., Jacobson, N. S., Follette, V. M., & Dougher, M. J. (Eds.). (1994). *Acceptance and change: Content and context in psychotherapy.* Reno, NV: Context Press.

Herman, J. (1992). *Trauma and recovery.* New York: Basic Books.

Horner, A. (1990). *The primacy of structure.* Northvale, NJ: Jason Aronson.

James, W. (1902). *The varieties of religious experience: A study in human nature.* Cambridge, MA: Harvard University Press.

Jung, C. (1953). *Two essays on analytical psychology.* Cleveland, OH: Meridian Books.

Koestler, A. (1967). *The creative act.* New York: Macmillan.

Kuhn, T. (1962). *The structure of scientific revolutions*. Chicago: University of Chicago Press.

Kurtz, E. (1979). *Not-God: A history of Alcoholics Anonymous*. Center City, MN: Hazelden.

Kurtz, E., & Ketcham, K. (1994). *The spirituality of imperfection*. New York: Bantam Doubleday Dell.

Loder, J. (1989). *The transforming moment*. Colorado Springs, CO: Helmers & Howard.

Miller, W. R., & C'de Baca, J. (2001). *Quantum change: When sudden insights and epiphanies transform ordinary lives*. New York: Guilford Press.

Neki, J. S. (1976). An examination of the cultural relativism of dependence as a dynamic of social and therapeutic relationships. *British Journal of Medical Psychology, 49*, 1–22.

Niebuhr, R. (1943). The serenity prayer.

Nowinski, J. (2004). Evil by default: The origins of dark visions. *Journal of Clinical Psychology, 60*, 519–531.

Pargament, K. (1997). *The psychology of religion and coping: Theory, research, practice*. New York: Guilford Press.

Piaget, J. (1952). *The origins of intelligence in children*. New York: International Universities Press. (Original work published 1936)

Piaget, J. (1968). *The construction of reality in the child*. New York: Basic Books. (Original work published 1954)

Piaget, J. (1970). Piaget's theory. In P. Mussen (Ed.), *Carmichael's manual of child psychology* (3rd ed., pp. 703–732). New York: Wiley.

Popper, K. (1966). *The open society and its enemies* (Vol. I). Princeton, NJ: Princeton University Press.

Pratt, J. B. (1946). *The religious consciousness: A psychological study*. New York: Macmillan.

Rambo, L. R. (1993). *Understanding religious conversion*. New Haven, CT: Yale University Press.

Rokeach, M. (1973). *The nature of human values*. New York: Free Press.

Sanderson, C., & Linehan, M. M. (1999). Acceptance and forgiveness. In W. R. Miller (Ed.), *Integrating spirituality into treatment* (pp. 199–216). Washington, DC: American Psychological Association.

Soper, D. W. (1951). At the end of self, God. In D. W. Soper (Ed.), *These found the way: Thirteen converts to Protestant Christianity* (pp. 173–175). Philadelphia: Westminster Press.

Spilka, B., Hood, R. W., Jr., Hunsberger, B., & Gorsuch, R. (2003). *The psychology of religion: An empirical approach* (3rd ed.). New York: Guilford Press.

Tiebout, H. (1944). Therapeutic mechanisms of Alcoholics Anonymous. *American Journal of Psychiatry, 100*, 468–473.

Tillich, P. (1951). *Systematic theology*. Chicago: University of Chicago Press.

van der Kolk, B. (Ed.). (1987). *Psychological trauma*. Washington, DC: American Psychiatric Press.

Watzlawick, P., Weakland, J., & Fisch, R. (1974). *Change*. New York: Norton.

Webster's third new international dictionary. (1981). Springfield, MA: Merriam-Webster.

Worthington, E. L. (2000). *Dimensions of forgiveness: Psychological research and theological perspectives*. Philadelphia: Templeton Foundation Press.

Yalom, I. (1980). *Existential psychotherapy*. New York: Basic Books.

10

EMERGING MODELS OF SPIRITUAL DEVELOPMENT: A FOUNDATION FOR MATURE, MORAL, AND HEALTH-PROMOTING BEHAVIOR

JARED D. KASS AND SUSAN LENNOX

The role of spiritual maturation in human development has not been fully explored. When Erikson (1963) identified religion as a foundational resource through which parents provide children with a sense of trust, and through which elders cope with impending death, he took a first step toward assigning a meaningful role to spirituality within developmental models. Subsequent steps include study of the health consequences of spiritual well-being among the elderly (Koenig, 1994; Moberg, 2001); religious faith across the life span (Worthington, 1989); religious coping (Pargament, 1997); and developmental mentoring (Daloz Parks, 2000). Nonetheless, spiritual maturation remains marginal in developmental literature. Clinebell (1995) criticized this marginalization, suggesting that spiritual development is a critical fulcrum through which mature attitudes and behaviors are shaped.

We thank Rabbi Michael Luckens for his review of the second section of this chapter (Spiritual Development: Conceptualizations From the Jewish Tradition), and Jennifer Crane for her work as research assistant.

Porpora (2001) highlights a societal need to understand spiritual development more fully. Although 95% of Americans believe in a Divine Being, only 50% report this belief to affect their systems of meaning or moral behavior. Data from the National Opinion Research Center and structured interviews suggest that most Americans have "an emotional detachment from the sacred." God is an abstraction, not an experienced reality through which matrices of meaning and behavior are developed (Porpora, 2001). These data support Fowler's (1981) rueful observation that few people achieve mature stages of faith. They may also help explain the modest empirical relationships found between spirituality and well-being (Wulff, 1997). Mature religious coping is beneficial (Pargament, 1997), but many people may not know how to achieve this. Consequently, Porpora (2001) suggests the need for a model of spiritual development that is accessible and compelling to adults in our society.

Currently, the field of human development lacks a comprehensive conceptual and methodological model of spiritual development. Aspects of this process have been studied through specific lenses, resulting in a pastiche of constructs rather than an integrated model. The purpose of this chapter is to take a tentative step toward articulating a more comprehensive framework through which spiritual development can be understood and studied. In the first section, we review current psychological models of spiritual development. In the second section, we examine a more comprehensive religious model, drawing on Maimonides' *Guide of the Perplexed*. In the third section, we present a case study that describes a young adult engaged in a process of spiritual development.

SPIRITUAL DEVELOPMENT: CONCEPTUALIZATIONS FROM PSYCHOLOGY

Several streams of inquiry have examined changes that take place in an individual during spiritual maturation. Five areas of investigation are discernible in the literature: maturation of conceptual processes that shape religious meaning; adherence to a moral and behavioral framework that contributes to social justice and individual well-being; maturation of God representations; capacity for core religious experience; and participation in the developmental challenges of the human life cycle as vehicles for spiritual growth.

1. *Maturation of conceptual processes that shape religious meaning*: Structural developmental research observes distinct stages in cognitive learning (Piaget, 1952) moral decision making (Gilligan, 1982; Kohlberg, 1981), and ego formation (Kegan, 1982; Loevinger & Blasi, 1980). In each area, advanced cognitive processes are more autonomous, tolerant of ambiguity, and sensitive to complex interdependent factors.

Fowler (1981) observed a similar maturational process during faith development. Initially, religious concepts and values are received from family and community. Following a conventional period of unreflective acceptance, individuals begin to think autonomously and to develop systems of meaning more congruent with their life experience. Individuals move from rigid concepts of "right and wrong" or "us and them" to more complex, inclusive universalizing modes of faith. Their relationship with God moves from socially constructed and consensual to authentically personal.

Similar patterns emerge in other research. Oser and Gmunder (1991) observed change in religious explanations of life crises. In early developmental stages, individuals see God as the sole cause of problems. Later, they replace God's agency with their own. Finally, they develop interdependent explanations, affirming personal agency while recognizing interdependence with God and other people. Allport (1957) and Genia (1995) found mature religious faith characterized by autonomous thought and human interconnectedness. In research on postconventional stages of ego development, Cook-Greuter (1994) identified cognitive processes that underpin and clarify universalizing faith. In these stages of higher order thinking, individuals are more aware of themselves as fluid selves embedded in a matrix of interconnections and display a heightened capacity for self-awareness regarding their behavior.

Fowler's model has received useful criticism. Its hierarchical structure appears to value moral relativism and lack of commitment to organized religion (see next section). However, the identification of the capacity for autonomous thought and the perception of universal human connectedness as measures of spiritual maturity are substantive contributions to the study of spiritual development in a religiously plural society.

2. *Adherence to a moral and behavioral framework that contributes to social justice and individual well-being:* Although adherence to such a framework is central to every religious tradition, this concept is not a focal criterion of maturity in the structural perspective. Fowler values social justice and behavioral self-regulation. However, his model has been read to suggest that they only emerge from postconventional, autonomous religious faith. Critics consider the limitations of this hierarchical structure to be serious, particularly because Fowler recognizes that few individuals reach advanced stages of his faith development model (Koenig, 1994; Moberg, 2001).

A robust model of spiritual development requires greater focus on adherence to moral and behavioral codes. Furthermore, it must recognize the reinforcement that organized religious communities provide for these goals. Rather than view behavioral self-regulation as *an outcome of* spiritual development, this model might better view behavioral self-regulation as *a foundation for* spiritual development. Recent models of Christian religious maturity contribute to a more comprehensive definition of spiritual development by emphasizing the significance of behavioral criteria and participation in congregational life (Benson, Donahue, & Erickson, 1993; Ellison, 1999; Malony, 1988).

3. *Maturation of God representations*: Object relations and social learning theories identify forces that shape an individual's images of God. Initially, these insights were used as proofs that God did not exist (Wulff, 1997). However, as this conclusion has been questioned, these insights have been used in pastoral counseling to help individuals overcome distorted, and distorting, God images (Clinebell, 1984).

Rizzuto (1979) is figural in this reformulation of object relations theory. Although early God representations generally are projections of parental figures (either punishing or beneficent), Rizzuto observes that the God representation is an autonomous, stable aspect of the psychic structure. Spero (1992) carries this formulation further. He uses Freud's pre-psychoanalytic writing to suggest evidence that the infant begins life with a potential for religious feeling built into the psychic architecture prior to the onset of representational activity. For Spero, God is real and not simply a projective object. Meissner (1996) synthesizes these approaches. He suggests that the job of a psychotherapist is to accept the presence of God representations and to help deconstruct distortions of those God images that emerge from maladaptive object relations. Thus, a central task in spiritual development is to examine one's images of God, to understand their meanings and origins, and to transcend distorted representations by replacing them with images congruent with a benevolent, loving God (Jordan, 1986).

Social learning theorists emphasize cognitive and cultural forces that shape God images (Poloma, 1995). Extending Proudfoot's (1985) work on religious attribution, Katz (1983) argues that all religious experience is culturally conditioned. Feminist and multicultural theorists lend support by observing that images of God reflect the gender and race of a society's dominant social group (Spretnak, 1982). However, many of these same theorists refuse to reduce God to a cultural construct. God is a primary source of resilience for African American families (Billingsley, 1992). The cultural shaping of God representations does not preclude God's a priori existence (Spretnak, 1991). Clinebell (1984) considers the social deconstruction of God images a valuable aspect of Christian spiritual development.

4. *Capacity for core religious experience*: Although James (1902/1958) introduced the psychological study of religious experience, Allport may be more responsible for recognition of its role in spiritual development. Investigating the disturbing positive relationship that had been found between religion and racial prejudice, Allport and Ross (1967) concluded that religion did not become a maturational force until its values became deeply internalized or *intrinsic*. One aspect of intrinsic religiosity is the experienced awareness of the presence of God.

Allport's research provided groundwork for studies by Hood (1975) and Batson and Ventis (1982) in which religious experience and the quest for personally meaningful spirituality were found to contribute to psychological well-being and maturation. Subsequently, Kass and colleagues found that *core spiritual experiences* have two elements: (a) a distinct event and a cognitive appraisal of that event, which results in personal conviction of God's existence; (b) the perception of a highly internalized relationship between God and the person (Kass, Friedman, Leserman, Zuttermeister, & Benson, 1991). When individuals experience God's presence and recognize this presence as a core foundation of self, their psychological resilience appears to increase (Easterling, Gamino, Sewell, & Stirman, 2000; Kass, 1995). Core religious experience cannot be engineered. However, receptivity to these experiences is enhanced through contemplative practices common to the world's religious traditions (Poloma & Gallup, 1991). A central effect of contemplative practices is the emergence of the perceptual capacity for *connective awareness* (Kass, 2001). Neurological correlates of this emergent perceptual capacity have been observed by Newburg and D'Aquili (2001) using spectral tomography.

5. *Participation in the developmental challenges of the human life cycle as vehicles for spiritual growth:* Erikson rooted his stage model in biological epigenetic forces more deeply than did Fowler. Consequently, neo-Eriksonian models focus on different aspects of spiritual development than Fowler's formulation. These models begin with Erikson's insight that the biological and social phases of the human life cycle are structured to produce psychological growth. Helminiak (1987) suggests that God is the foundation of the epigenetic developmental process. Human development and spiritual development are synonymous constructs and share the same goal: an autonomous individual capable of self-transcendence and authenticity. Theist, and specifically Christian, perspectives add depth to an understanding of this process. However, they do not change the developmental process itself. Meissner (1987) suggests that God is more integrally involved in the developmental process. Through Divine grace, God empowers the individual to mature spiritually as well as psychologically. Meissner describes eight phases of spiritual development analogous to Erikson's stages: faith–hope, contrition, penance–temperance, fortitude, humility, love of neighbor, service, and charity. Loder extends (1998) these ideas. He suggests that the developmental challenges that God has built into the life process contain the potential for the discovery of our spiritual identity and our capacity to embody Divine, altruistic love. Thus, these theorists extend Erikson's normative developmental insights to include maturational potentials of a deeply spiritual nature. When individuals learn to participate in the life process as a vehicle for spiritual maturation, the full range of human potential can be experienced and achieved.

Conclusion: The streams of inquiry that we have reviewed provide important perspectives on spiritual development. Together, they may identify most elements that our religious traditions consider salient. However, each model only highlights certain elements. None describes the rich interplay between elements that is crucial to this process. This complexity can be understood best through closer analysis of the lived experience of a religious tradition. Although any major religious tradition would illustrate our point, we will look at this holistic process through the lens of the Jewish tradition.

SPIRITUAL DEVELOPMENT: CONCEPTUALIZATIONS FROM THE JEWISH TRADITION

Judaism is "a way of life that endeavors to transform virtually every human action into a means of communion with God," explains Rabbi Louis Finkelstein (1999, p. 294), former chancellor of the Jewish Seminary of America. This process takes place through performance of *mitzvot* (good deeds) that elevate each aspect of daily life—including interpersonal relationships, parenting, sexuality, work life, diet, and preservation of health—to the domain of the sacred. The *mitzvot* include the moral imperatives of the Ten Commandments, the justice imperatives of the prophets, and a panoply of daily blessings and prayers. Together, the *mitzvot* comprise a code of behavior and a vehicle for elevated awareness called *halakhah* ("the way"). Through *halakhah*, communion with God becomes a daily, lived experience (Ariel, 1995). Thus, from the Jewish perspective, the highest state of spiritual development can be described as constant behavioral, cognitive, and affective immersion in one's relationship with God.

Maimonides (Rabbi Moses Ben Maimon, 1135–1204) is a key figure in the development of *halakhah*. He served as Chief Rabbi of Cairo and physician to the Sultan of Egypt; his ideas influenced many religious thinkers, including St. Thomas Aquinas (Heschel, 1982). His classic work, *The Guide of the Perplexed*, is a pillar of Jewish philosophy (Maimonides, 1963). The purpose of Jewish law, he explains, is to promote the welfare of body and soul, and to create social organizations that enhance health and well being through justice (book III, chap. 27). The achievement of these goals requires spiritual development, a process that he describes comprehensively.

Maimonides (1963) summarized a Jewish model of spiritual development near the end of *The Guide* (book III, chap. 54). He begins by quoting Jeremiah (9:22–23):

> Thus saith the Lord: Let not the wise man glory in his wisdom, neither let the mighty man glory in his might, let not the rich man glory in his riches; but let him that glorieth glory in this, that he understandeth and knoweth Me; That I am the Lord who exercise loving kindness, judgment, and righteousness, in the earth; For in these things I delight, saith the Lord.

In this beautiful passage, Jeremiah does not claim that wealth, power, and knowledge are inherently evil. However, these attributes should not be glorified. A human being's purpose, and highest potential, is to understand and to know God.

We achieve this developmental pinnacle through two methods. First, we govern our behavior by following the essential principles of *halakhah*: loving kindness (the Golden Rule), righteousness (commitment to fairness and social justice), and judgment (empowered action bringing loving kindness and justice into the world). Thus, *how we use* our wealth, power, and knowledge is a crucial moral and developmental fulcrum that must be approached self-reflectively. From a Jewish perspective, the quality of community that we build with others is a principal measure of spiritual development.

Second, we immerse ourselves psychologically in awareness of God's presence. For, Maimonides (1963) added, "God is very near to everyone who calls, If he calls truly and has no distractions; He is found by every seeker who searches for Him, If he marches toward Him and goes not astray" (book III, chap. 54, p. 638). This idea can make a challenging task seem overly easy. Our biggest distractions—desires for wealth, power, and knowledge—have a strong hold on our minds. Nonetheless, this statement is built on an insight central to Jewish spirituality: God can be known because "in its profoundest being, the soul of man is a part of the Divine" (Steinsaltz, 1980, p. 51). Maimonides considered the soul a point of access between humans and God. The soul's capacity for "rational intuition" brought "contact, assimilation, and (sometimes) identity with, not God, but the Active Intellect," which Maimonides considered God's formative manifestation in the world (Goodman, 1999, pp. 21–23).[1] In Maimonides's (1963) model of psyche and soul, "when the senses rest" and the mind is free from the distractions of daily life, the "imaginative faculty" can experience God's presence (book II, chap. 36).

God as *spiritual presence* is a figural concept throughout *The Guide* (Maimonides, 1963). Although written in the 12th century, it seems a surprisingly modern text. A key theme is the deconstruction of images that suggest God's corporeality, gender, or physical location (book I, chaps. 1, 46; book II, chap. 25). Maimonides shows that the Talmud does not support literal interpretation of these images (book I, chap. 46) and that the visions of prophecy cannot be perceived by the senses (book I, chaps. 49, 50; book II, chap. 46). These visions (whether internal or external) should be understood as images that God places in the mind of the prophet to illuminate qualities of God's being (book I, chap. 46). Drawing from Isaiah (12:3) and the Talmud, Maimonides suggests that a more useful image for understanding God is "an overflowing spring of water" (book II, chap. 12). For God is not a separate being in place and time. Rather, God is the eternal *I Am* (Exod., 3:14), the foundation of being (book I, chap. 63).

---

[1]Goodman explains that rabbis who find rationalism and mysticism incompatible often place Maimonides in their camp. However, the connection between the soul of man and God is central to Maimonides's ideas.

The Talmudic image of Divine *overflowing* (Maimonides, 1963, book II, chap. 12) taps a central paradox of Jewish spirituality. God is separate from physical reality (transcendent) and, at the same time, a pervasive inner presence (immanent; Mintz, 1984; Steinsaltz, 1980). Human consciousness has the capacity, at the core of psychological being, to apprehend and draw inspiration from God's presence. Maimonides's account of inspiration "is a serious and profound attempt to make conceptual sense of what [the 10th-century Muslim philosopher who influenced Maimonides] al-Farabi called higher-order thinking" (Goodman, 1999, p. 15). This capacity for higher order thinking (i.e., connective awareness) is the second means through which Jeremiah's admonition to know God can be achieved.

Thus, the Jewish perspective on spiritual development suggests a constant interaction between two methods of communion with God: adherence to *halakhah* (transformation of behavior through self-regulation and deeds governed by loving-kindness, righteousness, and judgment) and immersion in the apprehension of God's presence (transformation of cognitive and relational worldview through deconstruction of God images and higher order thinking during prayer and contemplative practice). The interaction between these elements becomes even more apparent in Maimonides's discussion of two additional topics: evil and the stages of spiritual growth.

Maimonides (1963) describes three categories of evil. The first type results from the underlying process that governs physical matter: *coming-to-be* and *passing-away*. Consequently, humans experience death, illness, and natural disasters (book III, chap. 12). He calls them evil because they are destructive. Yet their source is Divine providence: "Were it not for the passing-away of the individuals, the coming-to-be relating to the species would not continue." We cannot be "endowed with flesh and bones" and not be subject to the restrictions of physical existence. Maimonides develops this idea to emphasize that God does not create evil "as an essential act." Rather, evil stems from "a privation" consequent to the nature of material life. Therefore, the best way to cope with this type of evil is to affirm, rather than turn away from, one's relationship with God (book III, chap. 10).

Maimonides foreshadows existential and psychoanalytic thought when he describes ontological privation as a primary human experience. The centrality of this existential wound explains why the experience of connection with God is the primary therapeutic method that Judaism teaches. At the same time, Maimonides (1963) considers the central wound of privation as the cause of the other two forms of evil, both of which are the result of human action and free will (book III, chap. 17). The second type of evil is "actions that humans inflict on each other." A primary example is tyrannical domination of one person (or people) over another. The third type of evil is "actions that humans inflict on themselves." Primary examples are "the vices" of unregulated eating, drinking, and sexuality that he considers causal to physical and psychological ailments (book III, chap. 12). Fundamentally, these two types of evil are rooted in "ignorance." If humans perceived their underlying connection with God, and thereby overcame ontological privation, "they would refrain from doing any harm to themselves and others" (book III, chap. 11).

Maimonides (1963) describes a stage model of spiritual development (book III, chap. 51). These ascending stages can be summarized as unregulated behavior; adherence to *halakhah* that is unreflective and literal in its interpretation; adherence to *halakhah* that reflectively tries to understand essential meaning through nonliteral interpretation, scientific understanding, and rational thought; and a final stage that adds to the previous level the use of higher order thinking for full immersion in the experience of connection to God. Thus, Maimonides identifies advanced levels of spiritual development. However, behavioral adherence to *halakhah* remains foundational at every stage.

Maimonides's stage model is rooted in the Jewish conception of history. Personal and social history are "the meeting ground between God and man" (Hahn, 1993, p. 74). Even tragic circumstances contain the potential for spiritual development if we face these events in communion with God. This concept is illustrated in Frankl's method of logotherapy derived from his Holocaust experience (Frankl, 1959; Kass, 1996). When faced with human evil beyond his control, Frankl learned to ask not "Why is this terrible circumstance happening to me?" but rather, "What does life expect of me at this moment?" Frankl's response encapsulates Maimonides's approach to spiritual maturation. It offers a distilled strategy for meaningful life choices and a joyful relationship with God throughout the life span.

In summary, Maimonides presents an interactive, multidimensional *behavioral–cognitive–relational* model of spiritual development that integrates the five elements of spiritual growth discussed in the previous section. This model can be described operationally as the ability to embody loving-kindness, justice, and empowered action in one's relationship with self and others, through immersion in relationship with God.

CASE STUDY IN SPIRITUAL DEVELOPMENT

Although Maimonides offers a compelling model of, and rationale for, spiritual maturation, these ideas are not readily accessible in a society that has become emotionally detached from the sacred. Porpora's (2001) work suggests the need to translate these concepts into a format that is compelling to contemporary adults. The following case study reviews a student's participation in a transformative learning curriculum that has been taught to adult undergraduate and graduate students since 1987 (Kass, 2001). This curriculum is designed to help students understand the functional role of spiritual development and contemplative practice in human maturation. It illustrates a behavioral–cognitive–relational model of spiritual maturation by engaging them in a sequenced, experiential learning process using written self-inquiry assignments. Students with a broad range of religious beliefs (including atheism) participate in a multifaith learning group in which a particular religion is not espoused. Students are encouraged to identify and deepen their particular spiritual identity while learning to value other spiritual traditions. The data for this case study were derived from this student's written self-inquiry narratives.

Karen was a 26-year-old accountant studying for a master's degree. She grew up in a stable, loving Southern Baptist family. In her spiritual autobiography, written in the first weeks of class, she explained that religious life had been important to her when she was young but that she now felt estranged from her religion and spirituality.

> I always liked church. I enjoyed the community. I'm a social creature, so it provided an outlet for that . . . I was loved there. I was a member of the youth group; I played the piano for the children's choir. . . . Sometimes I would feel the Spirit, and at age 11 I was baptized. . . . As I got older I began to claim my beliefs and to argue for them in church. I never just accepted what people said. I knew what was true in my heart, my gut, my intuition. My mother taught me that. And I thank her for it. . . . When my Sunday school teacher came back from a mission trip in Poland and called the Catholic Church a work of the Devil, I got up and walked out. I stopped going to church regularly after that. . . . When I got to college, my roommate took me to the open house at the Baptist Student Union. Coincidence? Nothing is. I found a worship community. . . . Most of the students were questioning their heritage like I was. We communed with one another in Christ.

These activities produced new awareness about prejudice and social justice. "I saw another side of religion. The side you have to wrestle with, just like Jacob. . . . My journey became clearer and more difficult. How was I to accept, to claim my heritage and embrace my religion?" Although these were important times of friendship and engagement, she stopped going to church when she graduated. "I haven't been active in church since."

Karen enrolled in the class for two reasons. First, her previous religious activities had been oriented primarily to social justice and her own social needs. She wanted to explore her own spirituality in a deeper way. "I want to find my religious self and nourish her. . . . Why is this important to me? Because I am a Christian. And that to me means to be Christ-like." Second, she had become aware of inner turmoil that previous religious activities had not helped her explore. Spirituality had always been "her strength." Yet she needed "to renew that strength" in a deeper way "and learn how to heal wounds that are buried too deep within for any x-ray to find." Karen had begun to acknowledge "my own force of destruction: depression. Not just sadness, but feeling utterly morose. I've never contemplated suicide. But I have often felt a desire to live within myself. To stop interacting with the world."

These wounds focused on "being a woman, being feminine, feeling loved." Throughout childhood, she remembered people telling her she was pretty. "Then came adolescence! Does anyone come out unscathed!? I didn't. I was sooo tall. I had my growth spurt in the 6th grade. I was 5'6" . . . and the boys were all 5'!" Throughout high school, "I could never figure out the relationship thing. I had a few boyfriends, but it never lasted very long. . . . In college it just got worse. Everything was about sex appeal and that meant short skirts, tight clothes. Not me at all. . . . I still struggle with this issue. I have learned that how I feel is more important than what I think I look like. But I still base so much on looks. . . . This whole thing still confuses me."

Karen's depression reflected the collision of developmentally appropriate needs for intimacy with our culture's destructive pressure on women to be thin. Her depression also reflected a discontinuity between her previous religious development and her psychological life. These two aspects of her life were not in balance.

After writing a spiritual autobiography, the students chose a behavior or attitude (relevant to the well-being of self or others) that they wanted to change. Karen focused on depression. She then was asked to explore her specific behavioral responses to the stress in her life. "I like to eat comfort foods. That temporarily eases the situation, but it makes for more stress in terms of body image." Extending this exploration to her psychological responses to stress, she noticed a pattern: "I also tend to seek comfort from people. . . . I realize that I am addicted to certain people and the way they make me feel. I find myself needing to hear from or talk to certain people. I experience the high, the withdrawal and the rationalizations. Scary!"

Karen began to recognize the lengths that she would go to feel comforted. Her exploration of these themes soon suggested an underlying negative aspect of her worldview. "When I feel lonely or hurt . . . all my insecurities kick in and I feel as if I am in some way not good enough for the world." Asked about her relationship with God at times of stress, she reflected, "I think I forget about God in these times. I just ignore God because I know if I seek that source that I will have to deal with the real issue or pain and that seems much too difficult."

Through these explorations, Karen began to recognize that her depression, needs for comfort, and alienation from God were related aspects of a negative worldview through which her life seemed "overwhelming and unfulfilling." She realized, intellectually, that her relationship with God could serve as a more authentic form of comfort and as a stable foundation for a positive worldview. "I think it is my faith in a greater source of love that gives me the hope to continue to persist against this negative worldview." But she did not know how to enter into such a relationship with God: "I just wish I could get a mirror made by the greater source of love!"

To help the students learn how to enter into such a relationship, the class instructor introduced them to basic components of contemplative practice. Initially, they learned to calm their minds by focusing on "the stillness and peace" that can be found in the layer of awareness beneath their thought processes. Next, they learned to move to deeper layers of self where they could tap the "rational intuition" and, ultimately, sense their connection to God. To learn to enter this level of awareness, they were taught visualization techniques that helped them become receptive to symbolic messages from the core self.

During an early exercise, they were led in a guided visualization in which they walked down a country road. Afterward, they continued the journey on their own and were asked to find "an inner place of safety and comfort." This inner locale then served as a place where they could seek symbolic messages of guidance from their spiritual core. In her imaginative exploration, Karen climbed through kudzu "and jumped into a large hole" sliding down a wet surface. "The tunnel kept getting curvier. I was filled with adrenaline. The rush of the speed and also of the thrill of what might lie ahead." She described what she landed in:

> an underground lake. The water was cool and very clear . . . and came up to about my thigh. I began to wade ahead. After a while I saw a beam of light shining toward me, like the way the moon casts its rays across the ocean to you on the beach. . . . As I came closer to the light I could see the shore and an opening. I walked through the opening and was standing at the front gate of a large, white, Victorian farmhouse. Somehow I knew that this was my house. I walked through the gate into a quaint flower garden. I saw rockers and swings on a porch decorated with ferns and red geraniums.

This location became her place of contemplation.

In a subsequent exercise, the students were asked to return to their place of contemplation and to find someone or something (i.e., a symbolic figure) that might help them address the life issues they had been exploring. Having discussed Frankl's work, the students were asked to explore what life expected of them as a response to the difficulties they faced. In the garden outside her farmhouse, Karen noticed the following:

> many people—family and friends—gathering around me. Then a man approached and touched my hand. He said the most beautiful things to me. It touched my heart. I wish I could remember the exact words. . . . But it was something like, *Sing. They have come to hear you sing. It is the music that brings them here. It is your love that you share through your song. Sing for them. Sing for me. . . . Then you can begin to connect to the ultimate song of us all. Sing.* I was truly moved by what happened.

At the next class, Karen did sing. She sang a sacred song for the group that she had learned as a child. She sang with a strength that surprised us.

Her face rippled with emotion, warmth, and energy. This was a part of her that we had not met before. We learned that she had sung in church as a child, but had not been in touch with "the singing part" of herself in a long time. Her meditation had reconnected her; she had been singing all week. The more she sang, she reported, the more confident she felt about herself and her attractiveness to others. She spoke for several minutes about the profound meaning of this meditation—and how glad she was to have met, in her place of contemplation, this unknown man who knew that she needed to sing.

In the following weeks, Karen behaved in increasingly self-confident ways. She spoke up in class about her ideas and responded forcefully—and thoughtfully—to others. In addition, her meditations became increasingly deep. Her place of contemplation became both a haven and a point of embarkation for meaningful journeys into herself. Several weeks later, during another meditation, "I felt within myself a swelling light—light energy. I felt care, love, joy, pain, hurt, and suffering in my chest. . . . Then this light . . . filled my hands. It was so pink. It was alive and beautiful."

Reflecting on this experience, she felt that it symbolized her growth in self-esteem. "This image was telling me of this place I am at in my life. I feel empowered. . . . I feel the strength I need to accomplish my dreams. I feel loved and I am not afraid of being alone." In addition, there was a deeper recognition. During this meditation, she described how she felt:

> secure, and somehow known. I was not alone. I never felt as if I was separate. And whether the light energy was in my hands or all around me, it was all through me. That is how I see God in my life—ever present, knowing, sensing, being, loving, light energy. Maybe this is the product of the faith I've begun to embrace.

These meditative experiences were formative in Karen's spiritual growth. She understood that these explorations were imaginal and symbolic; nonetheless, their numinous quality felt palpable and real. Her relationship with God was beginning to feel alive in a way that she had never experienced.

Karen's spiritual life had undergone a shift that would be difficult to reverse. Nonetheless, such an experience can easily recede into memory unless it is translated into daily behavior and awareness. Daily prayer is a practice that anchors an individual in the awareness of relationship with God. In the next class, the students were asked to find an anchoring prayer that they could use on a daily basis, particularly during times of stress. Karen identified several traditional prayers that held meaning for her. These included the Our Father and Ave Maria. Still, she wanted to find a more personal prayer.

> This time when I went to the house. . . . I went inside and went from room to room shouting, "Is anyone home?" Finally I went through this door under the staircase. It led into a study and there sat a man in a large chair, legs crossed, smoking a pipe. I said, "I should've known you'd be in

here." It was the same man that had told me to sing in the first meditation, but he seemed older this time. I still didn't really see his face. I told him you'd sent me to find a centering prayer." After speaking with him, it came to me, *"Sing to me the song of us all."* I felt a wonderful sensation all over. I knew these were the words.

The meaning of her anchoring prayer became clear in her written reflections. In times of stress, she "gets lost, and loses touch with God's presence." At those moments, "I need to stop and listen to God's music more deeply." The phrase *Sing to me the song of us all* became a prayer asking God to guide her in a moment of doubt. It was also a personal reminder to stop and listen to God's music—to feel God's presence. In her first meditation, the wise man had told her to sing. This time, he had reversed the message. He had told her to anchor herself by listening to God's music. She did not need to nurture herself all the time. She could let God nurture her. All she needed to do was ask—and listen. Once again, the wise man had given her a great gift, and she knew it. "I ran to him and hugged him and asked how he always did that. He just smiled. Then I said, 'What would I do without you?' He replied (and I'll never forget this part), 'You'll never know.' " The tenderness of this moment moved Karen deeply. "I told him I was going to play. . . . I went out the back door and started picking flowers. . . . I lifted my arms and I felt all the energy of God flow through me into the sky."

Through the symbol of the wise man, she had experienced God's love and eternal presence in a profound way. In addition, she had found a first anchoring prayer for daily use. As she reflected on her growth, she noted that "when I get overly stressed I say the prayer and then listen for the song that comes to mind. It's funny what songs pop up!"

It is not easy to nourish our relationship with God in isolation. Our class had served as a formative spiritual community for Karen. By design, however, this community was temporary. Karen would need to find more permanent communities to nourish her spiritual growth. Consequently, we had spent considerable time earlier in class discussing the value of participation in a religious congregation, and how to identify congregations that stifle growth or abuse power.

In her final reflection, Karen observed:

I go to church again. I pray. I see God in those around me. I know God's love and feel the energy as I move through the world. I don't have profound epiphanies everyday, but I have joy. . . . I can't begin to express how good it is to be home again. The journey of the prodigal daughter has come to its fruition. She is home and she knows the blessings it has to offer. She will be a better witness to its abundance because of her journey. . . . George [a classmate] and I had a discussion last night after leaving class about bringing your own experience of spirituality, your own God, to the worship community and combining that with others. It is the combination of the two that is the joy.

This case study illustrates a method through which adults (in a multifaith educational context) can learn to conceptualize and experience the value of spiritual development. During the initial phase of this course, as Karen participated in autobiographical self-inquiry exercises, she began to recognize that her depression-related behavior was related to an underlying spiritual vacuum. She lacked (in her words) "a mirror made by a greater source of love." Without such a mirror, and in the midst of our culture's pressure on young women to be thin, she had developed a negative body image, low self-esteem, and unhealthy eating behaviors. Conceptual recognition of this vacuum helped her understand why and how deepening her spiritual life could become a constructive aspect of her development. Consequently, she was receptive to the experiential learning component of this curriculum, and actively engaged in progressively deeper psychospiritual explorations. As the course introduced key spiritual practices taught by our religious traditions, she began to experience how daily prayer—which anchors individuals in ongoing awareness of their relationship with God—could help her cope more effectively with daily stress and maintain a regimen of constructive behavior. Similarly, she began to understand how deeper, extended periods of contemplative exploration could help her discover interior levels of self where spiritual wisdom and guidance become accessible. In addition, she experienced how a spiritually engaged community could provide individuals with an environment that reinforces health-promoting and prosocial behaviors. As Karen developed basic components of a spiritually engaged lifestyle, her depression-related behavior diminished. She became more self-confident and self-regulating. Her worldview became more positive. Her relational experience of God deepened. She took a step toward reentry in her (Baptist) religious community. Perhaps most important, she began to realize the degree to which these behavioral, cognitive, and relational aspects of her life were interconnected. Each intellectual realization, and each deepening of her experience, constituted movement toward participation in spiritual life with an intellectual and personal understanding of its underlying logic and goals.

Karen's developmental process also illustrates the five components of spiritual maturation identified by research in the psychology of religion, as discussed in the first section of this chapter: *First, Karen experienced change in the conceptual processes through which she shaped religious meaning.* She entered the course spiritually adrift. As a child, she had accepted the religious beliefs taught within her community. However, when she concluded that some of these beliefs were prejudicial, she severed herself from her sense of spiritual connection to God. As her experience in this class helped her discover an internal source of spiritual meaning, and as her relationship with God took on more personally meaningful cadences, she could re-affirm the value of this relationship. In addition, she could begin to reenter the spiritual community of her birth, confident that her locus of spiritual meaning was now internal. *Second, Karen experienced increased behavioral self-regulation.* Although always committed to the ethical and moral principles of Christian life, Karen's depression had led to a harmful dysregulation of behavior. In effect, she could not maintain principles of behavior in which she believed and that she knew were good for her and others. Through a process of self-inquiry, in which she came to understand the psychospiritual dynamics of these health-defeating behaviors, she regained self-control. At the same time, she came to value the reinforcing effects of participation in a spiritually engaged community. *Third, Karen's capacity for core religious experience increased.* Her earlier religious education had not taught her about contemplative practices and the dynamics of prayer. Consequently, her inherent capacity for connective awareness had not been nurtured. By facilitating her use of the "rational intuition" (see discussion on Maimonides), she learned to explore an internal level of psychological awareness where numinous experience can take place. *Fourth, and closely related to the third area of development, Karen's deepening experience of God's presence led to a shift in her God image.* Where she had formerly conceptualized God as judging and distant, she developed a more loving and internalized God image. *Finally, Karen demonstrated a heightened ability to participate in the developmental challenges of the human life cycle as vehicles for spiritual growth.* She had experienced a collision between her developmentally appropriate needs for intimacy and our culture's destructive pressure on young women to be thin. The formation of internalized spiritual resources helped her meet this challenge constructively. At the same time, with spiritual resources available, this developmental challenge became a vehicle for further spiritual growth. Thus, she had taken the first step toward incorporating an idea central to the worldview of our spiritual traditions: The process of living, itself, contains the potential for spiritual maturation—and constitutes an experiential learning curriculum leading to that goal.

As discussed in the second section of the chapter, however, these five elements of spiritual maturation should not be viewed (or facilitated) in isolation. The world's religious traditions (presented here through the discussion of Maimonides) treat these elements as components of a multidimensional, interactive model. Each component is nurtured, and refined, by the other elements. The case study of Karen illustrates how an individual's behavior-in-the-world and her internal experience of relationship with God can, and should, become mutually informing. When developed holistically, these components lead to the maturational goals central to our religious traditions: *the ability to embody loving-kindness, justice, and empowered action in one's relationship with self and others, through immersion in relationship with God.*

From the viewpoint of psychological constructs of change, this multidimensional model integrates behavioral, cognitive, relational, and existential approaches. Where practitioners and researchers in applied psychology tend to favor one of these approaches and to disagree with proponents of the others, our religious traditions have developed an approach to maturation and healing that integrates them in a dynamic and indissoluble methodology.

Thus, our religious traditions have something to teach professional psychology about integrated applications of these approaches, as well as the central role that spiritual maturation can play in effecting positive change. At the same time, the field of psychology has developed a functional language and analytic concepts that can help our religious traditions (which have disagreed too often among themselves) to recognize their shared maturational goals and practices.

In conclusion, this chapter has presented a formulation of spiritual development as a multidimensional, interactive phenomenon through which the significance of its role in human development may be understood and studied more effectively. In addition, this chapter has helped to illustrate the mutual benefits of ongoing dialogue between our spiritual traditions and the field of psychology.

REFERENCES

Allport, G. W. (1957). *The individual and his religion*. New York: Macmillan.

Allport, G. W., & Ross, J. M. (1967). Personal religious orientation and prejudice. *Journal of Personality and Social Psychology, 5*, 432–443.

Ariel, D. (1995). *What do Jews believe: The spiritual foundations of Judaism*. New York: Schocken Books.

Batson, C. D., & Ventis, W. L. (1982). *The religious experience: A social psychological perspective*. New York: Oxford University Press.

Benson, P. L., Donahue, M. J., & Erickson, J. A. (1993). The faith maturity scale: Conceptualization, measurement, and empirical validation. In M. L. Lynn & D. D. Moberg (Eds.), *Research in the social scientific study of religion* (Vol. 5, pp. 1–26). Greenwich, CT: JAI Press.

Billingsley, A. (1992). *Climbing Jacob's ladder: Enduring legacies of African-American families*. New York: Simon & Schuster.

Clinebell, H. (1984). *Pastoral care and counseling: Resources for the ministry of healing and growth*. Nashville, TN: Abingdon Press.

Clinebell, H. (1995). *Counseling for spiritually empowered wholeness*. New York: Haworth Pastoral Press.

Cook-Greuter, S. R. (1994). Rare forms of self-understanding in mature adults. In M. E. Miller & S. R. Cook-Greuter (Eds.), *Transcendence and mature thought in adulthood: Further reaches of human development* (pp. 119–146). Lanham, MD: Rowman & Littlefield.

Daloz Parks, S. (2000). *Big questions, worthy dreams: Mentoring young adults in their search for meaning, purpose, and faith*. San Francisco: Jossey-Bass.

Easterling, L. W., Gamino, L. A., Sewell, K. W., & Stirman, L. S. (2000). Spiritual experience, church attendance, and bereavement. *Journal of Pastoral Care, 7*, 436–451.

Ellison, C. W. (1999). Spiritual maturity index. In P. C. Hill & R. W. Hood (Eds.), *Measures of religiosity* (pp. 201–204). Birmingham, AL: Religious Education Press.

Erikson, E. (1963). *Childhood and society.* New York: Norton.

Finkelstein, L. (1999). Nothing is ordinary. In R. Eastman (Ed.), *The ways of religion: An introduction to the major traditions* (pp. 293–300). New York: Oxford University Press.

Fowler, J. (1981). *Stages of faith: The psychology of human development and the quest for meaning.* San Francisco: Harper.

Frankl, V. (1959). *Man's search for meaning.* New York: Simon & Schuster.

Genia, V. (1995). *Counseling and psychotherapy of religious clients: A developmental approach.* Westport, CT: Praeger Publishers.

Gilligan, C. (1982). *In a different voice: Psychological theory and women's development.* Cambridge, MA: Harvard University Press.

Goodman, L. E. (1999). *Jewish and Islamic philosophy: Crosspollinations in the classic age.* New Brunswick, NJ: Rutgers University Press.

Hahn, H. (1993). Between God and man. In L. Kravitz & K. M. Olitzky (Eds.), *Pirke Avot: A modern commentary on Jewish ethics* (p. 74). New York: UAHC Press.

Helminiak, D. A. (1987). *Spiritual development: An interdisciplinary study.* Chicago: Loyola University Press.

Heschel, A. J. (1982). *Maimonides: A biography.* New York: Farrar, Strauss & Giroux.

Hood, R. W. (1975). The construction and preliminary validation of a measure of reported mystical experience. *Journal for the Scientific Study of Religion, 14,* 29–41.

James, W. (1958). *Varieties of religious experience.* New York: New American Library. (Original work published 1902)

Jordan, M. (1986). *Taking on the gods: The task of the pastoral counselor.* Nashville, TN: Abingdon Press.

Kass, J. (1995). Contributions of religious experience to psychological and physical well-being: Research evidence and an explanatory model. In L. VandeCreek (Ed.), *Spiritual needs and pastoral services: Readings in research* (pp. 189–213). Decatur, GA: Journal of Pastoral Care Publications.

Kass, J. (1996, Spring). Coping with life-threatening illnesses using a logotherapeutic approach, Stage II: Clinical mental health counseling. *International Forum for Logotherapy, 20,* 10–14.

Kass, J. (2001). *Mentoring students in the development of leadership skills, health-promoting behavior, and pro-social behavior: A rationale for teaching contemplative practices in university education.* Paper presented at the Colloquium on Contemplative Practice in Higher Education, Lesley University, Cambridge, MA.

Kass, J., Friedman, R., Leserman, J., Zuttermeister, P., & Benson, H. (1991). Health outcomes and a new measure of spiritual experience. *Journal for the Scientific Study of Religion, 30,* 203–211.

Katz, S. T. (Ed.). (1983). *Mysticism and religious traditions.* New York: Oxford University Press.

Kegan, R. (1982). *The evolving self: Problem and process in human development*. Cambridge, MA: Harvard University Press.

Koenig, H. G. (1994). *Aging and God: Spiritual pathways to mental health in midlife and later years*. Binghamton, NY: Haworth Press.

Kohlberg, L. (1981). *The philosophy of moral development*. San Francisco: Harper & Row.

Loder, J. E. (1998). *The logic of the spirit*. San Francisco: Jossey-Bass.

Loevinger, J., & Blasi, A. (1980). *Ego development*. San Francisco: Jossey-Bass.

Maimonides, M. (1963). *The guide of the perplexed* (S. Pines, Trans.). Chicago: University of Chicago Press.

Malony, H. N. (1988). The clinical assessment of optimal religious functioning. *Review of Religious Research, 30*, 3–17.

Meissner, W. W. (1987). *Life and faith: Psychological perspectives on religious experience*. Washington, DC: Georgetown University Press.

Meissner, W. W. (1996). The pathology of beliefs and the beliefs of pathology. In E. Shafranske (Ed.), *Religion and the clinical practice of psychology* (pp. 241–267). Washington, DC: American Psychological Association.

Mintz, A. (1984). Prayer and the Prayerbook. In B. W. Holtz (Ed.), *Back to the sources: Reading the classic Jewish texts*. New York: Simon & Schuster.

Moberg, D. O. (Ed.). (2001). *Aging and spirituality: Spiritual dimensions of aging theory, research, practice, and policy*. New York: Haworth Pastoral Press.

Newberg, A., & D'Aquili, E. (2001). *Why God won't go away: Brain science and the biology of belief*. New York: Ballantine Books.

Oser, F., & Gmunder, P. (1991). *Religious judgement: A developmental perspective*. Birmingham, AL: Religious Education Press.

Pargament, K. (1997). *The psychology of religion and coping: Theory, research, practice*. New York: Guilford Press.

Piaget, J. (1952). *The origins of intelligence in children*. New York: Norton.

Poloma, M. M. (1995). The sociological context of religious experience. In R. W. Hood (Ed.), *Handbook of religious experience* (pp. 161–182). Birmingham, AL: Religious Education Press.

Poloma, M., & Gallup, G. H. (1991). *Varieties of prayer: A survey report*. Philadelphia: Trinity Press International.

Porpora, D. V. (2001). *Landscapes of the soul: The loss of moral meaning in American life*. New York: Oxford University Press.

Proudfoot, W. (1985). *Religious experience*. Berkeley: University of California Press.

Rizzuto, A. M. (1979). *The birth of the living God: A psychoanalytic study*. Chicago: University of Chicago Press.

Spero, M. H. (1992). *Religious objects as psychological structures: A critical integration of object relations theory, psychotherapy, and Judaism*. Chicago: University of Chicago Press.

Spretnak, C. (Ed.). (1982). *The politics of women's spirituality*. New York: Anchor Books.

Spretnak, C. (1991). *States of grace: The recovery of meaning in the postmodern age*. San Francisco: Harper.

Steinsaltz, A. (1980). *The thirteen petalled rose: A discourse on the essence of Jewish existence and belief*. New York: Basic Books.

Worthington, E. L. (1989). Religious faith across the lifespan: Implications for counseling and research. *Counseling Psychologist, 17,* 555–612.

Wulff, D. M. (1997). *Psychology of religion: Classic and contemporary*. New York: Wiley.

11

THE EFFECTS OF RELIGIOUS PRACTICES: A FOCUS ON HEALTH

CARL E. THORESEN, DOUG OMAN, AND ALEX H. S. HARRIS

What are the effects of religious practices? Such a fundamental question raises a host of conceptual and definitional issues. For example, what constitutes a religious practice? What types of effects are of concern? What might Judeo-Christian perspectives contribute to the understanding of these effects?

In this brief chapter, we by necessity will focus on effects in one major area: health. We also focus on four major religious practices: attendance at religious services, prayer, meditation, and forgiveness. Doing so in no way implies that other religious or spiritual practices, such as music, are deemed less worthy of consideration. Rather, we do so in part because empirical evidence is available from controlled studies, in varying degrees of quantity and quality, on these topics (Koenig, McCullough, & Larson, 2001). We also recognize the probable contributions to health of other religiously motivated behaviors concerning such matters as diet; nutrition; sanitation; and refraining from alcohol and other substance abuse, smoking, and sexual promiscuity.

In our consideration of the health effects of some clearly recognizable religious *practices*, we briefly look at theoretical concepts (or lack of them) and empirical evidence that have guided how Judeo-Christian practices have been viewed in psychological research. We suggest some ways to expand and improve these scientific views in light of Judeo-Christian conceptions. We also discuss areas where religion and psychology might mutually learn from each other in a relationship of open dialogue and collaboration (Barbour, 2000; Jones, 1994).

Our focus is primarily on individuals (e.g., health outcomes and practice of religion by individuals). Although we do not address the role of community, we want to acknowledge its centrality, and how religious institutions as a part of the community represent valuable sources of "social capital" playing important roles in people's health and well-being (see Putnam, 2000). As empirical researchers, we also note our need for genuine modesty about what a scientific framework can and cannot provide in understanding religious practices and health. Much can be looked at empirically (with the sensitivity required in such matters), such as particular behaviors, cognitions, emotions and experiences situated within certain contexts. Yet some realms of religious experience, manifested in practices, will remain beyond our ability to capture them adequately with available scientific methods. Much remains to be known and with patience and understanding we will learn more, and in doing so we will also learn more about what we do not know.

COMMON THEMES AND DIVERSITY IN LIVING SPIRITUALITY

Religious and spiritual practices have long been a major, yet sometimes overlooked, concern of all Judeo-Christian religious institutions. Indeed, these practices can be seen as the primary vehicle by which a person comes to have faith in and to know and love God as the source of all life and, in addition, to love one's neighbor as one loves oneself. For Christians, these practices include seeking to embody the example and teachings of Jesus Christ as the son of God. Judeo-Christian scriptures also convey the wisdom imparted through great prophets and leaders, such as Abraham, Moses, and Isaiah in the Hebrew scriptures and Matthew, John, and Paul in the Christian New Testament. These sacred scriptures in effect have set the stage for a variety of spiritual practices based on beliefs, codes, rules, and attitudes about how and why one can "live one's religion" in daily life.

The personal spiritual experiences of Judeo-Christian mystics and saints, such as St. Augustine, St. Francis of Assisi, St. Teresa of Avila, and the Baal Shem Tov, have also powerfully influenced traditional understandings of the goals and benefits of practices. Expressed through narrative and anecdote, these figures' personal experiences and lived examples have illustrated the role of various practices in striving to live religious beliefs through transcending self-will, bearing suffering, and coming to know and accept the will of God (Thoresen, 2003; Oman & Thoresen, 2003a, 2003b).

Great variability exists among different denominations of Judaism and Christianity (and other major religions as well) in attitudes concerning the purpose and relative value of various practices. For example, Driskill (1999) pointed out that in comparison with Roman Catholicism, many mainline Protestant denominations have tended to avoid practices that have a more mystical, personal, meditative–contemplative, or experiential focus. Wuthnow (1998), a distinguished sociologist of religion, described the sharp decline of focus on personal spiritual practices within most American mainline churches and the growing number of "spiritual seekers" not formally affiliated with a church. Roof (1999) and Fuller (2001) also described Americans who seek a more personal experience with God outside of an organized religious context. For such persons, the God of organized religion is often perceived as "out there or up there" somewhere rather than "in here" (Roof, 1999, p. 60). Within the United States, an increasing variability also seems to be emerging, especially since the 1960s, among those who identify themselves as religious or as spiritual (e.g., Roof, 1999). Thoresen (2003) recently summarized the estimates from various studies, tentatively concluding that roughly 50% of Americans identify themselves as both religious and spiritual, 10% as only religious, 20% as only spiritual, and 20% as neither religious nor spiritual. These proportions may vary, however, in a particular region in either direction by as much as 15% or 20% (e.g., northern California vs. northern Alabama), and within each category (e.g., spiritual only) further diversity exists. For example, even among persons identifying themselves as neither religious nor spiritual, over half may engage in some religious or spiritual practices, such as frequently using prayer or attending religious services (Fuller, 2001), and fewer than 10% appear to be true atheists. It is clear that active interest in religious practices extends across almost all social and economic boundaries and does so among a majority of Americans.

CORRECTIVES FROM TRADITIONAL PERSPECTIVES

Several traditional religious perspectives may be especially useful for helping social science in general and psychology in particular to overcome earlier reductionistic tendencies and to develop more nuanced understandings of religious ways of thinking, acting, and living.

First, psychology can benefit by more fully recognizing the often purposeful and *conative* (goal-directed) nature of sincere religious involvement (Emmons, 1999). Such a view is reflected in a definition offered by Hill and colleagues (2000, p. 66):

> [Spirituality involves] the feelings, thoughts, experiences, and behaviors that arise from a search for the sacred. The term "search" refers to attempts to identify, articulate, maintain, or transform. The "sacred" refers

to a divine being, divine object, Ultimate Reality, or Ultimate Truth as perceived by the individual.

Hill et al. (2000) noted that pursuing a search for the sacred need not exclude searching for other objects, such as identity, belongingness, meaning, health, or wellness. Thus, in contrast to *spirituality* as a search for the sacred, Hill et al. (2000) view *religion* as a search for either sacred or nonsacred goals within a context that has seeking the sacred (i.e., spirituality) as its "primary goal" (p. 66). That is, spirituality and religion are both goal directed, and neither can be reduced to only doctrines or simple codes of conduct. In this context, we consider a practice as religious that has been regularly sanctioned in established social contexts as a useful or necessary tool to be employed in a search for the sacred. The four religious practices that we discuss below are sanctioned by Judeo-Christian traditions but are also widespread in other religious faiths.

Second, psychologists should recognize that scientific evidence does not require reductionistic views of human nature (Brown, 2002) and that the implications of religious views of human nature merit scientific exploration (see chap. 1, this volume). For example, from the Judeo-Christian perspective the human being is capable of continued spiritual growth. Such growth might involve coming to recognize that the "invisible qualities" of God may be "understood from what has been made" (Rom. 1:20, NIV), that "the kingdom of God is within you" if you seek it (Luke 17:21, NIV), and that ultimately you can be "transformed by the renewal of your mind" (Rom. 12:2, NIV). Scientifically exploring the consequences of such views of human nature demands new measures, concepts, and approaches. These overlap to some extent with those used in the emerging field of positive psychology (Snyder & Lopez, 2002; see also Antonovsky, 1987; McCullough & Snyder, 2000; Nottingham, Gorsuch, & Wrightsman, 1970).

Third, psychology should go beyond inadvertently truncated views of religious social support that emphasize dimensions such as material and emotional support, but fail to acknowledge the collective meaning-making functions of religion (chap. 7, this volume). For example, religious social support and socialization into shared meaning systems appear partly responsible for recent successes in fostering behavior (marital fidelity and increasing the age of initial sexual activity) that has dramatically reduced HIV infection in some developing countries (Green, 2001; 2003; see also chap. 6, this volume). By socializing adherents into specific shared meaning systems, religious communities may foster both quality and quantity of social support (Ellison & Levin, 1998), as well as enhanced psychological resources (Pargament, 1997). For example, religious affirmation of the reality of the sacred and of a loving God may provide for people of all ages a source of secure attachment that contributes to physical and mental health (Rowatt & Kirkpatrick, 2002). Similarly, adherents who affirm a loving God in action historically may gain emotional links to vivid and inspiring models of individually healthy actions and attitudes (Oman & Thoresen, 2003a; Silberman, 2003). For example, religious socialization may instill the attitude that, in the words of St. Francis, "it is in giving that we receive" (quoted in Easwaran, 1991, p. 30).

Finally, psychology must avoid overemphasizing physiological outcomes and must recognize that practices do not act in isolation from each other. For example, by focusing on short-term physiological outcomes, some researchers have concluded that contemplative prayer and meditation are functionally equivalent to progressive muscle relaxation (Smith, 1986). Focusing solely on immediate physical outcomes, however, ignores the purposeful and dynamic interrelatedness of religious practices as complementary tools or vehicles for leading an increasingly sanctified life within an often tumultuous world (Emmons, 1999; Hill et al., 2000). Practices displaying similar physiological correlates may possess sharply contrasting mental and cognitive correlates that shape a person's future life course in differing ways (Smith, 1986).

Emerging scientific concepts of health now emphasize the importance of looking beyond immediate physical correlates. Scientific conceptions of health have broken out of the exclusive mold of being only concerned with the physical realm of the body (Thoresen & Harris, 2002). Ryff and Singer (1998), for example, describe health much more as an overall state of mind than as a physical condition of the body. Health involves meaning and purpose, quality of relationships with others, perceived mastery and agency, self-evaluative processes, and the overall energy and enthusiasm needed to fulfill major life goals. The overlap of this expanding perspective of health with current views of spirituality merits careful attention when studying religious practices and health effects (Thoresen, 2003). More generally, any exclusive focus on physical correlates of isolated practices ignores the well-understood reciprocal influences between behavior, cognition, and the natural and social environment (Bandura, 1986), including possible transcendent contexts that may be unknowable by contemporary psychology (Oman & Thoresen, 2002).

Unfortunately, the theoretical and methodological consequences for science of the dynamic mutual influence of spiritual practices collectively over time has seldom been clearly articulated. As a prologue to our review of specific practices, we next discuss this deficit.

A MORE DYNAMIC SCIENTIFIC PERSPECTIVE ON EFFECTS OF PRACTICES

In everyday and in much scientific language, to speak of a religious practice as having "effects" is to comment on what is *caused* by the practice. Both science and the public possess an overarching interest in understanding causal effects. Granting this shared interest, it turns out that clarifying the possible causal effects of particular religious practices presents many challenges. Can a practice be adequately specified and measured? Can effects be reliably assessed and accurately attributed to a particular practice? Can potential confounding factors, such as age, gender, ethnicity, or other individual difference factors, be appropriately controlled? Is it possible and appropriate to treat a particular practice and its presumed effects separately from other religious practices and experiences, as if each were a freestanding, independent variable? (see discussion in Oman & Thoresen, 2002).

Randomized experiments in psychology are the scientific method of choice for generating reliable causal inferences. Randomizing participants to different experimental conditions usually ensures that any statistically significant outcome can be attributed to differences in the experimental variable (e.g., meditation) rather than to other factors, such as preexisting differences between individuals. Currently, however, we do not know to what extent we can experimentally influence perhaps the most defining feature of religion—spirituality defined as a search for the sacred. This is because so little experimental research has ever examined spirituality itself as an outcome measure (for exceptions see Astin, 1997; Oman, Thoresen, & Hedberg, 2003; Thoresen et al., 2001). Current experimental evidence sheds light primarily on components of religious practices that "make sense" *apart* from a spiritual search. Two practices we discuss later—forgiveness and meditation—have generated a growing experimental literature, perhaps because major components of these practices make sense when practiced apart from a spiritual search (note, however, that these practices may exert more powerful long-term effects if conducted as part of a spiritual search; see Oman & Thoresen, 2001; Smith, 1986).

In contrast, two other practices we examine, prayer and attendance at religious services, have generated much less experimental research, perhaps because researchers doubt whether such practices make sense separated from a spiritual framework (note that experimental intercessory prayer studies randomly assign participants to be the *beneficiaries* of prayers, but not to *offer* prayers).

In contrast to limited experimental evidence, many observational studies have explored correlates of religious practices. Such observational evidence, however, must be interpreted in light of the dynamic nature of lived religious practice. As already noted, in the real world ("in vivo"), people who engage in one practice (e.g., attending religious services) often engage in other practices (such as various types of prayer; see Poloma & Gallup, 1991b). The multiple dimensions of living religious practice tend to correlate with each other, as well as with measures of cognitive, affective, and other religious dimensions, such as a person's spiritual strivings (Emmons, 1999). Over time, these multiple dimensions of religious practice and experience may in part be "reciprocally determined" by each other. A person's choice to begin attending services, for example, may encourage religious support from others, which in turn may encourage increased attendance at services.

One important consequence of the evolving nature of lived religious practice is that an individual's religious practice may produce both (a) *direct effects* on a nonreligious outcome of interest, as well as (b) *indirect effects* mediated by other religious practices. To illustrate, meditating daily may directly lower blood pressure but also may produce cognitive and affective changes that enhance interest in attending religious services, resulting in more social support, which in turn reduces stress and further reduces blood pressure. This dynamic feature of religious practice is highlighted by Table 11.1, which illustrates that religious practices may not only influence nonreligious outcomes (e.g., physical health) but may also affect other dimensions of religious practice (e.g., religious coping). Many other factors may also be involved, such as a person's health status, personality style, interpersonal relationships, group affiliations, and the quality of one's social network (Bandura, 1986).

The dynamic nature of religious practices poses considerable challenges for observational research. For example, do we investigate *direct* causal effects, *interactional* effects, or *total* causal effects from religious involvement or from a particular religious practice? (Oman & Thoresen, 2002). Effects of a religious practice may also depend on nonreligious moderating factors, such as age, gender, ethnicity, personal difference factors, or even genetics (Boomsma, de Geus, van Baal, & Koopmans, 1999). Other practical challenges are posed by the need for a proper statistical analysis and for valid and sensitive assessment of religious practice (Miller & Thoresen, 2003). Thus, like other lifestyle factors that lack direct randomized experimental evidence (such as health effects from individual smoking, which cannot ethically or practically be subject to randomization), conclusions about the causal effects from religious practices are best assessed with a wide range of experimental and observational evidence over time (Levin, 1994). In the context of such multilevel methodologies (Cacioppo & Brandon, 2002; Cook, 1985), we see no clear reason to ignore the evidential force of religious experience itself. Especially relevant are the most cross-culturally universal features of religious experience, such as mystical experiences of human nature as deeply connected with the divine or sacred (Jones, 1994; Smith, 1976). We now turn to four common practices that have been linked to health and well-being.

ATTENDANCE AT RELIGIOUS SERVICES

Attending services is probably the most common public practice of religion. Embedded within the multifaceted construct of attendance lies a host of more specific practices and the experiences while attending services. These

TABLE 11.1

Selected Studies Documenting Effects From Specific Religious Practices
on Measures of Religion and Health

Practice	Type of effect		
	Other religious practices[a]	Mental health	Physical health
Attendance[b]	Religious coping (Pargament, 1997)[c]	Anxiety (Koenig et al., 1993) Depression (Braam et al., 2001)	All-cause mortality (Hummer et al., 1999) Circulatory mortality (Oman et al., 2002)
Prayer	Forgiveness (Poloma & Gallup, 1991b)	Happiness (Poloma & Pendleton, 1991)	Baroreflex sensitivity (Bernardi et al., 2001)
Meditation	Spiritual experiences (Astin, 1997) Spirituality (Oman et al., 2003)	Anxiety and panic (Kabat-Zinn et al., 1992) State and trait anxiety (Davidson, 2001)	Mortality (Alexander et al., 1989) Atherosclerosis (Ornish et al., 1990)
Forgiveness	Spiritual experiences (Thoresen et al., 2001)	Optimism (Thoresen et al., 2001)	Cortisol (Berry & Worthington, 2001)

Note. Studies indicated that the practice in the left column (column 1) were associated with improvements in other religious indicators (column 2) or health (columns 3 and 4). All associations were significantly positive (for other religion practices) or salutary (for health measures). Causation is not demonstrated by these data, however.
[a]The living practice of religion involves a dynamically evolving set of beliefs and practices in which each component is best understood in the context of all other beliefs and practices, and may influence health partly *through* its dynamic influence on other religious practices. Column 2 labelled "other religious practices" represents pioneering work on the effects of individual religious practices on other dimensions of spirituality and religiousness.
[b]Attendance represents a multiple set of practices (e.g., rituals, music, etc.), not a single practice.
[c]Pargament (1997, Appendix B) cites several studies reporting significant associations of attendance at services with various types of religious coping.

may range from deeply personal if not sacred experiences during church, including feeling directly connected with God, to casual conversations at the beginning and ending of services about many things, varying widely in their religious or spiritual significance. Some common practices engaged in during attending services include, among others, prayer, meditation, music in different forms, various rituals and ceremonies, biblical reading and listening to Scripture, and sermons or messages from religious leaders and laypersons. Many of these practices appear to facilitate observational or vicarious learning of spiritual ways of living from exemplars of virtue and compassion (Bandura, 2003; Oman & Thoresen, 2003b). The physical setting of services is often perceived as sacred (e.g., the house of God) and may contain crosses, icons, or other significant symbols that powerfully interact with particular practices to influence the effects on health and other outcomes. Indeed, along with family life (Mahoney, Pargament, Tarakeshwar, & Swank, 2001) and some forms of religious education, attending services could be viewed as the primary religious staging ground in which a person learns about what it means to be religious and to live more spiritually.

What is the evidence linking attendance with health effects? Given the multidimensionality of attendance as a practice and the nature of scientific studies to date, offering definitive answers is difficult. Reviews have presented encouraging yet cautious commentary about the positive effects of attending services regularly; they have also cited the serious limitations of published research (e.g., Koenig et al., 2001; Levin, 1994). Yet in many ways we know more scientifically about attendance and its health effects than any other religious practice.

Two recent reviews capture what we know to date. First, McCullough, Hoyt, Larson, Koenig, and Thoresen (2000) evaluated 29 independent prospective studies linking attendance and all-cause mortality (total N > 125,000). Although a great deal of variability in effects was found among these studies and several other factors also independently predicted less death (e.g., social support, married status, perceived good health), McCullough et al. reported 29% less mortality for frequent versus nonattendees (equivalent to seven more years of life). Second, Powell, Shahabi, and Thoresen (2003), using a Cochrane Library strategy, individually evaluated attendance–mortality studies and selected the "top" 11 studies that met stringent research design criteria. Of several hypotheses linking religious factors and health, only one predicting less total mortality with high attendance among community dwelling (nonclinical) populations was rated "persuasively supported." The reduction in relative mortality risk of weekly or more attendance versus nonattendance was 25%. Two recent well-controlled studies also reported that frequent attendance independently predicted reduced mortality across several specific causes of death, including cardiovascular and respiratory diseases, but not cancer (Hummer, Rogers, Nam, & Ellison, 1999; Oman, Kurata, Strawbridge, & Cohen, 2002).

Numerous studies also suggest that attendance is predictive of better mental health. Regular attendance has been associated, for example, with less depression (Braam et al., 2001), less anxiety (Koenig et al., 1993), less suicide, and less alcohol abuse. Positive correlations have also been consistently reported between attendance and other mental health variables, such as self-esteem, hope and optimism, life satisfaction, social support, and perceived meaning in life (see reviews in Koenig et al., 2001).

What might account for positive associations of attendance with health and survival (Oman & Thoresen, 2002)? Work by Strawbridge, Shema, Cohen, and Kaplan (2001) suggests enhanced social support and improved health behaviors may play a role. From 1965 to 1994, those attending weekly were significantly more likely, compared with infrequent attenders, to improve their poor health behaviors as well as to maintain good health behaviors (e.g., maintaining social connections and stable marriages, avoiding depression, exercising regularly, refraining from smoking).

Another proposed mechanism, supported by some evidence, is that frequent attenders have greater psychosocial and coping resources (Krause et al., 2001). To date, however, none of these proposed mechanisms, either singly or in combination, have fully accounted for the observed religion–health associations. This suggests that other unknown mechanisms may be involved (George, Ellison, & Larson, 2002). Lacking also has been evidence regarding possible moderating or mediating factors, especially other religious or spiritual practices. Possible harmful health effects associated with attendance (and other practices as well) have yet to receive the careful attention that they deserve. Various individual difference and cultural variables could clarify who may benefit the most, who might be harmed, and who might be unaffected by regularly attending services (see American Psychological Association, 2002).

Our review also suggests that many psychological variables have been "missing in action" in longitudinal studies on health effects of religious attendance (Thoresen & Harris, 2002). This may be due to studies that were started many years ago (e.g., 1960s) containing few psychological variables. Future attendance–health studies should clearly include more psychological variables, including personality, attachment style, types of coping, striving, and perceived meaning that may relate to religious self-understanding (Park & Folkman, 1997). Such factors could also be explored through longitudinal studies not only of what moderates health behavior changes (Strawbridge et al., 2001) but also of whether attendance moderates changes in other religious practices, such as religious social support, prayer, meditation, and forgiveness.

PRAYER

The practice of prayer is nearly universal across cultures. Reported frequency of prayer varies by ethnicity, denomination, and culture. Women and older persons generally pray more than men and younger persons. People also use prayer more frequently as a coping resource with more severe or intractable problems or those unresponsive to medical interventions. Prayer may take place in groups, individually in seclusion, or silently at many moments throughout the day (Oman & Driskill, 2003).

Writers on prayer have distinguished up to 21 types of prayer (McCullough & Larson, 1999). Several recent empirical studies distinguish between petitionary, ritual, conversational, and meditative forms of prayer (Poloma & Gallup, 1991b). One study also distinguished a fifth category, "contemplative prayer" (Cox, 2000).

Historically, unspecified forms of prayer have been assessed by questionnaire items (e.g., "how frequently do you pray?"), sometimes embedded in scales on private religiosity. Assessments rarely have measured subjective experience of prayer or used alternative time frames to measure frequency or intensity of prayer (e.g., "past week" vs. "do you pray?" or "how fervently or deeply?"). Differences between prayers offered at formal religious services, in small groups, and engaged in privately have seldom been clarified (see Krause, Chatters, Meltzer, & Morgan, 2000, for improved assessment). Among recent multidimensional scales, Poloma and Pendleton's (1991) 15-item scale offers psychometrically supported subscales for petitionary, ritual, conversational, and meditative prayer.

Many theological and spiritual traditions suggest that a person's relative involvement in different types of prayer may change over time as the person grows spiritually and becomes committed to new modes of "spiritual striving" (Emmons, 1999). For example, prayer that places a greater emphasis on communion with the sacred (meditative and contemplative prayer), compared with conversational prayer, has been more highly correlated with spiritual experience and several measures of well-being (Cox, 2000). Similarly, Poloma, and Gallup (1991a) found that meditative, but not other forms of prayer, predicted higher levels of forgiveness, even when other forms of prayer, demographics, and attending services were controlled. (We suspect that contemplative prayer would also show similar correlates.) Still, regardless of the distinctions among kinds of prayer, all types of sincere prayer may contribute to religious forms of coping with stress (Pargament, 1997) because all prayer involves relating in some way to a sacred and powerful being. It is understandable that theories of possible mechanisms linking prayer to health often only emphasize its stress-preventive and stress-buffering functions (Krause et al., 2000; McCullough & Larson, 1999).

Empirical findings relating frequency of prayer to measures of health and well-being have been inconsistent. Positive associations have been reported with some measures (e.g., purpose in life in recovering alcoholics or lower mortality) but not others (purpose in life among community-dwelling adults or happiness). Negative associations have also been reported, such as more depression and worse physical health. Reviewing these essentially cross-sectional designs, McCullough and Larson (1999) suggested inconsistencies may be due to several factors: use of single-item measures, differences between studies in control variables or sample sizes, or differences in outcomes studied or types of sample populations. Virtually unexamined are variables that could modify (moderate) effects of prayer, for example, age, baseline health, ethnicity, other religious factors, or individual differences measures (e.g., personality style).

Poloma and Pendleton (1991) exemplify a more sophisticated approach. Using a multidimensional measure, they found many significant associations between well-being and different types of prayer (petitionary, ritualistic, meditative, and conversational). Controlling for demographics, other religiosity measures, and other types of prayer revealed a negative association between happiness and ritualistic prayer. However, several positive prayer–well-being associations still remained significant.

By far the most controversial studies of prayer have examined distant intercessory prayer, a form of petitionary prayer directed toward the well-being of others. A recent, well-designed example is reported by Harris and colleagues (1999), who randomized coronary care unit patients into two groups. One group received usual medical care ($n = 524$) and another group ($n = 466$) were also "treated" by having several interdenominational Christians pray for their "speedy recovery with no complications." Using a predefined scoring system, the prayed-for group experienced a better coronary care "course" (i.e., significant yet modest reductions in some but not all medically related events while hospitalized). In the past few years, several studies of similar design have raised a storm of scientific and theological controversy without producing conclusive findings (Chibnall, Jeral, & Cerullo, 2001). It is interesting that at least one randomized controlled trial of distant intercessory prayer has reported that *engaging* in intercessory prayer produced significantly greater benefits in well-being for the intercessors (those praying) than for the persons being prayed for; thus, "regardless of whether intercessory prayer affects the health of those prayed for, it may at least have psychological benefits for those doing the praying" (Koenig et al., 2001, p. 132). From a Judeo-Christian perspective, praying "with a loving heart" for the welfare of others may indeed be a spiritually rich and health enhancing experience (James 5:13–17, KJV).

Current scientific evidence relating nonmeditative prayer to health is mixed but has produced some limited initial evidence for associations with health that appear relatively independent of other religious measures. The methodological simplicity of existing studies of prayer opens the possibility that future work may reveal more subtle or complex patterns that include indirect effects of nonmeditative prayer on health, perhaps mediated by spiritual growth, as suggested by many religious traditions (see also suggestions in Oman & Driskill, 2003).

MEDITATION AND HEALTH

Judaism and Christianity each possess contemplative prayer traditions, such as Kabbalah, Hesychasm, and Prayer of the Heart, that extend many centuries into the past. These Judeo-Christian forms of contemplative prayer have involved regular systematic disciplines or exercises that involve contemplation, clearing and calming the mind, or focusing the mind on a specific object (e.g., the breath, God, compassion, a holy name, or a prayer; see Driskill, 1999; Easwaran, 1991; Goleman, 1988; Keating, 1996; Smith, 1986). Such practices, often generically described as meditation, come in a variety of forms worldwide (e.g., concentrative vs. mindfulness and awareness methods), but all represent "in essence, the effort to retrain attention" (Goleman, 1988, p. 169). The word *meditation* is sometimes associated only with Eastern religions (e.g., Hinduism and Buddhism), more narrowly with Transcendental Meditation (TM), or more recently with Mindfulness Meditation (MM). Nevertheless, underlying common processes are shared by authentic meditative practices everywhere (Goleman, 1988; Schopen & Freeman, 1992).

Meditation studies have generally examined, with rare exceptions (e.g., Oman et al., 2003), variants of TM (Alexander et al., 1989) or MM (Kabat-Zinn, Massion, Kristeller, & Peterson, 1992). Virtually no studies have investigated meditation as a spiritual practice within a Judeo-Christian framework. Rather, with rare exception, most have been offered as secular methods. In addition, many have focused only on physiological outcomes and have suffered from various design flaws, including inadequate assessments, lack of a comparison group, or failure to control for other factors that could explain health effects (Murphy, Donovan, & Taylor, 1999; Seeman, Dubin, & Seeman, 2003).

Some well-designed studies do suggest that meditation offers a variety of physical and mental health benefits related to reduced somatic and mental arousal and improved stress management skills. For example, Alexander et al. (1989) demonstrated in a small sample of 73 older persons that two forms of meditation (TM and MM) produced much higher rates of survival over three years (100% and 88%) than did relaxation training (65%) or merely assessing participants over time (63%). It is important to note that the study demonstrated that the effects were not explained simply by becoming more relaxed.

Research in the affective neurosciences is beginning to suggest that meditation may be a crucial factor in altering brain processes, thereby changing physiological processes influencing major organ systems, such as immune, neuroendocrine, and cardiovascular functioning. Davidson (2001) reported that MM meditation increased activity in the left prefrontal cortex area and reduced activity in the right prefrontal cortex. The left area is often associated with positive emotions, such as feeling compassion, and the right area with increases in negative affect, such as fear. Also found were increased immune competence in dealing with an influenza vaccine as well as less cortisol and more positive emotions.

These and other studies strongly suggest that meditation may offer a powerful but generally ignored practice that can promote better health and well-being. However, they do not provide knowledge about meditation as a spiritual or religious practice nor its effects on spiritual factors. An expert panel recently noted that the spiritual dimensions of meditation interventions, when present at all (e.g., in the form of a focus phrase or prayer), have generally been ignored in research reports (Seeman et al., 2003). The meanings of words in which the mind is steeped may matter a great deal, however, according to religious perspectives that range from the Jewish scriptures ("As [a man] thinketh in his heart, so is he," Prov. 23:7) to the Buddha ("All that we are is the result of what we have thought" Dhammapada 1:1, quoted in

Easwaran, 1991, p. 39). That is, from a spiritual perspective, a person may "begin to resemble and actually become whatever we give our attention to" (Easwaran, 1991, p. 38).

In effect, meditation research has focused only on the physiological processes of meditation and ignored the context and content of meditation. The time seems ripe for psychologists to investigate how religiously or spiritually based meditation as a practice relates to health and to other spiritual practices and outcomes as well (Oman & Beddoe, 2003).

FORGIVENESS AND HEALTH

Is forgiveness a religious or spiritual practice? Christian and Jewish scriptures (i.e., New Testament, Torah) strongly advocate, sometimes demand, some form of forgiveness, suggesting that forgiveness qualifies as religious practice. Yet for many religiously active people, forgiveness may remain an abstract moral value but not a practice. This may happen because people morally rationalize why the offender deserves anger and resentment and not forgiveness (Bandura, 1986) or because they lack the needed skills to forgive.

What is forgiveness? Although consensus is lacking, most agree it is a process, not just a decision (Worthington, Sandage, & Berry, 2000). Most also agree that it requires patience, sustained effort, and courage. Because forgiveness is multifaceted, it defies crisp definitions. Most researchers agree what forgiveness is not: pardoning (currently a legal term), excusing (implies good reason for offence), condoning (implies justification), forgetting (implies diminished conscious memory), reconciling (a related process), and denying (implies unwillingness to acknowledge hurt). Definitions appear to share two major features: (a) a willingness to let go of one's attachment to negative thoughts, feelings, and actions toward offender (especially the right to blame and resent); and (b) a willingness to increase positive thoughts, feelings, and actions (e.g., empathic understanding) toward the offender and the possibility of reconciliation. Cultural, societal, and religious factors, often ignored empirically, are influential in whether and how people forgive (Sandage & Wiens, 2001). It is significant that empirical studies to date have not studied forgiveness explicitly as a spiritual or religious practice. Although secularly based studies offer encouraging evidence that aggrieved persons can forgive offenders, we do not know if spiritually oriented forgiveness influences health and well-being (Thoresen, Harris, & Luskin, 2000).

Several recent studies provide encouraging evidence that forgiving others may also influence health. For example, Witvliet, Ludwig, and Vander Laan (2001) demonstrated elevated physiological and emotional reactivity (e.g., blood pressure, heart rate, negative emotions) when memories of being hurt and grudges were mentally rehearsed compared with imagining empathy and forgiveness toward the offender. Thoresen et al. (2001) found forgiveness training effective, compared with wait control group, at improving forgiveness self-efficacy (confidence to take specific actions to forgive) and reducing perceived distress, negative health symptoms, and anger effects, all related to improved health. Significant increases in positive daily spiritual experiences were also found.

As noted, psychologists and others need to answer several questions about the religious and spiritual nature of forgiveness. For example, under what conditions would religiously framed forgiveness prove more effective than secular versions of forgiveness? Would these effects relate to improved health as well as spiritual growth and experiences (e.g., feeling God's presence, greater inner peace)? What may moderate and mediate any relationship between forgiveness and health, such as one's beliefs about God, other spiritual practices, or opportunities to observe spiritual models of forgiveness (Bandura, 2003; Oman & Thoresen, 2003b)? Given the centrality of forgiveness in the Judeo-Christian tradition and the growing global complexity coupled with conflict of modern life, we believe that spiritually based forgiveness deserves high priority on any list of needed studies by psychologists and other social scientists.

CLOSING COMMENTS

The empirical evidence linking religious practices to health, as we see it, is very promising, indeed encouraging, but clearly unproved. Undoubtedly religion is related in some ways to health, mostly for the better. We have raised a number of issues that deserve attention. One major problem in empirical studies concerns oversimplified, reductionistic approaches to religious and spiritual practices. Often, a practice has been studied outside of its religious or spiritual context. In such cases the practice has by design been stripped of any religious meaning or intention. Those studies of secularized versions of spiritual practices have indeed provided valuable information pertinent to health. We currently lack understanding of these practices when used explicitly as part of a person's religious or spiritual beliefs and goals, however. We have noted the changing nature of spirituality among the American public, in particular, the growing number of Americans who perceive themselves as spiritual but not religious (roughly 20%). This subgroup of Americans deserves careful study, especially to better understand their spiritual practices and effects on health. We also suspect along with Wuthnow (1998) and others (Driskill, 1999; Fuller, 2001; Roof, 1999) that not enough focused attention has been given to the teaching and learning of essential spiritual skills and practices within many Judeo-Christian communities (i.e., talking and telling is not synonymous with teaching or learning when it comes to practices).

The reductionistic perspective has been particularly at issue in the study of health, given the prominence of the biomedical model that defines health principally in terms of physiological processes and disease. Studies are needed that adequately deal with the more indirect and longer term effects of religious practices, given that health is influenced by many factors over time. We have noted, however, a growing positive health perspective that frames health in more holistic terms and shares with Judeo-Christian perspectives concern with meaning, purpose, and direction in life as well as positive human relationships and self-mastery skills. In addition, the crucial role of spiritual experiences, often ignored in current study, as process as well as outcomes of practices, remains relatively unexplored.

In the beginning of this chapter, we suggested four religious perspectives that health-relevant psychology and social science could benefit by more fully incorporating: more fully recognizing the purposeful, goal-directed dimensions of religion and spirituality; examining the influence of religious views of human nature, especially views of the individual as capable of spiritual growth; understanding religious social support in light of its shared meaning-making functions; and recognizing the dynamic causal interrelationships of religious practices. Our review of empirical research on the health effects of religious practices suggests that these perspectives are beginning to be incorporated into research, but their use is uneven and much progress is still required. For example, although a few studies now recognize prayer as multidimensional, very few longitudinal studies of nonmeditative prayer are available. Similarly, although studies of contemplative prayer and meditation are increasingly studying psychological as opposed to purely physiological outcomes, little attention has yet been given to cognitive context and effects from meditation that may mediate its interrelationships with other religious practices, as well as perhaps with health over the long term.

Our review provides highly suggestive but inconclusive evidence of causal effects of religious practices in improving health. However, the possibility of negative health effects from religious practices, as noted, merits continuing study (e.g., see chap. 13). Throughout history and at present, some have suffered serious abuse, sometimes death, by others acting in the name of a religion or as religious leaders. For examples, one has only to recall the Crusades and the Inquisition of centuries past or the tragedies of some extreme religious cults (e.g., Jonestown). Recently, the highly publicized controversies surrounding physical and sexual abuse by members of religious orders also speaks to egregiously harmful effects (Plante, 1999). Apparently a sizable segment of health professionals believe that spirituality and religion and their practices either have no effect or have harmful effects on health and well-being (Koenig et al., 2001). We believe that religion as a major social institution, along with others, such as education, law, and medicine, that provide professionally based care and service, have undoubtedly contributed at times to certain negative health effects for some people. We also believe that many have benefited, often immeasurably, by and through their religious and spiritual beliefs and practices.

We have raised a number of issues that deserve attention. One overarching concern merits comment: the possibility that psychology and religion might form a more collaborative and constructive partnership, each helping to bring out the best in the other (Barbour, 2000; Jones, 1994). If psychology is to make more helpful contributions and to benefit from improving its understanding of religious and spiritual experiences, then state-of-the-art psychology as a science must be incorporated in empirical research on religion and spirituality (Thoresen & Harris, 2002). In the same way, leading religious scholars and practitioners must also be engaged to work with psychologists and other social scientists in clarifying and enhancing practices.

REFERENCES

Alexander, C. N., Langer, E. J., Newman, R. I., Chandler, H. M., & Davies, J. L. (1989). Transcendental meditation, mindfulness, and longevity: An experimental study with the elderly. *Journal of Personality and Social Psychology, 57*, 950–964.

Antonovsky, A. (1987). *Unraveling the mystery of health: How people manage stress and stay well*. San Francisco: Jossey-Bass.

American Psychological Association. (2002). *Guidelines on multicultural education, training, research, practice, and organizational change for psychologists*. Washington, DC: Author.

Astin, J. A. (1997). Stress reduction through mindfulness meditation: Effects on psychological symptomatology, sense of control, and spiritual experiences. *Psychotherapy and Psychosomatics, 66*, 97–106.

Bandura, A. (1986). *Social foundations of thought and action*. Englewood Cliffs, NJ: Prentice Hall.

Bandura, A. (2003). On the psychosocial impact and mechanisms of spiritual modeling. *The International Journal for the Psychology of Religion, 13*, 167–174.

Barbour, I. G. (2000). *When science meets religion*. San Francisco: Harper.

Bernardi, L., Sleight, P., Bandinelli, G., Cencetti, S., Fattorini, L., Wdowczyc-Szulc, J., & Lagi, A. (2001). Effect of rosary prayer and yoga mantras on autonomic cardiovascular rhythms: Comparative study. *British Medical Journal, 323*, 1446–1449.

Berry, J. W., & Worthington, E. L., Jr. (2001). Forgivingness, relationship quality, stress while imagining relationship events, and physical and mental health. *Journal of Counseling Psychology, 48*, 447–455.

Boomsma, D. I., de Geus, E. J., van Baal, G. C., & Koopmans, J. R. (1999). A religious upbringing reduces the influence of genetic factors on disinhibition: Evidence for interaction between genotype and environment on personality. *Twin Research, 2,* 115–125.

Braam, A. W., van den Eeden, P., Prince, M. J., Beekman, A. T. F., Kivelae, S. L., Lawlor, B. A., et al. (2001). Religion as a cross-cultural determinant of depression in elderly Europeans: Results from the EURODEP collaboration. *Psychological Medicine, 31,* 803–814.

Brown, W. S. (2002). Nonreductive physicalism and soul: Finding resonance between theology and neuroscience. *American Behavioral Scientist, 45,* 1812–1821.

Cacioppo, J. T., & Brandon, M. E. (2002). Religious involvement and health: Complex determinism. *Psychological Inquiry, 13,* 204–206.

Chibnall, J. T., Jeral, J. M., & Cerullo, M. A. (2001). Experiments on distant intercessory prayer: God, science, and the lesson of Massah. *Archives of Internal Medicine, 161,* 2529–2536.

Cook, T. D. (1985). Postpositivist critical multiplism. In R. L. Shotland, & M. M. Mark (Eds.), *Social science and social policy* (pp. 21–62). Beverly Hills, CA: Sage.

Cox, R. J. (2000). *Relating different types of Christian prayer to religious and psychological measures of well-being.* Boston: Boston University Press.

Davidson, R. J. (2001, October). *Positive affect: Perspectives from affective neuroscience.* Paper presented at the Gallup Organization's Positive Psychology Summit Conference, Washington, DC.

Driskill, J. D. (1999). *Protestant spiritual exercises: Theology, history, and practice.* Harrisburg, PA: Morehouse.

Easwaran, E. (1991). *Meditation: A simple eight-point program for translating spiritual ideals into daily life* (2nd ed.). Tomales, CA: Nilgiri Press. Retrieved from http://www.nilgiri.org

Ellison, C. G., & Levin, J. S. (1998). The religion-health connection: Evidence, theory, and future directions. *Health Education and Behavior, 25,* 700–720.

Emmons, R. A. (1999). *The psychology of ultimate concerns: Motivation and spirituality in personality.* New York: Guilford Press.

Fuller, R. C. (2001). *Spiritual, but not religious: Understanding unchurched America.* New York: Oxford University Press.

George, L. K., Ellison, C. G., & Larson, D. B. (2002). Explaining the relationships between religious involvement and health. *Psychological Inquiry, 13,* 190–200.

Goleman, D. (1988). *The meditative mind: The varieties of meditative experience.* Los Angeles: Tarcher.

Green, E. C. (2001). The impact of religious organizations in promoting HIV/AIDS prevention. *The CCIH Forum,* 2-11. Retrieved May 25, 2004, from http://www.ccih.org/forum/0110-02.htm

Green, E. C. (2003, September). *Faith-based organizations: Contributions to HIV prevention.* Washington, DC: U.S. Agency for International Development and the Synergy Project, TvT Associates.

Harris, W. S., Gowda, M., Kolb, J. W., Strychacz, C. P., Vacek, J. L., Jones, P. G., et al. (1999). A randomized, controlled trial of the effects of remote, intercessory prayer on outcomes in patients admitted to the coronary care unit. *Archives of Internal Medicine, 159,* 2273–2278.

Hill, P. C., Pargament, K. I., Hood, R. W., Jr., McCullough, M. E., Swyers, J. P., Larson, D. B., & Zinnbauer, B. J. (2000). Conceptualizing religion and spirituality: Points of commonality, points of departure. *Journal for the Theory of Social Behaviour, 30,* 51–77.

Hummer, R. A., Rogers, R. G., Nam, C. B., & Ellison, C. G. (1999). Religious involvement and U.S. adult mortality. *Demography, 36,* 273–285.

Jones, S. L. (1994). A constructive relationship for religion with the science and profession of psychology: Perhaps the boldest model yet. *American Psychologist, 49,* 184–199.

Kabat-Zinn, J., Massion, A. O., Kristeller, J., & Peterson, L. G. (1992). Effectiveness of a meditation-based stress reduction program in the treatment of anxiety disorders. *American Journal of Psychiatry, 149,* 936–943.

Keating, T. (1996). *Intimacy with God: An introduction to centering prayer.* New York: Crossroad/Herder and Herder.

Kirkpatrick, L. A. (1999). Attachment and religious representations and behavior. In J. Cassidy & P. R. Shaver (Eds.), *Handbook of attachment: Theory, research, and clinical applications* (pp. 803–822). New York: Guilford Press.

Koenig, H. G., George, L. K., Blazer, D. G., Pritchett, J. T., & Meador, K. G. (1993). The relationship between religion and anxiety in a sample of community-dwelling older adults. *Journal of Geriatric Psychiatry, 26,* 65–93.

Koenig, H. G., McCullough, M. E., & Larson, D. B. (2001). *Handbook of religion and health.* New York: Oxford University Press.

Krause, N., Chatters, L. M., Meltzer, T., & Morgan, D. L. (2000). Using focus groups to explore the nature of prayer in late life. *Journal of Aging Studies, 14,* 191–212.

Krause, N., Ellison, C. G., Shaw, B. A., Marcum, J. P., & Boardman, J. D. (2001). Church-based social support and religious coping. *Journal for the Scientific Study of Religion, 40,* 637–656.

Levin, J. S. (1994). Religion and health: Is there an association, is it valid, and is it causal? *Social Science and Medicine, 38,* 1475–1482.

Mahoney, A., Pargament, K. I., Tarakeshwar, N., & Swank, A. B. (2001). Religion in the home in the 1980s and 1990s: A meta-analytic review and conceptual analysis of links between religion, marriage, and parenting. *Journal of Family Psychology, 15,* 559–596.

McCullough, M. E., Hoyt, W. T., Larson, D. B., Koenig, H. G., & Thoresen, C. (2000). Religious involvement and mortality: A meta-analytic review. *Health Psychology, 19,* 211–222.

McCullough, M. E., & Larson, D. B. (1999). Prayer. In W. R. Miller (Ed.), *Integrating spirituality into treatment: Resources for practitioners* (pp. 85–110). Washington, DC: American Psychological Association.

McCullough, M. E., & Snyder, C. R. (2000). Classical sources of human strength: Revisiting an old home and building a new one. *Journal of Social and Clinical Psychology, 19,* 1–10.

Miller, W. R., & Thoresen, C. E. (2003). Spirituality, religion, and health: An emerging research field. *American Psychologist, 58,* 24–35.

Murphy, M., Donovan, S., & Taylor, E. (1999). *The physical and psychological effects of meditation: A review of contemporary research with a comprehensive bibliography 1931–1996* (2nd ed.). Sausalito, CA: Institute of Noetic Sciences.

Nottingham, J., Gorsuch, R., & Wrightsman, L. (1970). Factorial replication of the theoretically derived subscales on the philosophies of human nature scale. *Journal of Social Psychology, 81,* 129–130.

Oden, T. C. (1984). *Care of souls in the classic tradition.* Philadelphia: Fortress Press.

Oman, D., & Beddoe, A. (2003, July). *Structuring meditation interventions to enable learning from spiritual exemplars.* Paper presented at the Summer Research Opportunity Program Symposium, Berkeley, CA.

Oman, D., & Driskill, J. D. (2003). Holy name repetition as a spiritual exercise and therapeutic technique. *Journal of Psychology and Christianity, 22,* 5–19.

Oman, D., Kurata, J. H., Strawbridge, W. J., & Cohen, R. D. (2002). Religious attendance and cause of death over 31 years. *International Journal for Psychiatry in Medicine, 32,* 69–89.

Oman, D., & Thoresen, C. E. (2001, August). *Using intervention studies to unravel how religion affects health.* Paper presented at the 109th Annual Convention of the American Psychological Association, San Francisco.

Oman, D., & Thoresen, C. E. (2002). "Does religion cause health?": Differing interpretations and diverse meanings. *Journal of Health Psychology, 7,* 365–380.

Oman, D., & Thoresen, C. E. (2003a). The many frontiers of spiritual modeling. *The International Journal for the Psychology of Religion, 13,* 197–213.

Oman, D., & Thoresen, C. E. (2003b). Spiritual modeling: A key to spiritual and religious growth? *The International Journal for the Psychology of Religion, 13,* 149–165.

Oman, D., Thoresen, C. E., & Hedberg, J. (2003, June). *A spiritual toolkit for compassion and effectiveness: A randomized intervention among health professionals.* Paper presented at the conference on Works of Love: Scientific and Religious Perspectives on Altruism, Villanova, PA.

Ornish, D., Brown, S. E., Scherwitz, L. W., Billings, J. H., Armstrong, W. T., Ports, T. A., et al. (1990). Can lifestyle changes reverse coronary heart disease? The lifestyle heart trial. *The Lancet, 336,* 129–133.

Pargament, K. I. (1997). *The psychology of religion and coping: Theory, research, practice.* New York: Guilford Press.

Park, C. L., & Folkman, S. (1997). Meaning in the context of stress and coping. *Review of General Psychology, 1,* 115–144.

Plante, T. G. (1999). *Bless me father for I have sinned: Perspectives on sexual abuse committed by Roman Catholic priests.* Westport, CT: Praeger Publishers.

Poloma, M. M., & Gallup, G. H. (1991a). Unless you forgive others: Prayer and forgiveness. In *Varieties of prayer* (pp. 85–106). Philadelphia: Trinity Press.

Poloma, M. M., & Gallup, G. H. (1991b). *Varieties of prayer.* Philadelphia: Trinity Press.

Poloma, M. M., & Pendleton, B. F. (1991). The effects of prayer and prayer experiences on measures of general well-being. In Spirituality: Perspectives in theory and research [Special issue]. *Journal of Psychology and Theology, 19*, 71–83.

Powell, L. H., Shahabi, L., & Thoresen, C. E. (2003). Religion and spirituality: Linkages to physical health. *American Psychologist, 58*, 36–52.

Putnam, R. D. (2000). *Bowling alone: The collapse and revival of American community.* New York: Simon & Schuster.

Roof, W. C. (1999). *Spiritual marketplace: Baby boomers and the remaking of American religion.* Princeton, NJ: Princeton University Press.

Rowatt, W. C., & Kirkpatrick, L. A. (2002). Two dimensions of attachment to God and their relation to affect, religiosity, and personality constructs. *Journal for the Scientific Study of Religion, 41*, 637–651.

Ryff, C., & Singer, B. (1998). The contours of health. *Psychological Inquiry, 9*, 1–28.

Sandage, S. J., & Wiens, T. W. (2001). Contextualizing models of humility and forgiveness: A reply to Gassin. *Journal of Psychology and Theology, 29*, 201–211.

Schopen, A., & Freeman, B. (1992). Meditation: The forgotten western tradition. *Counseling & Values, 36*, 123–134.

Seeman, T. E., Dubin, L. F., & Seeman, M. (2003). Religiosity/spirituality and health: A critical review of the evidence for biological pathways. *American Psychologist, 58*, 53–63.

Silberman, I. (2003). Spiritual role modeling: The teaching of meaning systems. *The International Journal for the Psychology of Religion, 13*, 175–195.

Smith, H. (1976). *Forgotten truth: The primordial tradition.* New York: Harper & Row.

Smith, J. C. (1986). Meditation, biofeedback, and the relaxation controversy: A cognitive–behavioral perspective. *American Psychologist, 41*, 1007–1009.

Snyder, C. R., & Lopez, S. J. (Eds.). (2002). *Handbook of positive psychology.* London: Oxford University Press.

Strawbridge, W. J., Shema, S. J., Cohen, R. D., & Kaplan, G. A. (2001). Religious attendance increases survival by improving and maintaining good health practices, mental health, and stable marriages. *Annals of Behavioral Medicine, 23*, 68–74.

Thoresen, C. E. (2003, August). *Seeking the spiritual in secular places.* Paper presented at the 111th Annual Convention of the American Psychological Association, Toronto, Ontario, Canada.

Thoresen, C. E., & Harris, A. H. (2002). Spirituality and health: What's the evidence and what's needed? *Annals of Behavioral Medicine, 24*, 3–13.

Thoresen, C. E., Harris, A. H. S., & Luskin, F. (2000). Forgiveness and health: An unanswered question. In M. E. McCullough, K. I. Pargament, & C. E. Thoresen (Eds.), *Forgiveness: Theory, research, and practice* (pp. 254–280). New York: Guilford Press.

Thoresen, C. E., Luskin, F., Harris, A. H. S., Benisovich, S. V., Standard, S., Bruning, J., & Evans, S. (2001). Stanford forgiveness project: Effects of forgiveness intervention on perceived stress, state and trait anger, and self-reported health. *Annals of Behavioral Medicine, 23*, SO37.

Witvliet, C. v., Ludwig, T. E., & Vander Laan, K. L. (2001). Granting forgiveness or harboring grudges: Implications for emotion, physiology, and health. *Psychological Science, 12,* 117–123.

Worthington, E. L., Jr., Sandage, S. J., & Berry, J. W. (2000). Group interventions to promote forgiveness: What researchers and clinicians ought to know. In M. E. McCullough, K. I. Pargament, & C. E. Thoresen (Eds.), *Forgiveness: Theory, research, and practice* (pp. 228–253). New York: Guilford Press.

Wuthnow, R. (1998). *After heaven: Spirituality in America since the 1950s.* Berkeley: University of California Press.

12

INTERGENERATIONAL TRANSMISSION OF RELIGIOUSNESS AND SPIRITUALITY

BRENDA A. MILLER

Families play a central role in the transmission of religious beliefs, values, and practices across the generations. Although the development of spirituality and religiousness may be self-driven or emerge from a more external and mystical source, such as in the transformative experiences described by Miller and C'de Baca (2001), the family is an important force to shape spirituality and religiousness of an individual. Families, however, do not operate in a cultural vacuum, but access religious institutions that provide a supportive organizational framework through which religious traditions are transmitted and supported.

This chapter explores how families transmit religiousness across the generations and support the continuity of religious traditions. First, the importance of religiousness to American families is described. Next, the chapter explores some potential theoretical bases for the transmission of religiousness across the generations addressing the questions of how and why this transmission may be influential. Examples of empirical studies that examine the intergenerational transmission of religious practices, beliefs, and values are reviewed. Also identified are roles and family structures that are relevant to the transmission of religiousness across the generations. Finally, the environmental influences on family transmission of religiousness are discussed.

Most of this chapter addresses how religiousness is transmitted from parent to the young, reflecting the research that has addressed this direction of influence. Less information exists regarding how extended family members influence the young. There is also little research on how adult family members influence the religious and spiritual course of other adult family members throughout the course of their lives. There is some limited information on how the younger generation influences the spirituality and religiousness of their parents, however.

In keeping with the definitions of spirituality and religiousness introduced by Miller in chapter 1, this chapter primarily examines the transmission of religiousness across the generations, given that this is the focus of most prior research. Spirituality as an indicator of one's own connection to the Divine may also be affected by family transmission, however. Where possible, this chapter explores the issue of how the spirituality of an individual is shaped by family forces.

IMPORTANCE OF RELIGIOUSNESS AND SPIRITUALITY IN FAMILIES TODAY

Despite the historical traditions of Judeo-Christian belief structures, some doubt whether these traditions are relevant to families today and whether families continue to transmit these religious perspectives and tenets. General population data suggest that spirituality and religiousness continue to occupy an important role for many within the general population. In 1998, approximately two thirds of the population reported membership in a church or synagogue, and this membership rate has remained relatively stable during the 1980s and 1990s (Gallup & Lindsay, 1999). More than half (60%) of the population identifies religion as "very important" in their lives, and 42% reported that religion is "increasing in influence" (Gallup & Lindsay, 1999). About 40% of the population reported attendance in the seven days prior to the 1998 survey (Gallup & Lindsay, 1999). Although such attendance rates have varied some over time (e.g., temporarily increasing to 47% shortly after September 11, 2001), Gallup commented that "there has been no persistent upward or downward trend over the past six decades" (2002, pp. 98, 277). Clearly, the overall belief in the importance of religiousness remains high.

Age, ethnicity, and gender all influence the importance of spirituality and religiousness for individuals. Older adults are more likely to engage in religious and spiritual practices, such as church attendance and prayer. Whereas among young adults (18–29 years old) approximately a third reported attending a church or a synagogue in the seven days prior to the survey, among seniors (65–74 years old) the attendance rate was slightly more than half (52%; Gallup & Lindsay, 1999). There is also evidence that religious practices such as prayer become more frequent with age (Levin & Taylor, 1997). To what extent cohort effects have an impact on religious involvement separately from developmental stages across the life span is a matter of debate (Chaves, 1989; Hout & Greeley, 1990). During the late 1960s and early 1970s, new challenges to the established religious organizations emerged and the "generation gap" (youth protesting the existing status quo and normatively rejecting authority) was part of the popular cultural understanding. During this time frame, a national study of Lutherans was conducted and the two youngest cohorts reported less religiosity (as measured by practices) than their parents (Johnson, Brekke, Strommen, & Underwager, 1974). Nonetheless, the young *believed* that they were religious. Comparing themselves to their parents' levels of religiousness, two thirds of the 15- to 18-year-olds and three fourths of the 19- to 23-year-olds perceived themselves as being as religious or more religious than their mothers and fathers.

The importance of religious involvement is more pronounced among certain ethnic groups. Based on analyses of five large national samples, African Americans reported significantly higher levels of religiosity compared with Caucasians (Taylor, Mattis, & Chatters, 1999). Also, national population data indicate ethnicity differences. According to the Gallup Poll (Gallup & Lindsay, 1999), a higher proportion of African Americans and Hispanics, compared with Caucasians (85%, 75%, and 58%, respectively) reported religion as very important. In examining religious practices, a similar pattern emerged. During the seven-day period before the survey, 55% of African Americans, 48% of Hispanics, and 39% of Caucasians reported attending church or synagogue. According to general population data collected by the General Social Surveys, cohort effects may be more pronounced among African Americans than European Americans (Sherkat, 2001). Church attendance data over a 26-year span (1972–1998) indicated that there was a decrease in church attendance for African Americans among younger cohorts for most denominations. In contrast, among Caucasians, neither substantial nor significant cohort variations in religious participation were noted (Sherkat, 2001). It must be kept in mind, however, that the overall rates of attendance for Caucasians was much lower than for African Americans and that despite changes in African American participation, the consistent finding was higher attendance rates for African Americans than Caucasians.

A number of studies suggest that women are more likely than men to incorporate religious involvement into their everyday lives. Women are more likely than men to report religion as very important to their lives (67% vs. 53%, respectively) and more likely to be a member of a church or synagogue (73% vs. 63%; Gallup & Lindsay, 1999). The 1988 National Opinion Research Center's General Social Survey showed that women were more likely than men to have prayer as part of their lives (Levin & Taylor, 1997). Differences between male and female religious involvement may be related to their differing social roles.

HOW DO FAMILIES INFLUENCE RELIGIOUSNESS AND SPIRITUALITY?

Despite the growing body of research findings that explore the impact of religiousness on various outcomes, theoretical frameworks that explain how religiousness is transmitted across the generations are limited. Although children who are raised by religious parents are exposed to religious influences throughout their childhood, adolescence is a developmental stage that many religious organizations target in an effort to exert an influence on the life course (Smith, Faris, & Denton, 2003). Exploring how and why religious organizations influence the young, Smith (2003) theorized that religious effects among (American) adolescents occur because of three larger dimensions: moral order, learned competencies, and social–organizational ties.

First, according to Smith, moral order is accomplished through moral directives of self-control and personal virtues, spiritual experiences that guide youth to moral commitments and constructive life patterns, and role models that provide examples and offer positive relationships to youth. Second, youth develop learned competencies within the religious organizations including such skills as leadership, being a productive member of the community, and coping skills. Smith argued that the religious teachings provide the young with an understanding of historical cultures and an appreciation of the fine arts such as music. Finally, Smith suggested that the third major dimension of religious influence occurs through social and organizational ties. Religious organizations provide youth with access to adult members of the community affording a wider range of human interaction that affords helpful information, resources, and opportunities. Religious organizations also provide relationship ties and dense networks that can provide a context in which negative approaches to life can be discouraged and positive ones encouraged. Religious organizations provide links to national and transnational religious organizations that allow experiences to reach beyond the immediate community. Although Smith described this theoretical framework for understanding effects of religious organizations on adolescents, these same elements may be equally relevant throughout the life span.

This theoretical framework may be helpful for thinking about how families ensure the transmission of religiousness across the generations. It is important that this theoretical framework identifies key assets that an individual develops within the religious traditions. The assets Smith identified are similar to those that others have described. A number of studies completed by Benson and colleagues at the Search Institute have identified developmental assets that are linked to thriving and successful adolescents (Benson, 1997; Benson & Leffert, 2001; Benson, Leffert, Scales, & Blyth, 1998; Leffert et al., 1998). These developmental assets can be grouped into external and internal domains. Asset types that are within the external domain are family and community support, youth empowerment, family and community boundaries and expectations, and constructive use of time (Leffert et al., 1998). Assets that are in the internal domain include commitment to learning, positive values, social competencies, and positive identity (Leffert et al., 1998). These assets have been identified as powerful predictors of thriving (Scales, Benson, Leffert, & Blyth, 2000); however, they have also been negatively related to risk behaviors (Leffert et al., 1998). These assets map well to the attributes associated with religious involvement for the young.

Spirituality and religiousness may provide both assets and means by which individuals develop a sense of coping with life experiences (Pargament, 1997). Religiousness and spirituality also help to define life courses and give meaning to life's journey. In both Jewish and Christian traditions, one of the primary responsibilities for parenting is to teach children appropriate behaviors and raise them according to religious tenets. For example, in Deuteronomy, the laws of Israel are being set forward and in these instructions are the messages to teach one's own children and grandchildren (Deut. 4:9). Likewise, in the New Testament, children are exhorted to obey their parents, and parents are cautioned to bring their children up according to the Holy Scriptures (Eph. 6:1–4).

Families have provided the context in which the Judeo-Christian religious beliefs, values, and practices have been perpetuated across the generations. Although organized religious institutions facilitate transmission of religious involvement, primary responsibility rests with parents and extended families to socialize and teach their children about religious traditions. For young children, exposure to the religious institutions does not occur unless parents arrange such opportunities. Families as units may have unique religious experiences and spiritual needs based on the interactions of the individuals comprising the family at any one time. Family members stimulate and react to each other. They may discuss each other's experiences. They must deal with each other's behaviors. Furthermore, the developmental stages of the family members may be expected to interact within the family unit to create different sets of demands and needs at any given point in time. For example, consider a two-parent family with two children, two years apart. The family dynamics when the children are 6 and 4 years old are different from when the children are 16 and 14 years old. Understanding how a family effectively promotes the transmission of religious beliefs, values, and practices given this ever-changing context and development is relevant to understanding how family resources may be available to assist individual family members cope with psychological or physical problems, set goals, develop their personalities, and meet life constructively.

The influence of the young on older family members also plays an important role in the religious involvement of adults. As individuals age and become more reliant on adult children for care and assistance, the ability of the elderly to maintain their religious involvement may be affected if there is not a supportive adult child who will assist in meeting these needs. Furthermore, the family traditions, roles, and rituals may help to sustain the religious practices, beliefs, and values of individual family members throughout their life span.

Finally, the ability of families to transmit religiousness across the generations may be embedded in the hard-to-define and little-understood concept of love. Judeo-Christian traditions recognize that love is central to the identity of the religious and crucial to the human experience. Judeo-Christian religions continually speak to the importance of loving, both in the intimacy of family units and in the expression of altruistic acts of love and kindness to individuals in the larger community. In this book, Kass and Lennox (chap. 10) reflect on Jewish beliefs expressed in the *halakhah* as described by Maimonides, including the concept of practicing loving kindness. Likewise, from the New Testament of the Bible comes the command to "Love one another" (John 13:34). Indeed, Jesus asserts that "all the Law and the Prophets" can be summarized by the two commands to "Love the Lord your God with all your heart and with all your soul and with all your mind" and "Love your neighbor as yourself" (Matt. 22:37–40). Love is widely acknowledged in other religious traditions and even in the popular media as a human motivator for change. It is this underlying construct, perhaps coupled with spiritual practices, that catalyzes the human motivation for change in many instances (Miller, 2000).

Although the importance of love is not unique to Judeo-Christian perspectives, it is particularly emphasized within Judeo-Christian teachings. Childhood understandings of love grow out of and are demonstrated through the family relationships experienced in the everyday lives of children. As individuals become older, family relationships provide additional opportunities to solidify and expand this understanding of love. For example, caring for aging parents by adult children requires new growth and understanding of the concept of love within the family. The family also becomes the metaphor for the larger religious community, expanding the bonds of loving connection beyond the family of origin. Also, this larger religious community provides a framework for developing an understanding of altruistic love as acts of compassion and kindness generated for individuals who are unknown to the religious group or outside the family of origin or even the religious congregational family. Ethical ways of living that are manifested in kindness and altruistic actions are defined by Judeo-Christian tenets. These ethical teachings encourage the expansion of love throughout the life span to include the myriad of relations that comprise the human experience.

EMPIRICAL EVIDENCE THAT FAMILIES TRANSMIT RELIGIOUSNESS ACROSS THE GENERATIONS

A recent review of adolescent data drawn from general population studies and corresponding measures of religiosity suggests that the effective transmission of parental values regarding religiousness has remained fairly constant over the past 20 years (Smith et al., 2003). The ability of parents to transmit religiousness across the generations is dependent on parents' ability to communicate accurately what they believe, the values they hold, and the practices that they have found to support their own spirituality and religiousness. Frequency of verbal communication regarding religious beliefs not only improved the adherence to the same beliefs by the offspring, but also improved the ability of offspring to understand and perceive accurately the parental belief structure (Flor & Knapp, 2001; Herzbrun, 1993; Okagaki & Bevis, 1999). Paternal religiousness as indicated by behaviors such as church attendance, frequent family religious discussions, and identification of personal values about religious experience and practice were related to agreement on practices between fathers and sons 9 to 12 years old (Clark, Worthington, & Danser, 1988). Similarly, maternal values and religious experience and practice were also related to agreement on practices.

Spiritual modeling is also recognized as an important mechanism for transmission of religiousness and spirituality (Oman & Thoresen, 2003). Central to the concept of spiritual modeling is *observational spiritual learning*, a term defined by Oman and Thoresen (2003). Framing a conceptual model for spiritual growth, these authors suggested that relevant skills for developing spiritual growth are learned through observing other persons who are exemplary in modeling spiritual practices. None of their examples of exemplary models included family members; however, family members can provide another potent source of spiritual modeling that produces either growth or stagnation.

Recent research addresses the concept that children respond more to parental modeling than parental instruction. In comparing parental desire for children to be religious with parental modeling, parental modeling is a more powerful predictor of children's religious behavior (Flor & Knapp, 2001). For young adults (18–25 years old), parental behaviors, such as participating in joint religious activities and opportunities to observe parental religious behaviors were identified as major mechanisms of parental transmission of values (Okagaki, Hammond, & Seamon, 1999).

Spiritual modeling across the generations may have powerful influences because the observer develops perceptions of the other's beliefs. In a study of young adults and their parents, if young adults believed that their parents valued religion, there was a greater likelihood that the young adults desired to adopt parental belief patterns; this relationship actually mediated the relationship between adult child and parent beliefs (Okagaki et al., 1999). There is evidence that parental religious practices continue to influence adult children at least during the early adult years. A national longitudinal study of randomly selected parents and adult children indicated that parental religiosity (measured by six items that capture behavioral aspects of religion) was the strongest predictor of 19-year-old adult children's religiosity (Myers, 1996).

This was true even controlling for adult offspring's characteristics such as college attendance, marital status, presence of children, and social involvement indicators (Myers, 1996).

Family love, an understudied but important dimension of family life, influences the transmission of religiousness and development of an individual's spirituality. There is some empirical evidence for how these constructs influence transmission. High levels of emotional support increase the correlation between fathers and adolescent religious consensus in a study of Jewish male and female adolescents (13–18 years old; Herzbrun, 1993). Among traditional fathers with sons, emotional support was the best predictor of religious consensus (Herzbrun, 1993). Among liberal fathers, emotional support was significant in predicting religious consensus only with daughters.

As youth age, specific features of the beliefs and cultural distinctiveness of the religious group with which parents identify may become more relevant to how effectively their religious involvement is transmitted to the next generation. Fundamentalist religious beliefs have been associated with increased importance parents place on religious faith keeping by the next generation, and the importance parents placed on the child's obedience to parental authority (Danso, Hunsberger, & Pratt, 1997). Among college students, fundamental beliefs were correlated with valuing obedience and parental emphasis on the importance for children's acceptance of parental religious faith (Danso et al., 1997). The relationship between fundamentalism and adherence to parental belief structures may be related to parental strictness. In a study of Canadian high school seniors, Hunsberger, Pratt, and Pancer (2002) reported that doubting religious tenets was negatively associated with (–0.16) with parental strictness. In a study of (mostly) high school seniors ($N = 939$) from 12 public and four Roman Catholic schools, religious doubts were negatively associated with parental warmth (–0.21; Hunsberger et al., 2002).

Parental acceptance and emotional attachment between child and parent may differentially influence the transmission of religiousness. Although data are limited, at least one study of families from rural Iowa with adolescents (13–16 years old) showed differential impact of maternal and paternal acceptance on transmission of religiousness. Mothers who exhibited acceptance were more likely to convey their religious beliefs and practices, compared with mothers who were less accepting (Bao, Whitbeck, Hoyt, & Conger, 1999). In contrast, fathers' religious beliefs and practices affected their daughter's religious beliefs more when there was low parental acceptance.

Children may still become religiously involved when emotional attachment is missing or in short supply in families, but the nature of that involvement may be affected. In a sample of adolescents (mean age 16) in Sweden, insecure attachments with mothers at Time 1 was associated positively with the Emotionally Based Religiosity Scale, an instrument designed to assess the affect-regulating function of religion and turning to or maintaining contact with one's religion to provide a sense of security (Granqvist, 2002). In contrast, insecure attachments with both mothers and fathers were found to be negatively associated with the Socialization-Based Religiosity Scale, an instrument designed to assess the degree to which individuals adopted parental religious standards (or lack thereof). Fifteen months later, a readministration of the questionnaires revealed that Time 1 measures of insecure attachment to mother, but not father, were positively associated with decreased religiosity at Time 2 (Granqvist, 2002).

Although most research on families and religion has examined the role of parents on children, there is also evidence that children have an impact on parental religiousness. According to a reanalysis of Gallup Poll data, 95% of all parents have a religious affiliation (Mahoney, Pargament, Tarakeshwar, & Swank, 2001). A number of other studies indicate that religious involvement is increased in families with children (Myers, 1996; Sherkat, 2001). In a recent random-digit-dial survey of upstate New York, higher rates of attendance were associated with the presence of children for both men and women (Becker & Hofmeister, 2001). Furthermore, there was some indication that for women, the presence of children may increase religious salience and religious salience may actually be the impetus for church attendance (Becker & Hofmeister, 2001).

WHICH FAMILY STRUCTURES AND PARENTAL ROLES INFLUENCE TRANSMISSION?

Numerous examples exist within the Old Testament of recognition of the important roles of both the mother and father in Jewish families. Children are exhorted to honor both fathers and mothers (Deut. 5:16) and obey both the father and mother (Deut. 21:18). Within the New Testament, children are exhorted to honor their father and mother (Luke 18:20; Mark 7:10). Recent empirical evidence suggests that maternal and paternal roles impact the transmission of religiousness differently. In several studies, maternal values were especially important predictors of youth's religious values (Dudley & Dudley, 1986; Gunnoe & Moore, 2002; Nelsen, 1990). In a study of parent–youth triads (youth 15–26 years old), mothers, compared with fathers, had greater influence on transmitting traditional religious beliefs (Acock & Bengtson, 1978). Interestingly, this study found no support for the hypothesis that the parent of the same sex as the child would have a stronger influence on the child's adoption of traditional religious beliefs, religious behaviors, or religiosity (Acock & Bengtson, 1978).

Other research gives further insight into the differences between maternal and paternal influences on religious affiliation and underscores the importance of maternal roles. The findings from a large ($N = 13,122$) study of parents and offspring (high school age) showed that if neither parent reported religious affiliation, the overwhelming majority (85%) of youth also reported no religious affiliation; if both parents reported a religious affiliation, the overwhelming majority (90%) reported a religious identity (Nelsen, 1990). If only mothers reported a religious identity, between 83% and 84% of youth still reported a religious affiliation. If only fathers reported a religious identity, however, between 43% and 53% of youth reported a religious identity (Nelsen, 1990). The substantial difference between the impact of mother only versus father only suggests that maternal influences on the religious identity of youth may have a separate and important impact on offspring's decisions about religious involvement. Findings from these studies may reflect a particular cohort of youth, however, rather than support a more universal pattern of maternal influence, given the era (1970s) in which the data were gathered. Young people in the late 1960s and early 1970s helped to define the meaning of "generation gap," and these findings of parental differences based on parental gender and roles may be related to the historical times.

Additional support for differences between maternal and paternal influence on their children's religious involvement was reported in a study conducted during the 1980s. In a study of college students in Australia (N = 836), college students identified the most important person to influence their religious beliefs as their mothers (27.2%) compared with their fathers (11.3%; Hunsberger & Brown, 1984). Maternal influence was greater than paternal influence for all religious orientations (i.e., Anglican, other Protestant, Roman Catholic, Orthodox, Jewish, Agnostic, Atheist, Personal Religion). Whether these findings are applicable to the youth in the United States needs to be investigated; however, these findings suggest that the maternal role may be more influential for moral and spiritual development of offspring, at least in some cultural groups.

The influence of maternal and paternal religiousness on offspring is also complicated by the degree of agreement in religiousness for the parents. A number of studies indicate that when parents hold similar religious values, beliefs, and practices, there is a stronger conveyance to the next generation (Hoge, Petrillo, & Smith, 1982; Okagaki & Bevis, 1999; Okagaki et al., 1999). The congruence from one generation to the next also differs according the age of the offspring. According to a study of parents and youth (15–26 years old), congruence of parental religious behavior was more highly predictive of youth religiosity than attitudinal measures such as traditional sexual norms, tolerance of deviance, and militarism (Acock & Bengtson, 1978). Agreement between parents and children (12–14 years old) regarding values may be related to salience of the parental message and the ease with which parents are able to verbalize the message (Cashmore & Goodnow, 1985). Another important component of the transmission may well reflect the redundancy of the message, however (Cashmore & Goodnow, 1985). Thus, verbal messages may become increasingly important as children move into early adolescence and require more than the continual emphasis on behaviors that may be sufficient for young children. As children move into adolescence, their need to explore beliefs and values increases in importance and is critical for reinforcing their earlier learned religious behaviors.

There is some evidence that two-parent households may provide a better family structure for transmitting religious involvement to children, perhaps because of the dramatic changes that can occur in home environments of children of divorce. The 1987 National Survey of Families and Households ($N = 13,017$) showed that parental divorce was associated with offspring switching religious identities (Lawton & Bures, 2001). It is surprising that this relationship between parental divorce and switching religious identity was reported regardless of whether the divorce had occurred during the individual's childhood or after the respondent became an adult (Lawton & Bures, 2001). This suggests that the impact of parental divorce on religious involvement is due to more than simply structural changes of the family. Perhaps personal changes that result in rethinking religious involvement occur regardless of the age of the offspring at the time of the parental divorce.

Two-parent households are not a better vehicle for transmitting religious involvement to children if family violence is present, however. Partner violence is another environmental crisis in families that can affect the ability of parents to transmit religious involvement. Some theorists have contended that Christianity is rooted in patriarchy that legitimizes male dominance and, by extension, male violence (Dobash & Dobash, 1979). In particular, these concerns have been raised in light of the defenders of "traditional" patriarchal family structures found in conservative denominations (Bartkowski, 1997).

To date, however, research studies do not support a link between religiosity and partner violence (Brinkerhoff, Brandin, & Lupri, 1992; Cunradi, Caetano, & Schafer, 2002; Ellison, Bartkowski, & Anderson, 1999). In a large national sample of men and women ($N = 13,017$), no positive relationship between conservative Protestant affiliation and acts of domestic violence existed (Ellison et al., 1999). In fact, attendance at religious services was inversely related to perpetration of abuse for both men and women. Neither was denominational homogamy or heterogamy linked to domestic violence. The only relationship to domestic violence was when the man was substantially more conservative than the woman. These findings were replicated in a National Study of Couples ($N = 1,440$). Neither male-to-female nor female-to-male violence differed by denominational homogamy or heterogamy (Cunradi et al., 2002). Another study has suggested a curvilinear relationship between church attendance and spousal violence with couples who report infrequent attendance (1–3 times per month) showing the highest levels of partner violence compared with nonattendees and frequent attendees (Brinkerhoff et al., 1992). In a national study of couples, men who were frequent religious attendees had significantly lower rates of perpetrating partner violence and significantly lower rates of victimization by partner compared with men who infrequently attended religious services (Cunradi et al., 2002). In the same study, women who were frequent attendees of religious services were less likely to be victimized compared with infrequent attendees.

WHAT ARE THE ENVIRONMENTAL INFLUENCES ON FAMILY TRANSMISSION?

The ability for families to transmit religiousness and support spiritual growth may be influenced by the social and historical events that are present during a child's youth. For example, the social upheaval and challenges to authority that occurred during the 1960s and 1970s presented a different historical context for transmitting religiousness. Among high school students attending a parochial school (Seventh Day Adventist), the more students identified their teachers and parents as perceiving religion as a code of laws with rigid boundaries, the more evident was rebellion toward religion (Dudley, 1978).

Cohort and historical trends may also affect the transmission rates of religious involvement. Sherkat (2001) argued that there is an evolution of sect–church–sect that provides a historical framework in which generations live through their religious practices and beliefs. His argument is that sects emerge in younger generations when religious experimentation and shifts in affiliation are most likely to happen and religious preferences are fluid. According to Iannaccone (1990), this is also a time when investments in human relationships within the structure of the church are lowest.

Peer influences are another component of the child's environment that adds complexity to understanding intergenerational transmission of religious involvement. In a study of 16- to 18-year-olds involved in churches from one of six denominations, separate structural equation models for male and female respondents indicated that parents were not a strong influence during the late adolescent years for religious involvement (Erickson, 1992). Among female and male adolescents, home religious behavior was a predictor of religious belief and commitment and adolescent's religious education. This home religious behavior appeared to be weakly linked to parents' religious influence for male respondents and to parents' level of religious activity for female respondents. For both male and female respondents, religious education was a predictor of religious worship behavior. The latter relationship was confounded, however, by attendance at Sunday school being both a measure of religious education and tied to appearing for religious worship behavior.

A more recent study suggests that among youth 17 to 22 years old, peer religiosity was a better predictor of their religiosity than was maternal religiosity (paternal religiosity was not measured), and friends attending church at 16 years of age was a strong predictor of later adolescent religiosity (Gunnoe & Moore, 2002). The question of how peers influence parental messages about spiritual beliefs, values, and practices and the ages at which peer messages begin to weaken parental messages needs further clarification.

Families connected to religious organizations may have support networks instrumental for addressing family needs or accessing what can be described as social capital or developmental assets (Benson & Leffert, 2001). In times of crisis or need, the members of the religious organization can provide support (e.g., problem solving, emotional, financial) and assistance (e.g., fulfill tasks and roles of family members). Religious organizations also provide families with social activities and events that promote the religious values and beliefs of the organization. Thus, the members of the religious organization may be described as a large, extended family surrounding the nuclear family. The role of the religious institution is particularly well noted in Black communities, where the church is described as meeting needs for social networks both historically and in the present (Moore, 1992).

Reports from other ethnic backgrounds reinforce the message that cultural context influences the integration of religion in everyday life for families. Among Native American communities, the incorporation of spirituality into everyday lives is emphasized by the culture and traditions. Often these communities combine Native spiritual traditions with Christian beliefs (Csordas, 1999; U.S. Department of Health & Human Services, 2001). With Amish culture and religion, the traditions extend into everyday family life through the adherence to the "old ways," including use of horse and buggies rather than mechanized means of transportation (Weaver-Zercher, 2001). For immigrant families struggling to identify with their new culture and maintain their religious traditions, the challenges for the successful transmission of religiousness are even more evident (Kim, 2002; Min, 2002).

CONCLUSION

Whether individuals are born with a predisposition for spiritual growth or religious involvement is a point of philosophical debate. Generally, individuals are raised by families, and these families vary on the level of religiousness to which they expose the young. Likewise, families continue to influence the religiousness and spirituality of an individual throughout his or her life. Introductions to spirituality or religiousness may occur early in life and may result in individuals experiencing further deepening of the connections to their spirituality or religious commitment throughout an individual's life. Individuals may also experience little spiritual connection or religious training in early life and may never engage in that aspect of self. Furthermore, a more dynamic process is also probable with connections and disconnections with one's spirituality or religiousness occurring along the life span.

Within a Judeo-Christian framework, the development of the individual's spiritual growth and religious identity is viewed both as a result of individuals seeking a relationship with the Divine and as a result of cultural and religious traditions. The role of family in developing the individual's spiritual growth and religious identity has received less attention. Yet the family is a primary source of social learning for the young, including many of the developmental assets described earlier. Family members continue to shape the behaviors and thoughts of the individual throughout the life span. Finally, the family is a powerful arena for experiencing and sharing love, and this love can be a powerful motivator for seeking and committing oneself to change throughout life. It is this latter construct that is especially framed within the family. The extent to which the religious traditions help families foster, maintain, and express this love may help to explain some of the impact of religiosity on positive human outcomes. The importance of family for guiding the individual through their spiritual development, providing social support for times of crisis, and celebrating the transitions through life is intertwined with the religious ceremonies and practices in Jewish and Christian religions.

Religious infrastructure can be conceptualized as the organizational infrastructure including the physical buildings, systems of communication, social networks, or clergy and church staff. Perhaps more important, however, this infrastructure is also what exists in the hearts and minds of the people who are drawn to participate in the religious organizations. Although not universally true, many individuals involved within their churches and synagogues seek to negotiate successfully their personal changes through life, to help others accomplish the same, and through service to others, build stronger and more resilient communities. Perhaps this resilience is built on the structures of developing a moral order, learned competencies, and social and organizational ties as suggested by Smith (2003). Similarly, the strengths of individual assets as described by Benson and his colleagues (1997, 1998, 2001; Leffert et al., 1998; Scales et al., 2000) can be fostered in a religious environment. Another potential conduit for fostering human change may be built on the foundations of love that are first created within the family unit and supported by the religious traditions. Judeo-Christian traditions may support this development and continuance of love, not only within the family, but with the larger community and with the Divine. Within Judeo-Christian traditions, families become central to providing an environment through which love can be learned and conveyed. Efforts to construct a different psychological approach for working with families need to explore love as another potential key element of human experience—one that varies in strength and intensity much as does spirituality and religiousness.

REFERENCES

Acock, A. C., & Bengtson, V. L. (1978). On the relative influences of mothers and fathers: A covariance analysis of political and religious socialization. *Journal of Marriage and the Family, 40,* 519–530.

Bao, W., Whitbeck, L. B., Hoyt, D. R., & Conger, R. D. (1999). Perceived parental acceptance as a moderator of religious transmission among adolescent boys and girls. *Journal of Marriage and the Family, 61,* 362–374.

Bartkowski, J. P. (1997). Disputes over spousal authority among Evangelical family commentators. *Journal for the Scientific Study of Religion, 36,* 393–410.

Becker, P. E., & Hofmeister, H. (2001). Work, family, and religious involvement for men and women. *Journal for the Scientific Study of Religion, 40,* 707–722.

Benson, P. L. (1997). *All kids are our kids: What communities must do to raise caring and responsible children and adolescents.* San Francisco: Jossey-Bass.

Benson, P. L., & Leffert, N. (2001). Childhood and adolescence: Developmental assets. In N. J. Smelser & P. G. Baltes (Eds.), *International encyclopedia of the social and behavioral sciences* (pp. 1690–1697). Oxford, England: Pergamon Press.

Benson, P. L., Leffert, N., Scales, P. C., & Blyth, D. A. (1998). Beyond the "village" rhetoric: Creating health communities for children and adolescents. *Applied Developmental Science, 2,* 138–159.

Brinkerhoff, M. B., Brandin, E., & Lupri, E. (1992). Religious involvement and spousal violence: The Canadian case. *Journal for the Scientific Study of Religion, 31,* 15–31.

Cashmore, J. A., & Goodnow, J. J. (1985). Agreement between generations: A two-process approach. *Child Development, 56,* 493–501.

Chaves, M. (1989). Secularization and religious revival: Evidence from US church attendance rates, 1972–1986. *Journal for the Scientific Study of Religion, 28,* 464–477.

Clark, C. A., Worthington, E. L., Jr., & Danser, D. B. (1988). The transmission of religious beliefs and practices from parents to firstborn early adolescent sons. *Journal of Marriage and the Family, 50,* 463–472.

Csordas, T. J. (1999). Ritual healing and the politics of identity in contemporary Navajo society. *American Ethnologist, 26,* 3–23.

Cunradi, C. B., Caetano, R., & Schafer, J. (2002). Religious affiliation, denominational homogamy, and intimate partner violence among U.S. couples. *Journal for the Scientific Study of Religion, 41,* 139–151.

Danso, H., Hunsberger, B., & Pratt, M. (1997). The role of parental religious fundamentalism and right-wing authoritarianism in child-rearing goals and practices. *Journal for the Scientific Study of Religion, 36,* 496–511.

Dobash, R. E., & Dobash, R. (1979). *Violence against wives: A case against the patriarchy.* New York: Free Press.

Dudley, R. L. (1978). Alienation from religion in adolescents from fundamentalist religious homes. *Journal for the Scientific Study of Religion, 17,* 389–398.

Dudley, R. L., & Dudley, M. G. (1986). Transmission of religious values from parents to adolescents. *Review of Religious Research, 28,* 3–15.

Ellison, C. G., Bartkowski, J. P., & Anderson, K. L. (1999). Are there religious variations in domestic violence? *Journal of Family Issues, 20,* 87–113.

Erickson, J. A. (1992). Adolescent religious development and commitment: A structural equation model of the role of family, peer group, and educational influences. *Journal for the Scientific Study of Religion, 31,* 131–152.

Flor, D. L., & Knapp, N. F. (2001). Transmission and transaction: Predicting adolescents' internalization of parental religious values. *Journal of Family Psychology, 15,* 627–645.

Gallup, G., Jr. (2002). *The Gallup Poll: Public opinion 2001.* Wilmington, DE: Scholarly Resources.

Gallup, G. J., & Lindsay, D. M. (1999). *Surveying the religious landscape: Trends in U.S. beliefs.* Harrisburg, PA: Morehouse.

Granqvist, P. (2002). Attachment and religiosity in adolescence: Cross-sectional and longitudinal evaluations. *Personality and Social Psychology Bulletin, 28,* 260–270.

Gunnoe, M. L., & Moore, K. A. (2002). Predictors of religiosity among youth aged 17–22: A longitudinal study of the national survey of children. *Journal for the Scientific Study of Religion, 41,* 613–622.

Herzbrun, M. B. (1993). Research note: Father–adolescent religious consensus in the Jewish community: A preliminary report. *Journal for the Scientific Study of Religion, 32,* 163–168.

Hoge, D. R., Petrillo, G. H., & Smith, E. I. (1982). Transmission of religious and social values from parents to teenage children. *Journal of Marriage and the Family, 44,* 569–580.

Hout, M., & Greeley, A. (1990). The cohort doesn't hold. *Journal for the Scientific Study of Religion, 29,* 519–524.

Hunsberger, B., & Brown, L. B. (1984). Religious socialization, apostasy, and the impact of family background. *Journal for the Scientific Study of Religion, 23,* 239–251.

Hunsberger, B., Pratt, M., & Pancer, S. M. (2002). A longitudinal study of religious doubts in high school and beyond: Relationships, stability, and searching for answers. *Journal for the Scientific Study of Religion, 41,* 255–266.

Iannaccone, L. R. (1990). Religious practice: A human capital approach. *Journal for the Scientific Study of Religion, 29,* 297–314.

Johnson, A. L., Brekke, M. L., Strommen, M. P., & Underwager, R. C. (1974). Age differences and dimensions of religious behavior. *Journal of Social Issues, 30,* 43–67.

Kim, J. H. (2002). Cartography of Korean American protestant faith communities in the United States. In P. G. Min & J. H. Kim (Eds.), *Religions in Asian America: Building faith communities* (pp. 185–213). Walnut Creek, CA: Altamira Press.

Lawton, L. E., & Bures, R. (2001). Parental divorce and the "switching" of religious identity. *Journal for the Scientific Study of Religion, 40,* 100–111.

Leffert, N., Benson, P. L., Scales, P. C., Sharma, A. R., Drake, D. R., & Blyth, D. A. (1998). Developmental assets: Measurement and prediction of risk behaviors among adolescents. *Applied Developmental Science, 2,* 209–230.

Levin, J. S., & Taylor, R. J. (1997). Age differences in patterns and correlates of the frequency of prayer. *The Gerontologist, 37,* 75–88.

Mahoney, A., Pargament, K. I., Tarakeshwar, N., & Swank, A. B. (2001). Religion in the home in the 1980s and 1990s: A meta-analytic review and conceptual analysis of links between religion, marriage, and parenting. *Journal of Family Psychology, 15,* 559–596.

Miller, W. R. (2000). Rediscovering fire: Small interventions, large effects. *Psychology of Addictive Behaviors, 14,* 16–18.

Miller, W. R., & C'de Baca, J. (2001). *Quantum change: When epiphanies and sudden insights transform ordinary lives.* New York: Guilford Press.

Min, P. G. (2002). A literature review with a focus on major themes. In P. G. Min & J. H. Kim (Eds.), *Religions in Asian America: Building faith communities* (pp. 15–36). Walnut Creek, CA: Altamira Press.

Moore, T. F. (1992). The African-American church: A source of empowerment, mutual help, and social change. In K. I. Pargament, K. I. Maton, & R. E. Hess (Eds.), *Religion and prevention in mental health: Research, vision, and action* (pp. 237–258). New York: Haworth Press.

Myers, S. M. (1996). An interactive model of religiosity inheritance: The importance of family context. *American Sociological Review, 61,* 858–866.

Nelsen, H. M. (1990). The religious identification of children of interfaith marriages. *Review of Religious Research, 32,* 122–134.

Okagaki, L., & Bevis, C. (1999). Transmission of religious values: Relations between parents' and daughters' beliefs. *Journal of Genetic Psychology, 160,* 303–316.

Okagaki, L., Hammond, K. A., & Seamon, L. (1999). Socialization of religious beliefs. *Journal for the Scientific Study of Religion, 20,* 273–294.

Oman, D., & Thoresen, C. E. (2003). Spiritual modeling: A key to spiritual and religious growth? *International Journal for the Psychology of Religion, 13,* 149–165.

Pargament, K. I. (1997). *The psychology of religion and coping: Theory, research, practice.* New York: Guilford Press.

Scales, P. C., Benson, P. L., Leffert, N., & Blyth, D. A. (2000). Contribution of developmental assets to the prediction of thriving among adolescents. *Applied Developmental Science, 4,* 27–46.

Sherkat, D. (2001). Investigating the sect-church-sect cycle: Cohort specific attendance differences across African-American denominations. *Journal for the Scientific Study of Religion, 40,* 221–234.

Smith, C. (2003). Theorizing religious effects among American adolescents. *Journal for the Scientific Study of Religion, 42,* 17–30.

Smith, C., Faris, R., & Denton, M. L. (2003). Mapping American adolescent subjective religiosity and attitudes of alienation toward religion: A research report. *Sociology of Religion, 64,* 111–133.

Taylor, R. J., Mattis, J. S., & Chatters, L. (1999). Subjective religiosity among African-Americans: A synthesis of findings from five national samples. *Journal of Black Psychology, 25,* 524–543.

U.S. Department of Health & Human Services. (2001). *Mental health: Culture, race, and ethnicity: A supplement to "Mental health: A report of the Surgeon General"* (DHHS Publication No. 0497-D-01). Washington, DC: U.S. Government Printing Office.

Weaver-Zercher, D. (2001). *The Amish in the American imagination.* Baltimore: John Hopkins University Press.

13

SPIRITUAL STRUGGLE: A PHENOMENON OF INTEREST TO PSYCHOLOGY AND RELIGION

KENNETH I. PARGAMENT, NICHOLE A. MURRAY-SWANK,
GINA M. MAGYAR, AND GENE G. ANO

And it came to pass, as soon as he came nigh unto the camp, that he saw the calf and the dancing; and Moses' anger waxed hot, and he cast the tablets out of his hands, and broke them beneath the mount. (Exod. 32:19)

He attacked first in the form of Desire, parading three voluptuous goddesses with their tempting retinues. When the Buddha-to-be remained unmoved, the Temptor switched to the guise of Death. . . . Mara was waiting for him with one last temptation. . . . Why not commit the whole hot world to the devil, be done with the body forever, and slip at once into the cool haven of perpetual nirvana? (Smith, 1958, pp. 94–95)

And about the ninth hour Jesus cried with a loud voice, saying . . . My God, my God, why hast thou forsaken me? (Matt. 27:46)

The phenomena of greatest interest to scientific disciplines are defined not only by the disciplines themselves, but also by larger social and cultural forces (Kuhn, 1962). Religion is one such societal force that can shape the direction of scientific inquiry. Although the field of psychology has generally neglected those phenomena of deepest concern to religious and spiritual communities, more recently this picture has begun to change. With the rise of a "positive psychology" has come greater attention to religiously rooted constructs, such as forgiveness, gratitude, evil, and hope (see Snyder & Lopez, 2002). Religious traditions, however, point to many other potentially valuable objects of study for psychology. This chapter introduces to psychology a phenomenon of particular interest to the Jewish and Christian world—spiritual struggles.

According to most religious traditions, the pathway leading to the sacred is neither straightforward nor painless. It is, instead, marked by obstacles, difficult terrain, wrong turns, and dead-ends. Struggles in the spiritual journey are widely accepted within the world's major religions. Even the greatest

245

religious figures experienced periods of profound conflict and struggle in their spiritual quests. The struggle may be interpersonal, as we see when Moses shattered the tablets containing the Ten Commandments on witnessing the people of Israel worshipping the Golden Calf. The struggle may be intrapsychic, as illustrated by the temptations of Siddhartha Gautama as he sat beneath the Bo tree on the epochal evening before he became the Buddha, the Enlightened One. Or the struggle may involve the Divine, as we hear in the words of Jesus Christ on the cross, crying out to God. Thus, spiritual struggles may take different forms. All struggles, however, grow out of an encounter between an individual and a situation that endangers or harms the ultimate spiritual destination, be it the promised land, self-realization, or union with God. From a Judeo-Christian perspective, all struggles involve more than an individual and a situation; they unfold in relationship to a Supreme Being.

In Jewish and Christian thought, spiritual struggles are not simply "life stressors," "life crises," or "critical transitions." Instead, they represent crucial moments in time, when matters of greatest value are at stake. Spiritual struggles are spiritual "forks in the road" that can lead to despair, hopelessness, and meaninglessness on the one hand, and renewal, growth, and transformation on the other.

Despite their significance within the religious world, spiritual struggles have received relatively little attention from psychologists. Perhaps because of their own relatively low levels of religiousness (Shafranske, 1996a), psychologists have underestimated the importance of a variety of religious and spiritual phenomena, including spiritual struggles. Furthermore, psychologists have tended to reduce religious and spiritual processes to other, presumably more basic, psychological, social, and physiological dimensions (Pargament, Magyar, & Murray-Swank, in press). Spiritual struggles, for instance, could be explained in terms of more fundamental intrapersonal or interpersonal conflicts.

The last 10 years have witnessed an upsurge of interest in religion and spirituality as a dimension of life that is significant and powerful in its own right. In this chapter, we focus on spiritual struggles as a phenomenon of interest for psychology as well as religion, one that can shed further light on not only the spiritual side of life but also the life of the person as a whole. Throughout the chapter, we integrate the insights and wisdom gleaned from Jewish and Christian traditions with emerging psychological research and theory. We begin by examining the meaning of spiritual struggles and present data indicating that spiritual struggles are not unusual. Next, we turn our attention to some of the factors that may lead to spiritual struggles. We then review an emerging body of research that points to the significant implications of spiritual struggles for psychological, social, and physical functioning. We conclude the chapter by reviewing examples of psychological and spiritual programs that have been designed to help people address and resolve their struggles.

THE MEANING OF SPIRITUAL STRUGGLE

Spirituality can be viewed as a resource that helps orient and sustain people through major life crises and transitions. In fact, a number of studies have shown that spiritual beliefs, practices, and relationships can buffer the impact of life events on health and well-being (Koenig, McCullough, & Larson, 2001; Pargament, 1997). Spirituality is not simply a method of preserving and protecting people from psychological, social, or physical harm, however. For many, it is an ultimate value in and of itself. Within Judeo-Christian traditions, the highest of all ends is "to know God." As Johnson (1959) put it, "It is the ultimate Thou whom the religious person seeks most of all" (p. 7).

From this perspective, life experiences cannot be understood outside of a spiritual context. Life events have an impact on people not only psychologically, socially, and physically but also spiritually. Furthermore, experiences that pose a threat to or damage the individual's spiritual beliefs, practices, values, and relationships may be especially disturbing because they endanger those aspects of life that the individual holds sacred. People do not simply acquiesce to these threats, however. In response to spiritual challenges, people struggle to hold on to their spiritual values or, if necessary, transform their spirituality. In this sense, spiritual struggle is a distinctive and potent phenomenon, a way of coping—not in a mundane or trivial sense, but in its most profound form, when no less than the soul may be at stake.

The process of struggle is not easy. Struggles are just that, struggles; they are marked by expressions of pain, anger, fear, doubt, and confusion—all signs of a spiritual system under strain and in flux. In short, we define spiritual struggles as efforts to conserve or transform a spirituality that has been threatened or harmed.

Spiritual struggles can take different forms. Within Judaism and Christianity, three types of spiritual struggle are commonplace: interpersonal, intrapsychic, and Divine. The Hebrew Bible and New Testament are replete with stories of conflicts among families, friends, tribes, and nations, from the mortal struggle between Cain and Abel (Gen. 4) and the conflict between the Pharaoh of Egypt and the people of Israel (Exod. 5:14) to the disputes among Jesus' disciples about who would be the greatest in the kingdom of heaven (Mark 9:34) and the clash between the apostles Peter and Paul about appropriate spiritual conduct and matters of ecclesiology (Gal. 2:11–21). Certainly, interpersonal spiritual struggles are not a thing of the past. Nielsen (1998) found that 65% of an adult sample reported some sort of religious conflict in their lives, and most of these conflicts were interpersonal in nature. In a focus group study of older adults, Krause, Chatters, Meltzer, and Morgan (2000) identified several types of negative interactions among church members, including gossiping, cliquishness, hypocrisy on the part of clergy and members, and disagreements with official church doctrine. These struggles may have been particularly painful because they violate expectations about how members of religious communities should enact their spiritual values with each other, as we hear in the words of one woman:

> They get off in a corner and talk about you and you're the one that's there on Saturday working with their children and ironing the priest's vestments and doing all that kind of thing and washing the dishes on Sunday afternoon after church. But they don't have the Christian spirit. (p. 519)

Spiritual struggles can take place intrapersonally as well as interpersonally. Major figures throughout Jewish and Christian history have articulated important questions and doubts about matters of faith. For example, Ciarrocchi (1995) pointed out that the Christian spiritual master, John Bunyan (1628–1688), one of the most important religious and literary figures of his time, often experienced "tormenting doubts about his personal salvation" (p. 35). Many people currently experience such intrapsychic spiritual struggles as well. For example, only 35% of a national sample of Presbyterians indicated that they had never had any religious doubts (Krause, Ingersoll-Dayton, Ellison, & Wulff, 1999). Intrapersonal struggles may center around matters of spiritual motivation as well as faith. In this vein, Ryan, Rigby, and King (1993) contrasted religiousness that is personally chosen and valued (identification) with a religiousness that grows out of social pressure and feelings of anxiety, guilt, and low self-esteem (introjection). The latter form of religiousness, they suggested, is "characterized by experiences of conflict and pressure" (p. 588). Exline (2003) has articulated a related intrapsychic spiritual struggle, the tension between the pursuit of virtuous behavior as encouraged by many religious traditions and the natural inclination to pursue human desires. Paradoxically, she noted, attempts to cultivate the virtues may only highlight human limitations and imperfections. Moreover, Exline concluded, the struggle between virtuous strivings and vices may not be easily resolved, given the limited human capacity for self-control and the temptations the environment provides for gratification of the appetites.

Finally, and perhaps most important, spiritual struggles may reflect a tension between the individual and the Divine. Leading figures in Judeo-Christian history did not hesitate to share their feelings with God and, at times, even to argue with God. In the Psalms of David, we hear many expressions of pain and frustration with God:

> My God, my God, why hast thou forsaken me? Why art thou so far from helping me, and from the words of my roaring? O my God, I cry in the daytime, but thou hearest not; and in the night season, and am not silent. (Psalms 22:1–2)

Today Jews and Christians generally view God as a loving, all-powerful Being who is directly involved in their lives, ensuring that goodness will be ultimately rewarded (Pargament & Hahn, 1986). Critical life events, however, can throw this view of God into question, leading to struggles with the Divine. Consider the painful doubts of a 14-year-old Nicaraguan girl:

> Many times I wonder how there can be a God—a *loving* God and *where* He is. . . . I don't understand why He lets little children in Third World countries die of starvation or diseases that could have been cured if they would have had the right medicines or doctors. I believe in God and I love Him, but sometimes I just don't see the connection between a loving God and a suffering hurting world. Why doesn't He help us—if He truly loves us? It seems like He just doesn't care. Does He? (Kooistra, 1990, pp. 91–92)

In response to pain and suffering, people may struggle to redefine their relationship with the Divine. Survey studies show that approximately 10% to 50% of various samples express negative emotions to God, including anger, anxiety, fear, and feelings of abandonment (e.g., Exline & Kampani, 2001; Exline, Yali, & Lobel, 1999; Fitchett, Rybarczyk, DeMarco, & Nicholas, 1999; Pargament, Koenig, & Perez, 2000).

To conclude this section, we emphasize several points. First, although spiritual struggles can reflect tension and turmoil in an individual's social sphere, personal life, or relationship with God, these struggles are not necessarily mutually exclusive. In fact, they may contribute to each other; conflicts with God may lead to interpersonal or intrapsychic spiritual conflicts. Spiritual conflicts with family, friends, or congregation could conceivably lead to conflicts with God and intrapersonal struggles. Consistent with this idea, researchers have found significant intercorrelations among indicators of interpersonal, intrapersonal, and Divine struggle (e.g., Pargament, Smith, Koenig, & Perez, 1998). Second, although spiritual struggles are not uncommon, it is important to remember that spiritual beliefs and practices are generally more a source of support and comfort than struggle and strain (e.g., Exline, Yali, & Sanderson, 2000; Pargament et al., 1998). Finally, we must emphasize that spiritual struggles should not be equated with spiritual deficiency. Consider this example: "I am told that God lives in me—and yet the reality of darkness and coldness and emptiness is so great that nothing touches my soul" ("Perspectives," 2001, p. 23). This quote comes from none other than Mother Teresa. As noted earlier, over the course of their lives, even the greatest religious figures have experienced spiritual struggles. How do we account for these struggles? What brings them about? We turn our attention now to some of the factors that may lead to spiritual struggles.

THE ROOTS OF SPIRITUAL STRUGGLE

Jewish and Christian writings point clearly to one root of spiritual struggle—the confrontation with painful life situations. For example, in the

Hebrew Bible, Job faced stressors of the most extreme kind. After losing considerably valuable property and possessions (Job 1: 13–17), learning that all of his children had been killed (Job 1:18), and becoming afflicted with festering sores that covered his whole body, Job faced all three types of spiritual struggle. He experienced interpersonal spiritual struggles with his friends (Job 3–27), which were particularly painful for him because their response to his suffering violated his expectations about how members of his spiritual community should be there for one another during times of trouble. As Job put it:

> A despairing man should have the devotion of his friends, even though he forsakes the fear of the Almighty. But my brothers are as undependable as intermittent streams, as the streams that overflow when darkened by thawing ice and swollen with melting snow, but that cease to flow in the dry season, and in the heat vanish from their channels. (Job 6:14–17, NIV)

Job also experienced intrapsychic spiritual struggles, such as religious doubts about ultimate justice in the world (Job 21:7–26). Finally, Job's afflictions led to spiritual struggles with the Divine. He stated:

> God assails me and tears me in his anger and gnashes his teeth at me; my opponent fastens on me his piercing eyes. . . . God has turned me over to evil men and thrown me into the clutches of the wicked. All was well with me, but he shattered me; he seized me by the neck and crushed me. He has made me his target. (Job 16:9, 11–12)

The New Testament also includes illustrations of spiritual struggles that grow out of extreme circumstances. While awaiting his arrest in the Garden of Gethsemane, Jesus experienced an interpersonal spiritual struggle after realizing that his disciples had fallen asleep when they were supposed to be praying (Matt. 26:36–46). While preparing for his impending crucifixion, Jesus also experienced an intrapsychic spiritual struggle manifested as tension between his own desire and the pursuit of God's will, although he ultimately desired to fulfill God's will.

> And he went forward a little, and fell on the ground, and prayed that, if it were possible, the hour might pass from him. And he said, Abba, Father, all things are possible unto thee; take away this cup from me: nevertheless not what I will, but what thou wilt. (Mark 14:35–36)

Finally, Jesus experienced spiritual struggles with the Divine, which can be heard in his anguish on the cross when he cried out, "My God, my God, why hast thou forsaken me?" (Matt. 27:46). Thus, Judeo-Christian perspectives suggest that distress and major life crises can elicit spiritual struggles.

Psychological research offers more systematic evidence of the link between struggles and stressful life experiences (Pargament, 1997). A significant number of people experience spiritual struggles when faced with major life stressors, particularly stressors of the most extreme kind. For example, in an extensive survey of 708 Holocaust survivors, Brenner (1980) found that 38% of the survivors who were observant Jews before the Holocaust became nonobservant after. In contrast, only a small percentage (4%) of all survivors first became observant after the Holocaust. One formerly observant survivor put it this way:

> I used to have a very personal, intimate relationship with God. I thought everything I did and every move I made God knew and was right there and He was participating in my life every step of the way. . . . That's the kind of person I was, and that's how observant I was then. Then the Nazis came, and where did He go? God was no longer near me. Disappeared. And I am no longer the person I was. (pp. 67–68)

Excruciating circumstances may not be the only factor that leads to spiritual struggles; whether life events elicit spiritual struggles may also depend on the character of the orienting system the individual brings to these experiences. The orienting system enables people to understand and deal with a variety of challenges and tasks in life (Pargament, 1997). It is made up of personality traits, worldviews, beliefs, attitudes, values, practices, emotions, and relationships. Spirituality is also a part of the orienting system. Some orienting systems, however, are stronger than others. People are most vulnerable to "disorientation," spiritual and otherwise, when they encounter life experiences that push them beyond the capacity of their orienting systems. Thus, spiritual struggles may grow out of orienting systems that are characterized by weakness and vulnerability in personal, social, and spiritual domains.

In the personal domain, research has shown that poorer mental health has been associated with spiritual struggles. For example, trait anger has been associated with feelings of alienation from God (Exline et al., 1999) and other negative feelings toward the Divine (Exline & Kampani, 2001). In a study of religious coping among college students dealing with a variety of life stressors, Ano and Pargament (2003) found that neuroticism significantly predicted spiritual struggles, even after controlling for other potentially relevant predictors. Thus, certain personality characteristics may make people vulnerable to spiritual struggles during times of distress.

In the social domain, spiritual struggles have been tied to a lack of social support and, more specifically, family-related problems. For instance, Kooistra and Pargament (1999) found that higher levels of religious doubting among Protestant adolescents were associated with higher levels of parental authoritarianism, harsher styles of discipline in the family, perceptions of greater insincerity or less commitment in the parents' religion, higher levels of conflict in the family environment, and more conflictual relationships with mothers.

Finally, spiritual struggles may grow most directly out of the individual's spiritual orientation—that is, the character of his or her general spiritual beliefs, practices, history, relationships, and values. Several limitations in the spiritual domain are worth noting. First, a narrow, undifferentiated spiritual orientation that does not adequately consider the darker side of life, such as evil and human suffering, may be vulnerable to problems. James (1902/ 1936) described this type of spiritual orientation as a "healthy-minded religion" (p. 125) and maintained that, although it has its advantages, it is ultimately incomplete

> because the evil facts which it refuses positively to account for are a genuine portion of reality; and they may after all be the best key to life's significance, and possibly the only openers of our eyes to the deepest levels of truth. (p. 160)

The failure to acknowledge the darker side of life leaves the individual both ill equipped to face painful experiences and ripe for spiritual struggle. Second, a spirituality that is not well integrated into the individual's life may be more prone to turmoil. Years of exposure to religious ideas and practices may contribute to "spiritual resistance" to challenging and threatening life events. Along these lines, Brenner (1980) found that pre-Holocaust observant survivors who had no Jewish religious education were four times more likely to become nonobservant than remain observant following the Holocaust. Third, spiritual struggles may grow out of insecure religious attachments, such as an anxious–ambivalent relationship with a God who is seen as inconsistent and unpredictable or an avoidant relationship with a God who is seen as distant, disinterested, and uncaring (Kirkpatrick, 1992). In the face of difficult life experiences, insecure religious attachments may lead to spiritual struggles in which the individual must wrestle with feelings of Divine abandonment, anger, anxiety, or guilt. Consistent with this notion, Belavich and Pargament (2002) studied 155 adults waiting for a loved one undergoing inpatient heart surgery and found that insecure attachments to God were related to greater levels of spiritual struggle.

Although limitations in one's spiritual orientation may lead to spiritual struggles, the problem here is not a lack of spirituality. Those who attach little importance to transcendent issues are likely to be spared spiritual turmoil. Spiritual struggles may have more to do with the quality of spirituality than the absolute level of spirituality. Still, even those with sturdy spiritual orienting systems are not immune to spiritual struggles. Recall the religious despair voiced by Mother Teresa and the struggles experienced by other seminal religious figures, such as Job and Jesus. Perhaps there is another possible factor that inevitably leads to spiritual struggles.

Judeo-Christian perspectives point to one other precursor to spiritual struggles. According to some Judeo-Christian perspectives, spiritual struggles in the form of a "dark night of the soul" are brought forth by God as a natural part of spiritual development (Saint John of the Cross, 1584/1990). The "dark night of the soul" involves an experience of spiritual "dryness" or desolation on the part of the individual that is initiated by God to move the person toward spiritual maturity. According to Saint John of the Cross (1584/1990),

> the Divine assails the soul in order to renew it and thus to make it Divine. . . . As a result of this, the soul feels itself to be perishing and melting away, in the presence and sight of its miseries, in a cruel spiritual death. . . . For in this sepulcher of dark death it must abide until the spiritual resurrection which it hopes for. (p. 104)

In this framework of spiritual development, the "dark night of the soul" is a "transitioning period of wrestling and struggling, which is clearly distinguished from the beginning excitement and joy [of spiritual childhood] and from the later sense of spiritual confidence that comes from a life of trials and walking with God" (Coe, 2000, p. 294).

In sum, spiritual struggles cannot be attributed to stressors or individual factors alone. Instead, struggles can be found in which people face critical life experiences that point to the limitations of their orienting systems and push them to consider new ways of thinking, acting, and relating to the world. From a Judeo-Christian perspective, spiritual struggles may be brought forth by God to move the individual toward spiritual maturity. Although this contention is beyond the realm of empirical science, the theological dimension of spiritual struggles raises important questions for the psychology of religion. For example, are struggles that are perceived to be brought forth by God more or less harmful than struggles arising from other factors? How might a "dark night of the soul" affect one's image of God, attachment to God, or religious commitment? Such questions remain to be explored. At this point, the reader might be asking, why all the bother about spiritual struggles? Do they, in fact, have any implications for health and well-being? We now shift our attention to this important question.

THE CONSEQUENCES OF SPIRITUAL STRUGGLE

Within Judeo-Christian traditions, spiritual struggles have been depicted both negatively and positively. Some sacred writings treat expressions of spiritual struggle critically. Consider a portion of the story of Moses. After leading the Jewish people out of Egypt, he reaches the limit of his tolerance when his followers complain about the lack of food and drink in the wilderness. At this point, God intervenes and tells Moses to speak to a rock, which will then pour out water for the people. Rather than speak to the rock as God had commanded, however, Moses, in a moment of weakened faith and anger with his people, hits the rock with his rod. God's response is swift and severe. Moses will lead his people to the Promised Land, but he will not be allowed to enter it himself (Num. 20:6–13).

In many instances, though, interpersonal, intrapsychic, and Divine struggles are accepted as steps toward spiritual reconciliation and growth.

For example, within the Book of Psalms, the psalms of lament are marked by a formal structure that moves from struggle to resolution (Capps, 1981). First, a complaint is lodged with or against God (e.g., "O my God. I cry in the daytime, but thou hearest not"; Psalms 22:2 KJV). The complaint is then followed by a confession of trust in God (e.g., "Our fathers trusted in thee: they trusted, and thou didst deliver them"; Psalms 22:4 KJV), a petition for deliverance, and words of assurance and praise of God (e.g., But be not thou far from me, O Lord: O my strength, haste thee to help me. . . . I will declare thy name unto my brethren: in the midst of the congregation will I praise thee"; Psalms 22:19, 22 KJV).

The account of the disciple Thomas in the New Testament provides another biblical example of strengthened faith after a period of profound disbelief and uncertainty. Following the crucifixion and death of Jesus, Thomas refused to believe that the resurrected Christ appeared to the other apostles. He declared, "Unless I see the mark of the nails in his hands and put my finger into the nailmarks and my hand into his side, I will not believe" (John 20:25, NAB). Thomas endured sadness, confusion, and undoubtedly castigation from the other disciples until Jesus appeared again a week later in the locked room. On this occasion, Thomas was present and exclaimed, "My Lord and my God," and believed that Jesus had risen from the dead. Although branded "Doubting Thomas," which serves as a reminder to Christians that even the most devoted often face periods of struggle and disbelief, he is also recognized for his devotion and loyalty to Christ and Christ's message (John 11:16). It is believed Thomas's faith was reinforced through Christ's resurrection and that he lived a life of missionary work and martyrdom in India.

From a psychological perspective, spiritual struggles can also be evaluated in positive or negative terms. Within many developmental theories, tension, conflict, or struggle of some kind are seen as a necessary ingredient for change. Piaget (1975), for instance, noted that a transformation in mental structures occurs only after disequilibrium, when the child's existing schemas prove to be inadequate to the tasks at hand. Psychologists of religion, from James (1902) to Batson (Batson, Schoenrade, & Ventis, 1993), have also commented on the importance of openness, curiosity, and flexibility as elements of a more mature faith. The deepest religious commitment, they maintain, is fashioned in the workshop of question and doubt.

However, according to some theories, there may be a price to be paid for spiritual struggles. The conflicts and inconsistencies that are a part of these struggles may produce dissonance and distress, particularly among those who view spirituality as central to their identity (Festinger, 1957). Struggles may induce shame, guilt, and alienation, especially among groups and communities that do not sanction open discussion of religious doubts and questions. Moreover, spiritual struggles embody fundamental questions about the ultimate benevolence, fairness, and meaningfulness of the world: Why do people in my religious community speak of love but fall so far short in practice? Why am I tempted to do things I know are wrong? How can a loving God allow innocent people to suffer? These are questions, among others, that cut to the heart of our assumptive worlds, shaking and perhaps shattering our sense of security and well-being (Janoff-Bulman, 1989).

Empirical studies have begun to shed some light on the implications of spiritual struggles for health and well-being. Clear links have been established between various forms of spiritual struggle and indices of distress. Focusing on interpersonal spiritual struggles, Krause, Ellison, and Wulff (1998) examined negative church interactions as they relate to psychological well-being in a national sample of clergy, elders, and rank-and-file members of the Presbyterian Church (USA). Clergy and elders who were involved in more negative interactions in the church reported greater psychological distress; similar effects were not found for members. In a study of church members and college students, reports of interpersonal religious conflict and conflict with the clergy and church dogma were associated with poorer mental health, including lower self-esteem, greater anxiety, and more negative mood (Pargament, Zinnbauer et al., 1998).

In terms of intrapsychic spiritual struggles, more religious doubts have been associated with greater anxiety and negative affect among adolescents and church members (Kooistra & Pargament, 1999; Pargament, Zinnbauer, et al., 1998), more depressed affect and less positive affect among Presbyterian leaders and members (Krause et al., 1999), and less happiness and life satisfaction in a national sample of adults (Ellison, 1991). Also noteworthy is a study by Ryan et al., (1993) who examined internal religious conflict among church members and college students by a scale of "introjected faith" (e.g., "I turn to God because I'd feel guilty if I didn't," "I attend church because others would disapprove if I didn't"). Higher levels of religious introjection were tied to greater anxiety and depression and to lower self-esteem, identity integration, and self-actualization.

Several studies have linked struggles with the Divine to emotional and physical distress. In a series of investigations by Exline and her colleagues, feelings of alienation from God were correlated with depression among college students and adult psychotherapy outpatients (Exline et al., 2000). Difficulty forgiving God in a college student sample was associated with greater anxiety, depressed mood, trait anger, and problems forgiving oneself and others (Exline et al., 1999). Pargament and his colleagues have also examined the relationships between several indicators of Divine struggle (e.g., feeling punished by God, feeling abandoned by God, feeling angry at God, questioning God's powers, attributing problems to the devil) and psychological distress. They reported that Divine struggles are related to less positive affect, more depressed affect, and less religious satisfaction among Presbyterians (Pargament, Ellison, Tarakeshwar, & Wulff, 2001); more psychological distress among victims of the 1993 Midwest floods (Smith, Pargament, Brant,

& Oliver, 2000); and more symptoms of PTSD and callousness among members of churches near the Oklahoma City bombing (Pargament, Smith, et al., 1998).

Particularly noteworthy are a few longitudinal studies in this area. In a study of medical rehabilitation patients, anger with God was predictive of poorer recovery over the four-month follow-up period, even after controlling for depression, social support, demographic factors, and level of independent physical functioning at admission (Fitchett et al., 1999). Furthermore, the effects of anger with God on recovery could not be explained by the patients' general level of anger because general anger failed to predict recovery. In the longitudinal study of medically ill elderly patients (Pargament et al., 2002), indices of Divine struggle at baseline predicted increases in depressed mood and declines in physical functional status and quality of life over the two-year period, after controlling for selective attrition, mortality bias, demographic factors, and baseline health and mental health. Perhaps most striking, spiritual struggles in this sample at baseline were predictive of increased risk of mortality (Pargament, Koenig, et al., 2001). Even after controlling for possible confounding or mediating variables, including demographics, physical health, and mental health variables, Divine struggles were tied to a 22% to 33% greater risk of dying over the two-year period.

All in all, these studies show that unmistakable signs of distress often accompany spiritual struggles. But what about the other possibility? Can we expect only pain and suffering from spiritual struggles? Can people gain a keener sense of themselves, the world, and the nature of God from spiritual struggle? Here the evidence is more meager, perhaps because relatively few researchers have attempted to assess the positive changes that may follow from spiritual struggles. Nevertheless, a few studies suggest that people may experience some gain as well as pain from their spiritual struggles.

Magyar, Pargament, and Mahoney (2000) examined the impact of perceived sacred violations (i.e., desecrations) of romantic relationships in a sample of college students. Desecration, they found, predicted more negative affect, more physical health symptoms, and more intrusive and avoidant thoughts and behaviors related to the event, even after controlling for the number of offenses committed in the desecration and the negativity of the impact of the betrayals. It is interesting, however, that equally strong correlations emerged between desecration and the subjective experiences of post-traumatic growth (PTG; e.g., feeling self-reliant, changing or reestablishing priorities in life, developing new interests) and spiritual growth (e.g., growing closer to God, feeling more spiritual). Similarly, in a sample of adults who belonged to churches close to the site of the Oklahoma City bombing, reports of spiritual struggle were linked with not only more symptoms of PTSD and callousness toward others, but, once again, greater stress-related growth (Pargament, Smith, et al., 1998). Finally, a similar pattern of findings emerged in the longitudinal study of medically ill elderly patients (Pargament, Koenig,

Tarkeshwar, & Hahn, 2002); signs of spiritual struggle were tied not only to declines in quality of life and physical functioning and greater risk of mortality but also to reports of greater spiritual growth. Thus, it appears that religion and spirituality may play an important role in positive interpretations and resolutions following challenging life events. Yet what, in particular, might Judeo-Christian traditions provide for their adherents that contribute to these emerging findings?

One of the most significant and powerful beliefs held by Jews and Christians is the emphasis and importance of life and living, as well as death. In the Jewish tradition, for instance, the faithful make an effort to pass on their spirit and gifts to loved ones, human kind, and the earth. Through a life well lived, an individual leaves a legacy of love and caring to future generations. Christians believe that Jesus' life represents the dying and rising that they are called to endure. When people suffer any kind of tragedy, crisis, or challenge, they experience the death portion of the Paschal mystery (The two aspects of the Paschal mystery are first, that by Christ's death He liberates believers from sin, and second, by His resurrection, He opens for believers the way to a new life; United States Catholic Conference, 1994). Over and over in the Scriptures, Christians read how Jesus' resurrection has changed the ending of the story. There is no death so final that life (hope) cannot rise forth from despair. It can take a long time, and people need to be disposed toward looking for it, yet Christians are taught that life can triumph over death. As the New Testament asserts, "unless a grain of wheat falls to the ground and dies, it remains just a grain of wheat; but if it dies, it produces much fruit"(John 12:24, NAB).

Another important dimension of Jewish and Christian faith lies in the conviction that growth, wisdom, and understanding are ends to be attained in and of themselves (Pargament, 1997). Thus, struggle may be a necessary precursor to transformation. Perhaps only through adversity can some people devote themselves to the discovery of new sources of significance, such as recognizing new priorities, pursuing a healthier lifestyle, developing more profound relationships, and, ultimately, creating a closer relationship with God. To experience the Divine, even at the cost of challenge and struggle, is the highest aim within Judaism and Christianity.

Social scientists of religion aspire to better understand how religion and spirituality exert their dynamic influence on growth and well-being following negative life events. Whereas the Judeo-Christian beliefs and practices described here offer theological explanations, additional studies are needed to examine the potential gains people may experience through their spiritual struggles. At this point, the overall pattern of findings suggests that spiritual struggles are a double-edged sword. They have a destructive, even deadly potential. At the same time, they may have the potential to bring people closer to wisdom, maturity, and a sense of connectedness with the transcendent.

Many questions remain. Must people go through a "dark night of the soul" before they are able to grow through their struggles? Do people simultaneously experience both "pain and gain" from their struggles? Perhaps most important, what determines whether struggles will lead ultimately to serious physical and psychological problems or personal growth and maturation? One part of the answer may lie in the factors that precipitated the struggle. Unexpected life events that seem to defy explanation and fundamentally shake the individual's orientation to the world are likely to be particularly problematic. The death of a child or a betrayal by a spouse would fall into this category. More predictable events (e.g., death or illness of an aging parent) and controllable events (e.g., moral lapses) may elicit spiritual struggles that are more easily integrated into a benevolent and meaningful view of oneself and the world. People who perceive their spiritual struggles in a larger spiritual context may also be more likely to grow from their experiences. For example, many people perceive their crises as "sent by God," spiritual tests or trials that challenge them to move farther along the path to the sacred. These kinds of benevolent religious appraisals of life stressors have been linked with reports of spiritual growth (e.g., Park & Cohen, 1993).

Whether spiritual struggles lead to positive or negative outcomes may also depend on the individual's ability to reach a satisfactory resolution to his or her struggles. An analysis from the longitudinal study of medically ill elderly patients is particularly relevant here (Pargament et al., 2002). The researchers speculated that the connection between spiritual struggles and declines in health might be due to the failure among some patients to resolve their struggles. To test this idea, they compared "chronic spiritual strugglers" (i.e., those who reported spiritual struggles at baseline and two years later) with those who experienced spiritual struggles at only one point in time and those who did not experience spiritual struggles at all. As predicted, the chronic spiritual strugglers were more likely to decline in their quality of life and, to a marginal degree, become more depressed and more physically dependent from baseline to follow-up in comparison to the other groups. Thus, the danger of spiritual struggles may lie less in the struggles themselves than in the risk of "getting stuck" in the struggles.

These findings, tentative as they are, underscore the importance of the individual's access to the personal, social, and spiritual resources that are necessary to resolve struggles before they become chronic. In this vein, Magyar et al. (2000) conducted a series of path analyses, revealing that positive religious coping mediated the associations between desecrations of romantic relationships among college students and spiritual growth, posttraumatic growth, and positive affect; students who made greater use of positive religious coping methods (e.g., sought spiritual support, benevolent spiritual appraisals) following a desecration were more likely to report positive transformations in their lives. It appears, then, that pastors, religiously sensitive psychologists, and other helping professionals may have a significant role to play in helping people resolve their spiritual struggles.

INTERVENTIONS THAT ADDRESS SPIRITUAL STRUGGLES

We have outlined various types of spiritual struggles, the factors that lead to struggle, and the implications of struggle for health and well-being. Now we turn our attention to the various ways that helping professionals have attempted to intervene with such struggles. Several books and articles have been written about integrating spirituality and religion into psychological treatment (Griffith & Griffith, 2002; Miller, 1999; Richards & Bergin, 1997; Shafranske, 1996b) and adapting psychological techniques for religious clients (McCullough, 1999; Propst, 1988; Worthington, Kurusu, McCullough, & Sandage, 1996). Here, we focus on those interventions that specifically target spiritual struggles. This work is in its infancy. With a few exceptions, the evidence in support of these interventions is anecdotal and based on case studies. Nevertheless, these approaches to treatment are promising. Furthermore, explicitly rooted in Judeo-Christian traditions of thought and practice, these interventions represent novel methods of change for the field of psychology.

Interventions to Address Intrapsychic Struggles

Several pastors and clinicians have developed interventions to deal with intrapsychic spiritual struggles. For example, Evangelical Renewal Therapy addresses the discrepancy between an individual's beliefs and behaviors (Saucer, 1991). Saucer encouraged repentance as the mechanism of change. There are five phases to the process of repentance: analysis of moral action, rebuke, confession, prayer, and recompense (e.g., making amends through corporal works of mercy). This approach was designed to help Evangelical Christians cope with the emotional distress and self-defeating behaviors that result from failures to live by their values. Saucer elaborated, "The client's mistakes are rebuked, prayed over, confessed, and expiated" (p. 1103).

Genia (1990) described an "interreligious encounter group" that attempted to address internal spiritual struggles through a group format. A primary goal of this group was to remain open and inclusive of individuals from various faith traditions. In addition, religious doubts and uncertainties were normalized with group members encouraged to voice their spiritual questions. The group intervention focused on enhancing religious development through the exploration of spiritual conflicts, the resolution of internal conflicts, solidification of a spiritual sense of identity, and the development of personal spiritual goals. Group members helped each other discover their own spiritual truths and answer difficult existential questions about death, freedom and responsibility, isolation, and meaninglessness.

Expressing doubts, questioning values, and fostering spiritual identity are particular ways to address intrapsychic religious conflicts. Richards and Bergin (1997) stressed the importance of this task in adolescent faith development: "Given that a major psychosocial task of adolescence concerns issues of identity . . . spiritual interventions that help adolescents affirm their sense of identity, worth and belonging, and clarify and internalize health values may be useful to them" (p. 251). In this vein, Dubow, Klein, and Pargament (2001) developed a psychoreligious program to help Jewish adolescents become more aware of, choose, and integrate Jewish values into their identities and lives. More specifically, the program, called "*Mi Atah*" (Hebrew for "Who Are You?") helps adolescents integrate into their lives several virtues: learning (the value of knowledge and the hard work required to get it), honesty (the value of being open and truthful with yourself, with others, and with God), *Teshuva* (repentance; the value of maintaining caring, respectful relationships with others and with God), and *Tikkun Olam* (the value of being a good person and repairing the world). This 12-week program used scenarios, role-plays, discussions, biblical verses, education about the Torah, and written exercises to address internal spiritual questions and conflicts faced by Jewish adolescents. The impact of the study was evaluated by comparing the Jewish adolescents pre- and postintervention on a measure of the salience of their Jewish identity and on written vignettes that were evaluated for the degree to which the students integrated Jewish values and resources in the process of solving common adolescent problems. Initial empirical results of this study were promising; the adolescents experienced significant increases in Jewish identity and integration of Jewish values and resources in the process of problem solving.

Struggles With the Divine

A number of interventions have focused on helping to repair or facilitate an individual's relationship with God or the transcendent. Some interventions address individuals' feelings of abandonment, guilt, anger, isolation, and distance in their relationships with God. For example, Zornow (2001), a Christian minister, created "Crying Out to God," a distinctive religiously based program that focuses on the psalms of lament. Through the process of lamenting, Zornow argues, the individual can restore a close connection with the Divine or the "I–Thou" relationship. He explained that the program is

> for those who are going, or have gone through suffering and find it difficult to worship or pray. . . . This spirituality of crying out to God takes

seriously the spiritual struggles of the sufferer and their prayer life. Its goal is to encounter God in the midst of fear, pain, distress, and turmoil. (p. 2)

Zornow's program helps others go through a five-step process of lamentation: the address, the complaint, petitioning, vow to praise, and waiting. Lamenting gives broad expression to painful spiritual struggles and attempts to restore a connection with a Divine presence.

Other interventions focus more specifically on spiritual struggles related to particular life events (e.g., cancer, abuse, abortion, serious mental illness). For example, Cole and Pargament (1999) addressed feelings of spiritual disconnection and conflictual feelings toward God among cancer survivors. In one session, participants explored their feelings of abandonment, guilt, anger, and closeness with this God and how these feelings related to their illness. Visualization, discussion, and an adapted version of the "two chair" Gestalt technique were implemented in this session. Cole and Pargament (1999) wrote,

> Through an imagined conversation with God, the individual is helped to reconstruct a relationship with the Sacred that integrates the negative affective response to the diagnosis and re-establishes a sense of trust, mutual affection and connectedness. (p. 403)

The results of this intervention revealed that pain severity decreased in the treatment group, whereas it increased in the control group. In addition, the level of depression remained the same in the spiritually focused group, whereas it increased in the control group.

The lack of control and helplessness that cancer survivors face in some ways parallels the spiritual struggles that survivors of abuse and other traumas encounter. For example, Garzon, Burkett, and Hill (2000) developed a 12-week group intervention for Charismatic Christian survivors of childhood sexual abuse. This intervention was designed to address struggles involving anger, forgiveness, shame, and trust. Various types of spiritual exercises and practices were used in the intervention, including Christian imagery, the concept of finding the "true self in Christ," redemptive suffering, and various forms of prayer. According to case studies, the four participants in this pilot project voiced satisfaction with the group.

Burke and Cullen (1995) developed a group intervention for women struggling with postabortion guilt, grief, and spiritual isolation. This Christian intervention used ritual, spiritual imagery, discussion, prayer, and "Living Scripture" to aid in the psychological and spiritual healing of abortion-related spiritual struggles. Living Scripture asks participants to imagine themselves as characters in various biblical stories. For example, in one session, the leader asks participants to visualize that they are the woman at the well in Samaria (John 4:4–30):

You are the woman carrying the water jug up to the well. You're feeling burdened. The weight of the earthen jug presses down on your shoulders. Your back and neck ache under the pressure. . . . Jesus looks deep into your eyes. He tells you about your life, where you've come from, who you've been with, what you're like. Jesus knows everything about you. (pp. 63–64)

Other spiritual exercises attempted to foster connection and reduce guilt. For example, one step focused on developing a spiritual relationship with an aborted child through a spiritual imagery exercise whereby the mother encounters Christ with the child and experiences reconciliation.

Finally, some clinicians have directed their attention to the spiritual struggles of those with serious mental illness. Kehoe (1998) has led and written about various Spiritual Beliefs and Values groups for seriously mentally ill clients (e.g., those diagnosed with schizophrenia, bipolar disorder, major depression). In these groups, participants raise religious or spiritual concerns and explore their beliefs and struggles in an interdenominational, open-ended format. She has described the themes that have occurred repeatedly over the past 15 years: hopelessness, anger, abandonment, God's role in the illness, and differentiating spirituality from delusions. Kehoe believes these groups represent a valuable forum that enables people with serious mental illness to explore and heal their spiritual struggles.

Interpersonal Spiritual Struggles

Interpersonal spiritual struggles have received somewhat less clinical attention, with some important exceptions. Fallot (2001) described interpersonal spiritual struggles experienced by individuals with serious mental illness. He stated that, "Religious organizations can offer significant antidotes to the stigma often connected to mental illness. Consumers describe the empowerment that attends a sense of acceptance and belonging in valued faith communities" (p. 114). Fallot continued by noting that, "Many consumers have felt rejected by these communities" (p. 115). He suggested ongoing efforts at collaboration between faith communities and mental health professionals.

Interpersonal spiritual struggles do not affect only those with serious mental illness. Many people face spiritual conflicts and estrangement from friends, families, and their communities. Therapists have only just begun to address these conflicts. For example, Butler, Gardner, and Bird (1998) commented on how God can be a resource for resolving marital tensions. Prayers to God, they noted, are incompatible with spousal hostility, contempt, and negativity. Joint prayers, they found, calm and soften the level of conflict in the marriage. As one couple put it, "We've knelt down and prayed and it's amazing . . . what it does in softening our hearts" (p. 462).

Interpersonal spiritual struggles represent an important area for future intervention work. There are many unanswered questions. How can we help marriages in which spiritual violations (e.g., infidelity) have occurred? How can we aid blended families struggling over the differences in religious backgrounds and traditions each individual brings to the family? How can we assist congregations struggling with tensions between cliques and subgroups? How can psychologists and other helping professionals work together to resolve spiritual rifts and tensions between various factions within the community? Answers to these questions may help to alleviate some of the most intractable, painful, and destructive of all interpersonal conflicts.

CONCLUSIONS

Within the Judeo-Christian tradition, we can find rich descriptions of many phenomena that are distinctively human. By attending more carefully to these phenomena, psychologists could develop a more complete picture of human nature, one that acknowledges our spiritual potential. In this chapter, we have drawn from Judeo-Christian thought to introduce one particularly important phenomenon of interest to psychology. Spiritual struggle is not to be confused with a secular psychological process. It is a distinctive form of tension and conflict that holds powerful spiritual meaning as well as significant implications for human functioning.

Spiritual struggles should be of interest to psychologists and religious communities. This conclusion is supported by a variety of empirical studies linking interpersonal, intrapersonal, and Divine spiritual struggles with indices of health and well-being. As yet, we do not understand the mechanisms that may explain these linkages. Spiritual struggles could be understood in terms of putatively more basic psychological, social, and physiological dimensions. Spiritual struggles have remained significant predictors of health and well-being, however, even after controlling for alternate explanations, such as trait anger, depression, negativity, and personality variables. Further studies may yield different results. At present, though, these findings are consistent with the conclusion George, Ellison, and Larson (2002) reached after their extensive review of the empirical literature on religion and health, namely, the religion–health connection cannot be fully explained by health practices, social ties, psychological resources, or belief structures. The alternative is to view spirituality, including spiritual struggles, as a significant dimension of human functioning in its own right (Pargament et al., in press).

Spiritual struggles are more than a response to trauma and transition. They are signs of crisis in and of themselves, signs of a spirituality under threat. As such, they are deeply disquieting, for they have to do with the most sacred of matters. Nonetheless, stories within Jewish and Christian literature remind us that crises of all kinds are not only sources of pain and suffering, they can be precursors to growth. We have reviewed some preliminary evidence that suggests this may also be the case for spiritual struggles. The task for religious professionals, psychologists, and other helping professionals, then, is not to eliminate spiritual struggles, but to help people anticipate and deal with their struggles before they become chronic and before they lead to significant damage. To do that, we need to learn much more about how struggles evolve and how we may best help people in the midst of their spiritual conflicts. Promising programs have been developed by clergy and religiously minded psychologists. Research in this area is just beginning. Empirical studies of intervention are currently few and far between. This is, however, an exciting and promising area for psychological and religious study.

Perhaps we also need to think more about how to equip people to deal with spiritual struggles before they occur. A critical part of this process may involve improvements in spiritual education. Psychological and religious communities could work more closely together to develop and evaluate educational programs that destigmatize spiritual struggles, essentially normalizing these struggles as a common and, at times, valuable part of spiritual experience. Better education of children and adolescents is another important direction. Unfortunately, religious education often ends at adolescence, just when youth are developing the capacity to deal with abstractions, inconsistencies, paradox, and the complexities embodied in spiritual struggles. Educational programs could address various spiritual explanations, practices, and resources for dealing with pain and suffering, grappling with doubt, and resolving interpersonal conflicts. With more differentiated, more flexible, and better integrated spiritual orientations, people may be better prepared to wrestle with their angels and their demons, emerging from their struggles strengthened rather than diminished.

REFERENCES

Ano, G. G., & Pargament, K. I. (2003). *Correlates of religious struggles: An exploratory study.* Unpublished master's thesis, Bowling Green State University, Bowling Green, OH.

Batson, C. D., Schoenrade, P., & Ventis, L. (1993). *Religion and the individual.* New York: Oxford University Press.

Belavich, T., & Pargament, K. I. (2002). The role of attachment in predicting religious coping with a loved one in surgery. *Journal of Adult Development, 9,* 13–29.

Brenner, R. R. (1980). *The faith and doubt of Holocaust survivors.* New York: Free Press.

Burke, T. K., & Cullen, B. (1995). *Rachel's vineyard: A psychological and spiritual journey of post-abortion healing.* New York: Alba House.

Butler, M. H., Gardner, B. C., & Bird, M. H. (1998). Not just a time-out: Change dynamics of prayer for religious couples in conflict situations. *Family Process, 37*, 451–475.

Capps, D. (1981). *Biblical approaches to pastoral counseling.* Philadelphia: Westminster.

Ciarrocchi, J. W. (1995). *The doubting disease: Help for scrupulosity and religious compulsions.* Mahwah, NJ: Paulist Press.

Coe, J. H. (2000). Musings on the dark night of the soul: Insights from St. John of the Cross on a developmental spirituality. *Journal of Psychology and Theology, 28*, 293–307.

Cole, B., & Pargament, K. I. (1999). Re-creating your life: A spiritual/psychotherapeutic intervention for people diagnosed with cancer. *Psycho-Oncology, 8*, 395–407.

Dubow, E., Klein, S., & Pargament, K. I. (2001). *Mi Atah: A psychoreligious program designed to integrate Jewish values into the lives of Jewish adolescents.* Unpublished manuscript, Bowling Green State University, Bowling Green, OH.

Ellison, C. G. (1991). Religious involvement and subjective well-being. *Journal of Health and Social Behavior, 32*, 80–99.

Exline, J. J. (2003). Stumbling blocks on the religious road: Fractured relationships, nagging vices, and the inner struggle to believe. *Psychological Inquiry, 13*, 182–189.

Exline, J. J., & Kampani, S. (2001, October). *Anger at God as a response to negative life events.* Paper presented at the annual meeting of the Society for the Scientific Study of Religion, Columbus, OH.

Exline, J. J., Yali, A. M., & Lobel, M. (1999). When God disappoints: Difficulty forgiving God and its role in negative emotion. *Journal of Health Psychology, 4*, 365–380.

Exline, J. J., Yali, A. M., & Sanderson, W. C. (2000). Guilt, discord, and alienation: The role of religious strain in depression and suicidality. *Journal of Clinical Psychology, 56*, 1481–1496.

Fallot, R. D. (2001). Spirituality and religion in psychiatric rehabilitation and recovery from mental illness. *International Review of Psychiatry, 13*, 110–116.

Festinger, L. (1957). *A theory of cognitive dissonance.* Stanford, CA: Stanford University Press.

Fitchett, G., Rybarczyk, B. D., DeMarco, G. A., & Nicholas, J. J. (1999). The role of religion in medical rehabilitation outcomes: A longitudinal study. *Rehabilitation Psychology, 44*, 1–22.

Garzon, F., Burkett, L., & Hill, J. (2000, August). *Women survivors of childhood sexual abuse: A Christian healing group intervention.* Paper presented at the 108th Annual Convention of the American Psychological Association, Washington, DC.

Genia, V. (1990). Interreligious encounter group: A psychospiritual experience for faith development. *Counseling and Values, 35*, 39–51.

George, L. K., Ellison, C. G., & Larson, D. B. (2002). Exploring the relationship between religious involvement and health. *Psychological Inquiry, 13*, 190–200.

Griffith, J. L., & Griffith, M. E. (2002). *Encountering the sacred in psychotherapy: How to talk with people about their spiritual lives*. New York: Guilford Press.

James, W. (1902/1936). *The varieties of religious experience: A study in human nature*. New York: Modern Library.

Janoff-Bulman, R. (1989). Assumptive worlds and the stress of traumatic events: Applications of the schema construct. *Social Cognition, 7*, 113–136.

Johnson, P. E. (1959). *Psychology of religion*. Nashville, TN: Abingdon Press.

Kehoe, N. C. (1998). Religious-issues group therapy. *New Directions for Mental Health Services, 80*, 45–55.

Kirkpatrick, L. A. (1992). An attachment-theoretical approach to the psychology of religion. *International Journal for the Psychology of Religion, 2*, 3–28.

Koenig, H. G., McCullough, M. E., & Larson, D. B. (2001). *Handbook of religion and health*. New York: Oxford University Press.

Kooistra, W. P. (1990). *The process of religious doubting in adolescents raised in religious environments*. Unpublished doctoral dissertation, Bowling Green State University, Bowling Green, OH.

Kooistra, W. P., & Pargament, K. I. (1999). Predictors of religious doubting among Roman Catholic and Dutch Reformed high school students. *Journal of Psychology and Theology, 27*, 33–42.

Krause, N., Chatters, L. M., Meltzer, T., & Morgan, D. L. (2000). Negative interaction in the church: Insights from focus groups with older adults. *Review of Religious Research, 41*, 510–533.

Krause, N., Ellison, C. G., & Wulff, K. M. (1998). Church-based support, negative interaction, and psychological well-being: Findings from a national sample of Presbyterians. *Journal for the Scientific Study of Religion, 37*, 725–741.

Krause, N., Ingersoll-Dayton, B., Ellison, C. G., & Wulff, K. M. (1999). Aging, religious doubt, and psychological well-being. *The Gerontologist, 39*, 525–533.

Kuhn, T. S. (1962). *The structure of scientific revolutions*. Chicago: University of Chicago Press.

Magyar, G. M., Pargament, K. I., & Mahoney, A. (2000, August). *Violating the sacred: A study of desecration among college students*. Paper presented at the 108th Annual Convention of the American Psychological Association, Washington, DC.

McCullough, M. E. (1999). Research on religion-accommodative counseling: Review and meta-analysis. *Journal of Counseling Psychology, 46*, 92–98.

Miller, W. R. (Ed.). (1999). *Integrating spirituality into treatment: Resources for practitioners*. Washington, DC: American Psychological Association.

Nielsen, M. E. (1998). An assessment of religious conflicts and their resolutions. *Journal for the Scientific Study of Religion, 37*, 181–190.

Pargament, K. I. (1997). *The psychology of religion and coping: Theory, research, practice*. New York: Guilford Press.

Pargament, K. I., Ellison, C. G., Tarakeshwar, N., & Wulff, K. M. (2001). Religious coping among the religious: The relationship between religious coping and well-being in a national sample of Presbyterian clergy, elders, and members. *Journal for the Scientific Study of Religion, 40,* 597–513.

Pargament, K. I., & Hahn, J. (1986). God and the just world: Causal and coping attributions to God in health situations. *Journal for the Scientific Study of Religion, 25,* 193–207.

Pargament, K. I., Koenig, H. G., & Perez, L. (2000). The many methods of religious coping: Initial development and validation of the RCOPE. *Journal of Clinical Psychology, 56,* 519–543.

Pargament, K. I., Koenig, H. G., Tarakeshwar, N., & Hahn, J. (2001). Religious struggle as a predictor of mortality among medically ill elderly patients: A two-year longitudinal study. *Archives of Internal Medicine, 161,* 1881–1885.

Pargament, K. I., Koenig, H. G., Tarakeshwar, N., & Hahn, J. (2002). *Religious coping methods as predictors of psychological, physical, and spiritual outcomes among medically ill elderly patients: A two-year longitudinal study.* Paper presented at the 110th Annual Convention of the American Psychological Association, Chicago, IL.

Pargament, K. I., Magyar, G. M., & Murray-Swank, N. (in press). The sacred and the search for significance: Religion as a unique process. *Journal of Social Issues.*

Pargament, K. I., Smith, B. W., Koenig, H. G., & Perez, L. (1998). Patterns of positive and negative religious coping with major life stressors. *Journal for the Scientific Study of Religion, 37,* 710–724.

Pargament, K. I., Zinnbauer, B. J., Scott, A. B., Butter, E. M., Zerowin, J., & Stanik, P. (1998). Red flags and religious coping: Identifying some religious warning signs among people in crisis. *Journal of Clinical Psychology, 54,* 77–89.

Park, C. L., & Cohen, L. H. (1993). Religious and nonreligious coping with the death of a friend. *Cognitive Therapy and Research, 17,* 561–577.

Perspectives. (2001, September 17). *Newsweek,* p. 23.

Piaget, J. (1975). *The equilibration of cognitive structures: The central problem of intellectual development.* Chicago: University of Chicago Press.

Propst, L. R. (1988). *Psychotherapy in a religious framework: Spirituality in the emotional healing process.* New York: Human Sciences Press.

Richards, P. S., & Bergin, A. E. (1997). *A spiritual strategy for counseling and psychotherapy.* Washington, DC: American Psychological Association.

Ryan, R. M., Rigby, S., & King, K. (1993). Two types of religious internalization and their relations to religious orientation and mental health. *Journal of Personality and Social Psychology, 65,* 586–596.

Saint John of the Cross. (1990). *The dark night of the soul: A masterpiece in the literature of mysticism by St. John of the Cross* (E. A. Peers, Trans.). New York: Image Books, Doubleday. (Original work published 1584)

Saucer, P. R. (1991). Evangelical renewal therapy: A proposal for integration of religious values into psychotherapy. *Psychological Reports, 69,* 1099–1106.

Shafranske, E. P. (Ed.). (1996a). Religious beliefs, affiliations, and practices of clinical psychologists. In E. P. Shafranske (Ed.), *Religion and the practice of clinical psychology* (pp. 149–164). Washington, DC: American Psychological Association

Shafranske, E. P. (Ed.). (1996b). *Religion and the clinical practice of psychology.* Washington, DC: American Psychological Association.

Smith, H. (1958). *The religions of man.* New York: Harper & Row.

Smith, B. W., Pargament, K. I., Brant, C., & Oliver, J. M. (2000). Noah revisited: Religious coping by church members and the impact of the 1993 Midwest flood. *Journal of Community Psychology, 28,* 169–186.

Snyder, C. R., & Lopez, S. J. (Eds.). (2002). *Handbook of positive psychology.* New York: Oxford University Press.

United States Catholic Conference. (1994). *Catechism of the Catholic Church.* New York: Doubleday.

Worthington, E. L., Kurusu, T. A., McCullough, M. E., & Sandage, S. J. (1996). Empirical research on religion and psychotherapeutic processes and outcomes: A 10-year review and research prospectus. *Psychological Bulletin, 119,* 448–487.

Zornow, G. B. (2001). *Crying out to God: Uncovering prayer in the midst of suffering.* Unpublished manuscript.

V
REFLECTIONS

14

IMPLICATIONS OF JUDEO-CHRISTIAN VIEWS OF HUMAN NATURE, MOTIVATION, AND CHANGE FOR THE SCIENCE AND PRACTICE OF PSYCHOLOGY

CARLO C. DiCLEMENTE AND HAROLD D. DELANEY

Societal and cultural influences have played an important role in the development of psychology as a science and profession. Despite William James's (1890) view that the emerging discipline of psychology should embrace wide-ranging explorations of human phenomena, psychological science grew up during the late 19th and early 20th centuries in the context of a scientific empiricism that was reductionistic and materialistic. Although never embraced by all, many psychological researchers believed in empirical inquiry as the foundation of psychological truths and the cornerstone of a science that could be significantly differentiated from its philosophical roots (Fowler, 1990; Hilgard, 1987). Method often turned into metaphysic (Robinson, 1981), that is, entities or phenomena that could not be observed empirically were presumed to be nonexistent. Although certain leaders in the field championed idiographic and qualitative approaches to understanding human phenomena (Allport, 1950; Rogers, 1961), many in psychological research pledged allegiance to an empiricism that seemed to reduce phenomena to the observable, quantifiable, and measurable. Moreover, the popular, Freudian psychoanalytic approach to viewing and treating psychological problems emphasized universal repressed basic human drives and emotions and various societal and personal mechanisms of defense that made a lasting mark on the profession of clinical psychology (Freedheim, 1992; Wulff, 1996). These influences clearly affected the psychological theories about human nature, motivation, psychopathology, and change that have developed over the past 120 years.

This view of science and restricted scope led psychological theories and research to emphasize observable, clearly defined, and operationalized variables, hypotheses verifiable by scientific empirical method, and problematic or pathological functioning (Fowler, 1990; Kimble, 1989). These elements made an impact on the development of psychology in terms of the content of what has been explored, the methods and measurements used in this exploration, the approaches to intervention and treatment, and the focus of training and practice. It would be misleading, however, to characterize all psychological theories and models as incorporating these narrow perspectives (Bergin, 1980). Moreover, as demonstrated in this volume's historical overview (chap. 2) and in many of the previous chapters, the precursors and roots of modern psychology draw upon insights from religious traditions reaching far back into recorded human history and thought. Nevertheless, empiricism, materialism, reductionism, and a focus on pathology have had a significant influence on how the science of psychology has developed, what it has examined, how it has gone about that exploration, and when and how it has seen fit to create interventions.

This chapter examines in depth the implications that an exploration into the Judaic and Christian perspectives on human nature, motivation, and change offered in this volume could or should have on the discipline of psychology in both its scientific explorations and practice. We highlight conclusions from the previous chapters and discuss what adaptations and accommodations would be needed in psychological inquiry, methodology, therapy, and training to address adequately and substantively the influence, insights, wisdom, and practices of Jewish and Christian traditions. It is an initial assumption of this chapter that psychology would be greatly enriched by taking into account the influence and wisdom of the Judeo-Christian traditions in human history to understand fully human nature, motivation, and change (Jones, 1994; Polkinghorne, 1996; Worthington, 1994). Concepts and traditions regarding religion and spirituality exist in many societies and among significant groups of individuals in those societies and, as such, represent an important aspect of human functioning for these individuals (Bergin, 1980). The focus of this chapter and this volume is limited to the Judaic and Christian traditions, but we believe that a similar exercise could be usefully undertaken for other influential and overarching religious and cultural traditions (Buddhist, Hindu, Muslim, and others).

A host of writers have addressed the interface between science and religion and, more specifically, between psychology and religion (Miller, 1999b; Roberts & Talbot, 1997; Shafranske, 1996). Many schemas have been proposed to describe this interface and to discuss the interactions (Haught, 1995; Russell, Murphy, Meyering, & Arbib, 1999). We use that offered by Ian Barbour (1997, 2000). He describes four potential interactions between science and religion: (a) *conflict*, (b) *independence*, (c) *dialogue*, and (d) *integration*. We discuss each in some detail, paying particular attention to how they are represented in the interaction between psychology and the Judeo-Christian teachings and traditions.

There is evidence of a conflicted relationship between scientific and religious worldviews both in psychology and among Judaic and Christian religious teachings. Psychology has often viewed religion as a repressive mechanism and as part of a societal control mechanism that interferes with personal growth (Kurtz, 1999; Wulff, 1996). Religious experiences have often been viewed as paranormal events that have been subsumed under the rubric of parapsychology or viewed as more pathological events (defense mechanisms or group histrionic events). That religious delusions and fantasies often are incorporated in paranoid and psychotic disorders contributes to the belief among psychologists that religion is related to problematic human development. However, religious leaders have often viewed psychology with suspicion. Pope Leo XIII's encyclical on modernism mentioned clearly the potential destructive effects of psychotherapy and psychological theories of human behavior (Gillespie, 2001). Current commentators have criticized on the one hand the implicit reductionism or deterministic components of scientific psychology and on the other hand the self-aggrandizing aspects of some self psychologies as conflicting with the Christian view of the person (Roberts, 1997; Vitz, 1997b). In the extreme form of this *conflict*, scientific psychology and Judeo-Christian perspectives are at odds and locked in a struggle to capture the minds and hearts of humanity. Both views cannot be right, and there is little room for compromise because the perspectives are viewed as diametrically opposed. The only possibility for rapprochement would be to have a psychology completely subservient to a Judeo-Christian perspective (a Jewish or Christian psychology) or to have a psychology that viewed religion and religious phenomena as aberrations that could be studied scientifically (an agnostic or atheistic psychology of religion). The majority of authors of this volume would reject both of these options.

The *independence* view of the relationship between the science of psychology and the Judeo-Christian perspective argues for a peaceful coexistence between these two superpowers contending that psychology and religion have two different ways of knowing and sources of truth, separate realms of inquiry and influence, and independent realities (Barbour, 2000). From this perspective, psychology and religion do not need each other, and trying to bring them together would pose significant problems for both (Ward, 1995). Although there are some common historical roots, it is clear that psychology and religion have developed very different traditions of scholarship and ways of seeking the truth. Theological exploration and biblical exegesis are not the same as psychological experimentation and evaluation of theories. Arguments from authority and the primacy of biblical truths do appear to be contrary to the skepticism and empiricism that mark psychology's struggle to be free from philosophy and to be identified as a natural science. However, understanding human phenomena may involve many methods of exploration (Koch & Leary, 1985), and spurious dichotomization should be avoided because significant similarities may exist in ways of knowing across the two disciplines (Barbour, 1997; Jones, 1994). Independence could allow for a mutual respect and an agreement to disagree and be different, but it creates parallel tracks of exploration and impedes any cross-fertilization and collaboration that could potentially enhance the science of psychology and the discipline of theology as well as the practice of psychology and religion (Barbour, 2000; Johnson & Jones, 2000).

Dialogue would enable the two separate endeavors of psychology and religion to communicate about findings, issues, problems, and potential solutions. The dialogue perspective often overlaps with the independence perspective in that the two arenas are viewed as separate, independent entities that join together in a dialogue that could be characterized anywhere from strained to polite to intimate. Dialogue encourages exploration of the Judeo-Christian perspective and the psychological theories about the person, motivation, and change so that there is a clear understanding of each other's views (Shafranske & Maloney, 1996). Such a dialogue would require some suspension of judgment until there was a clear understanding of the theories, views, and positions of each side of the dialogue. As in any dialogue, the problems that could occur include lack of a common language, emotional commitments, and strongly held positions that make listening problematic and promote debate rather than discussion (G. R. Collins, 2000; Myers, 2000). Dialogue can promote a deeper understanding of similarities and differences among perspectives, offer possibilities for collaboration, and promote a communion between the perspectives that enriches both. However, dialogue does not necessarily produce détente, should not eradicate real differences, and may lead to contention and possible irreconcilable differences (Johnson & Jones, 2000). Clearly it has been the aim of this volume to produce at minimum a dialogue that could enrich psychology's view of human nature, motivation, and change by exploring the Judaic and Christian perspectives. All of the chapters promote a dialogue that could enrich both psychology and religion.

Integration is Barbour's (1997, 2000) last perspective to describe the relationship between science and religion. It would probably result from collaboration between psychologists and religious professionals and from dialogue that discovered significant communalities and agreements. Integration assumes a compatibility of perspectives or common goals that provide the underpinnings for close collaboration and a "more systematic and extensive kind of partnership between science and religion" (p. 3). Theology and psychology, religious practice and psychotherapy would be integrated in a manner that would preserve the unique contributions of each perspective and yet be combined to create a psychospiritual perspective that could be used to examine both psychological assumptions and science as well as religious beliefs and practices. Although this appears to be a noble goal, it is not at all clear that it is feasible in reality (G. R. Collins, 2000). Many attempts at integration make one or the other of the perspectives predominant and the remaining one a handmaid (Johnson & Jones, 2000; Roberts, 2000; Talbot, 1997). Several studies of religious phenomena illustrate this sort of conceptual and methodological flaw (Slater, Hall, & Edwards, 2001; Sloan & Bagiella, 2002; Smith, 2001). If, however, there is a conviction that the reality of the nature of the human person and of motivation and change represents objective truth that can be uncovered both by the science of psychology and by the revelation of scripture, integration appears a more attainable goal (Jones, 1994; Worthington, 1994). Attempts to include a spiritual dimension in psychological models of human nature as well as attempts to integrate research on shame and guilt into religious perspectives represent efforts to integrate the two perspectives in a more substantive manner (Jones, 1997; Jung, 1933; Pargament, 1997). An overarching perspective that would be integrative and substantive remains elusive (chap. 2). Nevertheless, in several chapters in this volume, the authors have attempted to promote or create an integrated perspective incorporating Judeo-Christian presuppositions and values into analyses of phenomena of interest to psychology.

Notable examples include Baumeister's analysis (chap. 3) illustrating how the Judeo-Christian view of human nature that entails responsibility as moral agents could help promote socially responsible virtuous action and how psychological research on methods for training the moral muscle could help parents and religious groups promote resistance to temptation. Similarly, Evans (chap. 4) examines the self, arguing that viewing humans as creatures designed to be in relation to God helps us to understand important social dimensions of selfhood. In chapter 5, Bien illustrates how the great themes of biblical narratives can be useful in clinical work, especially in dealing with issues of meaning and purpose in life. In chapter 6, Jones and Hostler argue that viewing humans as embodied persons whose physicality is good is the natural result of Christian doctrines of creation and incarnation. Although this view leads to important differences with how some mainstream psychological theories view sexuality, it is consistent, for example, with data on predictors of satisfying sexual relationships. Worthington and Berry (chap.

8) argue that using religious perspectives in contrast to secular ones encourages psychology to regard virtues as more interdependent and to value "yieldedness" rather than self-control as a master virtue. Thoresen and colleagues (chap. 11) highlight the salutary effects on health documented in research that takes seriously the effects of practices such as prayer and forgiveness. Finally, Pargament and colleagues (chap. 13) explore the consequences of spiritual struggles, an important phenomenon in Judeo-Christian traditions that would likely be ignored by secular psychology without the leavening dialogue for which we are arguing. Each of the chapters in this volume highlights phenomena that could be understood and examined more fruitfully with greater dialogue and a better integration of psychological inquiry and the perspectives of the Judeo-Christian traditions.

PSYCHOLOGICAL SCIENCE AND RESEARCH

Much of the conflict and most of the barriers to both dialogue and integration lie in the arena of the scientific skepticism, assumptions, and the research methods used by psychology to establish truths. Criticisms by those representing Judaic and Christian perspectives emphasize that the assumptions of materialism, reductionism, and radical empiricism prevent psychology from appreciating and adequately addressing the spiritual aspects of human nature (Bergin, 1980; G. R. Collins, 2000; Roberts, 2000; Roberts & Talbot, 1997; see also chaps. 1, 2, and 8, this volume). On the opposite side the staunch defenders of empiricism and psychological science have argued that an antiscientific view underlies the religious perspective and hence it constitutes a threat to scientific psychology (Kimble, 1989; Myers, 2000; Ward, 1995). It is clear that if psychological science is equated with a reductionistic materialism that refuses to acknowledge any reality that could be called spiritual or entity that could be labeled soul, there is little room for discussion, let alone dialogue. Moreover, if scientific research in human nature reduces all phenomena to the least common denominator, there appears to be little room for uniqueness, choices, responsibility, and individual motivation (Bergin 1980; Evans, 1996; see chaps. 3 and 7, this volume).

For some chance at dialogue and even minimal integration to exist, the science of psychology needs to reassess its foundational assumptions and scientific methods. Early 20th-century conceptualizations of science and scientific method were the foundation of psychological science (Hilgard, 1987). The resolution of the conflict between James's broad view of psychology and the more narrow view of the early 20th-century behaviorists focused rather exclusively on the tangible, measurable, and manageable. Are these assumptions and perspectives current? Often physics, astronomy, biology, and chemistry are more open to theorizing about unseen phenomena than is psychology (Barbour, 2000; Russell et al., 1999). These disciplines entertain theoretical models (e.g., String Theory) of unseen dimensions, value conceptual explorations, and seem to avoid methodological dogmatism. Issues like the origin of the universe and creation appear to be less problematic arenas for a dialogue between science and religion than the nature of the human person (Russell et al., 1999). To facilitate dialogue, psychologists need to make some adjustments to their view of psychological science. There seem to be three major areas in which the science of psychology could profitably expand its vision and practice in order to be able to address Judaic and Christian views of the nature of the human person, motivation, and change.

1. The first area of discussion should be the epistemology of our science and scientific inquiry. What is the evidence that can be accepted to support the existence of a phenomenon? Does empirical validation have to include data-analytic techniques that always result in p values? How can we study second- or third-order constructs that may account for multiple first-order phenomena but be less directly observable? Should not our scientific skepticism include a thorough exploration of any value-laden assumptions that may hinder our exploration of phenomena of human nature that could be called spiritual? It is a hopeful sign that many of these questions and issues are currently being debated in the psychological literature (Gergen, 2001; Hunter, 1997; Sampson, 2000; Wilkinson & the Task Force on Statistical Inference, 1999).

Scientific inquiry needs theoretical perspectives that offer some models for understanding the phenomena of interest; an ability to observe and operationalize how the assumed mechanisms function; and an evaluation of the assumed theoretical view that can be replicated. In their arguments, many of the chapter authors in this volume seem to ask for a broadening of our epistemology (see especially chap. 6) in order to be able to better understand human nature, human interactions, spiritual dimensions of the human experience, and motivation and change. The psychological aspects of human nature are far more complex than even the most complicated biological mechanism or genetic structure precisely because of the interactions of biological, psychological, and social dimensions. The same is true of spiritual and religious aspects of human nature. Simplicity in the face of this complexity is not virtuous and can be misleading. The evidence base of psychology must expand to include less observable phenomena that nevertheless can be evaluated scientifically in some operational fashion. Data from the human experience over time should be incorporated into our models or should, at least, be examined and explained in our models of human nature (James, 1902/1985). Arguments and views about the human reality from scriptural sources should be evaluated and not simply dismissed (Jones, 1994; Miller, 1999b; Shafranske, 1996). The broad scope of the investigation of human nature found in many of the early psychologists should be recaptured to reverse the trend of an increasing narrowing of focus of scientific psychology.

2. Research design and analyses that are capable of capturing complex, interactive phenomena must be developed and used in psychological inquiry. Just because a concept is more elusive is no reason to abandon its scientific pursuit. We have always been impressed with the courage and ingenuity of Carl Rogers. He proposed a reduction in discrepancy between real and ideal self as a marker of successful psychotherapy (Rogers, 1954). Despite the difficulties, he created a way to operationalize this discrepancy using a card sort and measured it in a longitudinal, controlled trial that demonstrated effects. He was also the first behavioral scientist to develop, apply, and publish data using the method of recording interviews and rating the verbal interaction to assess elusive concepts such as warmth, congruence, and empathic understanding. Many of the constructs identified in the preceding chapters are complex and not easily measured (e.g., having a sense of calling from God [chap. 4], transformational change [chap. 9], or immersion in the apprehension of God's presence [chap. 10]). We need the best and brightest of our professions to define clearly what is the phenomenon and then to find creative and unique ways to measure the characteristic, event, or sequelae at the heart of the phenomenon (Hogan & Nicholson, 1988; Pargament, 1997). At the same time, we need to continue to develop analytic techniques that can address multiple influences, interactions, reciprocity in causality, shifting effects over time, micro- and macroprocessing of information, and sophisticated mediator and moderator analyses (MacCallum & Austin, 2000). There have been great strides in the area of data analysis that should provide researchers and scholars with new tools with which to address the complex questions raised in this volume (L. M. Collins & Sayer, 2001; Raudenbush, 2001). Latent variable analysis, multidimensional linear types of analytic techniques, and interactive and relational designs should enhance our ability to address some of these questions. A recent rebirth of qualitative techniques that avoid the criticisms of the early attempts of Titchener and colleagues to evaluate human experience from inside out (Hilgard, 1987) also can enhance our ability to create some common ground between the Judeo-Christian traditions and the science of psychology (Denzin & Lincoln, 1994).

3. Finally, there is the reality that psychology as science and profession and psychologists as scientists and professionals are culturally grounded in their own metaphysical, historical, and philosophical roots. The question is not whether we have limitations in these areas in terms of our theoretical assumptions and our approaches to personality, pathology, and therapy but what they are and how they affect our work. The challenge is to evaluate the impact of these limitations on our theorizing, conceptualization, observation, operationalizing, and measurement of phenomena and how they affect the development and implementation of our interventions. Human development, personality, health, and pathology are necessarily value-laden areas of research and intervention. To be able to create a dialogue and the potential for integration, psychologists—those who participate in the Judaic and

Christian traditions as well as those who do not—could fruitfully examine how their basic views of human nature and functioning affect their thinking and their behavior. At a more personal level, the minimal challenge for all psychologists is to delineate how they will manage their own personal views of religion in their science and practice and whether it will reflect a conflict, independence, dialogue, or integration perspective.

ASSESSMENT AND MEASUREMENT

In the arena of human personality, there have been many attempts to evaluate the various key characteristics that make us human. The history of personality theory research is replete with alternative ways of conceptualizing these characteristics. The widely varying methods used to evaluate them include, to cite just a few, the biographical analysis used by Allport, the Role Repertory measure of cognitive constructs developed by Kelly, the Rod and Frame tests of Witkin, and the experimental approaches to identify temperament-based dimensions of personality by Costa and McCrae (Pervin, 1990). The dimensions of human nature are many, subtle, and intricately intertwined. To evaluate the importance of many of the dimensions identified in previous chapters, researchers need to create measures that adequately assess the constructs of interest (Bergin, 1980; Gorsuch, 1984).

A well-established truism in psychological research is that what is found is completely dependent on what is assessed and how this is done. Shame or spirituality exists in psychological research precisely in the manner that each of these constructs is measured and evaluated. A single item or a complex statement could yield a very different view of the construct when compared with an observation, a series of observations, a complex set of questions, or a peer evaluation (Hogan & Nicholson, 1988). What we evaluate in our research is limited by our methods and measures. Although this truth seems self-evident in psychological research, the reality is that a review of the literature often reveals arguments and issues that seem to ignore this reality particularly when dealing with concepts or words that have common currency (Gorsuch, 1984; Jones, 1997; Pargament, 1997). Conflicts exist even in research in the arena of religious concepts (Slater et al., 2001). Clarification of what is meant and what is measured is most critical when dealing with concepts that are part of the perspective and teachings of the Judeo-Christian tradition because terms related to these concepts have multiple meanings and many connotations. There is an entire field of biblical exegesis that is dedicated to establishing the meaning of some of these concepts. Psychologists must be particularly careful and precise as they attempt to study and evaluate these concepts. Discussions of volition (chap. 3), virtues and vices (chap. 8), and spiritual struggle (chap. 13) illustrate some of the challenges involved.

There is also a question of how to incorporate concepts and insights from the Judeo-Christian tradition into the science and practice of psychology. Should we isolate some ideas and study them independently, or should we attempt to evaluate a larger, more comprehensive picture? As Thoresen et al. (chap. 11) make clear, the different dimensions of religious practice and experience are likely reciprocally determined by each other, for example, prayer may be modeled and encouraged by religious attendance, which may also result in more social support, which may encourage more attendance. Thus, separating direct and indirect effects of any one religious practice and appreciating the extent to which religious practices are informed by the larger belief system of individuals represent major challenges to researchers. To advance the dialogue and the potential for integration, one needs at minimum a sufficient explanation and exploration of the larger context of single traits, experiences, and emotions to be able to decide on the proper breadth or to discuss important limitations of any attempt to measure and evaluate these complex concepts and constructs independently of a larger context. The basic question is how to treat religion, spirituality, and spiritual experience in psychological science. Should these phenomena be treated as individual differences that can be assessed, along with a number of other traits and experiences, in an effort to evaluate unique contributions? Or should they be treated as a larger cultural phenomenon that would require a broader understanding and view of religion and spirituality? Maybe the answer is the prototypic one: It depends on the nature of the question and the objective of the research. Nevertheless, the larger picture and the cultural context appear to be critical for understanding the more isolated traits, states, and experiences (Hartup & Lieshout, 1995). There is a need to develop methods and measures that validly and reliably assess contexts and situations. The experience of spirituality, transformation, and virtue is contextual as well as personal. Terms such as *Christian* and *Jewish* do not represent a homogeneous experience or context. Surveys and measures that do not account for contextual and subgroup differences are unlikely to produce sound science or a sophisticated understanding of the role of religion and spirituality in the lives of individuals and groups.

The issue of what is the *proper perspective* for dialogue and possible integration raises more questions of how to incorporate religion and spirituality into psychology science and practice. Increasing dialogue and attempts at integration are needed. Yet the appropriate model or models for this dialogue and integration is an area of contention and disagreement (G. R. Collins, 2000; Myers, 2000; Powlison, 2000; Roberts, 2000). Some support the creation of a Judaic or Christian psychology that would give priority to being faithful to biblical revelation and at the same time "read it for what we and our contemporaries can recognize as *psychology*" (Roberts, 2000, p. 155). There is a tendency in the field to create separate psychologies for various types of problems or issues (feminist psychology, Black psychology, sports psychology, health psychology) or to identify psychological theories as separate psychologies (Freudian psychology, humanistic psychology, existential psychology; Freedheim, 1992). Creating a Judaic or Christian psychology could offer a way to create a psychological perspective that respects and protects the teachings and insights of the Judeo-Christian traditions from the detrimental assumptions of the mainstream psychological science and practice (Beck, 1999; Talbot, 1997; Vitz, 1997a). Most of the contributors to this volume agree with Myers (2000), however, in thinking that creating a separate Jewish or Christian psychology is not a particularly helpful or appropriate way to integrate Judeo-Christian perspectives into psychology. Using a label like Christian psychology would appear to equate the Christian perspective with a personality theory or a special-interest issue. It would also suggest a need for a Jewish psychology, a Muslim psychology, a Buddhist psychology, an atheistic psychology, and so forth. This can be demeaning to the value of the universal insights and cultural influence that are represented by the Jewish, Christian, and other religious perspectives. Regardless of the model for dialogue and integration chosen, fragmentation and piecemeal exploration of the insights and experiences derived from the Judaic and Christian perspectives also would not do them justice. There needs to be a balance between creating a separatist psychology and developing a psychology that can respect, understand, and possibly incorporate these religious experiences and traditions.

Another issue in the arena of measurement focuses on the source of the data. Much of the research that attempts to evaluate the experience of the individual relics on self-reports, which have been viewed as both a curse and a blessing in the history of psychology. Social psychological research has demonstrated how personal self-report and cognitive processing can be distorted (Gilbert, Fiske, & Lindzey, 1998). We have terms such as social desirability, observer bias, and so on that have consistently been used to undermine individuals' self-reports. There is, however, another perspective. With internal self-evaluations and reports of unverifiable events, there are few other sources of data than the report of the individual (Ajzen, 2001; Bandura, 2001). In this area, psychological science needs to evaluate how to get the most accurate or representative self-reports rather than call for an elimination of this data source. Additional sources of data, multiple points of assessment, better conceptualization, and evaluation of related factors could strengthen our evaluations of spiritual experiences (Hill & Pargament, 2003). Self-evaluations and self-reports are critical in the assessment of the phenomena of interest to the authors in this volume in order to create a dialogue or integration of scientific psychology and the Judeo-Christian perspective (Gorsuch, 1984). The constructs discussed in almost all the chapters in this volume cannot be studied without the careful and critical use of self-report.

PSYCHOTHERAPY AND PSYCHOPATHOLOGY

Probably one of the most difficult areas for dialogue and integration relates to how problems or pathology are defined and what constitutes proper remediation of serious psychopathology and the problems of normal life (Miller, 1999a; Shafranske, 1996). What is defined as abnormal, how religious themes are handled in defining delusional and psychotic symptoms, and how spirituality is viewed in defining positive mental and psychological health are arenas that can create conflict and controversy (Kurtz, 1999; Oman, 2002; Miller & Thoresen, 1999). Psychology and moral theology can disagree on a variety of issues, from gender roles and identity to guilt, forgiveness, responsibility, and choice (Gillespie, 2001). The dilemma of psychotherapy and spirituality is no less complicated. Kurtz (1999) outlined several critical differences in approaches taken to spirituality and some forms of psychotherapy revolving around self-sacrifice versus self-centeredness, empowerment versus powerlessness, self-help versus acceptance. There is evidence for both helpful and potentially problematic interactions between religion and health (Exline, Yali, & Sanderson, 2000; chap. 11).

Although the potential for differences and division is clear between psychology and religion, there already exist many ways that human behavior can be viewed within psychology, as demonstrated by the multiple theories of personality that have been proposed in the history of psychology (Hilgard, 1987). Differences turn into divisions when there exists a lack of mutual respect and an absence of dialogue. This turning of differences into divisions has happened as often within psychology and within religions as between the two. If psychology takes seriously the teachings offered in the biblical tradition, including the notion of spirituality and the strengths of the Judaic and Christian practices, then it can be open to examining the role of prayer, asceticism, faith, and spiritual practices on human development, growth, and pathology (Allport, 1950; Bergin, 1980; Jones, 1994; Jung, 1933). If religion takes psychology seriously, it can be open to reexamining some of its views of human nature and human functioning in light of psychological research and practice (Griffiths, 1997; Myers, 2000) and to exploring the beneficial as well as potentially detrimental effects of some aspects of religious experience and practice (Exline et al., 2000; Oman, 2002; Smith, 2001).

Early fears that psychology and psychotherapy would overwhelm religion and make religious beliefs and practices useless have not become reality (Gillespie, 2001). In fact, most measures of religion and spirituality such as religious attendance have remained steady over the past several decades and some, such as interest in growing spiritually, have risen dramatically (Gallup, 2002; Gallup & Jones, 2000). Likewise, many current perspectives within psychology on personality and social context address the issue of spirituality and religious beliefs (Miller, 1999b). Understanding religious beliefs and practices have become part of cultural diversity and competence. A number of the chapters in this volume attempt to provide a basis for dialogue in the areas of identity, volition, gender and sexuality, change, and motivation, as well as spiritual development, transformational learning, and the psychological effects of religious practices. The differences and disagreements in the areas of psychotherapy and psychopathology are real, and treading the boundary between psychology and the Judaic and Christian traditions in this arena is tricky. Conflict between moral and psychological perspectives is not a necessary conclusion, however, and mutual respect for differences can enrich both psychological science and religious views (Pargament, 1997).

EDUCATION, TRAINING, AND PRACTICE

Although there are some notable exceptions among training programs, the incorporation of the views and arguments made in this volume into the academic education and clinical training of psychologists is in its infancy (Miller, 1999b). In many academic programs discussion of religion and religious beliefs occurs most frequently in courses on professional ethics. In the ethical standards of psychologists, there is a clear message that scientists and practitioners must respect the ethnic, cultural, and religious beliefs and practices of research participants and psychotherapy clients (American Psychological Association, 2002; see also http://www.apa.org/ethics/code2002.html). In a related codicil, psychologists are admonished to be aware of their own beliefs and prejudices and not to allow them to be substituted for scientific and validated approaches (Koocher & Keith-Speigel, 1998). It is clear that we expect psychologists to be sophisticated in their understanding of religious and cultural aspects of human development and functioning (Bergin, 1980; Jones, 1994, O'Donohoe, 1989). The knowledge, understanding, and critical thinking that would make for this sophistication are not always present in the preparation of these psychologists, however. Personality theories are taught without acknowledging the issues related to spirituality and development of religious beliefs. Child development courses often fail to explore the impact of family religious practices and upbringing and the multigenerational nature of such influences. Clinical training is given with little regard to the questions of religious beliefs and how they would affect diagnosis and treatment plans. Discerning when and how to refer to spiritual counseling rather than psychotherapy is a skill that is often underdeveloped in clinical settings. In the training of young professionals, there is also a need for discussions of personal beliefs and how they could influence the individual's approach to psychopathology and treatment in terms of underestimating or overestimating certain aspects of religious beliefs or practices (Bergin, 1980, 1991). Religious and spiritual issues deserve as much or more concern as language, ethnicity, customs, and culture. Both in the academic preparations of clinical psychologists as well as other applied psychologists and in the practicum and internship experiences of these students, the reality and importance of the religious and spiritual schemas of the client and the therapist should receive much more attention.

SPECIFIC RECOMMENDATIONS

On the basis of the chapters in this volume, the following are specific recommendations that result from the reflections and discussions of the participants in this interesting and informative exercise. Although the recommendations are based on the work of the entire group, the authors of this chapter are responsible for the specific wording and content of the recommendations and not all participants may agree with all that follows.

1. Religion, spirituality, and other concepts from the Judaic and Christian traditions can best be understood in a multidimensional context as personal, cultural, and community dimensions that should be considered in our psychological theories of human development, human agency, psychological stress and coping, human motivation and change, physical and mental health, resiliency and well-being, human relationships and sexuality, virtues and vices, self-regulation, and social functioning.

2. Method and measures are critical to science. Advances in methods have often precipitated great leaps in scientific knowledge. If psychology is to explore the vast space of spirituality and religion, our approach to science must be open to a broad range of measures and methodologies, innovation in analytic techniques, and broader conceptual frames to guide our explorations.

3. Polarization and dichotomies interfere with dialogue and integration. Although extreme positions and describing polar opposites in exaggerated fashion often aid in clarifying positions and breaking new ground, it is the mark of more mature science to search for communalities, understand interactions, and bring into the mix the complexities of context. Psychological science with its current emphasis on integrating the biological, psychological, and social dimensions, its considerations of positive psychology, resilience, culture and context, and its growing sophistication in examining and understanding human agency and complex interactive causality seems better prepared to examine and understand Judaic and Christian traditions and practices.

4. Diversity, cultural awareness and competence, and individual and group differences are central to our psychological understanding of development, health, pathology, and treatment. Theories, treatments, and research and training of psychologists could profit greatly from an increased emphasis on religion and spirituality as an integral part of culture and community. It is only by attempting to understand the individual in a group or community and how the community influences personal virtues and values, cogni-

tion, motivation, and change that psychology will be able to address many of the experiences of religion and spirituality in the lives of individuals and communities.

5. There appears to be much room for collaboration and connection between the science and practice of psychology and the Judaic and Christian traditions. We must also add a note of caution: Belief and science are not the same. From the time of Galileo and before, there has been tension and often open conflict between religion and belief systems and scientific discovery. There are boundaries that must be respected and experiences that may never be understood completely.

6. It is hoped that this volume will move psychologists and religious professionals to greater mutual respect, greater realization of personal and perspective limitations, greater tolerance for the ambiguity that dialogue entails, and an increased appreciation for what we do not know as well as what we believe we do know. Humility is part of scientific skepticism. Truth is a common bond and goal.

REFERENCES

Ajzen, I. (2001). Nature and operation of attitudes. *Annual Review of Psychology, 52,* 27–58.

Allport, G. W. (1950). *The individual and his religion.* New York: Macmillan.

American Psychological Association. (2002). Ethical principles of psychologists and code of conduct. *American Psychologist, 57,* 1060–1073.

Bandura, A. (2001). Social cognitive theory: An agentic perspective. *Annual Review of Psychology, 52,* 1–26.

Barbour, I. G. (1997). *Religion and science: Historical and contemporary issues.* New York: HarperCollins.

Barbour, I. G. (2000). *When science meets religion.* New York: HarperCollins.

Beck, J. R. (1999). *Jesus and personality theory.* Downers Grove, IL: InterVarsity Press.

Bergin, A. E. (1980). Psychotherapy and religious values. *Journal of Consulting and Clinical Psychology, 48,* 95–105.

Bergin, A. E. (1991). Values and religious issues in psychotherapy and mental health. *American Psychologist, 46,* 394–403.

Collins, G. R. (2000). An integration view. In E. L. Johnson & S. L. Jones (Eds.), *Psychology and Christianity: Four views* (pp. 102–195). Downers Grove, IL: InterVarsity Press.

Collins, L. M., & Sayer, A. G. (Eds.). (2001). *New methods for the analysis of change.* Washington, DC: American Psychological Association.

Cronbach, L. J. (1975). Beyond the two disciplines of scientific psychology. *American Psychologist, 30,* 116–127.

Denzin, N. K., & Lincoln, Y. S. (Eds.). (1994). *Handbook of qualitative research.* Thousand Oaks, CA: Sage.

Evans, C. S. (1996). *Wisdom and humanness in psychology: Prospects for a Christian approach*. Vancouver, Canada: Regent College.

Exline, J. J., Yali, A. M., & Sanderson, W. C. (2000). Guilt, discord, and alienation: The role of religious strain in depression and spirituality. *Journal of Clinical Psychology, 56*, 1481–1496.

Fowler, R. D. (1990). Psychology: The core discipline. *American Psychologist, 45*, 1–6.

Freedheim, D. K. (Ed.). (1992). *History of psychotherapy: A century of change*. Washington, DC: American Psychological Association.

Gallup, G., Jr. (2002). *The Gallup Poll: Public opinion 2001*. Wilmington, DE: Scholarly Resources.

Gallup, G., Jr., & Jones, T. (2000). *The next American spirituality: Finding God in the twenty-first century*. Colorado Springs, CO: Victor.

Gergen, K. J. (2001). Psychological science in a postmodern context. *American Psychologist, 56*, 803–813.

Gilbert, D. T., Fiske, S. T., & Lindzey, G. (1998). *The handbook of social psychology* (4th ed.). New York: McGraw-Hill.

Gillespie, C. K. (2001). *Psychology and American Catholicism: From confession to therapy?* New York: Crossroads.

Gorsuch, R. L. (1984). Measurement: The boon and bane of investigating religion. *American Psychologist, 39*, 228–236.

Griffiths, P. J. (1997). Metaphysics and personality theory. In R. C. Roberts & M. R. Talbot (Eds.), *Limning the psyche: Explorations in Christian psychology* (pp. 41–57). Grand Rapids, MI: Eerdmans.

Hartup, W. W., & Lieshout, C. F. M. (1995). Personality development in social context. *Annual Review of Psychology, 46*, 655–687.

Haught, J. F. (1995). *Science and religion: From conflict to conversation*. Mahwah, NJ: Paulist Press.

Hilgard, E. R. (1987). *Psychology in America: A historical survey*. New York: Harcourt Brace Jovanovich.

Hill, P. C., & Pargament, K. I. (2003). Advances in the conceptualization and measurement of religion and spirituality. *American Psychologist, 58*, 64–74.

Hogan, R., & Nicholson, R. A. (1988). The meaning of personality test scores. *American Psychologist, 43*, 621–626.

Hunter, J. E. (1997). Needed: A ban on the significance test. *Psychological Science, 8*, 3–7.

James, W. (1890). *The principles of psychology*. New York: Holt.

James, W. (1985). *Varieties of religious experience*. Cambridge, MA: Harvard University Press. (Original work published 1902)

Johnson, E. L., & Jones, S. L. (2000). A history of Christians in psychology. In E. L. Johnson & S. L. Jones (Eds.), *Psychology and Christianity: Four views* (pp. 11–53). Downers Grove, IL: InterVarsity Press.

Jones, S. L. (1994). A constructive relationship for religion with the science and profession of psychology: Perhaps the boldest model yet. *American Psychologist, 49*, 184–199.

Jones, S. L. (1997). The meaning of agency and responsibility in light of social science research. In R. C. Roberts & M. R. Talbot (Eds.), *Limning the psyche: Explorations in Christian psychology* (pp. 186–205). Grand Rapids, MI: Eerdmans.

Jung, C. G. (1933). *Modern man in search of a soul* (W. S. Dell & C. F. Baynes, Trans.). New York: Harvest Books.

Kimble, G. A. (1989). Psychology from the standpoint of a generalist. *American Psychologist, 44*, 491–499.

Koch, S., & Leary, D. E. (1985). *A century of psychology as science*. New York: McGraw-Hill.

Koocher, G. P., & Keith-Spiegel, P. (1998). *Ethics in psychology: Professional standards and cases* (2nd ed.). New York: Oxford University Press.

Kurtz, E. (1999). Spirituality and treatment: The historical context. In W. R. Miller (Ed.), *Integrating spirituality into treatment: Resources for practitioners* (pp. 19–46). Washington, DC: American Psychological Association.

MacCallum, R. C., & Austin, J. A. (2000). Application of structural equation modeling in psychological research. *Annual Review of Psychology, 51*, 201–226.

Miller, W. R. (1999a). Diversity training in spiritual and religious issues. In W. R. Miller (Ed.), *Integrating spirituality into treatment: Resources for practitioners* (pp. 253–264). Washington, DC: American Psychological Association.

Miller, W. R. (Ed.). (1999b). *Integrating spirituality into treatment: Resources for practitioners*. Washington, DC: American Psychological Association.

Miller, W. R., & Thoresen, C. E. (1999). Spirituality and health. In W. R. Miller (Ed.), *Integrating spirituality into treatment: Resources for practitioners* (pp. 3–18). Washington, DC: American Psychological Association.

Myers, D. G. (2000). A levels of explanation view. In E. L. Johnson & S. L. Jones (Eds.), *Psychology and Christianity: Four views* (pp. 54–101). Downers Grove, IL: InterVarsity Press.

O'Donohue, W. (1989). The (even) bolder model: The clinical psychologist as metaphysician–scientist–practitioner. *American Psychologist, 44*, 1460–1468.

Oman, D. (2002). 'Does religion cause health?': Differing interpretations and diverse meanings. *Journal of Health Psychology, 7*, 365–380.

Pargament, K. I. (1997). *The psychology of religion and coping: Theory, research and practice*. New York: Guilford Press.

Pervin, L. A. (Ed.). (1990). *Handbook of personality theory and research*. New York: Guilford Press.

Polkinghorne, J. (1996). *Scientists as theologians*. London: SPCK.

Powlison, D. (2000). A biblical counseling view. In E. L. Johnson & S. L. Jones (Eds.), *Psychology and Christianity: Four views* (pp. 196–242). Downers Grove, IL: InterVarsity Press.

Raudenbush, S. W. (2001). Comparing personal trajectories and drawing causal inferences from longitudinal data. *Annual Review of Psychology, 51,* 501–526.

Roberts, R. C. (1997). Parameters of a Christian psychology. In R. C. Roberts & M. R. Talbot (Eds.), *Limning the psyche: Explorations in Christian psychology* (pp. 74–101). Grand Rapids, MI: Eerdmans.

Roberts, R. C. (2000). A Christian psychology view. In E. L. Johnson & S. L. Jones (Eds.), *Psychology and Christianity: Four views* (pp. 148–195). Downers Grove, IL: InterVarsity Press.

Roberts, R. C., & Talbot, M. R. (Eds.). (1997). *Limning the psyche: Explorations in Christian psychology.* Grand Rapids, MI: Eerdmans

Robinson, D. N. (1981). *An intellectual history of psychology.* New York: Macmillan.

Rogers, C. R. (1954). *Psychotherapy and personality change.* Chicago: University of Chicago Press.

Rogers, C. R. (1961). *On becoming a person.* Boston: Houghton Mifflin

Russell, R. J., Murphy, N., Meyering, T. C., & Arbib, M. A. (Eds.). (1999). *Neuroscience and the person: Scientific perspectives on divine action.* Vatican City State: Vatican Observatory Publications; and Berkeley, CA: Center for Theology and the Natural Sciences.

Sampson, E. E. (2000). Reinterpreting individualism and collectivism: Their religious roots and monologic versus dialogic person–other relationships. *American Psychologist, 55,* 1425–1432.

Shafranske, E. P. (Ed.). (1996). *Religion and the clinical practice of psychology.* Washington, DC: American Psychological Association.

Shafranske, E. P., & Maloney, H. N. (1996). Religion and the clinical practice of psychology: A case for inclusion. In E. P. Shafranske (Ed.), *Religion and the clinical practice of psychology* (pp. 561–586). Washington, DC: American Psychological Association.

Slater, W., Hall, T. W., & Edwards, K. J. (2001). Measuring religion and spirituality: Where are we and where are we going? *Journal of Psychology and Theology, 29,* 4–21.

Sloan, R. P., & Bagiella, E. (2002). Claims about religious involvement and health outcomes. *Annals of Behavioral Medicine, 24,* 14–21.

Smith, T. W. (2001). Religion and spirituality in the science and practice of health psychology: Openness, skepticism, and the agnosticism of methodology. In T. G. Plante & A. C. Sherman (Eds.), *Faith and health: Psychological perspectives* (pp. 355–380). New York: Guilford Press.

Talbot, M. R. (1997). Starting from Scripture. In R. C. Roberts & M. R. Talbot (Eds.), *Limning the psyche: Explorations in Christian psychology* (pp. 102–122). Grand Rapids, MI: Eerdmans.

Vitz, P. C. (1997). A Christian theory of personality. In R. C. Roberts & M. R. Talbot (Eds.), *Limning the psyche: Explorations in Christian psychology* (pp. 20–40). Grand Rapids, MI: Eerdmans.

Vitz, P. C. (1977). *Psychology as religion: The cult of self-worship.* Grand Rapids, MI: Eerdmans.

Ward, L. C. (1995). Religion and science are mutually exclusive. *American Psychologist, 50,* 542–543.

Wilkinson, L., & the Task Force on Statistical Inference. (1999). Statistical methods in psychological journals. *American Psychologist, 54,* 594–604.

Worthington, E. L., Jr. (1994). A blueprint for interdisciplinary integration. *Journal of Psychology and Theology, 22,* 79–86.

Wulff, D. M. (1996). The psychology of religion. In E. P. Shafranske (Ed.), *Religion and the clinical practice of psychology* (pp. 43–70). Washington, DC: American Psychological Association.

15

PSYCHOLOGY AS THE SCIENCE OF HUMAN NATURE: REFLECTIONS AND RESEARCH DIRECTIONS

WILLIAM R. MILLER AND HAROLD D. DELANEY

There was a time when psychological phenomena were seen only in spiritual terms. Then we went through a period in which spirituality was often seen in psychological terms. Now what?
—Gerald May (1992, p. 5)

TOWARD A SCIENCE OF HUMAN NATURE

The roots of psychology as a profession and as a discipline lie deep in spiritual soil. The etymological root *psyche* is the classic Greek concept of soul. Psychology is literally the study of the soul, the very essence of what it is to be human. Long before there were psychologists, people brought their psychic troubles to their spiritual leaders. Many still do.

It is ironic, then, that no aspect of humanity has been more neglected in psychology than the *psyche*. Psychologists study the development and influence of biological, hereditary, evolutionary, cognitive, affective, social, and behavioral aspects of human nature. A comprehensive psychological evaluation encompasses mental, emotional, sexual, interpersonal, vocational, motivational, perceptual, and social functioning, but rarely the health and welfare of the human spirit.

Yet perhaps psychology, as a profession and discipline, has not really strayed all that far from its Judeo-Christian roots. In Jewish thought, the soul is not a separable component, like a detachable sticker placed temporarily on

291

a material body. Such dualism is foreign to historic Judaism. Neither is dualism inherent in Christianity. The ancient Apostles' Creed affirms the resurrection of the body in a new form, not the extrication of an eternal black box within it. The Hebrew *ruach* and the Greek *pneuma*—both often translated as *spirit*—refer to the breath, the life force, the essence of the whole person. A Judeo-Christian understanding of human nature is fundamentally holistic, a unity of body, mind, and spirit.

In this regard, Thomas Merton (1960) described spiritual direction as concerned with the entire person, not some isolated part:

> There is a temptation to think that spiritual direction is the guidance of one's spiritual activities, considered as a small part or department of one's life. You go to a spiritual director to . . . take care of your spirit, the way you go to a dentist to . . . take care of your teeth, or to a barber to get a haircut. This is completely false. The spiritual director is concerned with the *whole* person, for the spiritual life is not just the life of the mind, or of the affections, or of the "summit of the soul"—it is the life of the whole person. (p. 14)

When understood in this way, the *psyche* is not so far removed from the historic subject matter of psychology.

To be sure, psychologists often study rather narrow sectors of human nature: prospective memory, schedules of reinforcement, behavioral response to specific drugs, cortical evoked potentials. Such is specialization in science. One hopes that by understanding thoroughly the component processes, a clearer picture of the whole (in this case, human nature) emerges.

Nevertheless, any sum-of-parts picture of human nature is incomplete. Psychology, we believe, is fundamentally about the whole person. Here we differ from the consensus definition of psychology as "the science of behavior." Of course behavior can be, and often is, defined broadly enough to include all of human experience—emotions, thoughts, dreams, goals, hopes, meaning, loves, and so on—but then what is the good of calling it all "behavior"? How is love behavior different from love, prayer behavior from prayer, or health behavior from health?

In the classic behaviorism of J. B. Watson (now called *naïve behaviorism*) behavior meant observable behavior, not subjective experiences and hypothetical constructs. The insufficiency of this approach is recognized by contemporary radical behaviorists, who are more concerned with perceptual representation, acceptance, and contextual meaning.

There are, however, perspectives within psychology that lie much closer to a Jewish or Christian understanding of the *psyche*. Humanistic and existential perspectives, the "third force" in clinical psychology, eschew a narrow focus on parts of the person, seeking instead to keep in view the whole meaning-making individual and to encompass and integrate all of human experience. Jungians adopt a similarly broad concept of the person, including transpersonal aspects of identity and meaning. Health psychologists who work at the interface of mind and body, as in the study of the complexities of psychoneuroimmunology, often have cause to step back and take an integrative perspective.

Conceptions of the person within modern holistic health lie closer still to Jewish and Christian understandings of human nature. Within medicine, specialization has led to ever-narrowing foci of scientists and practitioners, to the point that the patient in a hospital bed may be thought and spoken of primarily as a liver, a heart, or an infected foot. Holistic health is a rebound to this trend, challenging us to find ways to understand wellness and deliver care in a more integrated fashion. Not all medical care requires a whole-person perspective, but often integrative care is better medicine. At the simplest level, a medication prescribed by one physician may interact with a different medication prescribed by another provider or for another purpose. Hepatic problems resulting from alcohol abuse are associated with adverse effects in many other organ systems and are obviously linked to drinking behavior, which in turn can be influenced by a plethora of psychic factors (biological, psychological, social, spiritual, etc.). Focusing in on any one link may miss the bigger picture of the chains constraining the person's life.

One of the most important contributions of Judeo-Christian thought to our discipline, then, may be a challenge to rethink the nature of psychology itself. Whatever the value of analyzing component processes, we are reminded that our subject matter is the *psyche*, the whole person. Such a psychology is not best advanced by isolating spirituality for specialist study. We do not propose the creation of a National Institute on Spirituality. Instead, psychologists have a special role, as well as a distinctive perspective and voice, to keep in focus the human nature of persons. We have a unique, irreducible subject matter: the human *psyche* in all its complexity.

This is a legacy that we have from the very beginning of scientific psychology. William James was fascinated by the richness and varieties of human nature, including religion in particular, although he himself was not religious by belief or practice. If anything, James may be faulted for defining religion wholly in terms of human experience, without reference to institutional religion (Hauerwas, 2001). The "father of American psychology" was interested in the whole person, and especially in aspects that make an integrated whole of the parts. For James, psychology was the study of human nature.

Howard (1986) asked whether we dare develop a truly human science. The costs of not doing so are high. With behavior instead of personhood as a focus, we are in jeopardy of studying the brushstrokes and hues on a canvas without appreciating the art itself, let alone the artist. This is not to devalue careful study of the details of human nature. Psychology needs both microscope and telescope, the close-up and the panoramic view. The study of *psyche*, however, calls for a constant appreciation of the integrated whole. In this respect, psychology is not modeled on other sciences. The study of particular particles, compounds, cells, or organs is the stuff of science, without necessarily worrying about how it all fits together. Those who study the action of alcohol on neural membranes may never have seen a patient with alcohol dependence, nor is it essential that they do so. To understand the *psyche*, however, involves not only the integration of part processes but also consideration of higher order agentive and meaning processes that distinguish human nature. It is here that psychology has a special mission, and a message to carry to other sciences and professions. To miss this central focus and fascination with human nature is to sell our birthright as the science of *psyche* and to lose the unique heritage of our discipline.

What, then, are some broad outlines of a science of human nature? Surely one is a constant interest in how the parts fit together with the person in context. Not just the components, but relationships among different aspects of human functioning are of central interest. Another involves the classic balance between nomothetic and idiographic approaches to the study of people. What people have in common is surely of interest, after one filters out the noise of individual differences. Yet the science of *psyche* also bears responsibility to represent individual uniqueness as essential to humanity, and not mere nuisance variance. In this regard, the subject matter of psychology particularly includes those aspects that make us human, that define us individually and collectively as *homo sapiens*.

RESEARCH DIRECTIONS FOR A PSYCHOLOGY OF HUMAN NATURE

The chapters of this book offer a rich sampling of Judeo-Christian perspectives on psychology. Although they share some broad interpretational presuppositions outlined in chapter 1, the variety of perspectives represented make it clear that monotheistic viewpoints are not monolithic. No uniform research agenda emerges from spiritual and religious perspectives, even when one limits the religious scope to Judeo-Christian thought. To illustrate, whereas Baumeister argued that self-control could be considered the most basic underlying human virtue that will allow one to avoid the seven deadly sins of Christian theology (chap. 3), Worthington and Berry disagreed. They argued in chapter 8 that this is a wrong-headed idea resulting from a focus on evil and that in Christian theology the key is not effortful self-control; rather, loving and actively yielding to God is the master virtue. Similarly, whereas Kass and Lennox (chap. 10) discussed the idea of an autonomous individual as the shared goal of human development and spiritual development, Evans (chap. 4) and Brown and Miller (chap. 9) construed the goal of spiritual development instead as rooted in relation, indeed, in a submission, to a Divine other. Thus, whatever else may come of explicit incorporation of Judeo-

Christian perspectives into psychology, it is unlikely that this will lead to an inflexible, singular view of whatever topic is under investigation.

A second point that seems clear from these chapters is that the dialogue between Judeo-Christian perspectives and psychology promises to lead to a rich array of opportunities for empirical research. As Jones and Hostler argued in chapter 6, Judeo-Christian perspectives on psychology should offer a set of background assumptions such as are defined by other conceptual approaches, be they humanistic, existential, radical behaviorist, or evolutionary. Such background assumptions inform psychological research by suggesting questions of interest and providing an interpretational framework for making sense of results. The viability of a Judeo-Christian perspective as a player in psychological scholarship will hinge on the ability to generate "novel and significant hypotheses regarding measurable phenomena that yet in turn yield empirically powerful findings in comparison to competing explanatory systems" (p. 117, Jones & Hostler, this volume).

As one further product of the discussions that generated this volume, we highlight some specific research questions and directions that are raised by the chapter authors. Our comments here follow the order of chapters 3 through 13.

Baumeister

The provocative series of studies by Baumeister and his associates provide evidence supporting a willpower theory of self-control, rather than competing theories (e.g., Muraven, Tice, & Baumeister, 1998). Resisting temptation seems to use up a limited resource, temporarily rendering one less able to persist on other tasks or to engage in other acts of self-regulation (e.g., Baumeister, Bratslavsky, Muraven, & Tice, 1998). The avoidance of unnecessary temptation is common counsel in both Jewish (e.g., Proverbs) and Christian Scripture ("Lead us not into temptation," Matt. 6:13). This raises the question of the relative merits of minimizing exposure to temptation versus confronting and coping with such situations. Successful changers seem to avoid temptation early in the change process but then gradually reexpose themselves to previously risky stimuli as their self-control strengthens (DiClemente, 2003).

This work on self-control suggests various empirically testable interventions, many of which would be consonant with Judeo-Christian religious perspectives. Indeed, some useful and generalizable interventions might be derived from religious practice. That the moral muscle can be strengthened is, as Baumeister noted in chapter 3, simply a modern confirmation of centuries of advice on learning self-control or building character. Transcendental meditation, deeply rooted in Eastern religion, has been secularized and successfully applied with religious and nonreligious people alike (Benson &

Klipper, 1990; Kabat-Zinn, 1995). Similarly, other forms of meditation have a long history in Christian practice and are known by various names such as contemplative or "centering" prayer (Keating, 1994; Merton, 1969). Helping people of Jewish or Christian faith to practice religious disciplines (such as prayer, fasting, or scriptural study, cf. Evans, chap. 4) might both enhance their spiritual lives and serve more generally to strengthen their self-control muscles, much as has been found for secular exercises such as diet or posture control. Indeed, difficulty in maintaining religious practices is a common and sometimes distressing complaint among people of faith. Perhaps tailoring preventive and treatment interventions to address such religious practices as well as other behaviors could render them more appealing to religiously oriented people, enhancing adherence. Propst, for example, found that modifying cognitive therapy in response to clients' religious beliefs increased the efficacy of treatment for depression (Propst, 1996; Propst, Ostrom, Watkins, Dean, & Mashburn, 1992).

Evans

Complementing Baumeister's examination of the executive or volitional component of the self is Evans's analysis of the self's awareness of itself and its social character. That people's desire for favorable information from others about themselves is stronger than the desire for accurate information (Sedikides, 1993) is not surprising to those schooled in Judeo-Christian wisdom (e.g., "The heart is deceitful above all things"; Jer. 17:9). The strong empirical evidence that people overestimate their own abilities relative to others (see chap. 4) suggests a need for research on how to gain more accurate knowledge of oneself (and others) and the effects of doing so. The biblical exhortation "Do not think of yourself more highly than you ought, but rather think of yourself with sober judgment" (Rom. 12:3, NIV) is in the context of discussion about correctly discerning and using one's gifts. Instruments to assess spiritual maturity or spiritual gifts that are designed for use in conjunction with feedback from others are beginning to be used in religious organizations, but with unknown effects on self-knowledge or behavior (e.g., Ford, 1998). As Evans suggested, research is needed on the ways in which people gain a sense of calling from God and on factors, such as conceptions of God and others, determining the kinds of actions to which these motivations lead.

It seems fairly clear that the inner sense of self is shaped by social relations (see chaps. 3 and 4). What social factors (e.g., acceptance, feedback) best address insufficient or oversufficient self-esteem or promote self-actualization? A Christian perspective on the self, as illustrated by Kierkegaard, is that the identity of the self is always grounded in relation to something outside the self. Grounding the self in relation to the higher power of Alcoholics Anonymous, the ideal self of Rogers and Maslow, the Yahweh of Jewish scripture, or the Christ of the New Testament would appear to be a more stable criterion than one's peer group. Kierkegaard's exclamation "what an infinite accent falls on the self by having God as the criterion!" suggests that those who perceive their identity primarily in terms of a relation to God should be less affected than others by circumstances such as pressures toward social conformity. This is an empirically testable hypothesis.

Bien

In chapter 5, Bien mentioned that stories convey a sense of movement and that the basic Judeo-Christian story pictures a movement toward salvation and healing. Although research on narratives was not common in psychology throughout much of the 20th century, psychology and various social sciences and humanities disciplines, as well as theology, have in recent years begun to embrace narrative epistemologies, including life histories, discourse analysis, and other forms of qualitative research. One fruit of this research is the perspective it offers on the self, namely, the identity or self-awareness that complements the executive, decision-making dimensions discussed by Baumeister and the relational aspects of the self discussed by Evans. McAdams (1985, 1993) and others have argued that adult identity is basically a narrative of the self, a narrative that evolves and is internalized as we go through life constructing a self-defining life story. Some of this research most relevant to the current project is summarized in a book published by the American Psychological Association and edited by McAdams, Josselson, and Lieblich (2001). In particular, the question Bien raises of specific narrative themes within religious traditions that are positively or negatively related to health or well-being is addressed in this research. It turns out that the theme of *redemption*, central to Judeo-Christian thought but related to deliverance themes of other religions (James, 1902/1999, p. 552), regularly shows up in the life stories of adults whose lives are remarkable for their "generativity," that is, enfused with a "concern for and commitment to promoting the well-being of later generations" (McAdams & Bowman, 2001, p. 10; cf. Evans, chap. 4, section titled "Kierkegaard on Human Relationality", p. 83 this volume).

Stories also have long been an important method of teaching and conveying spiritual truths within world religions (Kurtz & Ketcham, 1992). The storytelling aspect of human nature has also been developed in narrative therapies (Freedman & Combs, 1996; White & Epston, 1990), a growing but largely unevaluated approach to psychotherapy. The importance of storytelling in human development and healing seems a fruitful avenue for future research. Helping adolescents construct a life story in the context of their faith traditions, for example, may strengthen some of the positive effects of religion on socially responsible behavior.

Jones and Hostler

Beyond these three analyses of the self based on self-regulation (chap. 3), self-awareness (chap. 4), and narrative (chap. 5), Jones and Hostler presented in chapter 6 a fourth perspective on human nature in their exploration of the role of sexuality in personhood. Modern evolutionary psychology views sexuality as grounded in adaptations to ancient environments, narrowing attention to the ways in which behavior promotes reproductive fitness, a view similar in some ways to a psychoanalytic view of sexuality as derivative from the interaction of an animalistic id with external prohibitions. In contrast to some secular stereotypes of religion, Jones and Hostler described a profoundly positive Jewish and Christian view of sexuality as an instantiation of a deeper spiritual truth that is embodied in marriage. Better marital functioning has been found "to be generally associated with more joint religious activities between couples as well as greater perceptions of marriage having spiritual characteristics and significance" (Mahoney et al., 1999, p. 333). Thus, Jones and Hostler here argued that "the strong relationship of religiousness, sexual fidelity, and relational stability and quality is to be expected and deserves much more extensive empirical exploration."

Maehr

Martin L. Maehr asserted in chapter 7 that religion offers meaning that may influence motivation, as appreciated in social theory at least from the time of Max Weber. The influence of religion on human motivation is brought more sharply into focus by the modern cognitive construal of motivation in terms of choice and decision making, a view highly compatible with Judeo-Christian perspectives on human nature. In particular, Maehr maintained that religion informs motivation through its effects on our sense of self, the purposes we try to achieve, and the action possibilities from which we choose. He raised interesting research questions—for example, what are the effects of religious education on personal and spiritual development, and why it is that minority students seem to fare better in Roman Catholic schools than in public schools. As Maehr noted, the role of the specifically religious nature of these schools has not typically been studied, but it should be. Given the markedly higher importance of religion among African Americans and Hispanics (populations often at higher risk for school failure) compared with Caucasians (cf. Brenda Miller, chap. 12), should we not ask how religion can be put into play in motivating an investment in school achievement? At the least, future studies of parochial schools, if not their public counterparts, should consider the plausible roles religion can play in framing achievement patterns. Also of interest is the effect of religion in promoting communal consciousness and collectivist rather than individualistic motivations. More broadly, Maehr asked how religion influences, for better or worse, not only patterns and aspirations with regard to achievement, but human development in general.

Worthington and Berry

After comparing and contrasting Jewish and Christian perspectives on virtue, Worthington and Berry suggested some specific and testable hypotheses. They predicted, for example, that Christians (relative to Jews or secular populations) will place lesser value on reason and prize more highly as virtues gratitude and yielding to God's control. They also posited that virtues develop in religion-congruent clusters rather than independently, and that this should be particularly true of individuals who are highly committed to their religion. In this regard, they also hypothesized that longtime adherents of Islam and Judaism would prize conscientiousness-based virtues to a greater extent and warmth-based virtues to a lesser extent than would longtime adherents of Christianity. However these specific predictions may fare with empirical testing, chapter 8 more generally called for research on the influence of religion on human conceptions and manifestations of virtues.

Brown and Miller

The phenomenon of transformational change is familiar within Judaism and Christianity in the lives of historic figures such as Moses and Saul. Although William James (1902/1999) was vitally interested in such sudden and discontinuous turnabouts, they have received relatively little attention within modern psychological science (Hardy, 1979; Loder, 1981; McAdams & Bowman, 2001; Miller & C'de Baca, 2001), perhaps because they have not been subject to experimental control. In chapter 9, Brown and Miller surveyed various perspectives on transformational change and their meaning in human identity. Like Evans, they discussed the need for a Divine "other" to complete a limited self. Like Worthington and Berry, they explored the role of surrender or yieldedness in such transformational change. There is parallel, too, to Bien's explication of the central role of narratives in human nature, because stories, whether fictional and biographical, convey both human limitations and potential for change. Here is a potentially fruitful area for qualitative research—to explore and understand more fully the discontinuous transformational changes in human life. The wedding of qualitative methods of narratives or interviews with content-analysis systems that permit blind coding and derivation of quantitative indices in this area is illustrated well by the work of McAdams and his colleagues (e.g., McAdams, Diamond, de St. Aubin, & Mansfield, 1997). These researchers found that the hallmark of the internalized life stories of highly generative adults is a prevalence of redemption imagery whereby bad scenes are transformed into good outcomes and one is motivated to a life of moral steadfastness and pursuit of goals to benefit society. This is the sort of rigorous testing of hypotheses that is needed in investigating transformational change from Judeo-Christian perspectives.

Kass and Lennox

Developmental psychology has focused largely on personality, cognitive, social, and, more recently, emotional development. In chapter 10, Kass and Lennox explored the less studied dimension of spiritual development. They began by reviewing various psychological models of spiritual development that in their view "share the same goal: an autonomous individual capable of self-transcendence and authenticity." They contrasted this with the historic Jewish perspective developed by Maimonides, which construes spiritual maturity as knowing God, in the sense of having one's actions embody loving kindness and righteousness and immersing oneself in the apprehension of God's presence. Maimonides's perspective on evil, similar to Plato's, is that it basically arises from ignorance, particularly regarding one's connectedness with God. Testable hypotheses follow, anticipating an inverse relationship between God-consciousness and human vices. This relationship is specifically asserted within the teachings of Alcoholics Anonymous, where enhancing God-consciousness is understood as an antidote to addiction (Tonigan, Toscova, & Connors, 1999).

Thoresen, Oman, and Harris

Members of Judeo-Christian religious communities are encouraged through biblical teaching, examples, and modeling to engage in practices such as prayer and meditation. Although these practices have spiritual ends as their goal, research has more typically examined effects on temporal outcomes such as longevity. Meta-analytic and epidemiologic reviews of dozens of prospective studies link religious involvement to reduced all-cause mortality, with effects equivalent to seven additional years of life for frequent attenders versus nonattenders (McCullough, Hoyt, Larson, Koenig, & Thoresen, 2000; Powell, Shahabi, & Thoresen, 2003). The mechanisms underlying this linkage are not well understood, however, and represent an important area for further research. Recent work suggests that religious involvement increases survival via marital stability, improved mental health, and lower rates of smoking and alcohol consumption (Oman & Thoresen, 2002; Strawbridge, Shema, Cohen, & Kaplan, 2001). A better understanding of such salutary effects may suggest ways in which they could be promoted within as well as outside religious communities.

In chapter 11, Thoresen and his colleagues particularly focused on religious practices that may promote health and longevity. The practice of transcendental meditation has been associated with higher survival rates, more positive emotions, and lower stress hormone production (Alexander, Langer, Newman, Chandler, & Davies, 1989; Davidson, 2001). Less studied are the effects of Judeo-Christian mystical and meditative practices such as contemplative or centering prayer; (e.g., Keating, 1994, 2002). Positive health effects have also been associated with religion-consistent practices such as selfless loving, acceptance, and forgiveness (Cole & Pargament, 1999; Sanderson & Linehan, 1999), and research is needed on how such practices can be effectively promoted within and outside faith contexts.

Research on the potentially positive effects of spiritual and religious practice should not be limited to the controlling of adverse behavior and outcomes. Also worthy of study are the elevating and edifying functions of spiritual practice and religious involvement, such as gratitude (Emmons & McCullough, 2003), inspiration, hope, joy, or transcending of habitual and limiting mindsets (Seligman, 1998). Maslow (1994) studied such peak experiences, and their nature and sequelae deserve further qualitative and quantitative empirical exploration.

As discussed elsewhere in this volume, research on the effects of spirituality and religion should consider the potential for both positive and negative influences in individual and collective human life. The effects of spiritual and religious involvement are not uniformly or inevitably benevolent, and the darker side of spirituality has long been recognized in both psychology and religion.

Miller

What factors influence the extent to which an individual manifests religiousness in adult life? Judeo-Christian traditions emphasize parental responsibility for instructing their children in the faith. In chapter 12, Brenda A. Miller highlighted parental religiousness as the most important predictor of their adult children's religiosity and reviewed various factors that moderate or enhance this relationship. Such facilitators include parental warmth and acceptance, the presence and religious congruence of both parents, and the frequency of communication about religious matters. She also explored the differing roles of mothers and fathers in intergenerational transmission of religious values, beliefs, and practices, an area in which additional research is needed. Greater knowledge of the processes that inspire intergenerational transmission would be of direct interest and help to parents who wish to bolster their children's faith as adults. The role of other adult figures besides parents in influencing children's spiritual development also deserves further study.

Pargament, Murray-Swank, Magyar, and Ano

After helpfully distinguishing among interpersonal struggles, intrapsychic struggles, and struggles with the Divine, Pargament and his colleagues described in chapter 13 how such spiritual struggles have their origin in the interaction between stressful life experiences and the individual's religious orienting system. As a complement to chapter 11 on positive health effects of spiritual and religious practices, they examined the deleterious effects of spiritual struggles on well-being. The "pain and gain" idea is the silver lining and suggests an empirical hypothesis worthy of further exploration: As Pargament and colleagues noted, "people who perceive their spiritual struggles in a large spiritual context may also be more likely to grow from their experiences." Pargament's own research explores the more general effects of "benevolent religious appraisals of life stressors" on health, complementing the work mentioned previously of McAdams et al. (2001) examining relationships between benevolent appraisals of stressors and generativity.

The *DSM–IV* (American Psychiatric Association, 1994) contained for the first time a diagnostic code for religious or spiritual problems, yet most mental health professionals know little about how to help people resolve such spiritual struggles. Faith crises are common for adolescents in religious families as they struggle with the transition from childhood comprehension of religion toward an adult faith. Parents, clergy, and supportive others may be uncertain how best to respond to such spiritual struggles and doubts, or they may respond in detrimental ways. There is also historic recognition that in adult spiritual development, it is common to encounter harrowing "dark nights of the soul." Pargament and his colleagues suggested that an important step for coping with spiritual struggles may be preparing people to deal with them before they occur. Prospective studies of spiritual development and direction could be helpful in clarifying how best to help people negotiate spiritual and religious struggles and to promote benevolent resolution rather than hurtful and harmful outcomes.

TOWARD A PSYCHOLOGY THAT INCLUDES SPIRITUALITY

Finally, we emphasize the need to develop a broader and clearer understanding of human spirituality that embraces but is not limited to religious issues and practices. There are many psychometrically sound instruments for measuring religiousness (Hill & Hood, 1999), but the measurement of spirituality is less well developed, although it is an active area of current research (e.g., Fetzer Institute, 1999; Koenig, McCullough, & Larson, 2001, chap. 33; Underwood & Teresi, 2002). Spirituality can be conceived and assessed as a multivariate construct, like personality or health, within which every individual can be located in multidimensional space (Miller & Thoresen, 1999). As Dallas Willard (2002, p. 45) has quipped, spiritual formation is like education: everyone gets one, though not necessarily a good one. Research to date on spirituality and health has focused primarily on religiousness, usually with relatively crude univariate, often single-item measures (Larson, Pattison, Blazer, Omran, & Kaplan, 1986; Weaver et al., 1998). An analogy, perhaps, would be to study the effects of personality on health by focusing on social extroversion. Extroversion is an important component of personality and is likely to be relevant to health (e.g., through social support, risk taking, etc.), but it is a modest sector within the richer domain of personality.

Psychology faces some substantial obstacles in implementing increased focus on religious and spiritual issues (e.g., as an aspect of diversity training of clinical psychologists; see chap. 14 of this volume). One of these is the well-documented underrepresentation of practicing religious people among psychologists. Within the U.S. population, 94% report that they believe in God (Gallup & Lindsay, 1999), with 83% self-identifying as Christian and 2% as Jewish (the Christian percentage includes those stating a religious preference of Protestant or Catholic, the Jewish percentage "includes Jews who define themselves as Jewish by religion as well as those who define themselves as Jewish in cultural terms"; U.S. Census, 2000, p. 62). Among members of the American Psychological Association, however, fewer than half professed belief in God (Regan, Malony, & Beit-Hallahmi, 1980; Shafranske, 1996, p. 154). Similarly, 72% of the general public endorsed the statement that "My whole approach to life is based on my religion," but fewer mental health professionals believed similarly, with psychologists (at 33%) having a lower level of endorsement of this statement than any other category of mental health professional (Bergin & Jensen, 1990). The picture is similar in beliefs of academic psychologists relative to faculty in other disciplines. A recent survey of 59 academic disciplines revealed that psychology was sixth from the bottom in the percentage of faculty endorsing any religion (Shafranske, 1996, p. 152).

Despite their lack of personal beliefs, psychologists must reckon with the fact that 72% of Americans agree with the statement, "My religious faith is the most important influence in my life" (Princeton Religious Research Center, 1994), with 40% indicating that they have had a life-changing religious or spiritual experience (Smith, 2002). Although many such experiences are reported in the context of Christian faiths (e.g., 39% of the U.S. population describe themselves as "born again" and as having had a conversion experience; Gallup & Lindsay, 1999), a minority of Americans identify themselves as spiritual but not religious. Furthermore, although the proportion of the population attending a church or synagogue at least weekly has remained roughly 4 in 10 for more than 60 years (Gallup & Lindsay, 1999), interest in spirituality whether religiously based or not, is clearly on the rise. For example, in 1944, 58% of the population expressed an interest in spiritual growth, whereas in 1998, 82% expressed a need to grow spiritually (Gallup & Lindsay, 1999). It is clear that spirituality is an aspect of human experience that psychology should no longer ignore.

One vital contribution of adding spirituality to the science and profession of psychology, we believe, is to enlarge and enrich the conception of the human person (cf. Assagioli, 1965). Understanding spiritual development expands one's appreciation of the complexity of human development. Whereas maturation of the brain, as reflected in intelligence and cognitive development, is reached relatively early in life, spiritual maturity is usually understood as peaking much later in adulthood. Assessing the spiritual and religious aspects of people can expand appreciation of human motivation, strengths, resources, and potential. Furthermore, one of the principal ways in which cultures differ from each other is in spiritual and religious heritage, and it is difficult to understand cultural differences without appreciating the profound influence of this aspect of human nature. Within some cultures and subcultures, including many in the United States, religion is central to identity, meaning, purpose, and the sense of self.

This is not to say that psychological science can capture all, or even the essence, of human spirituality and religion. As understood in Judaism and Christianity, God cannot be controlled as an independent variable. To study the behaviors or symbolism of the Seder or Eucharist does not begin to capture its transcendent meaning for Jews or Christians as a transaction with God. The penchant of science to explain (or to explain away as "nothing but") runs headlong into the Judeo-Christian appreciation of mystery (e.g., Evans, 1986). Although psychology may well enrich spirituality in various ways, and both religion and psychology concern a search for truth, their methodologies are quite different.

A psychology that ignores spirituality, however, necessarily promotes an incomplete understanding of the human person. Whatever the spiritual and religious inclinations of psychologists, our conception of people should not exclude this crucial domain of human experience, identity, and culture. It was perfectly natural for William James (1902/1999), himself a secular psychologist, to be fascinated with understanding religious experience as "a study of human nature." A century later, the spiritual side of humankind remains as a vital puzzle worthy of consideration within the science and practice of psychology.

REFERENCES

Alexander, C. N., Langer, E. J., Newman, R. I., Chandler, H. M., & Davies, J. L. (1989). Transcendental meditation, mindfulness, and longevity: An experimental study with the elderly. *Journal of Personality and Social Psychology, 57*, 950–964.

American Psychiatric Association. (1994). *Diagnostic and statistical manual of mental disorders* (4th ed.). Washington, DC: Author.

Assagioli, R. (1965). *Psychosynthesis*. New York: Penguin Books.

Baumeister, R. F., Bratslavsky, E., Muraven, M., & Tice, D. M. (1998). Ego depletion: Is the active self a limited resource? *Journal of Personality and Social Psychology, 74*, 1252–1265.

Benson, H., & Klipper, M. Z. (1990). *The relaxation response*. New York: Avon Books.

Bergin, A. E., & Jensen, J. P. (1990). Religiosity of psychotherapists: A national survey. *Psychotherapy, 27*, 3–6.

Cole, B. S., & Pargament, K. (1999). Spiritual surrender: A paradoxical path to control. In W. R. Miller (Ed.), *Integrating spirituality into treatment: Resources for practitioners* (pp. 179–198). Washington, DC: American Psychological Association.

Davidson, R. (2001, October). *Positive affect: Perspectives from affective neuroscience*. Paper presented at the Gallup Organization's Positive Psychology Summit Conference, Washington, DC.

DiClemente, C. C. (2003). *Addiction and change: How addictions develop and addicted people recover*. New York: Guilford Press.

Emmons, R. A., & McCullough, M. E. (2003). Counting blessings versus burdens: An experimental investigation of gratitude and subjective well-being in daily life. *Journal of Personality and Social Psychology, 84*, 377–389.

Evans, C. S. (1986). *The quest for faith: Reason and mystery as pointers to God*. Downers Grove, IL: InterVarsity Press.

Fetzer Institute. (1999, October). *Multidimensional measure of religiousness/spirituality for use in health research: A report of the Fetzer Institute/National Institute on Aging Working Group*. Kalamazoo, MI: Author.

Ford, P. (1998). *Discovering your ministry identity: Learning to be who you already are*. Saint Charles, IL: ChurchSmart Resources.

Freedman, J., & Combs, G. (1996). *Narrative therapy: The social construction of preferred realities*. New York: Norton.

Gallup, G., Jr., & Lindsay, D. M. (1999). *Surveying the religious landscape: Trends in U.S. beliefs*. Harrisburg, PA: Morehouse.

Hardy, A. (1979). *The spiritual nature of man*. Oxford, England: Oxford University Press.

Hauerwas, S. (2001). *With the grain of the universe*. Grand Rapids, MI: Brazos Press.

Hill, P. C., & Hood, R. W., Jr. (Eds.). (1999). *Measures of religiosity*. Birmingham, AL: Religious Education Press.

Howard, G. (1986). *Dare we develop a human science?* Notre Dame, IN: Academic Publications.

James, W. (1999). *The varieties of religious experience: A study in human nature*. New York: Modern Library. (Original work published 1902)

Kabat-Zinn, J. (1995). *Wherever you go, there you are: Mindfulness meditation in everyday life*. New York: Hyperion.

Keating, T. (1994). *Intimacy with God: An introduction to centering prayer*. New York: Crossroad.

Keating, T. (2002). *Open mind, open heart: The contemplative dimensions of the gospel*. New York: Continuum.

Koenig, H. G., McCullough, M. E., & Larson, D. B. (2001). *Handbook of religion and health*. New York: Oxford University Press.

Kurtz, E., & Ketcham, K. (1992). *The spirituality of imperfection: Modern wisdom from classic stories*. New York: Bantam Books.

Larson, D. B., Pattison, E. M., Blazer, D. G., Omran, A. R., & Kaplan, B. H. (1986). Systematic analysis of research on religious variables in four major psychiatric journals, 1978–1982. *American Journal of Psychiatry, 143*, 329–334.

Loder, J. E. (1981). *The transforming moment: Understanding convictional experiences*. New York: HarperCollins.

Mahoney, A., Pargament, K. I., Jewell, T., Swank, A. B., Scott, E., Emery, E., & Rye, M. (1999). Marriage and the spiritual realm: The role of proximal and distal religious constructs in marital functioning. *Journal of Family Psychology, 13*, 321–338.

Maslow, A. H. (1994). *Religions, values, and peak experiences*. New York: Viking Press.

May, G. G. (1992). *Care of mind, care of spirit*. San Francisco: HarperCollins.

McAdams, D. P. (1985). *Power, intimacy, and the life story: Personological inquiries into identity*. New York: Guilford Press.

McAdams, D. P. (1993). *The stories we live by: Personal myths and the making of the self*. New York: Morrow.

McAdams, D. P., & Bowman, P. J. (2001). Narrating life's turning points: Redemption and contamination. In D. P. McAdams, R. Josselson, & A. Lieblich (Eds.), *Turns in the road: Narrative studies of lives in transition* (pp. 3–34). Washington, DC: American Psychological Association.

McAdams, D. P., Diamond, A., de St. Aubin, E., & Mansfield, E. (1997). Stories of commitment: The psychosocial construction of generative lives. *Journal of Personality and Social Psychology, 72*, 678–694.

McAdams, D. P., Josselson, R., & Lieblich, A. (Eds.). (2001). *Turns in the road: Narrative studies of lives in transition*. Washington, DC: American Psychological Association.

McCullough, M. E., Hoyt, W. T., Larson, D. B., Koenig, H. G., & Thoresen, C. (2000). Religious involvement and mortality: A meta-analytic review. *Health Psychology, 19*, 211–222.

Merton, T. (1960). *Spiritual direction and meditation*. Collegeville, MN: Order of St. Benedict.

Merton, T. (1969). *Contemplative prayer*. New York: Herder & Herder.

Miller, W. R., & C'de Baca, J. (2001). *Quantum change: When epiphanies and sudden insights transform ordinary lives*. New York: Guilford Press.

Miller, W. R., & Thoresen, C. E. (1999). Spirituality and health. In W. R. Miller (Ed.), *Integrating spirituality into treatment: Resources for practitioners* (pp. 3–18). Washington, DC: American Psychological Association.

Muraven, M., Tice, D. M., & Baumeister, R. F. (1998). Self-control as limited resource: Regulatory depletion patterns. *Journal of Personality and Social Psychology, 74,* 774–789.

Oman, D., & Thoresen, C. E. (2002). Does religion cause health? Differing interpretations and diverse meanings. *Journal of Health Psychology, 7,* 365–380.

Powell, L. H., Shahabi, L., & Thoresen, C. E. (2003). Religion and spirituality: Linkages to physical health. *American Psychologist, 58,* 36–52.

Princeton Religious Research Center. (1994). *Religion in America 1993–1994.* Princeton: Author.

Propst, L. R. (1996). Cognitive–behavioral therapy and the religious person. In E. P. Shafranske (Ed.), *Religion and the clinical practice of psychology* (pp. 391–407). Washington, DC: American Psychological Association.

Propst, L., Ostrom, R., Watkins, P., Dean, T., & Mashburn, D. (1992). Comparative efficacy of religious and nonreligious cognitive–behavioral therapy for the treatment of clinical depression in religious individuals. *Journal of Consulting and Clinical Psychology, 60,* 94–103.

Regan, C., Malony, H. N., & Beit-Hallahmi, B. (1980). Psychologists and religion: Professional factors and personal beliefs. *Review of Religious Research, 21,* 208–217.

Sanderson, C., & Linehan, M. M. (1999). Acceptance and forgiveness. In W. R. Miller (Ed.), *Integrating spirituality into treatment: Resources for practitioners* (pp. 199–216). Washington, DC: American Psychological Association.

Sedikides, C. (1993). Assessment, enhancement, and verification determinants of the self-evaluation process. *Journal of Personality and Social Psychology, 65,* 317–338.

Seligman, M. E. P. (1998). *Learned optimism: How to change your mind and your life.* New York: Pocket Books.

Shafranske, E. P. (1996). Religious beliefs, affiliations, and practices of clinical psychologists. In E. P. Shafranske (Ed.), *Religion and the clinical practice of psychology* (pp. 149–162). Washington, DC: American Psychological Association.

Smith, T. W. (2002, October). *National Opinion Research Center survey research on religious change.* Paper presented at the initial Spiritual Transformation Scientific Research Program Conference, Philadelphia.

Strawbridge, W. J., Shema, S., Cohen, R. D., & Kaplan, G. (2001). Religious attendance increases survival by improving and maintaining good health behaviors, mental health, and social relationships. *Annals of Behavioral Medicine, 23,* 68–74.

Tonigan, J. S., Toscova, R. T., & Connors, G. J. (1999). Spirituality and the 12-step programs: A guide for clinicians. In W. R. Miller (Ed.), *Integrating spirituality into treatment: Resources for practitioners* (pp. 111–131). Washington, DC: American Psychological Association.

Underwood, L. G., & Teresi, J. A. (2002). The Daily Spiritual Experience Scale: Development, theoretical description, reliability, exploratory factor analysis, and preliminary construct validity using health-related data. *Annals of Behavioral Medicine, 24*, 22–33.

U.S. Census Bureau. (2000). *Statistical abstract of the United States: 2000.* Washington, DC: U.S. Department of Commerce.

Weaver, A. J., Kline, A. E., Samford, J. A., Lucas, L. A., Larson, D. B., & Gorsuch, R. L. (1998). Is religion taboo in psychology? A systematic analysis of religion in seven major American Psychological Association journals: 1991–1994. *Journal of Psychology and Christianity, 17*, 220–232.

White, M., & Epston, D. (1990). *Narrative means to therapeutic ends.* New York: Norton.

Willard, D. (2002). *Renovation of the heart: Putting on the character of Christ.* Colorado Springs, CO: NavPress.

AUTHOR INDEX

Numbers in italics refer to entries in the reference sections.

SUBJECT INDEX

Erikson, E., 185, 189
Ethical heroism, 85
Ethnicity, and religiousness, 228–229, 239, 214–215
European Americans, and religiousness, 229
Evangelical Renewal Therapy, 259
Evil, 88–90, 150–151, 153, 192–193. *See also* Sin; Virtue
Evolutionary psychology, 4, 119, 126
Executive function, 59, 77, 81
Existential perspectives, 60, 170–171, 260

Fall, Christian doctrine of. *See* Depravity
Faith, in determinism, 59–60
Faith and reason, Aquinas and, 37–38
Faith community. *See* Religious communities
Faith crises. *See* Spiritual struggle
Faith development, 21, 150, 186–187, 260, 301
Faith, leap of, 43, 59, 178
Family, 59, 126, 128–129, 161, 187, 212
    love, 234
    religious practices, coverage of in child development courses, 283
    spiritual struggles, and, 251
    structures, and transmission of religiousness, 237–238
    transmission of religiousness, and, 99–100, 227–228, 230–235, 240, 251
    violence, 237–238
Father. *See* Family; Parents; Parental roles
Fechner, Gustav, 43
Fetzer Institute, 21
Finkelstein, Rabbi Louis, 190
Fordham College, 47
Forgiveness, 149–150, 156, 177, 210, 212, 218–219, 282, 301
Fowler, J., 186–187, 189
Francis of Assisi, St., 35, 206, 208
Frankl, V., 193
Freedom, 32, 35, 37, 42, 57–61, 67–70, 84. *See also* Free will
Free will, 35–37, 44, 57–62, 67–68, 153. *See also* Determinism; Will
Freud, Sigmund, 4, 35, 40, 45, 110, 120–121, 136, 148, 173, 188
Fuller Theological Seminary, 49

Gandhi, Mahatma, 87
Gender

and *imago Dei*, 82–82n, 123, 125, 188, 191
    and religiousness, 211, 228–229
Generation gap, 229, 236
Genetic psychology, 45
Goals, 139–140, 207–208
God, 16–17, 19, 82, 88, 124, 191, 208, 245–258, 260–262
    as "other," 177–178
    as taboo within psychology, 15
    belief in, 14, 22, 36, 38–39, 48, 59, 88, 161, 186, 189, 207, 303
    immanence of, 48, 192
    self's relation to, 84–87
    transcendence of, 32, 96, 192
    views or representations of, 96, 107–108, 186–188
    William James's beliefs concerning, 43–44
God consciousness, assessment of, 19
God-relationship, 84–91, 154, 190–193, 195–198
God representation, 188, 200
Grace, 35, 41, 43, 106, 108, 174, 189
Gratitude, 149, 154–156, 245, 301
Great Awakening, 40
Greek and Roman world, 32–33, 147
Guided visualization, 196–198
Guilt, 17, 31–34, 80–81, 106, 151, 248, 254–255, 260–262

Halakhah, 190–193
Hall, G. Stanley, 45–46, 167
Health. *See also* Medicine; Mental health; Spiritual health
    and attendance at religious services, 211–214
    and forgiveness, 218–219
    and meditation, 216–218
    and prayer, 214–216
    and religious practices, 300–301
    and spirituality, 209
    and spiritual struggle, 255–256, 258
Health psychology, 293
Hegel, G. W. F., 172
Heidegger, Martin, 76
Hickok, Laurens P., 39
Hinayana Buddhism, 122
Hispanics, and religiousness, 229, 298
Historical-critical method, 105
Holistic health, 293
Holocaust survivors, 251–252

call to love God and neighbor, 85–86, 88, 154, 206, 232

Freudian view of, as alien to person, 120

God's nature, as fundamental aspect of, 86, 89, 107, 108, 123, 125, 208, 248–249

Judeo-Christian emphasis on, 232, 240

loving kindness (Golden Rule), 190–193, 200, 300

obligation resulting from being loved, 89

of neighbor, as stage of spiritual development, 189

passionate, 125, 152

perfect, 82

religious affection, as, 41

selfless, 17, 22, 301

and sexual longings, 127

and transmission of religiousness, 232, 234, 240

virtue of, 149, 156–159, 294

Loyola University, 47

Mahan, Asa, 42

Mahayana Buddhism, 122

Maimonides, 36, 186, 190–193, 200, 232, 300

Marriage, 125–126, 128–129, 213, 262–263, 298

Maslow, Abraham, 7, 14, 48, 85, 119, 171, 297, 301

Maturation process, in spiritual development, 186–187

McClelland, David, 135–137

McCosh, James, 39, 42

Measurement, in psychological research, 272, 279–281, 284, 302

Medicine, and religion, 48–49, 293

Meditation, 18–19, 65, 67, 88, 122–123, 160, 196–198, 209–212, 216–218, 220, 295–296, 300–301

Menninger, K., 8, 20, 49

Menschenbild, 16–19

Mental health, and spiritual struggle, 251, 262

Metanoia, 168–169

Methodism, 41n

Middle Ages, 32–38, 153

Midrash, 151

Mindfulness Meditation (MM), 216–217

Mishnah, 151–152

Mitzvot, 190

Modernism, 46, 118, 147–148, 273

Morality, 17, 31, 34, 81, 127, 156

Moral order, and religiousness, 230, 240

Moses, 18, 90, 105, 154, 167–168, 206, 245–246, 253, 299

Mother. *See* Family; Parents, Parental roles

Motivation, 78, 298–299

achievement, 136–137, 142

decision theory models of, 138–141

goals and purposes, 134, 138–142, 215

need to belong, 59, 79, 134

psychoanalytic perspectives on, 99, 120–121, 272, 298

role of religion in, 15, 19, 133–142, 152–162

role of values in, 6, 143–162

self-enhancement, 78, 97

sexual, 118–130

sociocultural origins of, 135, 142

spirituality and, 13, 248

yieldedness to God as, 156

Movement, in transformational change, 171–175

Naive behaviorism, 11, 292

Narrative therapies, 297

National Institute on Aging, 21

National Institutes of Health, 14

National Opinion Research Center, 186, 229

National Study of Couples, 237

National Survey of Families and Households, 237

Native Americans, and religiousness, 239

Natural law, 17

Neoplatonism, 34

"New self," Christian notion of, 153, 157–158

Niebuhr, Reinhold, 177

"Not God," 17, 20, 32

Object relations theory, 188

Obligations, and relatedness, 81, 89

Observational spiritual learning, 233

Observation of the self, 75–76

Ontotheology, 116–117

Orienting system, and spiritual struggle, 251–253

"Other," God as, 177–178

Pace, Edward, 47

Paradise, 83

Parapsychology, 273

Religion and psychology, 116–117, 153–162, 168, 186–190, 207–209, 273–276, 280–281, 284

Religiosity. *See* Religiousness

Religious communities, 18, 22, 137, 140–142, 187–188, 208–209, 232, 240, 249, 264

Religious concepts, defining, 279

Religious cultures, 137

Religious education, 238, 252, 264, 298

Religiousness, 13, 22, 44–45, 129, 207–208, 246, 248, 251–252, 298. *See also* Religious practices; Spiritual development; Spiritual struggle
of Americans, 14, 19, 48, 186, 207, 228–229, 303–304
assessment of, 14, 21–22
transmission of, 227–228, 230–235, 237–239, 301–302

Religious organizations, 230, 239–240, 296

Religious people, psychology's understanding of, 15, 156–157, 303–304

Religious practices, 160, 205, 229, 300–301. *See also* Spiritual disciplines; Transmission of religiousness
assessing effects of, 209–211, 280
effects on health, summary of, 212
Judeo-Christian perspective, 206–207
multiple dimensions, 210–211
negative effects, 220–221

Religious psychology, 45

Religious schools, 142, 238, 298

Renaissance, 38–39

Renunciation, 122

Repentance, 152–153, 168, 259

Reproduction, 119, 122n,125–128

Research agenda, 19–23, 87–90, 128–130, 294–295

Research design, in scientific psychology, 278

Resolution, of spiritual struggle, 258–259

Responsibility, 17, 18, 22, 44, 58, 64, 69, 146–147, 260, 275, 276

Resurrection of the body, Christian doctrine of, 125, 292

Revelation, divine, 87–88, 90

Rogers, Carl, 4, 7, 8, 14, 24, 48–49, 171, 278, 297

Romanticism, 147–148

Rosemead, 49

Rush, Benjamin, 41

St. Louis University, 47

Sartre, Jean-Paul, 60, 78

Saul, transformation of, 23. *See also* Paul, St.

Science and religion, dialogue between, 115–118, 273–276. *See also* Dialogue between psychology and religion

Scientific psychology, overview of implications for, 276–279

Search Institute, 230

Second Great Awakening, 41n

Secularism, 13–15, 46–49, 246, 303

Secular philosophy, 147–151

Self, 58–59, 134, 140. *See also* "New self"; Transformation
autonomy and the, 42, 83, 176
basic features of, 58–59
criterion for the, 86–87
and evolution, 61
ideal, 84–85, 278, 297
observation of, 75–76
and pride, 65
psychologies, 273
reality of, 76
relational, 73–93, 99, 296–297

Self-awareness, and standards, 77–78, 83

Self-concept, 58, 76, 141

Self-control, 62–70, 81, 151, 156–158, 178–180, 295–296

Self-deception, 78–79, 89

Self-esteem, 79–80

Selfhood, 58–59, 76–77, 87

Selfishness, 85, 127

Self-knowledge, inaccuracy of, 78–79

Self-perception, 78

Self-regulation, 58, 62–65, 137
and spiritual development, 187–188, 199–200

Self-reports, 281

Self-system, in transformational change, 174–175

Self-theory, 76

Sensibilities, Upham and, 41–42

Serenity prayer, 177

Sex therapy, 129

Sexton, Virginia Staudt, 47

Sexuality, 298
Augustine and, 33–34
Buddhist conceptualization of, 121–123
Christian conceptualization of, 123–128
as conceptualized in psychology, 118–121

Shalom, 18, 103–105

Sheen, Bishop Fulton, 46

virtue, contrasted with, 147–148
Vice, 146
Virtue, 17, 20, 146, 299
    Judeo-Christian perspective, 152–153, 155–157
    psychological perspective, 148–151
Virtue ethics, 150–151
Virtues and vices, classification of, 146, 159–160
Vocation from God, 85, 87–90, 135–136
Volition, 59, 62–65. *See also* Self-control

Watson, J. B., 46, 292
Weber, Max, 135–138

Webster's Third New International Dictionary, 169
Weltanschauung, 16
Wesley, John, 41n
Wheaton College, 48
Will, 41–42. *See also* Volition
Willpower, 62–67
Women, and religiousness, 229

Youth
    and religiousness, 230–231, 236, 238–239
    and spiritual struggle, 260

ABOUT THE EDITORS

William R. Miller, PhD, is a clinical psychologist who has been on the University of New Mexico psychology faculty since 1976. With a central interest in the psychology of change, he has been active in developing, testing, and disseminating evidence-based treatment methods, with a particular focus on addictions. He also has a longstanding interest in pastoral psychology and the interface of psychology with spirituality.

Harold D. Delaney, PhD, a psychologist with expertise in quantitative and methodology areas, has served on the University of New Mexico psychology faculty since 1975. The coauthor of a graduate text on experimental design, he also has interests in the history of psychology and the relationship between psychology and Christianity. Currently Dr. Delaney is directing a Templeton-funded research project on spiritual transformation.